AFRICAN POLITICAL, ECONOMIC, AND SECURITY ISSUES

THE AFRICAN GROWTH AND OPPORTUNITY ACT

TRADE AND INVESTMENT PERFORMANCE ANALYSIS

AFRICAN POLITICAL, ECONOMIC, AND SECURITY ISSUES

Additional books in this series can be found on Nova's website under the Series tab.

Additional e-books in this series can be found on Nova's website under the e-book tab.

AFRICAN POLITICAL, ECONOMIC, AND SECURITY ISSUES

THE AFRICAN GROWTH AND OPPORTUNITY ACT

TRADE AND INVESTMENT PERFORMANCE ANALYSIS

CARMAN HAYES
EDITOR

New York

Copyright © 2014 by Nova Science Publishers, Inc.

All rights reserved. No part of this book may be reproduced, stored in a retrieval system or transmitted in any form or by any means: electronic, electrostatic, magnetic, tape, mechanical photocopying, recording or otherwise without the written permission of the Publisher.

For permission to use material from this book please contact us:
Telephone 631-231-7269; Fax 631-231-8175
Web Site: http://www.novapublishers.com

NOTICE TO THE READER

The Publisher has taken reasonable care in the preparation of this book, but makes no expressed or implied warranty of any kind and assumes no responsibility for any errors or omissions. No liability is assumed for incidental or consequential damages in connection with or arising out of information contained in this book. The Publisher shall not be liable for any special, consequential, or exemplary damages resulting, in whole or in part, from the readers' use of, or reliance upon, this material. Any parts of this book based on government reports are so indicated and copyright is claimed for those parts to the extent applicable to compilations of such works.

Independent verification should be sought for any data, advice or recommendations contained in this book. In addition, no responsibility is assumed by the publisher for any injury and/or damage to persons or property arising from any methods, products, instructions, ideas or otherwise contained in this publication.

This publication is designed to provide accurate and authoritative information with regard to the subject matter covered herein. It is sold with the clear understanding that the Publisher is not engaged in rendering legal or any other professional services. If legal or any other expert assistance is required, the services of a competent person should be sought. FROM A DECLARATION OF PARTICIPANTS JOINTLY ADOPTED BY A COMMITTEE OF THE AMERICAN BAR ASSOCIATION AND A COMMITTEE OF PUBLISHERS.

Additional color graphics may be available in the e-book version of this book.

Library of Congress Cataloging-in-Publication Data

ISBN: 978-1-63463-068-9

Published by Nova Science Publishers, Inc. † New York

CONTENTS

Preface vii

Chapter 1 African Growth and Opportunity Act (AGOA): Background and Reauthorization 1
Brock R. Williams

Chapter 2 AGOA: Trade and Investment Performance Overview 21
United States International Trade Commission

Index 323

PREFACE

This book seeks to inform the discussion on the potential reauthorization of AGOA through analysis of the components of the AGOA legislation; U.S. import trends associated with AGOA; the impact of AGOA on African economies and U.S.-Africa trade; and the issues surrounding the reauthorization process.

Chapter 1 – The African Growth and Opportunity Act (AGOA) is a nonreciprocal trade preference program that provides duty-free treatment to U.S. imports of certain products from eligible sub-Saharan African (SSA) countries. Congress first authorized AGOA in 2000 to encourage export-led growth and economic development in SSA and improve U.S. economic relations with the region. Its current authorization expires on September 30, 2015.

In terms of tariff benefits and general eligibility criteria, AGOA is similar to the Generalized System of Preferences (GSP), a U.S. trade preference program that applies to more than 120 developing countries. AGOA, however, covers more products and includes additional eligibility criteria beyond those in GSP. Additionally, AGOA includes trade and development provisions beyond its duty-free preferences.

U.S. imports from AGOA beneficiary countries (AGOA countries) represent a small share (2%) of total U.S. imports and are largely concentrated in energy-related products. Oil is consistently the top duty-free U.S. import from AGOA countries, accounting for 77% of such imports in 2013. Despite remaining the top U.S. import under AGOA, U.S. oil imports from the region have fallen by more than half or nearly $30 billion, since 2011. Among non-energy products, apparel is the top export for a number of AGOA countries. U.S. apparel imports typically face relatively high tariffs and are excluded from duty-free treatment in GSP, but are included in the AGOA preferences giving AGOA countries a competitive advantage over other apparel producers. Still, only a handful of countries, primarily Lesotho, Kenya, and Mauritius, make significant use of the apparel benefits. Apart from apparel and energy products, South Africa accounts for the bulk of U.S. imports under AGOA. As the most economically advanced country in the region, South Africa also exports a much more diverse range of manufactured goods than other AGOA countries; vehicles in particular have become a major South African export under AGOA.

Most observers agree that AGOA has successfully led to increased and more diversified exports to the United States from sub-Saharan African countries. Despite this, Congress may wish to address a number of issues and challenges as it considers possible reauthorization of AGOA. Among these challenges is how current and potential AGOA beneficiaries can better utilize the AGOA program and its duty-free benefits. Studies suggest that even among some countries that do make significant use of the AGOA preferences, the lower-skill apparel production which AGOA has spurred has not led to the production of higher-skill manufactured products. Other issues relate to the nonreciprocal nature of the AGOA preferences. Some argue that the United States should focus more on two-way trade agreements with the region, particularly with more advanced countries such as South Africa, given improving economic conditions in Africa in recent years. The European Union (EU), for example, has negotiated Economic Partnership Agreements (EPAs) with several African countries that provide some reciprocal tariff benefits, potentially placing U.S. firms at a competitive disadvantage relative to European firms in some markets.

Chapter 2 – This report describes, reviews, and analyzes the trade and investment performance ofbeneficiary countries under the African Growth and Opportunity Act (AGOA) from 2000 to 2013. It also examines potential products for export to the United States or forintegration into regional and global supply chains and examines changes in the businessand investment climate in sub-Saharan Africa (SSA), as well as reciprocal tradeagreements between SSA and non-SSA partners and the relationship of theseagreements to the objectives of AGOA.

In: The African Growth and Opportunity Act
Editor: Carman Hayes

ISBN: 978-1-63463-068-9
© 2014 Nova Science Publishers, Inc.

Chapter 1

AFRICAN GROWTH AND OPPORTUNITY ACT (AGOA): BACKGROUND AND REAUTHORIZATION[*]

Brock R. Williams

SUMMARY

The African Growth and Opportunity Act (AGOA) is a nonreciprocal trade preference program that provides duty-free treatment to U.S. imports of certain products from eligible sub-Saharan African (SSA) countries. Congress first authorized AGOA in 2000 to encourage export-led growth and economic development in SSA and improve U.S. economic relations with the region. Its current authorization expires on September 30, 2015.

In terms of tariff benefits and general eligibility criteria, AGOA is similar to the Generalized System of Preferences (GSP), a U.S. trade preference program that applies to more than 120 developing countries. AGOA, however, covers more products and includes additional eligibility criteria beyond those in GSP. Additionally, AGOA includes trade and development provisions beyond its duty-free preferences.

U.S. imports from AGOA beneficiary countries (AGOA countries) represent a small share (2%) of total U.S. imports and are largely concentrated in energy-related products. Oil is consistently the top duty-free U.S. import from AGOA countries, accounting for 77% of such imports in 2013. Despite remaining the top U.S. import under AGOA, U.S. oil imports from the region have fallen by more than half or nearly $30 billion, since 2011. Among non-energy products, apparel is the top export for a number of AGOA countries. U.S. apparel imports typically face relatively high tariffs and are excluded from duty-free treatment in GSP, but are included in the AGOA preferences giving AGOA countries a competitive advantage over other apparel producers. Still, only a handful of countries, primarily Lesotho, Kenya, and Mauritius, make significant use of the apparel benefits. Apart from apparel and energy products, South Africa accounts for the bulk of U.S. imports under AGOA. As the most economically advanced country in the region, South Africa also exports a much more

---

[*] This is an edited, reformatted and augmented version of a Congressional Research Service publication R43173, prepared for Members and Committees of Congress dated July 24, 2014.

diverse range of manufactured goods than other AGOA countries; vehicles in particular have become a major South African export under AGOA.

Most observers agree that AGOA has successfully led to increased and more diversified exports to the United States from sub-Saharan African countries. Despite this, Congress may wish to address a number of issues and challenges as it considers possible reauthorization of AGOA. Among these challenges is how current and potential AGOA beneficiaries can better utilize the AGOA program and its duty-free benefits. Studies suggest that even among some countries that do make significant use of the AGOA preferences, the lower-skill apparel production which AGOA has spurred has not led to the production of higher-skill manufactured products. Other issues relate to the nonreciprocal nature of the AGOA preferences. Some argue that the United States should focus more on two-way trade agreements with the region, particularly with more advanced countries such as South Africa, given improving economic conditions in Africa in recent years. The European Union (EU), for example, has negotiated Economic Partnership Agreements (EPAs) with several African countries that provide some reciprocal tariff benefits, potentially placing U.S. firms at a competitive disadvantage relative to European firms in some markets.

INTRODUCTION

In 2000, Congress passed the African Growth and Opportunity Act (AGOA), a U.S. trade preference program, in order to help spur market-led economic growth and development in sub-Saharan Africa (SSA) and deepen U.S. trade and investment ties with the region.[1] Since its enactment, Congress has amended AGOA five times, making some technical changes and renewing the trade preferences through September 30, 2015.

According to the Assistant U.S. Trade Representative, (USTR) for Africa, "AGOA is the cornerstone of America's trade and investment policy with sub-Saharan Africa."[2] Economic conditions in Africa, however, have changed considerably since Congress passed the initial AGOA legislation. Annual real gross domestic product (GDP) growth in SSA was nearly a full percentage point lower than global GDP growth (2.3% vs. 3.2%) in the decade leading up to AGOA's passage (1990-2000).[3] Over the last 10 years, however, SSA's growth averaged 5.7 %, 2 points higher than the 3.7% world average. While the region still contains many of the world's poorest countries and faces significant economic challenges, some observers and policymakers argue that changing economic conditions warrant an evolution in U.S. policy toward SSA, focused more strongly on private sector investment and increasing two-way trade.[4] In recent years, SSA's growing economic potential and abundant natural resources have attracted other foreign investors, including state-supported enterprises from countries such as China, which is now the region's largest trading partner.

Some Members of Congress, the Obama Administration, and many African governments have highlighted the successes of AGOA and have called for an expedited reauthorization process. As part of this process, Congress may wish to consider whether AGOA, in its current form, is achieving the initial goals of the program, including whether it addresses effectively the changing economic circumstances in Africa. Most interested observers are positive about the AGOA preference program, but some have expressed concerns about specific provisions of the program, such as the lack of coverage for certain agricultural products, or would like to see the AGOA preferences granted to a broader range of least-developed countries beyond just Africa. Others would like to see a broader program that addresses concerns over U.S. businesses' ability to effectively compete in the region, though this could also be addressed in complementary legislation or Administrative initiatives.[5] This report seeks to inform the discussion on the potential reauthorization of AGOA through analysis of (1) the components of the AGOA legislation; (2) U.S. import trends associated with AGOA; (3) the impact of AGOA on African economies and U.S.-Africa trade; and (4) the issues surrounding the reauthorization process.

KEY PROVISIONS OF AGOA[6]

AGOA (Title I, P.L. 106-200), as amended, is a nonreciprocal preference program that provides duty-free access into the United States for qualifying exports from eligible SSA countries. Among the products that qualify for this duty-free treatment, apparel products have particular economic significance for several countries, in part due to special provisions granted to least-developed AGOA countries ("Third-Country Fabric Provision").[7] In addition to the tariff preferences, the AGOA legislation includes mandates for an annual meeting of U.S. and African government officials to discuss trade and economic issues—the AGOA Forum—as well as specific guidelines on U.S. development assistance directed toward SSA. Countries must meet specific eligibility requirements to qualify for these benefits.

Table A-1 in the Appendix, provides a list of SSA countries, as defined by AGOA. It highlights the 41 current AGOA beneficiary countries, and notes their eligibility status for other aspects of the AGOA preferences and GSP. It also lists U.S. imports under AGOA and GSP for each country and its GDP/capita—a rough measure of a country's level of economic development.

Unilateral Trade Preference Program

At the core of AGOA are the tariff benefits that provide duty-free access to the U.S. market for certain products from eligible SSA countries. In terms of these tariff benefits and country eligibility requirements, AGOA is essentially an expansion of the Generalized System of Preferences (GSP), a U.S trade preference program that applies to over 120 developing countries, including SSA countries. AGOA builds on GSP by providing preferential access to the U.S. market for more products, such as apparel, and sets out additional eligibility criteria. AGOA also includes other trade and development components, beyond preferences, that are not part of GSP.[8]

AGOA, like other U.S. trade preference programs, is nonreciprocal and unilateral. The preferences apply to U.S. imports and not to U.S. exports, so reauthorization only requires action by the U.S. government. These one-way preferences are granted to developing countries with the goal of enhancing export-led economic growth, and typically exclude items that may be considered import sensitive. This distinguishes them from other U.S. trade liberalization efforts such as free trade agreements (FTAs) or multilateral agreements through the World Trade Organization (WTO), which reduce and/or eliminate tariffs for both U.S.

imports and exports. AGOA included a provision requiring the President to explore potential FTA negotiations with interested AGOA beneficiaries, suggesting that Congress envisioned AGOA as a stepping stone to potential broader trade pacts with African countries. FTA negotiations with South Africa and its regional partners in the South African Customs Union (SACU) sprang from this mandate in AGOA, but were ultimately unsuccessful and suspended in 2006.[9]

Product Coverage

The tariff benefits provided by AGOA include all products covered by GSP, as well as additional products the President determines are not import-sensitive with regard to imports from SSA.[10] According to a report by the Government Accountability Office (GAO) in 2008, the U.S. Harmonized Tariff Schedule (HTS) includes some 10,500 individual tariff lines for U.S. goods imports, of which roughly 3,800 have no most-favored nation (MFN) tariff (i.e., all WTO members may export them to the U.S. duty-free).[11] GSP removes the tariff on an additional 3,400 products (4,800 for least-developed countries), and AGOA makes another 1,800 tariff lines duty-free, though a large share of these are included in the GSP benefits for least-developed countries (LDCs).[12] AGOA extends duty-free treatment to certain apparel and footwear products, which are not eligible under GSP (even for LDCs). Agricultural products subject to tariff-rate quotas (TRQ) remain ineligible for duty-free treatment under both AGOA and GSP.[13] AGOA beneficiaries are also exempt from certain caps on allowable duty-free imports under the GSP program ("competitive need limitations").[14]

Rules of Origin

Products from AGOA countries must meet certain rules of origin (ROO) requirements in order to qualify for duty-free treatment (see the textiles and apparel section for sector-specific rules of origin). First, duty-free entry is only allowed if the article is imported directly from the beneficiary country into the United States. Second, at least 35% of the appraised value of the product must be the "growth, product or manufacture" of a beneficiary developing country, as defined by the sum of (1) the cost or value of materials produced in the beneficiary developing country (or any two or more beneficiary countries that are members of the same association or countries and are treated as one country for purposes of the U.S. law) plus (2) the direct costs of processing in the country. Up to 15% of the required 35% of the appraised value may be of U.S. origin, and any amount of production in other beneficiary SSA countries may also contribute to the value-added requirement ("regional cumulation").[15]

Textile and Apparel Provisions

AGOA includes duty-free treatment for certain apparel and textile products, though some are subject to quantitative limitations. These provisions in AGOA are significant, because (1) apparel production has played a unique role in the development process of some countries; and (2) the duty-free benefits apply to a sector with relatively higher U.S. tariff rates than average overall U.S. tariff rates. Not all AGOA beneficiaries are eligible for the apparel provisions. Duty-free treatment for apparel products under AGOA requires beneficiary countries to adopt an efficient visa ("tracking") system to prevent unlawful transshipment—

production shipped through and exported from, but not actually produced in, a given country, often for particular tariff or quota benefits.[16]

Apparel production has been a significant component in some countries' economic development.[17] Unlike textile production, it typically requires low-skilled labor and minimal capital expenditures, allowing lesser-developed countries to become globally competitive. Some research suggests that success in low-skill and export intensive industries such as apparel may help lead to a more diversified manufacturing sector.[18] Nonetheless, the U.S. apparel sector is deemed "import sensitive," and has some specific safeguards. For example, in U.S. free trade agreements (FTAs), apparel tariff lines typically have "yarn forward" general rules of origin (which govern how much of the product must be made in the beneficiary country and longer tariff phase outs), and most preference programs either exclude these articles (GSP) or have caps on duty-free treatment (including AGOA).[19]

The existing general restrictions on U.S. imports of apparel make AGOA's preferential treatment for these product lines especially advantageous. The average U.S. applied tariff on apparel is 11.4% compared to an average for all products of 3.5%.[20] This relatively high preference margin may help explain how some AGOA producers, especially the LDCs, are competitive with lower-cost producers in Asia and elsewhere.[21]

Textile and apparel articles qualifying for duty-free treatment include

- Apparel assembled in one or more AGOA beneficiary countries from U.S. yarn and fabric;
- Apparel made of SSA(regional) yarns and fabrics, subject to a cap until 2015;
- Apparel made in a designated LDC of third-country yarns and fabrics, subject to a cap until 2015;
- Apparel made of yarns and fabrics not produced in commercial quantities in the United States (determination must be made that the yarn or fabric cannot be supplied by the U.S. industry in a timely manner, and to extend preferential treatment to the eligible fabric);
- Certain cashmere and merino wool sweaters;
- Textiles and textile articles produced entirely in an LDC SSA beneficiary country; and
- Certain handloomed, handmade, ethnic printed fabrics, or folklore articles (certain countries only).[22]

Third-Country Fabric Provision

AGOA's third-country fabric provision is a special rule that allows U.S. apparel imports from least-developed SSA countries to qualify for duty-free treatment even if the yarns and fabrics used in the production of the apparel are imported from non-AGOA countries. This provision, which was reauthorized in August 2012 (P.L. 112-163), is currently set to expire in September 2015, along with the overall AGOA program.

Eligibility

Eligibility for the AGOA trade preference program consists of two separate steps. First, the country must be included in a statutorily-created list of sub-Saharan African countries, described in AGOA (19 U.S.C. 3706). This list has been updated periodically by new legislation (e.g., the 112th Congress added South Sudan in P.L. 112-163).

The second step requires the President to determine annually which eligible countries, from those on the list of SSA countries defined by Congress, should become beneficiaries of the AGOA preferences. There are two different sets of criteria for the President's consideration in this process: Section 104 of AGOA (19 U.S.C. 3703) and Section 502 of the Trade Act of 1974, or GSP (19 U.S.C. 2462).

- **Section 104** is specific to AGOA and requires the President to consider a number of factors related to the prospective AGOA country's economy; rule of law; elimination of barriers to U.S. trade and investment; poverty reduction efforts; protection of worker rights; support of terrorist activities; and interference with U.S. national security and foreign policy efforts.
- **Section 502**, as amended, sets out the eligibility requirements of the Generalized System of Preferences (GSP), which must also be met by any AGOA beneficiary country. These also include a number of economic and political factors.

In two separate proclamations during the past year, President Obama has made changes to AGOA country eligibility.[23] The President reinstated AGOA eligibility for Mali and Madagascar, which is now effective. He also terminated AGOA eligibility for Swaziland, effective January 1, 2015, due to the country's failure to meet eligibility criteria related to worker rights.

Least-Developed Country Status

AGOA, like GSP, has additional benefits for least-developed beneficiary countries (LDCs). Under GSP, these countries qualify for duty-free treatment on an additional 1,400 products. Under AGOA, the additional benefits are more flexible rules governing the duty-free treatment of textiles and apparel. Unlike GSP, which provides the President broad latitude in determining LDC status, AGOA defines LDCs as countries with a per capita gross national product (GNP) of less than $1,500 in 1998 as measured by the World Bank.[24] Botswana, Namibia, and Mauritius are also explicitly granted LDC status in AGOA, despite GNP per capita levels above that threshold. This exemption is particularly economically significant for Mauritius; it is the fourth-largest exporter under AGOA (excluding oil trade) and exports primarily apparel products under the preference program.

AGOA Forum

AGOA requires the President, in consultation with Congress and the other governments concerned, to hold annually a United States-Sub-Saharan Africa Trade and Economic Cooperation Forum.[25] The purpose of the Forum, which is held in alternate years in the United States and Africa, is to "discuss expanding trade and investment relations between the

United States and Sub-Saharan Africa and the implementation of [AGOA] including encouraging joint ventures between small and large businesses." The 12th AGOA Forum took place in Addis Ababa, Ethiopia, from August 9-13, 2013, focusing on "Sustainable Transformation through Trade and Technology."

Technical Assistance and Capacity Building

Unlike other U.S. preference programs, AGOA directs the President to target U.S. government technical assistance and trade capacity building (TCB) in AGOA beneficiary countries.[26] This assistance is intended to encourage governments to (1) liberalize trade policy; (2) harmonize laws and regulations with WTO membership commitments; (3) engage in financial and fiscal restructuring; and (4) promote greater agribusiness linkages. AGOA also includes assistance for developing private sector business associations and networks among U.S. and SSA enterprises.[27] Technical assistance must be targeted to increasing the number of reverse trade missions; increasing trade in services; addressing critical agricultural policy issues; and building capabilities of African states to participate in the WTO, generally, and, particularly, in services. In FY2012, the most recent year for which data are available, the United States reported obligating approximately $94.6 million in TCB assistance to AGOA countries, down considerably from the previous five years during which TCB funding averaged over $600 million per year.[28] Of this amount in 2012, $12.4 million was obligated for physical infrastructure development, $25.8 million on trade-related agriculture projects, and $27.7 million on competition policy, business, environment, and governance.

In addition to these broad mandates, AGOA includes language pertaining to the following agencies:

- **Overseas Private Investment Corporation (OPIC).** Section 123 expresses the sense of Congress that OPIC should exercise its authority to support projects in SSA and directs OPIC to increase funds directed to SSA countries.
- **Export-Import Bank (Ex-Im Bank).** Section 124 of AGOA expresses the sense of Congress that the Ex-Im Bank should continue to expand its financial commitments to its loan guarantee and insurance programs to African countries and commends the Bank's sub-Saharan Africa Advisory Committee for its work in fostering economic cooperation between the United States and SSA. This committee's work was extended to September 30, 2014, in recent legislation reauthorizing the Ex-Im Bank (§23 of P.L. 112-122).[29]
- **United States Trade Representative (USTR).** Section 117 supports the creation of an Assistant USTR for Africa to serve as the "primary point of contact in the executive branch for those persons engaged in trade between the United States and sub-Saharan Africa," and the chief adviser to the U.S. Trade Representative (USTR) on trade and investment issues pertaining to Africa. This position previously had been established by President Clinton in 1998.
- **U.S. Foreign Commercial Service (CS).** Section 125 notes that the CS presence in SSA had been reduced since the 1980s and the level of staffing in 1997 (seven officers in four countries) did not "adequately service the needs of U.S. businesses

attempting to do business in sub-Saharan Africa."[30] Accordingly, the legislation required the posting of at least 20 CS officers in not less than 10 countries in SSA by December 31, 2001, "subject to the availability of appropriations."[31] According to data provided by the Department of Commerce for FY2014, there are now 15 CS officers in sub-Saharan Africa up from 5 in FY2012. These are located in Angola (4), Ethiopia (1), Ghana (1), Kenya (2), Mozambique (1), Nigeria (2), South Africa (3), and Tanzania (1).

- **U.S. Agency for International Development (USAID).** Aside from Millennium Challenge Corporation (MCC) compacts that include TCB, USAID funds much of the trade capacity building efforts related to AGOA($58 million of the $94.6 million mentioned above). In 2011, the Administration announced the African Competitiveness and Trade Expansion (ACTE) initiative, a trade and investment initiative with funding of up to $30 million annually, subject to appropriations.[32] ACTE supports the three African Trade Hubs, one of USAID's most oft-cited AGOA-related projects.[33] Based in Ghana, Kenya, and Botswana, the Trade Hubs attempt to help potential exporters become globally competitive and make full use of their AGOA benefits.[34] As part of the Administration's Trade Africa Initiative, the EastAfrica Trade Hub will be renamed the East Africa Trade and Investment Hub and will build on its current activities to expand two-way trade and investment between the United States and the East African Community.[35]

Annual Report to Congress

Originally, AGOA also required the President to submit an annual "comprehensive report on the trade and investment policy of the United States for sub-Saharan Africa." In a subsequent reauthorization of the AGOA trade preferences, this requirement was not extended. The most recent report was in 2008.

U.S. IMPORTS UNDER AGOA AND GSP[36]

U.S. imports from AGOA countries represent a small share of overall U.S. imports. In 2013, the United States imported $2,240 billion in goods, of which only $38.2 billion, or less than 2%, came from AGOA countries. 70% of these imports ($26.8 billion) received duty-free treatment, under either AGOA or GSP, though crude oil accounts for much of this. Among non crude oil U.S. imports, 39% received duty-free treatment under AGOA or GSP.[37]

Energy-related products (e.g., crude oil) dominate U.S. imports from SSA under AGOA and GSP, representing 82% of such imports in 2013, though these imports have fallen sharply in the past two years.[38] Given SSA's abundant natural resources and the already low U.S. tariff on oil ($0.05- $0.10 per barrel), much of this trade would likely occur regardless of the preference program. The discussion that follows focuses on non-energy trade between the United States and SSA. (See the text box below for more information on U.S. oil imports under AGOA.)

In 2013, U.S. imports from SSA under AGOA and GSP, excluding energy products, were $4.9 billion (**Figure 1**). This represents a more than three-fold increase (up from $1.3 billion) since 2001, the first full year of AGOA eligibility, although these imports have fallen slightly since 2011. Apparel products remain one of the largest non-oil import categories; however, these imports peaked in 2004 prior to the dismantling of the complex multilateral quota system, known as the Multifiber Agreement (MFA). The MFA limited U.S. apparel imports from certain countries, thus eliminating the extent of competition faced by AGOA apparel exporters. Though U.S. apparel imports still face relatively high tariffs, removal of these strict quantitative limitations reduced the AGOA countries' competitive advantage in producing apparel. U.S. apparel imports under AGOA, though very significant for some AGOA countries, represent only 1% of overall U.S. apparel imports. U.S. apparel imports totaled $80.4 billion in 2013, with $30.3 billion from China, $8.0 billion from Vietnam, and less than $1 billion total from AGOA beneficiaries (**Table 1**).

While U.S. apparel imports from AGOA countries have declined from their peak in 2004, imports of other products have been rising rapidly. Vehicle imports have seen strong growth, rising from $289 million in 2001 to nearly $2.2 billion in 2013. These and other more advanced manufactured products, such as chemicals, come almost exclusively from South Africa. Imports of products with more widespread origins have grown on a more modest scale. U.S. imports of food and agriculture products, including nuts, fruits, cocoa, sugar, beverages, and tobacco have increased from $136 million to $446 million during the same period.

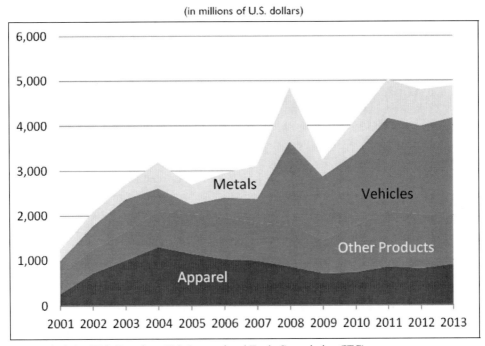

Source: Analysis by CRS. Data from U.S. International Trade Commission (ITC).
Notes: Imports for consumption basis. Metals defined as HTS chapters 76 and 72; vehicles as HTS chapter 87; apparel as HTS chapters 61 and 62; and energy as HTS chapter 27.

Figure 1. Non-Energy U.S. Imports from SSA under AGOA and GSP.

Table 1. U.S. Imports of Apparel Products by Country
(in millions of U.S. dollars, 2013)

Top Overall Countries	Import Value	Top AGOA Countries	Import Value
China	$30,319	Lesotho	$321
Vietnam	8,034	Kenya	309
Indonesia	4,998	Mauritius	190
Bangladesh	4,796	Swaziland	50
Mexico	3,813	Botswana	6

Source: Analysis by CRS. Imports for consumption data from U.S. ITC trade dataweb.
Notes: Imports for consumption basis. Apparel products defined as HTS chapters 61 and 62.

U.S. imports from SSA under AGOA and GSP are heavily concentrated in a few countries. **Figure 2** highlights the top exporters of non-energy products to the United States under both programs. Again, excluding energy products, U.S. preferential imports from South Africa totaled $3.7 billion in 2013, accounting for roughly three-quarters of all U.S. imports from SSA under AGOA/GSP. Other top non-energy exporters under AGOA/GSP are the major apparel producers: Kenya ($342 million); Lesotho ($321 million); and Mauritius ($199 million). Cote d'Ivoire was the fifth largest exporter under these preference programs, exporting largely cocoa products ($85 million). Aside from these top countries, however, the preferences are not heavily utilized. U.S. preferential imports were less than $1 million for over half of the 40 AGOA beneficiary countries in 2013.

IMPACTS OF AGOA

Through AGOA Congress set out to improve the economic development of SSA and increase U.S. trade ties with the region. A handful of countries have made strong use of the preference program and have increased employment in economic sectors that benefited from duty-free treatment under AGOA. For example, the government of Lesotho, one of the major apparel exporters under AGOA, estimates that employment in manufacturing rose from 19,000 in 1999 to 45,700 in June 2011.[40] A peer-reviewed economic study found a direct link between the AGOA preferences and increased U.S. imports from beneficiary countries, and concluded that these increased SSA exports were not merely diverted from other potential export destinations (e.g., the European Union).[41] This relationship was strongest for the apparel sector and other sectors with high U.S. import tariffs.

Despite these achievements, challenges remain, such as the limited number of countries making significant use of the preferences, and doubts as to whether AGOA countries have been able to translate these short-term preference benefits into transformative changes in their manufacturing capabilities and overall competitiveness.[42] As highlighted above, the majority of AGOA non-oil imports come from South Africa. Among the other countries that have made significant use of the preferences, apparel exports account for most of their AGOA exports. While the apparel sector has been acknowledged as a potential launching point for more advanced manufacturing industries, the manufacturing sectors in many AGOA beneficiary countries remain highly underdeveloped. One study asserts that AGOA apparel production is concentrated in the lowest-skill tasks with little knowledge transfer to local workers and that the global competitiveness of AGOA exporters still depends on their preferential treatment.[43]

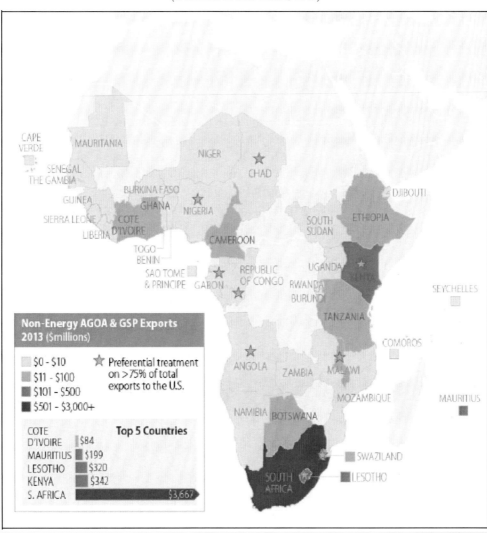

Source: Analysis by CRS. Data from U.S. ITC.
Notes: Imports for consumption basis. Energy products defined as HTS chapter 27. Stars represent preferential treatment on over 75% of total exports to the United States, including energy products. Map only includes countries eligible for AGOA benefits in 2013.

Figure 2. Top AGOA and GSP Exporters excluding Energy Products.

U.S. OIL IMPORTS UNDER AGOA AND GSP

Crude oil has been the top U.S. import from SSA under AGOA and GSP since AGOA's first full year of duty-free treatment in 2001 (**Figure 3**), The following are key facts regarding U.S. oil imports under AGOA and GSP.

- The top 5 AGOA-eligible oil exporters are Nigeria, Angola, Chad, Gabon, and Republic of Congo.
- Both AGOA and GSP grant duty-free status to U.S. crude oil imports.
- GSP only affords this treatment to least-developed countries (LDCs).
- Nigeria is not considered an LDC under GSP and so depends on AGOA for duty-free treatment of its crude oil exports to the United States. It is the only major AGOA-eligible oil exporter that is not considered an LDC under GSP.
- Crude oil prices have exceeded $100 a barrel in recent years. This high market value coupled with a very low U.S. import tariff, $0.05-$0.10 per barrel, makes AGOA and GSP's crude oil tariff benefit relatively insignificant.
- U.S. crude oil imports from SSA in 2013 were 57% lower than in 2011 (a nearly $30 billion decrease), which may be partially due to the increased U.S. production of shale oil, a direct competitor with oil from some SSA countries due to its similar composition.[39]

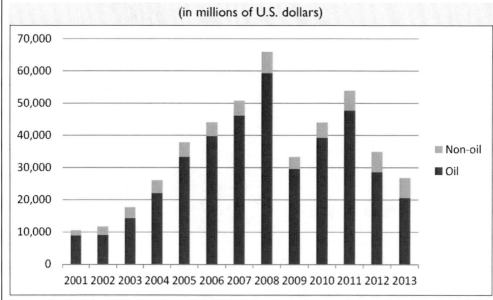

Source: Analysis by CRS. Data from U.S. ITC.
Notes: Imports for consumption basis. Oil defined as HTS 4-digit category 2709.

Figure 3. Oil Imports from SSA under AGOA and GSP.

In addition to AGOA's tangible goals related to economic development and trade, AGOA also supports the achievement of other strategic objectives. AGOA serves as a focal point for U.S. economic relations with SSA. If the recent period of high economic growth in much of SSA continues, the United States may have an increasing interest in the region's potential as a consumer market and destination for both U.S. exports and foreign direct investment (FDI). A study by McKinsey estimated that the number of African households making above $5,000 per year, the point where discretionary spending begins, would rise from 85 million in 2008 to 128 million in 2020.[44] Though AGOA focuses specifically on U.S. imports, it spurs dialogue between the United States and SSA countries on two-way trade and investment issues through the annual AGOA Forum. Through the eligibility criteria required for the program, the United States maintains some influence over the political and economic structure of the beneficiary countries. These strategic aspects of AGOA may become more important as other foreign countries, such as China, continue to increase their commercial and political ties with SSA.

Reauthorization Debate

AGOA's authorization is set to expire on September 30, 2015. President Obama,[45] some Members of Congress, officials from beneficiary countries, and various stakeholders support renewing the preferences. The United States Trade Representative (USTR), Ambassador Froman, in a speech at the AGOA Forum in August 2013, argued that this potential reauthorization provides an opportunity to "lay the foundation for AGOA 2.0," addressing some of its challenges and making it more compatible with the changing economic landscape in SSA.[46] In November 2013, the Administration requested four investigations of AGOA by the U.S. International Trade Commission (ITC), and the ITC held a subsequent hearing on the topic in January 2014.[47] The first report, published in April 2014, addresses AGOA's trade and investment performance.[48] The other three reports, which cover AGOA's impact on U.S. industries and consumers, rules of origin, and the EU-South Africa FTA, are confidential. Congress also recently sought greater study of the AGOA preference program. In December 2013, relevant committee leadership, bicameral and bipartisan, requested a GAO report to consider the effectiveness of AGOA including utilization of the preferences and its impact on two-way trade.[49] Ambassadors of the AGOA beneficiary countries have added their voices to the debate on AGOA, publishing a set of their recommendations for a potential renewal.[50] Press reports suggest that African countries' willingness to implement the WTO trade facilitation agreement reached at the Bali Ministerial in late 2013 may also affect support for AGOA reauthorization.[51] The following are some issues that may merit congressional consideration during AGOA's reauthorization debate.

- *Investor Uncertainty, Country Eligibility, and Length of Reauthorization.* Private sector actors have argued that uncertainty regarding the duration of AGOA preferences, both due to the eligibility reviews and periodic reauthorizations, hinders investment in the region. Some have called for a longer and uniform reauthorization (i.e., 10-15 years) for all AGOA preferences, including the third-country fabric provision, and for more transparency and greater consideration of economic implications during annual eligibility reviews.[52] On the other hand, changes to the eligibility criteria could decrease the potential leverage AGOA provides to encourage economic and political reform in beneficiary countries. Lengthened periods of authorization could also limit the incentive for more advanced economies, such as South Africa, to engage in more comprehensive trade liberalization efforts.

- *Intra-African Trade.* Intra-African trade and economic integration have been cited as a crucial but often absent component of economic development in the region.[53] Regional integration efforts are one way to improve these intra-African trade ties, and AGOA calls for "expanding U.S. assistance to sub-Saharan Africa's regional integration efforts." In the first decade of AGOA's enactment, African intra-regional trade stayed flat at around 10%.[54] It may be worthwhile to evaluate the impact, if any, that AGOA and corresponding U.S. development assistance has had in improving regional integration efforts and intra-African trade, and determine whether AGOA should further address these issues.[55]

- *Two-way Trade.* Like other U.S. preference programs, AGOA provides preferential access to the U.S. market with no reciprocal preferential U.S. access to the beneficiary countries. In light of economic improvements in the region, some observers are now calling for a greater focus on two-way trade in AGOA. This goal was included, however, in the original AGOA legislation mandating that the Administration seek out possible FTA partners among SSA nations. Subsequent negotiations with South Africa and its regional partners in SACU began in 2003, but were ultimately unsuccessful and postponed indefinitely in 2006. The European Union (EU), however, successfully concluded an Economic Partnership Agreement (EPA) providing reciprocal preferential tariff treatment to EU exports to South Africa, though it excludes a range of products.[56] Two relevant policy questions follow: (1) is the United States willing to negotiate less comprehensive and high-standard FTAs than it normally negotiates to gain more access to emerging markets like South Africa, or are countries in the region more prepared to engage in comprehensive, reciprocal trade talks; and (2) should AGOA include its own graduation process, which, like that for GSP, removes more economically advanced countries from the preference program once they reach a certain level of economic development (e.g., GDP/capita level)?

- *Country Participation.* Over half of the current AGOA beneficiaries exported less than $1 million to the United States under AGOA in 2013. Many of these are LDC AGOA countries that are eligible for duty-free treatment on apparel exports and enjoy the more flexible rules of origin ("Third-Country Fabric Provision"), giving them a significant competitive advantage over other producers. A handful of AGOA countries, particularly Kenya, Lesotho, and Mauritius, provide the bulk of apparel exports under AGOA. Should factors that helped these countries successfully utilize AGOA potentially be integrated into a revised AGOA framework to help spur similar success in other AGOA LDCs?

- *Trade Capacity Building (TCB).* Exporters in AGOA countries face numerous challenges. These include poor infrastructure, inadequate access to electricity, and skilled labor shortages. AGOA sets out broad aims for TCB, which are administered through different agencies, particularly USAID. Since 2001, $4 billion has been allocated to TCB funding in AGOA countries by various U.S. government agencies, particularly USAID and MCC. Yet discussions on AGOA often center on the need for more TCB funding. In 2011 GAO reported that USAID needed better evaluation of its TCB programs.[57] In addition to the effectiveness of TCB, another issue is whether a lack of TCB funding has been a major constraint in AGOA countries' ability to take advantage of the trade preferences. In 2012, TCB funding in AGOA countries dropped to $95 million from an average of $629 million over the previous five years, largely because no new MCC compacts with TCB components were initiated with an AGOA country in 2012.

- *Products Covered under AGOA Preferences.* AGOA and GSP provide duty-free access on U.S. imports of approximately 5,200 tariff lines, which together with the products already duty-free in the U.S. tariff schedule, grants AGOA beneficiaries duty-free access to roughly 86% of U.S. products. While a majority of products are covered under AGOA, some of the excluded products are competitively produced in AGOA countries, particularly agricultural products.[58] Though some agriculture products are included in AGOA, those subject to tariff-rate quotas (TRQs) are limited in the amount that may enter duty-free. Expanding the products covered under AGOA could allow a greater number of AGOA beneficiaries to make use of the trade preference program. Such a move, however, could prove politically sensitive in the United States, as most items excluded from U.S. preference programs are potentially import sensitive. AGOA exporters may also have difficulty meeting U.S. food safety standards for agricultural products. Expanding access to the U.S. agriculture market may also require additional TCB funding.

- *Duty-Free Quota-Free (DFQF) Beyond Africa.* AGOA's tariff benefits, which include apparel products, are broader than those provided by GSP. Some argue, including in the context of the current WTO Doha negotiations, that broader DFQF tariff preferences should be granted to all least-developed countries, not just those in Africa.[59] LDCs throughout the world face relatively high U.S. import tariffs given the particular items they export, such as apparel and agricultural products. For example, in 2013, U.S. import duties on all imports from Cambodia ($463 million) were higher than those from the France ($422 million).[60] Providing broader DFQF access to LDCs would erode some of the competitive advantage AGOA apparel producers currently receive. A recent study estimates that apparel exports from AGOA countries would fall considerably if AGOA-like benefits were expanded to all LDCs.[61] Other studies, however, estimate that a broader DFQF program could actually benefit AGOALDCs by including protected sectors such as agriculture, despite potential losses in apparel production.[62] In addition, proponents of DFQF argue that apparel products currently produced in AGOA countries could be targeted for exemption from a broader DFQF program.[63]

APPENDIX. AGOA BENEFICIARIES

TableA-1. AGOA and GSP Eligibility, U.S. Imports, and GSP/Capita, by Country

Country	GSP	GSP-Least Developed	AGOA	AGOA Third-Country Fabric Provision	U.S. Non-Energy Imports under AGOA/GSP* (thousand $s, 2013)	GDP/Capita ($s, 2012)
Angola	√	√	√		66	5,485
Benin	√	√	√	√	7	752
Botswana	√		√	√	5,929	7,191
Burkina Faso	√	√	√	√	67	634
Burundi	√	√	√		0	251
Cameroon	√		√	√	21,560	1,151
Cape Verde	√		√	√	159	3,838
Central African Republic	√	√			NA	473
Chad	√	√	√	√	0	885
Comoros	√	√	√		0	831
Democratic Republic of Congo	√	√			NA	272
Republic of Congo	√		√		41,009	3,154
Cote d'Ivoire	√		√	√	84,670	1,244
Djibouti	√	√	√		0	N.A.
Equatorial Guinea					NA	24,036
Eritrea	√				NA	504
Ethiopia	√	√	√	√	35,310	470
Gabon	√		√		224	11,430
Gambia	√	√	√	√	61	512
Ghana	√		√	√	34,673	1,605
Guinea	√	√	√		159	591
Guinea-Bissau	√	√			NA	539
Kenya	√		√	√	342,502	862
Lesotho	√	√	√	√	320,879	1,193
Liberia	√	√	√	√	3	422
Madagascar	√	√	√	√	NA*	447
Malawi	√	√	√	√	51,238	268
Mali	√	√	√	√	NA*	694
Mauritania	√	√	√		0	1,106
Mauritius	√		√	√	199,268	8,124
Mozambique	√	√	√	√	1,378	579
Namibia	√		√	√	566	5,668
Niger	√	√	√		52	383
Nigeria	√		√	√	5,403	1,555

Country	GSP	GSP-Least Developed	AGOA	AGOA Third-Country Fabric Provision	U.S. Non-Energy Imports under AGOA/GSP* (thousand $s, 2013)	GDP/Capita ($s, 2012)
Rwanda	√	√	√	√	782	620
Sao Tomei and Principe	√	√	√		36	1,402
Senegal	√		√	√	625	1,032
Seychelles	√		√		178	11,758
Sierra Leone	√	√	√	√	56	635
Somalia	√	√			NA	N.A
South Africa	√		√		3,667,783	7,508
South Sudan	√	√	√		0	862
Sudan					NA	1,580
Swaziland**	√		√	√	54,153	3,044
Tanzania	√	√	√	√	10,986	609
Togo	√	√	√		331	574
Uganda	√	√	√	√	1,578	547
Zambia	√	√	√	√	3,999	1,469
Zimbabwe					NA	788

Source: Analysis by CRS. Data from USTR, ITC, and Commerce Department.

Notes: Import data based on imports for consumption. Import data is only listed for AGOA-eligible countries (even if they remain eligible for GSP).

(*) Mali and Madagascar were ineligible for the AGOA preferences in 2013, but their eligibility was reinstated in 2014.

(**) Swaziland's eligibility will be removed, effective January 1, 2015.

End Notes

[1] Trade preference programs give nonreciprocal duty-free U.S. market access to select exports of eligible less-developed countries.

[2] Hearing Testimony by Florizelle Lizer, U.S. Congress, Senate Committee on Foreign Relations, Subcommittee on African Affairs, *Economic Statecraft: Embracing Africa's Market Potential*, 112th Cong., 2nd sess., June 28, 2012, S.Hrg. 112-604 (Washington: GPO, 2012), p. 12.

[3] Analysis by CRS. Data from International Monetary Fund, *World Economic Outlook*, April 2013.

[4] For example, in remarks leading up to President Obama's trip to Africa, USTR Michael Froman stated, "If we are to achieve sustainable development, it is our view that investment must be the driver." USTR, "Remarks by United States Trade Representative Michael Froman to the U.S. Global Leadership Coalition," press release, June 25, 2013 http://www.ustr.gov/about-us/press-office/press-releases/2013/june/remarks-united-states-trade-representative-michael-fr.

[5] For example, a bill has been introduced in the 113th Congress relating to efforts to increase U.S. exports to Africa (H.R. 1777 and S. 718) and the Administration has initiated programs such as Trade Africa, which centers on a potential trade and investment agreement with the East African Community.

[6] Some of this material was drawn from a previous CRS report by Vivian C. Jones.

[7] Apparel production is an important component of AGOA because it is seen as a manufacturing sector with relatively low technological and investment barriers to entry by newly industrializing countries and as having high job-generation potential for relatively low-skilled labor forces, both issues of relevance to many African countries.

[8] In addition to AGOA, there are four other U.S. regional preference programs that have different product coverage than GSP: the Caribbean Basin Economic Recovery Act (CBERA); the Caribbean Trade Partnership Act (CBTPA); the Andean Trade Preference Act (ATPA); and the Haitian Opportunity through Partnership Encouragement (HOPE) Act.[8]

[9] Observers cited several possible reasons for the unsuccessful FTA negotiations, including the capacity of SACU nations to negotiate a U.S.-style (comprehensive and high-standard) FTA, and disagreements between the parties on the scope and level of ambition of the negotiations.

[10] The AGOA trade preferences, including the portion covered by GSP, are in effect through September 2015, regardless of GSP's reauthorization.

[11] U.S. Government Accountability Office, *U.S. Trade Preference Programs Provide Important Benefits, but a More Integrated Approach Would Better Ensure Programs Meet Shared Goals*, GAO-08-443, March 2008, pp. 70-72.

[12] Ibid.

[13] TRQs are two-tiered tariffs. In-quota import quantities face one tariff, while above-quota import quantities face another, typically much higher, tariff.

[14] CRS Report RL33663, *Generalized System of Preferences: Background and Renewal Debate*, by Vivian C. Jones.

[15] §506A of P.L. 93-618, as added by §111 of P.L. 106-200, and amended by §7 of P.L. 108-274.

[16] For more information, see Department of Commerce, Office of Textiles and Apparel (OTEXA) Summary of AGOA textile and apparel provisions at OTEXA website, http://otexa.ita.doc.gov.

[17] Karina Fernandez-Stark, Stacey Frederick, and Gary Gereffi, *The Apparel Global Value Chain*, Duke Center on Globalization Governance and Competitiveness, November 2011.

[18] Paul Collier and Anthony Venables, *Rethinking Trade Preferences to Help Diversify African Exports*, Centre for Economic Policy Research, June 2007.

[19] A "yarn forward" rule means that, in order to qualify for trade benefits under an FTA, all products in a garment from the yarn stage forward must be made in one of the countries that is party to the agreement.

[20] World Trade Organization, *World Tariff Profiles—United States*, 2012.

[21] For a discussion of challenges faced by African firms, see Ann E. Harrison, Justin Yifu Lin, and L. Colin Xu, *Explaining Africa's (Dis)Advantage*, National Bureau of Economic Research, Working Paper 18683, January 2013.

[22] Department of Commerce, Office of Textiles and Apparel (OTEXA) Summary of AGOA textile and apparel provisions at OTEXA website, http://otexa.ita.doc.gov.

[23] The December 23, 2013, proclamation may be found at http://www.whitehouse.gov/the-press-office/2013/12/23/presidential-proclamation-african-growth-and-opportunity-act, and the June 26, 2014, proclamation may be found at http://www.whitehouse.gov/the-press-office/2014/06/26/presidential-proclamation-agoa. Additional information on the changes in eligibility status is available via USTR's website at http://www.ustr.gov/about-us/press-office/press-releases/2014/June/President-Obama-removes-Swaziland-reinstates-Madagascar-for-AGOA-Benefits.

[24] 19 U.S.C. §2462(a)(2) and 19 U.S.C. §3721(c)(3).

[25] Representatives from appropriate sub-Saharan African regional organizations and government officials from other appropriate countries in sub-Saharan Africa also could be invited, and generally are. African countries hosting the Forum must be nominated by their participant peers and be able to sponsor associated costs.

[26] Section 122 of P.L. 106-200 (19 U.S.C. §3732).

[27] Ibid.

[28] USAID, which administers the collection and dissemination of the data on TCB, includes portions of Millennium Challenge Corporation (MCC) compacts, such as infrastructure projects, in these figures. USAID reports the MCC funding in the year it is granted, though the distribution of the funds occurs over several years. No new MCC compacts with TCB components were initiated with AGOA countries in 2012, which explains the large drop in TCB funding. U.S. Agency for International Development, Trade Capacity Building Database, http://tcb.eads.usaidallnet.gov/.

[29] Export-Import Bank Reauthorization Act, 12 U.S.C. 635(b)(9)(B)(iii).

[30] AGOA, §125(a)(4).

[31] AGOA, §125(b).

[32] USAID, "U.S. Announces New African Trade Capacity Building Initiative at AGOA Forum," press release, June 9, 2011, http://www.usaid.gov/news-information/press-releases/us-announces-new-african-trade-capacity-building-initiative-agoa.

[33] For example, see Hearing Testimony by Earl W. Gast, U.S. Congress, Senate Committee on Foreign Relations, Subcommittee on African Affairs, *Economic Statecraft: Embracing Africa's Market Potential*, 112th Cong., 2nd sess., June 28, 2012, S.Hrg. 112-604 (Washington: GPO, 2012), p. 10.

[34] Each of the three regional Trade Hubs has its own website with information on its activities. For more information see West Africa, http://www.watradehub.com/aboutus; East Africa, http://www.competeafrica.org/; and South Africa, http://www.satradehub.org/.

[35] CRS Report IN10015, *Trade Africa Initiative*, by Nicolas Cook and Brock R. Williams.

[36] AGOA and GSP overlap in their product coverage so this discussion considers them jointly. Trade data in this section come from the U.S. International Trade Commission's dataweb, http://dataweb.usitc.gov/, and http://dataweb.usitc.gov/africa/trade_data.asp.

[37] Though only 39% of non-oil imports entered the United States under AGOA or GSP, nearly 90% of non-oil imports entered duty-free, because a large portion of products face no U.S. import tariff.

[38] Unless otherwise specified, energy-related products refers to HTS chapter 27.

[39] Sarah Kent, "Nigeria Bearing Brunt of U.S. Shale-Oil Boom," *The Wall Street Journal*, March 6, 2013.

[40] Central Bank of Lesotho, *Africa Growth and Opportunities Act (AGOA): Economic Impact and Future Prospects*, CBL Economic Review No. 131, June 2011, p. 3.

[41] Garth Frazer and Johannes Van Biesebroeck, "Trade Growth under the African Growth and Opportunity Act," *The Review of Economics and Statistics*, vol. 92, no. 1 (February 2010).

[42] Niall Condon and Matthew Stern, *The Effectiveness of African Growth and Opportunity Act (AGOA) in Increasing Trade from Least Developed Countries*, EPPI-Centre, Social Research Unit, Institute of Education, University of London, March 2011.

[43] Lawrence Edwards and Robert Z. Lawrence, *AGOA Rules: The Intended and Unintended Consequences of Special Fabric Provisions*, National Bureau of Economic Research, Working Paper 16623, December 2010.

[44] McKinsey Global Institute, *Lions on the Move: The Progress and Potential of African Economies*, June 2010, p. 22.

[45] The White House, "Remarks by President Obama at Business Leaders Forum," press release, July 1, 2013, http://www.whitehouse.gov/the-press-office/2013/07/01/remarks-president-obama-business-leaders-forum.

[46] USTR, "Remarks by United States Trade Representative Michael Froman to the AGOA Forum in Addis Ababa, Ethiopia on "The Future of U.S.-African Trade and Economic Cooperation," press release, August 12, 2013, http://www.ustr.gov/Froman-AGOA-Forum-on-The-Future-of-US-Africa-Trade-and-Economic-Cooperation.

[47] Testimony and submissions for the hearing can be found through the USITC's website or at http://agoa.info/downloads/hearings.html.

[48] http://www.usitc.gov/publications/332/pub4461.pdf.

[49] http://foreignaffairs.house.gov/press-release/bipartisan-congressional-leaders-push-increase-effectiveness-agoa-landmark-legislation.

[50] http://allafrica.com/download/resource/main/main/idatcs/00070593:d8333db143ebe828b7b54f7847dc5fb8.pdf.

[51] "Punke Hopeful on Trade Facilitation; Says U.S. to Press India at G20," *Inside U.S. Trade*, July 17, 2014.

[52] The Corporate Council on Africa, *Promoting Shared Interests: Policy Recommendations on Africa for the Second Term of the Obama Administration*, April 2013, p. 18.

[53] Africa's trade with itself accounts for only 11% of its total trade, compared with 50% in developing Asia and 70% in Europe. United Nations Conference on Trade and Development, *Intra-African Trade: Unlocking Private Sector Dynamism*, Economic Development in Africa Report 2013, July 2013.

[54] Brookings Africa Growth Initiative, *Accelerating Growth through Improved Intra-African Trade*, January 2012, p. 2.

[55] The Administration recently announced the Trade Africa initiative, which centers on a new trade and investment partnership with the East African Community (EAC). This may eventually include a bilateral investment treaty (BIT) and a trade facilitation agreement with the EAC. http://www.whitehouse.gov/the-press-office/2013/07/01/fact-sheet-trade-africa.

[56] GSP already includes language related to such occurrences, declaring a country ineligible if it "affords preferential treatment to the products of a developed country, other than the United States, which has, or is likely to have, a significant adverse effect on United States commerce." 19 U.S.C. §2462(b)(2)(C).

[57] U.S. Government Accountability Office, *The United States Provides Wide-ranging Trade Capacity Building Assistance, but Better Reporting and Evaluation Are Needed*, GAO-11-727, 2011, http://www.gao.gov/products/GAO-11-727.

[58] GAO, *Options for Congressional Consideration to Improve U.S. Trade Preference Programs*, Prepared Statement for Hearing, GAO-10-262T, November 2009, p. 4.

[59] Kimberly Ann Elliott, *Why Is Opening the U.S. Market to Poor Countries So Hard?*, Center for Global Development, January 2012.

[60] Calculated duties according to U.S. ITC tariff and trade dataweb.

[61] Brookings and United Nations Economic Commission for Africa, *The African Growth and Opportunity Act: An Empirical Analysis of the Possibilities Post-2015*, July 2013, p. 17.

[62] Antoine Bouet et al., *The Costs and Benefits of Duty-Free, Quota-Free Market Access for Poor Countries: Who and What Matters*, Center for Global Development, Working Paper 206, March 2010.

[63] Letter from Kimberly Elliott, Center for Global Development, to Michael Froman, USTR, June 24, 2013, http://www.cgdev.org/publication/supporting-multilateralism-and-development-us-trade-policy-duty-free-quota-free-market.

In: The African Growth and Opportunity Act
Editor: Carman Hayes

ISBN: 978-1-63463-068-9
© 2014 Nova Science Publishers, Inc.

Chapter 2

AGOA: TRADE AND INVESTMENT PERFORMANCE OVERVIEW[*]

United States International Trade Commission

ABSTRACT

- This report describes, reviews, and analyzes the trade and investment performance of beneficiary countries under the African Growth and Opportunity Act (AGOA) from 2000 to 2013. It also examines potential products for export to the United States or for integration into regional and global supply chains and examines changes in the business and investment climate in sub-Saharan Africa (SSA), as well as reciprocal trade agreements between SSA and non-SSA partners and the relationship of these agreements to the objectives of AGOA.
- The Commission found that U.S. imports from AGOA countries are dominated by imports entering under AGOA, and that these imports accounted for about 70 percent of all imports from AGOA countries during 2008–13. On average, crude petroleum accounted for almost 90 percent of these imports throughout the period. Excluding crude petroleum, U.S. imports under AGOA are concentrated in three sectors—transportation equipment (primarily passenger motor vehicles from South Africa), refined petroleum products, and apparel. These products accounted for 89 percent of U.S. non-crude petroleum imports under AGOA in 2013.
- The report's findings suggest that SSA participates in global supply chains (GSCs) primarily in supplying raw materials and primary inputs because of its abundant natural resources, including land, metals, and minerals. SSA involvement in manufacturing and other value-added production activities is generally limited, consisting of semiprocessed items or items with preferential access to third-country markets. Countries in SSA generally have little participation in downstream GSC activities because of weaknesses in production capacity, infrastructure and services, business environment, trade and investment policies, and industry institutionalization (private and public sector linkages and inter-industry coordination).

---

[*] This is an edited, reformatted and augmented version of USITC Publication Number 4461 (Investigation Number 332-542), issued April 2014.

- The Commission found, however, that several SSA countries are using regional integration, export diversification, and product value addition to implement economic development strategies. In particular, Burundi, Ethiopia, and Zambia are developing national strategies to increase export opportunities under AGOA. Supply-side constraints are the main obstacles to increasing and diversifying AGOA exports.
- The report's findings suggest that AGOA's impact on foreign direct investment (FDI) has been strongest in the apparel industry. Overall, the program's trade benefits and eligibility criteria appear to have motivated AGOA beneficiary countries to improve their business and investment climates. AGOA has had a positive impact on FDI inflows, particularly in the textile and apparel sector in Kenya, Lesotho, Mauritius, Swaziland, and Botswana, and also in South Africa's automotive industry. Some studies, however, suggest that reciprocal trade agreements may have certain advantages over unilateral trade preference programs such as AGOA.

ACRONYMS

Acronyms	Term
ACP	African, Caribbean, and Pacific
AGOA	African Growth and Opportunity Act
APHIS	Animal and Plant Health Inspection Service, U.S. Department of Agriculture
ATC	Agreement on Textiles and Clothing, World Trade Organization
AVE	ad valorem equivalent
BEA	Bureau of Economic Analysis, U.S. Department of Commerce
BIT	bilateral investment treaty
CAFTA-DR	Dominican Republic-Central America-United States Free Trade Agreement
CAGR	compound annual growth rate
CEMAC	Economic and Monetary Community of Central Africa
CES	constant elasticity of substitution
CGE	computable general equilibrium
CN	combined nomenclature
COCOBOD	Ghana Cocoa Board
COMESA	Common Market for Eastern and Southern Africa
CRIG	Cocoa Research Institute of Ghana
DFQF	duty-free/quota-free
DRC	domestic resource cost
DTC	Diamond Trading Company
EAC	East African Community
EBA	Everything But Arms (EU trade preference program)
EC	European Community
ECOWAS	Economic Community of West African States

EFTA	European Free Trade Association
EIU	Economist Intelligence Unit
EPA	economic partnership agreement
EPZ	Export Processing Zone
ESA	Eastern and Southern Africa
EU	European Union
FDI	foreign direct investment
FGI	Fung Global Institute
FMD	foot and mouth disease
FTA	free trade agreement
GAFTA	Greater Arab Free Trade Area
GCI	Global Competitiveness Index
GDP	gross domestic product
GSC	global supply chain
GSP	Generalized System of Preferences
GVC	global value chain
HS	Harmonized System (international tariff nomenclature)
IMF	International Monetary Fund
LAC	Latin America and the Caribbean
LDBC	lesser-developed beneficiary country (under AGOA)
LDBDC	less-developed beneficiary developing country (under GSP)
LDC	least-developed country
LPI	Logistics Performance Index
M&A	mergers and acquisitions
Mercosur	South American Common Market
MFA	Multi-Fiber Arrangement
MFN	most favored nation
MNC	multinational company
MRA	meta-regression analysis
NAFTA	North American Free Trade Agreement
NTR	normal trade relations
NTU	Nanyang Technological University
OECD	Organisation for Economic Co-operation and Development
OPEC	Organization of Petroleum Exporting Countries
PAFTA	Pan-Arab Free Trade Area
PPML	Pseudo-Poisson Maximum Likelihood
R&D	research and development
RCA	revealed comparative advantage
ROOs	rules of origin
RSC	regional supply chain
SACU	Southern African Customs Union
SADC	South African Development Community

SOE	state-owned enterprise
SPS	sanitary and phytosanitary
SSA	sub-Saharan Africa
TBTs	technical barriers to trade
TDCA	European Community-South Africa Trade Development and Cooperation Agreement
TRQ	Tariff-rate quota
UN	United Nations
UNCTAD	UN Conference on Trade and Development
UNECA	UN Economic Commission for Africa
UNIDO	UN Industrial Development Organization

COUNTRY ASSOCIATIONS

Common Market for Eastern and Southern Africa (COMESA)

Burundi, Comoros, Democratic Republic of the Congo, Djibouti, Egypt, Eritrea, Ethiopia, Kenya, Libya, Madagascar, Malawi, Mauritius, Rwanda, Seychelles, Sudan, Swaziland, Uganda, Zambia, Zimbabwe

East African Community (EAC)

Burundi, Kenya, Rwanda, Tanzania, Uganda

Economic and Monetary Community of Central Africa (CEMAC)

Cameroon, Central African Republic, Chad, Equatorial Guinea, Gabon, Republic of the Congo

Economic Community of West African States (ECOWAS)

Benin, Burkina Faso, Cabo Verde, Côte d'Ivoire, The Gambia, Ghana, Guinea, Guinea-Bissau, Liberia, Mali, Niger, Nigeria, Senegal, Sierra Leone, Togo

European Free Trade Association (EFTA)

Iceland, Liechtenstein, Norway, Switzerland

European Union (EU)

Austria, Belgium, Bulgaria, Croatia, Cyprus, Czech Republic, Denmark, Estonia, Finland, France, Germany, Greece, Hungary, Ireland, Italy, Latvia, Lithuania, Luxembourg, Malta, Netherlands, Poland, Portugal, Romania, Slovakia, Slovenia, Spain, Sweden, United Kingdom

Greater Arab Free Trade Area (GAFTA)

Bahrain, Egypt, Iraq, Jordan, Kuwait, Lebanon, Libya, Morocco, Oman, Palestine, Qatar, Saudi Arabia, Sudan, Syria, Tunisia, United Arab Emirates, Yemen

North American Free Trade Agreement (NAFTA)

Canada, Mexico, United States

Pan-Arab Free Trade Area (PAFTA)

Bahrain, Egypt, Iraq, Jordan, Kuwait, Lebanon, Libya, Madagascar, Morocco, Oman, Palestinian Authority, Qatar, Saudi Arabia, Sudan, Syria, Tunisia, United Arab Emirates, Yemen

South American Common Market

Argentina, Brazil, Paraguay, Uruguay, Venezuela

Southern African Customs Union (SACU)

Botswana, Lesotho, Namibia, South Africa, Swaziland

Southern African Development Community (SADC)

Angola, Botswana, Democratic Republic of the Congo, Lesotho, Madagascar, Malawi, Mauritius, Mozambique, Namibia, Seychelles, South Africa, Swaziland, Tanzania, Zambia, Zimbabwe

Sub-Saharan Africa.

EXECUTIVE SUMMARY

Introduction

The African Growth and Opportunity Act (AGOA) was signed into law on May 18, 2000, by President Clinton as part of the Trade and Development Act of 2000.[1] In a statement of policy in the Act, Congress expressed support for, inter alia, "encouraging increased trade and investment between the United States and sub-Saharan Africa," "reducing tariff and nontariff barriers and other obstacles to sub-Saharan African and United States trade," and "expanding United States assistance to sub-Saharan Africa's regional integration efforts."[2] The statement of policy also expressed support for negotiating reciprocal and mutually beneficial trade agreements, strengthening and expanding the private sector, and facilitating the development of civil societies and political freedom.[3] Authority to provide the principal trade preferences under AGOA is currently in effect through September 30, 2015.

Noting that the Administration is working with its partners in the region and Congress to renew and potentially modify AGOA, the United States Trade Representative (USTR), in a letter received on October 17, 2013, requested that the U.S. International Trade Commission (Commission or USITC) conduct four investigations and provide four reports on AGOA.[4] The present report focuses on AGOA's trade performance, utilization, and competitiveness factors; AGOA's effects on the business and investment climate in sub-Saharan Africa (SSA); and current or potential reciprocal trade agreements between SSA and non-SSA partners, as well as the relationship of these agreements to the objectives of AGOA. The USTR requested that the report cover the period 2000 through 2013.

More specifically, the USTR asked for the USITC's report to:

- Provide a review of the literature on the AGOA preference program, in terms of expanding and diversifying the exports of AGOA beneficiary countries to the United States, compared to preference programs offered by third parties such as the EU;
- Identify the non-crude petroleum sectors (i.e., manufacturing and agricultural) in AGOA beneficiary countries in which exports to the United States, under AGOA and under the U.S. Generalized System of Preferences program, have increased the most, in absolute terms, since 2000, and identify the key factors behind this growth;
- Describe the main factors affecting AGOA trade in the principal non-crude petroleum products that AGOA beneficiary countries export and that the United States principally imports from non-sub-Saharan African sources;
- Based on a review of literature, identify products with potential for integration into regional or global supply chains, and export potential to the United States under AGOA, as well as factors that affect AGOA beneficiary countries' competitiveness in these sectors;
- Identify and describe changes, if any, in the business and investment climates in sub-Saharan African countries since 2000, including removal of barriers to domestic and foreign investment;
- Describe U.S. goods and services-related investment trends in sub-Saharan African countries since 2000 and compare these trends with investments by other countries in sub-Saharan African countries, including investments by the EU, China, Brazil, and India. Identify any links between these investment trends and the AGOA program;
- Provide a list of reciprocal trade agreements that sub-Saharan African countries have completed or are under negotiation. For the reciprocal trade agreements that have entered into force and, to the extent information is available in the case of those that are pending or under negotiation, provide a brief description of areas covered or likely to be covered under the agreements; identify U.S. sectors/products impacted or potentially impacted, including any tariff differentials; and
- Provide examples of developing countries that have moved from unilateral trade preferences to reciprocal trade agreements, and any effects of the change for the developing country in terms of expansion and diversification of trade.

Major Findings and Observations

U.S. Imports from AGOA Beneficiary Countries

U.S. Imports from AGOA Countries Are Dominated by Imports Entering under AGOA

U.S. imports under AGOA accounted for about 70 percent of all imports from AGOA countries during 2008–13. Between 2001 and 2013, U.S. imports under AGOA increased by about 10 percent per year, from $7.6 billion to $24.8 billion. On average, crude petroleum accounted for almost 90 percent of U.S. imports under AGOA during 2001–13, with a sharp decline in 2009 because of the U.S. recession and volatility in the trend since then (figure ES.1). U.S. imports under AGOA of products other than crude petroleum increased steadily between 2001 and 2008, declined in 2009 due to the recession, and gradually recovered during 2010–13 (figure ES.2).

Excluding Crude Petroleum, U.S. Imports under AGOA Are Concentrated in Three Sectors

Three sectors—transportation equipment, refined petroleum products, and apparel—accounted for 89 percent of U.S. non-crude-petroleum imports under AGOA in 2013. The imports of transportation equipment primarily consisted of passenger motor vehicles from South Africa. About 88 percent of U.S. imports of refined petroleum products, such as distillate and residual fuel oils, were supplied by Nigeria and Angola. Major apparel suppliers in 2013 were Lesotho, Kenya, and Mauritius. Although apparel continues to be an important U.S. import under AGOA, imports have declined gradually as a share of all U.S. AGOA imports since the expiration of the World Trade Organization (WTO) Agreement on Textiles and Clothing in 2005. In 2005–13, the share of apparel imports decreased sharply, falling from 41 percent of U.S. non-crude-petroleum imports under AGOA in 2005 to 19 percent in 2013. Two countries— South Africa and Nigeria—represented 73 percent of all U.S. non-crude-petroleum imports under AGOA in 2013.

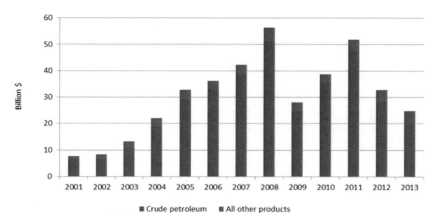

Source: USITC DataWeb/USDOC (accessed February 18, 2014).
Note: The data in this figure are based on the list of AGOA-eligible countries, which varies by year. For a complete list of AGOA- eligible countries by year, see table 1.1.

Figure ES.1. U.S. imports under AGOA, 2001–13.

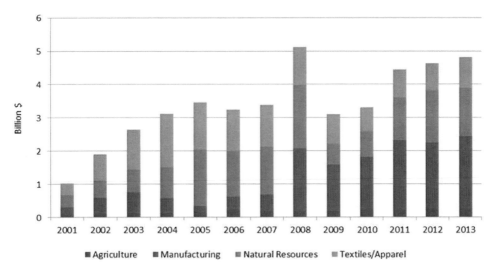

Source: USITC DataWeb/USDOC (accessed February 18, 2014).
Note: The data in this figure are based on the list of AGOA-eligible countries, which varies by year. For a complete list of AGOA- eligible countries by year, see table 1.1. "Agriculture" includes all agricultural products; "manufacturing" includes electronics, machinery, transportation equipment, chemicals, miscellaneous manufacturing, and special provisions items; "natural resources" includes energy products except crude petroleum, minerals and metals, and forest products; and "textiles/apparel" includes textiles, apparel, and footwear.

Figure ES.2. U.S. imports under AGOA, excluding crude petroleum, 2001–13.

Potential for SSA Integration into Regional and Global Supply Chains

SSA Countries' Participation in Global Supply Chains Can Have a Positive Effect on Their Economies

Regional and global supply chains are defined as cross-country production networks between multiple firms that supply interlinked economic activities necessary to bring a product from conception to consumption. Global supply chains (GSCs) and regional supply chains (RSCs) have spread rapidly over the past 30 years as technological advances in communications and transportation have enabled firms to take advantage of international cost differences. Integration into these chains by SSA countries can have a positive effect on their economic development by increasing the amount of value added locally, increasing employment and productivity, and raising per capita incomes.

Most SSA Participation in GSCs Is in Upstream Activities, Particularly Supplying Raw Materials and Primary Inputs

One of SSA's strongest competitive advantages is its abundant natural resources, including land, metals, and minerals. As a result, SSA participates in GSCs chiefly by supplying raw materials and primary inputs. SSA involvement in manufacturing, and especially GSC manufacturing, is generally limited. Manufacturing in SSA is usually of semiprocessed items and/or of items that have preferential access to third-country markets— e.g., via AGOA for the U.S. market and via Everything But Arms (EBA) for the EU.

A Number of Factors Affect the Potential Of SSA Countries to Participate in Global and Regional Supply Chains

The Organisation for Economic Co-operation and Development (OECD) identified five broad categories of factors that affect SSA participation in GSCs and RSCs: production capacity, infrastructure and services, business environment, trade and investment policy, and industry institutionalization (private and public sector coordination and inter-industry linkages). Countries with low levels of participation in downstream GSC/RSC activities generally have weaknesses in all five areas, although the importance of these factors for developing countries varies by sector.

A Small Number of Products Accounted for Most of the Growth in U.S. Imports from AGOA Beneficiary Countries under AGOA and GSP Provisions

The top 10 growth leaders among non-crude-petroleum products imported under AGOA and GSP during 2000–2013 accounted for over 90 percent of the positive growth in value over the period (table ES.1). The leading product group—motor vehicles—supplied about one-third of the growth and totaled $2.1 billion in 2013. Refined petroleum products followed, accounting for one-quarter of the growth and totaling $1.3 billion in 2013. Other major growth products, in descending order, were apparel; ferroalloys; aluminum mill products; cocoa, chocolate, and confectionery; miscellaneous inorganic chemicals; certain organic chemicals; edible nuts; and citrus fruit.

Table ES.1 Top ten U.S. imports from AGOA-eligible countries under AGOA/GSP (excluding crude petroleum) by leading growth product, 2000 and 2013

Product	2000	2013	Absolute growth 2000–2013
	Million $		
Motor vehicles	0.0	2,115.7	2,115.7
Refined petroleum products	1.4	1,297.2	1,295.8
Apparel	0.7	907.4	906.7
Ferroalloys	171.7	530.4	358.7
Aluminum mill products	56.6	189.3	132.7
Cocoa, chocolate, and confectionery	4.4	122.8	118.4
Miscellaneous inorganic chemicals	79.3	175.9	96.6
Certain organic chemicals	17.4	103.1	85.7
Edible nuts	0.5	62.3	61.8
Citrus fruit	0.0	61.7	61.7
All other	350.0	617.1	267.1
Total	682.1	6,182.9	5,500.8

Source: USITC DataWeb/USDOC (accessed February 18, 2014).

Despite Generally Low Rates of Participation in GSC/RSC Downstream Activities, Certain SSA Countries Are Moving to Higher Value-Added Production

SSA countries have participated in GSCs and RSCs in agriculture and agroprocessing (e.g., vegetables and vegetable agroprocessing in Kenya, floriculture in Uganda and Kenya, and cocoa production and processing in Ghana); extractive industries (e.g., petroleum activities in Nigeria and diamonds processing in Botswana); and manufacturing (e.g., automobile production in South Africa and apparel production in several countries). These successes may illuminate the trade policy and infrastructure changes SSA economies will need to make in order to increase their participation in higher-value added production and to become more integrated into GSCs. A review of literature suggests that SSA sectors with the greatest potential to further integrate into RSCs and GSCs are (1) agricultural products and foodstuffs, (2) leather and leather products, (3) textiles and apparel, and (4) extractive natural resource products, such as ferrous, petrochemicals, and platinum group metals.

SSA Export Potential to the United States

Sources Identified Primarily Agricultural Products, Handcrafts and Woodcrafts, and Leather and Leather Products As Potential Exports from AGOA Countries to the United States

Although a wide range of products with export potential from AGOA countries to the United States were identified, most fall into the broad categories of agricultural products, handcrafts and woodcrafts, and leather and leather products (table ES.2). These products were identified in AGOA country national development strategies, previous Commission reports, and the economic literature.

Products with Export Potential for AGOA Countries Benefit from Factors That Make Them Competitive in International Markets

Several factors support production and make certain sectors in AGOA countries internationally competitive. For example, agricultural products with potential for export growth to the United States take advantage of favorable climates, fertile soils, abundant and low-cost labor, policies and programs that support the sector, and the development of farmer cooperatives and other organizations.

In the handcraft and woodcraft sector, many SSA countries benefit from availability of abundant and distinctive raw materials (e.g., bamboo and clay), the prevalence of an artistic and creative culture, and supportive government policies. In the leather and leather products sector, certain AGOA countries benefit from an abundance of livestock herds, good climate and soil conditions that contribute to quality livestock and skins, and strong government support for the sector.

Despite These Advantages, AGOA Countries Face Many Impediments to Export Growth

Many factors weaken AGOA countries' ability to compete in global markets, including limited skilled labor, low levels of technological innovation, lack of scale economies, and high-cost and unreliable energy. Weak transportation infrastructure (especially poor rural roads and inefficient port facilities), and burdensome customs procedures, also harm the cost competitiveness of many potentially exportable products from SSA. Challenges meeting foreign standards restrict trade as well, especially the difficulties SSA agricultural producers have in complying with foreign sanitary and phytosanitary (SPS) requirements.

Table ES.2. Sectors with export potential in selected SSA countries

Country	Products/sectors	Source
Ethiopia	Textiles and apparel, leather products and footwear, home furnishings, cut flowers	Ethiopia Growth and Transformation Plan, 2010/11–14/15; economic literature
Ghana[a]	Basketry and related straw products, woodcraft and furniture, cashew nuts, shea nuts and shea butter	USAID West Africa study, 2011
Malawi	Oilseed products, sugar cane products, agroprocessing, light manufacturing	Malawi National Export Strategy, 2013–18
Mauritius	Jewelry, agroprocessing and seafood processing, light manufacturing, plastics, metal-based products, leather, handbags, fashion accessories	Mauritius National Export Strategy, 2013
Mozambique	Food and industrial crops, horticulture, oilseeds, leather and leather products, wood products, jewelry, cashews, grapefruit, rice, potatoes, paprika, and bananas	Mozambique Country Assistance Strategy, 2011–15; World Bank report, 2010
Rwanda	Horticulture, handcrafts, leather and leather products	Rwanda National Export Strategy, 2011
Senegal	Cotton, horticulture, cashews, mangoes, dairy products, bananas, woven textiles, fisheries, hibiscus tea, millet	World Bank report, 2010
Uganda[b]	Horticulture, dairy products, cereals, pulses, oilseeds, ingredients for pharmaceuticals and cosmetic industries, handcrafts, toys, jewelry, leather products, woodcrafts	Uganda National Export Strategy, 2008–12
West Africa	Cashews, peanuts, and shea nuts and shea butter	ECOWAS, 2010
SSA-wide	Bananas, cereal flours, corn, honey, coffee, cocoa, cotton, fruits, vegetables, cut flowers, cashews, sesame, shrimp and prawns, logs, hardwood lumber and wood products, petroleum products, liquefied natural gas, electricity, light industrial products, leather products, processed wood products, chemicals, aluminum, gold, copper, gemstones, cocoa butter and paste, prepared and preserved fish, acyclic alcohols, flat-rolled steel, liquefied natural gas, apparel, unwrought aluminum, wood veneer, shea butter, spices, tropical fruit, footwear, natural rubber, processed diamonds, textiles, wood furniture, peanuts	USITC, 2005; USITC, 2007; USITC, 2008; International Food and Agricultural Policy Council, 2010

Notes: [a] These sectors have been identified for West Africa more generally, including Burkina Faso and Mali.
[b] Exports from these sectors are targeted mainly to regional markets, such as countries within the EAC.

There Is a Range of Products That the United States Imports Principally from Non-SSA Countries, Even Though These Products Are Also Produced—and Exported Elsewhere—by SSA Countries

Sectors where AGOA exports and U.S. imports are both large, yet there is little bilateral trade, may have export potential to the United States under AGOA. These are sectors where AGOA countries are viewed as globally competitive by third countries, as well as where there is strong import demand in the United States. Major product categories that met these criteria in 2012 were fresh, chilled, and frozen fish, horticultural products (including cut flowers, bananas, and tropical fruit), sugar, certain apparel (e.g., T-shirts and sweaters), and gold.

Multiple Factors Explain the Limited Bilateral Trade Between AGOA Countries and the United States for Certain Products

In many cases, higher transport costs to the U.S. market relative to other markets are too much to overcome, especially in light of the distance and the lack of efficient trade linkages to the U.S. market from SSA. Also, SSA exports are often uncompetitive in the U.S. market without tariff preferences. Even where SSA exports have such preferences, the margin of the preferences is shrinking or disappearing as more countries supplying the U.S. market receive duty-free access through reciprocal trade agreements. In some cases, AGOA exporters are precluded from claiming preferences because of an inability to meet AGOA rules of origin or because of volume restrictions for certain products under the program. Other factors, such as historic commercial ties to other markets, difficulties meeting U.S. SPS requirements, and rapidly rising demand for raw materials in other markets, particularly China, coupled with foreign direct investment in SSA in extractive industries, also limit exports from AGOA countries to the United States.

Business Climate and Investment Trends in SSA

The Business and Investment Climate in SSA Has Improved Noticeably Since 2000, but Progress Has Been Uneven among Countries

The improved business and investment climate since 2000 can be attributed to better macroeconomic conditions, sounder governance, a less burdensome regulatory environment, and a more open trade and investment regime overall. At the same time, SSA remains a highly challenging place to do business, especially when compared with other emerging economies. Issues that continue to discourage investment in SSA countries include poor investor protection, slow removal of investment barriers, and insufficient infrastructure. Of the 49 SSA countries Rwanda, Sierra Leone, and Burundi (AGOA beneficiary countries) are among the best performers, making improvements across most measures. South Sudan and Djibouti (also AGOA beneficiaries) as well as Somalia and Eritrea (which have never been AGOA beneficiaries), are among the worst performers.

South Africa and Nigeria Are by Far the Largest Destinations for Foreign Direct Investment (FDI) in SSA

In 2012, South Africa and Nigeria accounted for more than half of all FDI in SSA (figure ES.3). FDI in South Africa is split roughly evenly between mining, manufacturing, and services, particularly financial services. The largest share of FDI inflows to Nigeria likely goes to the petroleum sector, although precise data are not available. The SSA countries experiencing the fastest FDI growth over 2000–2012 were Somalia, Comoros, Niger, and the Central African Republic, all starting from a very low base. Larger SSA economies experiencing particularly fast FDI growth in recent years included the Democratic Republic of the Congo, Mozambique, and Ghana. Important industry destinations for FDI in recent years include natural resources (petroleum and mineral extraction and downstream processing), certain manufacturing industries (textiles and apparel, footwear, automotive, and consumer products), infrastructure, and certain services (financial services and telecommunications).

The EU Is the Largest Source of FDI in SSA, Followed by the United States

The EU countries with the most greenfield FDI projects in SSA were the United Kingdom, Germany, France, and Portugal. FDI inflows from the EU as a whole accounted for almost two- thirds of total SSA FDI during 2003–07, but dropped to one-half in 2008–10. In contrast, the average U.S. share of FDI inflows increased from 7 percent (2003–07) to 12 percent of the total (2008–10); the share of Chinese inflows increased from 3 percent to 8 percent; and inflows from other sources (including India, Japan, Canada, the United Arab Emirates, Australia, Brazil, and other SSA countries) increased from 16 percent to 30 percent for the same periods. The largest SSA investors in other SSA countries were South Africa and Kenya.

The Number of New FDI Projects in SSA Countries in the Service Sector Is on the Rise

In the past, much of the FDI in SSA was focused on natural resource extraction, including mining, petroleum and natural gas extraction, and renewable energy. This pattern is changing, however: during 2007–12 the number of new FDI projects focused on resources declined, while the number of projects in the services and manufacturing sectors increased. Natural resources contributed to less than one-third of Africa's GDP growth between 2000 and 2012, with the service sector growing particularly fast as a share of GDP.

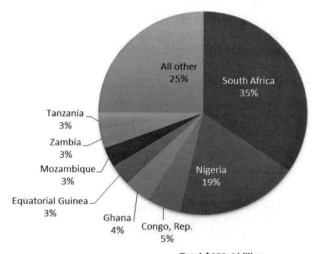

Source: UNCTAD, UNCTADStat database (accessed October 29, 2013).

Figure ES.3. Cumulative FDI position in destination SSA countries, 2012.

AGOA's Impact on FDI Has Been Strongest in the Apparel Industry

Although it is difficult to quantify AGOA's direct and indirect effects on FDI trends, the program's trade benefits and eligibility criteria appear to have motivated SSA countries, particularly AGOA beneficiary countries, to improve their business and investment climates. Moreover, AGOA has had a positive impact on FDI inflows, particularly in the textile and apparel sector in Kenya, Lesotho, Mauritius, Swaziland, and Botswana, and also in South Africa's automotive industry. However, observers have noted that the uncertainties associated with the short-term renewals of the program, and the changing eligibility of particular AGOA beneficiary countries, have limited AGOA's impact in attracting new investment to SSA.

SSA Reciprocal Trade Agreements

Reciprocal Trade Agreements Differ in Many Ways from Unilateral Trade Preference Programs

Unilateral trade preference programs imply a one-way flow of benefits, while reciprocal trade agreements generally involve a negotiated accord between countries in which each incurs benefits and obligations, generally for an indefinite period of time. In addition, the scope of reciprocal agreements is generally broader, addressing not only tariff reductions but also nontariff measures (NTMs) and other conditions relating to trade in goods and services such as quotas, customs procedures, and administrative policies. Unilateral trade preferences are generally temporary and can be removed with little warning, while reciprocal agreements establish more permanent trading rules, which are gradually codified into the laws of the member countries. According to the economic literature, unilateral programs tend to provide only modest benefits to beneficiaries because NTMs (such as administrative compliance costs and the transaction costs associated with rules of origin) are mostly not addressed. Further, dozens of bilateral, regional, and multilateral trade agreements have been signed over the last 20 years, lowering tariffs between trading partners and reducing the tariff advantages that beneficiary countries receive under unilateral preference programs. On the other hand, many reciprocal trade agreements encourage economic restructuring that ultimately promotes a more efficient use of resources and more permanent trading relationships.

The North American Free Trade Agreement (NAFTA) and U.S. Free Trade Agreements with Chile and Morocco Highlight Some Advantages of Reciprocal Agreements over Unilateral Ones

Mexico's participation in NAFTA negotiations can be viewed as the means chosen by the Mexican government to anchor policy commitments it had already made, both at home and abroad. In addition, NAFTA membership encouraged the government to make structural reforms in the economy. Mexico's experience with NAFTA implies that SSA countries, too, can use reciprocal trade agreements as a stimulus to enact economic reforms and compete globally. Such reforms may have many impacts, but one of the most important is to provide investors with the economic certainty needed to increase FDI. Chile's 2004 free trade agreement (FTA) with the United States had many such reforms, including lowered tariffs, codified rules for FDI, new protections for investors, and forums to address certain NTMs. Both average annual FDI inflows into Chile as well as exports more than doubled in the years following the implementation of the FTA. Morocco is another case in point: since it signed an FTA with the United States in 2004, both U.S. exports to Morocco and FDI in Morocco have increased significantly and Morocco's exports to the United States have more than doubled. These trends are likely linked to trade and investment rules imbedded in the agreement. Morocco is also the first country in North Africa to conclude a bilateral trade facilitation agreement with the United States, building on the FTA. Trade facilitation agreements between nations and FDI linkages can be enhanced with reciprocal trade agreements in effect.

SSA Countries, Often As Regional Blocs, Have Pursued Reciprocal Trade Agreements with Non-SSA Partners—Many with Asymmetrical Provisions

An important aspect of many of these trade agreements is regional integration of SSA countries. For example, the economic partnership agreements (EPAs) between the European Commission and African states and regions have African regional integration as an explicit goal. Similarly, the FTA between the European Free Trade Association (EFTA), a small European bloc, and the Southern African Customs Union (SACU) incorporates bilateral agricultural arrangements concluded with three of the EFTA states separately as well as the SACU states collectively. These agreements generally allow SSA partners to reduce tariffs over a longer period of time than the non-SSA partners. For example, under the EFTA-SACU FTA, EFTA tariff reductions or elimination took place immediately on the date of entry into force (in May 2008), while SACU tariff reductions or elimination will be complete by January 2015. Similarly, EPAs between the EU and SSA countries specify that EU tariff reductions are immediate and that African countries' reductions are to be phased in over many years—as many as 25 years for some products and countries.

Summary of the Economic Literature on AGOA Trade Performance

The Findings of Studies Estimating AGOA's Impact on Exports from SSA Vary, Ranging from Broad Positive Effects to No Effect, or to Positive Effects Only in Certain Sectors

Due to differences in study methodology, time periods assessed, and level of product aggregation, studies assessing the effect of AGOA on total exports found either that AGOA had no effect or else that the effects, while positive, were generally small. Another set of studies that looked at AGOA's effect on exports by disaggregated product categories found that AGOA helped to increase SSA exports of some products, but not others. For example, numerous investigations concluded that AGOA led to increased beneficiary country exports of apparel, with many emphasizing that increased apparel exports were largely due to AGOA's rules of origin for apparel (particularly the third-country fabric provision), which are more liberal than those of many other U.S. preference programs.

The Literature on AGOA's Role in Export Diversification Supports the Hypothesis That for Nonenergy Exports, AGOA Was Modestly Successful in Generating New Product Export Flows

More than a decade after the program's implementation, most U.S. imports under AGOA continue to be energy products. However, the literature concludes that AGOA has helped to generate exports of new products in several nonenergy product categories, including apparel, agriculture, and manufactures (e.g., plastics and miscellaneous chemical products). Again, there is some evidence to suggest that the diversification of apparel exports is largely due to more liberal rules of origin. Although the number of nonenergy products exported has increased, many of these new exports occurred in product groups that represented only a small share of a country's total exports.

Studies Analyzing the Effects of Other Unilateral Trade Preference Programs on SSA Exports Had Mixed Results: Some Found Increased Exports, Some Found No Effect, and Some Found Effects Only for Certain Sectors

Most studies analyzing the effects of other unilateral trade preference programs on SSA exports have dealt with the effects of EU trade preferences. Again, because of differences in study methodology, time period assessed, and level of product aggregation, studies analyzing total exports had mixed results: some suggested that preferences increased exports, while others found that preferences had a negative relationship with exports. Studies analyzing more disaggregated trade flows generally concluded that EU preferences had a positive effect on developing country export flows, but these effects varied by country and product sector. With respect to export diversification, EU programs were found to have increased the number of products exported in some sectors, while leading to greater export concentration in others. Aside from EU preferences, one analysis of China's trade preference program found that the program likely generated higher SSA exports for only one product category—"other primary products." This includes beverages, tobacco, oils and fats, and mineral fuels.

Studies Comparing EU and U.S. Unilateral Preference Programs Found That EU Programs Were Generally More Effective at Increasing Beneficiary Country Exports; U.S. Programs, at Diversifying Beneficiary Country Exports

While comparative analyses concluded that both U.S. and EU trade preferences helped to increase beneficiary country export flows, in general EU preferences had a greater effect on the value of exports. At the same time, the trade-generating effects of preferences depended greatly on the sector and beneficiary country in question. U.S. preferences were found to be more effective at increasing SSA apparel exports than EU preferences, but EU preferences were more effective at increasing SSA agricultural exports. At the same time, U.S. preferences were found to be more likely overall to generate an export of a new product than EU preferences, and U.S. preferences were found to increase the probability of exporting new products in more sectors than EU preferences.

Although AGOA Has Helped Generate Additional SSA Exports in Some Sectors, the Literature Concluded That the Program Could Be Further Improved

The literature offered several recommendations on how AGOA could be improved, based largely on results of empirical investigations. These recommendations covered changes to the program itself, including making AGOA permanent, extending AGOA to offer full duty-free/quota-free access to the U.S. market, and further relaxing AGOA's rules of origin. Other recommendations involved further assistance that the United States could offer that would help beneficiaries better take advantage of AGOA preferences, such as providing greater trade facilitation assistance, offering more capacity-building to help beneficiaries better comply with SPS rules, and promoting U.S. foreign direct investment in Africa. Finally, the literature identifies actions that beneficiary countries could take on their own that would improve their ability to take advantage of AGOA preferences, including reducing tariffs on imports of intermediate goods, investments in transportation infrastructure, improved rule of law, and improved protection of intellectual property rights.

SECTION 1. INTRODUCTION

Purpose and Scope

The African Growth and Opportunity Act (AGOA) was signed into law on May 18, 2000, by President Clinton as part of the Trade and Development Act of 2000.[5] In a statement of policy in the Act, Congress expressed support for, inter alia, "encouraging increased trade and investment between the United States and sub-Saharan Africa," "reducing tariff and nontariff barriers and other obstacles to sub-Saharan African and United States trade," and "expanding United States assistance to sub-Saharan Africa's regional integration efforts."[6] The statement of policy also expressed support for negotiating reciprocal and mutually beneficial trade agreements, strengthening and expanding the private sector, and facilitating the development of civil societies and political freedom.[7] Authority to provide the principal trade preferences under AGOA is currently in effect through September 30, 2015.

Noting that the Administration is working with its partners in sub-Saharan Africa (SSA) and in Congress to renew and potentially modify AGOA, the United States Trade Representative (USTR), in a letter received on October 17, 2013, requested that the U.S. International Trade Commission (Commission or USITC) conduct four investigations and provide four reports concerning AGOA.[8] This report—the first listed of the four—focuses on AGOA's trade performance, utilization, and competitiveness factors; AGOA's effects on the business and investment climate in sub-Saharan Africa; and current or potential reciprocal trade agreements between SSA and non-SSA partners, along with the relationship of these agreements to the objectives of AGOA. The USTR requested that the report cover the period 2000 through 2013.[9]

More specifically, the USTR asked for the USITC's report to:

- Provide a review of the literature on the AGOA preference program, particularly studies exploring whether AGOA has succeeded in expanding and diversifying the exports of AGOA beneficiary countries to the United States, compared to preference programs offered by third parties such as the European Union (EU);
- Identify the non-crude petroleum sectors (i.e., manufacturing and agricultural) in AGOA beneficiary countries in which exports to the United States under AGOA and under the U.S. Generalized System of Preferences (GSP) program have increased the most, in absolute terms, since 2000, and identify the key factors behind this growth;
- Describe the main factors affecting AGOA trade in the principal non-crude petroleum products that AGOA beneficiary countries export and that the United States principally imports from non-SSA sources;
- Based on a literature review, identify products with potential for integration into regional or global supply chains and export potential to the United States under AGOA, as well as factors that affect AGOA beneficiary countries' competitiveness in these products;
- Identify and describe changes, if any, in the business and investment climates in SSA countries since 2000, including removal of barriers to domestic and foreign investment;

- Describe U.S. investment trends related to goods and services in SSA countries since 2000, and compare these trends with investments by other countries in SSA countries, including investments by the EU, China, Brazil, and India. Identify any links between these investment trends and the AGOA program;
- Provide a list of reciprocal trade agreements that SSA countries have completed or that are under negotiation. For the reciprocal trade agreements that have entered into force and, to the extent information is available, for those that are pending or under negotiation, provide a brief description of areas covered or likely to be covered under the agreements, and identify U.S. sectors/products impacted or potentially impacted, including those affected by any tariff differentials; and
- Provide examples of developing countries that have moved from unilateral trade preferences to reciprocal trade agreements, and any effects of the change for the developing country in terms of expansion and diversification of trade.

As requested by USTR, the report covers SSA countries, as defined in AGOA, and where applicable, those AGOA beneficiary countries that are designated as lesser-developed beneficiary countries (LDBCs).

Approach and Sources of Information

In response to USTR's request, the Commission based this report on an analysis of trade and investment data, a review of the relevant literature (including previous Commission reports on SSA countries and AGOA), and information obtained from industry sources through telephone interviews and local field interviews. In addition, the report includes information drawn from a public hearing held by the Commission on January 14, 2014,[10] and written submissions received in response to a notice published in the *Federal Register*.[11]

The trade data used in this report to examine the trends in exports from AGOA beneficiary countries came from official statistics of the U.S. Department of Commerce as well as from the Global Trade Atlas database. To describe investment trends in SSA countries, foreign direct investment (FDI) data were largely drawn from UNCTADStat, the interactive database of the United Nations Conference on Trade and Development (UNCTAD); Eurostat and other foreign- government data sources; databases maintained by the U.S. Bureau of Economic Analysis (BEA); the Financial Times' FDI Markets database; and the Bureau van Dijk's Zephyr database. Other sources of information for the report included academic literature and publications from U.S. and foreign governments; regional organizations in SSA countries, such as the Common Market for Eastern and Southern Africa (COMESA) and the African Development Bank; and international institutions, including the International Monetary Fund (IMF), the Organisation for Economic Co-operation and Development (OECD), the World Bank, the World Trade Organization (WTO), and United Nations agencies, such as UNCTAD, the United Nations Economic Commission for Africa (UNECA), and the United Nations Industrial Development Organization (UNIDO).

Organization of the Report

The remainder of this section summarizes the AGOA program and describes beneficiaries and trade benefits under the program. Section 2 analyzes U.S. imports from AGOA beneficiary countries, identifies U.S. imports under AGOA and the GSP that increased the most in absolute terms since 2000, and discusses the factors behind this growth. Section 3 broadly examines the potential for SSA products to integrate into regional and global supply chains, describes current examples of SSA participation in these supply chains, and highlights other products with potential for integrating into these supply chains. Section 4 explores the SSA products with the greatest potential for exports to the United States, and identifies and analyzes products that SSA countries export but that the United States imports from other sources. Section 5 describes the business climate and investment trends in SSA, while section 6 provides a list and brief description of reciprocal trade agreements that SSA countries have completed or that are under negotiation. Section 6 also gives examples of developing countries that have moved from unilateral trade preferences to reciprocal trade agreements. Finally, section 7 offers a review of economic literature on AGOA that seeks to assess the program's success in expanding and diversifying exports to the United States, compared to preference programs offered by third countries.

There are 8 appendixes to this report. Appendix A contains a copy of the request letter from USTR, and appendix B reproduces the *Federal Register* notice announcing the institution of these investigations. Appendix C has a copy of the hearing schedule, and appendix D contains a summary of the positions of interested parties. Appendices E through H include statistical and text tables and figures that are referenced throughout the report.

Summary of the AGOA Program

AGOA authorizes the President to (1) designate an SSA country as a beneficiary SSA country if the President determines the country meets the eligibility requirements set forth by the authorizing legislation, and (2) grant certain unilateral trade benefits to designated beneficiary SSA countries.[12] In addition to authorizing the benefits, the Act established a U.S.-SSA Trade and Economic Cooperation Forum (AGOA Forum) to foster close economic ties between the United States and sub-Saharan Africa.[13]

AGOA also amended title V of the Trade Act of 1974 to extend additional benefits under the U.S. GSP program to beneficiary SSA countries, initially through September 30, 2008, and by authorizing the President to provide duty-free treatment for certain articles otherwise excluded from duty-free treatment under the GSP.[14] AGOA also provided duty-free treatment for certain textile and apparel articles. It did so under two provisions: (1) the Act's textile and apparel provisions (section 112) initially through September 30, 2008, and (2) a special rule for lesser- developed countries, which is also referred to as the "third-country fabric provision" because it allows beneficiary countries to use non-U.S., non-AGOA fabric (section 112(b)(3)(B)) in making apparel for export under AGOA, initially through September 30, 2004.[15]

Several major amendments have been made to AGOA since its enactment:

- On August 6, 2002, President Bush signed into law the Trade Act of 2002 (Public Law 107-210). The AGOA-related provisions in the 2002 Act, referred to as AGOA II, clarified and expanded the eligibility of products under the textile and apparel provisions. It also increased the cap on U.S. imports of apparel articles made with regional fabric or yarns.
- On July 12, 2004, President Bush signed into law the AGOA Acceleration Act of 2004 (Public Law 108-274), known as AGOA III. AGOA III extended preferential trade treatment to AGOA beneficiary countries through September 30, 2015; extended the third-country fabric provision through September 30, 2007; and provided additional Congressional guidance to the Administration on how to administer the textile and apparel provisions of the bill.[16] The 2004 amendments also expanded the definition of "lesser developed beneficiary sub-Saharan African country" to specifically include Botswana and Namibia, making them eligible for the third- country fabric provision.[17] However, AGOA III reduced the cap on U.S. imports of apparel articles made with third-country fabric or yarns.[18]
- On December 20, 2006, President Bush signed into law the Africa Investment Incentive Act of 2006 (Public Law 109-432), known as AGOA IV. AGOA IV extended the third-country fabric provision through September 30, 2012; increased the cap on U.S. imports of apparel articles made with third-country fabric or yarns for the one- year period beginning October 1, 2006, to 3.5 percent of all apparel articles imported into the United States in the preceding 12-month period; added an "abundant supply" provision;[19] designated certain denim articles as being in abundant supply; and added a textile provision for lesser-developed countries.[20]
- On October 16, 2008, President Bush signed into law an amendment to the AGOA textile and apparel provisions as section 3 of the Andean Trade Preference Extension Act (Public Law 110-436). The amendment continued to designate Botswana and Namibia as lesser-developed beneficiary SSA countries, and extended the designation to Mauritius.[21] It also revoked the abundant supply provision.[22]
- On August 10, 2012, President Obama signed into law amendments to AGOA (Public Law 112-163) that added South Sudan to the list of SSA countries, and extended the third-country fabric provision to September 30, 2015.[23]

Beneficiaries

AGOA Beneficiaries

The President is authorized to designate an SSA country as an eligible AGOA country if he determines that the country meets the eligibility criteria for designation as a beneficiary developing country under the U.S. GSP law and certain additional eligibility requirements under AGOA.[24] With regard to the AGOA eligibility requirements, the President must determine that the country: (1) has established, or is making continual progress toward establishing, a market-based economy, the rule of law, the elimination of barriers to U.S. trade and investment, poverty reduction, protection of internationally recognized worker rights, and efforts to combat corruption; (2) does not engage in activities that undermine U.S. national security or foreign policy interests; and (3) does not engage in gross violations of internationally recognized human rights or provide support for acts of international terrorism.[25] The President must terminate the designation of a country if he determines that an eligible SSA country is not making continual progress in meeting these requirements.[26]

AGOA defines "sub-Saharan Africa" to refer to 49 SSA countries, including South Sudan, added in 2012.[27] In his initial proclamation on October 2, 2000, after AGOA was enacted, President Clinton designated 34 SSA countries as AGOA-eligible countries.[28] The President is required to monitor, review, and report to Congress annually on the progress of each of the 49 countries in meeting the AGOA eligibility requirements in order to determine the current or potential eligibility of each country to be designated as a beneficiary.[29] Table 1.1 shows that the President, in 2013, determined that 39 of 49 potentially eligible countries in SSA were eligible for AGOA benefits.[30]

Textile and Apparel Beneficiaries

SSA countries determined to be eligible for AGOA benefits do not automatically qualify as eligible for preferences under the textile and apparel provisions. To be eligible for trade preferences under the textile and apparel provisions, AGOA beneficiary countries must have in place an effective visa system[31] to prevent unlawful transshipments and the use of counterfeit documents, as well as effective enforcement and verification procedures, and be separately designated to receive this tariff treatment.[32] In 2013, 27 AGOA beneficiary countries also qualified for the general textile and apparel provisions (table 1.1).

AGOA beneficiary countries that had a per capita gross national product of less than $1,500 a year in 1998, as measured by the World Bank, are accorded the status of LDBCs.[33] These countries may be eligible for additional preferential treatment for "lesser-developed countries"—under the third-country fabric provision and the textile provision described below—on the condition that such countries meet the textile and apparel provisions' requirements mentioned above. In 2013, 26 AGOA beneficiary countries were eligible for these additional textile and apparel benefits for LDBCs, including the third-country fabric provision. Although Botswana, Namibia, and Mauritius had a per capita gross national product of more than $1,500 in 1998, they are currently accorded AGOA LDBC status by statute.[34] South Africa is the only country that is eligible for trade benefits under the textile and apparel provisions, but not for AGOA LDBC trade benefits (table 1.1).

Trade Benefits under AGOA

Almost all products of AGOA beneficiary countries may enter the United States duty-free, either under AGOA, GSP, or a non-preference zero rate of duty. The latter duty rate applies to any country with which the United States has normal trade relations (NTR), formerly known as most-favored-nation status.[35]

AGOA and GSP

AGOA builds on the U.S. GSP program, a trade program designed to promote economic growth in developing countries.[36] The tariff benefits provided by AGOA include all products covered by the GSP.[37] Moreover, AGOA authorizes the President to grant duty free treatment to certain articles that are normally excluded from such treatment under the GSP if the President determines that such articles are not import-sensitive in the context of imports from beneficiary SSA countries.[38] Import-sensitive articles under GSP consist of watches; certain electronic articles; certain steel articles; footwear, handbags, luggage, flat goods, work gloves, and leather wearing apparel; certain semi-manufactured and manufactured glass products; and any other articles that the President determines to be import-sensitive in the context of the GSP.[39] As a result, very few products of AGOA beneficiary countries remain ineligible for duty-free treatment. Ineligible products currently include certain steel products, canned apricots and peaches, dried garlic, frozen fruit, and some leather and glass products.[40]

Table 1.1. SSA countries' eligibility for AGOA and AGOA textile and apparel provisions, 2001–13

	2001	2002	2003	2004	2005	2006	2007	2008	2009	2010	2011	2012	2013
Angola				X	X	X	X	X	X	X	X	X	X
Benin	X	X	X	$X^{a,b}$	$X^{a,b}$	$X^{a,b}$	$X^{a,b}$	$X^{a,b}$	$X^{a,b}$	$X^{a,b}$	$X^{a,b}$	$X^{a,b}$	$X^{a,b}$
Botswana	X^a	$X^{a,b}$	$X^{a,b}$	$X^{a,b}$	$X^{a,b}$	$X^{a,b}$	$X^{a,b}$	$X^{a,b}$	$X^{a,b}$	$X^{a,b}$	$X^{a,b}$	$X^{a,b}$	$X^{a,b}$
Burkina Faso					X	$X^{a,b}$	$X^{a,b}$	$X^{a,b}$	$X^{a,b}$	$X^{a,b}$	$X^{a,b}$	$X^{a,b}$	$X^{a,b}$
Burundi							X	X	X	X	X	X	X	X
Cameroon	X	$X^{a,b}$	$X^{a,b}$	$X^{a,b}$	$X^{a,b}$	$X^{a,b}$	$X^{a,b}$	$X^{a,b}$	$X^{a,b}$	$X^{a,b}$	$X^{a,b}$	$X^{a,b}$	$X^{a,b}$
Cabo Verde	X	$X^{a,b}$	$X^{a,b}$	$X^{a,b}$	$X^{a,b}$	$X^{a,b}$	$X^{a,b}$	$X^{a,b}$	$X^{a,b}$	$X^{a,b}$	$X^{a,b}$	$X^{a,b}$	$X^{a,b}$
Central African Republic	X	X	X										
Chad	X	X	X	X	X	$X^{a,b}$	$X^{a,b}$	$X^{a,b}$	$X^{a,b}$	$X^{a,b}$	$X^{a,b}$	$X^{a,b}$	$X^{a,b}$
Comoros								X	X	X	X	X	X
Congo, Dem. Rep.			X	X	X	X	X	X	X	X			
Congo, Rep.	X	X	X	X	X	X	X	X	X	X	X	X	X
Côte d'Ivoire		X	$X^{a,b}$	$X^{a,b}$							X	X	$X^{a,b}$
Djibouti	X	X	X	X	X	X	X	X	X	X	X	X	X
Equatorial Guinea													
Eritrea	X	X	X										
Ethiopia	$X^{a,b}$	$X^{a,b}$	$X^{a,b}$	$X^{a,b}$	$X^{a,b}$	$X^{a,b}$	$X^{a,b}$	$X^{a,b}$	$X^{a,b}$	$X^{a,b}$	$X^{a,b}$	$X^{a,b}$	$X^{a,b}$
Gabon	X	X	X	X	X	X	X	X	X	X	X	X	X
Gambia			X	X	X	X	X	$X^{a,b}$	$X^{a,b}$	$X^{a,b}$	$X^{a,b}$	$X^{a,b}$	$X^{a,b}$
Ghana	X	$X^{a,b}$	$X^{a,b}$	$X^{a,b}$	$X^{a,b}$	$X^{a,b}$	$X^{a,b}$	$X^{a,b}$	$X^{a,b}$	$X^{a,b}$	$X^{a,b}$	$X^{a,b}$	$X^{a,b}$
Guinea	X	X	X	X	X	X	X	X	X		X	X	X
Guinea-Bissau	X	X	X	X	X	X	X	X	X	X	X		
Kenya	$X^{a,b}$	$X^{a,b}$	$X^{a,b}$	$X^{a,b}$	$X^{a,b}$	$X^{a,b}$	$X^{a,b}$	$X^{a,b}$	$X^{a,b}$	$X^{a,b}$	$X^{a,b}$	$X^{a,b}$	$X^{a,b}$
Lesotho	$X^{a,b}$	$X^{a,b}$	$X^{a,b}$	$X^{a,b}$	$X^{a,b}$	$X^{a,b}$	$X^{a,b}$	$X^{a,b}$	$X^{a,b}$	$X^{a,b}$	$X^{a,b}$	$X^{a,b}$	$X^{a,b}$
Liberia								X	X	X	X	$X^{a,b}$	$X^{a,b}$	$X^{a,b}$
Madagascar	$X^{a,b}$	$X^{a,b}$	$X^{a,b}$	$X^{a,b}$	$X^{a,b}$	$X^{a,b}$	$X^{a,b}$	$X^{a,b}$	$X^{a,b}$				
Malawi	$X^{a,b}$	$X^{a,b}$	$X^{a,b}$	$X^{a,b}$	$X^{a,b}$	$X^{a,b}$	$X^{a,b}$	$X^{a,b}$	$X^{a,b}$	$X^{a,b}$	$X^{a,b}$	$X^{a,b}$	$X^{a,b}$
Mali	X	X	$X^{a,b}$	$X^{a,b}$	$X^{a,b}$	$X^{a,b}$	$X^{a,b}$	$X^{a,b}$	$X^{a,b}$	$X^{a,b}$	$X^{a,b}$	$X^{a,b}$	
Mauritania	X	X	X	X	X		X	X		X	X	X	X
Mauritius	X^a	X^a	X^a	$X^{a,b}$	$X^{a,b}$	$X^{a,b}$	X^a	$X^{a,b}$	$X^{a,b}$	$X^{a,b}$	$X^{a,b}$	$X^{a,b}$	$X^{a,b}$
Mozambique	X	$X^{a,b}$	$X^{a,b}$	$X^{a,b}$	$X^{a,b}$	$X^{a,b}$	$X^{a,b}$	$X^{a,b}$	$X^{a,b}$	$X^{a,b}$	$X^{a,b}$	$X^{a,b}$	$X^{a,b}$
Namibia	X^a	$X^{a,b}$	$X^{a,b}$	$X^{a,b}$	$X^{a,b}$	$X^{a,b}$	$X^{a,b}$	$X^{a,b}$	$X^{a,b}$	$X^{a,b}$	$X^{a,b}$	$X^{a,b}$	$X^{a,b}$
Niger	X	X	$X^{a,b}$	$X^{a,b}$	$X^{a,b}$	$X^{a,b}$	$X^{a,b}$	$X^{a,b}$	$X^{a,b}$		$X^{a,b}$	$X^{a,b}$	$X^{a,b}$
Nigeria	X	X	X	$X^{a,b}$	$X^{a,b}$	$X^{a,b}$	$X^{a,b}$	$X^{a,b}$	$X^{a,b}$	$X^{a,b}$	$X^{a,b}$	$X^{a,b}$	$X^{a,b}$
Rwanda	X	X	$X^{a,b}$	$X^{a,b}$	$X^{a,b}$	$X^{a,b}$	$X^{a,b}$	$X^{a,b}$	$X^{a,b}$	$X^{a,b}$	$X^{a,b}$	$X^{a,b}$	$X^{a,b}$
São Tomé and Príncipe	X	X	X	X	X	X	X	X	X	X	X	X	X
Senegal	X	$X^{a,b}$	$X^{a,b}$	$X^{a,b}$	$X^{a,b}$	$X^{a,b}$	$X^{a,b}$	$X^{a,b}$	$X^{a,b}$	$X^{a,b}$	$X^{a,b}$	$X^{a,b}$	$X^{a,b}$
Seychelles	X	X	X	X	X	X	X	X	X	X	X	X	X
Sierra Leone	X	X	X	$X^{a,b}$	$X^{a,b}$	$X^{a,b}$	$X^{a,b}$	$X^{a,b}$	$X^{a,b}$	$X^{a,b}$	$X^{a,b}$	$X^{a,b}$	$X^{a,b}$
Somalia													

Table 1.1. (Continued)

	2001	2002	2003	2004	2005	2006	2007	2008	2009	2010	2011	2012	2013
South Africa	X[a]	X[a]	X[a]	X[a]	X[a]	X[a]	X[a]	X[a]	X[a]	X[a]	X[a]	X[a]	X[a]
South Sudan													X
Sudan													
Swaziland	X[a,b]	X[a,b]	X[a,b]	X[a,b]	X[a,b]	X[a,b]	X[a,b]	X[a,b]	X[a,b]	X[a,b]	X[a,b]	X[a,b]	X[a,b]
Tanzania	X	X[a,b]	X[a,b]	X[a,b]	X[a,b]	X[a,b]	X[a,b]	X[a,b]	X[a,b]	X[a,b]	X[a,b]	X[a,b]	X[a,b]
Togo								X	X	X	X	X	X
Uganda	X[a,b]	X[a,b]	X[a,b]	X[a,b]	X[a,b]	X[a,b]	X[a,b]	X[a,b]	X[a,b]	X[a,b]	X[a,b]	X[a,b]	X[a,b]
Zambia	X[a,b]	X[a,b]	X[a,b]	X[a,b]	X[a,b]	X[a,b]	X[a,b]	X[a,b]	X[a,b]	X[a,b]	X[a,b]	X[a,b]	X[a,b]
Zimbabwe													

Source: USITC DataWeb/USDOC (accessed November 26, 2013), USDOC/OTEXA (accessed November 26, 2013), various *Federal Register* notices, and various Presidential Proclamations.

Note: X: Eligible for AGOA; [a]: Eligible for AGOA textile and apparel provisions; [b]: Eligible for additional AGOA textile and apparel benefits for LDBCs.

In 2012, qualifying goods from AGOA beneficiary countries were eligible to enter duty free under approximately 6,800 tariff lines (defined at the 8-digit level in the Harmonized Tariff Schedule of the United States, or HTS).[41] Of these, approximately 3,500 tariff lines were already covered by GSP, 1,500 tariff lines were already covered by GSP for least-developed beneficiary developing countries (LDBDCs),[42] and 1,800 tariff lines were covered exclusively by AGOA.[43]

Unlike GSP, for sugar, tobacco, peanuts, beef, and some dairy products where U.S. tariff rate quotas exist, AGOA beneficiary countries can export to the United States duty free within the allocated quota, although the shipments above the applicable quantitative limit are subject to the prevailing NTR over-quota duties.[44]

Although a large portion of AGOA-eligible items also qualify under the GSP, AGOA adds a number of other benefits—in particular, that it does not lapse if the GSP program experiences what have become frequent periodic expirations and lapses. Also, U.S. imports under AGOA are not subject to the GSP's competitive need limitations and GSP's country-income graduation requirements.[45]

Rules of Origin

The duty-free treatment provided by AGOA is subject to rules of origin requirements, which are the same as under GSP except for the textile and apparel provisions.[46] For non-apparel/textile items, the product must be imported directly from an AGOA beneficiary country into the customs territory of the United States, and must be the growth, product, or manufacture of an AGOA beneficiary country. Moreover, certain costs may not be less than 35 percent of the appraised value of the article at the time it enters the United States.[47] These costs are the sum of (a) the cost or value of the materials produced in one or more AGOA beneficiary countries or former AGOA beneficiary countries, plus (b) the direct costs of processing operations performed in those countries. Up to 15 percentage points of that 35 percent may be derived from U.S. parts or materials used to produce the product in a beneficiary SSA country or countries.[48] For qualifying AGOA textile and apparel products, the rules of origin requirements vary with the product.

AGOA Textile and Apparel Provisions

AGOA's textile and apparel provisions took effect on October 1, 2000, providing duty-free and quota-free treatment for certain eligible textile and apparel articles made in beneficiary SSA countries.[49] Like the other AGOA preferences, the textile and apparel provisions are scheduled to expire on September 30, 2015.[50]

Eligible textile and apparel articles must be made in qualifying SSA countries, and include:

- apparel made with U.S. yarns and fabrics;
- apparel made with SSA (regional) yarns and fabrics, subject to a cap;
- apparel made with yarns and fabrics not produced in commercial quantities in the United States;
- certain cashmere and merino wool sweaters; and
- eligible hand-loomed, handmade, or folklore articles, and ethnic printed fabrics.[51]

The Third-Country Fabric Provision

Under a special rule for lesser-developed countries, certain AGOA countries with LDBC status have access to additional preferential treatment in the form of duty-free access for apparel articles made from yarns and fabric originating anywhere in the world, subject to a cap.[52] This special rule is also referred to as the third-country fabric provision, and expires on September 30, 2015.[53]

Textile Provision for Lesser-Developed Countries

AGOA IV added a textile provision for lesser-developed countries, which extends preferential treatment to textiles and textile articles[54] originating entirely in beneficiary AGOA LDBCs. Beneficiary countries must meet the textile and apparel benefit eligibility requirements and incorporate textiles and textile articles into their visa systems.

Cap and Surge Mechanism

The duty-free cap on U.S. imports of apparel from AGOA beneficiary countries is filled on a first- come, first-served basis. If during any year the cap is met, the relevant apparel products from AGOA beneficiary countries may still enter the United States; however, they will be assessed the prevailing NTR duty rate (column 1-general rates set forth in the HTS) at the time of entry.[55] To date, the cap has never been reached.

In addition to the cap on apparel imports, AGOA includes a surge mechanism to protect U.S. industries from surges in apparel imports. AGOA requires the Secretary of Commerce to monitor apparel imports made of regional and third-country yarns and fabrics on a monthly basis to guard against disruptive import surges. If increased imports are determined to cause or threaten serious damage to the U.S. apparel industry, the President shall suspend the duty-free treatment for the article(s) in question.[56] To date, the surge mechanism has not been invoked.

SECTION 2. U.S. IMPORTS FROM AGOA COUNTRIES AND THE ROLE OF AGOA

Introduction

This section provides an overview of U.S. merchandise imports from designated AGOA beneficiary countries and discusses the role of AGOA in their trade with the United States. The overview covers the period 2000 to the present, although it focuses on 2008–13, the most recent six-year period for which data are available.[57] Trade data presented for 2000–2013 are based on the list of countries eligible for trade preferences under AGOA, which varies by year, as described in section 1.[58]

The first half of the section analyzes U.S. imports under AGOA by sector and by AGOA beneficiary country (hereafter "AGOA country"), and describes the importance of U.S. imports under AGOA as a share of total imports from AGOA countries. The second half of the section identifies the U.S. imports from AGOA countries that increased the most since 2000 under AGOA and the U.S. Generalized System of Preferences (GSP), and examines the factors behind this growth.

U.S. Imports from AGOA Countries

Total U.S. imports from AGOA countries grew at an average annual rate of 6.7 percent between 2000 and 2013, rising from $16.5 billion in 2000 to $38.2 billion in 2013 (figure 2.1).[59] Growth was most pronounced in the earlier part of this period: during 2000–2008, the value of U.S. imports from AGOA countries increased almost fivefold, reaching a record of close to $80 billion in 2008. Since then, U.S. imports from AGOA countries have fluctuated sharply.

The trend in total U.S. imports from AGOA countries closely tracks the trend in crude petroleum imports, which accounted for about 70 percent of total import value over this time period. The value of U.S. crude petroleum imports rose on average 14.6 percent annually between 2000 and 2013, although such imports became highly volatile after 2008. Both the quantity and price of U.S. imports of crude petroleum fell sharply in 2009 following the economic recession. These recovered in 2010 and 2011 as crude petroleum prices strengthened, but dropped again in 2012 and 2013 in response to weak U.S. demand and higher U.S. domestic production. The value of U.S. imports of all other products from AGOA countries increased between 2000 and 2013 at 1.7 percent annually. Imports of these products dipped in 2009 in response to the weak U.S. economy, but recovered to a record $20 billion in 2011 before falling again in 2012 and 2013. Chief among non-crude petroleum imports are motor vehicles, refined petroleum products, apparel, ferroalloys, and certain agricultural products.

The vast majority of U.S. imports from AGOA countries enter duty free, either under preference programs or under NTR (normal trade relations) duty-free tariff lines. U.S. imports from AGOA countries are dominated by imports entering under AGOA; between 2008 and 2013, U.S. imports under AGOA made up 70 percent of the value of all U.S. imports from AGOA countries (table 2.1). Other U.S. imports from AGOA countries also entered duty free under GSP; such imports represented about 8 percent of all imports over 2008–13.[60] Altogether, duty-free U.S. imports under AGOA, GSP, and NTR represented 94 percent of all U.S. imports from countries eligible for AGOA preferences during 2008–13. Major imports under GSP in 2013 included crude petroleum (from least-developed beneficiary developing countries, or LDBDCs); ferroalloys; aluminum plates, sheets, and strips; and cocoa paste. Major imports entering duty free under NTR included platinum, diamonds, cocoa beans, natural rubber, and acyclic hydrocarbons.

During 2001–08, duty-free U.S. imports from AGOA beneficiary countries grew under both preference programs as well as under NTR. However, in 2009, imports fell in all three categories because of the economic recession in the United States. Whereas duty free imports under AGOA and NTR rebounded in 2010 and 2011, imports under GSP dropped, primarily reflecting a sharp decline in imports of crude petroleum under GSP (for LDBDCs) from $8.1 billion in 2008 to $0.3 billion in 2011.[61] In 2012, U.S. imports under GSP went up slightly as imports of crude petroleum from GSP LDBDCs rose, while duty-free imports under AGOA and NTR fell sharply in 2012 and again in 2013. U.S. imports under AGOA fell because of a large decline in crude petroleum imports, especially from Nigeria. Duty-free imports under NTR also dropped because of significant declines in some NTR-free imports, such as platinum, diamonds, and petroleum gases and other gaseous hydrocarbons.

Duties are collected on some U.S. imports from AGOA beneficiary countries. In 2013, 9.1 percent of U.S. imports from AGOA countries entered dutiable under NTR. In addition, duties were collected on some imports that were eligible for duty-free treatment under AGOA, including certain crude and non-crude petroleum products. Of the total $12.9 million in import duties that AGOA beneficiary countries paid in 2012, about $10.8 million were collected on AGOA-eligible products.[62] Various factors may have contributed to this phenomenon; for example, these exports may not have met rules of origin requirements (e.g., tuna loins), exporters may not have submitted the required documents and/or requested preferential treatment, or shippers may have received refunds for duties paid at a later time.

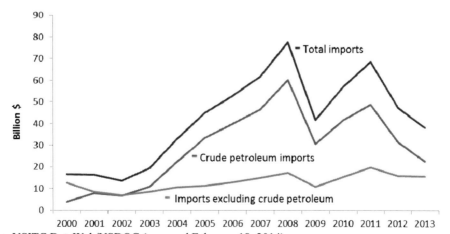

Source: USITC DataWeb/USDOC (accessed February 18, 2014).
Note: AGOA eligibility varies by year, and the list of AGOA countries is unique for each year. Table 1.1 provides a comprehensive list of AGOA eligibility by beneficiary country and year between 2000 and 2013.

Figure 2.1. U.S. imports from AGOA countries, 2000–2013.

Table 2.1. U.S. imports for consumption from AGOA countries, by special import program and rate provision status, 2001, 2005, and 2008–13

Program	2001	2005	2008	2009	2010	2011	2012	2013
				Million $				
NTR								
Dutiable	3,231.4	696.1	1,822.4	2,019.6	3,957.8	4,101.1	4,332.3	3,471.5
Duty-free	4,886.1	6,037.4	9,312.3	5,781.7	8,857.5	10,655.2	8,188.0	7,873.1
AGOA	7,579.2	32,743.1	56,373.7	28,050.3	38,664.8	51,883.1	32,747.7	24,797.9
GSP	586.9	5,403.3	9,885.2	5,659.0	5,605.1	1,956.8	2,144.2	2,017.9
Other[a]	41.3	57.5	96.6	70.3	41.3	42.8	44.5	47.7
Total	16,324.8	44,937.4	77,490.1	41,580.9	57,126.6	68,638.9	47,456.6	38,208.1
				% of total				
NTR								
Dutiable	19.8	1.5	2.4	4.9	6.9	6.0	9.1	9.1
Duty-free	29.9	13.4	12.0	13.9	15.5	15.5	17.3	20.6
AGOA	46.4	72.9	72.7	67.5	67.7	75.6	69.0	64.9
GSP	3.6	12.0	12.8	13.6	9.8	2.9	4.5	5.3
Other[a]	0.3	0.1	0.1	0.2	0.1	0.1	0.1	0.1
Total	100.0	100.0	100.0	100.0	100.0	100.0	100.0	100.0

Source: USITC DataWeb/USDOC (accessed February 18, 2014).

Notes: [a] "Other" includes imports under other programs, such as the Civil Aircraft Agreement. AGOA eligibility varies by year, and the list of AGOA countries is unique for each year. Table 1.1 provides a comprehensive list of AGOA eligibility by beneficiary country and year between 2000 and 2013.

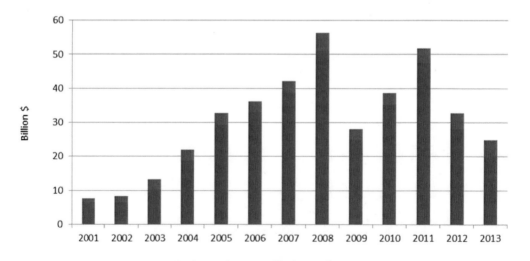

Source: USITC DataWeb/USDOC (accessed February 18, 2014).
Note: The data in this figure are based on the list of AGOA-eligible countries, which varies by year. For a complete list of AGOA- eligible countries by year, see table 1.1.

Figure 2.2. U.S. imports under AGOA, 2001–13.

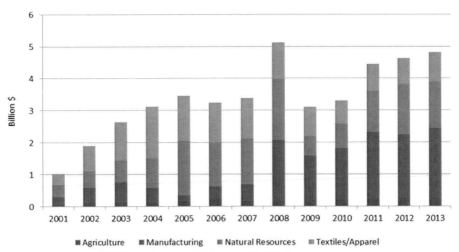

Source: USITC DataWeb/USDOC (accessed February 18, 2014).
Note: The data in this figure are based on the list of AGOA-eligible countries, which varies by year. For a complete list of AGOA- eligible countries by year, see table 1.1. "Agriculture" includes all agricultural products; "manufacturing" includes electronics, machinery, transportation equipment, chemicals, miscellaneous manufacturing, and special provisions items; "natural resources" includes energy products (except crude petroleum), minerals and metals, and forest products; and "textiles/apparel" includes textiles, apparel, and footwear.

Figure 2.3. U.S. imports under AGOA, excluding crude petroleum, 2001–13.

U.S. Imports under AGOA

U.S. imports under AGOA[63] increased from $7.6 billion in 2001 to $24.8 billion in 2013, and while volatile, grew roughly 10 percent annually on average (figure 2.2). During 2001–13, crude petroleum accounted for almost 90 percent of U.S. imports under AGOA.[64] U.S. imports under AGOA of products other than crude petroleum grew from $1 billion to almost $5 billion over this period (figure 2.3). U.S. imports under AGOA of manufactured goods, including electronics, machinery, transportation equipment, chemicals, and miscellaneous manufactured goods, experienced the largest growth after crude petroleum, increasing from $0.2 billion in 2001 to $2.2 billion in 2013. Imports of natural resources products under AGOA increased by $1.1 billion since 2001 (primarily made up of refined petroleum products) to reach $1.4 billion in 2013. Although U.S. imports of textiles and apparel under AGOA increased from 2001 to 2013, the value of these imports fell from a peak of $1.6 billion in 2004 to $0.9 billion in 2013. U.S. imports of agricultural products under AGOA rose slowly, remaining below $262 million annually.

U.S. Imports of Crude Petroleum under AGOA

Imports of crude petroleum under AGOA rose steadily during 2001–08, and then fluctuated sharply each year until 2013 (figure 2.2).[65] The growth in the value of crude petroleum imports under AGOA between 2001 and 2008 resulted from a combination of rising crude petroleum prices and growing global demand. Between 2001 and 2008, the average unit value of U.S. crude petroleum imports from AGOA countries rose from $25.54

per barrel to $103.28 per barrel, increasing roughly 22 percent annually on average. This trend reflected rising global demand (especially in emerging markets) and supply controls established by the Organization of Petroleum Exporting Countries (OPEC). In the same time frame, U.S. demand for crude petroleum also increased: the volume of U.S. imports from AGOA almost doubled, rising from 256 million barrels in 2001 to 496 million barrels in 2008 (close to 10 percent annually on average). As a result, the value of U.S. crude petroleum imports under AGOA increased 34 percent annually on average, rising from $6.5 billion in 2001 to $51.2 billion in 2008.

After 2008, U.S. imports of crude petroleum under AGOA entered a period of instability.[66] First, imports fell over 50 percent in 2009, dropping to $24.9 billion from $51.2 billion the previous year. This decline is associated with the economic downturn in the United States, which significantly curbed the U.S. demand for petroleum. At the same time, crude petroleum prices plummeted in response to plentiful global supplies, in part caused by a breakdown in discipline by certain OPEC members who failed to limit their production to OPEC-set levels.[67] Between 2009 and 2011, however, the value of U.S. imports of crude petroleum recovered quickly, mostly due to stronger petroleum prices as the per-barrel price of U.S. crude petroleum imports from AGOA countries rose from $64.40 to $112.90 over that period. Higher crude petroleum prices resulted from rising demand, reflecting the improvement in the global economy.

Finally, 2012 and 2013 again saw significant drops in U.S. imports of crude petroleum under AGOA, which fell to $20.0 billion in 2013 from $47.4 billion in 2011. This drop followed the increase in U.S. domestic crude production, coupled with lower domestic demand for petroleum products that reflected the continued weakness of the U.S. economy. In addition, production disruptions in Nigeria were reflected in a sharp drop in exports of Nigerian crude petroleum to the United States: these exports fell from $30.2 billion in 2011 to $9.9 billion in 2013.[68]

U.S. Imports under AGOA of Products Other than Crude Petroleum

U.S. imports under AGOA of products other than crude petroleum grew considerably in the 12 years following AGOA's launch, from $1 billion in 2001 to $4.8 billion in 2013 (table 2.2). These imports were highly concentrated in three sectors—transportation equipment, refined petroleum products, and apparel—accounting for about 89 percent of total U.S. imports under AGOA during 2001–13. U.S. imports under AGOA of agricultural products and of minerals and metals each accounted for an additional 5 percent share in this period.

Transportation equipment made up 44 percent of the value of U.S. non-crude petroleum imports under AGOA in 2013, and motor vehicles accounted for almost all of the imports in this sector. In 2001, U.S. imports of motor vehicles under AGOA totaled $238 million. In the following years, imports increased by about 20 percent annually, reaching a record $2.1 billion in 2013. U.S. imports of motor vehicles under AGOA consisted almost exclusively of passenger vehicle imports from South Africa, but also included $2.6 million in chassis and bodies from South Africa in 2013.

The United States has imported a variety of refined petroleum products under AGOA, mostly distillate and residual fuel oils and naphthas.[69] In 2013, refined petroleum products accounted for 26 percent ($1.2 billion) of U.S. imports under AGOA. Nigeria was the primary supplier, accounting for 76 percent of such imports, followed by Angola (12 percent). In addition, there were occasional small shipments under AGOA of low-octane gasolines and blend stocks from Cameroon, Chad, Gabon, and Ghana.

Apparel was the leading non-petroleum product category imported under AGOA at the beginning of the program, but has dropped in rank and value since then.[70] The United States imported apparel valued at $907 million under AGOA in 2013; Slacks and trousers ("bottoms"), men's cotton woven shirts, and knit tops were the largest categories of U.S. apparel imports under AGOA in 2013, and roughly two-thirds of apparel imports were cotton products. Lesotho, Kenya, and Mauritius were the largest suppliers, accounting for 90 percent of imports in 2013.

U.S. agricultural imports under AGOA accounted for about 5 percent of the value of all non- crude petroleum imports in 2013, a share that has been fairly constant since the beginning of the program. In 2013, agricultural imports reached $262 million, the highest level during 2001–13. Citrus fruit ($62 million), edible nuts ($58 million), wine ($52 million), and unmanufactured tobacco ($37 million) were the major categories of agricultural products imported in 2013, with imports of edible nuts and wine recording the fastest growth. U.S. imports of wine and unmanufactured tobacco under AGOA have grown steadily since 2001, while imports of citrus fruit peaked at $63 million in 2006 and have averaged $49 million per year in the past five years. U.S. imports of edible nuts under AGOA fluctuated until 2007, then increased during 2008–13, climbing by 265 percent over that six-year period. Edible nuts imports consisted primarily of shelled macadamia nuts from Kenya, Malawi, and South Africa and other shelled nuts from South Africa. Nearly all U.S. imports of both citrus fruit and wine under AGOA came from South Africa, and 96 percent of U.S. unmanufactured tobacco imports under AGOA were sourced from Malawi in 2013.[71]

The value of U.S. minerals and metals imports under AGOA grew from $91 million in 2001 to $203 million in 2013, accounting for 4 percent of the value of all U.S. imports under AGOA. The great majority of these imports of minerals and metals—$180 million worth—were standard ferromanganese from South Africa, an iron alloy that the United States imports to meet domestic demand for use in steel production. Unwrought manganese flake (often used in aluminum, welding, and other products) from South Africa accounted for an additional $23 million of U.S. mineral and metal imports under AGOA in 2013. Other mineral and metal imports amounted to about $0.2 million in 2013 and were primarily glassware and ceramic household products, 91 percent of which came from South Africa.

U.S. Imports under AGOA by Beneficiary Country

Just two countries, South Africa and Nigeria, represented 73 percent of all U.S. noncrude petroleum imports under AGOA in 2013; South Africa accounted for 54 percent and Nigeria for 20 percent (table 2.3). These two countries have been consistently large users of the AGOA program, primarily due to the size of South Africa's manufacturing sector and Nigeria's petroleum production. U.S. imports under AGOA from South Africa totaled $2.6 billion in 2013, of which $2.1 billion were motor vehicles, specifically automobiles. Ferromanganese also accounts for a large share of U.S. imports under AGOA from South Africa, totaling $180 million in 2013. Other major U.S. imports from South Africa under AGOA include chemicals, citrus fruit, wine and other fermented beverages, macadamia nuts, and base metals and chemical elements (primarily unwrought manganese flake). In 2013, the United States imported $941 million in refined petroleum products from Nigeria under

AGOA. Other major U.S. imports under AGOA from Nigeria in 2013 were hides, skins, and leathers ($0.9 million).

Table 2.2. U.S. imports under AGOA (excluding crude petroleum) by sector; 2001, 2005, and 2008–13

Sector	2001	2005	2008	2009	2010	2011	2012	2013
				Million $				
Transportation equipment	241.2	138.1	1,821.3	1,369.3	1,53s8.7	2,040.6	1,928.7	2,121.2
Motor vehicles	238.0	134.3	1,811.6	1,366.1	1,532.1	2,032.7	1,919.2	2,115.7
Refined petroleum products	278.9	1,625.8	1,550.4	513.9	621.5	1,063.4	1,348.0	1,236.1
Textiles and apparel	355.9	1,419.0	1,137.0	914.2	726.9	855.3	814.8	907.6
Apparel	355.9	1,419.0	1,136.9	914.0	726.9	855.0	814.5	907.1
Agricultural products	59.0	151.7	162.1	168.0	222.2	220.0	247.6	261.6
Citrus fruit	19.8	46.3	40.9	38.3	48.8	43.9	50.5	61.6
Edible nuts	7.3	26.6	15.9	18.9	44.2	53.6	64.5	58.0
Wine and certain other fermented beverages	4.1	27.4	30.3	26.5	29.8	30.7	45.1	51.8
Unmanufactured tobacco	8.2	5.6	11.9	28.9	32.3	39.9	40.8	36.8
Ethyl alcohol for nonbeverage purposes	11.4	19.4	23.5	17.4	22.9	17.0	17.0	16.8
Fruit and vegetable juices	0.8	4.6	11.0	13.5	13.4	11.8	10.8	8.1
Minerals and metals	91.2	73.6	370.3	95.6	146.2	212.7	221.3	202.9
Ferroalloys	28.1	62.8	367.4	87.4	141.9	204.5	197.4	180.0
Certain base metals and chemical elements	0.0	10.0	2.7	6.0	4.2	8.0	23.7	22.7
Chemicals and related products	3.8	44.7	78.0	41.2	44.4	52.7	63.3	62.3
Miscellaneous chemicals and specialties	0.0	32.7	73.8	38.1	40.5	47.5	54.4	60.7
Footwear	0.2	1.9	0.7	0.5	0.4	0.8	7.3	19.8
Miscellaneous manufactures	0.3	3.8	3.7	2.0	4.1	3.3	2.8	2.6
Forest products	0.1	0.2	0.1	0.1	0.0	0.1	0.1	0.1

Sector	2001	2005	2008	2009	2010	2011	2012	2013
				Million $				
Electronic products	0.0	0.1	0.0	0.2	0.0	0.1	0.0	0.0
Machinery	0.0	0.3	0.3	0.1	0.0	0.0	0.0	0.0
Total	1,030.6	3,459.2	5,123.8	3,105.2	3,304.5	4,449.0	4,634.0	4,814.1
				%of total				
Transportation equipment	23.4	4.0	35.5	44.1	46.6	45.9	41.6	44.1
Refined petroleum products	27.1	47.0	30.3	16.6	18.8	23.9	29.1	25.7
Textiles and apparel	34.5	41.0	22.2	29.4	22.0	19.2	17.6	18.8
Agricultural products	5.7	4.4	3.2	5.4	6.7	4.9	5.3	5.4
Minerals and metals	8.8	2.1	7.2	3.1	4.4	4.8	4.8	4.2
All other	0.4	1.5	1.6	1.4	1.5	1.3	1.6	1.8
Total	100.0	100.0	100.0	100.0	100.0	100.0	100.0	100.0

Source: USITC DataWeb/USDOC (accessed February 18, 2014).

Note: The data in this table are based on the list of AGOA-eligible countries, which varies by year. For a complete list of AGOA eligible countries by year, see table 1.1.

Table 2.3. U.S. imports under AGOA (excluding crude petroleum) by country 2001, 2005, and 2008–13

Country	2001	2005	2008	2009	2010	2011	2012	2013
				Million $				
South Africa	417.3	455.3	2,427.7	1,642.9	1,902.1	2,458.2	2,384.1	2,578.2
Nigeria	191.4	1,194.9	1,294.1	394.6	551.1	828.4	934.0	942.1
Kenya	55.1	272.1	252.2	205.0	220.6	288.3	287.7	336.5
Lesotho	129.5	388.3	338.8	277.0	280.3	314.3	300.6	320.8
Mauritius	38.9	146.8	97.3	98.7	117.9	156.0	160.0	187.9
Congo, Rep.	37.1	109.5	27.5	19.1	0.0	9.8	40.3	144.3
Angola	0.0	99.6	96.1	38.1	0.0	0.0	216.7	96.4
All other	161.3	792.7	590.1	429.8	232.5	394.1	310.4	207.4
Total	1,030.6	3,459.2	5,123.8	3,105.2	3,304.5	4,449.0	4,634.0	4,814.1
				% of total				
South Africa	40.5	13.2	47.4	52.9	57.6	55.3	51.4	53.6
Nigeria	18.6	34.5	25.3	12.7	16.7	18.6	20.2	19.6
Kenya	5.3	7.9	4.9	6.6	6.7	6.5	6.2	7.0
Lesotho	12.6	11.2	6.6	8.9	8.5	7.1	6.5	6.7
Mauritius	3.8	4.2	1.9	3.2	3.6	3.5	3.5	3.9
Congo, Rep.	3.6	3.2	0.5	0.6	0.0	0.2	0.9	3.0
Angola	0.0	2.9	1.9	1.2	0.0	0.0	4.7	2.0
All other	15.6	22.9	11.5	13.8	7.0	8.9	6.7	4.3
Total	100.0	100.0	100.0	100.0	100.0	100.0	100.0	100.0

Source: USITC DataWeb/USDOC (accessed February 18, 2014).

Note: The data in this table are based on the list of AGOA-eligible countries, which varies by year. For a complete list of AGOA- eligible countries by year, see table 1.1.

Table 2.4. AGOA utilization rates, including and excluding crude petroleum, by beneficiary country, 2013 (%)

Country	Utilization rate including all products	Utilization rate excluding crude petroleum	Country	Utilization rate including all products	Utilization rate excluding crude petroleum
Angola	67.4	11.0	Malawi	73.7	73.7
Benin	0.0	0.0	Mauritania	0.0	0.0
Botswana	2.1	2.1	Mauritius	55.6	55.6
Burkina Faso	0.1	0.1	Mozambique	1.8	1.8
Burundi	0.0	0.0	Namibia	0.0	0.0
Cameroon	13.3	13.3	Niger	[a]	[a]
Cape Verde	6.9	6.9	Nigeria	90.6	50.2
Chad	99.4	0.0	Rwanda	[a]	[a]
Comoros	0.0	0.0	São Tomé and Príncipe	0.0	0.0
Congo, Rep.	82.2	39.4	Senegal	0.1	0.1
Côte d'Ivoire	[a]	[a]	Seychelles	0.0	0.0
Djibouti	0.0	0.0	Sierra Leone	0.0	0.0
Ethiopia	16.4	16.4	South Africa	30.7	30.7
Gabon	88.5	12.6	South Sudan	0.0	0.0
Gambia	0.0	0.0	Swaziland	91.6	91.6
Ghana	0.9	1.1	Tanzania	14.7	14.7
Guinea	[a]	[a]	Togo	0.0	0.0
Kenya	77.9	77.9	Uganda	0.1	0.1
Lesotho	89.4	89.4	Zambia	[a]	[a]
Liberia	0.0	0.0	Overall	64.9	30.6

Source: USITC DataWeb/USDOC (accessed February 18, 2014).
Notes: [a] = Less than 0.05.

Other major sources of imports under the AGOA program include Kenya, Lesotho, Mauritius, the Republic of the Congo, and Angola. In 2013, U.S. imports under AGOA from Lesotho, the Republic of the Congo, and Angola each consisted of single product categories: over $321 million in apparel products from Lesotho, $144 million in refined petroleum products from the Republic of the Congo, and $96 million in refined petroleum products (exclusively distillate and residual fuel oil derived from petroleum or oils from bituminous minerals) from Angola.

The primary imports from Kenya under AGOA were apparel ($305 million in 2013); other major imports from Kenya were edible nuts ($24 million), cut flowers ($3 million), fruit and vegetable juices ($1 million), and sporting goods ($1 million). Major imports from Mauritius under AGOA included apparel ($187 million) and cereals ($0.5 million). Non-crude U.S. imports under AGOA by beneficiary country can be found in appendix E.

AGOA Utilization by Beneficiary Country

AGOA utilization, defined as U.S. imports under AGOA from a beneficiary country as a share of total U.S. imports from that country, was 65 percent in 2013 for trade in all products and across all countries (table 2.4).[72] In 2013, AGOA utilization (for all products) exceeded 90 percent for only three beneficiary countries: Chad (99 percent), Swaziland (92 percent), and Nigeria (91 percent).

The utilization rate exceeded 80 percent for an additional three countries: Gabon, Lesotho, and the Republic of the Congo. Meanwhile, South Africa, the largest source for U.S. imports under AGOA, had a utilization rate of just 31 percent in 2013. Also, 24 out of the 39 beneficiary countries in 2013 reported utilization rates of 10 percent or less, and 21 countries had utilization rates of 1 percent or less. Low utilization rates can stem from many different factors. For example, 12 countries with exports to the United States had no exports under AGOA. Also, countries supplying mostly products that are already duty free under NTR or under GSP have low utilization rates.

When crude petroleum imports are excluded from the calculation, the overall utilization rate falls to 31 percent. This difference in utilization rates indicates the importance of AGOA preferences for U.S. imports of crude petroleum from the region. For example, the utilization rate for Nigeria drops from 91 percent to 50 percent when crude petroleum is excluded from the calculation, and for Angola it drops from 67 percent to 11 percent. Of total U.S. imports from Chad, only crude petroleum receives AGOA preferences, so its utilization rate falls to 0 percent when crude petroleum is not considered.

AGOA/GSP Growth Products

During 2000–2013, a relatively small number of products accounted for the bulk of the growth in value, in absolute terms, of U.S. imports from AGOA beneficiaries under AGOA and GSP provisions.[73] Since AGOA was established as a program for SSA countries that builds on GSP, this section analyzes absolute growth in U.S. imports under both programs together. Table 2.5 presents a ranking of the top 25 "growth product" groups.

Not all products in these groups actually entered the United States under AGOA and/or GSP provisions; indeed, as shown in figure 2.4, the share of total U.S. imports from AGOA-eligible partners that entered under these provisions varied significantly from group to group during 2000–2013.

hese shares are determined largely by the duty status of non-AGOA/GSP products in a particular product group. For example, most of the U.S. imports from AGOA beneficiaries of products included in the cocoa, chocolate, and confectionery group consists of cocoa beans, which have a NTR duty rate of free and therefore do not enter under AGOA or GSP provisions. In contrast, most U.S. imports of products in the motor vehicles product group did enter under a trade preference program (under AGOA, in this case, because these goods are not GSP eligible).

Table 2.5. U.S. imports from AGOA-eligible countries under AGOA and GSP (excluding crude petroleum), by leading growth product, 2000–2013

Product	2000	2005	2010	2013	Absolute growth 2000–2013	Compound annual growth rate 2000–2013
	Million $					Percent
Motor vehicles	0.0	134.3	1,532.1	2,115.7	2,115.7	a
Refined petroleum products	1.4	1,784.3	621.5	1,297.2	1,295.8	76.6
Apparel	0.7	1,419.7	727.2	907.4	906.7	81.2
Ferroalloys	171.7	277.2	596.0	530.4	358.7	9.9
Aluminum mill products	56.6	153.9	160.2	189.3	132.7	10.6
Cocoa, chocolate, and confectionery	4.4	2.4	67.3	122.8	118.4	31.9
Miscellaneous inorganic chemicals	79.3	164.0	180.1	175.9	96.6	6.9
Certain organic chemicals	17.4	62.4	100.5	103.1	85.7	16.0
Edible nuts	0.5	30.7	48.8	62.3	61.8	48.7
Citrus fruit	0.0	46.4	48.8	61.7	61.7	a
Wine and certain other fermented beverages	0.1	32.1	38.6	61.4	61.3	68.6
Miscellaneous chemicals and specialties	0.2	32.9	40.8	60.7	60.6	64.7
Copper and related articles	7.6	6.6	7.3	57.8	50.2	18.4
Internal combustion piston engines, other than for aircraft	2.3	35.6	40.7	25.3	23.0	22.2
Certain base metals and chemical elements	0.2	10.6	5.5	23.0	22.8	46.0
Footwear	0.0	1.9	0.4	20.0	20.0	a
Ethyl alcohol for nonbeverage purposes	0.0	19.4	22.9	16.8	16.8	a
Prepared or preserved vegetables, mushrooms, and olives	1.1	5.2	11.2	16.5	15.3	25.0
Unmanufactured tobacco	24.1	36.2	37.2	37.7	13.6	3.8
Precious jewelry and related articles	22.4	56.0	24.3	33.5	11.1	3.4
Optical goods, including ophthalmic goods	3.3	7.3	15.5	12.4	9.1	11.6
Dried fruit other than tropical	0.0	2.4	10.1	8.7	8.7	a
Ships, tugs, pleasure boats, and similar vessels	5.1	11.2	16.3	13.0	7.9	8.1

Product	2000	2005	2010	2013	Absolute growth 2000–2013	Compound annual growth rate 2000–2013
Electric sound and visual signaling apparatus	0.6	2.7	0.1	7.6	7.1	24.3
Fruit and vegetable juices	1.4	4.9	13.4	8.4	6.9	15.8
All other	281.6	382.7	299.0	214.3	−67.3	a
Total	682.1	4,722.7	4,665.5	6,182.9	5,500.8	20.2

Source: USITC DataWeb/USDOC (accessed February 18, 2014).
Note: [a] = Not applicable.

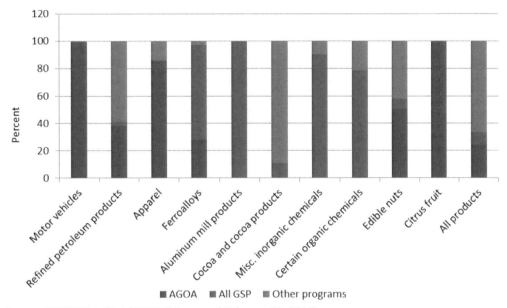

Source: USITC DataWeb/USDOC (accessed February 18, 2014).

Figure 2.4. Share of U.S. imports from AGOA beneficiaries under AGOA, GSP, and other provisions excluding crude petroleum), by leading growth product, 2000–2013.

The following section profiles each of the top 10 product groups in terms of the absolute growth of U.S. imports from AGOA beneficiaries under AGOA and GSP provisions during 2000–2013.[74] Each profile provides a description of the items in the product group; shows the shares of U.S. imports of these products under AGOA and GSP provisions in 2013; presents data on U.S. imports from AGOA beneficiaries under AGOA and GSP provisions, by major products and AGOA suppliers during 2008–13; and identifies key factors that contributed to growth during the period.

MOTOR VEHICLES

This product group includes passenger vehicles with the primary purpose of transporting people, rather than goods. These products include cars, sport- utility vehicles, and minivans, but not pickup trucks. This category also includes bodies for such vehicles, which made up less than one-half of 1 percent of imports in this category in 2013. The vast majority of motor vehicles imported into the United States under AGOA/GSP were from South Africa. These were primarily luxury cars produced by BMW and Mercedes. Nonpreferential U.S. imports in this category are subject to an NTR duty rate of 2.5 percent ad valorem.

Source: USITC DataWeb/USDOC (accessed February 26, 2014).

Motor vehicles: U.S. imports under AGOA and GSP, 2013 (share by value).

Motor Vehicles: Leading U.S. imports under AGOA and GSP, by product and key suppliers, 2000, 2005, 2008–13 (million $)

Product category (2012 HTS code)	Supplier	2000	2005	2008	2009	2010	2011	2012	2013
Vehicles for the transport of persons (8703)	South Africa	0	123	1,804	1,363	1,529	2,030	1,914	2,113
All other motor vehicles imported under AGOA/ GSP		0	11	7	3	3	3	5	3
Total motor vehicles imported under AGOA/ GSP		0	134	1,812	1,366	1,532	2,033	1,919	2,116

Source: USITC Data Web/USDOC (accessed November 26, 2013, and February 26, 2014).
Note: Due to rounding, sums may not match totals.

Major Factors in the Growth of Motor Vehicle Imports under AGOA/GSP

A South African government program of incentives for the motor vehicle industry helped to increase South African exports of motor vehicles, including to the United States. Before 1995, South Africa had an established motor vehicle industry, but very little trade in passenger vehicles, with only $110 million in exports and nearly $377 million in imports. However, the Motor Industry Development Programme (MIDP)—launched in 1995 and extended in 2013 as the Automotive Production and Development Programme (APDP)—created substantial incentives to invest in the South African motor vehicle industry and to produce both for export and for the domestic market. As a result, total South African imports and exports of passenger vehicles, excluding pickup trucks, increased significantly; exports to all markets reached nearly $3.3 billion in 2013, while imports reached nearly $5.5 billion.

The MIDP was designed to help South Africa's motor vehicle industry adjust to trade liberalization by offering incentives to rationalize production into a smaller range of products and gain economies of scale by increasing exports. To achieve these goals, the MIDP gradually reduced tariffs on imports of vehicles and components; imposed an export-import scheme that allowed vehicle and components exporters to earn tradable credits to offset duties on imported vehicles and components; offered a duty drawback program for exporters that provided import duty rebates for components and intermediate inputs used in exported vehicles; and provided a duty-free allowance on imported components of 27 percent of the value of vehicles produced for the domestic market.

In addition, the MIDP created an investment subsidy that offered import duty credits equal to 20 percent of the value of qualifying investments in buildings, plant and machinery, and tooling, over a five-year period. Since the implementation of the MIDP, substantial investments have been made in the South African motor vehicle industry. The MIDP's duty offsets encouraged global manufacturers, including BMW, Daimler, Ford, Toyota, and Volkswagen, to produce vehicles in South Africa for export, and to use the offsets earned by these exports to import other vehicles into South Africa. MIDP support for investments helped trigger over $300 million in investments from BMW and Daimler in vehicle manufacturing in South Africa.

Imports from car makers BMW and Daimler are the primary reason U.S. imports from South Africa increased from zero in 2000 to over $2.1 billion in 2013. Duty-free entry to the United States under AGOA was likely an important factor in BMW's decision to begin exporting passenger vehicles from South Africa to the United States in 2001 and Daimler's decision to export cars from South Africa to the United States in late 2007. However, Daimler has announced plans to produce the same car type it currently produces in South Africa in the United States in 2014, which would likely eliminate or significantly reduce Daimler's exports of passenger vehicles from South Africa to the United States.

Sources: BMW South Africa website, http://www.bmwplant.co.za/Content/frame_content.jsp@cont= http 3a 2f 2fhaf0gau02~5.htm (accessed January 13, 2014); Borgenheimer, "Motor Industry Development Program in South Africa," November 30, 2010; GTIS, Global Trade Atlas (accessed January 24, 2014); Hartzenburg and Muradzikwa, "Transfer of Technology for Successful Integration," 2002; Itano, "U.S. Pact Lifts South Africa Car Exports," July 9, 2003; Mercedes-Benz website http://www.mercedes- benzsa.co.za/corporate-structure/mercedes-benz-south africa/manufacturing-plant/ (accessed November 21, 2013); Pitot, "The End of MIDP" (accessed December 30, 2013); USITC DataWeb/USDOC (accessed November 26, 2013, and January 3, 2014).

REFINED PETROLEUM PRODUCTS

The products in this group are processed from crude petroleum; they include gasolines, kerosene, distillates, liquefied petroleum gas, asphalt, lubricating oils, diesel fuels, and residual fuel oils, among others. The primary refined petroleum products imported under AGOA are distillate and residual fuel oils and naphthas. The distillate fuel oils include diesel fuels and no. 1, no. 2, and no. 4 fuel oils, which are used primarily for space heating and electric power generation. Residual fuel oils, known as no. 5 and no. 6 fuel oils, are used for electric power production, space heating, vessel bunkering, and various industrial purposes. Naphthas are light distillates, blended with other materials to produce high-grade motor gasoline or jet fuel and also used as solvents and petrochemical feedstocks. Nigeria and Angola are the primary AGOA-eligible suppliers of U.S. imports of petroleum products; both are members of the Organization of Petroleum Exporting Countries (OPEC). The NTR rates of duty for refined petroleum products are about 0.04 percent ad valorem.

Refined Petroleum Products: Leading U.S. imports under AGOA and GSP, by product and key suppliers, 2000, 2005, and 2008–13 (million $)

Product category (2012 HTS code)	Supplier	2000	2005	2008	2009	2010	2011	2012	2013
Naphthas (2710.12.25)	Nigeria	0	320	645	258	357	561	533	645
	All other AGOA beneficiaries	0	78	14	3	0	55	21	0
Subtotal		0	398	659	261	357	616	554	645
Distillate and residual fuel oils (2710.19.06)	Angola	0	182	333	38	0	0	276	158
	Nigeria	0	753	511	48	32	76	114	170
	Cameroon	0	69	73	45	69	137	59	36
	All other AGOA beneficiaries	1	261	73	34	0	18	63	163
Subtotal		1	1,265	990	165	101	231	512	527
All other refined petroleum products imported under AGOA		0	121	138	88	164	216	341	125
Total refined petroleum products imported under AGOA		a1	1,784	1,787	514	622	1,063	1,407	1,297

Source: USITC DataWeb/USDOC (accessed November 26, 2013, and February 26, 2014).
Note: Due to rounding, sums may not match totals. [a] U.S. import data show a small shipment of refined petroleum products from Benin to the United States in 2000. This is likely a misclassification, as Benin had no refinery capacity during 2000–2013. This shipment may have originated in Nigeria, the only AGOA-eligible country with refineries capable of producing goods for export in 2000.

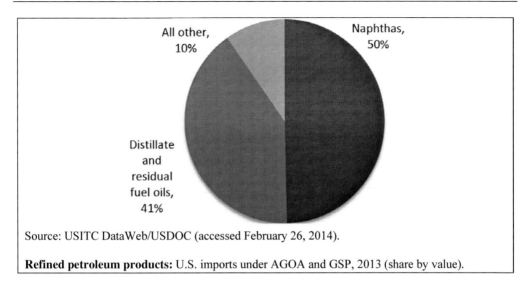

Source: USITC DataWeb/USDOC (accessed February 26, 2014).

Refined petroleum products: U.S. imports under AGOA and GSP, 2013 (share by value).

Major Factors in the Growth of Refined Petroleum Product Imports under AGOA/GSP

Rising, though volatile, prices for crude petroleum, the feedstock used by refineries to produce refined petroleum products, contributed to the increase in value of U.S. imports of petroleum products from AGOA-eligible countries during 2000–2013, despite a decline in the quantity of these imports over the same period (see below).

The average price of U.S. imports of crude petroleum products from AGOA-eligible countries (primarily Nigeria and Angola) increased from $23 per barrel in 2000 to $128 in 2013. The volatility of crude petroleum prices in this period is the result of OPEC production and price limits, supply disruptions in Nigeria due to continued civil unrest, strikes in Angola and Nigeria by crude petroleum field workers over working conditions, tensions between the West and Iran, increased demand in countries such as India and China, and an embargo on Syrian crude petroleum.

By value, U.S. imports of refined petroleum products from AGOA-eligible countries peaked in 2005, reaching a record high of $1.8 billion, then fell through the rest of the period to $1.3 billion in 2013—still much higher than the $279 million in 2001. While the value of U.S. imports of these goods from AGOA-eligible countries showed an overall increase during 2000–2013, the quantity declined from 12.8 million barrels in 2000 to 10 million barrels in 2013.

During 2000–2013, Nigeria was a net importer of refined petroleum products. Although Nigeria has four refineries, their capacity utilization rate hovers around 16–18 percent. These rates are low due to operational failures, fires, and sabotage, mainly of pipelines leading from the wellhead to the refineries. The four refineries have a combined crude petroleum distillation capacity of 445,000 barrels per day, an amount which could satisfy Nigerian demand for these products if the refineries operated at full or near- full capacity.

Angola has a single refinery, built in 1955 by Petrofina (a Belgian energy company that is now a subsidiary of Total). With a capacity of 39,000 barrels per day, this refinery cannot process the heavy crudes produced in Angola, only the lighter crudes that are imported. Consumption of refined petroleum products in Angola remains low due to low levels of economic development. Thus Angolan production is mainly exported, primarily to the United

States and the EU. Angola currently accounts for less than 0.5 percent of total U.S. imports of refined petroleum products.

Sources: *Oil and Gas Journal*, "Worldwide Refining Capacities Report," December 2, 2013; U.S. Department of Energy, *Country Analysis Brief: Angola*, February 5, 2014; U.S. Department of Energy, *Country Analysis Brief: Nigeria*, December 30, 2013.

APPAREL

This product group includes a wide range of knit, woven, and other apparel, such as suits, coats, tops, trousers, underwear and nightwear, dresses, ski apparel, and swimwear. The largest categories of U.S. apparel imports under AGOA in 2013 were "bottoms," including men's trousers. Roughly two-thirds of total U.S. apparel imports under AGOA were cotton products. Lesotho, Kenya, Mauritius, and Swaziland accounted for the vast majority of all U.S. imports under AGOA in 2013. The NTR rates of duty for these goods range from 2.6 to 32 percent ad valorem.

Apparel: Leading U.S. imports under AGOA and GSP, by product and key suppliers, 2000, 2005, and 2008–13 (million $)

Product category (2012 HTS code)	Supplier	2000	2005	2008	2009	2010	2011	2012	2013
Bottoms (6103.43, 6104.62, 6104.63, 6203.42, 6204.62, 6204.63)	Lesotho	0	195	170	142	161	191	186	191
	Kenya	0	197	164	120	111	134	147	154
	Swaziland	0	75	65	52	44	37	31	21
	All other AGOA Beneficiaries	0	214	161	137	40	37	27	27
Subtotal		0	680	560	450	356	399	389	393
Shirts (6105.10, 6105.20, 6109.10, 6109.90, 6205.20)	Mauritius	0	85	69	63	76	117	130	153
	Lesotho	0	25	40	39	39	53	53	55
	Kenya	0	15	16	10	8	26	25	40
	All other AGOA Beneficiaries	0	55	61	42	10	15	15	15
Subtotal		0	179	186	154	133	212	224	263
Sweaters (6110.20, 6110.30)	Lesotho	0	137	101	70	54	48	42	48
	Kenya	0	19	36	35	46	45	35	53
	Swaziland	0	45	33	24	29	16	12	9
	All other AGOA Beneficiaries	0	173	68	52	21	27	14	17
Subtotal		0	374	238	181	151	137	103	126
All other apparel products imported under AGOA		<1	<1	187	154	129	87	108	99
Total apparel products imported under AGOA		<1	1,420	1,137	914	727	855	815	907

Source: USITC DataWeb/USDOC (accessed November 26, 2013, and February 26, 2014)
Note: Due to rounding, sums may not match totals.

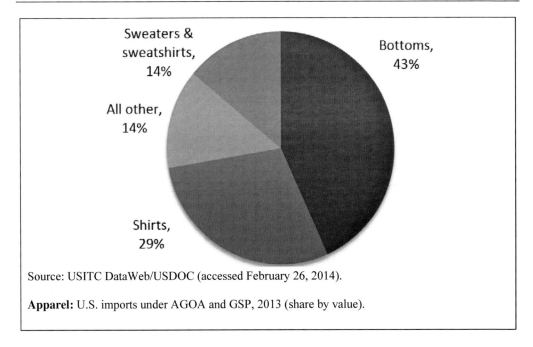

Source: USITC DataWeb/USDOC (accessed February 26, 2014).

Apparel: U.S. imports under AGOA and GSP, 2013 (share by value).

Major Factors in the Growth of U.S. Apparel Imports under AGOA/GSP

Duty-free access to the U.S. market under AGOA, combined with a liberal rule of origin for apparel for certain lesser-developed beneficiary countries (LDBCs), was a major factor in the growth of U.S. apparel imports from AGOA countries. Rapid growth occurred mainly from 2000 to 2005, when U.S. imports under preferences grew from $726,000 to $1.4 billion. Investors from quota-constrained suppliers, such as China and Taiwan, invested in factories in AGOA countries to take advantage of the quota-free access to the U.S. market. In addition to the duty-free, quota-free U.S. market access, certain AGOA beneficiaries received a special third-country fabric exemption, which allowed AGOA countries to use fabric sourced from anywhere and still qualify for AGOA preferences. Over 93 percent of U.S. imports of apparel (by value) under AGOA entered under this "third-country fabric provision" in 2013.

The end of developed-country textile and apparel import quotas in 2005 undermined U.S. apparel imports from AGOA countries. Before 2005, quotas limited the amount of lower-cost apparel from quota countries that could enter the U.S. and other developed-country markets, while AGOA beneficiaries had quota-free access to the U.S. market. After 2005, U.S. imports of apparel under AGOA fell, in part from the rise in U.S. market shares of Asian apparel suppliers that obtained new quota-free access to the U.S. market and displaced less competitive AGOA country suppliers. Some Asian investors with apparel facilities in AGOA countries closed them after 2005. During 2005–13, U.S. imports of apparel under AGOA decreased on average by 7 percent per year, to $907 million in 2013.

Uncertainly caused by last-minute and short-term renewals of the AGOA third-country fabric provision may have also contributed to the decline in U.S. apparel imports under AGOA since 2005, since buyers place orders for apparel 6–12 months in advance. In addition, the provision has been renewed for periods of only three to four years, which industry sources state does not provide the certainty needed to make new investments or place new or increased orders in the region.

Sources: USITC, *Sub-Saharan Africa: Factors Affecting Trade Patterns*, 2007; DOC, ITA, OTEXA, "U.S. Imports under Trade Preference Programs" (accessed February 3, 2014); USITC Data Web/USDOC (accessed November 26, 2013); GTIS, Global Trade Atlas database (accessed March 7, 2014); USITC, hearing transcript, January 14, 2014, 9, 20 (testimony of Somduth Soborun, ambassador of Mauritius to the United States); ACTIF, "Impact of AGOA on the Textile Industry," November 2010; ACTIF, "Competitiveness of the SSA Textile Sector," 2010.

FERROALLOYS

Products in this group are alloys of various metals and iron that are used in steelmaking and other ferrous metallurgy. Alloying elements are needed to achieve desired physical properties in finished steel products. The principal ferroalloys imported from AGOA-eligible countries are ferromanganese, silicomanganese, and ferrochromium. Because of its abundance of suitable ore and well-developed infrastructure, South Africa is a major world producer and exporter of these alloys and is the only AGOA beneficiary country with the current capability to produce them. NTR duty rates for these ferroalloys range from 1.5 to 3.9 percent ad valorem.

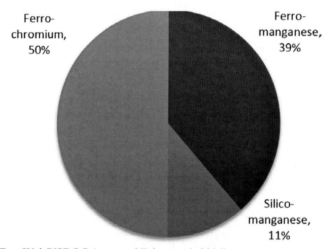

Source: USITC DataWeb/USDOC (accessed February 6, 2014).

Ferroalloys: U.S. imports under AGOA and GSP, 2013 (share by value).

Ferroalloys: Leading U.S. imports under AGOA and GSP, by product and key suppliers, 2000, 2005, 2008–13 (million $)

Product category (2012 HTS code)	Supplier	2000	2005	2008	2009	2010	2011	2012	2013
Ferromanganese (7202.11, 7202.19)	South Africa	20	98	446	114	195	246	238	205
	Zambia	0	0	0	1	0	0	0	0

Product category (2012 HTS code)	Supplier	2000	2005	2008	2009	2010	2011	2012	2013
Subtotal		20	98	446	114	196	246	238	205
Silicomanganese (7202.30)	South Africa	44	61	283	60	145	161	133	60
Ferrochromium (7202.41, 7202.49)	South Africa	94	118	308	103	254	247	228	264
Ferrosilicon (7202.21)	South Africa	14	0	0	<1	<1	2	6	1
Total ferroalloy imports under AGOA		172	277	1,037	277	596	656	605	530

Source: USITC DataWeb/USDOC (accessed November 26, 2013, and February 26, 2014).
Note: Due to rounding, sums may not match totals.

Major Factors in the Growth in Ferroalloy Imports under AGOA/GSP

Higher prices and volume growth contributed to the rise in the value of U.S. imports of ferrochromium and ferromanganese from South Africa during 2000–2013. The average unit values of these ferroalloys increased by 150 percent and 128 percent, respectively, over the period, and the quantities increased by 11 percent and 41 percent, respectively. Higher prices reflected stronger global demand for these alloys as global steel production grew rapidly— 89 percent by volume during 2000–2013. Prices for these ferroalloys peaked in 2008 and fell throughout the rest of the period, but still stayed above their prices from the early 2000s.

Rising prices also accounted for the increased value of U.S. imports of silicomanganese from South Africa during 2000–2013, as a 138 percent increase in the average unit value of these imports more than offset a 42 percent drop in their quantity. Supply factors in South Africa contributed to the drop in the volume of silicomanganese imports. The production of ferroalloys depends on the availability of suitable ore and of large amounts of competitively priced electricity. Production of ferroalloys in South Africa has been hampered in recent years by restrictions on the availability of electricity, as the state energy group, Eskom, negotiated agreements with the ferroalloy producers to buy back previously contracted supplies of electricity. This disruption has resulted in reduced production and some furnaces being shut down. The quantity of U.S. imports of silicomanganese from South Africa declined by 63 percent from 2008 through 2013.

During the same period, as global steel production increased rapidly, steel production in the United States declined from a peak level of 102 million metric tons in 2000 to 87 million metric tons in 2013. Because the United States relies on imports of these ferroalloys to meet domestic demand for steel production, this decline in steel production lowered U.S. demand for imports of certain ferroalloys during the period.

Sources: USITC DataWeb/USDOC (accessed November 20, 2013, and November 26, 2013); World Steel Association, Crude Steel Production, 1980–2012 (accessed January 24, 2014); International Manganese Institute, About Mn: Production (accessed January 24, 2014); *American Metal Market*, January 2008–November 2013.

ALUMINUM MILL PRODUCTS

Products in this group are rolled, extruded, or drawn from unwrought forms of aluminum or aluminum alloys into various forms, such as bars, wires, sheets, and pipes. Aluminum mill products are intermediate inputs for a wide range of downstream finished products in the construction, electric power, electronic equipment, machinery, packaging, and transportation equipment sectors. The vast majority of aluminum mill products imported into the United States under AGOA/GSP are aluminum plates, sheets, and strips from South Africa. NTR duty rates for these products range from 2.7 to 6.5 percent ad valorem.

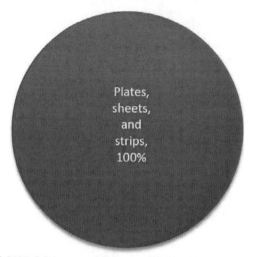

Source: USITC DataWeb/USDOC (accessed February 26, 2014).

Aluminum mill products: U.S. imports under AGOA and GSP, 2013 (share by value).

Aluminum mill products: Leading U.S. imports under AGOA and GSP, by product and key suppliers, 2000, 2005, 2008–13 (thousand $)

Product category (2012 HTS code)	Supplier	2000	2005	2008	2009	2010	2011	2012	2013
Plates, sheets, and strips (7606)	Ghana	2,309	0	0	0	0	0	0	0
	South Africa	50,302	150,920	155,246	97,452	156,849	190,428	195,778	188,793
Subtotal		52,611	150,920	155,246	97,452	156,849	190,428	195,778	188,793
All other aluminum mill product imports under AGOA		3,993	2,938	3,133	1,574	3,395	4,748	4,867	502
Total aluminum mill product imports under AGOA		56,604	153,857	158,379	99,025	160,243	195,175	200,645	189,295

Source: USITC DataWeb/USDOC (accessed November 26, 2013, and February 26, 2014).
Note: Due to rounding, sums may not match totals.

Major Factors in the Growth of Aluminum Mill Products under AGOA/GSP

Higher prices and volume growth contributed to the increased value of U.S. imports from South Africa during 2000–2013. The volume of U.S. imports of aluminum plates, sheets, and strips from South Africa under AGOA/GSP provisions rose strongly, growing by 37,643 metric tons (174.2 percent) between 2000 and 2013. However, the value of these imports rose even more strongly, growing by $138.5 million (275 percent). London Metal Exchange (LME) prices for unwrought aluminum have risen significantly (by about $650–$700 per metric ton) since the mid-2000s, due principally to expanding global demand, particularly from China.

U.S. demand for aluminum plates, sheets, and strips is driven by the various downstream aluminum-consuming industries (e.g., aerospace, appliances, construction, packaging, and transportation). During 2000–2013, the share of domestic consumption of these flat-rolled aluminum products accounted for by U.S. imports from all sources rose from 13 percent to 16 percent.

Before the AGOA program began, South Africa was well positioned to capitalize on AGOA provisions to export high-quality aluminum mill products to the U.S. market because it (1) was a long-established roller and extruder of aluminum, (2) has ready access to both domestically smelted unwrought aluminum and domestically generated aluminum waste and scrap as feedstock, and (3) has the largest and most sophisticated aluminum industry in sub-Saharan Africa.

In addition, Hulett Aluminium (Hulamin), South Africa's sole producer of aluminum flat-rolled products, upgraded its production capabilities and expanded capacity at its melting and rolling facilities during 1999–2000, reportedly to meet growing domestic and global demand for plate products. These investments enabled Hulamin to quadruple its sales volumes to 200,000 metric tons annually by summer 2006; diversify and enhance its product mix; reduce its per-unit production costs; and increase exports of its higher-quality/higher-value output. Further facility upgrades and expansions undertaken during 2006–09 were expected to raise Hulamin's potential annualized sales volumes to 250,000 metric tons.

Sources: AFSA, "Aluminum Industry in SA, Overview," n.d.; AMM.com, "Pricing," n.d.; Hulamin, "Hulett Alumium to Expand Capacity," October 11, 2006; Hulamin, "Hulett Corporate—History," http://www.hulamin.co.za/about_hulamin/history.htm; Hulamin, "Hulett Rolled Products—Home" http://www.hulaminrolledproducts.co.za; Hulamin, "Official Opening of Rolled Products Expansion," December 11, 2009; *Metal Bulletin*, "Hulett Aluminum to Boost Rolled Product Output by 9%," February 21, 2005; *Metal Bulletin*, "Hulett Aluminium to Raise Rolling Capacity by 20%," October 12, 2006; *Metal Bulletin*, "Hulett Invests for Growth," January 11, 2001; WBMS, "Aluminum, U.S.A., 2. Semi Manufactures," December 2003–December 2012.

COCOA, CHOCOLATE, AND CONFECTIONERY

Cocoa products are derived from cocoa beans, which are processed into intermediate products including paste, butter, and powder. Final products include chocolate and other food preparations containing cocoa products. The principal products imported under AGOA are cocoa paste and powder from Côte d'Ivoire and Ghana.

The NTR duty rates for cocoa paste and cocoa powder covered by preferences for AGOA countries are less than 0.5 percent ad valorem.

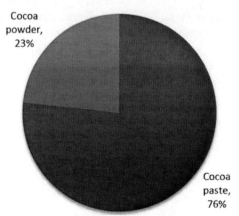

Source: USITC DataWeb/USDOC (accessed February 26, 2014).
Note: Chocolate and confectionery made up less than 1 percent of imports.

Cocoa, chocolate, and confectionery: U.S. imports under AGOA and GSP, 2013 (share by value).

Cocoa, Chocolate, and Confectionery Products: Leading U.S. imports under AGOA and GSP, by product and key suppliers, 2000, 2005, and 2008–13 (thousand $)

Product category (2012 HTS code)	Supplier	2000	2005	2008	2009	2010	2011	2012	2013
Cocoa paste (1803.20)	Côte d'Ivoire	0	0	0	0	0	42,745	83,785	71,818
	Cameroon	2,646	19	5,571	10,753	30,428	35,960	32,594	21,104
	All other AGOA beneficiaries	1,260	1,056	1,194	717	3,129	1,310	503	774
Subtotal		3,906	1,075	6,765	11,470	33,557	80,015	116,883	93,697
Cocoa powder (1805.00)	Ghana	48	36	235	7,548	32,943	29,136	31,445	16,813
	Côte d'Ivoire	0	0	0	0	0	5,384	9,964	11,716
	Nigeria	0	0	0	4	0	0	0	0
Subtotal		48	36	235	7,552	32,943	34,520	41,409	28,529
Chocolate and confectionery products (1806,1704)	South Africa	313	1,045	307	434	696	654	794	221
	All other AGOA beneficiaries	144	224	31	73	66	63	77	327
Subtotal		457	1,268	338	507	761	717	871	549
Total cocoa, chocolate, and confectionery imports under AGOA		4,410	2,379	7,338	19,529	67,262	115,252	159,163	122,775

Source: USITC DataWeb/USDOC (accessed November 26, 2013, and February 26, 2014).
Note: Due to rounding, sums may not match totals.

Major Factors in the Growth in Cocoa Product Imports under AGOA/GSP

Rising U.S. and global demand for cocoa- containing products bolstered demand for cocoa paste and powder. Rising global incomes were major factors in the cocoa product demand increase, as was recognition of its health benefits. U.S. producers source intermediate cocoa products from a variety of origins, including AGOA countries.

U.S. imports of cocoa, chocolate, and confectionery from AGOA-eligible partners under AGOA/GSP provisions rose substantially during 2000–2013, from 5,546 metric tons (valued at $4.4 million) in 2000, to 37,516 metric tons (valued at $122.8 million) in 2013. The rise in import values outpaced quantity increases for the various cocoa products, largely the result of cocoa bean price increases during the period.

The growth in demand for cocoa-containing products has contributed to an increase in global cocoa bean and product prices. According to International Cocoa Organization data, the average monthly price for cocoa beans rose from about $1,500 per metric ton in January 2005 to about $2,400 per metric ton in December 2012. Prices exceeded $3,500 per metric ton some months in 2010, largely the result of supply disruptions caused by civil strife in Côte d'Ivoire. Concerns about supply risk in Côte d'Ivoire, by far the world's leading producer of cocoa beans, have been long-standing and persistent. Other factors contributing to the long-term rise in cocoa product prices include improvements in quality (at the farm level, in transportation, and in storage) and the establishment of sustainability and social programs related to cocoa production. For example, the industry in Ghana is directed by the state cocoa board, COCOBOD, which implemented measures to improve product quality, increase farm yields, and raise farm gate prices.

Cocoa bean processing capacity in certain AGOA countries has increased. Some AGOA country governments have prioritized their cocoa industries and introduced incentives to facilitate the development and expansion of downstream value-added cocoa processing. Major transnational cocoa firms, such as Archer Daniels Midland, Cargill, and Barry Callebaut, as well as local operators, have established and expanded cocoa-processing facilities in the region, with the greatest concentration in Côte d'Ivoire and Ghana. Cocoa-processing capacity has risen by 50 percent in Côte d'Ivoire during 2008–12 and by 250 percent in Ghana during 2005–12. Africa has accounted for an increasing share of global cocoa processing in recent years, from 14 percent in 2005/06 to an estimated 19 percent in 2012/13. Despite this growth, AGOA cocoa product industries are facing increasing competition from growing processing capacity in Asia (Indonesia) and Latin America (Brazil).

Sources: Callebaut, "Barry Callebaut Inaugurates Second Cocoa Bean Processing Line," February 8, 2007; Cargill, "Cargill Celebrates Five Years in Ghana," November 5, 2013; George, "Structure and Competition," November 21, 2012; *Financial Times*, "Processing Capacity Grinds Cocoa Industry," December 17, 2012; ICCO, *Annual Report*; ICCO, Quarterly Bulletin of Cocoa Statistics; ICCO, "Statistics," http://www.icco.org/; TCC, *Cocoa Barometer 2009*, 2009; TCC, *Cocoa Barometer 2010*, 2010; TCC, *Cocoa Barometer 2012*, 2012.

MISCELLANEOUS INORGANIC CHEMICALS

Inorganic chemicals in this group include elemental metals, such as silicon, and simple compounds of these metals and oxygen, sulfur, nitrogen, or chlorine. They are used as inputs in the production of a wide variety of precursor chemical products, which are then used to make consumer goods, energy storage and generation devices, and electronics, among other things. Although a variety of inorganic chemicals are imported into the United States from AGOA beneficiary countries, the primary chemicals are silicon metal, manganese dioxide, and vanadium oxides and hydroxides. Silicon metal is used in the production process for lubricants and resins. Manganese dioxide is used primarily in producing dry-cell batteries, and vanadium oxides and hydroxides are used as an upstream catalyst in the production process for fertilizer. NTR rates of duty for these inorganic chemicals range from 4.7 to 5.5 percent ad valorem.

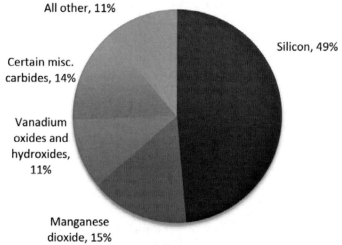

Source: USITC DataWeb/USDOC (accessed February 26, 2014).

Miscellaneous inorganic chemicals: U.S. imports under AGOA and GSP, 2013 (share by value).

Miscellaneous Inorganic Chemicals: Leading U.S. imports under AGOA and GSP, by product and key suppliers, 2000, 2005, and 2008–13 (million $)

Product category (2012 HTS code)	Supplier	2000	2005	2008	2009	2010	2011	2012	2013
Silicon, containing by weight less than 99.99 percent of silicon (2804.69)	South Africa	31	51	89	54	83	114	97	86
Manganese dioxide (2820.10)	South Africa	17	0	19	29	36	45	33	27
Vanadium oxides and hydroxides (2825.30)	South Africa	6	42	34	8	22	32	24	19
Certain miscellaneous carbides (2849.90)	South Africa	11	57	48	10	28	31	20	25

Product category (2012 HTS code)	Supplier	2000	2005	2008	2009	2010	2011	2012	2013
Other miscellaneous inorganic chemicals	South Africa	14	15	14	8	10	31	43	20
	All other AGOA beneficiaries	0	0	0	<1	0	<1	<1	<1
Subtotal		14	15	14	8	10	31	43	20
Total miscellaneous inorganic chemicals imports under AGOA		79	164	205	109	180	252	216	176

Source: USITC DataWeb/USDOC (accessed November 26, 2013, and February 26, 2014).
Note: Due to rounding, sums may not match totals.

Major Factors in the Growth of Miscellaneous Inorganic Chemical Imports under AGOA/GSP

Higher prices accounted for the increase in the value of U.S. imports of silicon metal (metallurgical or chemical grade) from South Africa during 2000–2013, since import volumes declined irregularly over the period. From 2000 to 2013, the quantity of silicon metal imported from South Africa fell by 16 percent, but the average unit value rose almost 150 percent, from $1,090 per metric ton to almost $2,700 per metric ton. South Africa is estimated to be the sixth- largest producer and fourth-largest exporter of silicon metal in the world, but is the largest among AGOA countries. U.S. producers of chemicals such as silanes and silicones are the primary consumers of silicon metal, with the U.S. aluminum casting industry being the second-largest. U.S. consumption of silicon metal is influenced by the demand for downstream chemical products, such as certain rubbers, resins, and lubricants, and for airplane and automobile aluminum parts.

Higher prices and volume growth contributed to the increase in the value of U.S. imports of manganese dioxide from South Africa during 2000–2013. The quantity imported from South Africa rose by 7 percent over the period, but the average unit value rose more—from $1,408 per metric ton in 2000 to $2,046 per metric ton in 2013, or by 45 percent. South Africa has the world's largest identified manganese deposits (about 75 percent of the global total) and is the world's largest exporter of manganese ore, from which manganese dioxide is produced. It is the second-largest global exporter of manganese dioxide, behind China. The United States must import to meet domestic demand, primarily from dry cell battery makers. Increases in demand for batteries during 2000–2013, as well as for manganese dioxide, have been small but consistent from year to year.

Volume growth and much higher prices contributed to the increase in U.S. imports of vanadium oxides and hydroxides from South Africa during 2000–2013. The quantity of vanadium oxides and hydroxides imported from South Africa grew 12 percent over the period, but the average unit value grew much more—from $4,739 per metric ton in 2000 to just more than $13,000 per metric ton in 2013, or by 176 percent. South Africa is the world's second-largest producer of vanadium, behind China, and available data shows that South African vanadium production increased significantly during 2000–2012 (almost 30 percent). South Africa is the third-largest global exporter of vanadium oxides and hydroxides, behind China and Russia. Makers of sulfuric acid are the primary U.S. consumers of vanadium oxides and hydroxides. Demand for sulfuric acid is influenced by the demand for fertilizer, which fluctuates based on economic factors in the agricultural sector.

Sources: USITC DataWeb/USDOC (accessed January 2014); BIT Fondel, "Silicon Metal," February 7, 2014.; CPM Group, "Manganese Market Outlook," February 2012; SEMI, "Metallurgical-Grade Silicon Making Inroads in PV," February 4, 2014; Shakhashiri, "Chemical of the Week: Phosphoric Acid, H3PO4," February 6, 2008; Shakhashiri, "Chemical of the Week: Sulfuric Acid, H2SO4," September 17, 2007; Suresh, "Sulfuric Acid," July 2012; Suresh, Schlag, and Inoguchi, "Inorganic Color Pigments," February 2011; USDOI, USGS, *Mineral Commodity Summaries: Manganese*, January 2013; USDOI, USGS, *Mineral Commodity Summaries: Silicon*, January 2013; USDOI, USGS, "Silicon," December 2013; USDOI, USGS, *Mineral Commodity Summaries: Vanadium*, January 2013; USDOI, USGS; "Vanadium," October 2013; USITC, *Electrolytic Manganese Dioxide from Australia and China*, 2008; USITC, *Shifts in U.S. Merchandise Trade 2006*, 2007; Westbrook Resources, "(Si) Atomic Number 14," n.d., http://www.wbrl.co.uk/silicon-metal.html (accessed February 7, 2014).

CERTAIN ORGANIC CHEMICALS

The organic chemicals in this group are used as inputs in the production of a variety of products, including adhesives, coatings, dyes and pigments, pharmaceuticals, plastics, and rubber. Although a wide variety of organic chemicals are imported into the United States from AGOA beneficiary countries, the primary chemicals imported under the AGOA/GSP programs are methyl ethyl ketone (MEK) and nonaromatic esters of acrylic acid. MEK is used as a solvent in adhesives and coatings, while nonaromatic esters of acrylic acid are used in the production of paints, coatings, adhesives, plastic sheet, and other products. The NTR rates of duty for MEK and nonaromatic esters of acrylic acid are 3.1 and 3.7 percent ad valorem, respectively.

Certain Organic Chemicals: Leading U.S. imports under AGOA and GSP, by product and key suppliers, 2000, 2005, and 2008–13 (million $)

Product category (2012 HTS code)	Supplier	2000	2005	2008	2009	2010	2011	2012	2013
Methyl ethyl ketone (2914.12.00)	South Africa	3	10	13	10	25	39	29	33
Nonaromatic esters of acrylic acid (2916.12.50)	South Africa	0	21	27	14	25	26	20	19
All other certain organic chemicals imported under AGOA		14	32	43	29	50	55	53	51
Total certain organic chemicals imports under AGOA		17	62	84	53	101	120	102	103

Source: USITC DataWeb/USDOC (accessed November 26, 2013, and February 26, 2014).
Note: Due to rounding, sums may not match totals.

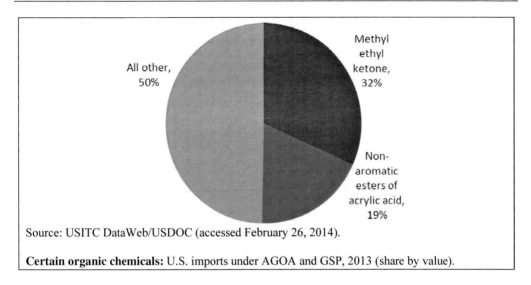

Source: USITC DataWeb/USDOC (accessed February 26, 2014).

Certain organic chemicals: U.S. imports under AGOA and GSP, 2013 (share by value).

Major Factors in the Growth of Certain Organic Chemical Imports under AGOA/GSP

The value of organic chemical imports of this type grew faster than the quantity of such imports over the period, primarily due to higher unit values resulting from increased costs of crude petroleum and other feedstocks. For example, while the volume of U.S. MEK imports from South Africa during 2000–2013 grew from 6,800 to 23,200 metric tons, or 242 percent, value grew by 865 percent.

U.S. demand for nonaromatic esters of acrylic acid by paints and coatings industries grew during 2000–2013 due to increases in demand for downstream products, such as architectural paints and coatings, and automotive lacquers.

Decreased U.S. production of MEK during 2000–2013 stimulated a rise in MEK imports from various countries, including AGOA beneficiary South Africa. Two U.S. MEK production plants were shuttered in 2004 and 2008. Although U.S. imports of MEK grew during 2000–2013, overall U.S. demand for MEK fell due to a variety of factors, including increased use of powder-based and water-based coatings. Many users also switched to higher solids concentrations to reduce solvent usage because organic solvents such as MEK contribute to air and water pollution.

South African production of organic chemicals in this group grew over 2000–2013. A major production facility was opened in 2004 by Sasol, a South African company, to take advantage of South Africa's abundant coal resources as a low-cost feedstock in the production of certain organic chemicals, including nonaromatic esters of acrylic acid.

Sources: *Chemical Week*, "Sasol Starts Up Acrylates Complex," April 7/14, 2004, 40; *Chemical Week*, "Shell Closes Louisiana MEK Plant," September 29/October 6, 2004, 62; Greiner and Funada, "Methyl Ethyl Ketone (MEK)," 2012, 11, 13; Glauser, "Acrylic Acid, Acrylate Esters and Superabsorbent Polymers," 2012, 20; USITC DataWeb/USDOC (accessed December 2013–March 2014).

EDIBLE NUTS

The United States imports various edible nuts from AGOA-eligible countries, including cashews, macadamia nuts, kola nuts, peanuts, pecans, and nut mixtures. However, cashews, the most heavily imported nut category from AGOA-eligible countries, are duty free under NTR. The vast majority of edible nuts imported under AGOA/GSP are macadamia nuts from Kenya, South Africa, and Malawi. NTR duty rates for macadamia nuts are less than 0.5 percent ad valorem.

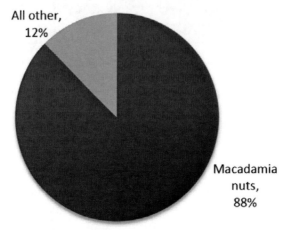

Source: USITC DataWeb/USDOC (accessed February 26, 2014).

Edible nuts: U.S. imports under AGOA and GSP, 2013 (share by value).

Edible Nuts: Leading U.S. imports under AGOA and GSP, by product and key suppliers, 2000, 2005, and 2008–13 (thousand $)

Product category (2012 HTS code)	Supplier	2000	2005	2008	2009	2010	2011	2012	2013
Macadamia nuts (0802.61, 0802.62)	Kenya	0	4,355	2,856	3,634	15,328	23,573	29,756	24,516
	South Africa	0	18,328	9,726	11,620	20,339	19,787	26,217	26,954
	Malawi	61	5,128	2,112	1,931	4,869	4,898	4,222	3,093
	Swaziland	0	0	0	0	120	179	170	0
	Mozambique	67	158	129	0	184	0	0	0
Subtotal		127	27,969	14,823	17,185	40,840	48,438	60,366	54,563
All other edible nuts imported under AGOA		404	2,687	6,861	4,137	7,923	7,810	9,357	7,787
Total edible nut imports under AGOA		532	30,656	21,684	21,322	48,763	56,248	69,722	62,350

Source: USITC DataWeb/USDOC (accessed November 26, 2013, and February 26, 2014).
Note: Due to rounding, sums may not match totals.

Major Factors in the Growth of Edible Nut Imports under AGOA/GSP

In terms of both value and volume, U.S. imports of edible nuts under AGOA/GSP provisions registered a dramatic rise since the implementation of AGOA, from 117 metric tons (valued at $532,000) in 2000 to 5,161 metric tons (valued at $62.3 million) in 2013. Most of this rise was accounted for by imports of macadamia nuts, which accounted for 88 percent of the value of imports of edible nuts under AGOA/GSP in 2013. The rise in value exceeded the growth in quantity over the period; unit values increased by 165 percent, driven by demand.

U.S. and global demand for macadamia nuts has been growing owing to the health benefits attributed to edible nuts, including macadamias. Intermittent weather-related supply constraints on Australian production, the traditional leading global exporter, during 2000–2013 contributed to an increase in both the quantity and value of exports of macadamia nuts from AGOA countries. Currently, the principal AGOA exporters are South Africa, which is the leading global producer of in- shell and shelled macadamia nuts combined; Kenya, a relative newcomer to the macadamia nut trade; and Malawi, which is expected to substantially increase exports in the coming years.

The growth of the South African macadamia nut industry has been aided mainly by the industry- funded South African Macadamia Growers' Association (SAMAC). Export competitiveness in South Africa has been enhanced by SAMAC's focus on improving quality, as many growers and processing facilities have attained accreditation under quality control programs. In addition, the largest South African macadamia nut company, Green Farms Nut Company, entered a joint venture in 2010 with the Australian producer Suncoast Gold and formed the world's largest macadamia nut marketing company, Green & Gold Macadamias. Another South African producer, Stahmann Farms Enterprises, joined the venture in October 2012.

A substantial rise in production and exports in Kenya has been attributable mainly to a combination of expanded acreage, quality improvement, international certifications, and value chain enhancement.

The Malawi government targeted the macadamia nut industry for development in the mid-1990s and received assistance from the African Development Bank.

Sources: ADF, "Macadamia Smallholder Development Project," April 2009; BIF, Equal Exchange, and Irish Aid, *Malawian Macadamias 2010–2020*; *Farmer's Weekly*, "Making a Mountain out of Macadamias," February 11, 2013; Equatorial Nut Processors, "About Us," 2013; Equatorial Nut Processors, "Our Certifications," 2013; GTIS, Global Trade Atlas database; International Nut & Dried Fruit, *Global Statistical Review 2007–2012* (accessed February 11, 2014); Horticultural Crops Development Authority, "Macadamia," February 21, 2014; Mbora, Jamnadass, and Lillesø, *Growing High Priority Fruits and Nuts in Kenya*, n.d.; Republic of South Africa, DAFF, *A Profile of the South African Macadamia*, 2012; Republic of South Africa, DAFF, National Agricultural Marketing Council, *International Trade Probe*, March 2013; South African Macadamia Nut Growers' Association, "Overview of the South African Macadamia Industry" (accessed January 30, 2014); Ten Senses, "Fair Trade Products," 2011; Twin, "Developing the Macadamia Sector in Malawi" (accessed February 19, 2014); USAID, *Kenya National AGOA Strategy*, June 2012; USDA, FAS, *Kenya: Macadamia Annual Report*, October 1, 2009; USAID, "Ten Senses Africa Ltd.," February 21, 2014; USDA, FAS, *Republic of South Africa: Tree Nuts Annual*, November 20, 2009.

CITRUS FRUIT

Various fresh citrus fruits are imported from AGOA- eligible countries, including oranges, lemons, and grapefruit. The majority of citrus fruit imported under AGOA are navel oranges from South Africa. Fresh oranges are not eligible for duty-free treatment under GSP. NTR duty rates for fresh oranges are 2 percent ad valorem.

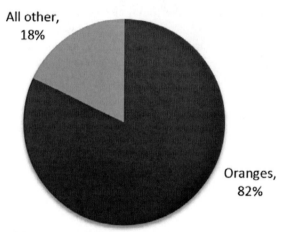

Source: USITC DataWeb/USDOC (accessed February 26, 2014).

Citrus fruit: U.S. imports under AGOA and GSP, 2013 (share by value).

Citrus Fruit: Leading U.S. imports under AGOA and GSP, by product and key suppliers, 2000, 2005, and 2008–13 (million $)

Product category (2012 HTS code)	Supplier	2000	2005	2008	2009	2010	2011	2012	2013
Oranges (0805.10)	South Africa	0	31	34	31	39	38	40	51
All other citrus fruit imported under AGOA		0	15	7	8	10	6	11	11
Total citrus fruit imports under AGOA		0	46	41	38	49	44	51	62

Source: USITC DataWeb/USDOC (accessed November 26, 2013, and February 26, 2014).
Note: Due to rounding, sums may not match totals.

Major Factors in the Growth of Citrus Fruit Imports under AGOA/GSP

Growth in the value of U.S. imports of oranges has been driven by increases in both import quantity and price. Despite rising import volume, the United States is only South Africa's sixth-largest export market for oranges, behind the EU, Russia, and several Middle Eastern countries. South Africa ranks as the world's second-largest exporter of citrus fruit after Spain and is the largest Southern Hemisphere exporter, capitalizing on its production niche as an off-season supplier for Northern Hemisphere markets.

Agricultural market deregulation in South Africa in the 1990s resulted in increased citrus plantings and more exports. South African citrus was approved for export to the United States in 1997.

Duty-free status under AGOA in 2001 allowed South African producers to get a foothold in the U.S. market at a time when the only major Southern Hemisphere competitor, Australia, did not have preferential access for oranges. Today, nearly all U.S. orange imports from major Southern Hemisphere producers (including Australia, Chile, South Africa, and Peru) enter duty-free under FTAs or AGOA, so the South African industry considers AGOA preferences vital to its continued success in the U.S. market.

The South African citrus industry has worked closely with importers and U.S. government agencies to make sure that their products meet U.S. market standards. South African citrus is eligible for preclearance from USDA's Animal and Plant Health Inspection Service (APHIS), under which exports are inspected and treated before leaving South Africa, expediting the clearance of the product on arrival at the U.S. port of entry. The South African industry has also received foreign direct investment from U.S. companies like Sunkist to help increase exports to growing markets. The industry has adapted to increased global competition by planting varieties popular in export markets and improving quality through better management practices.

Demand factors have also helped drive increased U.S. imports of South African oranges. The United States is a large producer of oranges for fresh consumption, but domestic production supplies the bulk of the market only from about November through June; off-season imports from mostly Southern Hemisphere suppliers dominate during July–October. U.S. consumer demand for these off-season citrus imports—also referred to as "summer citrus"—is growing.

Since 2000, total orange imports have grown more than 150 percent, with more than 80 percent of this total volume arriving in the July–October window. As the largest Southern Hemisphere exporter, South Africa has positioned itself as one of the United States' primary off-season citrus sources. In fact, the Western Cape Citrus Producers Forum has developed and implemented a marketing campaign specifically targeting the U.S. summer citrus market. Major U.S. retailers including Walmart, Costco, and Whole Foods all source fruit from South Africa.

Sources: GTIS, Global Trade Atlas database (accessed March 3, 2014); Freshful-SHAFFE Secretariat, "Minutes," April 22, 2013; Western Cape Citrus Producers Forum, "Summer Citrus," 2013; USDA, FAS, *South Africa: Citrus Annual Report*, May 15, 1999; USDA, FAS, *Republic of South Africa: Citrus Annual*, May 24, 2002; USDA, FAS, *Republic of South Africa: Citrus Annual*, December 14, 2012; USDA, FAS, *Republic of South Africa: Citrus Annual*, December 20, 2013; USDA, FAS, PSD database (accessed March 3, 20114); Nelson, "South African Citrus," May 4, 2012; Nelson, "South Africa Ships," December 3, 2013; Wilkinson, "King Citrus," July 8, 2013; USDA, NASS, *Citrus Fruits: 2013 Summary*, September 19, 2013; USDA, AMS, *Fresh Fruit and Vegetable Shipments 2000*, March 2001; USDA, AMS, *Fresh Fruit and Vegetable Shipments 2013*, February 2014.

SECTION 3. POTENTIAL FOR SSA INTEGRATION INTO REGIONAL AND GLOBAL SUPPLY CHAINS

Introduction

Regional and global supply chains are cross-border production networks joining multiple firms that supply interlinked economic activities that are needed to bring a product or service from conception to consumption.[75] Because firms contribute economic value through these activities, the chains are often referred to as value chains.[76] Although sub-Saharan Africa (SSA) is endowed with abundant natural resources, little domestic processing of these resources occurs within SSA. As a result, SSA's position along the global supply chain is primarily as a supplier of raw materials or primary products that undergo little value addition or domestic processing within SSA. According to South Africa's minister of trade, the challenge for Africa:

> is not just to integrate ourselves into VCs [value chains]—we are already integrated into VCs—but to elevate our place in those VCs. We are at the moment largely integrated into GVCs [global value chains] as producers and exporters of primary products. We are producers and exporters of dirt out of the ground, which is going to support ID [industrial development] somewhere else.[77]

Potential for further integration into regional or global supply chains therefore generally refers to the ability of firms within SSA to increase the economic value of what they produce and export (i.e., "moving up the value chain"). This can be accomplished by boosting domestic downstream processing of raw materials or primary commodities to produce intermediate or semifinished goods that are used to produce other goods (e.g., processing leather into leather upholstery for car seats, or processing cotton into textiles to produce apparel), or to produce final goods that are consumed within SSA or abroad (e.g., foodstuffs like beverages).

This section looks at the potential for SSA integration into regional and global supply chains by first providing an overview of global supply chains and a description of SSA's participation in them. The section then examines recent examples of value-added products in SSA that have been integrated into regional and global supply chains, including cut and polished diamonds in Botswana, cocoa in Ghana, and agroprocessed goods and apparel in southern Africa. It then presents products that have been identified by researchers, SSA governments, and other stakeholders as having potential for integration into regional and global supply chains. Based on a review of literature, these sectors include agricultural products and foodstuffs, leather and leather products, textiles and apparel, and minerals processing and extractive industries beyond merely supplying raw materials.

Source: Compiled by USITC staff.

Figure 3.1. Example of a simple supply or value chain.

Overview of Regional and Global Supply Chains

The activities occurring in a supply chain can be grouped into a series of broad sequential stages (figure 3.1). Moving upstream to downstream, a typical supply chain includes research and development (R&D) and/or product design; manufacturing, which includes all production stages from raw materials production to finished goods assembly; and marketing and retail sales activities.[78] A supply chain can also be considered a value chain, because firms contribute economic value as they move downstream. For some supply chains several firms are involved in the production phases, whereas for others a single firm carries out most production activities internally, while purchasing raw materials and some services from external suppliers.[79]

Global supply chains (GSCs) are value chains where one or more of these activities take place across international borders. An often cited example of a GSC is the production of Apple's iPod.[80] In this case, most R&D, management, and marketing are U.S.-based; the hard drive is designed in Japan; parts are produced in Asian countries, including Japan, Taiwan, the Republic of Korea (Korea), China, the Philippines, and Singapore; and final assembly is carried out in China by Taiwanese-owned manufacturers.

For some GSCs, participation is primarily among firms in countries that are geographically close to one another, such as countries within North America or the European Union (EU).[81] In such cases the chains are referred to as regional supply chains (RSCs). Production of the Learjet is an example of a North American-based RSC.[82] The Learjet, produced by a Canadian-owned firm, is assembled in the United States using fuselages built in Mexico and U.S.-designed engines built in Canada.[83] Only the wings come from outside North America. Firms operating in an RSC benefit from the ability to better meet customer and local pricing preferences, to lower inventory costs and exchange rate risk, to lower the cost of regulatory compliance, and to take advantage of regional trade preferences, such as those offered by the North American Free Trade Agreement (NAFTA) and the EU.[84]

Several factors have led to the rapid growth of GSCs over the past 30 years.[85] GSCs have enabled firms to take advantage of international cost differences (historically, lower wage costs in particular) by locating distinct activities in different countries based on their respective comparative advantage. But to take advantage of cost differences between countries, firms needed technological changes to improve communications (primarily through advances in telecommunications and the Internet) and to lower the cost of moving products across international borders. Thus GSCs have developed because of (1) improvements in international logistics, essential for fragmented GSCs, resulting from the development of comprehensive logistic firms;[86] (2) lower transportation costs; (3) lower tariffs and nontariff measures brought about by trade agreements; and (4) improvements in intellectual property rights protection and contract enforcement, which reduced risk for lead firms[87] to outsource.[88] To paraphrase one author, technological advances made GSCs feasible, and wage differences made them profitable.[89] While most participants in GSCs are developed and emerging economies, research has shown that participation by developing countries can have a positive effect on their economies (box 3.1).

> **BOX 3.1. WHY PARTICIPATION IN GSCS IS IMPORTANT FOR DEVELOPING COUNTRIES**
>
> Integration into GSCs is important for developing countries because it can boost economic growth by adding greater value to domestic industries, increasing employment, increasing productivity, and raising incomes.[a] According to the United Nations Conference on Trade and Development (UNCTAD), the amount of value added locally through GSC trade "can be very significant" relative to the size of a developing country's domestic economy. UNCTAD calculates that value-added trade contributes 28 percent to a developing country's gross domestic product (GDP), on average, versus 18 percent for developed countries.[b] UNCTAD concludes that participation in GSCs generates employment, provides a chance for industrial upgrading, and appears to correlate positively with GDP growth rates.[c] A World Bank study found that Asia's rising participation in GSCs correlated with its growing industrialization, which created millions of better-paying jobs that brought workers out of agriculture and the informal sector.[d]
>
> However, participation in GSC trade does not automatically trigger development gains. Countries must work to link to GSCs in a way that brings sustainable improvements in welfare. The Organisation for Economic Co-operation and Development (OECD) asserts that to support broad development goals, GSC trade must also (1) be brought into the overall national economic development agendas; (2) create general linkages to the local economy and build domestic capacity; and (3) improve employment by increasing the workforce, creating better jobs, and improving working conditions.[e] Also, the level of engagement of foreign firms plays an important role in the amount of gains that can be derived from GSCs. Developing countries derive greater benefits when these firms aid in workforce development, form links with domestic firms, and work with local institutions to develop the domestic industry.[f]
>
> Notes:
> [a] UNCTAD, Global Value Chains and Development, 2013, 1; Bamber et al., "Connecting Local Producers," 2013, 7; OECD, "Interconnected Economies," 2013, 32–33, 156.
> [b] UNCTAD, Global Value Chains and Development, 2013, iii.
> [c] UNCTAD, Global Value Chains and Development, 2013, 1, 20.
> [d] Dinh et al., Light Manufacturing in Africa, 2012, 22.
> [e] OECD, Interconnected Economies, 2013, 32.
> [f] Bamber et al., "Connecting Local Producers," 2013, 8.

GSCs operate in the production of a wide variety of goods, including electronics, semiconductors, toys, housewares, apparel, pharmaceutical products, certain agricultural products, minerals, metals, and oil. Manufacturing industries have been at the forefront of the development of GSCs because their products often have component parts that can be easily broken into discrete production phases in different countries, as the above iPod example illustrates.[90] Indeed, increased trade in intermediate and semifinished products between lead firms and their worldwide suppliers has been an important feature of the "GSC age."[91] Extractive industries (mining, oil, and gas) have long supplied raw materials to GSCs. However, in the past decade extractive industries have begun employing their own production GSCs by establishing and expanding the use of specialization and outsourcing of some production functions.[92] Some products are more apt to be made in RSCs than GSCs. These include products that are heavy, bulky, and expensive to transport; that spoil quickly, such as fresh agricultural products; that require lead firms and suppliers to collaborate closely on product development, like automobiles; that must meet strict regional standards; and that need to be delivered "just in time."[93]

Several factors affect the ability of developing countries to participate in GSCs and RSCs. The OECD identified 14 such factors and organized them into five broad categories:[94]

- **Production capacity**, which covers human-capital factors (including the cost, availability, and skill of labor), standards and certification, and "national innovation systems," including both the flow of information between parties and spending on innovation and R&D;
- **Infrastructure and services**, which covers the cost and quality of transportation, information and telecommunications, water, and energy supplies;
- **Business environment**, which includes "macro-economic stability and public governance," ease of opening a business, and access to financing;
- **Trade and investment policy**, which covers market access, export and import procedures, and border transit times (all of which can be referred to as trade facilitation measures) as well as tariffs and industry-specific policies (designed to support specific industries in participation and upgrading in GSCs); and
- **Industry institutionalization**, which the OECD defines as both (1) the ability of the private sector and public institutions to coordinate and (2) inter-industry coordination and maturity. Characteristics of industry maturity include experience of firms participating in GSCs and the establishment of influential industry associations to reduce transaction costs for meeting requirements.[95]

The importance of each of these factors varies by sector (table 3.1). In addition, a country's location, size, and stage of development also affect participation in GSCs.[96]

Table 3.1. Top five factors affecting the competitiveness of developing countries in GSCs, by sector

Sector GSC	Production capacity	Infrastructure and services	Business environment	Trade and investment policy	Industry institutionalization
Agriculture	• Human capital • Standards and certifications	• Transportation infrastructure and services	• Access to finance		• Industry maturity
Extractive industries	• Human capital • National innovation systems	• Energy infrastructure and services	• Public governance • Access to finance		
Manufacturing	• Human capital • Standards and certifications • National innovation systems	• Transportation, energy, and water services and infrastructure		• Policy and facilitation	

Source: Bamber et al., "Connecting Local Producers," 2013, 14–22.

Many developing countries have successfully integrated themselves into GSCs. Countries in East and Southeast Asia have been particularly successful at linking to manufacturing GSCs, largely by creating business-friendly environments.[97] Generally these countries have good production capacity, strong human capital (especially high worker productivity), and adequate infrastructure and services (including integrated transportation networks and a consistent supply of energy), as well as access to a reliable supply of inputs.[98] Their governments have also established policies that positively supported the countries' business environments, industry institutionalization, and trade and investment, allowing local firms to take advantage of the opportunities GSCs offered to industrialize.[99] They also created environments where local firms could upgrade within the GSCs, taking over more complex functions.

SSA's Participation in Regional and Global Supply Chains

According to the International Trade Centre, a joint agency of the World Trade Organization and the United Nations, one approach to assessing the extent of SSA integration into GSCs is to examine the share of SSA's total imports accounted for by intermediate goods and the share of SSA's total exports accounted for by transformed or finished goods. It assumes that an increase in the former share reflects greater domestic processing of imported inputs into final goods (and thus an increase in domestic value-added activities over time) that are consumed either in SSA or abroad. An increase in the latter share reflects greater domestic processing of either domestic or imported inputs into final goods (and thus an increase in domestic value-added activities over time) that are consumed in foreign markets. The International Trade Centre found that between 1995 and 2010, the share of imports of intermediate goods in SSA's total imports declined slightly (although it increased in value terms), but the share of exports of transformed or finished goods in SSA's total exports increased. Taking these trends together, the Center concluded that SSA has been moderately successful in establishing domestic processing industries that are based on a greater share of domestically produced inputs, and that it has also been moderately successful moving up the value chain by boosting exports of value-added products without increasing its reliance on imported inputs to process domestically.[100]

Despite evidence of moderate success in exporting some high-valued products, SSA's participation in GSCs occurs primarily in supplying raw materials. Most SSA economies continue to export primary commodities and import finished goods for consumption.[101] SSA involvement in manufacturing and other value-added production activities, and especially GSC manufacturing, is generally limited.[102] Manufacturing in SSA usually involves semiprocessed items and/or items that have preferential access to third-country markets via such measures as the United States' African Growth and Opportunity Act (AGOA) or the EU's Everything But Arms (EBA).[103]

Reasons for low SSA participation in downstream GSC activities can be inferred using the OECD- identified factors affecting GSC participation discussed above.[104] First, SSA generally lacks skilled human capital. For example, the productivity of Africa's large rural labor force is very low, both when measured by value added per worker and by yields.[105] Moreover, SSA generally has poor transportation and communications infrastructure, as indicated by some of the measures in the World Bank's Logistics Performance Index (LPI), as well as inadequate utilities.[106] Macroeconomic policies have been improving in SSA, but the business environment for many SSA countries is unfavorable because of broad concerns about public governance, including corruption, and limited access to financing. Most SSA countries have cumbersome trade and investment policies, especially those affecting export and import procedures. Because of long border transit times, exports from SSA take longer and cost more than from most other regions of the world; for example, the SSA average export time is almost triple the OECD average, and export costs are double.[107] USITC research found that the time, cost, and uncertainty of SSA overland transport to ports of export hurt SSA countries' ability to integrate into regional and global supply chains, which require production of time-sensitive goods or of items that require multiple stages of transportation.[108] Finally, many SSA countries have poor private sector and public sector coordination.

The reasons for low GSC participation are also illustrated by the World Economic Forum's global competitiveness index (GCI).[109] The vast majority of SSA countries rank in the bottom half of the GCI's country rankings, based on such factors as infrastructure, innovation, macroeconomic environment, technological readiness, access to finance through financial market development, and adequate human capital through higher education and training.[110]

SSA Success Stories in GSC Participation

Despite generally low rates of participation in GSC downstream activities, some SSA countries have successfully moved into production activities with greater value added (see below).[111] One area of success has been agriculture/agroprocessing (e.g., vegetables and vegetable agroprocessing in Kenya, floriculture in Uganda and Kenya, and cocoa production and processing in Ghana). A second area of some success has been extractive industries (e.g., upstream oil GSC activities in Nigeria and diamond processing in Botswana). A third is manufacturing (e.g., automobiles production in South Africa and apparel production in many SSA countries). These examples may point to trade policy and infrastructure changes that could help SSA economies increase their participation in higher-value-added production and become more integrated into GSCs.[112] They also illustrate that to participate in GSCs, SSA countries must be competitive in some, but not necessarily all, of the key factors affecting GSC participation in a particular industry (table 3.1).[113]

SSA countries with more advanced economies typically have higher downstream participation in GSCs across multiple industries. For example, South Africa, SSA's dominant manufacturer, and Mauritius have diverse economies and export a variety of manufactured goods.[114] These countries are also the top two destinations for foreign investment in SSA.[115] Reportedly, Mauritius has attracted over 32,000 offshore entities that are primarily focused on global commerce with India and China and regional commerce with South Africa.[116] South Africa and Mauritius rank highest among the SSA countries on the GCI—close to the average Southeast Asian level—indicating that they are competitive in many of the factors that make countries successful in GSCs.[117] South Africa, in particular, has good transportation, communications, and energy infrastructure and services, as well as well-developed legal and finance sectors.[118]

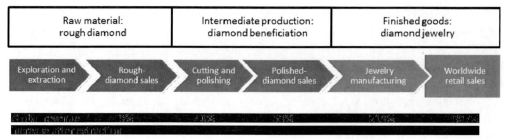

Source: Spektorov et al., The Global Diamond Report 2013, August 27, 2013, 5; UNECA, Making the Most of Africa's Commodities, 2013, 89.

Figure 3.2. Diamond jewelry global value chain.

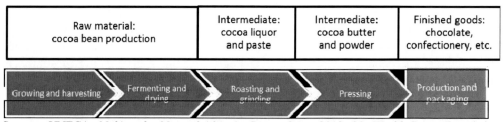

Sources: UNECA, *Making the Most of Africa's Commodities*, 2013, 95; World Cocoa Foundation, Cocoa Value Chain, (accessed January 8, 2014).

Figure 3.3. Cocoa/chocolate global value chain.

Four examples of SSA GSCs and RSCs illustrate the factors that have contributed to their successful development. The case of diamond exports by Botswana highlights how public governance (i.e., how a government exerts its authority) and public-private coordination can move a country into intermediate GSC production. Cocoa exports by Ghana show how industry institutionalization and standards can both improve the quality and value of a primary input that financially benefits the producer and, with different policies, can increase downstream production in a GSC to capture more value in the cocoa GSC. The example of Zambeef illustrates how a lead African firm based in Zambia can help others integrate into an RSC. The example of apparel production in southern Africa shows how labor cost differentials and open market access can lead to the development of an RSC.

Botswana: Diamonds

Traditionally, SSA diamond-producing countries have operated in rough diamond stages of the diamond GSC (figure 3.2).[119] While rough diamonds have substantial value, downstream diamond jewelry retail values are estimated to be three to four times that of the rough stone.[120] The middle stage of jewelry production involves cutting and polishing stones ("diamond beneficiation"). These activities do not add as much value as the jewelry stage, but do generate additional value and create employment opportunities. This stage of production historically occurred outside of Africa, mostly in Antwerp, Belgium, and more recently in new low-cost centers like Mumbai, Dubai, and Shanghai.[121] However, the government of Botswana, with support from De Beers, has moved Botswana's private sector downstream in the diamond GSC.[122]

In Botswana, where diamond mining is the major driver of economic growth, the government has sought to increase domestic participation in the downstream stages of the diamond GSC, including cutting and polishing stones, jewelry making, diamond trading, and complementary businesses.[123] De Beers, a leading firm in the diamond industry and the major mining operator in Botswana, has supported government efforts in recent years.[124] Initially the focus was on increasing domestic diamond beneficiation by controlling access to the diamonds from the mines jointly operated by the government and De Beers;[125] a policy required diamond traders wanting access to rough diamonds to set up in-country downstream processing.[126] As of 2012, close to 20 percent of Botswanan diamonds were cut domestically, and about 3,000 workers were employed in diamond beneficiation, making it the largest manufacturing sector in the country.[127] Additional downstream jobs are expected from the relocation to Botswana of the sales functions of the international branch of DeBeer's Diamond Trading Company (DTC) in 2013.[128] This includes relocating DTC aggregation, quality assurance, and sight preparation operations to Botswana.[129]

Ghana: Cocoa

West Africa is the world's major cocoa bean supplier, and includes the world's top three exporters: Côte d'Ivoire, Ghana, and Nigeria.[130] These countries participate in the cocoa and chocolate GSC as suppliers of raw materials (cocoa beans) (figure 3.3). In Ghana, where cocoa is a major driver of economic growth, the government has taken measures to ensure a consistently high-quality cocoa bean. The government-controlled Ghana Cocoa Board (COCOBOD) plays a central role in supporting Ghana's global competitiveness in cocoa. It works to exercise quality control for export beans (including grading, inspection, and treatment to prevent pests), conduct R&D (especially into high-yielding cocoa plants and pest and disease control),[131] and provide extension services for farmers.[132] These efforts have helped to expand Ghana's cocoa production and develop high-quality, premium-priced beans.[133]

Besides creating a premium cocoa bean, Ghana is also seeking to participate in the intermediate stages of the cocoa GSC by producing cocoa liquor and paste, which are sought by European buyers for use in manufacturing finished chocolate and confectionery.[134] Support for expanding and improving intermediate cocoa processing comes both from the private sector and the government. A number of local and foreign firms (including Archer Daniels Midland and Cargill) conduct downstream activities to produce intermediate cocoa products in Ghana. Local processing firms have established strong business relationships with many of their foreign buyers. As a result, Ghanaian producers receive support from many of their foreign buyers, including advice on purchasing materials and equipment, technical assistance, and, in some cases, forward contracts enabling better production planning and risk management.

The Ghanaian government has set a target to increase intermediate cocoa processing to 40 percent of production. To help achieve this goal, export processing zones (EPZs) have been established that are reportedly attracting investments from foreign cocoa grinders. The government has also created incentives for domestic producers, including price discounts, allowing access to imported processing machinery, enforcing EPZ benefits, and extending credit payment. While the cocoa industry still faces constraints, including an unreliable electricity supply, poor infrastructure, and inadequate access to capital, evidence suggests that Ghana is successfully increasing its intermediate production; the share of domestically processed cocoa exports doubled between 2007 and 2011 to account for roughly one-quarter of total cocoa exports.[135]

Zambia: Meat Products

Zambeef Products PLC (Zambeef) is a vertically integrated agribusiness that is part of an expanding South African lead RSC for consumer meat products in SSA. Zambeef was established in 1994 as a small beef slaughterhouse and retailer in Zambia.[136] However, over the past 20 years its business has expanded to the production, processing, distribution, and retailing of beef, chicken, and pork, as well as a number of other agricultural products.[137] An important factor in Zambeef's expansion has been its relationship with Shoprite, a South African supermarket chain (figure 3.4).[138] In 1995, Shoprite expanded into Zambia and contracted with Zambeef to manage its in-store meat counters.[139] When Shoprite broadened its operations to Nigeria (2005) and Ghana (2007), Zambeef also entered these markets to manage Shoprite's meat counters.[140] However, besides participating in Shoprite's RSC, Zambeef has expanded its own RSC by opening four stores in West Africa. In order to support both sets of stores, Zambeef is now expanding its supply chain in the region by establishing Nigerian operations that will include a feed lot, processing plant, and cold storage.[141]

Southern Africa: Apparel

In the mid-2000s, South African apparel firms established an RSC in which they manufacture apparel in Lesotho and Swaziland for the South African market (figure 3.5).[142] Head offices in South Africa handle the relationships with South African retail buyers and are responsible for product design, sourcing of inputs, and logistics. Most fabric, the primary input, is supplied by Asia; however, some is regionally supplied from South Africa, Mauritius, or Lesotho.[143] South African apparel firms located production facilities in Lesotho and Swaziland to take advantage of several factors:[144] (1) the lower cost of production (especially labor and overhead); (2) more flexible labor markets; (3) duty-free access under the Southern African Customs Union (SACU) for the finished clothes; and (4) proximity, as Lesotho and Swaziland's apparel industries are located in industrial zones near their borders with South Africa. Also, the changing needs of South African retailers encouraged the establishment of these RSCs. First, these retailers wanted to diversify their supplier base, especially after the South African government placed quotas on Chinese apparel imports in 2007–08. Second, some retailers wanted suppliers who could provide quicker and more flexible production runs with a higher fashion content.

Source: Zambeefplc.com website http://www.zambeefplc.com/zambeefplc/what-we-do/ (accessed January 23, 2014); Rabbobank, *Looking for Delta*, 2013, 31.

Figure 3.4. Zambeef's involvement in RSCs.

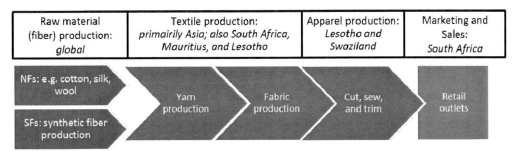

Source: Gereffi and Memedovic, *The Global Apparel Value Chain*, 2003, 5; USITC, *Textiles and Apparel*, January 2004, 1-2. Note: "NFs" are natural fibers; "SFs" are synthetic fibers.

Figure 3.5. South African apparel RSC.

Potential Participation in Regional and Global Supply Chains: Review of the Literature

A review of literature suggests that SSA sectors with the greatest potential to further integrate into RSCs and GSCs are (1) agricultural products and foodstuffs, (2) leather and leather products, (3) textiles and apparel, and (4) extractive natural resource products. Research shows that SSA already has factors that could enable it to be competitive in light manufacturing, including low-wage labor (enough to offset its lower labor productivity compared with Asian competitors), abundant natural resources, preferential access to high-income markets like the United States and EU, and sufficiently large local or regional markets. Large local or regional markets allow emerging SSA producers to develop capabilities and hone their skills in quick- response, high-volume production in those regional markets before selling into global markets.[145]

These sectors' potential for supply chain integration has garnered interest from governments and other stakeholders. For instance, a study being undertaken by UNCTAD (a UN body that addresses trade and development issues and provides technical assistance to developing countries) is intended to identify potential SSA supply chains in agroprocessing, textiles and apparel, and leather. The study will reportedly identify constraints to forming supply chains in these sectors, and identify and promote regional cooperation among industry associations active in these sectors.[146] In December 2013, UNCTAD, in collaboration with the Commonwealth Secretariat and other stakeholders, organized a workshop to discuss and share ongoing research in identifying potential RSCs in the sectors noted above.[147]

However, the development of light manufacturing in SSA faces several challenges. According to some researchers, broad impediments that continue to hamper the development of light manufacturing in SSA include (1) problems with the availability, cost, and quality of inputs, including lack of access to industrial land with developed infrastructure; (2) lack of access to finance; (3) inadequate or absent skills in the workforce; and (4) poor trade logistics (i.e., high costs for transporting goods to and from market).[148]

Agricultural Products and Foodstuffs

Based on a review of literature, the agricultural products and foodstuffs sector (collectively, the agroprocessing sector) has the greatest potential to integrate into regional supply chains within SSA.[149] According to one study by the UN Industrial Development Organization (UNIDO), rising incomes, greater urbanization, and changing consumer preferences within SSA have increasingly shifted consumption away from undifferentiated staple crops toward more fruits, vegetables, vegetable oils, fish and meats, dairy products, and other processed foods.[150] As a result, the study found that domestic and regional SSA markets will drive demand for value- added agricultural products and foodstuffs. Indeed, domestic markets and intra-SSA trade were found to account for more than three-quarters of the value of SSA's agricultural market.[151] Moreover, demand for food in SSA is expected to double between 2010 and 2015 to $100 billion. This will include demand for processed foods like bread, biscuits, and snack products, offering greater opportunities for SSA producers in domestic and regional markets.[152] Indeed, the growth of supermarket chains, retail outlets, and food service industries across SSA already reflects these trends.[153]

The agricultural products and foodstuffs sector must meet several competitive challenges if it is to further develop and integrate into regional supply chains across SSA. According to UNIDO, a key challenge is developing backward linkages with small-scale farmers in regional supply chains.[154] Principal impediments that these farmers face include (1) limited access to markets outside of local villages; (2) the variable availability and quality of the agricultural goods they produce, which impedes their ability to find a buyer; (3) poor access to inputs, including machinery and packaging; (4) lack of access to finance; and (5) inadequate access to market information within their own country.[155] According to the same study, other factors that limit access to regional markets, and thus the producers' potential to integrate into regional supply chains, include high transport costs; unreliable systems of contract enforcement; and insufficient information on the quantity, quality, and price of agricultural products in neighboring countries.[156]

Nonetheless, SSA countries, often under the leadership of regional associations, are developing policies to promote industrial development and greater domestic value addition in agricultural products and foodstuffs, which in turn could lead to greater participation in RSCs and GSCs.[157] For instance, a recent program launched in West Africa by the UN Economic Commission for Africa (UNECA), the Economic Community of West African States (ECOWAS), and other stakeholders aims to develop the agricultural sector by analyzing and developing value chains for strategic commodities, including rice (in Côte d'Ivoire, Ghana, Mali, and Senegal), maize (Benin, Côte d'Ivoire, Ghana, and Mali), and livestock (Mali).[158] In East Africa and southern Africa, efforts are underway to develop value chains for cassava, coffee, cereals, horticultural products, and cotton under the EU's "All ACP Commodities Program."[159] According to the Common Market for Eastern and Southern Africa (COMESA), as a result of Zambia's national cassava strategy, a number of small and medium-sized businesses in Zambia have reportedly begun to process cassava into flour, and livestock feed and chips, creating domestic market linkages between cassava producers, millers, and food and livestock firms. The strategy is expected to serve as a stepping stone to the development of a regional agroprocessing strategy focusing on roots and tubers.[160] Similarly, recognizing the low levels of domestic value added to agricultural products in West Africa, ECOWAS has prioritized the development of its agribusiness sector under a regional integration framework.[161] Likewise, trade ministers of the Southern African Development Community (SADC) have targeted the agroprocessing sector for development and increased value addition.[162]

Leather and Leather Products

The leather and leather products sector also has the potential to further integrate into RSCs and GSCs. According to one International Trade Centre study, several SSA countries, including Ethiopia, Mali, and Nigeria, increased domestic processing and exports of leather and leather products between 1995 and 2010.[163] The sector has garnered attention across SSA as a way to add value to local resources and sell leather products such as shoes and handbags into regional and international markets. In fact, Ethiopia is one of the largest producers and exporters of leather and leather products in SSA, and has targeted the sector for further development, as described below in section 4.

The sector faces several supply-side constraints that will likely continue to impede the development of RSCs. According to one study, poor disease control, lack of quality processing of raw hides and skins, and bans on imported processed leather contribute to a shortage of quality processed leather in Ethiopia.[164] Other competitive factors affecting the sector include lack of refrigeration at slaughtering facilities, long transport distances, and poor road conditions to tanneries.[165] Other SSA countries likely face similar obstacles.

Textiles and Apparel

As mentioned above, Lesotho and Swaziland have been integrated into regional production networks by several South African apparel firms to supply the South African market since the mid-2000s.[166] However, the sector has the potential for further integration into RSCs, primarily in East Africa and southern Africa. According to one Commission report, greater integration into RSCs could help facilitate access to materials, product specialization, production sharing, and speed to market.[167] In addition, cross-country integration could also enable producers to access larger apparel markets or reduce costs associated with transport, storage, border delays, and tariffs.[168] One industry observer notes that additional regional sourcing opportunities exist, particularly in the quick-response, fashion, and short-run segment, where regional suppliers have a potential competitive advantage compared to Asian apparel suppliers.[169]

The textiles and apparel sector faces numerous competitive challenges. According to one Commission report, SSA generally suffers from an insufficient base of apparel manufacturing through which to develop and sustain upstream production of yarn, fabric, and other inputs.[170] Another study characterizes the textile sector as the "weak link" in the SSA cotton-textile-clothing value chain.[171] Other competitive challenges facing upstream production of inputs include lack of knowledge of regional or international market opportunities, too little reliable electricity at competitive rates, insufficient clean water and wastewater treatment facilities, and inadequate transportation infrastructure, among others.[172]

Despite these challenges, efforts continue to develop textile and apparel regional supply chains in other parts of SSA. For instance, in 2009 COMESA launched the development of a cotton-to- clothing supply chain strategy to improve coordination within the sector. One initiative under the strategy aims to strengthen collaboration in the areas of research and policy between Malawi, Mozambique, Zambia, and Zimbabwe. Another initiative under the strategy aims to develop linkages in cotton and yarn between Zimbabwe and Mauritius.[173]

Minerals Processing and Extractive Industries

Processed minerals and other downstream products related to extractive resources have longer-term potential for integration into GSCs; most identified efforts, however, are currently in the nascent stages. In addition, efforts are being made across resource-rich countries within SSA to identify and develop mineral-based RSCs, although prospects appear mixed. For instance, South Africa is developing a strategy to strengthen regional industry linkages and develop value chains in the following sectors: (1) ferrous (including iron ore, ferroalloys, and steel);[174] (2) platinum group metals; (3) titanium and titanium pigments; (4) coal-, gas-, and oil- based polymers; and (5) mining equipment.[175] According to one study, how neighboring countries will respond to South Africa's regional strategy remains unclear, since value-added processing activities will likely be concentrated in South Africa.[176] In East Africa, the East African Community (EAC) is drafting a framework to develop value chains in the mineral processing, petrochemicals and gas processing, iron, and steel sectors.[177] In West Africa, ECOWAS has echoed similar commitments to develop regional industrial and mining policies and action plans.[178]

Despite its abundant natural resources, several factors continue to impede the development of mineral-based value chains within SSA. According to one study by UNECA, barriers to developing upstream linkages (including industries to support mining activities) include the lack of domestic capacity to supply upstream inputs, such as consulting, technical, or scientific services; lack of access to capital; and a shortage of local workers with technological expertise.[179] Impediments to developing downstream linkages (such as mineral processing or "beneficiation" activities) include a lack of the large economies of scale needed to be competitive in mineral processing, due in part to the absence of local manufacturing that would consume such products, as well as the inability of local firms to penetrate established mineral- based value chains primarily dominated by large multinational corporations. According to the same report, poor infrastructure conditions across SSA, including deficient and fragmented road networks and inadequate and expensive electricity supply, inhibit the development of both upstream and downstream linkages.[180]

SECTION 4. AGOA COUNTRY EXPORT POTENTIAL TO THE UNITED STATES

Introduction

While section 3 of this report identifies African products with potential for integration into regional and global supply chains, this section presents products that have been identified as offering the greatest potential for AGOA beneficiary countries to expand their exports to the United States. Two approaches were used to identify products. The first was to review published reports that identify products with export potential for SSA countries, including SSA countries' national export development strategies, previous USTR-requested Commission studies on SSA export competitiveness, and other economic literature, including academic studies and reports from international development institutions such as the World Bank. The second approach was to identify products that AGOA countries currently export and that are imported by the United States, but mainly from non-AGOA countries, such as fish products, cut flowers, and certain apparel products. For products identified under both approaches, the section describes AGOA countries' competitive strengths and weaknesses, along with other trade impediments that could hinder sales to the U.S. market.

Products with Export Potential for AGOA Countries: A Review of Published Research

Products Identified in National Export Development Strategies

Country governments and stakeholders across SSA have identified export sectors to develop as part of broader economic development strategies. These strategies include regional integration among SSA countries, which has the potential to create important export opportunities for SSA goods; export diversification to complement traditional export sectors; and product value addition for goods consumed domestically or exported. For example, the national export strategies from certain SSA countries, such as Rwanda, Uganda, and Malawi, identify a number of products with potential for growth and diversification (table 4.1). The products listed include agricultural and horticultural products, handcraft and woodcraft products (e.g., basketry, mats, and home furnishings), and leather and leather products (e.g., footwear and handbags).

Table 4.1. Products with export potential and factors affecting competitiveness in those sectors in selected SSA countries

Country	Products/sectors	Positive factors	Negative factors
Ethiopia[a]	Textiles and apparel	Government support to attract private investment in the sector.	Unreliable and inadequate electricity supply; underutilized mill capacity; limited access to credit; onerous customs procedures.
	Leather products and footwear	Abundance of livestock herds; good climatic and soil conditions contribute to quality livestock and skins; government support for the sector.	Poor disease control among livestock herds and weak veterinary services; lack of quality processing of raw hides and skins; bans on imported processed leather; lack of refrigeration at slaughtering facilities; long transport distances; poor road conditions to tanneries.
	Home furnishings	Not identified.	Not identified.
	Cut flowers	Not identified.	Not identified.
Ghana[b]	Handcrafts (basketry and related straw products, leather products, smock weaving)	Abundant and low-cost labor; low capital investment; relatively simple production processes.	Limited availability and rising costs of raw materials like straw and imported dies; limited storage facilities for inputs and final products; lack of suitable and readily available cargo trucks to transport baskets to the Accra market and for export.

Table 4.1. (Continued)

Country	Products/sectors	Positive factors	Negative factors
	Woodcraft and furniture	Abundant and low-cost labor.	Limited availability and high cost of raw materials (wood); low productivity; lack of credit to expand business; insufficient market demand/lack of market information.
	Cashew nuts (including cashew kernels and cashew apple processing)	Abundant and low-cost labor; climatic conditions conducive to growth of cashew nut trees.	High input costs; lack of processing facilities for both cashew nuts and cashew apples; high incidence of bush fires that destroy cashew crops; poor conditions of feeder roads linking farms to paved highways.
	Shea and shea butter	Climatic conditions and weather patterns conducive to shea nut production; policies and programs to support the sector.	Low rates of collection of shea production; high transport costs and costs incurred due to other delays that reduce the prices offered to farmers, thereby discouraging collection.
Malawi[c]	Oilseed products (cooking oil, soaps, lubricants, paints, varnishes, meals and flours, biofuel, animal feed, fertilizer, snacks and confectionary derived from sunflowers, groundnuts [peanuts], soya, and cotton)	Easy access to smallholder value-addition processes such as oil extraction from sunflower seed varieties; short growing seasons and low input requirements for sunflowers; groundnuts widely grown and adaptable to numerous environments; established groundnut farming methods that rural Malawians are familiar with; suitable soil and climatic conditions in low-lying areas of the country to grow cotton.	Low prices for raw sunflower crop acts as disincentive for farmers to produce; low crop yields, inefficient production techniques, poor storage techniques, and limited storage capacity; inability to control level of aflatoxin (a carcinogenic fungus) in groundnuts; poor yields for soya crops; lack of reliable market linkages between farmers and potential trading partners.
	Sugarcane products (sugar, high-value sugar through branding, sugar confectionary [syrups, sweets, caramel], sweetener, ethanol, spirits, cane juice, fertilizer, animal feed, cosmetics)	Low labor costs; large economies of scale in sugar production in the Shire Valley and the lakeshore; established sectoral knowledge and expertise; programs in place to help develop smallholder sugarcane farming in a way that reduces the risk of land disputes and allows community development.	Lack of a regulatory framework to develop sugarcane products sector, including for cultivation; high transportation costs; high irrigation and water usage costs; lack of milling capacity.

Country	Products/sectors	Positive factors	Negative factors
Malawi[c]	Manufactures (beverages; agroprocessing [dairy and maize, wheat, horticulture, and pulse value addition]; plastics and packaging, assembly)	Good soil and climatic conditions allow key upstream inputs (e.g., maize, horticulture, and oilseeds) to grow well in order to develop supply chains for the beverage and agroprocessing sectors; close proximity to regional markets with rapidly growing demand.	Lack of affordable and reliable energy supply; lack of market linkages between manufacturing and agriculture for agroprocessing and beverage sectors; lack of skilled labor and access to finance.
Mauritius[d]	Jewelry (metal, diamonds, pearls, semiprecious stones, imitation jewelry, and accessories)	Well-developed air transport infrastructure; goods are non-perishable, lightweight and have little volume, and hence relatively easy to airfreight; skilled human resources; established training institutions offer programs in design.	Lack of developing a brand image in gold and diamond jewelry products.
	Agroprocessing and seafood processing	Large maritime exclusive economic zone with an abundant stock of various fish species; well-developed port infrastructure including cold storage.	Lack of Mauritius-flagged fishing vessels to confer Mauritius country of origin to qualify for duty-free access under AGOA.
	Light manufacturing, plastic and metal-based products (e.g., cutlery, hardware, fabricated metal, plastic items, etc.)	Geographic location, well-developed transport infrastructure, including quality port facilities.	Lack of branding.
	Leather, handbags, and fashion accessories	Skilled human resources.	Lack of export strategy for small enterprises.
Mozambique[e]	Major crops (cashew, coconut, cotton, sugar, tobacco); Horticulture (grapefruit, cut flowers, vegetables); Basic food crops (maize, rice, cassava); Diversification crops (beans,	Abundant land resources with a wide range of fertile soils and climatic conditions that permit cultivation of a wide variety of crops; irrigation potential based on abundant surface water resources; coastal access; geographically well-positioned to sell to growing markets, including the Middle East and India.	Low productivity; low level of technological innovation; inability to meet foreign requirements for sanitary and phytosanitary (SPS) control; limited agroprocessing capabilities; high costs for seeds and other production inputs for export crops; ineffective producer organizations; high transport costs; limited export development services, including finance, and assistance with post-harvest management,

Table 4.1. (Continued)

Country	Products/sectors	Positive factors	Negative factors
	pulses, oilseeds, groundnuts)		complying with foreign import regulations.
	Leather and leather products	Abundant livestock herds and low-cost labor.	Lack of backward linkages to local hides, skins, and tanning.
Rwanda[f]	Horticulture (fruits, vegetables, and flowers, with focus on developing value-added products, including juices and dried fruits/chilies)	Availability of abundant labor; good climatic growing conditions.	Lack of adequate land to achieve economies of scale; lack of knowledge around proper crop cultivation and fertilizer and pest management; lack of knowledge of export procedures and requirements.
	Handcrafts (basketry and mats; embroidery and woven products; hand-loomed textiles and other products; ceramics and pottery; leather and leather products; wood products; jewelry	Availability of abundant and unique raw materials (e.g., bamboo, reeds, clay, animal skins, banana fiber, etc.); prevalence of artistic and creative culture; diversity of goods produced based on wide geographic footprint of production; presence of government policies to support the sector.	Supply-side constraints, including the following: (1) limited access tobecause of poor transportation and supply/logistics systems raw materials; (2) fragmented, unstructured, or individualized production systems; (3) low production levels; (4) low levels of specialization; (5) inconsistent product standardization; (6) low product development (design and quality); (7) limited knowledge of ways to access and develop market.
Uganda[g]	Fruits and vegetables (dried fruits, fruit juices and concentrates, fruit pulp processing, flour processing for bakery industry, fruit canning, and vegetable purees and chutneys)	Organized industry associations; cold storage infrastructure at Kampala airport; inexpensive labor; plentiful land resources; high-quality fruits and vegetables.	Lack of scale economies among small-scale, subsistence farmers; poor post-harvest handling practices (sorting, packing, loading); lack of processing technology and value addition, with the exception of a few companies that largely depend on imported pulp and concentrates; lack of adequate research to support value addition.
	Dairy products (including powdered milk, yogurt, ghee, and butter)	High-quality dairy products; good regulatory and legal framework; established institutional network, including research and development institutions; existence of a dairy processors association.	Poor animal husbandry practices; poor-quality milk-handling facilities in collection centers; high input costs (water, power, transport, packing); lack of adequate cold storage and transportation chain; limited success adding value to cheese, yogurt, and butter.
	Cereals, pulses, and oilseeds (including maize, beans, rice,	Organized industry associations; existence of cooperatives to help	Overdependence on rain-fed agriculture; limited scale economies due to subsistence

Country	Products/sectors	Positive factors	Negative factors
	chickpeas, sesame seeds, sunflower, soybeans)	farmers organize; stable support institutions; plentiful land resources; diverse subsector plant varieties.	farming and poor production methods; poor sorting at harvest stage; improper drying of seeds, resulting in poor quality and low prices; limited value addition (e.g., animal feed, breakfast cereals); dominance of informal trade.
	Natural ingredients for pharmaceuticals and cosmetic industries	Wide variety of natural ingredients grown in Uganda; sector initiative supported by biotrade program sponsored by UN Conference on Trade and Development (UNCTAD); private sector investment in the sector, although from a small base; indigenous knowledge of natural ingredients sector.	Lack of national production and processing standards; limited value addition, with over 70 percent of production sold as raw material; low levels of processing technologies; inadequate information on commercial plant species.
	Handcrafts (basketry, mats, ceramics, beads, pottery, hand textiles and woven products, toys, jewelry, bags, ornaments, leather products, and woodcrafts)	Availability of abundant and unique raw materials (e.g., raffia, barkcloth, banana fiber, animal skins, etc.); rich and diversified culture producing a wide variety of handcrafts; indigenous knowledge of sector; current and potential domestic market based on the tourism sector.	Unstructured and individualized production systems; limited investment; limited technical skills, capacity, and technology; limited resources for production, distribution, and marketing.

Sources: [a] USAID, East Africa Trade Hub, "AGOA Strategies Chart Course for Increased Exports," December 4, 2013; Government of Ethiopia, *Growth and Transformation Plan 2010/2011–2014/2015*, 2010; Dinh et al., "Light Manufacturing in Africa," 2012; Abebe, "Textiles FDI Booming," November 24, 2013. [b] West Africa more generally, including Burkina Faso and Mali. See USAID, West Africa Trade Hub, *Exports, Employment, and Incomes in West Africa*, 2011; [c] Government of Malawi, *National Export Strategy 2013–2018*, 2013; [d] Chemonics International, *Mauritius National AGOA Strategy*, 2013; Enterprise Mauritius website, http://www.source mauritius.com (accessed February 10, 2014); [e] USAID, *Removing Obstacles to Growth in Mozambique*, 2004; USAID, *Mozambique Country Assistance Strategy 2009–14*, 2009; African Development Bank, *Republic of Mozambique Country Strategy Paper 2011–2015*; [f] Government of Rwanda, *Rwanda Handcraft Strategic Plan*, 2009; Government of Rwanda, *Rwanda National Export Strategy*, 2011; and [g] Exports are mostly focused on regional markets. See Government of Uganda, *The Uganda National Export Strategy 2008–12*, 2007.

Note: As of this writing, Ethiopia has not published its AGOA export strategy, but it has identified home furnishings and cut flowers as priority sectors.

In many cases, the main competitive factors affecting the export potential of SSA countries in these sectors have also been identified, and are included in table 4.1. These strategies and sectors address exports generally, but many of them could also be targeted at increasing exports to the United States under AGOA.

Other SSA national development plans include specific steps to develop AGOA export strategies to increase export opportunities under the program. For example, Burundi is developing a country export strategy expected to be completed by early 2014.[181] The country is identifying strategic export sectors to develop, and reportedly plans to use AGOA's third-country fabric provision to help develop its nascent apparel manufacturing sector. Zambia is also committed to developing its domestic textiles and apparel sector to take greater advantage of AGOA preferences, and has reportedly called for the development of an industrial strategy to address the sector.[182]

Products Identified by the Commission

Previous USTR-requested Commission reports on SSA reviewed and identified export opportunities and barriers in AGOA-eligible countries. A 2005 Commission report used "revealed comparative advantage" (RCA) to help identify sectors in 37 AGOA-eligible countries with potential for export growth.[183] An RCA index identifies the extent to which a country has captured world market share for a particular good it exports compared to the extent to which it has captured world market share for all traded goods. RCA indices help identify a country's exports that are internationally competitive based on past export performance, as well as products that could be competitive based on past export growth.[184] RCAs were calculated for 37 AGOA-eligible countries using export data for 1998–2003 classified at the Harmonized System (HS) 4-digit level. The RCA analysis found a broad range of products with potential for export growth in a number of sectors. These included products in the agriculture, forestry, fisheries, and agroprocessing sectors (such as bananas, cereal flours, corn, honey, coffee, cocoa, cotton, fruits, vegetables, cut flowers, cashews, sesame, shrimp and prawns, logs, hardwoodlumber, and wood products); energy-related industries (including downstream petroleum products, liquid natural gas, and electricity); manufacturing (including light industrial products, leather products, processed wood products, and chemicals); and minerals and metals (including aluminum, gold, copper, and gemstones).

Two Commission reports in 2007 and 2008 identified factors that affect the competitiveness of certain products in global export markets. These products were selected by USTR and viewed as having significant potential for export diversification and growth in sub-Saharan Africa.[185] Agricultural products identified in these reports were cashews, cocoa butter and paste, cut flowers, fish, coffee, shea butter, spices, and tropical fruit; mining and manufacturing products identified were acyclic alcohol, flat-rolled steel, liquid natural gas, apparel, unwrought aluminum, wood veneer, footwear, natural rubber, processed diamonds, textiles, and wood furniture.[186] For each of these products, the reports identified the key factors affecting increased exports. Although a range of factors were identified, common to many products were demand growth and rising prices, increased investment, policies to promote the sector, regional integration, and certain improvements in infrastructure.

A 2009 Commission report focused on the effects of infrastructure conditions on SSA export growth and competitiveness for different agricultural products (coffee, shea butter, and pineapples and bananas) and manufacturing products (natural rubber and downstream products, and textiles and apparel). Some of the impediments to SSA export growth identified in the report were poor road infrastructure, the limited availability and high cost of vehicles for harvesting and shipping, unreliable and high-cost energy, and inefficient agricultural processing facilities.[187]

A witness at the Commission's hearing in connection with the current investigation said that technical assistance, capacity building, and other marketing efforts provided under AGOA have helped SSA countries increase exports of products that already faced low or no duties, including birdseed from Ethiopia and shea butter from West Africa.[188] A 2005 Commission report and the 2007 and 2008 Commission reports also identified shea in describing factors affecting trade trends in SSA.[189] The reports noted that the West African region, with the largest concentration of shea nut trees in SSA, has the potential to increase exports of both shea nuts and processed shea nut vegetable fat (shea butter) to markets in the United States and Europe.[190]

Products Identified in the Economic Literature

A World Bank guide on value-chain concepts and analysis pointed to several criteria for the selection of sectors, including sectors identified as national priorities for development because of their large impact on rural incomes and employment, the likelihood of attracting investment, previous sector assessments, and other qualitative input from industry experts or other stakeholders.[191] Using several of these criteria, a USAID-funded project drew up an initial list of products with export potential for Senegal, including cotton and horticultural products, cashews, mangoes, dairy products, bissap (hibiscus tea), fonio (a small-seeded millet variety), bananas, woven textiles, and fisheries. Following additional analysis, the list of sectors selected for intervention was eventually narrowed down to cashews, bissap, and mangoes.[192]

According to the same World Bank study, an alternative (or complementary) quantitative approach to RCA analysis is to compare a country's costs for producing a good domestically (so- called domestic resource cost, or "DRC") with world prices for the same good. This approach is useful in determining whether or not a country can competitively increase exports of that good. It is also useful because cost data broken down along different stages of a product's value chain can be used to identify potential inefficiencies in each link and therefore areas to target for improvement.[193] A DRC analysis carried out in Mozambique found that cashews and grapefruit were the most competitive of the sectors and crops studied, but that rice, potatoes, paprika, and bananas could be more competitive if technical assistance or additional agricultural inputs were available.[194]

A 2011 study by the Economic Community of West African States (ECONWAS) identified cashews, peanuts, and shea, among other agricultural products, as having export potential for many countries in West Africa.[195] A study by the International Food and Agricultural Policy Council identified exports to the United States under AGOA as a potential niche market for SSA peanut producers, especially exports of value-added peanut products, such as peanut snack foods.[196] Other studies showed the potential of nut exports under AGOA to improve incomes and employment in SSA. For instance, a USAID study estimated that every $1,000 of income generated from cashew production in central Ghana creates 120 jobs in the country and $1,430 in additional income per household in the local economy.[197] The study also found that shea production in Ghana had similar multiplier effects on additional household income. However, many of these studies also noted that these potential export sectors face challenges, such as poor infrastructure conditions, low-quality products, and a lack of technical assistance.

Handcrafts and woodcraft products, including baskets, woven mats, wood carvings, and home furnishings, have export potential to the United States due to the AGOA program. A study by USAID identified wood carvings and straw handcrafts as products offering Ghana opportunities to increase and diversify trade.[198] The sector enjoys widespread appeal across SSA, given its potential to reduce poverty in rural communities by boosting local employment and incomes, particularly among women. This study estimates that every $1,000 of income generated from basket producers in the Upper East region of Ghana creates 160 jobs and $580 in additional household income in the local economy, and that production of woodcrafts in Ghana had similar multiplier effects on job creation and additional household income.[199]

A body of economic literature has focused on identifying sectors in SSA that would benefit from regional integration. This research does not specifically identify sectors with potential for export growth, but addresses a key related question about which sectors would benefit the most from trade liberalization through regional integration. According to the United Nations Economic Commission for Africa (UNECA), increased regional trade has the potential to increase industrialization and structural transformation.[200] Indeed, regional integration has the potential to boost intra-African trade and create substantial export opportunities for SSA industrial and agricultural goods alike. Lowering barriers to trade within SSA is expected to result in increased trade within SSA, particularly for agricultural and food products. A UNECA study using a computable general equilibrium (CGE) model estimated that reducing tariffs, either under a regional free trade agreement (FTA) or a continental FTA, could boost intra-SSA trade by up to 52.3 percent ($34.6 billion). SSA exports of agricultural and food products—primarily wheat, cereals, raw sugar, milk and dairy products, and other processed foods, such as meat, sugar, and other food products—would be expected to increase the most in percentage terms. In terms of value, SSA exports of industrial products, including textiles and apparel, and leather products; petroleum products; mineral and metal products; and other manufactured goods would increase the most as a result of regional integration.[201]

Another quantitative approach to identify potential export opportunities is based on the concept of "product space,"[202] which draws on network science to determine how close products are to each other in terms of the production capabilities required to produce them, as well as how complex or sophisticated they are from the same point of view. This analysis also works to show the effect on countries' economic development of expanding the range and sophistication of products. A study by Hidalgo using this approach found that regional integration in southern Africa and East Africa, including Kenya, Mozambique, Rwanda, Tanzania, and Zambia, could lead to new production and export opportunities in the agricultural and foodstuff sector, as well as in textiles and apparel.[203]

Products That AGOA Countries Export and That the United States Principally Imports from Non-SSA Sources

Identification of Products

Since 2000, the United States has imported a range of products (other than crude petroleum) principally from non-SSA countries, even though these products are produced and exported by SSA countries as well. In 2012, for example, global cut flower exports by AGOA countries (excluding South Africa) were valued at $894 million. While cut flower imports by the United States were $968 million, AGOA countries supplied less than $3 million (0.3 percent) of this total (table 4.2). Similarly, several categories of apparel (HS 6109 and 6110) were exported by AGOA countries in 2012 at a value of $376 million; U.S. global imports of these goods exceeded $19 billion in value, but only 0.8 percent were sourced from AGOA countries.

Identifying sectors where AGOA exports and U.S. imports are large and yet there is little bilateral trade is important in assessing export potential to the United States under AGOA. These are sectors where AGOA countries are viewed as globally competitive by third countries, as well as sectors where there is strong import demand in the United States, provided that impediments to trade can be overcome. If the impediments can be overcome, these sectors offer potential for future export growth and higher rates of utilization of the program going forward.

Table 4.2. Selected products exported by AGOA countries and which the United States imports from non-AGOA countries, 2012[a]

HS 4	Product	AGOA exports to world	U.S. imports from world	U.S. imports from AGOA	AGOA share of U.S. imports
		Million $			Percent
0302	Fresh and chilled fish, excl. fillets	124.6	1,214.1	0.5	0.05
0303	Frozen fish, excl. fillets	447.9	531.6	2.4	0.45
0304	Fish fillets	529.4	4,644.2	9.2	0.20
0306	Crustaceans, live, fresh and chilled	159.4	5,104.6	3.2	0.06
0307	Molluscs, live, fresh and chilled	513.3	769.9	0.8	0.10
0603	Cut flowers	893.9	968.2	2.6	0.27
0708	Leguminous vegetables, fresh or chilled	217.2	152.4	0.0	0.02
0713	Leguminous vegetables, dried	316.9	482.1	2.1	0.44
0803	Bananas	412.7	2,084.0	0.0	0.00
0804	Tropical fruit	185.7	1,798.4	0.0	0.00
1701	Cane or beet sugar	826.9	2,282.8	15.7	0.69
4403	Wood in the rough	1,210.9	160.0	0.9	0.53
6109	T-shirts, singlets, tank tops, knitted or crocheted	198.8	5,255.2	41.9	0.80
6110	Sweaters, pullovers, sweatshirts, knitted or crocheted	176.8	13,817.3	106.0	0.77
7108	Gold, unwrought, semimanufactured or in powder	1,155.7	16,259.6	26.3	0.16
8411	Turbojets, turbopropellers, gas turbines, and parts	174.9	18,921.8	2.2	0.01

Source: GTIS (accessed March 4, 2014).

Notes: [a] HS 4-digit products for which AGOA-eligible countries' exports to the world and U.S. imports from the world are greater than $100 million, and AGOA countries' share of U.S. imports is less than 1 percent; excluding South Africa and petroleum and petroleum products.

The preferences afforded by the AGOA program are but one of the factors that shape U.S. importers' decisions whether to source a product from third countries or from SSA countries. For example, if an agricultural product exported from SSA is unable to meet U.S. sanitary and phytosanitary (SPS) regulations, it will not be allowed to enter the country, regardless of its tariff benefits under AGOA. The remainder of the section gives an overview of this and other factors that often lead U.S. importers to select non-SSA suppliers, followed by case studies that describe product-specific situations in more detail.

Factors Affecting SSA Export Competitiveness in the U.S. Market

Higher Transportation Costs to the U.S. Market

Transportation costs for AGOA products to the U.S. market reflect several factors, including distance to market, perishability of products, freight rates, and reliability of trade linkages. Each of these factors directly impacts the cost and timeliness of delivery of goods to U.S. consumers, with slower delivery times generally increasing transportation costs.

Distance to market plays an important role in determining transportation costs. For example, the United States is further from AGOA beneficiary countries than European countries, and the transportation cost differentials are substantial: container shipments to the United States reportedly take two weeks longer than shipments to European ports, and cost on average an extra $1,000 per standard 40-foot container.[204] World Bank cost estimates show that an additional day's travel time for a container from Africa offsets between 0.5 and 2.5 percentage points of tariff preferences.[205] Reducing delays in trading times would increase SSA's competitiveness in products where timely shipments are important, and increase the region's shares of manufactured products—particularly apparel, footwear, furniture, and leather products—in its total exports.[206]

Transportation costs are also a function of supply chain efficiencies. Countries such as Kenya and Uganda have made investments in infrastructure and customs administration that have increased exports—including exports of perishable agricultural products such as fresh flowers, fresh fish, and leguminous vegetables—especially to the EU.[207] SSA producers without a continuous cold chain continue to export perishable goods as well, but they must ship to nearby markets to reduce spoilage.

Established and efficient trade linkages are also important for keeping transportation costs low. For products such as cut flowers and apparel, African producers benefit from regular, direct flights to Europe which allow for fast delivery. Such flights often do not exist for AGOA exporters to the United States. Suppliers of similar goods in the Western Hemisphere (e.g., Colombia and Ecuador for cut flowers and Caribbean nations for textiles and apparel) take advantage of regular flights and efficient supply routes to U.S. consumers.

Inability to Compete in the U.S. Market without Tariff Preferences

Preferential tariff programs, including AGOA, are designed to boost the competitiveness of SSA suppliers to the U.S. market to offset such disadvantages. However, factors both related and unrelated to the programs themselves can lessen the benefits of those programs—for example, the inability of SSA suppliers to comply with AGOA rules of origin, and the existence of similar means of preferential access under FTAs or other programs for competing suppliers.

Some SSA exports to the U.S. market, such as sugar, tobacco, meat, and dairy products, continue to be subject to tariff rate quotas (TRQs) limiting export volumes eligible for duty-free treatment. For example, SSA countries producing sugar are eligible for duty-free treatment under U.S. raw sugar import quotas, but only under low-volume quotas granted to specific countries.[208] Over-quota imports from AGOA beneficiaries are subject to normal trade relations (NTR) rates of duty, which are prohibitively high in most cases. In contrast, Mexico received duty-free treatment for more than 1.9 million metric tons of raw sugar exports to the United States in fiscal year 2013 under access provisions of the North American Free Trade Agreement (NAFTA).[209] Some other products, such as certain canned fruit, are considered to be sensitive agricultural products and have never been eligible for tariff preferences under AGOA.

SSA exports to the U.S. market under preferential programs generally have no advantage over those of other suppliers that also enjoy such preferential access. An example is cut flowers from Colombia, which first received duty-free treatment under the Andean Trade Preference Act (1991) and subsequently under the U.S.-Colombia FTA (implemented 2012). As indicated in section 6, over time SSA exports to the U.S. market have been gradually facing a shrinking tariff preference margin vis-à-vis other suppliers as the United States concludes more reciprocal trade agreements with non-SSA trading partners. This tariff preference erosion is a narrowing of the gap between low (or zero) tariffs on U.S. imports from SSA countries and higher tariffs paid by other suppliers.

AGOA rules of origin are based on those in the U.S. GSP program. To be eligible for AGOA benefits, products must be grown, produced, or manufactured in one or more of the beneficiary countries and exported directly from an AGOA beneficiary country to the United States. Moreover, unless "wholly obtained" from a single AGOA country,[210] goods are subject to a 35-percent value-content rule and must undergo a double substantial transformation to count toward that figure.[211] According to industry sources, some SSA industries, such as tuna processing, have difficulty achieving the 35 percent value addition and therefore cannot export to the United States duty-free under AGOA (see below).

Historic Commercial Ties and Market Orientation

Resilient commercial ties, supported perhaps by a common language or a past colonial relationship, support a strong market orientation toward Europe for many SSA countries. Longstanding commercial ties have led to European investment in SSA industries, such as fish processing and vegetable farms, as described in more detail below. Furthermore, most SSA countries have had duty-free access to the EU under the Lomé Convention since 1976, giving SSA countries an incentive to export certain goods to the EU.[212] In contrast, the United States' historic trading partners are primarily in the Western Hemisphere, the Middle East, and East Asia, particularly NAFTA partners Mexico and Canada and countries with U.S. FTAs in place.

Small producers in emerging economies, such as those in SSA countries, are sometimes unable to meet the large orders required to service the U.S. market. Because of historic trade ties with Europe, SSA producers of textiles and apparel are often better matched to supply European fashion houses seeking small batches, as is the case for Mauritian apparel producers shipping to France.

Demand for Raw Materials from Rapidly Growing Developing Countries

Certain developing countries, such as China and India, have invested heavily in Africa's extractive industries to secure raw materials for their rapidly industrializing economies (more details are provided in section 5 of this report). For example, China invested $3 billion in coal and iron mines in Tanzania in 2011. An expanded port in Bagamayo, Tanzania, will export mineral ores and agricultural products to Asia from Tanzania, Zambia, and the Democratic Republic of the Congo.[213] China extends foreign debt forgiveness and loans to secure access to natural resources. In return for Chinese investment in development infrastructure, AGOA countries provide licenses to Chinese firms to extract natural resources in Africa. Mineral products account for nearly 80 percent of China's imports from Africa.[214] China is Africa's largest single-country trading partner, with two-way trade reaching $200 billion in 2012.[215]

Sanitary and Phytosanitary (SPS) Restrictions

For agricultural products, such as fresh produce and beef, African producers are often unable to meet U.S. SPS requirements and are thus unable to export to the United States. At the Commission hearing, African governments stated that U.S. stakeholders could help African producers meet U.S. SPS standards by expanding capacity-building efforts on food safety, as well as animal and plant health. In addition, SPS restrictions could be streamlined to facilitate more exports from Africa to the U.S. market without sacrificing consumer safety.[216] One person testifying at the hearing cited macadamia nuts and shea butter as success stories in capacity building and cooperation between U.S. and African governments to meet SPS standards.[217]

Case Studies

The following section sets out several product-specific case studies that illustrate the factors affecting the ability of AGOA countries to export to the U.S. market.[218] The products covered by these case studies were chosen because they provide good examples of the many barriers and logistical difficulties that SSA producers face in exporting to the U.S. market, which in turn affect the potential for expanding AGOA exports to the United States. U.S. and global imports of these products from AGOA countries and the world are shown in table 4.3.[219]

Beef

In 2012, AGOA countries exported $98.2 million in fresh and frozen boneless beef, but none to the United States.[220] The factors preventing beef exports to the United States include U.S. SPS requirements and the U.S. beef TRQ. U.S. regulations prohibit imports of fresh or frozen beef from countries or zones in which foot and mouth disease (FMD) is present, or which otherwise pose an undue risk of introducing FMD into the United States.[221] Further, AGOA provides for duty free access within the beef quota, but does not provide for duty free access over the quota volume.

Namibia was the largest AGOA country beef exporter in 2012, followed by Botswana and Swaziland. The EU was the largest market for these exports that year, followed by Norway. AGOA countries also exported smaller amounts of beef to regional trade partners such as Egypt. African producers have benefited from preferential market access in the EU since 1976.[222] Currently, the EU grants duty-free, quota-free access to beef from Namibia, Botswana, and Swaziland (as well as other countries), subject to EU SPS restrictions. This is more liberal access than is granted under AGOA.[223] In addition, some African exporters, such as Botswana, can reportedly get a higher price for beef in the EU than in closer export markets, such as South Africa.[224] Norway grants duty-free access to boneless beef imports within a TRQ from Southern African Customs Union (SACU) countries under the free trade agreement between the European Free Trade Association (EFTA) states and SACU.

In 2012, the United States imported $3.1 billion of beef, mainly from FTA partners Canada, Australia, and Mexico.[225] New Zealand also shipped significant amounts to the U.S. market. U.S. regulations prohibit imports of fresh or frozen beef from countries or zones in which FMD is present, which includes much of SSA. EU regulations allow imports of fresh or frozen beef from countries or zones in which FMD is present, as long as it is controlled through vaccination backed up by control of animal movement and traceability.

Copper

In 2012, AGOA-eligible countries exported $6.5 billion of copper ores and concentrates, unwrought forms, and waste and scrap of copper to the world;[226] U.S. imports were less than $3,000 from AGOA-eligible sources in that year. These upstream materials must undergo various degrees of further processing to be suitable inputs for manufacturing copper mill products, castings, and chemical compounds.[227] The factors affecting trade in copper include developing country demand for raw materials and historic commercial ties.

Zambia was the largest AGOA-eligible copper exporter in 2012, followed by South Africa, Namibia, Mauritania, and the Republic of the Congo. China was the largest market for exports from AGOA-eligible countries in 2012, followed by the EU, Korea, India, and Egypt. China and India have too little domestic copper to meet the consumption needs of their rapidly industrializing economies and have sought supplies worldwide, including from AGOA countries.[228] Chinese mining firms in particular have invested heavily in Zambia, dating back to the late 1990s.[229]

Furthermore, AGOA-eligible countries have well-established commercial ties, particularly trade and investment ties, and common legal systems and languages with their respective former Western European colonial powers.[230] South Africa's copper shipments to the EU market benefit from duty preferences under the European Union-South African Trade and Development Cooperation Agreement.[231] Other AGOA-eligible countries are in various stages of finalizing or have finalized economic partnership agreements (EPAs) with the EU.[232] British mining firms already have a foreign direct investment (FDI) presence in Namibia's copper mining industry and in South Africa's copper mining industry.[233]

Although a major producer of mined copper,[234] the United States imports copper principally from western hemisphere, FTA-partner countries. In 2012 the top-four sources of U.S. imports of mined copper—Chile, followed by Canada, Mexico, and Peru—were eligible for duty-free treatment under the U.S.-Chile FTA, NAFTA, and U.S.-Peru FTA, respectively. In the western hemisphere, the copper industry is characterized by long-established corporate and commercial ties, including an especially prominent U.S. FDI mining presence in Peru, along with some Canadian FDI mining presence in the United States.[235] Due to these existing trade and investment linkages, AGOA-eligible countries ship only very small amounts of copper to the United States.

Table 4.3. Select products that AGOA beneficiary countries export, but that the United States principally imports from non-AGOA countries, 2012 (million $)

Product	Global exports from AGOA countries	U.S. imports from AGOA	U.S. imports from rest of world
Boneless beef	98	0	3,083
Copper	6,547	a	5,605
Fresh fish and shellfish	598	a	1,399
Miscellaneous fresh vegetables	302	a	2,168
Women's and girls' cotton blazers	4	a	48

Source: USITC DataWeb/USDOC (accessed March 5, 2014); GTIS, Global Trade Atlas database (accessed March 5, 2014).

Note: [a] Less than $20,000.

Certain Fresh and Frozen Fish and Shellfish

In 2012, AGOA beneficiary countries exported over $598.3 million in certain fresh and frozen fish and shellfish, but less than $20,000 worth went to the United States.[236] In 2012, the United States imported $1.4 billion in these goods. Canada, China, Russia, Thailand, and Indonesia were the principal suppliers to the U.S. market. Major factors affecting trade in these products include historic commercial ties and AGOA's rules of origin, which follow the value-content method rather than the tariff shift method.[237]

Over half of AGOA countries' exports of these products went to the EU, with the remaining shipments going to China, Japan, and Hong Kong. South Africa, Senegal, and Mauritius were the largest AGOA exporters. Due to Africa's nearness to the European market, European fishing fleets are very active in African waters. African nations routinely grant fishing permits to EU vessels to fish in their waters, and some European companies perform basic processing of fish in SSA countries.[238] Much of the fish imported by the EU likely qualifies for its trade preference program.

Mauritius, Seychelles, Ghana, and Senegal have export-oriented tuna canning facilities, most of which are owned by major European brands. Under AGOA rules of origin, the fish caught by a European flagged vessel (a "third country" vessel) are not considered to be wholly the product of a beneficiary AGOA country and thus must undergo a double substantial transformation to meet a 35 percent value addition to the cost of the raw fish. U.S. Customs has held that the substantial transformation of raw tuna occurs when it is cut, trimmed, and packed, and that canning in itself is not an additional transformation, so it does not meet the double substantial transformation standard. As a result, the value of the raw tuna may not be included in the 35 percent calculation for tuna caught by a third country's vessels. Because the cost of raw tuna averages about 60 percent of the cost of the finished canned product, relying solely on the canning process to provide the required 35 percent value-content from beneficiary countries is risky, since the price of raw tuna is volatile.[239] As a result, very little tuna canned in AGOA beneficiary countries enters the United States under AGOA.

Industry sources indicate that AGOA countries could be potentially competitive sources of canned tuna in the U.S. market if AGOA's rules of origin were modified.[240] Several participants at the Commission hearing recommended a change to tariff-shift rules for tuna.[241]

Miscellaneous Fresh Vegetables[242]

AGOA countries exported fresh vegetables, such as green beans, peas, peppers, eggplant, squash, asparagus, okra, and sweet corn valued at $302 million in 2012; U.S. imports of these products from AGOA countries were less than $10,000 that year. The EU was by far the largest export market for these countries, though there is also notable intra-African trade in these goods. The factors affecting trade in these products include high transport costs related to perishability, historic commercial ties and FDI, and, to a lesser extent, U.S. SPS requirements.

Among AGOA producers, Kenya was the largest exporter of miscellaneous fresh vegetables, accounting for over two-thirds of AGOA exports, followed by Senegal, South Africa, Ethiopia, and Zambia. Since the 1990s, several African countries have diversified their production into in-demand products in the EU where African producers can take advantages of preferential market access.[243]

Fresh vegetables are perishable products requiring specific export infrastructure. The value of these products is greatly impacted by their handling after harvest; therefore, successful exporters must have efficient, sanitary, and refrigerated supply chains in place, which raises costs. Most fresh vegetables are shipped via airfreight over regular, established air routes.[244] Proximity to the EU and preferential market access give AGOA countries a pricing advantage over many western hemisphere suppliers in the EU market. Shipments to the EU are also the result of an investment relationship between European firms and African growers, as many African export-oriented vegetable farms were financed by European investors to supply the European market.

U.S. import demand for miscellaneous fresh vegetables is high; the United States imported $2.2 billion in 2012. NAFTA partners Canada and Mexico accounted for over 80 percent of total U.S. imports, with smaller shipments from other FTA partners such as Peru and Guatemala. High transport costs render most African countries uncompetitive in the U.S. market compared with closer producers such as Mexico, Canada, and Guatemala. The only types of vegetables for which AGOA countries would likely be competitive in the U.S. market are either highly differentiated products, such as a unique vegetable variety, or vegetable products with a particular certification (e.g., fair trade and organic).

Lastly, though not a binding constraint, U.S. imports of "new" fruit or vegetable products are allowed only after a pest risk analysis by the U.S. Department of Agriculture's Animal and Plant Health Inspection Service (APHIS) to prevent the entry of quarantined pests. These are conducted only if the National Plant Protection Organization in a source country requests an assessment first.[245] Many AGOA countries have thus far not applied for such analyses for the above products.[246]

Women's and Girls' Cotton Blazers[247]

AGOA countries exported $4.2 million of women's and girls' cotton blazers in 2012, but less than $4,000 to the United States. Women's blazers are a higher-value product with complicated construction, often containing lining fabric and extra seams. Relevant factors affecting trade in this product include distance to market and historic commercial ties.

Mauritius was the leading AGOA exporter of this product, shipping over $3.9 million in 2012 to the EU, primarily to the United Kingdom, France, and Belgium. Mauritius produces more high- quality, fashionable garments than other AGOA suppliers, and the Mauritian industry's reputation for quality and reliability ensures it is competitive with major Asian producers.[248] AGOA apparel producers receive preferential market access to the EU similar to that extended under AGOA, including an exemption for the use of third-country fabric.[249] Moreover, selling to Europe is a better match for Mauritius than selling to the United States, as EU markets place smaller orders and Mauritian factories are generally smaller and more specialized. In addition, Mauritian firms have long had a special relationship with France and share a common language.

According to industry sources, for higher-fashion (i.e., non-basic) items, speed to market becomes increasingly important, as these items quickly lose value if they reach retail outlets past their season. Shipping times by boat to the EU from Africa are generally two weeks shorter than those to the United States. Further, there are direct flights to several European cities from Mauritius, which allows air shipment.

In 2012, the United States imported over $814.8 million in apparel under AGOA. Basic apparel items such as slacks and trousers ("bottoms"), men's cotton woven shirts, and knit tops were the largest categories making up these imports. However, for women's and girls' cotton blazers, the United States reported minimal imports under AGOA. On the other hand, the United States imported $47.9 million of women's and girls' cotton blazers in 2012 from lower-cost Asian suppliers such as China, Vietnam, Indonesia, and the Philippines.[250]

SECTION 5. BUSINESS CLIMATE AND INVESTMENT TRENDS IN SUB-SAHARAN AFRICA

Introduction

The business and investment climate in AGOA-eligible countries, and in sub-Saharan Africa (SSA) more broadly, has improved since 2000. Global investors have responded, increasing foreign direct investment (FDI) inflows into SSA almost sixfold between 2000 and 2012. This significant increase contrasts with a slight overall decline in global FDI flows over the same period. However, FDI in SSA accounted for only 2.0 percent of global FDI between 2000 and 2012, and still presents significant challenges for investors.[251] As discussed later in this section, AGOA has been one factor in higher FDI flows to SSA, although several other factors also contributed to the region's progress.

South Africa and Nigeria were by far the largest FDI beneficiary countries in SSA, followed by the Republic of the Congo and Ghana. As a group, the members of the European Union (EU) are the largest investors in Africa, particularly the United Kingdom, Germany, and France. The United Kingdom and France maintain close economic ties to a number of former colonies, and Germany has extensive FDI in Africa's manufacturing sector, particularly in the automotive industry in South Africa. China and India have significantly expanded their investment in SSA since 2000, while Brazil does not have a large investment footprint in SSA. Natural resources (mining and petroleum), manufacturing, and services are all important sectors for foreign investment in SSA; however, the AGOA program has contributed more to investment in the apparel sector than to other SSA industries.

This section reviews several measures of the business and investment climate in SSA, and discusses changes in those measures over recent years. The section then presents a review of investment trends in the region, highlighting the primary destination countries, source countries, and industries for investment in SSA. Finally, the section addresses the possible links between AGOA and foreign investment in SSA since 2000.

Changes in the SSA Business and Investment Climate

The business and investment climate for a given country or set of countries is the set of location-specific factors shaping the incentives for firms to invest and operate.[252] An attractive business and investment climate is not just about generating profits for firms, but also about reducing uncertainty and minimizing costs and risks.[253] To evaluate the business and investment climate in SSA, this report employs five metrics that determine business and investment opportunities as well as risks in the region: macroeconomic variables, governance, business regulatory environment, trade and investment policy regime, and competitiveness.

As shown below, because of better macroeconomic conditions, sounder governance, a less burdensome regulatory environment, and a more open trade and investment policy regime, the business and investment climate in SSA has improved noticeably overall since 2000. However, the progress has been uneven among SSA countries. As a group, SSA remains among the more challenging places to do business, and the investment environment is less favorable than in Pacific Asia and in Latin America and the Caribbean (LAC). A number of issues, including poor investor protection, slow reduction of investment barriers, and insufficient infrastructure, continue to hinder business and investment.

Of 49 SSA countries, Rwanda, Sierra Leone, and Burundi (AGOA beneficiary countries) have made improvements by most metrics, while Somalia and Eritrea, which have never been eligible for AGOA benefits, experienced deteriorations in most metrics. This pattern suggests that designation as AGOA eligible may be related to improvement in the business and investment environment.

Macroeconomic Variables

The macroeconomic conditions in most SSA countries generally have improved or remained stable since 2000. The 2013 IMF Regional Economic Outlook acknowledged SSA's strong economic performance and predicted that this phenomenon would continue into the near future.[254] According to the World Bank's World Development Indicators (WDI), during 2000–2012, the economy of SSA as a group grew at an average annual rate of 11.8 percent—5.0 percentage points higher than the world average (table 5.1). SSA's gross domestic product (GDP) nearly quadrupled during the period, from $342 billion in 2000 to $1.3 trillion in 2012.

During this time, out of 49 SSA countries,[255] 44 grew at an average annual rate of more than 6 percent; 28 of them achieved a double-digit average annual growth rate. Equatorial Guinea (24.8 percent), Angola (23.4 percent), Ghana (19.1 percent), Chad (18.9 percent), Zambia (16.7 percent), Sierra Leone (16.1 percent), and Nigeria (15.6 percent) were among the fastest- growing economies in SSA, while Gambia (1.3 percent), Zimbabwe (4.1 percent), and Seychelles (4.4 percent) were among the slowest-growing. South Africa, the largest economy in the region, achieved an average annual growth rate of 9.3 percent.[256]

Table 5.1. Economic indicators, by selected region

	SSA	East Asia and Pacific (developing only)	Latin America and Caribbean (developing only)	World
GDP (nominal, billions $, 2012)	1,306.00	10,289.70	5,823.60	71,918.40
GDP, average annual growth rate (%, 2000–2012)	11.80	16.20	8.70	6.90
GDP per capita (nominal, $, 2012)	1,433.40	5,245.10	9,190.40	10,206.40
Exports of goods and services (billion $, 2011)	476.02	3,270.70	1,125.20	22,534.80
Exports (annual growth) (%, 2000–2011)	13.7	16.5	9.3	9.9
Share of global exports (%, 2011)	2.1	14.5	5.0	100

Source: World Bank, World Development Indicators (accessed December 10, 2013); USITC calculation.

SSA's exports of goods and services also grew steadily, by an average annual growth rate of 13.7 percent during 2000–2011[257]—about 4 percentage points faster than the world average. The value of SSA exports quadrupled, from $116 billion in 2000 to $476 billion in 2011. Meanwhile, the goods and services trade deficit remained, on average, around 1 percent of GDP.[258]

In contrast to the double-digit inflation rate frequently experienced by SSA countries before 2000, during 2000–2012, a period of robust economic growth, the inflation rate for SSA as a group was mostly kept at a single-digit level, averaged around 6.3 percent annually. In 2012, 25 of the 49 SSA countries had an annual inflation rate below 5 percent.[259] In addition to tighter monetary policies that contributed to lower inflation rates,[260] SSA also trimmed down external debt significantly. As a percentage of gross national income, SSA's external debt stocks fell by 83.8 percent on average during 2000–2011.[261] As a result, interest payments on external debt have been falling, lightening the financial burden on SSA countries and allowing more resources to be allocated to economic development.

The indicators above suggest improved macroeconomic conditions in SSA, which may be one reason for the region's improved environment for business and investment. However, SSA still lags behind the world, and behind even other developing regions, in most macroeconomic variables (table 5.1). The size of the SSA economy remained small in 2012, contributing only 1.8 percent of global GDP.[262] The income level in SSA was low, with GDP per capita of $1,433 in 2012. SSA's exports underperformed as well, accounting for only 2.1 percent of global goods and services exports in 2011. These facts could be perceived unfavorably by investors, but also could suggest the potential for future growth.

Governance

The World Bank defines governance as "the traditions and institutions by which authority in a country is exercised,"[263] including "a) the process by which governments are selected, monitored, and replaced, b) government's capacity to effectively formulate and implement sound policies, and c) the respect of citizens and the state for the institutions that govern economic and social interaction among them."[264] Governance is an important measure of the business and investment climate. A country with good governance is more attractive to business and investment, because it provides a predictable, accountable, stable, and transparent political environment, and allows investors and business owners to participate in the policy development and implementation process. On the other hand, a country with bad governance is more likely to deter business and investment, as the lack of transparency, efficiency, and capacity within the public sector often contributes to bureaucratic red tape, unexpected delays, and poor services. Such a situation creates a difficult business environment with high operating costs and risks.[265]

The World Bank publishes the Worldwide Governance Indicators (WGI), which have evaluated governance in 215 countries since 1996.[266] The WGI consists of six composite indicators of broad dimensions of governance ranked and covers all 49 SSA countries. According to the WGIs, most SSA countries have made some progress in improving their governance during 2000–2012 (table 5.2). Over this period, 43 out of 49 SSA countries improved at least one of the six measures of governance. Angola, the Democratic Republic of the Congo, Liberia, and Rwanda were among the top performers, making improvements across all six dimensions, while Benin, Gabon, Madagascar, Mali, Mauritania, and São Tomé and Príncipe were among the worst performers, experiencing deteriorations in all six areas of governance during 2000–2012 (see appendix G, table G.1 of this report).[267]

The areas in which SSA countries improved the most are "political stability and absence of violence/terrorism," "rule of law," "voice and accountability," and "regulatory quality." This trend reflects the subsiding civil wars and violent conflicts in the region, as well as the movement toward establishing democratic political systems and rule of law on the continent.[268]

However, according to the WGIs, corruption continues to pose a big challenge for business owners and investors, as only 14 SSA countries made progress in curbing corruption, while the remaining 35 SSA countries experienced various degrees of deterioration in control of corruption.[269] As 26 SSA countries were ranked in the bottom 25th percentile of "government effectiveness" worldwide in 2012, and only 17 SSA countries improved their performance in this indicator over 2000–2012, considerable progress is still needed in most SSA countries.

Business Regulatory Environment

While the metric of governance captures a country's overall political climate, the business regulatory environment reflects the transparency and ease of business-specific regulatory procedures, and associated start-up and operation costs for local firms. The less burdensome the regulatory procedures are, the more efficient and less costly for business operations, making the country attractive for business and investment. The analysis below uses the World Bank's Doing Business Indicators to measure the business regulatory environment and the progress that has been made in SSA countries. Launched in 2002, the Doing Business project provides objective measures of business regulations and their enforcement in 11 measures across 189 economies.[270] Based on 10 of the 11 measures, it provides an overall ranking of the ease of doing business for each economy.[271] In 2013, the Doing Business Indicators covered 47 SSA countries.[272] Three SSA countries were ranked in the top 50, and 33 SSA countries were ranked in the bottom 50 in terms of ease of doing business (appendix G, table G.2). The top 3 SSA countries were Mauritius, Rwanda, and South Africa.

SSA countries have made promising advances in improving their business regulatory environments. The World Bank reported that among the 50 economies with the greatest improvements in the world since 2005, the largest share, one-third, is in SSA.[273] According to the Doing Business Indicators, Burkina Faso, Mali, Rwanda, Sierra Leone, and Uganda were the top SSA performers, having made improvements in 9 out of 10 measures during 2006–13.[274] Most SSA countries have streamlined regulatory procedures and shortened the time required to conduct business activities. A majority of SSA countries successfully reduced the costs of getting electricity, dealing with construction permits, and registering property, and made improvements in getting credit. About 27 SSA countries made improvements in paying tax and reduced the tax rate as a share of profit. However, only a handful of SSA countries reduced the cost of exports and imports; 9 SSA countries made improvements in protecting investors; and 5 SSA countries reduced the cost of enforcing contracts. Of 47 SSA countries, 8 had no regulatory procedures in place for closing a business, and 10 made improvements in one or more components of resolving insolvency (table 5.3 and appendix G, table G.2).

Table 5.2. The Worldwide Governance Indicators, and the number of SSA countries that improved over 2000–2012

WGI	Measures	# of countries improved
Political stability and absence of violence/ terrorism	Captures perceptions of the likelihood that the government will be destabilized or overthrown by unconstitutional or violent means, including politically motivated violence and terrorism.	29
Rule of law	Captures perceptions of the extent to which agents have confidence in and abide by the rules of society, and in particular the quality of contract enforcement, property rights, the police, and the courts, as well as the likelihood of crime and violence.	25
Voice and accountability	Captures perceptions of the extent to which a country's citizens are able to participate in selecting their government, as well as freedom of expression, freedom of association, and a free media.	22
Regulatory quality	Captures perceptions of the ability of the government to formulate and implement sound policies and regulations that permit and promote private sector development.	22
Government effectiveness	Captures perceptions of the quality of public services, the quality of the civil service and the degree of its independence from political pressures, the quality of policy formulation and implementation, and the credibility of the government's commitment to such policies.	17
Control of corruption	Captures perceptions of the extent to which public power is exercised for private gain, including both petty and grand forms of corruption, as well as "capture" of the state by elites and private interests.	14

Source: World Bank, Worldwide Governance Indicators 2013 (accessed December 17, 2013); USITC calculations.

Table 5.3. SSA country improvements in doing business, 2006–13

Doing Business indicators	Component	Number of countries improved
Starting a business	Procedures (number)	33
	Time (days)	38
	Cost (% of income per capita)	42
	Paid-in min. capital (% of income per capita)	26
Dealing with construction permits	Procedures (number)	11
	Time (days)	23
	Cost (% of income per capita)	36
Getting electricity[277]	Procedures (number)	3
	Time (days)	15
	Cost (% of income per capita)	44
Registering property	Procedures (number)	10
	Time (days)	22
	Cost (% of property value)	35
Getting credit	Strength of legal rights index (0–10)	20
	Depth of credit information index (0–6)	14
	Public registry coverage (% of adults)	18
	Private bureau coverage (% of adults)	10
Protecting investors	Extent of disclosure index (0–10)	5
	Extent of director liability index (0–10)	8
	Ease of shareholder suits index (0–10)	5
	Strength of investor protection index (0–10)	9
Paying taxes	Payments (number per year)	13
	Time (hours per year)	13
	Total tax rate (% profit)	27
Trading across borders	Documents to export (number)	15
	Time to export (days)	35
	Cost to export (US$ per container)	4
	Documents to import (number)	17
	Time to import (days)	37
	Cost to import (US$ per container)	3
Enforcing contracts	Time (days)	16
	Cost (% of claim)	5
	Procedures (number)	18
Resolving insolvency	Time (years)	1
	Cost (% of estate)	1
	Outcome (0 as piecemeal sale and 1 as going concern)	0
	Recovery rate (cents on the dollar)	8

Source: USITC calculations based on World Bank, Doing Business Indicators 2013 (accessed December 17, 2013).

Even with clear signs of progress, then, SSA still lags behind other regions. Whereas 66 percent of 47 SSA countries were ranked in the bottom 25th percentile of the ease of doing business in 2012, only 16 percent of 25 Asia-Pacific economies and 13 percent of 32 LAC countries were in the bottom group. The business regulatory environment of SSA as a whole remains among the least business-friendly in the world.

Trade and Investment Policy Regimes

A country's trade and investment policy regime matters to business owners and investors. Open trade and investment policy regimes not only encourage trade and investment, but also foster regional economic integration, encourage market expansion, and generate business and investment opportunities. Moreover, trade and investment tend to be intrinsically interlinked.[275] An open trade policy promotes greater trade, which in turn attracts greater investment inflows. Likewise, an open investment policy encourages greater FDI inflows, which in turn increase the likelihood of trade.

Measures of the overall openness of a SSA country's trade and investment policy regime are composites of the metrics used to calculate the Heritage Foundation's Economic Freedom index—"Trade Freedom" and "Investment Freedom." Based on the trade-weighted average tariff rate and nontariff barriers (NTBs), the Heritage Foundation's Trade Freedom index is a composite measure of the absence of tariffs and NTBs that affect imports and exports of goods and services.[276] The higher the score, the less restrictive is a country's trade policy regime. A score of 100 means no restrictions. From 2000 to 2013, 42 out of 48 SSA countries improved their "Trade Freedom" scores on average by 21.9 points. By reducing tariff rates and/or NTBs, most SSA countries became more open to trade, scoring an average of 67.1 in 2013. Mauritius, Zambia, Namibia, Botswana, Burundi, Rwanda, South Africa, and Mozambique are among the most open-to-trade SSA countries (appendix G, table G.3).

The Heritage Foundation's Investment Freedom index measures the restrictions a country imposes on the flow of investment capital, including different rules for foreign and domestic investment; restriction on access to foreign exchange, payments, transfers, and capital transactions; as well as the transparency of investment regulations. Similar to the Trade Freedom index, the higher the score, the less restrictive is a country's investment policy regime. A score of 100 means no restrictions. Compared to the progress made in "Trade Freedom," improvements in "Investment Freedom" were modest. From 2000 to 2013, 25 out of 48 SSA countries improved their "Investment Freedom" scores, but on average by only 5.4 points. The average score of "Investment Freedom" for 48 SSA countries was 45.8 in 2013, suggesting that investment barriers remain significant in these countries. Mauritius, scored at 90, by far is the most investment-friendly country in the region. It was followed by Benin, Botswana, and Ghana, which each scored 70 (appendix G, table G.3). South Africa, one of the leading recipients of FDI in the region, scored 45 points in 2013, a decline of 25 from the 70 points it scored in 2000. In 2013, South Africa initiated a major investment policy change. Box 5.1 addresses changes under way in South Africa's investment policy regime.

Competitiveness

The four sets of metrics used in the foregoing discussion—involving macroeconomic variables, governance, business regulatory environment, and trade and investment policy regime—are all crucial components of a country's business and investment climate. However, other factors may be equally critical for business operations and investment decisions, such as infrastructure, market efficiency, technological advancement, and innovation. All factors together contribute to a country's level of competitiveness, as well as the potential for sustained business growth, and it is to these factors that this section turns.[278]

BOX 5.1. SOUTH AFRICA'S 2013 INVESTMENT LEGISLATION

The South African government recently made changes to its regulatory framework for foreign investment, drawing a mixed reaction from the investment community. The South African government published the draft of its 2013 Promotion and Protection of Investment Bill ("Investment Bill") for public comment on November 1, 2013.[a] The bill was introduced as part of an overhaul of the regulatory framework for foreign investment, following a government review of its policy on bilateral investment treaties (BITs) and the decision to withdraw from its BITs with Belgium, Luxembourg, Spain, Germany, and Switzerland. South Africa also indicated that it will terminate the remaining BITs with other countries, and the Investment Bill will replace these BITs with domestic legislation that sets out the rights and obligations of the government, and of all investors, both local and foreign.[b]

The response to South Africa's attempt to update its investment regime has been mixed. While some commentators applauded such action as reflecting the government's commitment to the rule of law, others are concerned about the negative effects that the unilateral termination of South Africa's BITs may have on investor confidence. The investment community has contended that the protection offered to foreign investors under the Investment Bill is of a lower standard than what the BITs provided. For its part, the South African government has argued that the Bill contains ample clarity, transparency, and certainty, and provides adequate protection to all investors, including foreign investors.[c]

Notes:
[a] The draft of the bill is available at http://www.tralac.org/files/2013/11/Promotion-and-protection-of-investment-bill-2013-Invitation-for-public-comment.pdf.
[b] Tralac Trade Law Center, "South Africa's Promotion and Protection of Investment Bill," November 20, 2013.
[c] Ibid.

First published in 2004, the World Economic Forum's Global Competitiveness Index (GCI) takes into account 12 important factors in its measure of overall competitiveness, and offers the most comprehensive and integrated snapshot available of national business and investment environments in the global context.[279] In 2009, the methodology of GCI went through a major revision, making it impossible to directly compare recent data to pre-2009 data, so this discussion will concentrate on the 2009–2013 results. In 2013, GCI covered 144 countries and territories, including 34 SSA countries. According to the 2012–13 GCI, the average GCI score for SSA was 3.57, lower than the Latin America and the Caribbean (LAC) average (3.97) and the Southeast Asia average (4.46).[280] SSA scored the lowest in 10 factors and second lowest in "institutions" and "labor market efficiency," where SSA scored slightly higher than LAC (figure 5.1). The gaps between SSA and the other two regions were biggest in "market size," "infrastructure," and "technological readiness."

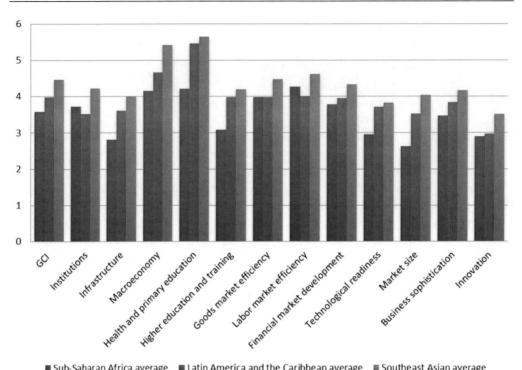

■ Sub-Saharan Africa average ■ Latin America and the Caribbean average ■ Southeast Asian average
Source: WEF, World Bank, and AfDB, *Africa Competitiveness Report 2013*, 2013.

Figure 5.1. GCI and 12 pillar scores of sub-Saharan Africa, Latin America and the Caribbean, and Southeast Asia, 2012–13.

In 2012–13, of 34 SSA countries, 8 were ranked between 50th and 100th out of the 140 countries rated, and 14 were ranked in the bottom 15 in the world (figure 5.2). South Africa, Mauritius, Rwanda, Seychelles, and Botswana, which have been AGOA beneficiary countries since 2000, were the most competitive economies in the region. Among 12 pillar factors of competitiveness, SSA performed relatively better in "labor market efficiency," "institutions," and "financial market development," and worse in "health and primary education," "higher education and training," and "technological readiness." A full list of SSA country rankings in each pillar factor can be found in appendix G, table G.4.

Overview of SSA Investment Trends

For most of the period from the 1970s through the end of the 1990s, total annual FDI flows into SSA remained close to $5 billion (not adjusted for inflation), even as FDI into Latin America and East Asia expanded rapidly. As a result, the SSA share of total FDI flows to developing countries declined from 25 percent early in the 1970s to 5 percent in 1999.[281] At the same time, the sources of FDI into SSA became more diverse. Before the mid-1990s, the principal source countries for FDI into Africa were France, the United Kingdom, the United States, and Japan. However, between 1994 and 1998 additional countries became important investors, and combined FDI flows from Canada, Italy, the Netherlands, Norway, Portugal, and Spain accounted for almost 25 percent of overall FDI inflows. China, India, Malaysia, and Taiwan also began to invest significant amounts in Africa, and FDI began to diversify away from natural resources to the food and beverages, textiles and apparel, and financial and other services sectors. African governments also began to privatize infrastructure assets, leading to a marked increase in FDI in infrastructure, including electric power, railways, and telecommunications.[282]

Increased political stability, liberalized FDI regulations in many SSA countries, and increasing regional integration, which expands the potential market for foreign investors in any one country, all encouraged new investment during the 1990s.[283] FDI inflows to SSA grew at an average annual rate of 16 percent, from $6.8 billion in 2000 to $41.0 billion in 2012 (figure 5.3), contrasted with a global annual decline of 0.37 percent over the same period.[284]

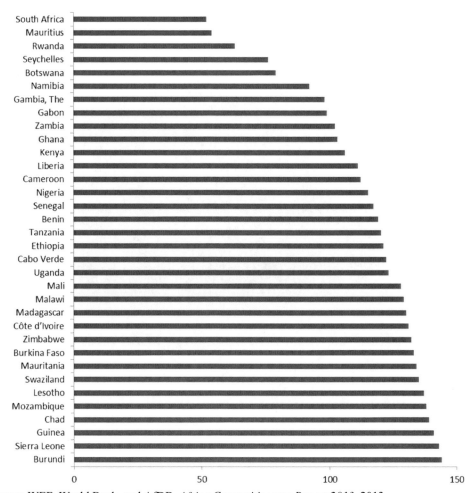

Source: WEF, World Bank, and AfDB, *Africa Competitiveness Report 2013*, 2013.
Note: According to the figure, South Africa was the most competitive and Burundi was the least competitive.

Figure 5.2. The rankings of sub-Saharan African countries in global competitiveness index, 2012–13 lowest score = most competitive).

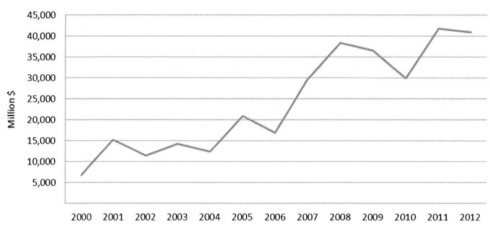

Source: UNCTAD, UNCTADStat database (accessed October 29, 2013).

Figure 5.3. FDI inflows to SSA, 2000–2012.

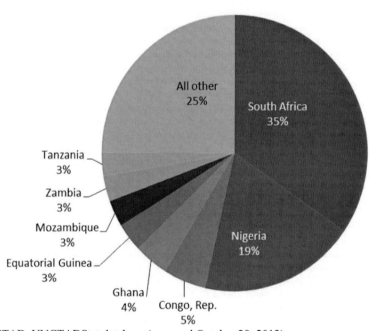

Source: UNCTAD, UNCTADStat database (accessed October 29, 2013).

Figure 5.4. FDI position in SSA countries, 2012.

The years since 2000—the AGOA period—have seen continued growth of FDI into SSA. FDI inflows into SSA during 2000–2012 represented 2.0 percent of global FDI inflows, compared with an average of 1.3 percent during the 1990s. Natural resources projects have continued to account for the majority of this investment, by value, but investor interest in other sectors has been increasing. For example, in 2012 nearly 25 percent of total greenfield FDI projects[285] in SSA were in consumer-related industries, up from 7 percent in 2008. Countries that were eligible for AGOA at some point during the period (i.e., all SSA countries except for Equatorial Guinea, Somalia, Sudan, and Zimbabwe) accounted for 97 percent of overall SSA FDI position.[286] Private capital flows have increased relative to foreign aid as a share of overall capital flows to SSA since 2002. During 2002–12, while foreign assistance more than doubled, rising from $18.1 billion to $42.5 billion, private capital flows to SSA nearly quintupled, rising from $14 billion to $67 billion, with FDI accounting for about three-quarters of the total.[287]

South Africa and Nigeria were by far the largest SSA recipients of foreign investment in 2012, as measured by cumulative FDI position (figure 5.4), and were also the two largest economies in SSA, as measured by GDP. However, a number of other countries have attracted higher amounts of FDI relative to their GDP, including Liberia (30.3 percent of GDP), Republic of the Congo (17.3 percent), Equatorial Guinea (15.6 percent), and São Tomé and Príncipe (14.8 percent). In comparison, FDI averaged 1.6 percent of GDP for South Africa and 3.4 percent of GDP for Nigeria.[288] The SSA countries experiencing the fastest FDI growth on an average annual basis were Somalia, Comoros, Niger, and the Central African Republic, all starting from a very low base. Larger SSA economies experiencing particularly fast growth of FDI inflows included the Democratic Republic of the Congo (38 percent), Mozambique (35 percent), and Ghana (32 percent).[289]

SSA Country Recipients of FDI

South Africa

FDI inflows to South Africa between 2007 and 2011 were dominated by investment from the United Kingdom, followed by Switzerland, Germany, and the United States (figure 5.5). South Africa is the most advanced economy in sub-Saharan Africa, with close links to several other markets in SSA, a relatively large and expanding domestic market, an abundance of tourist attractions, and extensive mineral wealth. Foreign investors are particularly attracted to banking, telecommunications, tourism, real estate, mining, and manufacturing.[290]

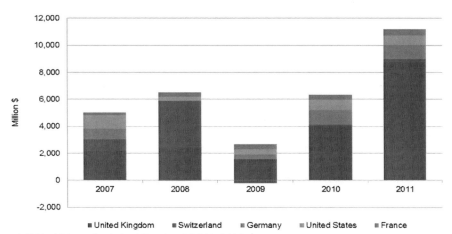

Source: AfDB, *African Statistical Yearbook 2013*, 2013.
Note: FDI inflows are negative when more money is divested from a country than is invested in that year.

Figure 5.5. FDI inflows to South Africa, by major source country.

Historically, South Africa has attracted FDI mainly into natural resources, especially mining (particularly in gold and diamonds), which accounted for a third of total inbound FDI position in both 2001 and 2009 (table 5.4). However, South Africa's mining sector has grown slowly compared to other countries with strong mining industries, due, in part, to investor uncertainty over labor unrest and potential nationalization.[291] Inbound FDI patterns in South Africa are changing, with broader geographic origins and with non-mining industries attracting investment from countries other than Europe and the United States in recent years.[292]

FDI position in the manufacturing sector increased from $10.7 billion in 2001 to $29.1 billion in 2009 (latest available). Since 2008, a number of manufacturing multinational companies (MNCs) have expanded their activities in South Africa, particularly in the automotive sector. Daimler AG invested $290 million into its South Africa operations and BMW invested a similar amount to expand its facilities, focusing on the export market. South Africa's auto assembly industry also includes Ford, General Motors, Volkswagen, Toyota, and Nissan. The South African government has offered incentives for FDI in the automotive industry, which contributes significantly to the country's export earnings, employment base, and technology transfer opportunities.[293]

The service sector accounted for a larger share of FDI in South Africa than either the primary or manufacturing sectors in 2001 and in 2009. FDI stock in services rose from $18.6 billion in 2001 to $39.8 billion in 2009, most prominently in financial services. South Africa has a highly developed financial services industry with well-capitalized and well-regulated local banks.[294]

The South African government released its National Development Plan in November 2011, detailing an effort to diversify the economy over 20 years. The plan contained broad policy guidelines to attract both domestic and foreign investment into certain industries, including financial services, mobile telecommunications, business process outsourcing, and infrastructure development.[295]

Table 5.4. South Africa: Distribution of inward FDI position, by industry, 2001 and 2009 (million $)

Sector/industry	2001	2009
Mining and quarrying	14,888	34,780
Manufacturing	10,733	29,066
Total services	18,569	39,794
Finance, insurance, real estate and business services	*15,667*	*28,195*
Transport, storage and communication	*1,059*	*7,793*
Wholesale and retail trade, catering and accommodation	*1,817*	*3,738*
Community, social and personal services	*26*	*68*
Construction	211	244
Agriculture, forestry and fishing	78	112
Electricity, gas and water	4	3
Total	44,483	104,000

Source: Unpublished data obtained from South African Reserve Bank (SARB) Research Unit and SARB Quarterly Bulletin, various issues, cited in Sauvant, Mallampally, and McAllister, Inward and Outward FDI Country Profiles, 1060.

Table 5.5. Nigeria, selected greenfield FDI projects in the coal, oil, and natural gas sector, 2003–13

Investing company	Number of reported projects	Total reported capital investment (million $)
Total (France)	7	3,400
ExxonMobil (United States)	5	2,600
Eni SpA (Italy)	4	400
Royal Dutch Shell (Netherlands)	3	5,000
ONGC (India)	2	4,000
Skipper Energy (Mauritius)	2	775
Indian Oil (IOC)	2	3,500
CityView	1	1,000

Source: Financial Times, FDIMarkets database (accessed January 14, 2014).

Note: Other multinational oil companies with oil and gas extraction projects in Nigeria with no capital investment values reported include Afren (United Kingdom), Chevron (United States), Energy Equity Resources (UK), Eni (Italy), Korea National Oil (KNOC), Kulczyk Oil Ventures (Canada), Nexen (Canada), Petrobras (Brazil), and Statoil (Norway). These data include both oil and gas extraction and related projects.

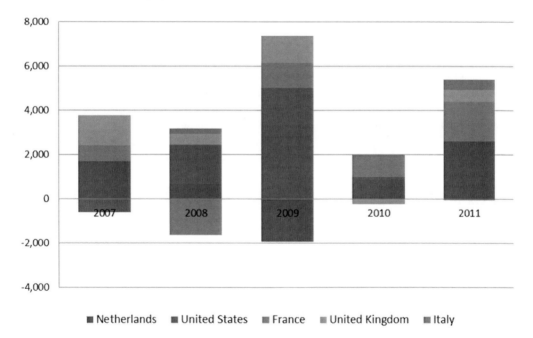

Source: AfDB, *African Statistical Yearbook 2013*, 2013.

Note: FDI inflows are negative when more money is divested from a country than is invested in that year.

Figure 5.6. FDI inflows to Nigeria, by major source country, 2007–11 (million $).

Nigeria

Nigeria received $50 billion in net FDI inflows between 2004 and 2011, the second-largest destination among SSA countries after South Africa.[296] Global petroleum companies are active investors in Nigeria, both in oil and gas extraction projects and in related areas such as refineries and pipelines (table 5.5). The Netherlands is one of the largest investors in Nigeria, likely reflecting Shell Oil's investment in the petroleum sector and related industries (figure 5.6).[297]

Mauritius

Mauritius is one of the most FDI-friendly countries in SSA. Although a small economy, it is the third-largest SSA country in terms of FDI inflows from the United States, and has a highly diverse group of source countries compared with other SSA countries (figure 5.7). From 2004 to 2011, Mauritius received significant FDI inflows from South Africa, other African countries (including North Africa), South Asia, as well as from the United States, the United Kingdom, and France. Investors are attracted to Mauritius for its open economy and strong regulatory system. Mauritius ranked first among African countries in the World Bank's Doing Business scale, and 20th out of all countries listed. It is also known for a highly educated and bilingual (French and English) population.

Significant FDI in Mauritius began in the 1980s with the creation of export processing zones (EPZs). The EPZs offered preferential access to the European market for textiles and other products, attracting investment from Asian companies interested in exporting apparel to Europe. Manufacturing, including apparel, was the main destination for FDI in the 1980s and1990s. More recently, however, the economy has attracted FDI in other sectors, and in 2011 the service sector drew the largest share of FDI inflows (69 percent), led by real estate (38 percent); finance and insurance (13 percent); and accommodation and food services (12 percent). Construction accounted for 28 percent of total inflows in 2011. Manufacturing, agriculture, forestry, and fishing together received only 3 percent of total FDI inflows in 2011.[298]

SSA Country Sources of FDI

The sources of FDI inflows to SSA have changed over time. The EU has remained the leading source of FDI inflows to SSA during the AGOA period, but the EU's share has declined in recent years as FDI increased from the United States, China, and other sources (figure 5.8).[299] Between 2003 and 2007, the EU accounted for 66 percent of overall FDI inflows to SSA, compared with the United States (7 percent) and China (3 percent). However, during 2008–10, the EU share declined to 50 percent while the shares from the United States, China, and other FDI sources all increased.

In addition to China, other Asian countries are also increasing FDI in SSA. The potential of West Africa's palm oil industry is leading to increased investment from Malaysia and Indonesia, both important producers of palm oil in Southeast Asia.[300] Also, Taiwanese firms have invested in the textile and apparel industries in a number of SSA countries, mostly to take advantage of AGOA trade preferences (see below).

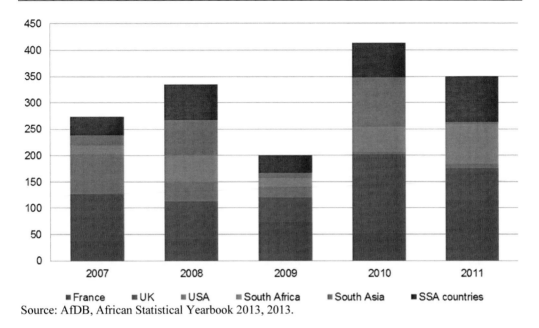

Source: AfDB, African Statistical Yearbook 2013, 2013.

Figure 5.7. FDI inflows to Mauritius, by major source country, 2007–11 (million $).

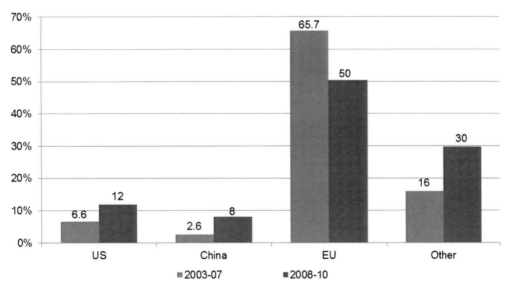

Sources: MOFCOM; UNCTAD, UNCTADStat database; USDOC, BEA; EC, Eurostat (accessed January 8, 2014).

Figure 5.8. Shares of FDI inflows into SSA, 2003–07 vs. 2008–10, by source region.

There are few official government data sources that report FDI inflows into SSA by source and destination countries and by industry. Commercial databases provide data for individual greenfield FDI projects (from 2003) and for cross-border acquisitions of African firms. According to these sources, greenfield FDI projects accounted for three quarters of new FDI in SSA during 2003–13, with the remainder being acquisitions by foreign firms. Data for the values of particular acquisitions and FDI projects are reported only sporadically, but it is possible to count the number of projects reported by source country, destination country, and industry. Such information is necessarily incomplete, but does provide some insight into the most prevalent investment sectors in SSA throughout most of the AGOA period.[301]

For both greenfield FDI projects and mergers and acquisitions, EU countries have accounted for about one-third of all projects during 2003–13, followed by other SSA countries and the United States (figure 5.9).[302] The number of greenfield FDI projects from all source countries has increased significantly since 2008. In addition to being the largest destination for greenfield FDI in SSA, South Africa is one of the largest outbound investors in other SSA countries, accounting for 322 of 656 (49 percent) FDI projects originating in SSA countries.

U.S. Investment in SSA

In 2012, the United States' cumulative FDI position in SSA was $28.6 billion; the three largest destinations for U.S. investment were Nigeria, Mauritius, and South Africa (table 5.6). Before 2001, South Africa was a leading SSA destination for U.S. investment, but since then U.S. FDI in Nigeria, Mauritius, and other SSA countries has grown significantly (figure 5.10). U.S. firms are continuing to invest in Africa. For example, GE reportedly planned to announce $1 billion of investment into Africa in 2013 alone. Illustrative GE projects include a $250 million project that broke ground in June 2013 in Calabar, Nigeria, that will manufacture and service power- generating equipment, and a tentative agreement to build a 1,000 MW natural gas-fired power plant in Ghana, signed the same month.[303]

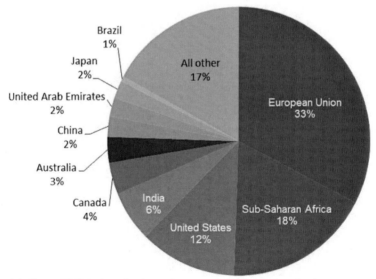

Source: Financial Times, FDIMarkets database; Bureau van Dijk, Zephyr database.

Figure 5.9. Greenfield FDI projects and M&A deals by source, 2003–13.

Table 5.6. United States: FDI outflows to SSA, 2000–2012, and FDI position in 2012

Country	2000	2001	2002	2003	2004	2005	2006	2007	2008	2009	2010	2011	2012	U.S. FDI position 2012
						Million $								
Total SSA	816	1,861	−705	2,228	1,164	1,452	5,103	3,494	2,220	8,904	5,523	3,048	1,546	28,576
Nigeria	137	−192	588	173	676	−846	144	−596	1,772	5,170	81	157	2,762	8,152
Mauritius	−9	29	−121	−13	184	−20	323	1,326	−265	654	1,179	−50	−86	7,062
South Africa	346	−86	125	232	480	82	159	1,000	306	1,088	447	621	250	5,502
Ghana	−24	91	−31	4	120	−4	729	(D)	(D)	205	−313	328	461	3,629
Angola	79	342	−263	−36	−22	98	280	−99	789	54	1,974	707	−3,011	1,245
Liberia	−218	−60	−260	47	62	149	−128	207	61	12	228	109	−19	1,019
Mozambique	1	8	3	1	(D)	(D)	4	−3	−2	(D)	127	(D)	(D)	619
Tanzania	20	−21	−3	−7	−3	−6	(D)	(D)	(D)	(D)	(D)	(D)	(D)	319
Kenya	−19	(D)	7	7	−7	40	−109	2	7	62	3	5	−145	259
Cameroon	(*)	−1	(D)	(*)	−32	36	−11	−52	2	−50	48	−4	6	203
Gabon	73	2	−182	11	61	−166	−17	130	−439	4	327	94	78	157
Zambia	5	2	−5	−4	−3	(*)	15	5	−1	3	18	−3	(*)	144
Côte d'Ivoire	−8	−64	40	20	60	54	−23	−88	−166	31	−13	−10	−25	118
Uganda	−5	−1	2	(*)	−4	1	1	(D)	(D)	3	6	1	−3	100
Other SSA countries	333	2,139	−1,418	1,823	8	2,216	4,800	3,090	142	2,646	4,995	2,270	−1,466	14,922

Source: USDOC, BEA, Balance of Payments and Direct Investment Position Data (accessed November 12, 2013).

Notes: FDI inflows are a measure of new investment in a single year. Inflows are negative when more money is divested from a country than is invested in that year. FDI position (or stock) is a measure of cumulative investment over time. (*) = Less than $0.5 million dollars; (D) = Data suppressed to avoid disclosure of individual company information.

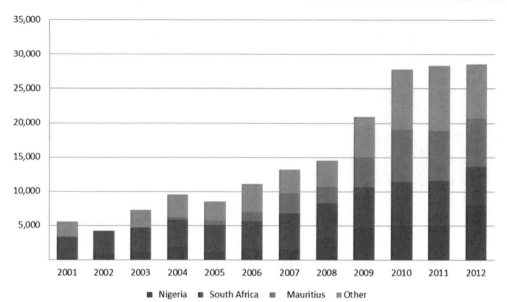

Source: USDOC, BEA, Balance of Payments and Direct Investment Position Data (accessed November 12, 2013).

Figure 5.10. U.S. direct investment position in AGOA countries, 2001–12.

Limited data are available for FDI by industry. Overall in 2012, 57 percent of the U.S. FDI position in Africa was directed to the mining sector (including petroleum), 15 percent in holding companies, and 6 percent in manufacturing.[304] For South Africa, the largest shares of U.S. FDI go to manufacturing (42 percent) and professional, scientific, and technical services (10 percent), with mining accounting for only 1 percent. In Nigeria, 45 percent of the U.S. FDI position is in mining (including petroleum).[305] Although further disaggregated industry data are not available, historically a large share of the FDI flows into Angola has been petroleum-related. That has begun to change in recent years, with more FDI going to services and consumer products manufacturing since 2008.[306]

Official U.S. data do not provide an industry breakdown for FDI in Mauritius. Even though Mauritius is one of the largest SSA recipients of U.S. FDI, commercial databases record only 12 greenfield FDI projects or acquisitions from the United States to Mauritius between 2000 and 2013.[307] U.S.-based companies often use Mauritius as an export platform to capture regional markets, benefiting from Mauritius's membership in SADC and COMESA. Mauritius also has a significant offshore financial sector, which serves as a major route for foreign investors to access India and other points in South Asia. As a result, a large share of U.S. FDI outflows to Mauritius is likely to be destined for final FDI projects in India.[308] Outbound FDI from Mauritius to India was estimated at $43 billion during April 2000–September 2010, or 42 percent of total FDI inflows to India during that period.[309] U.S. investors recorded FDI outflows to African holding companies of $3.4 billion in 2012.[310] Data for specific country destinations for those investments are not available, but given the investment patterns between Mauritius and India, a significant share of those funds may be invested in Mauritius.

Based on the number of FDI projects, Ghana, Liberia, and Mozambique appear to be the largest destinations after South Africa for non-petroleum-related FDI, although official data for FDI inflows by sector are not available for those countries. Nigeria is also a significant destination for non-petroleum-related FDI. As noted above, although the mining and petroleum industries account for almost one-half of all of the U.S. FDI position, U.S. investors also have significant interests in business services, downstream oil industry projects, communications, and consumer products in Nigeria.[311]

Overall, as measured by the number of greenfield FDI projects, U.S. investors in SSA have principally focused on software and IT services; business services; and coal, oil, and natural gas. In the manufacturing sector, the principal areas are consumer products, food and beverage, and automotive manufacturing (figure 5.11).[312] In the coal, oil, and natural gas sector, 33 of the 56 projects are oil and gas extraction projects. The others are fossil fuel electric power; natural, liquefied, and compressed gas; other electric power generation (coal, oil, and natural gas); other petroleum and coal products; petroleum refineries; and support activities for mining and energy.

EU Investment in SSA

Official statistics from the European Union report data for only two individual SSA countries: Nigeria and South Africa. In 2012, the FDI position in South Africa was $76.8 billion (41 percent of the overall EU position in SSA) and in Nigeria was $35.9 billion (19 percent).[313] The share of the EU FDI position in both countries has dropped since their peak levels in 2009 and 2010 (figure 5.12). On the other hand, the EU direct investment position in Central and Southern Africa increased at an average annual rate of 14.3 percent, from $42.7 billion in 2001 to $186.1 billion in 2012 (table 5.7).

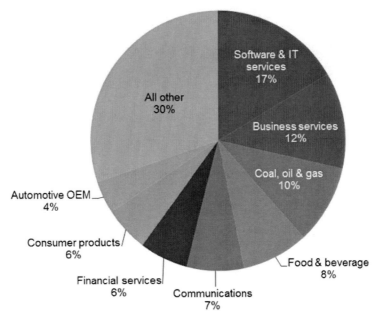

Source: Financial Times, FDIMarkets database.
Note: OEM – original equipment manufacturer.

Figure 5.11. U.S. greenfield FDI projects in SSA, 2003–13.

Table 5.7. EU: Outward FDI position in SSA, 2001–12

Country	2001	2002	2003	2004	2005	2006	2007	2008	2009	2010	2011	2012	CAGR %
						Million $							
Africa	53,845	66,969	104,899	134,247	141,480	169,378	213,882	224,629	287,292	291,044	272,873	291,882	16.6
Central and South Africa	42,656	51,506	81,659	104,511	112,420	131,009	158,898	165,218	199,283	218,333	179,279	186,059	14.3
Nigeria	NA	NA	14,744	14,363	17,681	24,201	32,584	36,525	39,824	37,271	33,066	35,889	10.4
South Africa	20,730	28,171	45,853	49,732	57,217	56,048	79,768	76,849	103,500	99,060	71,850	76,819	12.6

Source: EC, Eurostat database (accessed December 16, 2013).
Note: NA = Not available.

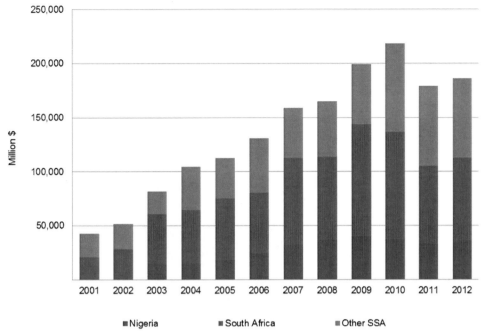

Source: EC, Eurostat database (accessed December 16, 2013).

Figure 5.12. EU FDI in SSA, 2001–12.

According to other data sources, during 2003–13, the United Kingdom accounted for 39 percent of greenfield FDI projects from the EU into SSA, followed by Germany, France, and Portugal (figure 5.13).[314] In addition, 38 percent of all the United Kingdom's projects were invested in five countries: South Africa, Nigeria, Kenya, Tanzania, and Ghana. All of these countries are former British colonies; each country accounted for between 6 and 8 percent of all UK FDI projects in SSA. In South Africa, more than half of all UK-based greenfield FDI projects were destined for the service sector, with the largest areas reported as financial services, business services, and software and IT services.[315]

Portuguese FDI in SSA focuses on Portugal's former colonies of Angola and Mozambique, with 130 and 12 projects, respectively, out of a total of 149 projects in those countries during the period. In Angola, 94 of those are financial services projects, primarily new bank branches opened by several large Portugal-based banks. However, these projects are not likely to represent significant financial outlays. In Mozambique, many projects are in the manufacturing sector, including several from Cimpor, a large cement company.[316]

German firms, with almost as many individual FDI projects as Portuguese firms, were much more focused on South Africa (86 projects), followed by Nigeria (12 projects) and Kenya (13 projects). In South Africa, auto industry projects accounted for one-third of the total, including 11 by Volkswagen; chemicals investments accounted for another 18 projects. Other Germany- based FDI projects in SSA are scattered among a wide variety of industries.[317]

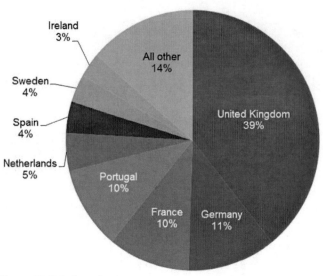

Source: Financial Times, FDIMarkets database.

Figure 5.13. Greenfield projects in SSA, by EU member, 2003–13.

FDI projects from France are diversified among 30 SSA countries, with South Africa, Nigeria, and Senegal accounting for the largest shares. France-based companies have invested in a wide variety of industries in SSA. The coal, oil, and natural gas sector is the largest (17 percent of all projects); oil and gas extraction projects account for half of these. Telecommunications is next, followed by business services, financial services, computer and IT services, and food and tobacco.[318]

The United Kingdom was also the largest acquirer of existing SSA companies. However, the Netherlands and Luxembourg, which did not appear among the largest greenfield investors, also numbered among the primary investors (see appendix G, table G.11). This is likely due to the role of those two countries as offshore financial centers, so that companies investing from the Netherlands and Luxembourg may actually be based elsewhere.

Brazilian Investment in SSA

Brazil is not a large investor in SSA, compared with other source countries discussed here, with total FDI position in the region equal to $200 million in 2010 almost entirely in Angola (latest available). This is only a tiny share of Brazil's global FDI position (table 5.8). Brazil's FDI into Africa targets strategic sectors, such as mining, energy, and infrastructure. Brazilian technology and expertise in infrastructure construction, tropical agriculture and agribusiness, biofuels, hydrocarbons exploration, mining, and telecommunications have created opportunities for Brazilian investors in SSA.[319]

Companhia Vale do Rio Doce (Vale), the Brazil-based mining company, is one of the country's largest investors in SSA (box 5.2). Vale accounted for 11 of the 32 greenfield projects recorded from Brazil to SSA between 2003 and 2013, six in the petroleum sector and five in the metals industry. Vale also acquired a majority stake in a joint venture with assets in the Simandou iron ore mine in Guinea for $2.5 billion. Vale's coal mine in Mozambique is its biggest operation outside Brazil.[320]

Box 5.2. Vale's FDI in Sub-Saharan Africa

Companhia Vale do Rio Doce (Vale), a Brazil-based global mining company, began an active expansion program in Africa in 2004. Vale's Africa focus will help the company to meet the demand for mineral resources from fast-growing China and India, as those countries continue to urbanize, increase the penetration of durable goods such as automobiles, and expand their infrastructure.[a] As of 2010, Vale had invested $2.5 billion into Africa (from all global operations, not necessarily from Brazil directly), and had plans to invest an additional $20 billion into Africa over the coming five years. In December 2013, however, the company announced that it was significantly cutting its annual global investment budget to $14.8 billion, from $18 billion in 2011, so the expected investment in Africa may not materialize.[b]

As of January 2014, Vale was active in six countries in SSA: Angola, the Democratic Republic of the Congo, Guinea, Malawi, Mozambique, and Zambia. The company was also reportedly exploring additional possibilities in other SSA countries.

- *Angola*: Vale is currently conducting exploration activities focused on copper.
- *Democratic Republic of the Congo*: Together with its joint venture partner, African Rainbow Minerals Ltd. (ARM), Vale is currently planning for future cobalt and copper operations.
- *Guinea*: Vale acquired a 51 percent stake in Guinea-owned BGS Resources (BGSR) for $500 million in 2006, with a further $2 billion depending on future developments. Vale's goal is the development of BGSR's concessions in the Simandou iron ore project. In addition to mining, the project envisions upgrading a local rail network. As of January 2014, licensing at Simandou was under review by the Guinean government and mining activities were suspended.
- *Malawi*: The railroad Vale is building from its Moatize coal mine in Mozambique will pass through part of Malawi on its way to the Port of Nacala in northern Mozambique. The railroad may also connect to Vale's copper operations in Zambia.
- *Mozambique*: The Moatize coal project entered full operation in 2012, and is expected to reach 11 million tons of coal production per year. The Moatize II project is scheduled to start producing in 2015, which will increase total production to 22 million tons per year. In addition to the mining operations, Vale is building the Nacala corridor, a 137-mile railroad from the port of Nacala, and also restoring the Sena Railway to the port of Beira. Total investment is expected to be in the range of $6 billion. Vale is also exploring additional Mozambique projects related to coal, phosphates, and natural gas.
- *Zambia*: Through its joint venture with ARM and Zambia's state-owned mining company ZCCM, Vale is mining for copper at the Lubambe mine, which has an annual production capacity of 45,000 tons of copper concentrate. The joint venture is expected to invest about $1 billion over five years.

Sources: Vale website, http://www.vale.com/EN/aboutvale/across-world/Pages/default.aspx (accessed January 23, 2014); Financial Times, FDIMarkets database; Bureau van Dijk, Zephyr M&A database; MacDonald, "Vale: Eyes $7B in Planned Africa Investments," February 6, 2013.

Notes:
[a] Campbell, "Vale Now Active in Southern, Central and West Africa," September 2, 2011.
[b] MiningReview.com, "Vale Plans to Invest up to US$20 Billion in Africa," October 28, 2010; Jamasmie, "Vale Slashes Investment Budget," December 2, 2013.

Table 5.8. Brazil: Outward FDI position, 2001–10 (billion $)

	2001	2002	2003	2004	2005	2006	2007	2008	2009	2010
World	50	54	55	69	79	114	140	156	165	181
Developing economies	42	45	44	48	50	79	100	111	69	80
Africa	0.42	0.16	0.11	0.13	0.14	0.03	0.11	0.16	0.2	0.2
Angola	0.27	0.03	0.02	0.03	0.02	0.02	0.1	0.14	0.1	0.2

Source: Central Bank of Brazil and UNCTAD's FDI/TNC database for 2007 and 2008, cited in Sauvant, Mallampally, and McAllister, *Inward and Outward FDI Country Profiles*, 2013, 669.

Petrobras, Brazil's state-owned oil company, has invested in petroleum extraction projects in Angola and Nigeria (project values not reported) and also invested $200 million in a biomass power project in Nigeria.[321] Petrobras is actively pumping oil in Angola and Nigeria and involved in petroleum exploration in Benin, Gabon, Libya, Nigeria, and Tanzania.[322]

Brazilian multinational construction firms have also been active in Africa. Odebrecht has been involved in Africa since at least the 1980s. Early projects included the construction of the Capanda dam in Angola and the country's first shopping mall in Luanda. Camargo Corrêa, another Brazil-based construction company, is building housing in Ghana. The construction firm Andrade Gutierrez has worked on projects ranging from ports to housing and sanitation projects in Angola, the Republic of the Congo, and Guinea. Unlike most Chinese construction firms, Brazilian construction firms are not state-owned and rely, to some extent, on credit lines to African governments from the state-owned Brazilian Development Bank (BNDES) and Banco do Brasil to fund their foreign operations. Brazilian credit lines to African countries target mostly infrastructure development and are generally tied to procurement of services and equipment in Brazil. Brazilian construction companies reportedly hire most of their labor force locally (Odebrecht is said to be the largest private employer in Angola).[323] Brazilian agricultural and consumer products firms are also interested in Africa, but few deals have been signed to date.[324]

Chinese Investment in SSA

Many Chinese investors in SSA are state-owned enterprises (SOEs), but as much as one-half of total investment comes from private-sector companies. Official Chinese FDI data may underestimate FDI in Africa, since the statistics often fail to include smaller, private sector companies involved in wholesale and retail trade and textiles. In general, Chinese private sector companies focus investing in the manufacturing and service sectors, while SOEs are more likely to invest in construction and resource extraction.[325] According to an UNCTAD estimate, as of 2006, there were about 700 Chinese-based firms operating in Africa.[326] That number is likely to be significantly higher in 2014. Most Chinese FDI in SSA has been greenfield investment (see appendix G, table G.13). During 2000–2013, only five Chinese acquisitions of SSA companies were reported, one each in Chad, the Democratic Republic of the Congo, Ghana, Mauritius, and South Africa (Standard Bank).[327]

FDI from China and from OECD countries has taken different paths, for two principal reasons. First, Chinese SOEs are able to operate on a longer time horizon than many OECD-based multinational firms, as many of their FDI projects are funded by the Chinese government with preferential access to capital, whereas most FDI from OECD countries is funded through stock markets or other private capital at market rates. Second, most OECD FDI is constrained by a number of international agreements affecting labor rights, the environment, product specifications, and the U.S. Foreign Corrupt Practices Act, whereas Chinese SOEs have far fewer restrictions to observe.[328]

Financing for many large infrastructure investment projects from China follows a model of "tied aid" that Western countries have largely abandoned. As described in one article, these projects generally follow a pattern: China's Export-Import Bank provides a line of credit, usually at subsidized interest rates, with the funds tied to the use of Chinese inputs and labor. Chinese SOEs bid on substantial infrastructure or resource extraction projects. The funds most often are transferred directly from the Export-Import Bank as payment to the Chinese firms, never going to African countries directly. The funding is repaid to the Chinese government in the form of commodity exports resulting from the project, from the African countries to China.[329]

South Africa was by far the largest destination for FDI outflows from China during 2003–10 (latest available data). However, Chinese investment in South Africa was driven almost entirely by a single transaction: the 2008 acquisition by the Industrial and Commercial Bank of China of a 20 percent stake in South Africa's Standard Bank, valued at $4.75 billion.[330] Nigeria ranked second, followed by Zambia and the Democratic Republic of the Congo, two countries that have attracted significant Chinese FDI in the mining industry (table 5.9).

Table 5.9. China: FDI outflows to SSA destinations, 2003–10

Country	2003	2004	3005	2006	2007	2008	2009	2010	Total
Million $									
South Africa	9	18	48	41	454	4,808	42	411	5,830
Nigeria	24	46	53	68	390	163	172	185	1,101
Zambia	6	2	10	87	119	214	112	75	626
Congo, Dem. Rep.	0	12	5	37	57	24	227	236	598
Niger	NA	2	6	8	101	0	40	196	352
Sudan	NA	147	91	51	65	-63	19	31	341
Ethiopia	1	0	5	24	13	10	74	59	186
Kenya	1	3	2	0	9	23	28	101	167
Madagascar	1	14	0	1	13	61	43	34	166
Angola	0	0	1	22	41	-10	8	101	164
Other SSA	29	56	72	78	95	186	335	454	1,305
SSA total	70	298	292	417	1,359	5,416	1,100	1,883	10,836

Source: Government of China, Ministry of Commerce.

Notes: SSA total calculated by the Commission by removing data for North African countries from the total provided by China's Ministry of Commerce. NA = Not available.

Table 5.10. Significant industry and country destinations for Chinese FDI in SSA, 2007

Industry	Identified destination countries
Oil and gas	Angola, Nigeria, and Sudan
Mining	Ethiopia, Sudan, Zambia, Kenya, and Uganda
Agriculture	Cotton in Zambia, Mali, and Uganda; poultry in Ghana; sugar in Madagascar; coffee in Kenya
Telecommunications	Angola, Ethiopia, Madagascar, Nigeria, Republic of the Congo, and Uganda
Utilities	Ethiopia
Financial services	Madagascar and South Africa
Apparel and footwear	Ethiopia, Ghana, Madagascar, Mauritius, and Kenya
Agroprocessing	Nigeria, Zambia, and Uganda
Construction and infrastructure	Angola, Ethiopia, Nigeria, Zambia, Republic of the Congo, Mali, South Africa, Uganda, Cameroon, Namibia, and Tanzania
Import/export and retail	Widespread activity throughout SSA reflecting small, private-sector Chinese firms

Source: Kaplinsky and Morris, "Chinese FDI in Sub-Saharan Africa," 2009, 557.

Table 5.11. India: FDI outflows, 1996–2010

Region/ economy	1996–2002	2002–09	2009–10	1996–2002	2002–09	2009–10
	Shares in %			Million $		
World	100	100	100	7525	75,985	10,623
Developing economies	65	48	68	a	36,498	7,239
Africa	10	12	14	750	9,321	1521
Nigeria	0	0	NA	7	301	NA
Sudan	NA	2	NA	NA	1,191	NA
West Africa	0	1	0	29	542	11
Central Africa	NA	0	NA	NA	85	NA
East Africa	9	8	14	638	6,342	1,430
Mauritius	8	8	13	618	6,165	1,426
Kenya	0	0	NA	13	149	a
Southern Africa	0	0	1	29	154	72
South Africa	0	0	1	22	118	69

Source: Department of Economic Affairs, Indian Ministry of Finance, cited in Sauvant, Mallampally, and McAllister, *Inward and Outward FDI Country Profiles*, 2013, 872–73.

Notes: NA = Not available. This table relies on investment approval data, since the Indian government does not publish a geographic breakdown of outward FDI flows. Data are by fiscal year (April 1–March 31).

Studies by the African Economic Research Consortium identified the most significant industry destinations for Chinese FDI in 20 SSA countries (table 5.10). Based on data from 2007, industries of particular note included oil and gas, mining, agriculture, services (particularly telecommunications, but also utilities and financial services), apparel and shoes, and agroprocessing.[331]

Much of the infrastructure investment is related to FDI in the extractive industries (both petroleum and mining) and metals. Examples include an oil pipeline and related port facilities in Sudan; a deepwater port, railroad track, and a hydroelectric power plant linked to an iron mine in Gabon; and the refurbishment of Angola's rail network, linked to petroleum extraction in that country, with potential links between Angolan ports and Zambia's copper mines.[332] In the metals industry, Chinese FDI in Mozambique's aluminum industry, driven by higher demand for aluminum from China, significantly increased overall FDI in that country. China has also invested heavily in Zambia's copper industry, particularly the Lumwana Mine and the Konkola Deep Mining Project.[333]

Indian Investment in SSA

Africa accounted for 14 percent of Indian FDI outflows in 2009–10, up from 10 percent during 1996–02 (table 5.11).[334] Mauritius ranked third among all destinations for outbound FDI flows from India during 2002–09, the only SSA country to appear among India's top 15 destinations, attracting just over 8 percent of total outflows during the period.[335]

Particularly large investments included acquisitions by three India-based mobile telecommunications companies in Zambia, South Africa, and the Republic of the Congo. Indian firms also acquired large African companies in oil and gas services, mining, steel production, and business services (see appendix G, table G.14).[336] Indian companies also recorded 309 greenfield FDI projects between 2003 and 2013 (see appendix G, table G.15). The largest number of projects went to South Africa (68), followed by Nigeria (35), Kenya (32), and Tanzania (26). The largest share (15 percent) was invested in financial services, primarily in South Africa and Tanzania. Telecommunications and software and IT services were also important industry destinations for Indian investors, with 38 and 29 projects, respectively, followed by automotive manufacturing and the coal, oil, and natural gas sector.[337]

SSA Countries' Investment in SSA

As noted above, SSA countries account for a significant share of overall FDI into the region, with South Africa being the leading investor. Kenyan firms ranked second as intra-SSA investors, with 145 outbound FDI projects in SSA. Together, South Africa and Kenya comprised 71 percent of all intra-SSA FDI projects during 2003–12.[338] SSA investors are more likely than investors from other regions to focus on the services and manufacturing sectors, rather than on natural resources extraction or processing. Manufacturing projects, in turn, tend to focus on less capital-intensive and lower-technology industries.[339] Table 5.12 highlights greenfield FDI projects and acquisitions by SSA countries in other SSA countries. For 2003–12, the top three country destinations for South Africa's FDI in SSA were Nigeria, Ghana, and Namibia.[340]

Investment in SSA by Industry

In the past, much of the FDI in SSA was focused on natural resource extraction, including mining, petroleum and natural gas extraction, and renewable energy. This pattern is changing, however: during 2007–12 the number of new FDI projects focused on resources declined, while the number of projects in the services and manufacturing sectors increased (figure 5.14).[341] Natural resources contributed to less than one-third of Africa's GDP growth between 2000 and 2012, with the service sector growing particularly fast as a share of GDP.[342] In an effort to illustrate this change, UNCTAD has recently tracked the share of greenfield FDI projects focused on sales to African consumers. UNCTAD defined the consumer sector as a basket of manufacturing and service sector industries that include financial services; food, beverages, and tobacco; textiles, clothing, and leather; transport, storage, and communications; and motor vehicles. The share of overall greenfield FDI projects in these sectors has increased steadily since 2008, reaching almost 25 percent in 2012.[343]

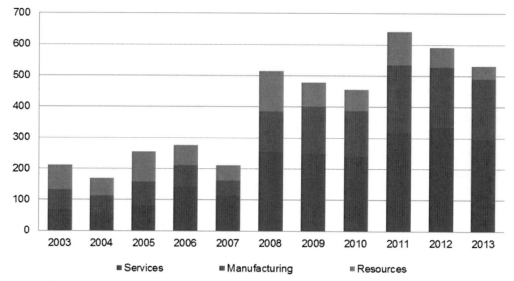

Source: Financial Times, FDIMarkets database (accessed January 14, 2014).
Note: Data are available only beginning in 2003.

Figure 5.14. Number of greenfield FDI projects in SSA, by sector, 2003–13.

Table 5.12. Number of greenfield FDI projects and mergers and acquisition transactions in SSA by SSA-based investors, by selected industry, 2003–13

Industry	2003	2004	2005	2006	2007	2008	2009	2010	2011	2012	2013	Total
Metals, mining and agriculture	10	6	7	13	7	8	6	16	11	5	4	93
M&A	6	3	3	7	4	3	1	4	1	2	0	34
Greenfield	4	3	4	6	3	5	5	12	10	3	4	59
Chemicals, rubber, plastics, non-metallic manufacturing	5	3	2	1	3	7	5	3	13	6	7	55
M&A	3	1	1	0	1	4	1	1	0	1	1	14

Industry	2003	2004	2005	2006	2007	2008	2009	2010	2011	2012	2013	Total
Greenfield	2	2	1	1	2	3	4	2	13	5	6	41
Food, beverages, tobacco	1	2	2	2	1	14	5	8	17	18	13	83
M&A	0	0	0	0	0	3	1	1	1	1	1	8
Greenfield	1	2	2	2	1	11	4	7	16	17	12	75
Textiles, apparel, leather	5	2	0	1	1	1	0	1	3	1	6	21
M&A	1	1	0	1	0	0	0	0	0	0	0	3
Greenfield	4	1	0	0	1	1	0	1	3	1	6	18
Machinery manufacturing	0	1	2	0	6	6	5	4	3	1	8	36
M&A	0	1	0	0	4	2	0	1	0	0	0	8
Greenfield	0	0	2	0	2	4	5	3	3	1	8	28
Financial services and real estate	6	12	13	23	17	91	72	49	73	42	49	447
M&A	1	6	3	7	5	14	3	4	7	1	2	53
Greenfield	5	6	10	16	12	77	69	45	66	41	47	394
Communications, business, and computer services	9	8	14	25	7	10	18	23	33	53	34	234
M&A	6	8	10	19	7	7	6	5	4	4	4	80
Greenfield	3	0	4	6	0	3	12	18	29	49	30	154
Wholesale, retail, distribution	0	0	5	3	1	5	2	1	3	2	3	25
M&A	0	0	4	2	1	5	2	1	3	2	3	23
Greenfield	0	0	1	1	0	0	0	0	0	0	0	2
Transportation	1	1	1	6	0	1	3	1	1	9	1	25
Greenfield	0	0	0	2	0	1	2	0	1	7	1	14
M&A	1	1	1	4	0	0	1	1	0	2	0	11
Tourism	3	2	1	1	1	11	0	3	1	2	7	32
M&A	0	1	1	0	1	2	0	0	1	0	2	8
Greenfield	3	1	0	1	0	9	0	3	0	2	5	24
Construction	0	0	1	1	0	5	4	3	8	3	13	38
M&A	0	0	1	1	0	0	0	1	1	0	0	4
Greenfield	0	0	0	0	0	5	4	2	7	3	13	34

Sources: Bureau van Dijk, Zephyr M&A database; Financial Times, FDIMarkets database; Commission calculations.

The service sector accounts for the majority of greenfield FDI projects in SSA, led by financial services and communications (table 5.13). The metals sector includes both metals mining and metals processing; the latter is a manufacturing industry. Other prominent manufacturing industries are food and tobacco and automotive manufacturing. Along with greenfield FDI, mergers and acquisitions (M&A) are the other source of foreign investment in SSA. Metals, mining, and agriculture; financial services; and wholesale and retail trade account for the largest shares of foreign acquisitions of existing SSA companies (figure 5.15).

Table 5.13. Number of greenfield FDI projects in SSA, by industry, 2003–13

Industry	Number of projects	Share of total %
Financial services	779	18
Communications	401	9
Metals	367	8
Business services	332	8
Coal, oil, and natural gas	290	7
Food and tobacco	257	6
Software and IT services	247	6
Transportation	158	4
Automotive OEM	146	3
Industrial machinery, equipment, and tools	123	3
Hotels and tourism	101	2
Other	1,136	26
Total	4,337	100

Source: Financial Times, FDIMarkets database (accessed January 14, 2014).

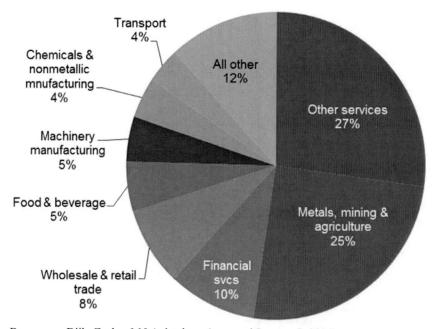

Source: Bureau van Dijk, Zephyr M&A database (accessed January 7, 2014).

Figure 5.15. M&A deals in SSA, by industry, 2000–2013.

Natural Resources (Petroleum, Metals, and Minerals)

Some of the highest-value investment projects in SSA involve oil and gas extraction, many by Asian-owned petroleum companies. However, FDI in the natural resources sector also includes significant investment in downstream petroleum industry projects, including construction of pipelines and refineries (table 5.14).[344]

Chinese state-owned companies are also particularly active investors in the SSA mining industry, especially in iron ore mines in Guinea, Sierra Leone, and Liberia, and likely to remain so for the foreseeable future. Combining production by China-based mining companies with production by companies based elsewhere, Guinea in particular could become one of the world's largest sources of iron ore by 2020.[345] During 2003–12, almost one-half of SSA greenfield FDI projects in the resource sector (including coal, oil, natural gas, metals, and minerals) were focused on downstream manufacturing and services activities, rather than on resource extraction (table 5.15).[346]

Table 5.14. Key Asian investment in SSA's downstream oil and gas industry

Destination country	Company	Project	Expected start-up date	Notes
South Africa	Sinopec (China)	Mthombo refinery, Port Elizabeth	2016	$10 billion project planned by Sinopec, PetroSA (South Africa), and Industrial Development Corp. (South Africa)
South Africa	Petronas (Malaysia)	Engen Petroleum	2013	Petronas is currently in talks to sell its stake in Engen Petroleum to PetroSA
Sudan	CNPC (China)	Khartoum refinery	2000	50/50 joint venture between CNPC and the Sudanese Ministry of Energy and Mining
South Sudan, Kenya, Rwanda	Toyota (Japan)	Oil pipeline	NA	$4 billion project. Dual pipelines running from South Sudanese oilfields to Kenya port of Lamu and from Rwanda to Mombasa
Uganda	CNOOC (China)	Hoima refinery	NA	In talks to develop a 30,000 barrel/day refinery in conjunction with a crude oil export pipeline as part of an upstream development in Lake Albertine
Uganda	China Export-Import Bank (China)	Dar Es Salaam pipeline	2014	Domestic pipeline connecting gas-rich Mtwara to Dar es Salaam, Tanzania
Tanzania	KOGAS (Korea)	Maputo gas pipeline	2014	Joint venture by KOGAS and ENH (Mozambique) to pipe gas for power and industry in Maputo, Mozambique

Source: BMI, *Asian Investment in Africa*, 2013.
Note: NA = Not available.

Table 5.15. Greenfield FDI projects: Mining and oil and gas extraction vs. downstream activities, 2003–13

Coal, oil and natural gas			Metals and minerals		
Activity	Number of projects	Share of total %	Activity	Number of projects	Share of total %
Oil and gas extraction	115	40	Gold ore and silver ore mining	94	20
Coal mining	24	8	Copper, nickel, lead, and zinc mining	69	15
			Other mining	122	26
Nonextractive activities	151	52	Nonextractive activities	178	38
Total	290	100	Total	463	100

Source: Financial Times, FDIMarkets database (accessed January 14, 2014).

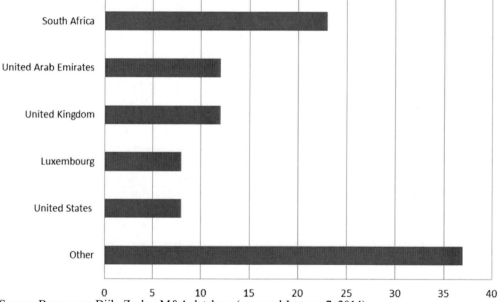

Source: Bureau van Dijk, Zephyr M&A database (accessed January 7, 2014).
Note: Reflects countries making acquisitions outside of their home country.

Figure 5.16. Number of foreign acquisitions in SSA agriculture, by 2000–2013.

In the minerals sector, examples of SSA countries receiving recent investment, or expansion of existing projects, include:

- *Mauritania:* 100 percent acquisition of Sphere Minerals by Glencore Xstrata (UK).
- *Burkina Faso and Mali:* Golden Rim (Australia) and Royal Falcon Mining (United Arab Emirates) plan to invest $6.9 million in minerals exploration.
- *Tanzania:* 100 percent acquisition of Mantra Resources by Atomredmetzoloto (Russia).

- *Eritrea:* Nevsun Resources (Canada) has invested in the Bisha Project, a gold, copper and zinc mine, and Chalice Gold (Australia) has agreed to sell a 60 percent stake in the Zara Gold project to SFECO Group (China), pending due diligence investigation.[347]

West Africa has also seen extensive recent investment in iron ore mining. Mauritania was exporting iron ore as of 2012, and additional deposits of interest to international mining companies are located in Guinea, Liberia, Gabon, Mauritania, Nigeria, Sierra Leone, the Republic of the Congo, Cameroon, and Côte d'Ivoire. Global mining companies BHP Billiton (Australia), Vale (Brazil), Rio Tinto (Australia), and Chinalco (China) are all active in SSA.[348] A number of SSA countries have made recent changes to their mining laws, raising taxes on mining companies, increasing the government ownership share in joint venture mining companies, or otherwise seeking to retain more revenue from mining projects. Angola, Tanzania, Guinea, and Mozambique have all passed new mining laws since 2010.[349]

Agriculture

Agricultural investment in SSA has focused primarily on grains, sugarcane, and palm oil plantations. South Africa is the largest destination for acquisitions in the agriculture sector (21 percent of all deals), followed by Kenya (9 percent), Côte d'Ivoire (7 percent), and Tanzania (6 percent).

Investment in SSA agricultural projects comes from diverse corners of the globe. Investors from South Africa, UAE, and OECD countries account for a large share of agriculture investment projects in SSA (figure 5.16). The Gulf countries account for 22 percent of total foreign land acquisitions in Africa, compared with 12 percent for India and 3 percent for China. Some of Southeast Asia's largest agricultural firms are among the investors, including Olam International (Singapore), Wilmar International (Singapore), Golden Agri Resources (Indonesia), and Sime Darby (Malaysia). Palm oil companies are showing increased interest in Africa, as expanded production in Indonesia becomes limited by land and labor availability. Vietnamese companies have also recently started acquiring land in different countries for rice cultivation, including Sierra Leone and Nigeria.

Infrastructure

The entire SSA region requires investment in infrastructure as a critical factor in economic growth. The lack of inland transportation infrastructure inhibits intra-regional trade, forcing SSA countries to rely more on trade with the EU, the United States, and developed countries in other regions. Among other SSA countries, Kenya is investing in updated rail infrastructure, which should help to lower costs to inland investments in Kenya and neighboring Uganda, where Kenya is a leading investor.[350] Historically, developed countries have provided significant funding for African infrastructure as financial assistance rather than through commercial investment, often through international development banks, such as the World Bank. The United States has been a major contributor to investment in trade-related infrastructure through its foreign aid programs.[351]

In recent years, China has provided by far the largest share of resources invested in SSA infrastructure. Most of the companies involved are state-owned, and much of the funding is provided as export credits. In contrast to development banks and financial assistance from OECD countries, Chinese financial flows to SSA more often have been directed to large infrastructure projects, which have succeeded in significantly improving the infrastructure in a number of SSA countries, as measured by the World Economic Forum's infrastructure rankings. However, while the number of SSA infrastructure projects financed by Chinese investment has significantly improved the overall level of infrastructure in the region, SSA is experiencing some backlash against Chinese practices, with Chinese companies accused of poor quality, little regard for environmental protections, and not enough hiring of local workers.[352]

India, Japan, and the Republic of Korea (Korea) have also begun to actively invest in SSA infrastructure, with an eye to securing resources. East Africa, and Ethiopia in particular, has received Indian investment in developing its road and rail capacity and connections with Djibouti. India has also invested in power and transport projects in Mozambique. In June 2013, Japan announced $32 billion in funding for Africa over a five-year period (with an undefined portion set for infrastructure), in addition to a May 2013 commitment of $2 billion to develop infrastructure around Africa's natural resources. Investment will focus on countries that can provide resources for Japanese industry or markets for Japanese products. Korea has increased its foreign aid to Liberia, focusing on infrastructure improvements, and Korean companies are increasingly seeking investment opportunities in SSA.[353]

One recently announced investment project in the infrastructure sector is the Reykjavik project, a $4 billion investment by a group of partners from the United States and Iceland to develop about 1,000 MW of geothermal energy in Ethiopia. A consortium of private investors is also actively studying more than 50 wind power sites in Ethiopia, which would produce close to 10,000 MW of electric power, in collaboration with U.S. engineers, manufacturers, and financiers.[354]

Table 5.16. FDI transactions in SSA manufacturing, 2003–13

	Greenfield	M&A	Total
South Africa	449	134	583
Nigeria	204	23	227
Kenya	119	8	127
Angola	102	2	104
Mozambique	84	5	89
Ghana	80	3	83
Uganda	63	8	71
Tanzania	57	3	60
Ethiopia	47	6	53
Zambia	47	4	51
Other	354	50	404
Total	**1,606**	**246**	**1,852**

Source: Financial Times, FDIMarkets database (accessed January 14, 2014); Bureau van Dijk, Zephyr M&A database (accessed January 7, 2014).

Manufacturing

Commercial databases recorded more than 1,800 foreign investment transactions in the manufacturing sector during 2003–13, of which almost 90 percent were greenfield FDI projects (table 5.16). South Africa, in particular, has witnessed strong investment in the automotive and heavy equipment manufacturing industries. These investments are partly due to the elimination of U.S. tariffs under AGOA, which has made South Africa an attractive location from which to export these products to the United States.[355] South Africa has also seen strong manufacturing investment in coal, petroleum processing, and chemicals. In Nigeria, the coal and petroleum processing sector was the most popular destination for FDI manufacturing projects, followed by food, beverages, and tobacco. In Kenya, destinations for manufacturing FDI include food, beverages, and tobacco; automobiles; consumer electronics; and other consumer products.[356] By source country, the largest investors in the SSA manufacturing sector (by number of projects) were the United States and the United Kingdom, followed by India (figure 5.17). Chinese and Indian companies have begun to invest in the automotive sector, particularly in non-passenger-car segments such as commercial vehicles and motorcycles.[357]

Textiles and Apparel

In the textiles and apparel industry (including footwear), commercial databases recorded 85 greenfield FDI projects and seven acquisitions between 2003 and 2013. South Africa was the recipient for about one-third of these transactions, followed by Ghana, Nigeria, and Ethiopia. According to many observers, the apparel industry has been the principal and most direct beneficiary of the AGOA program, largely due to AGOA's liberal rules of origin (ROOs) in the form of the third-country fabric rule. The rule permits African countries to source yarn and fabric inputs from any country and to export the apparel made from this fabric to the United States duty free. This creates opportunities for foreign investors, particularly from Taiwan and China, to access the U.S. market through SSA, but the investment is likely to quickly disappear if the AGOA program is discontinued.[358] The footwear sector has also attracted investment under AGOA, particularly in Ethiopia. The government of Ethiopia has introduced policies aimed at attracting investment to this sector, leveraging assistance from the U.S. Agency for International Development and other sources. They have succeeded in reaching out to individual footwear companies, and, according to one observer, the industry is beginning to develop.[359]

Lesotho, Kenya, Mauritius, and Swaziland were the principal sources of textile and apparel exports to the United States under AGOA in 2012.[360] Most of the production companies in Lesotho and Swaziland are owned by investors from Taiwan, with the remainder owned by South African-based firms.[361] African and Middle Eastern countries were the sources of many small-scale FDI projects.[362] The Ethiopian apparel industry has also received recent investment from India, China, and Turkey (for the EU market).[363]

Following the introduction of AGOA in 2000, Asian investors increased their FDI in Lesotho's textile and apparel industries, from $118 million in 2000 to $123 million in 2004. Most of the increase was due to investment in a denim mill, the first textile operation in Lesotho, by Nien Hsing Textile Co. (Taiwan). Nien Hsing invested in Lesotho to take advantage of opportunities to export to the United States under AGOA.[364] The mill produces fabric and yarn for use in local apparel production, and also exports fabric to countries within SSA and outside the region.[365]

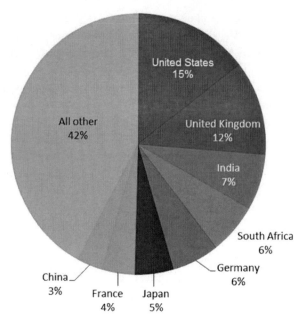

Source: Bureau van Dijk, Zephyr M&A database; Financial Times, FDIMarkets database; Commission calculations.

Figure 5.17. Greenfield FDI projects and M&A deals in manufacturing, by source country, 2003–13.

By 2005, Chinese investors had established textile and apparel subsidiaries in Ghana, Kenya, Lesotho, Madagascar, Malawi, Mauritius, Namibia, Nigeria, Tanzania, and South Africa. These companies are a source of exports to the United States and the EU, but Chinese companies reportedly also are making some longer-term investments in SSA. For example, in August 2012, China Garments announced plans to invest $40 million in Zimbabwe to form a joint venture with the Zimbabwe Cotton Company, to gain access to a steady cotton supply.[366]

While Asian investors are primarily interested in apparel assembly for export to the United States and the EU, South African investors in Lesotho and Swaziland tend to focus on exporting to South Africa. Their FDI is motivated by avoiding the higher labor costs and stronger labor unions in South Africa, so the AGOA program is less important for the future of those investments. Exports from neighboring countries to South Africa are duty free under the Southern African Customs Union agreement.[367]

Mauritius and Madagascar also have strong apparel industries that export principally to the EU and South Africa, and in Mauritius, 90 percent of the companies are locally owned, so AGOA is only a minor factor in apparel-related FDI to these countries. Mauritius-based firms, in particular, are increasing their focus on the South African market as European economic problems reduce the value of Mauritius' apparel exports to that region. Madagascar lost its AGOA eligibility on January 1, 2010, and experienced a sharp drop in apparel exports to the United States, at the same time as its exports to South Africa increased.[368]

AGOA was an important factor in the revival of Kenya's textile industry, with FDI rising from $16 million in 1999 to $162 million in 2004; Kenya's apparel exports rose from $44 million to $226 million during the same period. As of 2006, there were about 35 textile mills in the country, and Kenya was exporting yarn, fabrics, and other textiles. The textile firms, mostly located in the export processing zone, are primarily owned by investors from India, Sri Lanka, and Bangladesh, with some local ownership.[369] PVH, owner of the Calvin Klein and Tommy Hilfiger brands, recently opened a Nairobi buying office.[370]

There has been more than $300 million of FDI in Ethiopia's textile industry in 2012 and 2013, much of it from Europe, Turkey, and India. Most of this FDI is focused on exports to Europe, so is not directly related to AGOA. Many Turkish spinning and weaving factories have relocated from Turkey to Ethiopia because of the low costs of energy and labor, and are exporting their production back to Europe. The Ethiopian government is also offering new financial incentives to investors.[371]

West Africa's largest country, Nigeria, was once a major textile producer. The industry effectively collapsed after an influx of cheap textiles from China, combined with the failure of the Nigerian industry to modernize their equipment. However, the Nigerian government has earmarked close to $500 million to upgrade to new equipment and to sell off land and buildings at subsidized rates in an effort to revive the industry. According to one observer, a longer-term AGOA program would help to revive the West African textile and apparel industry by giving confidence to long-range investors. In addition, because West Africa is the closest part of Africa to the United States, U.S. investors reportedly would be willing to consider the region.[372]

Services

The SSA telecommunications services industry has attracted significant investment from around the world. The industry recorded 104 acquisitions from 2000 through 2013, with a combined reported value of $11.9 billion (values are not reported for all transactions). By number of deals, South Africa is both the biggest investor and the biggest destination country in this industry. By value, the United Kingdom is the largest investor, at just under $5.0 billion, primarily in South Africa. The United Kingdom is followed by Kuwait, which invested $1.3 billion in Sudan, and the Netherlands, with $1.3 billion, invested primarily in Ghana.[373]

In addition to reported merger and acquisition (M&A) transactions, China-based ZTE and Huawei have been active in SSA as greenfield investors in telecommunications. ZTE has invested in nine projects in Angola, Rwanda, Nigeria, the Democratic Republic of the Congo, Zambia, Ethiopia, and Kenya, with four of the projects (in Ethiopia, Kenya, Zambia, and Angola) reported to be focused on telecommunications manufacturing, rather than services. Huawei has invested in 10 projects (all reported as services) in South Africa, Angola, Nigeria, Côte d'Ivoire, Zimbabwe, Ethiopia, and Kenya.[374]

As of 2006, South Africa and Mauritius had developed call-center outsourcing industries, made possible by improvements in telecommunications infrastructure. Other countries beginning to develop call center industries include Ghana, Kenya, and Senegal. In most cases, these countries import capital goods from Europe, including computers and telecommunications equipment. SSA call centers generally serve multinational companies based in developed countries, but the call center functions are usually outsourced to locally owned firms, so are not themselves identified as foreign investment.[375]

AGOA's Impact on FDI Trends

With reduced investment risks, growing consumer markets, expanded business opportunities, and higher rates of return on investment, FDI in SSA has expanded rapidly since 2000.[376] Although it is difficult to quantify AGOA's direct and indirect effects on FDI trends over these years, AGOA's trade benefits and eligibility criteria appear to have incentivized and motivated SSA countries, particularly AGOA beneficiary countries, to improve their business and investment climates. Rwanda, Sierra Leone, and Burundi, all long-time AGOA beneficiary countries, have experienced the most improvements in their business and investment climates since the advent of the program.

Several observers view AGOA as having a positive influence on FDI in SSA. South Africa's ambassador to the United States stated that

> South Africa, based on the liquidity developed through AGOA, has been able to invest in infrastructure, and it was particularly through investments from the United States, for example, in our energy infrastructure that we have been able to make gains. General Electric has just built for us 143 locomotives. The hospitality industry has just bought 77 hotels in South Africa alone . . . and those are the kind of strides that we make that show that it is a win-win situation we're speaking about and no longer a unilateral gift to Africa. Our NDP, our National Development Plan, has poised us to graduate agriculture to a new level, and that is why U.S. companies like John Deere from exporting the odd implement has now set up a presence in South Africa from which to export its implements across the African continent.[377]

A number of reports have supported the notion that preferential access to the U.S. market under AGOA has been important for attracting investment to SSA. According to a report by the African Union, $1 billion in FDI from the United States to SSA was directly linked to AGOA, and overall FDI inflows to AGOA beneficiary countries increased by 77 percent from 1999–2000 (just before AGOA) to 2004–2005.[378] A study by the United Nations Industrial Development Organization that looked into FDI determinants and location decisions in SSA found "taking advantage of AGOA" was a leading factor, followed by "taking advantage of EBA," suggesting that foreign investors used SSA as an export platform to penetrate the U.S. and EU markets through preferential access.[379] In another survey, about three-fourths of respondents viewed AGOA as "important" or "very important" to SSA investment and trade, and strong linkage between AGOA and increasing FDI inflows was reported in those countries where Asian investment in the textile and apparel sector has increased.[380]

Another report on AGOA, commissioned by the South African government, attributed South Africa's growth in automotive exports to a combination of South African government policies to attract automotive investment, preferential market access to the United States and the EU, and a depreciation of the rand.[381] A similar point was expressed at the USITC public hearing on AGOA, with an observer noting that the tariff elimination under AGOA boosted U.S. auto imports from South Africa, resulting in increased investment in South Africa's automotive sector.[382]

Anecdotal news reports confirm the linkage between AGOA and FDI, especially in the textile and apparel industry in SSA. CNN reported that the textile and apparel industry in Lesotho, one of the largest in SSA, was boosted in recent years by the influx of Asian investors who have taken advantage of the AGOA program.[383] *Business Daily Africa* reported that in early 2012, facing uncertainty over the potential expiration of AGOA's third-country fabric provision, the level of capital investment in Kenya's textile and apparel industries shrank by 9.4 percent from its 2011 level.[384] After Madagascar lost its AGOA eligibility on January 1, 2010, FDI inflows in 2010 suffered a 24.2 percent decline, and its $600-million-a-year textile and apparel industries collapsed.[385]

Although the importance of AGOA to investment in SSA has been acknowledged, various studies and observers have also pointed out the limitations of the program. For example, most respondents to a survey of investors did not report a strong link between AGOA and increasing FDI inflows in industries outside of textiles and apparel.[386] Another observer pointed out that South Africa's allowing six major bilateral investment treaties (BITs) with other trading partners to lapse indicates a decline in the investment environment, and expressed the view that signing additional BITs with SSA partners would do more to improve that environment than does AGOA.[387]

According to some observers, the short-term authorizations of the AGOA program and the uncertainty of its future make it difficult for the gains to be sustained through long-term investment and the creation of new regional value chains.[388] Witnesses at the USITC hearing in connection with this investigation noted that the uncertain status of the program appears to be driving some existing investors to exit from Africa.[389] The short-term AGOA renewals may actually have been detrimental to FDI in the region, and witnesses called for a 15-year renewal of AGOA, to attract investment into sectors that are more capital-intensive than apparel manufacturing. According to one witness, an investor generally needs significant time to amortize an investment: "Typically, you're looking at 10 to 15 years to recoup your investment in a major new manufacturing plant. If you don't have the time horizon [under the AGOA program] to amortize your plan, why would you invest in Africa?"[390]

SECTION 6. RECIPROCAL TRADE AGREEMENTS: A COMPARISON WITH UNILATERAL TRADE PREFERENCE PROGRAMS

Introduction

Since the 1970s, exports from sub-Saharan Africa (SSA) have benefited from unilateral (one- way) trade preference programs that increase market access to developed economies through lower tariffs. South Africa has also signed reciprocal trade agreements with industrialized countries, but such agreements are rare in SSA. Reciprocal agreements, including free trade agreements (FTAs), are generally far more comprehensive in scope than unilateral trade preferences. Typically, FTAs reduce or eliminate tariffs on most trade in goods between the parties, establish rules of origin, and address such issues as customs procedures, sanitary and phytosanitary (SPS) measures, investment rules, and dispute settlement. Developing countries around the world have used reciprocal trade agreements to lock in prior reforms, increase exports and inward investment, and promote further integration with their trading partners.

By contrast, some of the reciprocal trade agreements entered into by SSA countries primarily focus on tariff reductions and border issues (e.g., customs) and include only a cursory treatment of issues such as intellectual property rights, SPS measures, and technical barriers to trade (TBTs). In many agreements between SSA countries and developed countries, the timing of tariff concessions is asymmetrical. Tariffs on SSA exports are reduced or eliminated immediately, while tariff concessions by SSA countries have a long phase-in period. Although a few reciprocal trade agreements involve only a single SSA country (e.g., EU-South Africa, Turkey-Mauritius), many of the agreements are regional (e.g., European Free Trade Association (EFTA)-Southern African Customs Union (SACU)). This is particularly true for the economic partnership agreements (EPAs) that the EU has been negotiating with certain African regional blocs.[391]

This section begins with a comparison of unilateral trade preference programs (e.g., AGOA and GSP) and reciprocal trade agreements (e.g., FTAs). The next section presents case studies of developing countries that have transitioned from unilateral trade preference programs to reciprocal trade agreements. They include Mexico and the North American Free Trade Agreement (NAFTA), Chile and its bilateral U.S. and EU FTAs, and Morocco and the U.S.- Morocco FTA.[392]

The final section of the section provides information on the reciprocal trade agreements that have been entered into by SSA countries, including the parties involved, timing, and, where known, the tariff advantage conferred relative to SSA imports of U.S. products. The section concludes with a discussion of negotiations on EPAs between the EU and various SSA countries and regions. Some SSA countries have not yet concluded negotiations on an EPA but continue to benefit from unilateral preferences.

Unilateral Trade Preference Programs versus Reciprocal Trade Agreements

Overview

Since the late 1960s and 1970s, developed countries such as Australia (in 1966), member states of the EU (1971), Japan (1971), Canada (1974), and the United States (1976) have provided a system of unilateral trade preferences in the form of reduced duties or duty free entry to goods from low-income countries as a way to encourage economic development and political stability. Such programs generally follow the rationale adopted by the United Nations Conference on Trade and Development (UNCTAD) in 1968.[393] The U.S. GSP program was authorized by the Trade Act of 1974 and made effective January 1, 1976.[394]

The United States, EU, and Japan receive over two-thirds of the value of imports covered under all national GSP programs.[395] However, in recent years, several rapidly growing economies, including China, Korea, Russia, Taiwan, and Turkey, have established their own GSP programs. The United States has also established several regional unilateral trade preference programs including AGOA, the Andean Trade Preference Act (ATPA), and the Caribbean Basin Economic Recovery Act (CBERA).

Overtime, certain developed countries have changed their relationships with trading partners by replacing unilateral trade programs with reciprocal trade agreements, such as FTAs. A key difference between the two is that a reciprocal trade agreement, as the term implies, involves a negotiated agreement between parties where each incurs benefits and obligations generally for an indefinite period of time. The following section highlights some of the other practical differences between unilateral trade preference programs and reciprocal trade agreements, which are summarized in table 6.1. The second half of this section examines, in a case study format, selected examples of trading partners that transitioned from unilateral trade preferences to reciprocal trade agreements.

Table 6.1. Principal differences between unilateral trade preference programs and reciprocal trade agreements

	Unilateral trade preferences	**Reciprocal trade agreements**
Nature and level of benefits	Benefits are extended by one country to another country or group of countries without receiving a similar level of benefits in return.	The benefits extended are those in an agreement negotiated between two or more countries, with each country receiving a similar level of benefits.
Framework	Unilateral preferences of the GSP type generally follow the approach adopted by UNCTAD in 1968 and endorsed by GATT and the WTO, which is to help developing countries gain easier access to developed country markets through tariff preferences.	Reciprocal trade agreements generally address trade issues identified by the participating countries which they find to be in their best interests. Agreements must be notified to the WTO.
Countries involved	Benefits are extended by individual developed countries generally to a broad range of developing countries in accordance with criteria established by the developed country.	Agreements generally involve two or more countries with mutual economic or political interests, which may reflect historical trade relationships, integrated industries, complementary economies, common borders, or other considerations.
Trade benefits involved	Benefits are principally in the form of tariff preferences such as duty-free treatment or reduced duties for eligible goods from beneficiary countries.	Benefits generally include the reduction or elimination of duties but also may include the reduction or elimination of nontariff barriers that affect trade in goods and services, intellectual property protection, simplified customs procedures, and so forth. Benefits may take effect when the agreement enters into force or over a multi-year transitional period.
Duration, modification, termination	Generally the developed country providing the benefit will specify the duration of the benefit and reserve for itself the right, at any time, to modify or terminate a benefit, including with respect to a country or product eligible for benefits. Benefits are often provided for a period of 5 years or less, and either terminate at that time or are extended at the discretion of the developed country.	Generally the parties to the agreement will negotiate the term of the agreement, including rights and obligations regarding modification and termination; in practice, most reciprocal agreements remain in effect for an indefinite period of time.

Source: USITC staff.

Scope

In practice, the scope of reciprocal trade agreements is generally broader than unilateral trade preference programs. Reciprocal trade agreements typically address not only tariff reductions but also nontariff measures and other conditions relating to trade in goods and services such as quotas, customs procedures, and administrative policies. Although reciprocal trade agreements can vary in scope, the NAFTA, for example, shows a list of 22 sections dealing with topics ranging from government procurement to agriculture and SPS measures, investment, and dispute settlement, and side agreements on labor and the environment.[396] By contrast, unilateral trade preference programs generally have been limited to tariff preferences (and sometimes more liberal access under TRQs), even when the political objectives of the preference programs are ambitious. For example, AGOA is designed to promote trade between the United States and SSA countries, but it also aims to encourage investment and economic development in the SSA region.[397]

Temporary versus Permanent Nature

Most programs providing unilateral trade preferences are temporary, and must be extended by the country providing the preferences in order to continue. They can be eliminated with little warning to recipient countries. Even unilateral trade preference programs designed to be more permanent in nature have sunset provisions. In the case of the U.S. Caribbean Basin Initiative (CBI), for example, the expansion of CBI benefits under the U.S.-Caribbean Basin Trade Partnership Act (CBTPA) expires in 2020.[398] Uncertainty about renewal can lead to underinvestment in benefiting industries, or to overcapacity if preferences are removed for long periods. By contrast, reciprocal trade agreements establish more permanent trading rules that are gradually codified into the laws of the member countries. Consequently the trading relationships between economic actors are also more permanent.

Product and Country Eligibility

Eligibility for unilateral trade preference programs is typically subject to some form of regular review, and recipient countries can lose their trade preferences either in full or for specific products. By contrast, product and country eligibility rules are generally reassessed only as agreed to by the parties to the reciprocal trade agreement.

Product Eligibility

Under unilateral trade preference programs, the developed country offering the program has the right to designate the products eligible for preferential treatment as well as to modify or withdraw that treatment for specific products. For example, under the U.S. GSP program legislation, the President can remove a product from GSP eligibility, such as in response to petitions submitted by interested parties in an annual review, or when imports of a product from a beneficiary country exceed the so called competitive need limit, which happens when U.S. imports of the product exceed a dollar or import share threshold.[399] For example, Chile was restricted in 2002 from exporting additional volumes of methanol to the United States under GSP because methanol imports exceeded the competitive need limit. However, after Chile entered into a free trade agreement with the United States in 2003, methanol from Chile was allowed to enter the United States duty free.[400]

A similar feature was recently added to the EU's GSP program. Starting in January 2014, the EU's GSP program suspends tariff preferences for a product when the average value of

EU imports of that product from the beneficiary country exceeds 17.5 percent of the total value of EU imports of that product from all GSP beneficiaries for three consecutive years (14.5 percent in the case of textiles and clothing).[401]

Country Eligibility

GSP beneficiary countries can also be subject to full graduation from the program, if a review determines that they have made sufficient strides to become a competitive and developed economy.[402] For example, Switzerland withdrew its GSP benefits in March 1998 for The Bahamas, Bermuda, Brunei Darussalam (Brunei), the Cayman Islands, Cyprus, the Falkland Islands, Hong Kong, Kuwait, Mexico, Qatar, the Republic of Korea (Korea), Singapore, and the United Arab Emirates. Similarly, the United States graduated Hong Kong, Korea, Singapore, and Taiwan from its GSP program in 1989.[403]

Unilateral trade preference programs often include noneconomic eligibility criteria, such as the degree to which the beneficiary country meets international standards of human rights, intellectual property rights, or labor standards. Programs often provide for periodic reviews of beneficiary country compliance. For example, in 1988, Chile was removed from the U.S. GSP program because U.S. officials determined that Chile's labor practices did not meet internationally recognized standards.[404] In June 2013, President Obama removed Bangladesh from the list of countries eligible for preferential tariffs under the U.S. GSP program because he determined that Bangladesh had not shown sufficient progress on workers' rights and safety.[405] By contrast, although the United States may require partners to meet certain basic criteria before negotiating an FTA, such requirements are not generally reviewed on an annual basis.[406]

U.S. AGOA legislation requires the President to determine initially and then annually whether SSA countries meet eligibility requirements that range from progress toward a market-based economy and the rule of law, to poverty reduction, the elimination of barriers to U.S. trade and investment, the protection of internationally recognized worker rights, and efforts to combat corruption.[407] In some cases, these requirements can be difficult for beneficiary countries to meet.[408] By contrast, while reciprocal trade agreements generally allow a party to withdraw or terminate an agreement, in practice this rarely happens.

Modest Benefits of Unilateral Trade Preferences

Although the economic literature often finds robust effects of FTAs on developing-country partners, it also finds that in many cases, unilateral trade preferences provide only modest benefits to recipient countries. For example, the literature is mixed on AGOA's effectiveness in promoting trade because the program maintains volume restrictions for sensitive U.S. sectors such as sugar.[409] Economic research also addresses short- and long-run effects, concluding that while unilateral trade preferences promote exports from low-income countries in the short term, they may actually decrease exports in the long run because of the ongoing effects of program-induced distortions in the beneficiary countries. These distortions are largely administrative costs associated with technical compliance with the trade preference rules.[410]

In addition, because of the narrow focus of unilateral trade preference programs, NTMs are not covered. NTMs, however, can serve as substantial trade barriers. Gravity modeling of the EU's Everything But Arms (EBA) program—the EU GSP program for least-developed countries— highlights the negative impact of NTMs such as transaction costs associated with rules of origin.[411] These NTMs offset the tariff benefits of unilateral trade preferences, particularly for the poorest beneficiary countries with few products to export. An example is Lesotho, which receives duty-free access under the EBA, yet exports almost nothing to the EU. Research suggests that NTMs, such as restrictive rules of origin and complex administrative arrangements, constrain the growth of Lesotho's exports.[412] Lesotho's capacity to produce tradable goods is likely limited by other factors as well, including a low-skilled work force, poor customs administration, high energy costs, poor physical infrastructure, limited government capacity for reform, and a lack of access to capital for small and medium-sized businesses.[413] None of these factors are directly addressed by tariff preferences in unilateral trade preference programs.

Finally, because unilateral trade preference programs rely on tariff preferences alone, the advantages these programs grant to recipient countries can dwindle over time. Dozens of bilateral, regional, and multilateral trade agreements have been signed over the last 20 years, lowering tariffs between trading partners and reducing the tariff advantages beneficiary countries receive under programs such as GSP, AGOA, and CBERA. In addition, successive rounds of multilateral trade negotiations at the WTO have consistently lowered tariffs on all products to most-favored nation (MFN) countries.[414] This reduction in the margin of tariff preferences is commonly known as "preference erosion" or "tariff erosion."

Economic research indicates that tariff erosion is particularly a problem for low-income African, Caribbean, and Pacific (ACP) countries, exacerbated because these countries tend to specialize in only a few products for export (e.g., textiles and apparel or certain agricultural goods). The ACP countries normally have a very low capacity to expand their exports to other products due to limited and inefficient capital markets, obstacles to labor mobility, and the absence of safety nets and training for displaced workers.[415] The WTO reports that Norway's GSP program, which benefits least-developed countries and 14 other developing countries, is well utilized, but has not produced any major increase in exports from those countries since 2008.[416] The stagnation is largely attributed to Norway signing reciprocal trade agreements with other trading partners, thereby eroding tariff preferences under its own GSP program.[417]

The case of Norway is more the rule than the exception. Recipient countries under most unilateral trade preference programs are adversely affected by tariff erosion. EU imports of beef from ACP countries, particularly Botswana, have declined since 2010. This decline is likely related to increased access to the EU market for beef from the EU's other trading partners. In 2009, to settle trade disputes with the United States over hormone-treated beef, the EU opened a tariff-rate quota for high-quality beef totaling 20,000 metric tons (mt).[418] Total duty- free quantities under the quota, now open to Argentina, Australia, Brazil, Canada, New Zealand, Paraguay, the United States, and Uruguay, increased to 48,200 mt in January 2012.[419] Beef from developed nations now receives duty-free status along with ACP countries. As a result, Botswana's beef exports to the EU have no tariff advantage to help them compete against high- quality, lower-cost beef in the EU market.[420]

Locking in Policy Reforms with Reciprocal Trade Agreements

Citing the weak benefits to recipient countries associated with trade preference programs, some economists recommend that beneficiary countries negotiate reciprocal trade agreements instead, because many reciprocal trade agreements encourage economic restructuring that ultimately causes resources to be used more efficiently within beneficiary countries. For example, recent empirical research comparing the two approaches concludes that reciprocal trade agreements are preferable, because they "lock in" needed domestic reforms and enhance a government's ability to commit to policies that may be unpopular with powerful domestic interests.[421]

The next section will review an example of one such commitment to lock in reforms—Mexico's membership in NAFTA. Other case studies follow, providing examples of transition from unilateral trade preferences to reciprocal trade agreements. Although direct economic effects are often difficult to quantify, each of the case studies shows that reciprocal trade agreements have largely resulted in increased trade and diversification of trade between the parties.

Case Study 1: The United States and Mexico

Mexico was a beneficiary country of the U.S. GSP program starting in 1976, the first year of the program. According to trade analysis, Mexico was the second-largest beneficiary of the U.S. GSP program in its early years because it exported many products to the United States that were subject to MFN tariff rates of more than zero.[422] Mexico benefited despite the fact that its exports were heavily impacted by competitive need limitations and discretionary removal from the program by U.S. policymakers.[423]

Since the U.S. GSP program was created, per capita gross domestic product in Mexico grew annually (in real terms) by 1.2 percent on average from 1976-2012.[424] But the average growth rate has increased slightly over the last twenty years, rising from 1.0 percent between 1976–1993 to 1.4 percent from 1993–2012. Many factors have played a role in Mexico's development, including increased development of natural resources, government and educational reforms, and proximity to the large U.S. economy. However, a significant factor was Mexico's inclusion in NAFTA with Canada and the United States, beginning in 1994. NAFTA spurred a significant increase in trade among the partner countries.[425] Between 1994 and 2012, Mexico's exports to the United States increased from $50 billion to $278 billion, and its trade balance with the United States shifted from a $1.3 billion deficit to a $61.7 billion surplus.[426]

Mexico diversified its trade within the region following NAFTA's implementation, with Mexican exports shifting toward manufactured goods. The country also increased vertical specialization and intra-firm trade among the NAFTA partners. While many factors contributed to the trend, NAFTA membership boosted foreign investment flows to Mexico and significantly improved productivity in that country.[427] Average annual foreign direct investment (FDI) inflows into Mexico over the five-year period after NAFTA was implemented (1994–98) were $11.0 billion, compared to an annual average of $3.9 billion during the five years prior to NAFTA (1989–93).[428]

One difficulty in quantifying the economic impact of NAFTA on Mexico is that the Mexican government began the process of liberalizing its trade and investment policies before NAFTA negotiations began. Mexico joined GATT in 1986, capping its maximum tariffs at 50 percent.[429] Then in the mid-1980s Mexico began phasing out import license requirements for nearly all imports, so that when NAFTA negotiations started, import licenses were only required on 230 of the 12,000 separate goods in the Mexican tariff schedule.[430] In addition, other economic shocks affected Mexico at the same time that NAFTA was finalized, including a severe financial crisis in 1994 (which resulted in a devaluation of the Mexican peso), other free trade arrangements NAFTA partners signed in the 1980s and 1990s, and a global economic recovery in the latter half of the 1990s. Even taking these major developments into account, NAFTA still played an important role in increasing regional trade and financial flows.[431]

In hindsight, Mexico's negotiation of NAFTA can be viewed as a means of anchoring prior policy commitments by the Mexican government. After Mexico's GATT accession, its revisions to laws governing FDI in 1993,[432] its debt restructuring in the 1989 Brady Plan, and its industry privatization between 1989 and 1992, the Mexican government finally created a policy environment in which gradual reductions in tariffs and NTMs with the United States and Canada could provide efficiency gains through the reallocation of domestic resources.[433] In the end, the FTA with its North American neighbors ensured that Mexico's policy decisions could not be easily undone.

For Mexico, NAFTA underpinned the government's efforts to press ahead with structural reforms in the economy. In turn, these reforms allowed Mexican businesses to respond more quickly and forcefully to competitive pressures from overseas, such as competition from Asian and Latin American companies, to provide goods and services in global markets. Mexico's experience in NAFTA demonstrates that developing countries can use reciprocal trade agreements as a stimulus to enact economic reforms that may be necessary to compete globally.[434] These reforms have many impacts, but one of the most important is to offer investors the economic stability needed to support increased FDI.[435]

Case Study 2: The United States and Chile

Like Mexico, Chile was a beneficiary country of the U.S. GSP program beginning with the program's inception in 1976. From the outset, Chile benefited significantly from the program because nearly all of Chile's exports to the United States under GSP would otherwise have been subject to non-zero MFN rates; in 1979, for instance, this affected $233 million out of $251 million in Chilean exports to the United States.[436] But Chile's preference margins—the difference between the preferential U.S. tariffs Chilean products faced and those faced by Chile's competitors outside of the GSP program—were among the lowest for countries receiving U.S. GSP treatment, thereby limiting Chile's trade advantage under GSP.[437]

Chile's economic development has slowed somewhat from the rapid growth rates of the 1980s and early 1990s, but rates of growth continue to be solid. Per capita GDP grew 5.8 percent annually (in real terms) between 1986 (the first year of Chile's OECD data) and 1994. From 1994 to 2003, real per capita GDP grew 3.4 percent annually, rising slightly to 3.7 percent from 2003 to 2012.[438] Many factors played a role in Chile's economic growth over the entire period, including government reforms to labor markets, pension markets, worker training, and educational systems, as well as longstanding mining and agricultural endowments.[439]

Yet another factor in the pace and timing of Chile's economic development was the government's policy of signing reciprocal trade agreements with its trading partners. Chile's 2004 FTA with the United States had many benefits, including lowered tariffs, codified rules for FDI, new protections for investors, and forums to address certain NTMs.[440] Between 2003 and 2012, Chile's exports to the United States more than doubled, growing from $3.7 billion to $9.4 billion, primarily consisting of copper, fruit, fish, and wood products.[441] Average annual FDI inflows into Chile over the five years after the U.S.-Chile FTA was implemented (2004–08) were $10.0 billion, compared to an annual average of $4.9 billion during the five years prior (1999–2003).[442]

Despite signing a number of reciprocal trade agreements over the past decade and expanding the value of total exports, Chile has not diversified its export portfolio. In fact, according to data from Chile's industrial association, SOFOFA, the number of products Chile exports has fallen steadily from 5,302 in 2005 to 4,938 in 2010.[443] Indeed, in 2013, copper still accounted for a large share–approximately 32 percent–of Chilean exports, in value terms.[444] The Chilean government anticipated that Chile's manufacturing exports would increase under its free trade agenda. But an increase in exports has yet to materialize because manufacturers still face technical barriers to trade related to quality standards. SOFOFA is now working closely with the Chilean government and the National Standardization Institute to develop norms and standards for a wide range of sectors to help them enter markets in Europe, North America, and Asia.[445]

For Chile's agricultural sector, however, reciprocal trade agreements have allowed exporters to make inroads into closed markets.[446] Under the U.S.-Chile FTA, Chile and the United States have worked to develop a system of equivalence to replace the quarantine treatment for fruit currently in place.[447] Several Chilean fruit exporters reported that the FTA with the United States—a country with stringent SPS risk analysis procedures—accelerated the authorization of their products to enter the U.S. market.[448]

An OECD report on Chilean fruit exports concludes that reciprocal trade agreements like the U.S.-Chile FTA can also stimulate trade in new products. Econometric analysis conducted by the OECD in 2013 indicated that the mere presence of an FTA, even without a preferential margin, increases the probability of exporting at least one new product by approximately 2 percent relative to other countries. The development of new commercial contacts between the trading partners may explain why this occurs.[449] A majority of Chilean fruit exporters interviewed for the OECD study (53 percent) agreed that FTAs, such as the U.S.-Chile FTA, have the capacity to promote trade in new products, although other factors such as consumer demand play a role.[450] Moreover, 62 percent of the exporters noted that FTAs stimulate innovations in processes or outputs, particularly in improving logistical connections between the trading partners.[451]

Case Study 3: EU and Chile

In addition to the U.S.-Chile FTA, the Chilean government has embarked on several other reciprocal trade agreements. The EU-Chile Association Agreement ("Agreement") entered into force on February 1, 2003.[452] A study funded by the EU Commission performed a product-level analysis that compared the trade benefits of the Agreement to Chile's benefits under the EU GSP program before 2003. Using 2009 data, the study concluded that EU imports from Chile would have been €500 million ($700 million) lower per year if Chile's goods had been subject to the EU's GSP program rather than the Agreement. The difference is equal to 15 percent of the value of trade under the Agreement.[453] The impact of the Agreement on EU imports, relative to the GSP program, is largest for wine, at €206 million ($288 million) or 36 percent of actual wine imports; fruits, at €151 million ($211 million) or

15 percent of actual fruit imports; and fish, at €55 million ($77 million) or 15 percent of actual fish imports.[454]

Economic research by the OECD on Chile's fruit trade, using both econometrics and a survey of exporters, concluded that Chile's agreement with the EU positively impacted Chile's exports of those goods.[455] While the econometric analysis focused only on the impacts of tariff reductions, the study also noted that the ability to comply with SPS measures appears equally important to Chilean exporters in boosting fruit exports to FTA trading partners. The SPS chapters of Chile's FTAs effectively determine whether an agricultural product can be shipped to the trading partner. Although those chapters do not generally go beyond what is offered under the WTO's SPS agreement, they often ensure closer contacts between regulatory agencies through the creation of technical committees and ad hoc committees that resolve procedural issues for specific products.[456]

In Chile's trade agreements with the EU, with Colombia, and with other members of the Trans- Pacific Strategic Economic Partnership (P-4) Agreement (with Brunei, New Zealand, and Singapore), there is a commitment among the signatories to apply SPS equivalence beyond WTO requirements.[457] The Chilean government is working to develop mechanisms that will gradually incorporate the SPS equivalence principle for a specific product or group of products. Chile is also working toward incorporating the principle of mutual recognition of SPS standards in its agreement with the EU.[458]

Case Study 4: The United States and Morocco

Since the U.S.–Morocco free trade agreement (FTA) was signed in 2004, U.S. imports from Morocco have more than doubled, increasing from $385 million in 2003 to $932 million in 2012.[459] Much of the increase was in mined products such as fertilizers and chalk. Annual U.S. FDI in Morocco has also quadrupled over the same period, totaling $613 million in 2012.[460] This investment is likely linked to trade and investment rules provided in the agreement for both signatories. In particular, the agreement requires that investor rights be backed up by an effective, impartial, and fully transparent procedure for dispute settlement. Submissions to dispute panels and panel hearings will be open to the public, and interested parties will have the opportunity to submit their views.[461]

In addition, Morocco recently became the first country in North Africa to conclude a bilateral trade facilitation agreement with the United States, building on the FTA. In November 2013, U.S. Trade Representative Michael Froman and Morocco's Minister of Economy and Finance Mohamed Boussaid signed a trade facilitation agreement to modernize customs practices, including provisions covering Internet publication, transit, and transparency of penalties. Morocco is also the first North African country to endorse joint principles on investment and on trade in information and communications technology services.[462] Such trade facilitation agreements between nations, as well as FDI linkages, can be enhanced with reciprocal trade agreements in effect; many reciprocal trade agreements establish rules for customs cooperation and trade facilitation among parties, and some even create committees to encourage more progress in this area.[463]

Reciprocal Trade Agreements in Sub-Saharan African Countries

Overview

For several years, individual SSA countries and blocs of SSA countries have been actively involved in seeking reciprocal trade agreements with non-SSA country partners.[464] The overarching purpose of these agreements is for economic growth through increased trade, investment, and integration into regional and global markets. These agreements deal primarily with trade in goods and rules of origin, although some address nontariff provisions involving such issues as SPS measures, TBTs, and intellectual property rights. However, other areas, such as customs procedures and investment, are rarely covered in these agreements. Many reciprocal trade agreements involving SSA countries are asymmetrical in nature, meaning that the trade concessions by African countries or regions are less extensive and/or take place much later than trade concessions offered by the partner countries or regions. A list of reciprocal trade agreements that SSA countries have completed or are in advanced stages of negotiatin is provided in table 6.2. In addition, information on several potential agreements reportedly being negotiated by SSA countries is presented in table 6.3.

Table 6.2. Reciprocal trade agreements involving SSA countries (in force or provisional)

Agreement	Participants	Details of agreement	Effective date	Coverage
EU-South Africa Trade Development and Cooperation Agreement	EU, Republic of South Africa	Primarily goods trade; some development	Trade-related articles provisionally applied 2000, fully entered into force 2004, liberalization completed 2012	Goods; limited treatment of TBTs and intellectual property rights; encourages investment and development
Free Trade Agreement between the European Free Trade Association (EFTA) States and the Southern African Customs Union (SACU) States	Iceland, Liechtenstein, Norway, Switzerland, Botswana, Lesotho, Namibia, South Africa, Swaziland	Combination of regional agreement and concessions between individual members	May 2008	Goods; limited treatment of SPS, TBTs, intellectual property rights; encourages cooperation on investment
Preferential Trade Agreement between the Common Market of the South (Mercosur) and the Southern African Customs Union (SACU)	Argentina, Brazil, Paraguay, Uruguay, Botswana, Lesotho, Namibia, South Africa, Swaziland	Reciprocal but less than a full FTA	2009	Goods; limited treatment of TBTs and SPS
Free Trade Agreement between the Republic of Turkey and the Republic of Mauritius	Turkey, Mauritius	Goods trade	June 2013	Goods; limited treatment of SPS and TRIPS

Table 6.2. (Continued)

Agreement	Participants	Details of agreement	Effective date	Coverage
EU Economic Partnership Agreements	EU, Cameroon	Provisional[a]	Negotiated: provisional October 2009	Goods; limited treatment of investment, intellectual property rights, SPS, and TBTs
	EU, Côte d'Ivoire	Provisional[a]	Negotiated: provisional 2009	Goods; limited treatment of SPS and TBTs
	EU, Ghana	Framework of an agreement	Negotiated, not yet entered into force	Goods; limited treatment of SPS and TBTs
	EU, East African Community (EAC) (Burundi, Kenya, Rwanda, Tanzania, and Uganda)	Framework of an agreement	Negotiated, not yet entered into force	Goods
	EU, Eastern and Southern African States (ESA) (Madagascar, Mauritius, Seychelles, and Zimbabwe)	Provisional[a]	Negotiated: provisional May 2012	Goods, calls for provisions on investment
	EU, Southern African Development Community (SADC) (Botswana, Lesotho, Mozambique, Namibia, and Swaziland have participated in negotiations)	Provisional[a]	Interim agreement signed June 2009 by Botswana, Lesotho, Swaziland, Mozambique[b]	Goods; limited treatment of SPS and TBTs; pledge to negotiate on investment
Pan-Arab Free Trade Area (PAFTA)	Algeria, Bahrain, Egypt, Iraq, Jordan, Kuwait, Lebanon, Libya, Morocco, Oman, Qatar, Saudi Arabia, Sudan, Syria, Tunisia, United Arab Emirates, Yemen, Palestinian Authority	Goods; elimination of duties	1998; Least developed states to eliminate duties by 2010	Goods

Source: Compiled by USITC from the following texts:

"Agreement on Trade, Development and Cooperation between the European Community and Its Member States, of the One Part, and the Republic of South Africa, of the Other Part," 1999

"Free Trade Agreement between the EFTA States and the SACU States," 2006

"Preferential Trade Agreement between the Common Market of the South (Mercosur) and the Southern African Customs Union (SACU)," 2009

"Free Trade Agreement between the Republic of Turkey and the Republic of Mauritius," http://www.mcci.org/trade_agreements_turkey.aspx (accessed January 28m 2014)

"Interim Agreement with a View to an Economic Partnership Agreement between the European Community and Its Member States, of the One Part, and the Central Africa Party, of the Other Part," 2009

"Stepping Stone Economic Partnership Agreement between Côte d'Ivoire, of the One Part, and the European Community and Its Member States, of the Other Part," 2008

"Stepping Stone Economic Partnership Agreement between Ghana, of the One Part, and the European Community and Its Member States, of the Other Part," 2007

"Agreement Establishing a Framework for an Economic Partnership Agreement between the European Community and Its Member States, on the One Part, and the East African Community Partner States on the Other Part," 2007

"Interim Agreement Establishing a Framework for an Economic Partnership Agreement between the Eastern and Southern Africa States, on the One Part, and the European

Community and Its Member States, on the Other Part," 2009

"Interim Agreement with a view to an Economic Partnership Agreement between the European Community and Its Member States, of the One Part, and the SACU EPA States, of the Other Part," 2009

"Agreement to Facilitate and Develop Trade among Arab States," 1981.

Notes: [a] Trade preferences of interim agreements are provisional on continued progress toward a comprehensive EPA. [b] Namibia participated in negotiations but did not sign the agreement.

Table 6.3. Potential agreements under negotiation by SSA countries

Agreement and partners	Comments
Senegal, China	Bilateral cooperation agreements signed in 2011.
Democratic Republic of the Congo, Turkey	Negotiations begun
Cameroon, Turkey	Negotiations begun
Ghana, Turkey	Negotiations begun
Seychelles, Turkey	Negotiations begun
Ethiopia, China	"*Agreement on Economic and Technical Cooperation Between the Government of the People's Republic of China and the Government of the Federal Democratic Republic of Ethiopia*" signed June 2010
Ethiopia, Sudan	Ethiopia-Sudan trade cooperation agreement
Kenya bilateral agreements	Kenya reportedly has bilateral trade agreements with Argentina, Bangladesh, Bulgaria, China, Egypt, Hungary, India, Iraq, the Netherlands, Pakistan, Poland, Romania, Russia, Korea, and Thailand. Negotiations are underway with Belarus, the Czech Republic, Iran, and Kazakhstan. These are not reciprocal
Tunisia, West African Economic and Monetary Union (WAEMU): customs union	Negotiations are underway
SACU, India, Brazil, South Africa	Negotiations are underway

Sources: Republic of Turkey, Ministry of Economy, "Turkey's Free Trade Agreements" (accessed January 9, 2014); Ministry of Foreign Affairs of the People's Republic of China, "China and Ethiopia" (accessed January 8, 2014); Focus Africa, "Ethiopia" (accessed January 15, 2014); Export Promotion Council of Kenya, "Trade Agreements" (accessed January 8, 2014); AllAfrica.com, "Tunisia and WAEMU to Sign Free Trade Agreement" (accessed January 16, 2014); Bilaterals.org, "IBSA" (accessed February 6, 2014).

Specific Agreements

European Community-South Africa Trade Development and Cooperation Agreement (TDCA)

One of the most comprehensive trade agreements in Africa is the Trade, Development and Cooperation Agreement (TDCA) between the EU and the Republic of South Africa (RSA).[465] The TDCA was signed in 1999. The trade-related articles became provisionally effective in 2000, and the TDCA was fully implemented in 2004. It covers trade in goods, although the parties also reaffirmed their commitments under the General Agreement on Trade in Services (GATS) and the Agreement on Trade-Related Aspects of Intellectual Property Rights (TRIPs). The EU and South Africa agreed to improve on protection provided under these treaties where appropriate. Further, the parties agreed to cooperate in promoting and encouraging investment, not only in South Africa but in the entire Southern African region. Lastly, the EU and South Africa encouraged trade in services and pledged to examine ways to harmonize SPS standards and regulations. A detailed description of tariff commitments under the TDCA is included in Appendix H.

A potential impact of the TDCA is to put the United States at a disadvantage vis-à-vis the EU in the South African market. However, any tariff disadvantage is likely small. Just over half of South Africa's tariff lines have zero duties under normal trade relations (NTR), sometimes called most-favored nation (MFN) status. Many products with NTR tariffs of over 20 percent (including some vehicles and parts) did not receive duty free treatment under the TDCA. Also, according to information provided by the government of South Africa, 75 percent of imports from the United States were duty-free in 2012, and a further 10 percent of imports had no tariff disadvantage relative to imports from the EU under the agreement.[466] Nonetheless, certain U.S. goods are disadvantaged against EU goods entering South Africa. In 2012, roughly 15 percent of South African imports from the United States faced NTR duties for which the EU received duty-free treatment, as outlined in the tabulation below:

U.S. tariff disadvantage vis-à-vis the EU (percent)	Major products	Percent of South Africa's imports from the United States
Tariff 5% or less	Machinery parts, relays, iron and steel	1
Tariff >5% and <10%	Peas, beans, fruits, and nuts	6
Tariff >10% and <15%	Valves, control panels, tools, and machinery parts	4
Tariff >15% and <20%	Bearings, electrical motors, generators, some automobiles	3
Tariff >20% plus non-ad valorem tariffs	Prepared foods, appliances, spirits	1

Source: Government of South Africa, "Analysis of RSA Imports from the US," January 22, 2014.

Free Trade Agreement between the European Free Trade Association (EFTA) States and the Southern African Customs Union (SACU) States

This agreement covers trade in goods between an individual EFTA state and an individual SACU state, and trade in goods between an individual EFTA state and the SACU as a whole.[467] Preferential tariff reductions or eliminations by the EFTA states took place on May 1, 2008, when the agreement entered into force, and tariff concessions by the SACU states are to be fully implemented by January 1, 2015. Three separate agricultural arrangements were negotiated between the SACU states collectively with Iceland, Norway, and Switzerland/Liechtenstein.[468]

Under the agreement, concessions offered by SACU states include duty reduction or elimination on most industrial products in the international Harmonized System (HS) chapters 25–98, and certain processed agricultural products as specified in the agreement; and duty elimination on products of two HS 4-digit headings from Iceland, along with the immediate or progressive elimination of duties on agricultural products from Switzerland/Liechtenstein.[469]

Meanwhile, concessions offered by EFTA states include immediate duty elimination on most industrial products (with the exception of goods in chapters 35 and 38 listed in Annex II); treatment no less favorable than that accorded to the EU for processed agricultural products; duty elimination by Iceland for many basic agricultural products; duty reduction or elimination by Norway on many basic agricultural products and a 500 metric ton tariff-rate quota (TRQ) for beef originating in Botswana or Namibia; and duty reduction or elimination by Switzerland and Liechtenstein for many basic agricultural products (many with seasonal restrictions or TRQs).

The EFTA-SACU trade agreement provides for duty-free access into the SACU market for a large number of products that the United States currently exports to SACU countries and that account for a substantial share of U.S. exports to the region. This duty-free access creates tariff disadvantages for U.S. producers compared to EFTA producers in the SACU market for those products. Sectors in which EFTA producers have a tariff advantage include pharmaceuticals, chemicals, and machine parts.[470]

Mercosur-SACU

The Preferential Trade Agreement between the Common Market of the South (Mercosur) and SACU was signed in December 2008, but is not currently in effect.[471] Article 2 notes that, as a preferential agreement, it is to be viewed as the first step toward a free trade agreement. The agreement covers a wide range of products but is not all-inclusive for either side. With limited exceptions, rules of origin allow for articles produced in any Mercosur or SACU country to receive preferential tariffs. For the most part, the Mercosur-SACU agreement does not result in a tariff disadvantage for the U.S. products that accounted for the majority of the value of U.S. exports to SACU countries in 2012. Notable exceptions include certain front-end loaders classified in HS 8429.51 and parts for construction equipment classified in HS 8431.49.[472]

Turkey-Mauritius FTA

The Turkey-Mauritius FTA entered into force on June 1, 2013, and reduces or eliminates duties on imports of most industrial and agricultural products between the parties. Specific concessions offered by Turkey included the immediate elimination of duties on most industrial products from Mauritius, and elimination of duties on specified textiles and apparel (mainly classified in HS chapters 61 and 62) over four years. Meanwhile, specific concessions offered by Mauritius include immediate elimination of duties on some industrial products from Turkey, while some products with NTR duties of 10 percent are reduced to zero over four years, and other products with duties of 25 percent are reduced to zero over five years. However, more than 100 HS 6-digit products are excluded from the agreement, including most agricultural products. An exception is Turkey's elimination or reduction of tariffs for some agricultural products (e.g., certain fresh and canned tuna) imported from Mauritius within a TRQ. Additionally, Mauritius committed to reduce duties on certain agricultural products with NTR tariffs of 10 percent to zero over four years (e.g., certain fisheries and dairy products), and committed to reduce duties on certain products with NTR tariffs of 25 percent to zero over five years (e.g., certain cheeses and canned tuna).

EU Economic Partnership Agreements

The 2000 Cotonou Agreement superseded the Lomé Conventions between the European Community and countries of Africa, the Caribbean, and the Pacific (ACP). This agreement covers the period March 2000–February 2020, although it was revised in 2001 and 2010, primarily to take into account changes in regional integration and security. The Cotonou Agreement called for the negotiation of reciprocal, WTO-compatible economic partnership agreements (EPAs) to enter into effect no later than January 2008.[473] Like the Cotonou Agreement, individual EPAs have economic development as a primary goal, as well as the reduction and eventual elimination of poverty in the ACP states and the integration of the ACP states into the world economy. For reasons of EU negotiating efficiency and to encourage regional cooperation, SSA countries were strongly encouraged by the EU Commission to negotiate their EPAs in groups rather than separately.[474] The EU has entered into negotiations for EPAs with five African regions: West Africa, Central Africa, Eastern and Southern Africa (ESA), the Eastern African Community (EAC), and the Southern African Development Community (SADC).[475]

EPAs are designed to include a broad range of provisions on trade in goods and services and to be WTO-compatible.[476] However, the reciprocal trade agreements are asymmetrical, with most products of ACP countries receiving duty-free, quota-free (DFQF) access to the EU market immediately, while preferential access to ACP markets for EU products is phased in over a long period (up to 25 years). EPAs also allow ACP countries to exclude sensitive products from liberalization.[477] However, EPAs include an "MFN clause" that will result in ACP countries giving the EU the best trade access afforded any other trading partner. Most EPAs that have been negotiated are "interim" agreements dealing only with trade in goods; they do not address services, nor do they address rules of origin and other trade barriers. To date, no SSA negotiating region has concluded an EPA. Interim agreements have been negotiated with the countries of the EAC, one country in Central Africa, 4 of the 12 ESA countries, 2 countries in West Africa, and 4 of the 7 countries in the SADC.[478] Information on the current status of the EPAs is presented in table 6.4.

The EU proposed in 2011 that preferential market access for ACP countries granted since January 2008 be rescinded for countries that have not concluded an EPA by January 2014.[479] Least-developed countries, including Burundi, Comoros, Lesotho, Mozambique, Rwanda, Tanzania, Uganda, and Zambia, would continue to receive DFQF access under the EU's existing Everything But Arms (EBA) program. For other SSA countries, including Cameroon, Ghana, Côte d'Ivoire, Kenya, and Swaziland, failure to ratify and implement EPAs would reportedly result in tariffs reverting to GSP levels, with far higher tariffs and stricter rules of origin for exports to the EU.[480]

Table 6.4. Status of EPA negotiations

SSA countries	Type of agreement	Status
Cameroon (Central Africa)	Interim EPA	Signed in 2009, not ratified.
Madagascar, Mauritius, Seychelles, and Zimbabwe (ESA)	Interim EPA	Provisionally applied May 2012. Negotiations continue.
Burundi, Kenya, Rwanda, Tanzania, and Uganda (EAC)	Partial interim EPA	Agreement reached in 2007, but has not been ratified and is not in effect. Negotiations continue.
Botswana, Lesotho, Mozambique, and Swaziland (SADC)	Interim EPA	Signed in 2009, not ratified. Negotiations continue.
Namibia (SADC)	Interim EPA	Participated in negotiations through 2009, but did not sign.
Côte d'Ivoire (West Africa)	Interim EPA	Negotiated 2007, signed 2008, not ratified.
Ghana (West Africa)	Interim EPA	Negotiated 2007, not signed or ratified.

Source: EU Commission, "Overview of EPA Negotiations," updated October 16, 2013.

Also, according to the EU Commission's latest reform of the GSP, which took effect in January 2014, middle-income countries, such as Botswana and Namibia, will no longer qualify for GSP treatment if EPAs are not signed.[481] These countries would revert to far higher MFN tariffs on their exports to the EU.[482] In the case of Namibia, exporters would face an average 19.5 percent duty on exports to the EU. Dutiable exports from Namibia to the EU currently total nearly €300 million ($398 million) annually; additional duties paid would likely be more than €58 million ($77 million).[483] Botswana and Namibia could lose substantial market access advantage and export revenue if an EPA is not implemented.

With limited progress on many EPAs, the deadline for the remaining African countries to ratify and implement comprehensive EPAs was delayed by the EU in early 2013 to October 1, 2014.[484] As the October deadline draws closer, several SSA countries are gradually increasing efforts to complete their EPAs with the EU. The Secretary General of the East African Community (EAC), which includes Burundi, Kenya, Rwanda, Tanzania, and Uganda, has been stressing the benefits of an EPA to EAC members. In particular, he has noted its transparency and predictability, the 25-year tariff phaseout for sensitive EAC imports, the ability of EAC members to negotiate with the EU rather than having rules imposed on them, and favorable rules of origin for textiles. The EAC is currently on track to meet the EU-imposed deadline.[485] As noted, the Government of Ghana has signed an interim EPA. But the European Commission has not indicated whether such an agreement would be enough for Ghana to retain its EU trade preferences.

According to some observers, hesitancy among SSA countries to ratify EPAs is the result of the EU's negotiating posture and uncertainty about the perceived benefits of such agreements by African parties.[486] For many SSA countries, tariffs generate a significant share of government revenues.[487] For example, potential tariff losses of an EPA have been estimated at between 2 percent and 16 percent of government revenues for countries in West Africa.[488] SSA countries may therefore be reluctant to spend the time and resources to complete an EPA when the net additional benefits are perceived to be quite modest.[489] As noted, the poorest beneficiary countries already benefit from the EU's EBA preferences, including DFQF access to the EU market, even if they do not sign an EPA. NTR tariffs are very low or free for many raw materials and hydrocarbons; therefore, resource-rich African countries may not feel significantly disadvantaged by revisions to or removal from tariff preferences under an EPA. Further, allowing SSA countries to exempt up to 20 percent of trade from liberalization may lock these countries into current production and trading patterns.[490]

An additional complicating factor is that EU negotiators focus on regional cooperation among ACP countries rather than bilateral discussions between the EU and each recipient country.[491] But in most cases, Africa's regional blocs have trouble negotiating with one voice. Within each region, countries with different levels of development face very different consequences of not concluding an EPA.[492] Consequently, the beneficiary countries are unable to set common negotiating priorities, and talks eventually break down.

SECTION 7. AGOA TRADE PERFORMANCE: A REVIEW OF THE LITERATURE

Now that AGOA has been in force for over a decade, there have been numerous economic analyses that have attempted to evaluate how it has impacted trade between sub-Saharan Africa (SSA) and the United States. The value of exports from the region to the United States has unequivocally grown between 2000 and 2013, but what part did AGOA play in this growth? And how did AGOA's role in stimulating exports from SSA compare to the role of trade preference programs offered by third parties, such as the European Union (EU)?

This section reviews literature aimed at answering the following five questions:

- To what extent are beneficiary countries using the preferences granted under AGOA?
- To what extent can the observed growth in trade be attributed directly to AGOA, and has this growth been only an increase in the volume of already traded products, or has the program helped to diversify exports by creating trade flows in new products?
- How effective have the unilateral tariff preference programs of other countries been at both increasing and diversifying SSA exports?
- How does the effect of AGOA in expanding and diversifying exports compare to the effect of trade preference programs offered by other parties, such as the EU?
- After having examined the effectiveness of AGOA, what recommendations does the literature make on how the program might be improved?

Based on the body of literature reviewed in this section, which is summarized in table 7.2 at the end of the section, the following broad conclusions are made about the AGOA program:

- Utilization rates (defined as the ratio of imports claiming preferences to imports of products eligible for preferences) for AGOA and other similar unilateral tariff

preference programs covering SSA are very high on average (greater than 85 percent in most cases), but vary by country and sector.
- AGOA's estimated impact on trade flows from SSA varied due to differences in study methodology, time period assessed, and level of aggregation, with some studies finding a positive total effect, some finding no effect, and some finding positive effects only in particular sectors.
- Various studies agreed that AGOA preferences led to increased SSA exports of apparel for some beneficiaries, with countries exporting higher volumes of apparel products and also diversifying into exports of new apparel products. Many of these studies emphasized that these gains were due to AGOA's less restrictive rules of origin for apparel, requiring only a single transformation.
- When considering nonenergy products, AGOA was successful at generating new product export flows. However, many of these new exports occurred in product groups that represented only a small share of a country's total exports.
- Other unilateral trade preference programs were also estimated to have varying effects in generating additional SSA exports due to variations in study methodology, time period, and level of aggregation. Some studies found that other unilateral preference programs did increase exports, some found no effect, and some found effects only for certain sectors. With respect to diversification, EU programs were found to increase the number of products exported in some sectors, but to decrease the number of products exported in other sectors.
- In general, EU unilateral preference programs were found to be more effective at increasing beneficiary country exports, while U.S. preference programs seemed to be more effective at diversifying beneficiary country exports. However, this may not be true for all countries or sectors; U.S. preferences were found to be more effective at both increasing and diversifying SSA apparel exports than EU preferences (as noted above, this was largely due to less stringent rules of origin in place under AGOA than under EU preference programs during the time periods analyzed). But EU preferences were more effective in increasing SSA agricultural exports.
- Although AGOA has helped generate additional SSA exports in some sectors, the literature concluded that the program could be further improved by making AGOA permanent, offering capacity-building assistance, offering full duty-free/quota-free access to beneficiary countries, and further relaxing rules of origin, among other recommendations.

Utilization of AGOA Preferences

Calculating the utilization of preferences under AGOA is complex.[493] Particularly problematic is the fact that AGOA-eligible countries receive preferential tariffs under overlapping programs— specifically the Generalized System of Preferences (GSP) and GSP for least-developed beneficiary developing countries (LDBDCs).[494] Because many products are eligible for preferential access under two regimes, a program's preference utilization rate must be calculated by including all regimes that offer the best available tariff rate. Calculating preference utilization in this way is done under the assumption that in the absence of one overlapping program, all imports would enter under the other (i.e., if AGOA countries could not also utilize GSP, then all imports would enter under AGOA instead of some under AGOA and some under GSP). In their 2012 analysis of utilization rates for the unilateral preference programs of four industrialized countries, Keck and Lendle found that the ratio of imports claiming AGOA preferences[495] to imports of products eligible for AGOA preferences in 2008 was 92 percent.[496] This utilization rate is higher than those of many U.S. bilateral free trade agreements, including U.S. free trade agreements (FTAs) with Australia, Israel, Singapore, and Morocco, as well as the Dominican Republic-Central America-United States FTA (CAFTA-DR).[497]

While this overall utilization rate is high, it potentially masks country and product heterogeneities that have been noted in previous works. In their 2004 analysis using 2002 data, Brenton and Ikezuki noted that while average utilization rates for AGOA were over 80 percent (comparable to similar EU program utilization rates), one-third of countries had rates below 20 percent, and 37 percent of countries had rates greater than 80 percent.[498] Analyzing data from 2005, Brenton and Hoppe found that overall combined AGOA/GSP utilization had risen to 95 percent.[499] Utilization rates continued to be highly variable by country, however, with 11 out of 37 beneficiaries achieving utilization rates of at least 98 percent, while five countries did not use the preferences at all.[500]

Using data disaggregated at the Harmonized System (HS)[501] 8-digit level from 2003, Dean and Wainio found that utilization rates varied widely between beneficiary countries and sectors. With respect to non-agricultural products, among AGOA countries eligible for AGOA but not GSP-LDBDC, all countries except for Eritrea, Gabon, and Mauritius showed combined GSP/AGOA utilization rates of at least 75 percent.[502] For AGOA countries eligible for GSP- LDBDC, average nonagricultural combined GSP/AGOA utilization was estimated at above 50 percent, but countries tended to either almost fully utilize their preferences or else not use them at all.[503] This dichotomy also existed with respect to apparel. Among the 20 countries eligible for AGOA apparel benefits, five did not utilize their benefits at all, but 12 countries had apparel preference utilization rates above 80 percent, and six of these had utilization rates of at least 95 percent.[504] Finally, in agricultural products, 14 countries had estimated GSP/AGOA utilization rates above 90 percent, but two did not use the preferences at all.[505]

Bureau, Chakir, and Gallezot came to similar conclusions in their 2007 analysis of unilateral preferences for agricultural and food products, finding that in 2002, AGOA's utilization rate for agricultural products was 85 percent.[506] However, the authors noted that despite the fact that most U.S. agricultural imports from eligible countries enter under preferential schemes, export flows remain small (with the exception of South Africa), leaving the authors questioning whether use of the preferences in itself constitutes success.[507]

Each of these authors offer several possible explanations for these variable utilization rates. A primary explanation is that countries not utilizing the preferences are simply not exporting products that are covered by the program. For example, Brenton and Ikezuki noted that for nine beneficiary countries, fewer than 5 percent of their exports were eligible for benefits under AGOA.[508] Dean and Wainio further explored this question of coverage by distinguishing between product types. They found that although overall non-agricultural product coverage by GSP/AGOA was estimated at virtually 100 percent for many countries, it was lower for others, given their export portfolios—examples included Benin, Mauritania, and Sierra Leone.[509] Combined coverage of agricultural products, however, approached 100 percent for all countries.[510] At the same time, AGOA significantly improved product coverage as compared to GSP—Mattoo, Roy, and Subramanian estimated that 72 percent of U.S. imports from sub- Saharan Africa would be covered under AGOA, up from 17 percent under GSP (largely due to petroleum product coverage in AGOA).[511]

Despite the fact that most exports from beneficiary countries were covered by AGOA, the value of these covered preferences was estimated to be low. This was partially due to the fact that U.S. most-favored-nation (MFN) tariffs are low: in 2001, the year AGOA was implemented, two- thirds of tariff lines (representing 84 percent of U.S. imports) faced U.S. applied MFN tariffs of less than 5 percent.[512] Taking into account the preference margin on each country's exported basket of goods in 2005, Brenton and Hoppe estimated that for 26 out of 37 AGOA beneficiary countries, AGOA preferences were valued at less than 2 percent of the value of that country's total exports to the United States.[513] The value of AGOA preferences exceeded 10 percent of the total value of exports to the United States for only 8 beneficiaries. Both Dean and Wainio and Brenton and Ikezuki used similar methodologies but different years of data, and similarly concluded that the value of AGOA preferences varied across countries. However, one major conclusion from both of these studies was that most of the value of preferences under AGOA was due to preferential access for apparel.[514]

Utilization of Comparable Tariff Preference Regimes

As noted in the previous section, preference utilization under AGOA is generally high, and in some cases is higher than utilization rates for U.S. bilateral trade agreements. When compared with other unilateral preference regimes aimed at developing countries granted by other developed countries, AGOA's average utilization rate is high (table 7.1). Average overall utilization rates of programs for which sub-Saharan African countries are eligible are all at least 70 percent, and all but one are within four percentage points of each other. (These programs include AGOA; the EU's GSP-Least Developed Countries [LDC]; the EU's GSP non-LDC for African, Caribbean, and Pacific [ACP] countries; Canada's GSP-LDC; and Australia's GSP-LDC.)[515] This suggests that while AGOA achieved the highest overall "best regime" utilization rate in 2008, the rate was not unusual compared to similar programs.

Table 7.1. Preference utilization rates of selected nonreciprocal preference regimes for which SSA countries are eligible, 2008

Program[519]	Importer country	Utilization rate[520] (percent)
AGOA	USA	92
GSP (LDC, ACP)	EU	87
GSP	USA	86
GSP (LDC)	Canada	86
GSP (non-LDC, ACP)	EU	86
GSP	EU	77
GSP (LDC)	Australia	70
GSP	Canada	66
GSP	Australia	58

Source: Keck and Lendle, "New Evidence on Preference Utilization," September 3, 2012, 27.

Two earlier studies focused on EU-granted preferences, which are of the greatest value with respect to beneficiary countries in sub-Saharan Africa, given current trade volumes. These studies corroborated the high utilization rates found by Keck and Lendle. In their 2009 study of EU preference utilization using 2001 data, Candau and Jean also grouped beneficiary countries according to overlapping preference schemes. They found that overall utilization rates for LDCs in sub-Saharan Africa were 92 percent, and were 94 percent for non-LDCs in the region.[516] Even when various product groupings were considered, the results suggested that EU preferences for sub-Saharan Africa were used for the vast majority of imports—utilization rates were greater than 88 percent in all product groups examined, both for SSA LDCs and non-LDCs.[517] Additional work specifically with respect to preferences on agricultural goods by Bureau, Chakir, and Gallezot confirmed that sub-Saharan Africa's utilization of EU preferences in this sector was high, estimated at 95–96 percent in 2002.[518]

Role of AGOA in Increasing and Diversifying Exports

Section 2 shows that exports from AGOA-eligible countries are increasing, and the previous section explains that beneficiaries are (on average) using the preferences granted by AGOA. However, neither of these facts directly links this export growth to the AGOA program. One tool that trade economists commonly use to evaluate the impact of trade policy changes, such as AGOA, is the gravity model, and variations of this framework comprise the bulk of the literature summarized in this section.[521] In general, two approaches are used to model the effect of trade preferences in this gravity framework—either a dummy variable is used to indicate that preferences were in effect for a certain country in a given year, or else the margin of tariff preferences for a specific product under a given agreement is included in the model. Both approaches are seen in the literature covered in this section.

Additionally, when assessing the value of a trade agreement, economists increasingly measure trade effects not only on aggregate export values, but also on whether trade agreements have helped countries to export new products. These two effects are commonly referred to as trade intensification and trade diversification, respectively, and the literature with respect to both will be summarized in the following sections.[522]

Role of AGOA in Increasing Exports
Regarding trade intensification, various post-implementation empirical investigations have attempted to measure the value of additional exports of already traded products created by AGOA preferences. On the whole they conclude that at the aggregate level, AGOA's impact has been either positive (but typically small) or insignificant. At the sector and country-specific levels, however, significant and positive impacts have unequivocally been measured. For this reason, therefore, the discussion below is presented by examining AGOA's effect in raising the volume of beneficiary country exports into effects on total trade versus more disaggregated approaches.

Effect on Total Trade
Conclusions on AGOA's effect on total exports are mixed, mostly due to variations in study methodologies and in the time period analyzed. Four studies were identified in which overall affects from AGOA were estimated to be positive, while three studies found no

statistically significant effect. Nouve's 2005 analysis on trade data from 1996–2004 using a gravity model[523] found that AGOA had a statistically significant and positive effect on beneficiary country exports to the United States, estimating that every dollar increase in exports under AGOA led to a spillover effect of an additional $0.16 to $0.20 in overall SSA exports to the United States.[524] Lederman and Özden analyzed AGOA beneficiary country export flows at the HS 2-digit level from 1997 to 2001 using a gravity model that included average AGOA utilization rates by product instead of AGOA policy dummy variables.[525] They found that participation in the program led to 5 percent higher exports for the average beneficiary country.[526]

Two studies that did not use a modeling framework also supported the conclusion that AGOA did help to increase beneficiary country exports. A survey based assessment of the program's performance by Karingi, Páez, and Degefa found that a majority of private sector respondents from various beneficiary countries believed that AGOA was very important to their trade and economic links, while a quarter reported that it was not important.[527] At the same time, only about half of the firms surveyed reported that they had directly benefited from AGOA.[528] Brenton and Hoppe concluded that only a small share of sub-Saharan Africa's increased exports to the United States could be attributed to AGOA because most export growth under the program was crude oil, which would have been shipped even if the program had not existed.[529]

In contrast to the papers highlighted above, three studies in the literature found that AGOA was not responsible for increased beneficiary country exports to the United States. Analyzing aggregate nonoil export data from 1995–2005 using a gravity model, Zappile found no statistically significant effect from AGOA on total nonoil exports.[530] Using a gravity model[531] on data from 1997–2004, Seyoum also found no link between AGOA and total exports (although the results pointed to significant effects in certain sectors, discussed in the following section).[532] Lastly, Tadesse and Fayissa's gravity model using aggregate trade data from 1991–2006 found no statistically significant effect from AGOA on total exports. However, this study found significant effects at the product level, which is discussed in the following section.[533]

Although four studies found positive effects and three found no effect of AGOA on aggregate AGOA beneficiary country export levels, Condon and Stern's 2011 literature review (which encompasses many of the works described above) points out a further consideration in assessing the overall benefits of the program. They note:

- The majority of the studies reviewed in the synthesis were conducted during the early years of AGOA and there is little evidence in the synthesis based on data beyond 2005. AGOA is still a relatively young initiative and supply responses from LDCs can take years to materialize, thus it is important that the impact of AGOA continues to be analyzed.[534]

Effect on Disaggregated Trade

While the conclusions in the aggregate trade effects literature are mixed, disaggregated trade and sector-specific analyses have more consistent findings. Specifically, these studies found that AGOA helped to increase SSA exports in some sectors and products, but not others. Furthermore, much of the disaggregated effects literature is critical of analyses that focus on aggregated trade effects for two reasons. First, authors pointed out that estimations of aggregated effects are misleading, since trade preferences are granted at the product level and thus do not provide the same margin of preference for every product. Secondly, some of the aggregated analyses do not take into account zero trade flows—an approach that has been shown to substantially bias trade effects estimates.[535] Cipollina, Laborde, and Salvatici made one of the most definitive statements arguing against using aggregated approaches that included dummy variables to represent preference programs, stating that this approach "cannot catch the variability of margins across countries and products, and it is likely to lead to an overestimation of the impact of the preferential scheme and cannot provide an accurate assessment of policies that (by definition) often discriminate among products."[536]

In their 2008 paper, Tadesse and Fayissa conducted both aggregated and disaggregated (at the HS 2-digit level) analyses of trade data from 1991–2006 using a Tobit[537] specification of the gravity model. They highlighted the results of the disaggregated model because of its ability to capture product heterogeneities. They found that AGOA was responsible for statistically significant increases in exports to the United States in 19 of 99 product categories (including vegetables, fruits and nuts, coffee/tea/spices, beverages, plastics, fabrics, apparel, and tin). However, they also found that AGOA had no effect on export levels of the majority of product categories (including oilseeds, cocoa, ores, rubber, ceramics, and vehicles) and was even associated with reduced export flows in some cases.[538]

Using a slightly different approach, Frazer and Van Biesebroeck came to similar conclusions. These authors used a triple difference-in-differences model[539] disaggregated to the HS 6-digit level on trade data from 1998 to 2006, and assigned all products to one of five categories: apparel, agricultural, mineral, petroleum, and manufacturing. They found that AGOA did cause increased exports of agricultural goods, manufactures, and apparel products, but not of petroleum and mineral products.[540] The authors also tested whether the increased post-AGOA export flows to the United States were simply the result of trade diverted from Europe. They found no evidence that increased exports to the United States resulted in lower exports to Europe, and in fact noted that AGOA was associated with increased exports of manufactures to Europe—likely the result of spillover effects.[541]

Like Tadesse and Fayissa, Seyoum analyzed the effects of AGOA at both aggregate and disaggregated levels. Although Seyoum found no evidence of increased overall exports due to AGOA, the author also analyzed the effects of AGOA on the three sectors with the largest exports under AGOA—energy, textiles and apparel, and minerals—using a variation of the gravity model on data from 1997–2004. Seyoum's results suggested that AGOA had a positive and significant impact only on exports of textiles and apparel; effects on energy and minerals were not significant.[542] The author provided several explanations for this result. First, most beneficiary countries already enjoyed substantial preferences due to GSP, so AGOA may not have significantly changed their market access. Second, many products that were not already duty-free prior to AGOA had very low MFN tariff rates (particularly in energy products), so the preferences under AGOA did little to stimulate increased exports. Lastly, with only four years of trade data since the program's implementation available at the time of the study, it may have been too early to determine whether beneficiary countries could successfully take advantage of the program.[543]

Cooke analyzed the effects of AGOA on trade from 1996–2009, using different levels of product aggregation, but for only a limited number of product categories (restricted to HS chapters 1, 2, 25, 26, and 50–63). The author used a triple differences-in-differences type approach that included preferential tariff margins to compare the ratio of U.S. imports from beneficiary countries to the rest of the world's imports from beneficiary countries. The author concluded that AGOA led to a statistically significant increase in exports of both apparel and non-apparel products in the categories included in the regressions—all other things being equal, AGOA raised beneficiary country exports of these products to the United States by 38.3–57.8 percent.[544] However, the volume effects were generally small, and greater for apparel products than for non-apparel products.[545]

Although Nouve's 2005 analysis was conducted using aggregated data, the author pointed out that given his results and the theoretical underpinnings of the gravity model, AGOA was more likely to raise exports of certain kinds of goods. He found that for highly substitutable products (such as commodities), AGOA would have no effect or even a negative effect on exports from beneficiary countries to the United States.[546] Nouve suggested that for this reason, one way for countries to benefit from the program would be to make their exports more distinctive in the U.S. market.[547]

Effects of AGOA Increase with Time

Another dimension of analysis of AGOA is its effect over time. Although many of the studies focused on the average effects of AGOA on beneficiary country exports, several of the studies also found evidence that the trade-increasing effects of AGOA grew over time. Tadesse and Fayissa's analysis found that since AGOA's implementation, the previous year's export levels were found to be highly significant determinants of exports of various product groups in the following year, suggesting that experience gained in exporting a particular product tends to expand future exports.[548] Each additional year exporting under AGOA resulted in a 2.5 percent increase in exports of essential oils and resinoids, a 1.6 percent increase in exports of coffee/tea/spices, a 4.5 percent increase in plastics exports, and a 4.9 percent increase in wood and wood article exports, just to name a few.[549] Frazer and Van Biesebroeck found even larger time effects in their estimations. They estimated that apparel effects grew from a 22 percent increase in 2002 to a 44 percent increase by 2006.[550] While the effects were not as large for non-apparel products, their growth rates also increased over time, from just a 6 percent increase in exports due to AGOA in 2001 to a 24 percent increase by 2006.[551]

Sector-Specific Findings

Although the previous section mentioned how the implementation of AGOA affected export flows of various disaggregated products, the following section explores sector-specific findings in greater detail.

Apparel

Because the greatest trade responses were seen in apparel, it follows that much of the literature has specific findings with respect to this sector. Frazer and Van Biesebroeck found that AGOA had a substantial impact on exports of apparel. Their model estimated that AGOA raised beneficiary country exports of apparel to the United States by a substantial 42 percent.[552] The authors also determined what portion of the growth in apparel was due to AGOA by multiplying this effect by pre-AGOA export levels, concluding that AGOA was responsible for 35 percent of the total growth in apparel exports.[553] However, they noted that these effects varied widely by country. The effect of AGOA on apparel exports was only positive and significant for 14 beneficiary countries; for the remainder, AGOA was either not significant or was even negative and significant in two cases.[554] Moreover, even among the countries where AGOA led to significantly increased exports of apparel products, the range of this increase varied substantially from a low of 9 percent to a high of 155 percent.[555] Overall, the authors concluded that while apparel exports increased substantially due to AGOA, these benefits were not widespread among beneficiary countries.

Several other authors, including Cooke, Tadesse and Fayissa, and Seyoum, supported the conclusions reached by Frazer and Van Biesebroeck. Although their investigations do not contain as much detail as Frazer and Van Biesebroeck, these authors all found that AGOA had a positive and significant effect on apparel exports.[556]

Rules of Origin

While some authors concluded that apparel exports were in fact stimulated by AGOA, several others stressed that these gains were primarily the result of AGOA's comparatively less restrictive rules of origin under its third-country fabric provision. Using panel data on beneficiary country apparel exports to Europe and the United States over 1996–2004, De Melo and Portugal-Perez estimated a model that disentangled beneficiary country apparel export responses caused by apparel tariff liberalization from those caused by rules of origin simplification under AGOA. Although the effects varied slightly depending upon the model's specification, under their preferred estimator,[557] the authors found that simplified rules of origin (single transformation) led to a 168 percent increase in apparel exports by the seven largest AGOA apparel exporters, while tariff removal alone caused only a 44 percent increase in exports.[558]

Though their findings did not come from an empirical model, Brenton and Hoppe concluded that simple data analysis leads to the conclusion that all growth in apparel exports under AGOA must have been due to the third-country fabric provision.[559] They pointed out that apparel exports from countries under the provision more than doubled from 2001 to 2005, while exports from countries not eligible for the provision actually declined over the same period.[560]

While all sources agreed that AGOA significantly raised apparel exports to the United States, not all authors concluded that this was an overall positive development. For example, Nouve's results suggested that the increase in beneficiary country apparel exports experienced under AGOA actually had a negative effect on total exports from the region. The author suggested that this result pointed to a reallocation of resources away from other export sectors toward textiles and apparel in order to sustain export gains in that sector, which may have had a positive or negative effect on the economy as a whole, depending upon the country.[561]

Agriculture

Frazer and Van Biesebroeck also contributed to the literature on AGOA's effect on beneficiary country agricultural exports to the United States. They estimated that AGOA raised beneficiary country exports of agricultural goods to the United States by 8 percent, and found that 15 percent of the total growth in exports of agricultural products since AGOA's implementation could be attributed to the act.[562] While these effects were smaller than in other sectors examined, the benefits were more widespread; nearly two-thirds of AGOA beneficiaries experienced significant positive increases in their agricultural exports as a result of AGOA.[563]

The only other post-implementation work that included specifics on the performance of agriculture comes from Nouve and Staatz, who estimated a gravity model (using an AGOA dummy variable) on trade in agricultural products using data from 1998–2002. They found that although the estimated effects were positive, they were not statistically significant.[564] The authors offered several possibilities for this finding, including the fact that with only two years of post-implementation data, impacts did not have sufficient time to materialize.[565]

Manufactures

Two studies provided a separate analysis of AGOA's effects on exports of manufactured goods (including chemicals). Frazer and Van Biesebroeck found that AGOA raised beneficiary country manufacturing exports to the United States by 15 percent, and estimated that 20 percent of the total growth in such exports (which rose more than 70 percent from AGOA's implementation through 2006) could be directly attributed to AGOA.[566] Moreover, the authors found that for 35 of the 41 countries analyzed, AGOA had a statistically significant, positive effect on manufactures exports.[567] Additionally, for these countries where the effect was positive, AGOA increased these exports by an average of 17 percent.[568]

Tadesse and Fayissa's results with respect to manufacturing exports were twofold. First, they estimated the effect of AGOA on total manufacturing exports, concluding that AGOA did result in a positive and statistically significant increase in exports of this category.[569] Subsequently, the authors conducted their analysis at the HS 2-digit level and found some specific manufactured products for which AGOA caused statistically significant increases in beneficiary country export flows to the United States, including pharmaceuticals, miscellaneous chemical products, and plastics.[570]

Role of AGOA in Diversifying Exports

Besides increasing the volume of trade between beneficiary countries and the United States, an additional goal of the AGOA program was to help diversify exports from the region. Export diversification—defined as the process of moving into exports of new goods, and sometimes referred to as trade initiation or creation—makes poorer countries less susceptible to external economic shocks by reducing their dependence on a limited number of products.[571] As a region, Africa still largely exports mostly primary products, including minerals, raw materials, and primary agricultural goods. A 2012 analysis from the U.N. Economic Commission for Africa found that over the period 1998–2009, Africa's exports were less diversified than those of any other region of the world.[572]

Given the importance of export diversification in a country's development process, it is not surprising that a sizable body of literature has examined AGOA's role in helping the region to diversify its exports. As with export expansion, the aggregate effects of AGOA on export diversification seem unimpressive, but mask significant diversification effects in certain countries and industries.

Aggregate beneficiary country export statistics do not initially appear to support the conclusion that AGOA has helped to diversify the region's exports. Páez et al. emphasized that 10 years after the Act's implementation, diversification of AGOA exports remained a challenge. They noted that through 2010, 90 percent of U.S. imports under AGOA were energy-related products.[573]

Within the other 10 percent of AGOA exports, however, the literature supports the conclusion that AGOA has had a statistically significant effect on the diversification of exports into new products. Frazer and Van Biesebroeck found that AGOA helped to diversify beneficiary country exports in various sectors. Moreover, they found that these trade diversification effects not only varied by product, but also that the probability of exporting a new product increased over time. For apparel products, the probability of exporting a new product rose from 1.8 percent in 2002 to 3.0 percent in 2006.[574] For non-apparel goods, AGOA increased the probability of exporting a new product from 0.5 percent in 2001 to 1.9 percent in 2006.[575] When the non- apparel diversification effects were broken down into more specific sectors, the authors found that AGOA increased the probability of exporting a new agricultural product by more than one-half and raised the probability of exporting a new manufactured product by two-thirds.[576] Given these effects, the authors concluded, "While AGOA countries export notably fewer products than most other countries, this gap decreased tremendously following the Act. This large increase in the probability of exporting is consistent with the AGOA effect growing over time."[577]

Tadesse and Fayissa reported these effects on a more disaggregated level, disentangling AGOA's trade creation effects (these authors' term for diversification) from its trade intensification effects (increase in existing exports) by identifying the HS 2-digit product categories that went from no export flows before AGOA implementation to positive export flows afterward, with one observation for each country-product pair per year. The analysis found that AGOA had significant trade initiation effects across 24 of 99 different product categories (including vegetables, milling products, miscellaneous chemical products, plastics, cotton, knitted fabrics, knit apparel, and non-knit apparel).[578] However, the majority of these newly created exports occurred in products that represented a small proportion of a country's total exports. Interestingly, AGOA resulted in both trade initiation and trade intensification in just 13 of 99 categories.[579] Overall, their results led the authors to conclude that the trade initiation effect of AGOA was much greater than its intensification effect.

One sector-specific analysis by de Melo and Portugal-Perez supported the export diversification findings of the two investigations outlined above. In their analysis of the apparel sector, they estimated the effect of AGOA (specifically, the third-country fabric provision) on the diversity of apparel exports to the United States, using a model specified at the HS 6-digit level. The authors estimated that AGOA's third-country fabric provision helped to increase the varieties of apparel exported by between 39 and 61 percent.[580] The authors stressed that this increase in export diversification was not due to tariff preferences granted under the program, but rather to a relaxing of the rules of origin for apparel products. They hypothesized that the reduced costs of complying with AGOA's simplified origin rules (as compared to the rules under GSP, for example) freed up firms' resources and allowed them to expand their export product lines, leading to the increased diversification.[581]

Raw data analysis by Brenton and Hoppe also reinforced the conclusions that AGOA had helped some countries diversify their exports, but mostly through increased apparel exports. They noted that exports of apparel have grown much faster than exports of other non-oil products, and that countries that had historically exported few apparel products (such as Botswana, Tanzania, and Uganda) had all increased their apparel exports.[582]

Survey-based evidence also supports the empirical analyses presented above. Karingi, Páez, and Degefa noted that 39 percent of private sector respondents in their survey reported diversification in their enterprise or sector due to AGOA.[583] But even with this evidence that AGOA was responsible for increased export diversification, it is not clear that this diversification was due to new firms entering the export market. Although firm-level transaction data were not available to answer this question, the 2012 Karingi, Páez, and Degefa survey found that the companies that were able to take advantage of the benefits of AGOA were in general larger firms that were already exporting.[584] This finding was indirectly supported by Brenton and Hoppe's 2006 work, where they noted that small firms have a more difficult time complying with rules of origin provisions, such as those in place under AGOA.[585]

Role of Other Unilateral Tariff Preference Programs in Increasing and Diversifying Exports

As noted in section 6 of this report, the United States is not the only country to grant unilateral tariff preferences like those available under AGOA and the U.S. GSP to developing African economies. In fact, 13 countries currently operate GSP programs similar to that of the United States, including Australia, Canada, the EU, and Japan. Various other unilateral preference regimes also exist outside of the GSP.[586] This section focuses on recent analyses of non-U.S. preference regimes, and their effects on expanding and diversifying exports. Studies evaluating EU trade preference programs make up the bulk of this section for two main reasons. First, the EU remains the primary export destination for sub-Saharan Africa's goods (due both to colonial ties and the region's relative proximity to the EU).[587] Second, beneficiary countries in sub- Saharan Africa have a long history of utilizing various trade preference programs for their exports to the EU, including GSP preferences, GSP preferences for LDCs (designated as "Everything But Arms" or EBA, since 2001), and ACP preferences under the now defunct Yaoundé, Lomé, and Cotonou agreements.

Role of Other Unilateral Tariff Preference Programs in Increasing Exports

As with the AGOA literature examined in the previous section, literature on the effectiveness of other preference programs in increasing trade can be divided into analyses that consider effects on total exports (mostly using policy dummy variables) and those that use more disaggregated approaches (typically involving preference margins). Another similarity of the "other programs" literature to the AGOA literature is that authors came to mixed conclusions about the effectiveness of such programs (i.e., some concluded that these programs increased trade, while others concluded that they did not). However, in contrast to the work discussed in the previous section, one study attempted to analyze the wide range of estimates on trade effects by conducting a meta-analysis on study results. We examine each of the three approaches (total trade, disaggregated, and meta-analysis) in turn.

Effects on Total Trade

Persson and Wilhelmsson's 2006 analysis covered perhaps the longest time period in analyzing how EU preferences affected developing-country export flows. The authors used EU import data from 1960–2002 to estimate a gravity model, augmenting it with a time trend and controlling for EU enlargement while also differentiating countries covered by overlapping programs. Because the data ended in 2002, the trade effect estimates from the regressions are for the GSP-LDC program, which was the precursor to EBA. Additionally, they estimated trade effects for ACP preferences under both the Lomé and Yaoundé agreements. Their results indicated that preferences for ACP-only (Lomé) countries raised exports by 30 percent, and preferences for countries benefiting from both ACP and GSP-LDC raised exports by 33 percent.[588] The GSP program alone was not found to have a significant effect on developing-country exports.[589]

In their 2009 analysis, Gradeva and Martínez-Zarzoso analyzed total trade data from 1995–2005 using a variety of estimators. Their results consistently found a negative and statistically significant relationship between a country participating in EBA and export performance, suggesting that participation in the program was actually associated with lower exports to the EU.[590] However, the estimations also found a positive and statistically significant relationship between the interaction of EBA preferences and the amount of official development assistance received in the previous year and exports in the current year, suggesting that trade preferences alone were not enough to spur increased exports, but when coupled with other development assistance did lead to export growth.[591] The authors concluded that aid and trade preferences were complements and should be used in tandem by developed countries in their global development strategies.[592]

Although Pishbahar and Huchet-Bourdon's 2008 study focused on the agricultural sector, the analysis was done on total agricultural trade and was not disaggregated at the product level. The authors used a gravity model to estimate how 11 different trade agreements (both bilateral and unilateral) had affected EU agricultural imports from beneficiary countries over the period 2000–2004. Although most agreements were found to increase total agricultural export flows, the authors found that both EU GSP and EBA were associated with reduced beneficiary country agricultural exports to the EU.[593] They offered several possible explanations for this result, including rules of origin and more administrative constraints under EBA than under the alternative Cotonou ACP preferences.[594]

Effects on Disaggregated Trade

Much of the more recent analyses eschew the total trade approaches described above because of their tendency to bias the overall estimation results. Using disaggregated data instead, these recent analyses focus more on trade effects by product and sector, with varying study periods, estimation strategies, and program coverage. These analyses conclude that the trade effects of EU trade preference programs vary significantly by sector or product.

Nilsson and Matsson conducted their analysis at a highly disaggregated level (HS 8-digit tariff line) and modeled preferences using product preference margins. They concluded that EU trade preferences played a positive role in increasing developing-country exports. In their 2009 analysis of data from 2003–07, the authors used a gravity model[595] to investigate the impact of the preferential margin on EU preferential imports, on both global and regional levels. Not only were EU preferences found to increase preferential imports on average, but effects were also positive and significant for all developing-country partner groups, with the exception of countries that had a bilateral FTA with the EU.[596] Using regression estimates, the authors then calculated the contribution of trade preferences toward explaining total EU imports from the various developing-country regions. For ACP LDC countries, the authors found that preferences alone explained 19 percent of total imports, while for ACP non-LDCs, preferences explained 10 percent of EU imports from the region.[597]

Cirera, Foliano, and Gasiorek used an even more disaggregated dataset in their analysis, and concluded that EU preferences have only a small impact on trade. Their 2011 analysis used import data from 2002–08 disaggregated at the Combined Nomenclature (CN)[598] 10-digit level, and listed the actual regime of entry of a product, in contrast to other analyses, which assume the entry regime is based on which offers the most beneficial tariff. The authors estimated trade effects using various measures of preferences, and the results varied depending upon the choice of preference margin. However, their results suggested that the now-defunct ACP preferences under Cotonou were more effective at raising exports than other regimes, and that the effectiveness of EBA depended upon how the margin was defined.[599] The authors concluded that while EU trade preferences had a positive but small impact on beneficiary country exports, GSP and EBA appeared less effective at raising exports than ACP preferences or FTAs.[600] The authors offered several potential explanations for this result, including more stringent rules of origin under GSP[601] and the possibility that since FTAs are negotiated bilaterally, preferences are more likely to reflect a country's export basket.[602]

In their 2013 analysis, Cipollina, Laborde, and Salvatici estimated a gravity model[603] with 2004 cross-sectional trade data disaggregated at the HS 8-digit level. They did not differentiate import regimes, but assumed that imports from all countries entered under the lowest available rate (which would cover EBA, GSP, and ACP preferences). The authors computed a relative preference margin as a ratio of the tariff applied to beneficiary countries versus a weighted average of the tariffs applied to their competitors. They computed this weighted average as a constant elasticity of substitution (CES) index—not the MFN rate—in order to account for beneficiary countries' comparative advantage with respect to their competitors.[604] Their results suggested that EU trade preferences in general (including EBA, GSP, ACP, and bilateral agreements) have different impacts across sectors, and these impacts are not necessarily related to the size of the preference margin.[605] Sectors where EU preferences resulted in large trade responses included ceramics and glassware, textiles,[606] and footwear.[607]

Additionally, the authors noted that in many cases, preferences for agricultural products did not have a significant impact, likely due to either preference scheme compliance costs or other preference regime restrictions, such as rules of origin requirements.[608] Overall, the authors noted that EU trade preferences generated additional beneficiary country exports representing about 3 percent of total EU imports, but that these increased imports from beneficiaries also displaced imports from non-beneficiaries.[609] Earlier work from these authors came to similar conclusions.[610]

Various other studies also used a disaggregated analysis, but focused their investigations on a particular sector or set of products. In their 2011 analysis using data from 1995–2006, Aiello and Cardamone focused on the effects of the EU's EBA program with respect to five agricultural goods.[611] The authors used a gravity model which included the margin of preference for each specific product to represent the effect of the preference program, and differentiated LDC preferences pre- and post-2001 in order to isolate the effect of EBA.[612] The analysis found mixed results with respect to how EBA had affected the exports of these products from ACP countries. EBA did not have a statistically significant effect on exports of coffee or molluscs, and it was associated with reduced exports in the case of cloves, but it was found to have a positive and statistically significant effect on exports of vanilla beans and crustaceans.[613] Although the authors did not draw any overarching conclusions on the overall effectiveness of EBA from these product case studies, they emphasized that their approach shows that EBA preferences have been effective in increasing exports of some products but not others. They concluded that studies like theirs may be useful in diagnosing why this is the case (they suggest nontariff barriers and rules of origin as possibilities).[614]

Cardamone also followed this case study approach in a gravity model setting, but using monthly import data on various fresh fruits over 2001–04. In line with the conclusions of Aiello and Cardamone, the author found that EU preference programs benefited some products but not others. For example, EU GSP was found to have a positive and significant effect on EU imports of apples and grapes, but a negative effect on EU pear and mandarin imports.[615] The author concluded that the impact of preferential margins on trade flows differs depending upon the commodity, which could be due to nontariff barriers or quality standards demanded by the importer.[616]

Aiello and Demaria conducted a broader sectoral analysis in their 2010 paper, investigating the effects of various EU preference programs on beneficiary country agricultural exports over the period 2001–04. The authors used specific program preference margins in a gravity analysis of the effects of various EU trade preference programs (including GSP, EBA, and ACP), using a variety of different estimators.[617] Their results suggested that GSP and EBA had a positive and significant effect on total beneficiary country agricultural exports, while the effects of the other programs varied across estimators.[618] When the authors examined trade effects in different agricultural sectors, their results suggested that GSP was correlated with a significant rise in exports of live trees, sugar, fruits, tropical fruits, and residues from the food industry, while EBA only had a positive significant effect on beneficiary country exports of lacs-gums.[619]

Although the bulk of the non-U.S. preference program literature concentrates on the effectiveness of EU preference programs, one recent paper analyzed the effectiveness of China's new unilateral preference program (begun in 2005, extended in 2008) on SSA exports to China. In their 2013 analysis, Co and Dimova used the triple difference-in-differences estimation technique of Frazer and Van Biesebroeck to analyze trade flows from 2002–10 at the HS 6-digit level. Their results indicated that while trade effects of Chinese preferences were heterogeneous by country and product group, they were only positive and significant for "other primary products," a category that includes beverages, tobacco, animal and vegetable oils and fats, inedible crude materials, and mineral fuels.[620] The authors concluded that outside of this product category, Chinese trade preferences have not contributed to increased imports from SSA.

Meta-Analysis Approach

In contrast to the studies examined above, Cipollina and Pietrovito's 2011 analysis combined all the estimates they could collect from the literature regarding the effect of EU trade preference programs on developing-country exports into one meta-analysis. Their goal was to determine why different studies purporting to investigate the same phenomenon could yield such widely varying results. They constructed a Meta-Regression Analysis (MRA) model that accounted for differences in 36 studies on EU preferential trade regimes and estimated the average preference program effect on trade, separated into two groups of studies: those that used a dummy variable to symbolize trade preference and those that used the preference margin instead.

Their analysis suggested that EU preferential trade agreements do, on average, positively impact trade flows, but that those impacts varied according to an author's chosen specification. On average, papers that used dummy variables to indicate the presence of preferences predicted that preferences increased trade by 2 percent in a fixed-effects[621] setting and by 22 percent in a random-effects setting.[622] Papers using preference margins estimated that a 10 percent increase in preference margin was associated with increased exports of 0.6 percent and 0.7 percent, respectively, for the fixed- and random-effects specifications.[623]

However, the authors cautioned against comparing estimates from the two analyses, stressing that one represented aggregate effects while the other was an elasticity based on tariff preference margins. Singling out the EBA program, the meta-analysis found that a 10 percent increase in the preference margin under this program increased trade by 2 percent, but analyses using dummy variables indicated that EBA decreased trade by 28 percent.[624] Taking into account all of the results of the meta-analysis, the authors concluded that when analyzing the effect of a particular preferential trade agreement (such as EBA), aggregating the data and using a dummy variable to simulate the presence of preferences tended to bias the results and underestimate the impact of the agreement in question.[625]

Role of Other Unilateral Tariff Preference Programs in Diversifying Exports

Various authors have also analyzed the role of EU trade programs in helping to diversify developing-country exports. In his 2003 analysis, Brenton expressed skepticism that EU trade preference programs were an effective tool in helping beneficiary countries diversify their export basket, given that for many developing countries, trade preferences resulted in preference margins of less than 1 percent.[626] The author argued that strict rules of origin in EU preference programs likely acted as a constraint to LDC export diversification,[627] since many countries eligible for preferences did not claim them.[628]

Other authors found more specific results using econometric estimation. Using Tobit and probit [629] estimation on HTS 6-digit trade data from 1994–2005, Gamberoni concluded that the extent to which an EU unilateral trade preference program led to export diversification was dependent upon both the program and the sector analyzed.[630] The author's results suggested that while EU GSP increased the number of products exported to the EU by beneficiary countries, GSP-LDC/EBA[631] had no statistically significant effect on the number of products exported, and ACP actually led to greater export concentration (i.e., fewer products exported) over time.[632] The author noted that this result for ACP preferences "supports the hypothesis that preferences could lock countries into existing structural capacities, rather than encourage export diversification."[633] However, when the author analyzed trade-creating effects for agriculture and textiles separately from total exports, ACP preferences were shown to increase the probability of exporting a new agricultural product by 7 percent; GSP was estimated to have similar magnitudes of probability for trade creation, while GSP-LDC showed no statistically significant diversification effect.[634] With respect to textiles, GSP was estimated to increase the probability of exporting a new product by 2 percent, while GSP-LDC and ACP preferences showed no statistically significant trade diversification effect.[635] The author noted that this result for GSP-LDC with respect to textiles in particular supported the idea that rules of origin under this regime at the time of the analysis[636] prevented countries from taking advantage of available preferences.[637]

Although their 2011 analysis did not single out any particular EU preference program, Cipollina and Salvatici concluded that EU trade preferences in general have an ambiguous impact on developing countries' export diversification. The authors analyzed trade data for 2004 at the HS 6-digit level using relative preference margins in a gravity model setting.[638] Although their model estimated that preferences on average have a positive and significant impact on export diversification, the impacts varied greatly by sector. Out of 16 sectors analyzed, preferences were found to have positive, significant impacts only on the number of products traded in 6 categories: animals and animal products, vegetable products, fats and oils, prepared foodstuffs, plastics, and vehicles.[639] For 7 of the sectors analyzed, EU trade preferences were found to actually result in significantly greater export concentration.[640] Based on these results, the authors concluded that EU preferences would likely lead to developing-country export diversification in agricultural goods, but discourage diversification of industrial good exports.[641]

In their 2013 work, Persson and Wilhemsson came to the overall conclusion that the extent of export diversification under unilateral trade preferences varies by preference program. However, using a long time series of data (1962–2007), the authors arrive at slightly different conclusions about which programs were more effective at increasing the number of products exported. Using a gravity model[642] to analyze various measures of diversification, the authors found that all GSP program variations (including GSP and GSP-LDC) were associated with statistically significant increases in the number of products exported, while ACP preferences at first led to an increase in the number of products exported, but over time led to greater export concentration.[643] At the same time, using various export diversification indices, the authors also demonstrated that while GSP programs led to countries exporting a greater number of products, most programs did not result in statistically significant differences in export earnings over time.[644] In other words, although beneficiaries were exporting more products, the value of exports remained concentrated in the same products over time.

Comparative Effectiveness of AGOA and Other Unilateral Preference Programs in Increasing and Diversifying Exports

As noted in the previous two sections, the literature regarding the effectiveness of many types of unilateral trade preferences (AGOA and otherwise) present a range of different conclusions based upon the study methodology, time period, and, in some cases, the sector under investigation. For this reason, it is difficult to make "apples-to-apples" comparisons of the aforementioned studies in order to determine in what ways one particular preference regime was more or less successful than a similar regime offered by a different country. In order to investigate comparative successes, this section examines studies that specifically analyze multiple preference regimes in a comparative setting, with respect to both trade intensification and trade diversification effects.

Intensification

Effects on Total Trade

Cipollina, Laborde, and Salvatici specifically compared the effects of U.S. and EU trade preferences in a gravity setting. Using cross-sectional data from 2004 in a gravity model[645] where an explicit measure for preference margin is calculated on a country-pair basis at the HS 8-digit level, the authors estimated how both U.S. and EU preferential trade policies affected beneficiary country export flows, with respect to both intensification and diversification.[646] While the trade intensification effects varied by product sectors, the results suggested that in most cases, EU and U.S. trade preferences both positively impacted trade flows.[647] However, the effect of preferences tended to be larger for products with greater price competition (i.e., products with higher price elasticities) rather than greater quality competition.[648] Overall, the authors concluded that in most cases, EU preferences were more effective at increasing trade than were U.S. preferences.[649] The authors noted that this finding was likely due to the fact that EU imports were more responsive to price changes than were U.S. imports, particularly when it came to imports of live animals and animal products, animal or vegetable fats and oils, and ceramics and glassware.[650]

A 2013 analysis from the European Commission Director General for Trade office by Davies and Nilsson came to a similar conclusion regarding the trade intensification effects of the respective EU and U.S. trade preference regimes. The authors estimated a gravity model on low-income and middle-income country export data from 2007–10, using policy dummies to examine total beneficiary country export flows and export flows with mineral fuels excluded. The authors found no statistically significant relationship between EU or U.S. trade policy and total exports of AGOA beneficiary countries.[651] However, when trade flows excluding mineral fuels were examined, the authors estimated that for AGOA beneficiary countries, EU trade policy led to two times more non-mineral fuel exports than U.S. policy.[652] Earlier work by Nilsson based on trade flows from 2001–03 also concluded that EU policy had been more successful in generating developing-country exports than U.S. policy. His 2005 gravity model analysis concluded that EU policy generated 35 percent more developing-country exports over that period, and that the effects were even higher for low-income countries.[653] Additionally, the analysis showed that both distance and colonial ties to an EU member state also had significant, statistically positive effects on export flows—results which help explain the stronger trade relationship between the EU and SSA as compared to the U.S. trading relationship with the region.[654]

Sector-Specific Findings

Although the foregoing analyses concluded that EU policy has been better at increasing developing-country trade flows, various other authors came to different conclusions when examining the trade effects of different sectors. For instance, Collier and Venables argued that for trade preference programs to be effective at raising manufacturing exports, they needed to be designed to be consistent with international trade in fragmented tasks. The authors emphasized that restrictive rules of origin prevent countries from exploiting their comparative advantage in fragmented tasks.[655] In order to illustrate the trade-creating effects of more flexible rules of origin, they compared U.S. and EU apparel imports from SSA over the period 1991–2005 using both triple difference-in-differences and quadruple difference-in-differences[656] approaches. The triple difference-in-differences approach results suggested that the AGOA apparel provision created about seven times more apparel exports to the United States relative to the EU, and the quadruple difference-in-differences estimates confirmed the finding that AGOA apparel treatment had a large, statistically significant impact on apparel exports.[657] The authors concluded that trade policy needs to take into account rules of origin that do not discourage specialization, and that AGOA's special apparel provision has demonstrated its effectiveness at increasing trade in apparel products vis-à-vis EU trade policy through 2005.[658] It is worth noting here that the EU has since relaxed its apparel rules of origin for LDCs, requiring only single transformation to confer origin—similar to AGOA.[659]

In their 2013 analysis, de Melo and Portugal-Perez also focused on how differences in rules of origin between U.S. AGOA and EU EBA affected trade flows. The authors modeled the relationship between apparel exports from AGOA beneficiary countries at the HS 4-digit level (where rules of origin are specified) and preferential access under the various rules of origin contained within both the EBA and AGOA agreements over the period 1996–2004. Controlling for other factors and recognizing that preference margins under the two regimes were similar, the authors found that the single transformation rule under AGOA was associated with a 168 percent increase in apparel exports from the seven largest AGOA apparel exporters.[660] In other words, the authors found that a U.S. rules of origin change under AGOA had caused increased beneficiary country exports, but the lack of a similar simplification in EU rules under EBA during that time period meant that the EU program produced no corresponding export increase.[661]

The 2008 analysis of Di Rubbo and Canali focused on the comparative effect of trade preferences on developing-country agricultural exports. The authors used a gravity model to investigate the comparative effect of EU trade policy versus U.S. trade policy on such exports from 1996–2005, subdividing these effects by country income level and time period (with a structural break between 2000 and 2001 to account for various trade reforms). The model's results suggested that the EU's trade policies have created more developing-country agricultural exports than have U.S. policies, but this effect varied substantially by country income group; EU policies seemed to be most effective at increasing exports from upper-middle income countries, followed by low-income countries, then lower-middle income countries.[662] Specifically, the authors calculated that EU trade policy led to 69 percent more agricultural exports from developing countries over 1996–2000, and 73 percent more agricultural exports over 2001–05.[663] These effects were even higher for the low-income country group to which most nations in SSA belong: EU policy led to 76 percent greater agricultural exports from low- income countries than did U.S. policy over 1996–2000, and to 81 percent greater agricultural exports than did U.S. policy over 2001–05—the period when AGOA came into effect.[664]

The findings of Bureau, Chakir, and Gallezot provide some possible explanations as to why EU policy was more effective in increasing developing-country agricultural exports. The authors focused solely on comparing the way developing countries utilized U.S. and EU trade preferences in the agricultural sector. The authors pointed out that developing countries have similarly high preference utilization rates for both U.S. and EU programs, but that preference schemes overlap such that developing countries can export to the EU and United States under various regimes. To determine why a certain regime was chosen, the authors estimated a probit model that accounted for the preferential tariff of a regime, the degree of processing of the product, and the size of the export flow. The results of this regression offered some insights into why EU preferences were found to be more effective at raising agricultural exports than U.S. preferences. First, the authors noted that for the EU on average, agricultural imports with higher degrees of processing were more likely to utilize preferences, while U.S. agricultural imports with a higher degree of processing were more likely to enter the United States under MFN treatment, suggesting that complying with U.S. rules of origin on processed agricultural products was either difficult or cost more than the gains from utilizing available preferences.[665] Second, the authors noted that beneficiary country exports under AGOA were in very small volumes, so that even though utilization was high, the authors questioned whether the preferences alone were successful in creating trade.[666]

Diversification

While various studies compared the effectiveness of EU and U.S preferences programs on trade intensification, fewer comparisons exist that explore the issue of how the programs affect SSA trade diversification. Nicita and Rollo gave one reason why this may be the case, stating that "one important feature of export growth in sub-Saharan Africa is that export diversification has been largely absent.... In 2011, more than three-quarters of export growth in sub-Saharan Africa was in products and destinations that were already exported in 2001."[667] In spite of this low trade diversification for the region over the period, one analysis was identified that compared EU and U.S. trade policy with respect to diversification, and one analysis specifically compared the efficacy of EBA and AGOA in diversifying SSA textile exports.

Without reporting results specific to each program, Cipollina, Laborde, and Salvatici concluded that U.S. trade preference programs are more successful than European ones at helping to diversify exports of trading partners. Using data from 2004, the authors estimated a highly disaggregated model, with trade in products defined at the HS 8-digit level and including all U.S. and EU preference programs. The authors found that U.S. preferences significantly increased the probability of exporting in every sector except for mineral products.[668] In contrast, although EU trade preferences significantly increased the probability of exports in most categories, they also decreased the probability of exports of hides and skins, wood, and footwear.[669] Additionally, they estimated that U.S. trade preferences increased the probability of a positive export flow in any given product by between 7 and 28 percent, while EU probabilities were found to be slightly smaller at between 3 and 23 percent.[670]

The rules of origin-centric analysis from de Melo and Portugal-Perez quantified the comparative effectiveness of AGOA and EBA at increasing the number of apparel products exported by beneficiary countries through 2004. Using a negative binomial regression model and product data at the HS 6-digit level, the authors found that the less-restrictive rules under AGOA during the time period in question[671] were associated with an increase in the number of products exported of between 39 and 61 percent.[672] While the authors noted that export diversification also took place with respect to products shipped to the EU, the magnitude of the diversification was less than for the U.S. market.[673]

Although their work does not uniquely deal with the United States and the EU, Nicita and Rollo's 2013 analysis offer some insights as to why EU programs seem to be better at increasing trade flows from SSA, while U.S. programs are more effective at diversifying their trade. The authors noted that export diversification requires not only expansion into new products, but also the survival of pre-existing export flows. For this reason, they investigated both the probability of new export flows and the probability of survival of existing flows using probit estimation. Their analysis specified data at the HS 6-digit level at two points in time, separating exports into primary, intermediate, and consumer goods, and taking into account both relative and direct market access.[674] The authors found that direct market access changes (such as reduced tariffs under AGOA) are important only for new export flows—in other words, reduced tariffs lead to greater export diversification.[675] Since EBA did not offer further reduced tariffs (indeed, it was a continuation of the EU's GSP-LDC program), Nicita and Rollo's work would suggest that few new export flows would manifest under the EBA program. However, relative market access (tariff advantages over competitor countries) matters for both new export flows and the survival of existing flows, suggesting that for sub-

Saharan Africa, keeping its tariff advantages in the U.S. market relative to other developing countries is now paramount to sustained exports.[676]

Recommendations on How to Improve AGOA

Given the literature's findings on AGOA's effectiveness and authors' hypotheses as to why they found the results they did, it is unsurprising that many authors offered recommendations on how the program could be improved. The empirical literature focuses on the factors that authors perceived as the greatest constraints to increased trade, given the results of their estimations. Seyoum provided some of the most comprehensive recommendations, based on both the author's own results and suggestions from other sources. The author made three major recommendations: improving supply capacity (including seeking out foreign direct investment (FDI) and capacity-building assistance); making AGOA permanent and binding; and improving the business climate of beneficiary countries (including improved rule of law and protection of intellectual property rights).[677] Additionally, the author advocated expanding the list of eligible products, ending country eligibility requirements to aid beneficiary countries in formulating long-term export strategies, and increasing trade assistance to improve both institutional and trade capacity.[678] Brenton and Ikezuki made similar broad-based recommendations, including recommending that AGOA should be made permanent or at least have a longer horizon, that all countries should be made eligible for clothing preferences with liberal rules of origin, that all products should be made duty-free/quota-free, and that beneficiary countries should address domestic constraints on trade and investment.[679]

Other authors were more focused in their recommendations, building them on particular estimation results. Tadesse and Fayissa focused on their result of increasing trade gains over time due to AGOA, advocating that policymakers should concentrate on ways to build on the trade-initiation momentum of the agreement.[680] They suggested that investments in networked communication, efficient transportation hubs, and training and capacity building would all be means to arrive at that result.[681] In contrast, Frazer and Van Biesebroeck advocated for wider product inclusion under AGOA. In formulating their recommendation, they combined two results—that AGOA helped to increase trade in various products and that at the time of the study, imports of non-oil products not included under AGOA were four times larger than imports of non-oil products that were covered by AGOA—to suggest that further liberalization on the part of the United States could greatly impact beneficiary countries' GDP.[682] Concluding his 2005 study, Nouve suggested that trade gains under AGOA would be substantially greater if beneficiary countries made an effort to maintain and promote the distinctiveness of their products, based on his finding that less substitutable goods benefit more under AGOA.[683]

Condon and Stern's 2011 review of AGOA-related literature summarized the findings of a wide variety of works and concluded the following: (1) AGOA should be extended to cover all products, including full duty-free, quota-free access for sensitive agricultural goods; (2) AGOA preferences should be made permanent to allow firms to plan for the future and make investments accordingly; and (3) AGOA would be more effective with less restrictive rules of origin, which would allow firms more flexibility in sourcing inputs in order to exploit their comparative advantage in low-cost labor.[684] Brenton and Hoppe also strongly emphasized

Condon and Stern's third finding, noting that rules of origin are preventing LDCs from becoming integrated into global production networks.[685]

Results from Mevel et al.'s joint Brookings-U.N. Economic Commission for Africa (UNECA) CGE modeling exercises also pointed to a number of recommendations for policymakers. The authors recommended that the program be extended beyond 2015 because they found that ending it would result in export losses and reduced employment in beneficiary countries.[686] They also recommended that the program be extended to grant full duty-free/quota-free access for eligible countries, given that their simulations suggested that such access would have little adverse impact on U.S. producers.[687] Aside from recommendations directed at the United States, the authors also stressed the importance of various reforms by the beneficiary countries themselves, including reducing tariffs on imports of intermediate goods in order to better take advantage of preferences granted by AGOA, and pursuing greater economic integration on the African continent in order to increase the region's competitiveness. The latter would need significant investments in trade facilitation to be successful, and the authors suggested that the U.S. should consider including trade facilitation and trade assistance in any new incarnations of the program.[688]

In their 2010 assessment looking back at AGOA's first decade of implementation, Páez et al., of UNECA, made various recommendations, including helping beneficiary countries comply with sanitary and phytosanitary (SPS) rules, reducing supply-side constraints (such as poor infrastructure), and a longer time horizon for the agreement in order to reduce firm uncertainty.[689] However, many of the authors' comments focused on easing the regulatory burden for African firms wishing to comply with AGOA. The authors noted that some sources estimate that benefits accrued by African countries under AGOA would have been five times higher if rules of origin were less stringent.[690] Additionally, the authors stressed that "in this myriad of preferences offered, AGOA appears to be one of the more stringent schemes, burdening beneficiaries with compliance requirements and unpredictable market access opportunities for their products."[691]

Survey-based opinions from Karingi, Páez, and Degefa were in a similar vein, with three-quarters of respondents recommending increased technical assistance and capacity building on standards and SPS measures.[692] In fact, respondents reported that complying with U.S. SPS regulations was one of the principal regulatory impediments preventing firms from accessing the benefits of the program.[693] Other recommendations included extending benefits beyond the 2015 expiration date, relaxing social and political criteria for countries emerging from conflict, providing greater support for small firms so that they can access the program's benefits, expanding the list of eligible products, and promoting U.S. investment in Africa.[694]

A summary of the literature on the effectiveness of AGOA and other similar unilateral tariff preference programs in this section is presented in table 7.2.

Table 7.2. Summary of the literature on the effectiveness of AGOA and other similar unilateral tariff preference programs

Author	Title	Years	Model	Findings	Impact
Utilization of Preferences					
Keck and Lendle 2012	"New evidence on preference utilization"	2008	Raw data analysis	AGOA's preference utilization rate was estimated at 92 percent. Utilization rates of similar programs directed toward LDCs was also estimated to be high. EU programs for LDCs or EU programs designated for ACPs all had estimated utilization rates of 86 percent or higher.	
Brenton and Ikezuki 2004	"The initial and potential impact of preferential access to the U.S. market under the African Growth and Opportunity Act"	2002	Raw data analysis	Average AGOA utilization rates were over 80 percent, but one-third of countries had utilization rates below 20 percent while 37 percent of countries had utilization rates greater than 80 percent.	
Brenton and Hoppe 2006	"The African Growth and Opportunity Act, exports, and development in Sub-Saharan Africa"	2005	Raw data analysis	AGOA utilization was estimated at 95 percent, but utilization rates are highly variable by country. Eleven of 37 beneficiaries were estimated to have utilization rates of at least 98 percent, but five countries did not utilize preferences at all.	
Dean and Wainio 2006	"Quantifying the value of U.S. tariff preferences for developing countries"	2003	Raw data analysis	All non-LDBDCs except three had estimated utilization rates of at least 75 percent for non-agricultural products. For LDBDCs, average the average utilization rate for non-agricultural products was above 50 percent. For agricultural exports, 14 countries were estimated to have utilization rates above 90 percent, but two did not use preferences at all.	
Bureau et al. 2007	"The utilization of trade preferences for developing countries in the agri-food sector"	2002	Raw data analysis	AGOA preference utilization rates for agricultural goods were estimated at 85 percent in 2002. SSA utilization of EU preferences on agricultural goods in the same year was estimated at 95–96 percent.	

Author	Title	Years	Model	Findings	Impact
Candau and Jean 2009	"What are EU trade preferences worth for Sub-Saharan Africa and other developing countries?"	2001	Raw data analysis	EU preference program utilization is high. In 2001, utilization rates for LDCs in SSA were estimated at 92 percent, while utilization rates for non-LDCs in SSA were estimated at 94 percent.	
Cooke 2011	"The impact of trade preferences on exports of developing countries: the case of the AGOA and CBI preferences of the USA"	1996–2009	Triple difference-in-differences type regression, HS-6 level for selected HS chapters	Overall, AGOA raised beneficiary country exports of selected products to the United States by 38.3-57.8 percent. AGOA led to statistically significant increases in exports of both apparel and non-apparel product categories, but the effects were small and greater for apparel than for non-apparel.	

Effects of AGOA

Author	Title	Years	Model	Findings	Impact
Nouve 2005	"Estimating the effects of AGOA on African exports using a dynamic panel analysis"	1996–2004	Dynamic panel gravity model using Difference and System GMM estimators	AGOA had a significant and positive effect on beneficiary country exports to the United States. Every dollar increase in exports under AGOA led to spillover effects of an additional $0.16 to $0.20 in exports. Trade flows of highly substitutable products would either not be affected by AGOA or be affected negatively. Less substitutable products would likely experience positive effects from AGOA. Further, exports of capital-intensive industries have benefitted more from AGOA than have exports of labor-intensive industries.	Positive
Lederman and Ozden 2004	"U.S. trade preferences: all are not created equal"	1997, 2001	Gravity model, disaggregated at the HS-2 level, using product program utilization rate as AGOA instrument	Participation in AGOA led to a five percent increase in exports for the average beneficiary country	Positive

Table 7.2. (Continued)

Author	Title	Years	Model	Findings	Impact
Brenton and Hoppe 2006	"The African Growth and Opportunity Act, exports, and development in Sub-Saharan Africa"	2005	Raw data analysis	Effects from AGOA had to be small, since most trade growth was in crude oil, which would have been shipped even in the absence of AGOA. All growth in apparel exports must have been due to the third country fabric provision, as exports from countries not eligible actually declined over the period examined.	Positive, but small
Zappile 2011	"Nonreciprocal trade agreements and trade: does the African Growth and Opportunity Act (AGOA) increase trade?"	1995–2005	Gravity model, aggregated trade data and AGOA dummy	AGOA had no statistically significant effect on aggregate beneficiary country nonoil exports.	No effect
Seyoum 2007	"Export performance of developing countries under the African Growth and Opportunity Act: experience from U.S. trade with Sub-Saharan Africa"	1997–2004	ARIMA variation of the gravity model, using AGOA dummy on aggregated trade data; separate models for textiles and apparel, energy, and minerals	AGOA had no effect at the aggregate level, but did have a positive and significant effect on exports of textiles and apparel. Effects on both energy and minerals were not significant.	No aggregate effect, positive effect on textiles and apparel
Tadesse and Fayissa 2008	"The impact of African Growth and Opportunity Act (AGOA) on U.S. imports from Sub-Saharan Africa (SSA)"	1991–2006	Tobit specification of the gravity model using AGOA dummy var; models estimate at both	In the aggregate, AGOA did not have a statistically significant effect on beneficiary country exports to the United States. At the HS-2 level, AGOA was responsible for a statistically significant increase in exports to the United States in 19 of 99 product categories, including vegetables, fruits and nuts, coffee/tea/spices, beverages, plastics, fabrics,	No aggregate effect, mixed effects by product

Author	Title	Years	Model	Findings	Impact
			aggregated and disaggregated (HS-2) levels	apparel, and tin. Further, trade increasing effects of AGOA grew over time. Manufacturing sectors experiencing positive trade effects as a result of AGOA included pharmaceuticals, miscellaneous chemical products, and plastics. Additionally, AGOA had significant trade initiation effects in 24 of 99 different product categories, including vegetables, milling products, miscellaneous chemicals, plastics, cotton knitted fabrics, knit apparel, and non-knit apparel.	
Condon and Stern 2011	"The effectiveness of African Growth and Opportunity Act (AGOA) in increasing trade from least developed countries: a systematic review"	Various	Literature review	Exports from AGOA countries have increased substantially since the program's implementation, and countries are utilizing the preferences. AGOA did have a positive impact on beneficiary country exports of apparel, but outside of apparel there is little evidence that AGOA helped to increase trade.	Positive for apparel, not conclusive for other sectors
Frazer and Van Biesebroeck 2010	"Trade growth under the African Growth and Opportunity Act"	1998-2006	Triple difference-in-differences regression, disaggregated at HS-6 level	AGOA had a positive effect on exports of agricultural goods, manufactures, and apparel, but trade effects for petroleum and mineral products were not significant. Additionally, positive trade effects grew over time. AGOA raised beneficiary country apparel exports by 42 percent on average, but effects were positive for only 14 beneficiaries. AGOA was estimated to raise agricultural product exports by 8 percent on average, and nearly 2/3 of beneficiaries experienced a significant positive increase in agricultural exports due to AGOA. In manufactures, AGOA was estimated to result in a 15 percent increase in beneficiary country exports, with significant positive effects for 35 beneficiaries.	Mixed, depending upon product group and country

Table 7.2. (Continued)

Author	Title	Years	Model	Findings	Impact
Karingi et al. 2012	"Report on a survey of AGOA's past, present, and future prospects: The experiences and expectations of Sub-Saharan Africa"	2011	Survey	AGOA helped diversify beneficiary country exports, and the probability of exporting a new product increased over time - particularly in apparel. A majority of private sector respondents from beneficiary countries believed that AGOA was very important to their economic and trade links, but only about half of firms reported that they had directly benefitted from AGOA. Also, 39 percent of private sector respondents reported diversification in their sector or enterprise due to AGOA.	Majority positive
de Melo and Portugal-Perez 2013	"Preferential market access design: evidence and lessons from African apparel exports to the US and the EU"	1996–2004	Panel estimation with various specifications	Simplified rules of origin under the third country fabric provision was correlated with a 168 percent increase in apparel exports by the seven largest AGOA apparel exporters. Furthermore, the third-country fabric provision helped to increase the varieties of apparel exported by between 39 and 61 percent.	Positive for apparel
Nouve and Staatz 2003	"Has AGOA increased agricultural exports from Sub-Saharan Africa to the United States?"	1998–2002	Fixed effects gravity model, using AGOA dummy	AGOA was estimated to have a positive effect on agricultural exports, but not a statistically significant one.	Positive, but not statistically significant
Páez et al. 2010	"A decade (2000-2010) of African-U.S. trade under the African Growth and Opportunity Act (AGOA): challenges, opportunities and a framework for post-AGOA engagement"	2000–2010	Descriptive analysis	Through 2010, 90 percent of U.S. imports under AGOA were energy-related products, suggesting that there has been little overall product diversification.	Little product diversification

Author	Title	Years	Model	Findings	Impact
Other preference programs					
Gamberoni 2007	"Do unilateral preferences help export diversification?"	1994–2005	Tobit and probit estimation	Export diversification effects of preferences are dependent upon the program and sector. GSP improved export diversification, EBA did not have a statistically significant effect on export diversification, and ACP preferences were estimated to have an anti-diversification effect. The analysis also estimates sector-specific diversification effects for agriculture and textiles.	GSP-LDC did not increase diversification, ACP led to increase export concentration
Persson and Wilhemsson 2013	"EU trade preferences and export diversification"	1962–2007	Gravity model using fixed effect Poisson Pseudo Maximum Likelihood (PPML) estimator	EU trade preference programs vary in their effect on export diversification of beneficiary countries. GSP and EBA were found to increase export diversification, while ACP preferences were first associated with export diversification, but resulted in greater product concentration by the end of the period of analysis. However, although GSP led to increased product diversification, most GSP programs did not lead to significant diversification of overall export earnings.	GSP-LDC increased diversification, but ACP led to increased concentration
Brenton 2003	"Integrating the least developed countries into the world trading system: the current impact of EU preferences under Everything but Arms"	2001	Raw data analysis	Low take-up of EBA preferences in their first year of implementation suggest that either countries do not see value in the preferences or else have difficulty in complying with the requirements of accessing preferences. For the range of developing countries analyzed, EBA preferences were found to have either no relevance, low relevance, or high relevance based on a country's export basket. However, even for countries with high relevance, take-up was nearly non-existent for ACP countries.	

Table 7.2. (Continued)

Author	Title	Years	Model	Findings	Impact
Aiello and Cardamone 2011	"Analysing the impact of Everything But Arms initiative using a gravity model"	1995–2006	Gravity model, fixed effects negative binomial estimator; programs modeled by margin of preference	Effects of EBA were found to be mixed among the five products analyzed, suggesting that the trade-stimulating effects of EBA were heterogeneous by product and, by extension, country. EBA was found to increase exports of crustaceans and vanilla, had no effect on exports of coffee or molluscs, and reduced exports of cloves.	Mixed, based on product
Cardamone 2011	"Trade impact of European Union preferences: an analysis with monthly data"	2001–2004 (monthly data)	Gravity model, fixed effects Poisson estimator; programs modeled by margin of preference	GSP preferences were found to have a positive and marked effect on EU imports of apples and grapes, but were estimated to have a negative effect on imports of pears and mandarins.	Mixed, depending upon product and regime
Gradeva and Martinez-Zarzoso 2009	"Trade as aid: the role of the EBA-trade preferences regime in the development strategy"	1995–2005	Various gravity specifications using EBA dummy, but Heckman selection model is preferred estimator	The authors found a statistically significant negative relationship between EBA and exports from LDCs. At the same time, they find a significant positive relationship between the interaction of EBA participation and amount of development aid received in the previous year and current year exports, suggesting that trade preferences alone are not enough to positively impact export performance, but coupled with aid can be successful.	EBA negative EBA plus official development assistance positive
Cipollina and	"Trade impact of EU preferential policies: a	Range covering	Meta regression analysis	Combined estimates imply that PTAs cause a substantial increase in trade flows, but these flows	Varied based on specification

Author	Title	Years	Model	Findings	Impact
Pietrovito 2011	meta-analysis of the literature"	1970s–2000s		vary widely depending on the estimation method used. Approaches using dummy variables to signify preferences result in a wide range of estimates, both positive and negative. Approaches using margins of preferences estimate more modest PTA effects, but significant and positive effects nonetheless.	
Co and Dimova 2013	"Preferential market access into the Chinese market: how good is it for Africa?"	2002–2010	Triple differences regression	Chinese preferences led to greater SSA exports of "other primary products," but did not have a significant effect on trade in any other category.	Mixed, based on product
Cipollina et al. 2013	"Do preferential trade policies (actually) increase exports? An analysis of EU trade policies"	2004	Gravity model using a PPML estimator, preferences modeled as relative margins vs. competitors	EU preferences have different impacts across sectors, which are not necessarily related to the size of the margin. EU preferences have large impacts on the ceramics, glassware, textiles, and footwear industries, but agricultural preferences in many cases do not seem to have any impact. Overall, EU preferences seem to have generated additional trade flows of around 3 percent of total EU imports.	Mixed, based on product
Aiello and Demaria 2010	"Do trade preferential agreements enhance the exports of developing countries? Evidence from the EU GSP"	2001–2004	Gravity model using preferential margins, using five different estimators	Results indicate that EU GSP has a positive and significant impact on exports of agricultural goods from beneficiary countries. Similar results emerged for EBA. However, at the product level, results are mixed.	For total ag exports: GSP and EBA positive. Product effects are mixed
Cirera et al. 2011	"The impact of GSP preferences on developing countries' exports in the European Union: bilateral gravity modelling at the product level"	2002–2008	Gravity model using preference margins, PPML estimator	Estimated trade effects vary depending upon how the preferences under various regimes are measured. ACP preferences were effective at raising trade regardless of how they were measured, but EBA's effectiveness depended upon how the margin was defined.	ACP positive EBA (effect dependent upon pref. definition)
Pishbahar and Huchet-	"European Union's preferential trade	2000–2004	Gravity model using preference	EBA and GSP were estimated to have a negative and significant impact on beneficiary country	EBA negative GSP negative

Table 7.2. (Continued)

Author	Title	Years	Model	Findings	Impact
Bourdon 2008	agreements in agricultural sector: a gravity approach"		program dummies	agricultural exports to the EU. However, Cotonou preferences were associated with higher beneficiary country exports.	Cotonou positive
Cipollina and Salvatici 2011	"Trade impact of European Union preferences"	2004	Heckman selection gravity model using preference margins	EU preferences generally have a positive impact on trade, but various sectors are affected differently. For manufactures, preferences have increased trade on the intensive margin, but has reduced the number of products exported. For agriculture, intensive margin impacts have been smaller, but the number of products exported has increased.	Intensive effects positive, but vary in magnitude. Extensive effects are mixed.
Nilsson and Matsson 2009	"Truths and myths about the openness of EU trade policy and the use of EU trade preferences"	2003–2007	Gravity model using a PPML estimator and preference margins	EU preferences have had a positive and significant impact on preferential trade flows for all developing country groups except FTA partners. Additionally, 19 percent of EU imports from ACP LDC countries are due to preferences, while 10 percent of imports from ACP non-LDC countries are due to preferences.	ACP LDC positive ACP non-LDC positive
Comparative studies					
Persson and Wilhemlsson 2006	"Assessing the effects of EU trade preferences for developing countries"	1960–2002	Gravity model augmented with time trend, using dummies	Preferences raised exports from ACP only (Lome) countries by 30 percent, raised exports from LDC non-ACP countries by 21 percent, and raised exports from LDC and ACP countries by 33 percent.	
Cipollina et al. 2010	"Do preferential trade policies (actually) increase exports? A comparison between EU and US trade policies"	2004	Zero-Inflated Poisson (ZIP) specification of gravity model, measure of preference margin	Both U.S. and EU preferences positively impact beneficiary country exports. EU preferences are more effective at increasing trade in most cases. U.S. preferences significantly increase the probability of exporting in almost all cases (between 7 percent and 28 percent). EU preferences increased import concentration in three product	LDC positive GSP (none) ACP positive

Author	Title	Years	Model	Findings	Impact
				sections, but increased the probability of exporting in many cases, ranging from 3 percent to 23 percent.	
de Melo and Portugal-Perez 2013	"Preferential market access design: Evidence and lessons from African apparel exports to the US and the EU"	1996–2004	Log-linear model under various specifications, with LAD as preferred estimator	EBA and AGOA offer similar tariff preferences for apparel, but simplified U.S. rules of origin under AGOA were associated with a 168 percent increase in beneficiary country apparel exports. The AGOA rules of origin simplification also resulted in an increase in the number of products exported of between 39 and 61 percent.	U.S. preferences better at diversification, EU preferences better at intensification
Collier and Venables 2007	"Rethinking trade preferences: How Africa can diversify its exports"	1991–2005	Triple difference-in-differences	In a relative setting utilizing two different approaches, the authors find that the AGOA apparel provision created around 7 times more apparel exports to the United States relative to apparel exports to the EU.	AGOA RoOs improved both trade amount and number of apparel products compared to EBA
Davies and Nilsson 2013	"A comparative analysis of EU and US trade preferences for the LDCs and the AGOA beneficiaries"	2007–2010	Gravity model, total trade dummy variables	EU and U.S. trade preference regimes had no effect on total exports, but EU trade policy was found to generate approximately twice the non-mineral fuel imports from AGOA beneficiary countries as did U.S. trade policy.	AGOA apparel provision significantly increased apparel exports
Gil-Pareja et al. 2012	"Do nonreciprocal preference regimes increase exports?"	1990–2008 (at 3-year intervals)	Various specifications, but two-stage Helpman, Melitz, and Rubinstein (HMR) gravity model is preferred	Using various specifications, the authors investigate whether unilateral preference regimes have a positive impact on trade flows. They find that on average, they do, but these effects vary by program: ACP-EU, EBA, GSP-EU, GSP-US, GSP-Canada, GSP-Japan, GSP-Norway, GSP-Russia, GSP-Switzerland are all found to have a positive and significant effect on total exports, while AGOA is not found to have a statistically significant impact on total exports from beneficiary countries.	EU preferences generated more trade than AGOA

Table 7.2. (Continued)

Author	Title	Years	Model	Findings	Impact
Di Rubbo and Canali 2008	"A comparative study of EU and US trade policies for developing countries: The case of agri-food products"	1996–2005	Generalized least squares gravity model with country-specific binary variables	EU trade policy with respect to agricultural goods from developing countries was found to increase exports more than U.S. trade policy. These differences varied by income group. Over the period 2001-2005, EU policy raised low-income ag exports by 81 percent, lower-middle by 63 percent, and upper-middle by 91 percent compared to U.S. policy.	AGOA does not have a statistically significant relationship with total beneficiary country exports
Bureau et al. 2007	"The utilisation of trade preferences for developing countries in the agri-food sector"	2002	Bivariate and multinomial probit models	On average, EU agricultural imports with a higher degree of processing were more likely to utilize preferences, while U.S. imports with a higher degree of processing were less likely to utilize preferences. Additionally, smaller shipments to both are less likely to utilize preferences.	EU trade policy raised developing country agricultural exports more than U.S. policy
Nicita and Rollo 2013	"Tariff preferences as a determinant for exports from Sub-Saharan Africa"	2000–2001, 2010-11	Comparative static approach using probit estimation	Changes in direct market access affects the probability of initiating trade in a new product, but relative market access is important to ensure that a country continues to export that product.	Processed agricultural goods are less likely to utilize U.S. preferences; the opposite is true for the EU.
Nilsson 2005	"Comparative effects of EU and US trade policies on developing country exports"	2001–2003	Gravity model	EU trade policy resulted in around 35 percent more trade flows in total from developing countries as compared to U.S. trade policy over this period. These effects were higher with respect to low-income and upper-middle income countries, but were not significant for lower-middle income	(no specific U.S. or EU effects reported)

Author	Title	Years	Model	Findings	Impact
Nilsson 2005	"Comparative effects of EU and US trade policies on developing country exports"	2001–2003	Gravity model	EU trade policy resulted in around 35 percent more trade flows in total from developing countries as compared to U.S. trade policy over this period. These effects were higher with respect to low-income and upper-middle income countries, but were not significant for lower-middle income countries. Colonial ties and distance were also major determinants of higher trade flows.	EU trade policy resulted in higher developing country exports vis-à-vis U.S. policy

Source: Compiled by USITC staff.
Note: More information about each article appears in the bibliography for section 7 of this report.

APPENDIX A. REQUEST LETTER

EXECUTIVE OFFICE OF THE PRESIDENT
THE UNITED STATES TRADE REPRESENTATIVE
WASHINGTON, D.C. 20508

SEP 3 0 2013

The Honorable Irving Williamson
Chairman
U.S. International Trade Commission
500 E Street SW
Washington, DC 20436

DOCKET NUMBER
2986

Office of the Secretary
Int'l Trade Commission

Dear Chairman Williamson:

First, let me thank you for the Commission's excellent work. The ITC is a key partner for USTR and I look forward to working with you on our many areas of common interest. I am writing today regarding the African Growth and Opportunity Act (AGOA).

The United States promotes trade and investment with sub-Saharan Africa and supports economic development through preference programs like AGOA. Since its enactment in 2000, AGOA has created opportunities to increase U.S.-sub-Saharan African trade and investment. As the Administration works with its partners in the region and Congress to renew and potentially modify AGOA, it is vital to have accurate factual information to (i) assess the impact AGOA has had on the economies of sub-Saharan Africa, and (ii) identify factors that have impacted trade, investment, and the economic climate in the region.

Therefore, pursuant to section 332(g) of the Tariff Act of 1930, and the authority delegated by the President to the United States Trade Representative (USTR), I request that the U.S. International Trade Commission (the Commission), conduct four investigations and provide four reports as follows:

Investigation 1: That the Commission conduct an investigation and provide a report addressing the following topics for sub-Saharan African countries, as defined in AGOA, and, where applicable, those AGOA beneficiary countries that are designated as a lesser developed beneficiary country (LDBCs), covering the period 2000–13:

1. AGOA trade performance, utilization and competitiveness factors. Specifically, the report should:

    - Provide a review of the literature on the AGOA preference program, in terms of expanding and diversifying the exports of AGOA beneficiary countries to the United States, compared to preference programs offered by third parties such as the EU.

    - Identify the non-crude petroleum sectors (i.e., manufacturing and agricultural) in AGOA beneficiary countries in which exports to the United States, under AGOA and under the U.S. Generalized System of Preferences program, have increased the most, in absolute terms, since 2000, and identify the key factors behind this growth.

Chairman Williamson
Page Two

- Describe the main factors affecting AGOA trade in the principal non-crude petroleum products that AGOA beneficiary countries export and that the United States principally imports from non-sub-Saharan African sources; and

- Based on a review of literature, identify products with potential for integration into regional or global supply chains, and export potential to the United States under AGOA, as well as factors that affect AGOA beneficiary countries' competitiveness in these sectors.

2. AGOA's effects on the business and investment climate in sub-Saharan Africa. Specifically, the report should:

    - Identify and describe changes, if any, in the business and investment climates in sub-Saharan African countries since 2000, including removal of barriers to domestic and foreign investment; and

    - Describe U.S. goods and services-related investment trends in sub-Saharan African countries since 2000 and compare these trends with investments by other countries in sub-Saharan African countries, including investments by the EU, China, Brazil, and India. Identify any links between these investment trends and the AGOA program.

3. Current or potential reciprocal trade agreements between sub-Saharan African and non-sub-Saharan African partners and the relationship of these agreements to the objectives of AGOA. Specifically, the report should:

    - Provide a list of reciprocal trade agreements that sub-Saharan African countries have completed or are under negotiation. For the reciprocal trade agreements that have entered into force and, to the extent information is available in the case of those that are pending or under negotiation, provide a brief description of areas covered or likely to be covered under the agreements; identify U.S. sectors/products impacted or potentially impacted, including any tariff differentials; and

    - Provide examples of developing countries that have moved from unilateral trade preferences to reciprocal trade agreements, and any effects of the change for the developing country in terms of expansion and diversification of its trade.

I anticipate that this report will be made available to the public in its entirety. Therefore, the report should not contain any confidential business or national security information. This report should be delivered <u>six months</u> from the date of this letter.

In addition, to further inform USTR's analysis, I request that the Commission provide three confidential reports, as follows:

Chairman Williamson
Page Three

Investigation 2: That the Commission conduct an investigation and provide a confidential report containing an assessment of the economic effects of providing duty-free treatment for imports of products from AGOA beneficiary countries on U.S. industries producing like or directly competitive products and on U.S. consumers. The report should include an assessment of the economic effect on U.S. industries and consumers of imports of articles already eligible for duty-free treatment under AGOA, as well as an assessment of the probable economic effect on U.S. industries and consumers of the extension of duty-free treatment to the remaining articles in chapters 1 through 97 of the Harmonized Tariff Schedule of the United States (HTS). The assessment should take into account implementation of U.S. commitments in the World Trade Organization and should be based on the HTS in effect during 2013 and trade data for 2012.

This report should be delivered six months from the date of this letter.

Investigation 3: That the Commission conduct an investigation and provide a confidential report that, to the extent practicable, identifies possible changes to the rules of origin under AGOA that could have the potential to promote regional integration and increase exports to the United States, and the leading manufactured or processed goods (non-petroleum) which might benefit from such changes.

This report should be delivered seven months from the date of this letter.

Investigation 4: That the Commission conduct an investigation and provide a confidential report containing, to the extent practicable, an assessment of the impact of the EU-South Africa Free Trade Agreement on U.S. exports to South Africa. This analysis should also identify the U.S. sectors/products with potential for increased U.S. exports if South Africa were to reduce its MFN tariffs for those U.S. products to the tariff levels of the EU-South Africa FTA.

This report should be delivered six months from the date of this letter.

In accordance with Office of the U.S. Trade Representative (USTR) policy on implementing Executive Order 13526, as amended, entitled "Classified National Security Information" and published January 5, 2010, I direct you to mark or identify as "confidential," for a period of ten years, such portions of the Commission's reports and its working papers that deal with the assessments and analyses, as identified by USTR, provided in the three confidential reports. Consistent with this Executive Order, this information will be classified on the basis that it concerns economic matters relating to the national security of the United States. USTR also considers the Commission's three confidential reports to be inter-agency memoranda that will contain pre-decisional advice and be subject to the deliberative process privilege.

Chairman Williamson
Page Four

I also request kindly that you submit outlines of these confidential reports as soon as possible to enable an appropriate USTR official with original classification authority to provide you with further written guidance on their classification, including the extent to which portions of the reports will require classification and for how long.

The Commission's assistance in this matter is greatly appreciated.

Sincerely,

Ambassador Michael B. G. Froman

APPENDIX B. *FEDERAL REGISTER* NOTICE

International Trade Commission

[Investigation No. 332–542, Investigation No. 332–544, Investigation No. 332–545, Investigation No. 332–546]

AGOA: Trade and Investment Performance Overview; AGOA: Economic Effects of Providing Duty- Free Treatment for Imports, U.S. AGOA Rules of Origin: Possible Changes To Promote Regional Integration and Increase Exports to the United States; EU-South Africa FTA: Impact on U.S. Exports to South Africa

AGENCY: United States International Trade Commission.

ACTION: Institution of investigations, scheduling of public hearing, and opportunity to provide written submissions.

SUMMARY: Following receipt of a request dated September 30, 2013 (received October 17, 2013) from the United States Trade Representative (USTR) under section 332(g) of the Tariff Act of 1930 (19 U.S.C. 1332(g)), the U.S. International Trade Commission (Commission) instituted four investigations for the purpose of providing the requested information: investigation No. 332–542, *AGOA: Trade and Investment Performance Overview;* investigation No. 332–544, *AGOA: Economic Effects of Providing Duty-Free Treatment for Imports;* investigation No. 332–545, *U.S. AGOA Rules of Origin: Possible Changes to Promote Regional Integration and Increase Exports to the United States;* and investigation No. 332–546, *EU- South Africa FTA: Impact on U.S. Exports to South Africa.*

DATES: December 13, 2013: Deadline for filing requests to appear at the public hearing.
December 17, 2013: Deadline for filing pre-hearing briefs and statements.
January 14, 2014: Public hearing.
January 21, 2014: Deadline for filing post-hearing briefs and statements.
January 21, 2014: Deadline for filing all other written submissions.
April 17, 2014: Transmittal to USTR of Commission reports on investigation Nos. 332–542, 332–544, and 332–546.
April 30, 2014: Transmittal to USTR of report on Commission investigation No. 332–545.

ADDRESSES: All Commission offices, including the Commission's hearing rooms, are located in the United States International Trade Commission Building, 500 E Street SW., Washington, DC. All written submissions should be addressed to the Secretary, United States International Trade Commission, 500 E Street SW., Washington, DC 20436. The public record for these investigations may be viewed on the Commission's electronic docket (EDIS) at https://edis.usitc.gov/edis3-internal/app.

FOR FURTHER INFORMATION CONTACT: For information with respect to specific investigations:

(1) Investigation No. 332–542, Project Leader Joanna Bonarriva (202–205–3312 or *Joanna.Bonarriva@usitc.gov*) or Deputy Project Leader Joanne Guth (202–205–3264 or *Joanne.Guth@ usitc.gov*);

(2) Investigation No. 332–544, Project Leader Kathryn Lundquist (202–205– 2563 or *Kathryn.Lundquist@usitc.gov*) or Deputy Project Leader Andrew David (202–205–3368 or *Andrew.David@ usitc.gov*);

(3) Investigation No. 332–545, Project Leader Deborah McNay (202–205–3425 or *Deborah.McNay@usitc.gov*) or Deputy Project Leader Heidi Colby-Oizumi (202–205–3391 or *Heidi.Colby@ usitc.gov*);

(4) Investigation No. 332–546, Project Leader David Riker (202–205–2201 or *David.Riker@usitc.gov*) or Deputy Project Leader Kyle Johnson (202–205–3229 or *Kyle.Johnson@usitc.gov*).

For information on the legal aspect of each of these investigations, contact William Gearhart of the Commission's Office of the General Counsel (202–205–3091 or *william.gearhart@usitc.gov*). The media should contact Margaret O'Laughlin, Office of External Relations (202–205–1819 or *margaret.olaughlin@ usitc.gov*). Hearing-impaired individuals may obtain information on this matter by contacting the Commission's TDD terminal at 202–205–1810. General information concerning the Commission may also be obtained by accessing its Internet server (http://www.usitc.gov). Persons with mobility impairments who will need special assistance in gaining access to the Commission should contact the Office of the Secretary at 202–205–2000.

Background: As requested, the Commission has instituted four investigations for the purpose of providing four reports as follows:

Investigation No. 332–542, AGOA: Trade and Investment Performance Overview

In its first report (investigation No. 332–542), the Commission will, as requested by the USTR, address the following topics for sub-Saharan African countries, as defined in the African Growth and Opportunity Act (19 U.S.C. 3701 et seq.) (AGOA), and, where applicable, those AGOA beneficiary countries that are designated as lesser developed beneficiary countries, covering the period 2000–13:

- AGOA trade performance, utilization and competitiveness factors, including (1) a review of the literature on the AGOA preference program, in terms of expanding and diversifying the exports of AGOA beneficiary countries to the United States, compared to preference programs offered by third parties such as the EU; (2) identification of non-crude petroleum sectors (i.e., manufacturing and agricultural) in AGOA beneficiary countries in which exports to the United States, under AGOA and under the U.S. Generalized System of Preferences program, have increased the most, in absolute terms, since 2000, and the key factors behind this growth; (3) a description of the main factors affecting AGOA trade in the principal non-crude petroleum products that AGOA beneficiary countries export and that the United States principally imports from non- sub-Saharan African sources; and (4) based on a review of literature, identification of products with potential for integration into regional or global supply chains, and export potential to the United States under

AGOA, as well as factors that affect AGOA beneficiary countries' competitiveness in these sectors.
- AGOA's effects on the business and investment climate in sub-Saharan Africa, including (1) the identification and description of changes, if any, in the business and investment climates in sub-Saharan African countries since 2000, including removal of barriers to domestic and foreign investment; and (2) a description of U.S. goods and services-related investment trends in sub-Saharan African countries since 2000 and a comparison of these trends with investments by other countries in sub-Saharan African countries, including investments by the EU, China, Brazil, and India, and identification of any links between these investment trends and the AGOA program.
- Current or potential reciprocal trade agreements between sub-Saharan African and non-sub-Saharan African partners and the relationship of these agreements to the objectives of AGOA, including (1) a list of reciprocal trade agreements that sub-Saharan African countries have completed or are under negotiation, a brief description of areas covered or likely to be covered under the agreements, and identification of U.S. sectors/products impacted or potentially impacted, including any tariff differentials; and (2) examples of developing countries that have moved from unilateral trade preferences to reciprocal trade agreements, and any effects of the change for the developing country in terms of expansion and diversification of its trade.

The Commission will deliver this first report to the USTR by April 17, 2014. The USTR also stated that it intends to make this report public.

Investigation No. 332–544, AGOA: Economic Effects of Providing Duty-Free Treatment for Imports

In its second report the Commission will, as requested by the USTR, provide an assessment of the economic effects of providing duty-free treatment for imports of products from AGOA beneficiary countries on U.S. industries producing like or directly competitive products and on U.S. consumers. The report will include an assessment of the economic effect on U.S. industries and consumers of imports of articles already eligible for duty-free treatment under AGOA, as well as an assessment of the probable economic effect on U.S. industries and consumers of the extension of duty-free treatment to the remaining articles in chapters 1 through 97 of the Harmonized Tariff Schedule of the United States (HTS). The assessment will take into account implementation of U.S. commitments in the World Trade Organization and will be based on the HTS in effect during 2013 and trade data for 2012.

The Commission will provide this second report to the USTR by April 17, 2014. The USTR stated that this report will be classified.

Investigation No. 332–545, U.S. AGOA Rules of Origin: Possible Changes to Promote Regional Integration and Increase Exports to the United States

As requested by the USTR, in its third report the Commission will, to the extent practicable, identify possible changes to the rules of origin under AGOA that could have the potential to promote regional integration and increase exports to the United States, and the leading manufactured or processed goods (non-petroleum) which might benefit from such changes.

The Commission will provide this third report to the USTR by April 30, 2014. The USTR stated that this report will be classified.

Investigation No. 332–546, EU-South Africa FTA: Impact on U.S. Exports to South Africa

As requested by the USTR, in its fourth report the Commission will, to the extent practicable, provide an assessment of the impact of the EU- South Africa Free Trade Agreement on U.S. exports to South Africa.

This analysis will also identify the U.S. sectors/products with potential for increased U.S. exports if South Africa were to reduce its MFN tariffs for those U.S. products to the tariff levels of the EU-South Africa FTA.

The Commission will provide this fourth report to the USTR by April 17, 2014. The USTR stated that this report will be classified.

The USTR indicated that those sections of the Commission's three confidential reports that relate to assessments and analyses will be classified. The USTR also indicated that he considers the Commission's three confidential reports to be inter-agency memoranda that will contain pre- decisional advice and be subject to the deliberative process privilege.

Public Hearing: A public hearing in connection with these investigations will be held at the U.S. International Trade Commission Building, 500 E Street SW., Washington, DC, beginning at 9:30 a.m. on January 14, 2014. Requests to appear at the public hearing should be filed with the Secretary no later than 5:15 p.m., December 13, 2013. All pre-hearing briefs and statements should be filed no later than 5:15 p.m. December 17, 2013; and all post-hearing briefs and statements should be filed no later than 5:15 p.m. January 21, 2014. All such briefs and statements should otherwise comply with the filing requirements in the ''Submissions'' section below. In the event that, as of the close of business on December 13, 2013, no witnesses are scheduled to appear at the hearing, the hearing will be canceled. Any person interested in attending the hearing as an observer or nonparticipant should contact the Office of the Secretary at 202–205–2000 after December 13, 2013, for information concerning whether the hearing will be held.

Written Submissions: In lieu of or in addition to participating in the hearing, interested parties are invited to file written submissions concerning any of the four investigations. Each written submission should identify the one or more of the four investigations to which the submission relates. All written submissions should be addressed to the Secretary, and should be received not later than 5:15 p.m., January 21, 2014. All written submissions must conform to the provisions of section 201.8 of the Commission's *Rules of Practice and Procedure* (19 CFR 201.8). Section 201.8 and the Commission's Handbook on Filing Procedures require that interested parties file documents electronically on or before the filing deadline and submit eight (8) true paper copies by 12:00 noon eastern time on the next business day. In the event that confidential treatment of a document is requested, interested parties must file, at the same time as the eight paper copies, at least four (4) additional true paper copies in which the confidential information must be deleted (see the following paragraph for further information regarding confidential business information). Persons with questions regarding electronic filing should contact the Secretary (202–205–2000).

Any submissions that contain confidential business information (CBI) must also conform with the requirements of section 201.6 of the Commission's *Rules of Practice and Procedure* (19 CFR 201.6). Section 201.6 of the rules requires that the cover of the document and the individual pages be clearly marked as to whether they are the "confidential" or "non-confidential" version, and that the confidential business information be clearly identified by means of brackets. All written submissions, except for confidential business information, will be made available for inspection by interested parties. In his request letter the USTR said that it is the intent of his office to make the Commission's report in the first investigation, No. 332–542

AGOA: Trade and Investment Performance Overview, available to the public in its entirety, and asked that the Commission not include any confidential business information or national security classified information in the report that it sends to the USTR. Any confidential business information received by the Commission in this investigation and used in preparing this report will not be published in a manner that would reveal the operations of the firm supplying the information. The Commission may include some or all of the confidential business information submitted in the course of investigation Nos. 332–544, 332–545, and 332–546 in the reports it sends to the USTR in those investigations. The Commission will not otherwise publish any confidential business information in a manner that would reveal the operations of the firm supplying the information.

By order of the Commission.
Issued: November 13, 2013.

Lisa R. Barton,
Acting Secretary to the Commission.
[FR Doc. 2013–27575 Filed 11–18–13; 8:45 am]
BILLING CODE 7020–02–P

APPENDIX C. CALENDAR OF HEARING WITNESSES

Those listed below appeared as witnesses at the United States International Trade Commission's hearing:

Subject: AGOA: Trade and Investment Performance Overview
AGOA: Economic Effects of Providing Duty-Free Treatment for Imports
U.S. AGOA Rules of Origin: Possible Changes to Promote Regional Integration and Increase Exports to the United States
EU-South Africa FTA: Impact on U.S. Exports to South Africa
Inv. Nos.: 332-542, 332-544, 332-545, and 332-546
Date and Time: January 14, 2014 - 9:30 a.m.

Sessions were held in connection with these investigations in the Main Hearing Room (room 101), 500 E Street, S.W., Washington, DC.

Embassy Witnesses

Embassy of the Republic of Mauritius
Washington, DC
His Excellency Somduth Soborun, Ambassador of the Republic of Mauritius to the United States

Embassy of the Federal Democratic Republic of Ethiopia
Washington, DC
His Excellency Girma Birru, Ambassador of the Federal Democratic Republic of Ethiopia to the United States

Embassy of the Republic of South Africa
Washington, DC
His Excellency Ebrahim Rasool, Ambassador of the Republic of South Africa to the United States

Embassy of the Republic of Kenya
Washington, DC
Her Excellency Ambassador Jean Kamau, Charge D'Affaires of the Republic of Kenya to the United States

Panel 1

Organization and Witness
Common Market of Eastern and Southern Africa ("COMESA")
Dennis Matanda, Head of Government Relations, Manchester Trade Limited, Inc.

New Markets Lab ("NML")
Washington, DC
Katrin Kuhlmann, President and Founder, Senior Advisor, Corporate Council on Africa

Manchester Trade Limited, Inc.
Washington, DC
Stephen Lande, President

Progressive Economy
Washington, DC
Edward Gresser, Director

Africa Business Initiative
U.S. Chamber of Commerce
Washington, DC
Scott Eisner, Vice President

National Foreign Trade Council, Inc.
Washington, DC
J. Daniel O'Flaherty, Vice President

Panel 2

Organization and Witness

American Sugar Alliance
Arlington, VA
Don Phillips, Trade Adviser

Covington & Burling LLP
Washington, DC
Dr. Witney Schneidman, Senior International Advisor

African Coalition for Trade Inc.
Washington, DC
Paul Ryberg, President

African Cotton and Textile Industries Federation ("ACTIF")
Nairobi, Kenya
Jaswinder Bedi, Chairman

American Apparel & Footwear Association ("AAFA")
Arlington, VA
Stephen Lamar, Executive Vice President

National Chicken Council
USA Poultry & Egg Export Council
    Washington, DC
William P. Roenigk, Consultant
Kevin Brosch, Principal, DTB Associates

McDermott Will & Emery
Washington, DC
on behalf of

California Cling Peach Board
Rich Hudgins, President and Chief Executive Officer, California Canning Peach Association
Carolyn B. Gleason)
) – OF COUNSEL
Pamela D. Walther)
-END-

APPENDIX D. POSITIONS OF INTERESTED PARTIES

Introduction

The following summaries of the positions of interested parties are based on information provided at a public hearing held on January 14, 2014, in Washington, DC, and material submitted to the Commission in conjunction with investigation Nos. 332-542, *AGOA: Trade and Investment Performance Overview;* 332-544, *AGOA: Economic Effects of Providing Duty-Free Treatment for Imports;* 332-545, *U.S. AGOA Rules of Origin: Possible Changes to Promote Regional Integration and Increased Exports to the United States*; and 332-546, *EU-South Africa FTA: Impact on U.S. Exports to South Africa*. The summaries express the views of the submitting parties and not those of the Commission, whose staff did not attempt to confirm the accuracy of, or make corrections to, the information provided. The full text of the hearing transcript and written submissions associated with the investigations can be found by searching the Commission's Electronic Docket Information System.[695]

Embassy of the Republic of Madagascar[696]

In a written submission to the Commission related to all four Commission investigations, Andriantiana Ulrich, Minister of Foreign Affairs, Embassy of the Republic of Madagascar, addressed the four AGOA reports generally and recommended that the United States do the following: (1) extend AGOA for 10 years; (2) extend AGOA's third country fabric provision immediately; (3) extend AGOA and consider a partnership structure to create a more favorable investment climate; (4) remove quotas on all U.S. imports of agricultural products from Sub- Saharan Africa (SSA) except sugar; (5) revise the rules of origin under AGOA for canned tuna; (6) consider a "Support Programme Imports (EIAO)" to encourage African countries benefiting from AGOA to further develop their exports and allow U.S. importers to increase the volume of items made by countries under AGOA to be at least equivalent to those entering the United Statesd from Bangladesh and Cambodia; and (7) provide a substantial grant by way of assistance and capacity building for eligible African countries.

Embassy of the Republic of Mauritius[697]

In written submissions and in hearing testimony, Ambassador Somduth Soborun of the Republic of Mauritius said that his submission related to all four investigations. Ambassador Somduth stated that at the African Union Ministers of Trade meeting in Addis Ababa, Ethiopia, on October 24, 2013, Ministers also adopted a unanimous AGOA declaration directing that the African Ambassador's Working Group in Washington continue to actively engage the U.S. Administration and Congress on ways forward for a reauthorization of AGOA for a period of at least 15 years. The Ambassador said that this would ensure that trade with the United States takes place on a predictable, reliable, and legally secure basis in order to inspire investors' confidence.

Ambassador Soborun said that the AGOA rules of origin related to canned tuna should be revisited. He indicated that it is almost impossible for African canned tuna to meet the AGOA rules of origin, which is largely determined by the flag of the vessel that catches the fish rather than the nation where the fish is processed and canned. He noted that some SSA countries are exporting canned tuna to the EU, but exports to the U.S. are extremely low despite the fact that canned tuna is eligible for duty-free entry under AGOA. If the rule were relaxed, he said exports of canned tuna to the United States under AGOA would increase, thereby benefitting AGOA- eligible countries.

The Ambassador also recommended that the Third-Country Fabric Rule for apparel and textiles, which has been the subject of renewal every two or three years, should be made coterminous with the life of a reauthorized AGOA. He stated this provision has been solely responsible for AGOA's success in the apparel industry and that 95 percent of the apparel and textile products produced under AGOA are dependent on the Third-Country Fabric rule.

To conclude, Ambassador Soborun made the following recommendations: (1) reauthorize AGOA before October 2014 for at least 15 years to guarantee the predictability and certainty required for long-term investment and economic growth; (2) make the Third-Country Fabric rule coterminous with the life of AGOA; (3) relax stringent U.S. sanitary and phytosanitary (SPS) standards that prohibit small African agricultural exporters; (4) increase U.S.-provided capacity building and technical assistance; (5) promote U.S. investment in Africa; (6) renew AGOA in line with and supportive of President Obama's *Power Africa Initiative*; and (7) have congressional delegations make periodic trips in the context of AGOA.

Embassy of the Republic of Cabo Verde[698]

In a written submission, Dr. Jose Luis Rocha, Deputy Minister of Foreign Affairs, Republic of Cabo Verde, reported that his submission related to three of the Commission's investigations, Nos. 332-542, *AGOA: Trade and Investment Performance Overview;* 332-544, *AGOA: Economic Effects of Providing Duty-Free Treatment for Imports; and* 332-545, *Rules of Origin: Possible Changes to Promote Regional Integration and Increase Exports to the United States.* The Deputy Minister stated that Cabo Verde wants AGOA benefits to be extended in order to expand its trade and investment connections with the United States.

However, Dr. Rocha stated that there are a number of legal and regulatory issues that impede the ability of Cabo Verde to utilize the market access provided by AGOA. He suggested the following ways to improve the program: (1) liberalize and stabilize rules of origin; (2) provide duty-free, quota-free (DFQF) access for more products; (3) increase U.S. trade capacity building assistance (e.g., registration, quality inspection, and certification of products); (4) provide incentives for U.S. companies to invest in SSA; (5) cooperate better with regional trade organizations; and (6) support more maritime shipping lines between the United States and Cabo Verde.

Dr. Rocha also listed the following supply side issues as posing challenges for Cabo Verde's use of AGOA: (1) limited understanding of AGOA by Cabo-Verdean businesses and farmers; (2) the limited scale of Cabo-Verdean production; (3) institutional weaknesses in the area of export control; (4) transport challenges; and (5) the high cost of water and energy. He also indicated that the following U.S.-imposed hurdles increase the difficulty for Cabo Verde to export to the United States under AGOA: (1) restrictive SPS requirements, (2) non-tariff barriers such as excise taxes, and (3) complex and restrictive AGOA rules of origin.

Embassy of the Federal Democratic Republic of Ethiopia[699]

In a written submission and in hearing testimony, Ambassador Girma Birru of the Federal Democratic Republic of Ethiopia and the co-chair of the AGOA Ambassadors Working Group in Washington, DC. stated his submission related to all four investigations. Ambassador Birru said that AGOA remains the central pillar of U.S.-Africa trade and economic cooperation and contended that it should be reauthorized.

Ambassador Birru stated that AGOA has made a significant impact on exports from SSA countries and has helped to generate jobs in both Africa and the United States. The Ambassador noted that energy-related products continue to constitute the major share of AGOA exports to the United States, but products from the textile and apparel sector have also gained visibility and prominence in U.S-Africa trade and AGOA has offered meaningful opportunities for eligible African countries to transform their economies. However, the Ambassador indicated that few AGOA countries have made use of the opportunity due to supply constraints, mostly related to the lack of infrastructure and institutional capabilities. Ambassador Birru noted that during the 2013 AGOA forum, African Ministers of Trade requested that the United States consider developing an AGOA compact with those countries that are taking steps to increase their AGOA exports to ensure that they receive the needed support to make the necessary policy and program changes to overcome supply side constraints.

The Ambassador noted the importance of the role of AGOA in regional integration and the relevance of the economic partnership agreements (EPAs). He stated that Africa is the least integrated region in the world and intra-regional trade is also the lowest in the world. He contended that regional integration efforts are one way to improve intra-African trade ties and noted that AGOA calls for expanding U.S. assistance to SSA regional integration efforts. He stated that the reauthorization of AGOA will promote regional integration by ensuring that the program continues to play a constructive economic role in supporting regional integration. Finally, the Ambassador asserted that graduation would be punitive and may be counterproductive to economic growth and regional integration.

Embassy of the Republic of Kenya[700]

In hearing testimony related to all four investigations, Ms. Jean Kamau, charge d' affairs, Republic of Kenya, reported that AGOA remains an important pillar for Africa's development and its contribution to the global economy. From Kenya's position, according to Ms. Kamau, AGOA has had a profoundly beneficial effect on Africa and the United States. Ms. Kamau said that the recommendations contained in the AGOA declaration should be adopted and should form the basis of future legislation for the reauthorization of AGOA. Finally, she stated that AGOA should be extended for an additional 15 year period.

Embassy of the Federal Republic of Nigeria[701]

In a written submission related to all four investigations, Professor Abe Adefuye, Ambassador and Head of Mission, Republic of Nigeria, reported that trade and investment with SSA under AGOA has been generally satisfactory. However, he said that Nigeria's performance has been below expectations due to internal problems related to initial political instability, inadequate infrastructure, poor micro-economic management, and the inability to diversify Nigeria's economy away from the capital intensive oil sector.

Ambassador Adefuye stated that the United States is gradually diversifying its investments in Nigeria from oil and gas to other non-oil sectors such as power, energy, agriculture, hospitality, housing, and healthcare, among others. The Ambassador indicated that Nigeria can only increase its non-oil exports under AGOA through the following measures: (1) developing national- and state-level AGOA strategies that leverage Nigeria's competitive and comparative advantages outside oil and gas; (2) cultivating more land to increase agri-business; (3) moving away from traditional exports of primary commodities and diversifying into value-added products; (4) improving Nigeria's ranking in the Doing Business Index to increase the inflow of FDI; and (5) promoting good governance.

The Ambassador stated that it is imperative to re-assess apparel rules of origin under AGOA because they are not just constraints on sourcing, but they also force producers to use higher cost fabrics and materials. He suggested that the United States consider the concept of cumulation as a way of dealing with stringent textile rules of origin. He also suggested that the U.S. government relax the rules or origin on fish and fish products to allow effective market access.

Embassy of the Republic of South Africa[702]

In a written submission and hearing testimony related to all four investigations, Ambassador Ebrahim Rasool, Republic of South Africa, recommended that AGOA be reauthorized for a period of 15 years and that the duration of the Third-Country Fabric Rule be made coterminous with AGOA. He said that AGOA should be transformed into a tool for economic integration with the United States rather than the one-way policy tool the United States originally envisioned, but he acknowledged that inadequate infrastructure, especially transport, energy, and water, continue to inhibit regional and international integration.

However, the Ambassador reported that because of AGOA, South Africa has been able to invest in its own infrastructure, primarily through investments from the United States. He said that the stage is now set for the United States to export not only capital goods, but also household appliances and other white goods into South Africa. AGOA, according to the Ambassador, has made the United States South Africa's second most important export partner as South Africa remains the largest market for U.S. goods on the African continent.

In its post-hearing submission, South Africa focused on the anti-dumping duties that it imposes on chicken cuts from the United States.[703] The submission indicated that South Africa's anti-dumping measures against U.S. chicken exports were scheduled to expire in 2005, but were extended an additional 5 years following the filing of a petition by the South African poultry industry and a ruling by the South African International Trade Administration Commission (ITAC). The submission noted that the importer appealed the decision to the

Supreme Court of Appeal (SAC) in 2007, that the SAC ruled in favor of the importer, and that the SAC then suspended the order to enable ITAC to carry out new "sunset review" investigations. The submission indicated that the ITAC imposed across-the-board punitive duties on poultry imports from the United States in February 2012, because U.S. chicken producers had failed to provide requested information during the original anti-dumping investigation conducted by ITAC's predecessor, the Board on Tariff and Trade, as well as during subsequent sunset reviews undertaken by ITAC.

African Coalition for Trade (ACT)[704]

In a written submission and in hearing testimony related to all four investigations, Mr. Paul Ryberg, President, African Coalition for Trade (ACT), described ACT as a non-profit trade association of African private sector entities engaged in trade with the United States under AGOA. Mr. Ryberg stated that AGOA is recognized as the cornerstone of U.S. trade and economic policy concerning Africa and that AGOA should be renewed for at least 15 years to provide the stability required by investors. Mr. Ryberg noted U.S. imports from Africa have increased by 123 percent since 2000. He indicated that he would focus on the development of trade in non-extractive products as a barometer of what AGOA has achieved and reported that non-extractive imports under AGOA grew by 138 percent, particularly in agricultural products, motor vehicles, apparel, and footwear. Mr. Ryberg further explained that 36 of the 38 AGOA beneficiaries eligible for duty-free treatment in 2012 took advantage of the program and that AGOA created hundreds of thousands of direct jobs and millions of indirect jobs.

Mr. Ryberg said that the third-country fabric rule is the most important AGOA rule of origin and that delays by Congress to renew this provision have already caused uncertainty and forced U.S. importers to shift orders out of Africa. He indicated that this rule accounts for more than 90 percent of AGOA apparel trade and said that it is essential for AGOA's apparel industry that this provision be extended. He expressed the view that without the third-country fabric rule, African apparel manufacturing would be decimated.

Mr. Ryberg offered several other recommendations: (1) that AGOA's rule of origin for canned tuna be changed to allow for tuna caught by non-African fishing boats either by creating a special rule of origin, such as a simple "tariff shift" standard, or by a special derogation allowing duty-free treatment for a limited volume of "non-originating" tuna; (2) that any proposal to "graduate" countries from AGOA should include rules of origin that provide that the remaining AGOA-eligible countries will continue to be able to "cumulate" with the graduated counties in satisfying AGOA rules of origin; and (3) that excluded agricultural products such as sugar, beef, and cotton should be added to AGOA-eligible products.

African Cotton & Textile Industries Federation (ACTIF)[705]

In hearing testimony related to all four investigations, Mr. Jaswinder Bedi, Chairman, African Cotton & Textile Industries Federation (ACTIF), said that ACTIF is the only Pan-African organization that represents the full cotton textile and apparel value chain. Mr. Bedi stated ACTIF's membership represents the entire cotton-textile-apparel value chain from across Africa, including cotton farmers, ginners, spinners, fabric manufacturers, and garment producers.

Mr. Bedi stated that it is undisputable that AGOA has been successful in spurring economic development and reducing poverty in Africa. He also stated that one of the challenges that has prevented AGOA from accomplishing all that its creators hoped for is the fact that heretofore AGOA has been authorized for only a few years at a time. This series of short-term renewals, according to Mr. Bedi, has deterred investors by compounding the risks already inherent in investing in Africa. Mr. Bedi noted that most investors require at least a ten-year horizon to amortize a major investment. Mr. Bedi strongly recommends that Congress renew AGOA for a 10–15 year period. He offered six suggestions as Congress looks to renew AGOA: (1) AGOA should be reauthorized for a sustained period because investors require stability and predictability; (2) the AGOA third-country fabric provision should be extended for the full term of AGOA's renewal; (3) the same terms of access should apply to all AGOA-eligible countries; (4) Congress should reiterate AGOA's policy of encouraging the administration to negotiate regional FTAs with the AGOA beneficiaries; (5) AGOA should create additional incentives for U.S. buyers to source apparel from Africa; and (6) Congress should renew AGOA well in advance of the September 30, 2015 expiration.

African Diplomatic Corps[706]

Ambassador Girma Birru, of Ethiopia, and Ambassador Somduth Soborun, of Mauritius, submitted a joint written submission on behalf of the African Diplomatic Corps relating to all four investigations. They stated that AGOA has come to be widely acknowledged as a very important milestone in the growing trade and investment relations between AGOA-eligible countries and the United States, but also stated that there are a number of systematic problems in some countries that have contributed to the underutilization of AGOA. They also included a list of the common constraints faced by AGOA-eligible countries.

Their submission listed possible modifications to the AGOA rules of origin for canned tuna, which they said is currently determined by the flag of the vessel that catches the fish rather than the nation where the fish is processed and canned. They also provided information on third-country fabric rules and regional integration. In addition, the submission noted that the negotiation of reciprocal free trade agreemetnts (FTAs) between the United States and African countries should remain one of AGOA's objectives. In their view, the current process of AGOA reauthorization does not necessarily provide the basis for an appropriate framework to address concerns on EPAs or FTAs between the United States and African countries. They noted that among the AGOA beneficiary countries, South Africa is the only country to have an FTA with the EU and they said that the South Africa-EU FTA is a unique situation, that it should be viewed on its own merits, and that it should not be an excuse to propose fundamental changes and derail the process of reauthorizing AGOA.

American Apparel & Footwear Association (AAFA)[707]

In hearing testimony related to all four investigations, Stephen Lamar, Executive Vice President, American Apparel & Footwear Association (AAFA), said that AAFA is the public policy and political voice of the apparel and footwear industry. He indicated that AAFA's members produce and sell clothing and shoes all around the world, including Africa. According to Mr. Lamar, the AAFA was among the earliest supporters of AGOA and AAFA's members have used AGOA since its enactment. He stated that AGOA has had the most impact on AAFA's apparel members but is now becoming increasingly important for its footwear members as well, particularly in Ethiopia. Mr. Lamar made four recommendations: (1) that AGOA be renewed as soon as possible; (2) when AGOA is renewed, that it should be renewed on the longest possible basis and recommended a 15-year renewal because it creates the kind of certainty that can lead to long-term trade and investment decisions; (3) that the third-country fabric provision should be renewed for the entire length of the program; and (4) that the third-country fabric provision should be extended equally to all AGOA-eligible countries.

American Automotive Policy Council (AAPC)[708]

In a written submission, the American Automotive Policy Council (AAPC) focused its comments on two of the investigations, Nos. 332-542, *AGOA: Trade and Investment Performance Overview* and 332-544, *AGOA; Economic Effects of Providing Duty-Free Treatment for Imports*. The Council said that it is an association representing the common policy interests of its member companies, including the Chrysler Group LLC (Chrysler), Ford Motor Company (Ford), and General Motors Company (GM). The Council said that it shares the goal of AGOA to assist the economies of SSA and to improve economic relations between the United States and the region. It said that its member companies have supported the success of AGOA since its launch in 2000 and two-way auto trade continues to grow steadily, and it said that it is crucial for the United States to extend this program beyond 2015.

AAPC noted that Ford is an active participant in South Africa's automobile industry, and that Ford manufactures light commercial vehicles and diesel engines for local consumption and export. AAPC also noted that Ford maintains a parts distribution center and an on-site modification center, as well as a supplier incubation facility and training simulation facility. The Council said that GM produces vehicles and parts in South Africa and Kenya and is the largest motor vehicle manufacturer, assembler, and distributor in the East Africa region. The submission indicated that GM maintains numerous auto parts warehouses, a conversion and distribution center, and a sales and marketing center. The Council stated that Chrysler is the second largest importer of vehicles in South Africa where it distributes vehicles, parts, and accessories to its authorized franchised dealer network in South Africa, Botswana, and Namibia. The submission also noted that the Chrysler Group distributes vehicles, parts, and accessories through its general distributor network in Kenya, Tanzania, Mauritius, Mozambique, Uganda, Zambia, and Zimbabwe. AGOA, according to AAPC, is currently used by one of its members and allows Ford to import diesel engines it manufacturers in South Africa into the United States for assembly into the new North America Transit Van manufactured in Kansas City. AAPC also said that Chrysler took advantage of AGOA until

2010 to source component parts from South Africa for use in vehicles manufactured in the United States.

Business Leadership South Africa (BLSA)[709]

In a written submission to the Commission, Mr. Thero Setiloane, Chief Executive Officer, Business Leadership South Africa (BLSA), said that BLSA is an independent association whose members represent South Africa's big business leadership and major multinational investors. Mr. Setiloane noted that his comments would focus on investigation No. 332-542, *AGOA: Trade and Investment Performance Overview*. BLSA, according to Mr. Setiloane, made three points in its submission: (1) BLSA supports an urgent, seamless 15-year extension of AGOA, (2) BLSA is not opposed to a negotiated, mutually beneficial free trade agreement between the United States and South Africa, and recommends a clause in a reauthorized AGOA to implement a framework for regional FTAs; and (3) BLSA proposes that a trade and investment facilitation component be included in AGOA legislation to institutionalize the benefits of the many U.S. programs that assist African trade facilitation.

CBI Sugar Group and the Mauritius Sugar Syndicate[710]

In a joint submission, the sugar industries of the CBI Sugar Group, the Philippines, the Dominican Republic, and Mauritius, focused their comments on two of the investigations, Nos. 332 542, *AGOA: Trade and Investment Performance Overview* and 332-544, *AGOA: Economic Effects of Providing Duty-Free Treatment for Imports*.[711] The submission recommended that sugar should continue to be excluded from AGOA. The submission said that recent experience with the reform of the EU sugar regime has proven that including sugar in duty-free initiatives actually does more harm than good to developing countries. The submission said that granting DFQF access to African sugar under AGOA risks destroying the U.S. Sugar Program, which is already vulnerable because of NAFTA. It also asserted that adding another major source of DFQF sugar to the U.S. market would risk further depression of the U.S. market price at a time when it is already at record low levels due to NAFTA.

Coalition of Services Industries (CSI)[712]

In written submissions to the Commission, Mr. Peter Allgeier, President of the Coalition of Service Industries (CSI), reported that CSI's comments are related to one of the four investigations, No. 332-542, *AGOA: Trade and Investment Performance Overview*. He indicated that CSI is primarily a policy advocacy association that works on behalf of U.S.-based global services industries. Mr. Allgeier stated CSI supports the expansion of trade and investment between the United States and countries participating in AGOA and a renewal of AGOA.

Mr. Allegier said that, despite the continued dominance of U.S.-AGOA imports by petroleum products, Africa's exports of non-oil products have more than tripled since AGOA's inception. He also said that SSA has diversified its exports, especially in services, including business and information and communication technology services. Mr. Allgeier identified five key issues CSI would like raised at the AGOA forum in 2014: (1) increased interest in trade in services, especially economic infrastructure services; (2) digital trade in services; (3) investment protection; (4) trade facilitation; and (5) intellectual property protection. He cited a recent World Bank sponsored event entitled "Trade in Services Africa," where services were identified as a key to growth and job creation in Africa.

Mr. Allgeier stated that as African countries become larger players in the global market, AGOA should include enhanced rules on trade facilitation. These enhanced rules, according to Mr. Allgeier, would be one of the most cost effective investments AGOA countries and international donors could make to improve economic competitiveness and support Africa's participation in global supply chains. Mr. Allgeier explained that international trade in services is vital for expanding and diversifying the markets of AGOA participants and thereby creating new and better paying jobs. He contended that the renewal of AGOA creates the opportunity to implement policies and capacity building support to improve the services sectors of AGOA countries.

The Common Market for Eastern and Southern Africa (COMESA)[713]

In a written submission and in hearing testimony related to all four investigations, Mr. Dennis Matanda stated that he was testifying on behalf of Mr. Sindiso Ngweya, Secretary General, The Common Market for Eastern and Southern Africa (COMESA). Mr. Matanda stated that COMESA is very supportive of AGOA and considers it vital to economic growth and poverty-reduction in Africa via regional integration. He also stated that AGOA has helped create many jobs and generated substantial investment in Africa, including in key economic sectors within COMESA. He included arguments presented by the DC Ambassadors' Working Group and the African Union requesting a conterminous extension of AGOA and its third-country fabric provision.

Mr. Matanda noted that 14 COMESA members are also AGOA-eligible and nine qualify for textile and apparel benefits. Mr. Matanda indicated that although U.S. imports from COMESA consist mainly of oil, such imports also include woven and knit apparel, spices, tea and coffee, and textiles. Mr. Matanda asserted that Africa's textile and apparel sector offers the best prospect for expanding production to the U.S. market. He listed a number of U.S. apparel companies active in the region including: Gap, Old Navy, Wal Mart, Vanity Fair, Target, and Calvin Klein. He noted that these companies are active in a number of AGOA beneficiaries, especially Kenya, Mauritius, and Madagascar before the latter lost its eligibility in 2009. He also said that delays to renew AGOA have led to serious dislocation in the industry as buyers have cancelled important Christmas orders over concerns that AGOA's duty-free provisions will lapse. Further, Mr. Matanda also stated that if products subject to U.S. tariff rate quotas such as groundnuts, sweetened cocoa, leaf tobacco, cotton, and sugar were fully admissible into the United States under AGOA, trade in agricultural products would be significantly enhanced. Mr. Matanda urged the Commission to carefully study the manner in which tariff-rate quotas inhibit trade under AGOA.

Mr. Matanda stated that U.S. imports from AGOA-eligible countries would increase if those countries developed agricultural processing capabilities, such as producing edible oils. He said that the most effective ways for Africa to be inserted into global supply chains and distribution networks is through modernization of the rules of origin. If these rules were changed, according to Mr. Matanda, producers and suppliers would be part of the global value chain based on tasks where Africa has a competitive advantage. He also noted that COMESA opposes South Africa's graduation from AGOA despite South Africa's considerable market access barriers to U.S. investment and exports.

Esquel Mauritius Ltd (EML)[714]

In a written submission, Mr. John Cheh, Vice Chairman and Chief Executive Officer, Esquel Mauritius Ltd (EML), said that he will focus exclusively on three of the four investigations, Nos. 332-542, *AGOA: Trade and Investment Performance Overview;* 332-544, *AGOA: Economic Effects of Providing Duty-Free Treatment for Imports;* and 332-545, *U.S. AGOA Rules of Origin: Possible Changes to Promote Regional Integration and Increase Exports to the United States.* According to Mr. Cheh, EML is a wholly owned subsidiary of the Esquel Group, one of the world's leading producers of premium cotton shirts for international brands such as Nike, Ralph Lauren, Tommy Hilfiger, J. Crew, Brooks Brothers, Hugo Boss, and Lacoste. He noted that EML has manufactured apparel products in Mauritius for more than 30 years and that EML originally invested in Mauritius in response to the quota system under the Multi-Fiber Agreement (MFA). Notwithstanding the end of the MFA, the Esquel Group remained in Mauritius because of quality workmanship and special AGOA duty-free privileges. Maintaining the Third Country Rules of Origin, according to Mr. Cheh, is essential for EML to maintain its manufacturing and export business in Mauritius. He stated that EML strongly supports extension of this provision until 2030.

Mr. Cheh stated that the present rules of origin allowing the use of third-country fabric provide African exporters and U.S. buyers with significant benefits and said that the most recent delay in the renewal of the third-country fabric provision in 2012 negatively impacted U.S. imports under AGOA. He noted that such imports only recovered starting in January 2013 following the renewal of the third-country provision in August of 2012 and have continued to improve through the first nine months of 2013. He also explained that if the third-country provision is not renewed or extended in 2015, it would drastically reduce Mauritius' export competitiveness and result in serious consequences for its textile and apparel industry.

Mr. Cheh cited other areas where AGOA can be improved, including: trade capacity building, education, and health and safety. He also commented that the United States could work with Mauritius to develop an "AGOA Regional Centre" for SSA with a wide mandate to focus on several objectives: (1) help improve AGOA countries' understanding of the U.S. market and its supply chain; (2) lower administrative burdens to improve the clearance of goods and establish acceptance of electronic documents for entry; (3) assist the private sector in the development of the logistics industry in AGOA countries; (4) facilitate financial services to improve capital flow for infrastructure investments; (5) improve training for local labor and professionals; and (6) coordinate U.S. foreign aid projects.

Ms. Katrin Kuhlmann[715]

In a written submission and in hearing testimony related to all four investigations, Katrin Kuhlmann, president, New Markets Lab and Senior Advisor to the Corporate Council on Africa (CCA), said that New Markets is a nonprofit membership based organization founded to build economic opportunity in developing markets through legal and regulatory reform and that CCA was founded to promote trade and investment between the United States and Africa. She stated that she focused her comments on trade and investment policy, legal and regulatory reforms, value chain development, and African regional integration.

Ms. Kuhlmann reported that value chains are becoming more complex, within and outside Africa, and production and processing involve an increasing number of actors, locations, and countries. Ms. Kuhlmann noted that access to essential services is becoming increasingly integral to well-functioning trade and value chains. She stated that both New Markets and CCA focus on increasing opportunities in services trade. She indicated one particular focus of New Markets Lab is work with the International Fund for Agricultural Development that looks at law and regulations from the perspective of scaling up interventions to develop agricultural value chains.

Ms. Kuhlmann said that EPAs are problematic because the EU has shifted away from comprehensive preferences for many countries, yet maintains preferences for the poorest developing countries. This new policy, according to Ms. Kuhlmann, has met with heavy criticism and resistance by African policymakers. She stated that EPAs create benefits for European companies, but their ability to increase and diversify African trade is questionable. She stated that U.S. and European trade policies vis-à-vis SSA are unlikely to have much impact unless they complement African initiatives to build regional markets.

Leading Women of Africa (LWA)[716]

In a written submission, Madelein Mkunu, CEO and President, Leading Women of Africa, said that LWA was founded as a Pan African forum to promote women's economic empowerment in support of its 21st Century goals for sustainable development. She indicated that her submission would focus on investigation No. 332-542, *AGOA: Trade and Investment Performance Overview*. Mrs. Mkunu said that AGOA has assisted women in Africa by providing duty-free access to U.S. markets for product lines where women are employed or own small businesses. She urged that AGOA's renewal be done with the appropriate modifications to accommodate 21st century trade between the United States and the participating African nations so that African countries can continue to open their economies and build free markets. She indicated that AGOA's renewal is vital to generating: (1) tangible and profitable investments; (2) job creation and opportunity for under-educated youth and women; (3) skills transfer; (4) market access for women; and (5) economic growth. Ms. Mkunu expressed support for the renewal of AGOA for at least 15 years to ensure investor confidence for the trade and investment that has already benefited the women of SSA.

Manchester Trade[717]

In a written submission and in hearing testimony, Mr. Stephen Lande, President of Manchester Trade, indicated that he submitted Manchester Trade's recently developed "Blueprint for AGOA" as a pre-hearing submission. Mr Lande noted that his comments would address three of the Commission's investigations, Nos. 332-542 *AGOA: Trade and Performance Overview*; 332-545, *U.S. AGOA Rules of Origin: Possible Changes to Promote Regional Integration and Increase Exports to the United States*; and 332-546, *EU-South Africa FTA: Impact on U.S. Exports to South Africa*. Mr. Lande, stated that actual trade between AGOA and the United States is much lower than anticipated and has failed to meet its potential except for machinery, motor vehicles, fruits and vegetables, and garments usually incorporating Chinese yarns and fabric. Mr. Lande stated these results are not surprising given the supply constraints, particularly inadequate infrastructure and manufacturing and processing capacity.

Mr. Lande expressed the view that removal of an AGOA beneficiary country should be used as a last resort and should only be taken if the following conditions are met: (1) the U.S. action does not have a negative effect on current U.S. investors or a dampening impact on future investments; (2) the U.S. action does not harm innocent parties such as small African apparel producers that rely on AGOA; and (3) the action is supported by African countries.

With regard to investigation No. 332-544, Mr. Lande said that it is important that Congress and the Obama Administration consider including agricultural products currently excluded from AGOA, particularly TRQ products where South Africa has export potential (e.g., groundnuts, sugar, leaf tobacco). As for investigation No. 332-545, he said that current rules of origin do not assist in confronting the real challenges of AGOA since the development level of many beneficiaries does not allow them to add 35 percent value-added even when cumulated. He suggested that AGOA's rules of origin be amended to provide duty-free entry for supply chain products with sufficient African content, even if the content is added before the final stage of production. Mr. Lande recommended that the United States consider designating willing economic communities for AGOA eligibility rather than individual countries. With regards to investigation no. 332-546, Mr. Lande said that the starting point for this investigation must be an analysis of the impact on trade. He also said that U.S. exports will experience a greater substantial negative impact if South Africa is graduated from AGOA.

Manganese Metal Company (MMC)[718]

In a written submission, Buks Botes, Marketing Manager, Manganese Metal Company (MMC), said that his submission would focus on three of the investigations, Nos. 332-542, *AGOA: Trade and Investment Performance Overview*, 332-544, *AGOA: Economic Effects of Providing Duty- Free Treatment for Imports*, and 332-546, *EU-South Africa FTA: Impact on U.S. Exports to South Africa*. Mr. Botes said that MMC is a producer of electrolytic manganese metal (EMM) and is located in the town of Nelspruit, in the Mpumalanga province of South Africa. Mr. Botes expressed support for the renewal of AGOA and he noted that there is no U.S. production of EMM, with China and South Africa being the world's only major producers. According to Mr. Botes, EMM is used by U.S. industry as a key alloying element for the production of various grades of steel, stainless steel, foundry alloys, aluminum alloys, copper alloys, welding rods, and selected manganese-based chemicals.

Mr. Botes stated that due to the duty-free benefits of AGOA, South African material can be competitively priced in a U.S. market dominated by Chinese-produced material. He stated that it is very important for U.S. EMM buyers to have a second source of supply in order to reduce country-risk and to increase competitiveness between suppliers. Mr. Botes stated that if the current AGOA program is not renewed beyond September 2015 or if South Africa is no longer a beneficiary country, it is highly likely that MMC will be driven out of the U.S. market and even cease production, negatively impacting U.S. business.

Mr. Botes explained that despite benefits of duty-free treatment provided by the EU South Africa FTA, the U.S. market is far more important to MMC. He reported that over the years, the share of MMC's sales to the United States has increased due to the relative advantage that MMC enjoys in the U.S. market, where its Chinese competitors are subjected to a 14 percent import duty.

National Chicken Council (NCC), USA Poultry and Egg Export Council (USAPEEC)[719]

In a written submission and in hearing testimony, Mr. William Roenigk, Senior Consultant, National Chicken Council (NCC), said that his comments would address investigation No. 332-542, *AGOA: Trade and Investment Performance Overview*. Mr. Roenigk said that NCC represents U.S. companies that produce and process over 95 percent of the chickens in the United States, and that the USA Poultry and Egg Export Council (USAPEEC) is a national trade association representing the interests of the U.S. poultry and egg export industry. Mr. Roenigk said that USAPPEEC members account for nearly 90 percent of total U.S. poultry and egg exports. He indicated that unless South Africa lifts anti-dumping duties on U.S. poultry, described below, and allows trade to resume fairly and without restraint, NCC and USAPEEC will strongly oppose any further extension of AGOA benefits to South Africa.

Mr. Roenigk noted that since 2000, South Africa has imposed antidumping duties on U.S. poultry. Prior to 2000, according to Mr. Roenigk, the U.S. industry enjoyed a South African export market of nearly 55,000 metric tons annually. He contends that South Africa initiated an antidumping case against U.S. poultry imports as a protectionist measure. He noted that South Africa is a net importer of poultry meat and the imposition of antidumping duties meant that South African domestic prices increased to four times the world price. Mr. Roenigk stated that since the imposition of antidumping duties, U.S. poultry has been totally shut out of the South African market.

Mr. Roenigk said that domestic poultry producers assumed that the U.S. government would immediately mount a challenge at the World Trade Organization (WTO). He stated that, despite constant requests that the case be pursued at the WTO, no action was taken. Mr. Roenigk also stated that in 2007 South Africa's imposition of antidumping duties on U.S. poultry was determined by the South African Supreme Court to be illegal under South African law. He noted that South African antidumping authorities simply declined to implement the Court's ruling and continued to impose antidumping duties on U.S. products.

National Foreign Trade Council (NFTC)[720]

In a written submission and hearing testimony, Mr. Dan O'Flaherty, Vice President, National Foreign Trade Council (NFTC), said his comments would address investigation No. 332-542, *AGOA: Trade and Investment Performance Overview*. He said that the NFTC is an association of 200 U.S.-based multinational corporations engaged in international trade and investment. Mr. O'Flaherty stated that AGOA preferences benefit both U.S. companies that source in Africa and African exporters. He stated that while reciprocity should remain the ultimate goal of AGOA, more adjustment time is required. The NFTC, according to Mr. O'Flaherty, supports renewal of AGOA, but is of the view that useful changes can be made to the statute.

Mr. O'Flaherty stated that the NFTC supports reducing U.S. content requirements, including changing the rules of origin to qualify significant intermediate African value-added even when the final product is exported from elsewhere. Additionally, he noted that NFTC supports allowing the designation of Africa's regional economic commitments (RECs) as AGOA beneficiaries provided that the REC's meet the eligibility requirements. Finally, Mr. Flaherty reported that a significant sector of the U.S. business community supports reciprocity for South Africa, as well as other countries in the region.

Mr. O'Flaherty identified three useful changes to AGOA: (1) designate REC's as eligible for AGOA benefits if they accept U.S. conditions; (2) enhance capacity-building in eligible countries; and (3) modify current AGOA rules of origin which currently require 35 percent of a product be made in an AGOA-beneficiary country for eligibility. Mr. O'Flaherty asserted that AGOA should be renewed for a period of 2 years, during which the Executive Branch and Congress can review the advice of the Commission, GAO, and private sector organizations to develop a stronger AGOA.

National Pork Producers Council (NPPC)[721]

In its written submission, the National Pork Producers Council (NPPC) said that it represents a federation of 43 state producer organizations and thus the domestic and global interests of 67,000 U.S. pork operations. The NPPC focused its comments on investigation No. 332-542, *AGOA: Trade and Investment Performance Overview*. The NPPC asserted that extending AGOA for more than five years, or worse, making it permanent, would be a serious mistake. In its written submission, NPPC noted that non-reciprocal free trade programs can be useful short term tools to assist developing countries compete in foreign markets, but dependence on preference programs for long or indefinite periods is unwise.

The NPPC said that its concerns focus particularly on South Africa because it is a major recipient of U.S. foreign economic assistance and trade benefits under AGOA, while its pork market is closed to U.S. producers. South Africa, according to the NPPC, blocks U.S. pork exports based on unscientific and unjustifiable concerns about porcine reproductive and respiratory syndrome, trichinae, pseudorabies, and other issues. The Council asserted that South Africa is not meeting the AGOA Section 104 requirement that it establishes or makes substantial progress toward establishing "the elimination of barriers to U.S. trade and investment." It also stated that AGOA is a one-way free trade agreement where the U.S. allows imports under AGOA to enter duty- free, while U.S. exports typically face myriad non-tariff measures that limit or block U.S. exports. The NPPC stated that it does not oppose the renewal of GSP and does not oppose an extension of AGOA for a period of five years or less. The Council would prefer to resolve these trade barriers at a technical level. The Council noted that the extension of GSP or AGOA to South Africa would remove any incentive for that country to move toward a reciprocal trade relationship with the United States. However, according to the NPPC, given the de facto ban on U.S. pork exports and the lack of progress in opening the market, U.S. pork producers may have no choice but to come out in opposition to AGOA.

Progressive Economy[722]

In a written submission and in hearing testimony, Edward Gresser, Director, Progressive Economy, said that Progressive Economy is a project of the Global Works Foundation and a non-partisan non-profit section 501(c)(3) organization. The Progressive Economy project is a research project meant to deepen understanding of U.S. trade policy and the global economy, with a special focus on supporting development and the reduction of poverty through trade. Mr. Gresser noted that his presentation would focus on investigation No. 332-542, *AGOA: Trade and Investment Performance Overview*.

Mr. Gresser offered the following observations about AGOA: (1) AGOA is a central element of U.S.-Africa economic relations and should be renewed in a timely fashion, (2) AGOA's market access provisions in clothing and manufacturing have yielded less benefits than commonly thought, whereas the enhanced dialogue, Trade Hubs, and other features meant to raise awareness of U.S. market opportunities and policy rules have probably done more, and (3) infrastructure and trade logistics are the greatest challenge to Africa's ability to take advantage of global market opportunities.

Mr. Gesser asserted that Africa's major successes in exporting to the United States have resulted mainly from the improved information on the U.S. market that African businesses, governments, and farm groups built up through AGOA's Ministerial conferences, Trade Hubs, and other dialogues. He also said that the effects of additional market access appear to be concentrated in the automotive industry, while the clothing program viewed as the centerpiece of the program in 2000 has produced only modest results.

Rocky Mountain District Export Council (RMDEC)[723]

In a written submission to the Commission, Rocky Mountain District Export Council (RMDEC) said that its comments would focus on investigation No. 332-542, *AGOA: Trade and Investment Performance Overview*. RMDEC stated that it is a trade advisory group to the U.S. Department of Commerce's International Trade Administration. The Council added that its mission is to educate and promote exports, exporting, and trade policy. RMDEC stated that its regional stakeholders for AGOA include multinational corporations, small and medium enterprises, and individual entrepreneurs, primarily in the agricultural and extractive industries. The Council said that the following factors impede trade, investment, and the economic climate in SSA: (1) lack of infrastructure; (2) a need for institutional capacity building; (3) a lack of policies, programs, and projects that advance corporate social responsibility; and (4) a lack of support for micro trade opportunities.

To overcome these impediments, Rocky Mountain suggests: (1) more support for energy infrastructure development; (2) support for training in leadership, best business practices, and technical English, with a complement of U.S. loans or grants devoted to capacity building; (3) support for public health, schools, agriculture and animal husbandry to differentiate U.S. efforts from those of its competitors; (4) inclusions of micro-finance in the AGOA effort; and (5) pursuit of responsible trade, not exploitation. The Council concluded by asking that the U.S. government consider supporting AGOA's ongoing trade shows being held across the United States to promote mutual trust.

Dr. Witney Schneidman[724]

In a written submission and in hearing testimony, Dr. Witney Schneidman, Senior International Advisor for Africa, Covington & Burling LLP and Nonresident Senior Fellow, African Growth Initiative, Brookings, said that his comments relate to three of the Commission's investigations, Nos. 332-542, *AGOA: Trade and Investment Performance Overview*; 332 545, *Rules of Origin: Possible Changes to Promote Regional Integration and Increase Exports to the United States*, and 332-546, *EU-South Africa FTA: Impact on U.S. Exports to South Africa*.

As concerns investigation No. 332-542, Dr. Schneidman indicated that the overriding concern is how investments by the EU, China, Brazil, and India have overshadowed the presence of U.S. firms in Africa. He stated that as a non-reciprocal preference program, AGOA has done little to advance the interests of U.S. companies. Dr. Schneidman suggested a zero tax on repatriated income from investments in productive areas would encourage U.S. companies to become more active in Africa.

Further, Dr. Schneidman indicated that the United States can offer more programs like those offered by the Millennium Challenge Corporation to strengthen regional integration and supply chains, which would increase exports to the United States. Dr. Schneidman also expressed the view that it would be a mistake to graduate South Africa from AGOA in 2015. He indicated that the Congressional Research Service reported that preferential imports from South Africa totaled $3.7 billion in 2012, accounting for roughly three-quarters of all U.S. imports from SSA under AGOA/GSP.

Dr. Schneidman stated it is important to note that the EU has adopted a trade policy toward Africa predicated on EPAs, which is negative for Africa, undermines regional integration, and discriminates against FDI and trade that does not originate in the EU. He recommended that USTR raise objections to the EPAs in the context of the Transatlantic Trade and Investment Partnership negotiations, but also in a formal discussion with the African Union. The African Union, according to Dr. Schneidman, should be encouraged to request the EU to postpone the deadline of October 1, 2014 when African nations are required to sign interim agreements.

U.S. Chamber of Commerce[725]

In a written submission and in hearing testimony, Mr. Scott Eisner, Vice President, African Affairs, U.S. Chamber of Commerce, said that the Chamber is the world's largest business federation representing the interests of more than three million businesses, state and local chambers, and industry associations. Mr. Eisner stated that the Chamber's comments address investigation No. 332-542, *AGOA: Trade and Investment Performance Overview*. Mr. Eisner stated that AGOA remains the cornerstone of U.S. trade and investment policy toward SSA. He remarked that AGOA's expiration provides the opportunity to review its integral role within U.S.-African relations and to readjust the legislation to reflect Africa's changing economic and political environment.

Mr. Eisner said that new products should be included in AGOA, the Agreement should be extended for a longer period of time, and that AGOA's third-party fabric provision should be changed. He also stated that some of the U.S. government's aid to Africa should be directed to build Africa's technical capacity under AGOA. Further, Mr. Eisner stated that AGOA's pending expiration undermines business and investor certainty, which is already affecting business decisions and trade, and said that if AGOA were to expire, many of the significant gains made by African economies would be undermined.

Mr. Eisner stated AGOA eligibility requirements must include factors that foster greater two-way trade such as intellectual property protections, customs regimes, and regulatory and legal standards. He also said that each AGOA eligible country must begin to implement sound trade practices in order to enhance bilateral and multilateral trading relationships. Finally, Mr. Eisner proposed that AGOA benefits for eligible countries be extended beyond 2015 to provide greater predictability and stability to U.S.-Africa trade.

United States Fashion Industry Association (USFIA)[726]

In a written submission, Julia Hughes, President, United States Fashion Industry Association (USFIA), said that USFIA represents textile and apparel brands, retailers, importers, and wholesalers based in the United States. She indicated that she would concentrate on two of the investigations, Nos. 332-542, *AGOA: Trade and Investment Performance Review*, and 332-545, *U.S. AGOA Rules of Origin: Possible Changes to Promote Regional Integration and Promote Exports to the United States*. USFIA member companies, according to Ms. Hughes, continue to source from textile and apparel producers in SSA. Ms. Hughes noted that these companies want to maintain partnerships on the African continent and she made the following recommendations: (1) AGOA should be renewed on a seamless basis as soon as possible and no later than 2014; (2) AGOA should be reauthorized for a 15-year period; (3) the third-country fabric provision should be renewed for the full duration of the AGOA renewal; (4) all AGOA beneficiary countries should benefit from AGOA's third-country fabric provision; and (5) trade capacity building programs should be expanded.

Universal Leaf Tobacco Company, Inc. (Universal)[727]

In a written submission, Mr. H. Michael Ligon, Vice President, Universal Leaf Tobacco Company (Universal), said that his company's business is based on its core function as a reliable, service-oriented international link between leaf tobacco growers and product manufacturers. He stated that Universal conducts business through its affiliates in Malawi,

Mozambique, South Africa, Tanzania, Zambia, and Zimbabwe. Mr. Ligon indicated that his submission would focus on investigation Nos. 332-542, *AGOA: Trade and Investment Performance Overview*, and 332-544, *AGOA: Economic Effects of Providing Duty-Free Treatment for Imports.*

Mr. Ligon stated that although AGOA is an extremely important trade preference program that has helped improve the economic and diplomatic relationships between the United States and the countries of SSA, it is undermined by, *inter alia*, tariff-rate quotas (TRQs) applied to many agricultural products. According to Mr. Ligon, only a small amount of leaf tobacco imports into the United States from Africa enters under AGOA. He noted that this is because the U.S. TRQ on leaf tobacco provides only a small duty free quota to imports from Malawi and other SSA exporters. Likewise, he noted that other SSA exporters are excluded from the U.S. market by high tariffs and limited volumes.

Further, Mr. Ligon said that AGOA should be renewed in an expeditious manner because it would be imprudent to wait until September 2015 as it would cause uncertainty. He also recommended that AGOA be improved by expanding access for products subject to TRQs. He stated that the AGOA legislation does not provide for TRQs on agricultural products, but rather they exist separately. Mr. Ligon asserted that leaf tobacco should be exempt from the over- quota tariff.

World Cocoa Foundation (WCF)[728]

In a written submission to the Commission, Mr. William Guyton, Vice President, World Cocoa Foundation (WCF) said that his submission concerns two of the investigations, Nos. 332-542, *AGOA: Trade and Investment Performance Overview* and 332-544, *AGOA; Economic Effects of Providing Duty-Free Treatment for Imports*. Mr. Guyton noted WCF's support for AGOA's renewal and expansion. Mr. Guyton contended that AGOA reached its objectives of expanding U.S. trade and investment with SSA, stimulating regional economic growth and economic integration, and facilitating SSA's integration into the global economy and has emerged as a critical element of U.S. policy in the region.

Mr. Guyton stated that the World Cocoa Foundation welcomed the increase in U.S.-SSA trade and indicated that more than $1 billion in cocoa beans and products are imported from SSA into the United States annually. He also noted that the United States continues to import more cocoa beans and products from SSA than any other agricultural product. Mr. Guyton urged the Commission to document AGOA's vital role in expanding and diversifying exports from AGOA beneficiary countries to the United States and to explain the economic benefits of expanded trade with SSA for U.S. and African producers, workers, farmers, and consumers to USTR, Congress, and the American people.

APPENDIX E. U.S. IMPORTS UNDER AGOA

Table E.1. U.S. imports for consumption under AGOA (excluding crude petroleum), by beneficiary country, 2001, 2005, and 2008–13

Country	2001	2005	2008	2009	2010	2011	2012	2013
			Thousand $					
Angola	a	99,583.4	96,057.7	38,055.9	0.0	0.0	216,742.1	96,386.9
Benin	0.0	0.0	0.0	0.0	0.0	0.0	0.0	0.0
Botswana	0.0	30,043.7	15,803.0	12,361.7	11,558.5	15,478.5	10,426.7	5,856.1
Burkina Faso	a	0.0	0.0	0.0	1.7	1.7	5.0	186.24
Burundi	a	a	0.0	0.0	0.0	0.0	0.0	0.0
Cameroon	15,259.2	69,153.1	72,737.8	45,099.6	69,409.4	137,372.0	65,148.1	36,426.7
Cabo Verde	0.0	2,115.4	0.0	0.0	145.6	154.0	116.9	146.4
Central African Republic	0.0	a	a	a	a	a	a	a
Chad	0.0	108,103.5	0.0	0.0	0.0	17,529.9	0.0	0.0
Comoros	a	a	0.0	0.0	0.0	0.0	0.0	0.0
Côte d'Ivoire	a	a	a	a	a	0.0	29,901.5	229.3
Congo, Dem. Rep.	a	0.0	0.0	0.0	0.0	0.0	a	a
Djibouti	0.0	0.0	0.0	16.8	0.0	0.0	0.0	0.0
Eritrea	0.0	a	a	a	a	a	a	a
Ethiopia	215.3	3,646.4	9,391.5	6,723.4	6,875.1	10,886.5	18,294.1	31,711.3
Gabon	0.0	0.0	19,202.8	15,857.0	0.0	0.0	0.0	17,339.8
Gambia	a	0.0	0.0	0.0	5.3	1.4	0.0	0.0
Ghana	33,092.4	49,926.9	31,493.6	2,303.3	2,052.8	72,731.1	16,988.1	2,811.0
Guinea	0.0	0.0	0.7	1.1	a	0.0	2.5	5.6
Guinea-Bissau	0.0	0.0	0.0	0.0	0.0	0.0	0.0	a
Kenya	55,090.2	272,131.1	252,243.0	204,981.6	220,636.1	288,273.4	287,737.5	336,534.8
Lesotho	129,522.8	388,344.3	338,796.8	277,046.4	280,341.6	314,311.2	300,609.0	320,806.9
Liberia	a	a	0.0	0.0	0.0	0.0	0.0	0.0

Country	2001	2005	2008	2009	2010	2011	2012	2013
Madagascar	92,145.3	273,193.1	277,050.7	210,003.9	[a]	[a]	[a]	[a]
Malawi	12,057.3	32,375.2	26,680.4	39,734.3	47,190.6	56,145.6	46,307.1	47,084.2
Mali	0.0	0.0	3.9	61.6	3.6	1.6	20.6	[a]
Mauritania	0.0	0.0	0.0	[a]	0.0	0.0	0.0	0.0
Mauritius	38,899.5	146,807.5	97,291.5	98,747.2	117,910.9	155,982.1	160,030.0	187,894.6
Mozambique	0.0	2,827.7	129.1	0.0	183.6	688.6	29.5	1,361.8
Namibia	0.0	53,058.4	6.2	0.0	5.3	12.8	215.6	0.0
Niger	0.0	24.3	0.7	2.8	[a]	0.0	1.2	0.3
Nigeria	191,368.7	1,194,923.9	1,294,141.2	394,603.6	551,064.9	828,360.0	934,024.2	942,087.2
Congo, Rep.	37,112.7	109,513.7	27,473.5	19,081.2	0.0	9,843.2	40,267.4	144,815.1
Rwanda	265.2	0.5	5.3	62.9	10.5	17.3	7.9	9.4
São Tomé and Principe	0.0	0.0	0.0	0.0	0.0	0.0	0.0	0.0
Senegal	0.0	9.2	10,228.9	1,585.1	6.7	2.7	5,634.0	11.0
Seychelles	0.0	0.0	0.0	0.0	0.0	0.0	0.0	0.0
Sierra Leone	0.0	0.0	0.0	0.0	0.0	0.0	0.0	0.0
South Africa	417,256.3	455,315.6	2,427,689.9	1,642,892.5	1,902,140.4	2,458,159.6	2,384,108.7	2,578,238.1
South Sudan	[a]	[a]	[a]	[a]	[a]	[a]	[a]	0.0
Swaziland	8,314.0	160,462.3	125,386.6	94,718.2	92,798.4	77,121.1	62,373.3	53,940.0
Tanzania	15.7	2,811.7	1,527.3	1,006.2	1,850.1	5,130.9	10,445.8	10,359.7
Togo	[a]	[a]	0.0	0.0	0.0	0.0	44,448.4	0.0
Uganda	0.0	4,854.3	472.6	221.9	344.8	786.9	64.5	55.9
Zambia	9.8	0.0	4.8	6.7	0.4	10.3	6.8	8.3
Total U.S. imports under AGOA excluding crude petroleum	1,030,624.5	3,459,225.1	5,123,819.3	3,105,174.9	3,304,536.0	4,449,002.3	4,633,956.3	4,814,126.9

Source: USITC DataWeb/USDOC (accessed February 18, 2014).

Notes: The data in this table are based on the list of AGOA eligible countries, which varies by year. For a complete list of AGOA eligible countries by year, see table 1.1. Data on U.S. imports for consumption under AGOA reported in this table exclude imports under HTS 2709 (crude petroleum) and rate provision code 11 (imports into U.S. Virgin Islands). [a] = Country was not AGOA eligible in this year.

APPENDIX F. PRODUCT SPACE METHODOLOGY AND DATA

Summary of Product Space and Complexity Analysis

Background

This appendix provides additional information on the product space and complexity analysis, which has become an increasingly applied approach to identify potentially competitive products. Work begun by Ricardo Hausmann and César Hidalgo has expanded the analysis of countries' export capabilities while illuminating the evolution of countries' productive structures and the implications of those structures for economic development.[729] Their work, here referred to as "product space and complexity analysis," draws on network science to determine how close products are to each other in terms of the production capabilities required to produce them, as well as how complex or sophisticated they are from the same point of view. The analysis covers all goods trade data, including manufactured goods, agricultural goods, and natural resources.[730] This analysis also shows the effect on countries' economic development of expanding the range and sophistication of products.

One insight from product space and complexity analysis is that it is important to calculate how close products are to each other—that is, how many capabilities are shared in the production of any two products.[731] This is determined by measuring "proximity"—the minimum probability that a country exports product 1 given that it exports product 2, or vice versa—which formalizes the intuitive idea that the ability of a country to produce one product depends on its ability to produce other products. Proximity and other related indicators provide insights into the possible ease with which a country producing product 1 will be able to move into producing product 2. The product space is the network connecting products based on their proximity, or how close they are to each other, and, therefore, the potential of exporting closely related products.

In examining what products countries export over time, research shows that countries tend to diversify by developing products that are close in the product space to those they already export.[732] The researchers show empirically that countries move from products that they already create to others that are "nearby"[733] in terms of the productive knowledge and capabilities that the products require. Their work has also shown that countries that develop successfully do so by exporting a diverse range of products, while countries that have lagged in development usually export a limited range of products. They theorize that producing a diverse range of products helps grow a nation's productive capabilities and the knowledge needed to produce new products.[734]

Economic complexity analysis examines which countries export a product, and then examines which other products are also exported by the countries that export the original product. The results determine a product-specific level of complexity or sophistication (i.e., more complex products are exported by only a few countries, which also export other complex products as well as a wide range of products; and less complex products are exported by many countries who also predominantly export a relatively limited range of products).[735] For example, complexity analysis has shown that not only do few countries export x-ray machines, but those countries also export a diverse range of other products, including other products that few countries export. On the other hand, it has also shown that many of the world's least-developed countries export only products (such as raw materials and agricultural products) that other countries with similarly limited export profiles also export.[736]

Product space and complexity analysis allows researchers to see relationships in the product export patterns that are not necessarily immediately obvious using other traditional methods of analysis (e.g., factor accumulation, technology differences, or supply chain).[737] One of their insights is that "input-output relationships do not explain proximity—i.e., products do not tend to be strongly connected to other varieties up or down the value chain." For example, one might think that exporting apparel is related to exporting textiles because those products are linked in a supply chain, but countries that are large apparel exporters may not actually also be large textile exporters. However, countries that are large apparel exporters may also be large wiring harness exporters, as the productive knowledge needed to produce apparel is more similar to the productive knowledge needed to produce wiring harnesses than it is to the productive knowledge needed to produce textiles.[738] Consequently, developing countries with the productive knowledge to produce apparel might be well advised to move into producing wiring harnesses before moving into producing textiles.[739]

Analysis of the product space and of a country's current export profile provides insight into potential avenues for development strategies. This analytical approach and these metrics can be used as an initial step or component, along with other analytical approaches, in a country- and product-focused process of identifying potentially competitive products and policies to advance economic development. Various entities assessing potential export products and opportunities for economic development are starting to turn to product space and economic complexity analyses.[740]

For example, the Government of Malawi's Ministry of Industry and Trade, in its *National Export Strategy 2013–2018*, began its nine-step assessment with a trade and market analysis that applies product space to Malawi exports. The goal was to provide a "road map for developing Malawi's productive base to allow for both export competitiveness and economic empowerment."[741]

After identifying potentially competitive products, the document assessed the economic environment, supportive institutions, and competencies, skills, and knowledge needed in order to develop an overall production development strategy to address appropriate constraints or build capabilities. Similarly, in a study for the German Marshall Fund, César Hidalgo applied these analytical approaches to identify new industrial export and production opportunities for Southern and Eastern African countries, both individually and as a regional grouping.[742]

Hidalgo noted in this study that the alternative approach provided by the product space analysis "allows us to make predictions about the products that a country can make in the future, since the ability of a country to produce a product in the future depends, through the local presence of capabilities, on the products that it is currently making."[743]

The African Development Bank also used product space analysis as an initial step in its *Comparative Study on Export Policies in Egypt, Morocco, Tunisia, and South Korea*.[744] In this study, Hausmann and Bustos used product space and complexity analyses to understand the structural transformation of Egypt, Morocco, and Tunisia, and then to compare them to China, the Republic of Korea, and Thailand. The report aimed to provide "policy recommendations on how these countries could improve their exports in the strategic industries."[745] Yet another example is a study by the Millennium Challenge Corporation and the Government of Liberia.

In helping Liberia and its development partners to identify the constraints on growth in Liberia, as well as the most binding constraints on diversity and investment, the researchers used product space analysis to "examine whether a lack of information on profitable opportunities constrains diversity and investment in Liberia."[746]

Selected Product Space and Complexity Data and Variables[747]

The product space and complexity analysis methodology produces several metrics that can help researchers identify potentially competitive products for export and economic development.

The terms describing these metrics allow researchers to classify products by their relatedness, complexity, and potential for future growth. The metrics *density* and *product complexity* are two measures that could point to areas for further research into potentially competitive products for AGOA-eligible countries because they can be used to predict extensive margin growth (e.g., diversification or expansion into new products) as a result of expanding or acquiring additional capabilities based on a country's current capabilities. The ability to expand capabilities, however, is affected by a variety of policies or market factors (e.g., domestic or international policies, domestic or international regulations, infrastructure constraints), and detailed product-specific analysis of relevant policies and market factors would be required to determine the viability of expanding into these product areas.

Density

Density measures how "close" a product is to a country's current productive capabilities. That is, products with a high density for a particular country are very close (i.e., their production involves many similar shared capabilities) to the products that the country already exports (e.g., men's shirts and women's shirts).

Product Complexity

The Product Complexity Index (PCI) measures how complex a product is by seeing how many countries export the product, and whether the product is also exported by countries that export other complex products. For example, the few countries that export x-ray machines also tend to export other complex machinery (that are exported by relatively few countries) as well as a diverse range of products.

Thus, x-ray machines have a relatively high PCI. On the other hand, many countries export light manufacturing products, but they tend to have a much more limited range of exports (that are exported by many countries, including those that export x-ray machines). Thus, footwear has a relatively low PCI.

Selected SSA Country Data and Results

To identify shared production capabilities among products, it is optimal to use internationally comparable production data. Since internationally comparable and sufficiently detailed production data are not available, export data, which reflect production capabilities and for which there are internationally comparable data, are used as a proxy for production. Product space analysis, complexity analysis, and associated metrics for this appendix were constructed using international trade data at the HTS (Harmonized Tariff Schedule) 4-digit level of aggregation.

Services trade data are not included because of the lack of sufficiently detailed and internationally comparable services trade data by industry. Natural resource products also were excluded in compiling the list of closest products based on density, as these products rely on geographic natural endowments that are not easily acquired by countries. The HTS 4-digit categories are identified with accessible labels[748] for ease of interpretation and reading. In some instances, the label appears distant from a country's production capabilities. These categories, nevertheless, may include a wide variety of products that are exported or capable of being exported by SSA countries when examined at a more disaggregated level, or may reflect data anomalies (e.g., reexports or exports of products destined for refurbishing or repair).

Potentially competitive products include both products a country does not export as well as those the country may export in some quantity, but not enough[749] to be considered globally competitive. While this analytical approach provides, among other things, insight into potentially competitive products, it does not in and of itself identify the specific missing capabilities, policy constraints, or policy or economic environment changes that would be necessary to expand into these potentially competitive products. Also, although the identified products are specific to a particular export country, they are not specific to a destination or market; i.e., these are potentially competitive products for global export, and not specifically to the U.S. market or specifically under the AGOA program.

For this analysis, the product space and complexity analysis data are presented for 21 countries: Angola, Cameroon, Chad, Côte d'Ivoire, the Republic of the Congo, Ethiopia, Gabon, Ghana, Kenya, Liberia, Mali, Mauritania, Mauritius, Mozambique, Nigeria, Senegal, South Africa, Tanzania, Togo, Uganda, and Zambia (tables F.1 through F.21 and figures F.1 through F.21).[750] These data are intended to illustrate the initial output using product space and complexity analysis—products that would warrant additional analysis to determine opportunities, constraints, and overall viability for production and exports. They are not meant to be interpreted as specific products that should be exported by AGOA-eligible countries; the products identified have not undergone additional analysis or vetting for country-specific production and export viability. This analytical approach and these metrics are most effective when supplemented by other analytical approaches, in a country- and product-focused process of identifying potentially competitive products.[751]

For each of the 21 SSA countries, there is a table and a figure providing product space and economic complexity metrics and export data. The first, second, and third columns of each table provide the rank, name, and HTS 4-digit code of the 15 most potentially competitive products based on the density metric defined above. These 15 products represent the 15 products closest to the country's current export profile or basket that are not currently competitively exported, as described above. The fourth and fifth columns list exports for the country and for all AGOA-eligible countries for 2012; these data provide context as to whether the country is exporting the product (though not globally competitively) or not, and whether other AGOA countries are exporting the same or similar products. Each corresponding figure plots the actual values for density and complexity (both defined above) for these 15 products.[752]

The density value is a country- and product-specific metric. That is, the density value for a given product—say, non-fileted frozen fish—is different for different countries; for example, it is different for Angola than for Mozambique. This difference is because the density value is relative to each country's current specific export products and related capabilities. The complexity value, on the other hand, is a product-specific metric. The level of product complexity for a specific product—say, copper wire—does not differ for different countries. Products that appear near the lower right-hand quadrant represent products that are both closer to the country's current production capabilities and relatively less complex; products in the upper left-hand quadrant represent products that are not as close to the country's current production capabilities and are also relatively more complex.[753] Decisions on which products would ultimately be more useful for production, export, and economic development would require researchers to identify the related constraints to production and export for each country, as well as the overall strategic value of these products in supporting economic development and increased income.

Summary of Identified Products

Despite the wide variety of the products identified as potentially competitive for the AGOA- eligible countries below, several sectors are prominent on the list. Sectors that emerge often across countries are agricultural and animal products, textile inputs and other textile products, apparel, footwear, accessories, processed wood products, processed metal products, low-tech manufactured products, construction products, and chemicals. Specific products in each of these sectors are listed below. As noted above, these are areas of potential competitiveness for these countries, for which additional detailed analysis would provide better insight into feasibility and product-specific issues.

- A large number of identified products are in the **agricultural and animal products** sector. These included unprocessed fruits, vegetables, or plants (such as cassava, tropical fruits, pepper, grapes, ginger, dried legumes, honey, bananas, cut flowers, and raw tobacco); processed fruits, vegetables, and nuts (such as cocoa paste and powder, dried, preserved, or frozen fruit and vegetables, sugar, fruit juice, and wine); processed animal products (such as hides and fur skins, and prepared animal hair), and fish products (such as processed fish and non-fileted frozen fish).
- **Textile inputs** were also identified, including wool and heavy pute woven cotton. **Other textile** products include carpets, blankets, and conveyor belt textiles. **Apparel** items include shirts, socks/hosiery, coats, and undergarments. Footwear parts were identified as a potentially competitive product in the **footwear** sector. Various **accessories** that could be potentially competitive include hat shapes (or forms) and neckties.
- **Processed wood** products that could be competitively produced include plywood, plaiting products, wood carpentry, shaped wood, and other wood articles. Similarly, **processed metal** products include copper wire, aluminum wire and bars, and metal clad products.
- Several **low-tech manufactured** products that were listed include plastic pipes, twine and rope, netting, jewelry, metal-clad watches, and watch cases and parts.
- A variety of **chemicals** are identified as potentially competitive products for a number of countries, although South Africa accounts for a large number of these products.
- Some **construction**-related products also emerge for several countries, including building stone, curbstones, and rock wool.

Comparison with Review of Literature in Sections 3 and 4

At an aggregate level, several of the sectors and products identified by the product space and complexity analysis shown above are broadly similar to those mentioned in this report as having export potential and targeted for further development. For example, several of the product groups listed in the literature as having potential for integration into regional or global supply chains (presented in section 3 of this report) overlap with the product space analysis presented here. These include agricultural products and foodstuffs, as well as textile and apparel products. Additionally, several sectors identified and targeted by country governments and stakeholders across SSA for further development as part of broader economic development strategies[754] (presented in section 4 of this report) overlap with the product space analysis here. These include agricultural (particularly horticultural) products, and handcraft and woodcraft products (e.g., basketry, mats, and home furnishings).

Table F.1. Angola: Potentially competitive products based on product space metric

Density Ranking[a]	Product	HTS-4 code	Angola exports, 2012[b]	All AGOA country exports, 2012[b]
			Actual $	
1	Raw Tobacco	2401	0	1,507,457,515
2	Non-fillet Frozen Fish	0303	45	850,988,814
3	Antiknock	3811	145,741	7,284,069
4	Yachts	8903	41,775	69,626,380
5	Butter	0405	0	8,508,921
6	Ginger	0910	0	53,875,138
7	Dried Legumes	0713	0	361,812,983
8	Building Stone	6802	282,733	24,243,031
9	Acyclic Alcohols	2905	0	241,922,048
10	Saturated Acyclic Monocarboxylic Acids	2915	98,298	45,736,167
11	Netting	5608	10,741	5,004,878
12	Safety Glass	7007	99,421	42,635,101
13	Metal-Clad Products	7114	0	1,082,545
14	Further Prepared Bovine & Equine Hides	4107	0	20,328,594
15	Aluminum Wire	7605	0	2,913,145

Source: Growth Lab, Harvard CID, and The Observatory (product space/density data, including HTS labels), accessed December 19, 2013; GTIS (export data), accessed January 15, 2014.

Notes: Does not include Natural Resources sector, as defined by Growth Lab.

[a] Ranked from closest to farthest products among the closest 15 products (i.e., 15 products nearest to the country's current capabilities) for all HTS 4-digit codes.

[b] Includes inter-African trade.

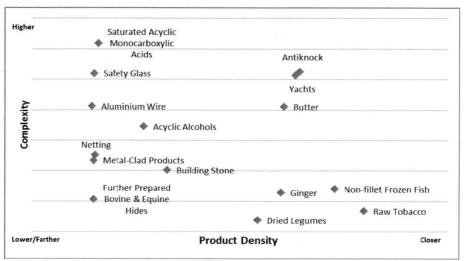

Source: Growth Lab at the Harvard Center for International Development and The Observatory, http://atlas.cid.harvard.edu/ (product space and complexity data, including HTS labels).

Figure F.1. Angola: Product space and complexity metrics related to potentially competitive products.

Table F.2. Cameroon: Potentially competitive products based on product space metric

Density ranking[a]	Product	HTS-4 code	Cameroon exports, 2012[b]	All AGOA country exports, 2012[b]
			Actual $	
1	Cocoa Paste	1803	57,201,397	1,226,596,440
2	Cassava	0714	414,124	36,217,158
3	Cocoa Powder	1805	220,694	299,751,380
4	Plywood	4412	6,174,598	85,299,294
5	Shaped Wood	4409	5,997,401	32,624,726
6	Wood Carpentry	4418	846,605	48,970,037
7	Tropical Fruits	0804	9,791,460	317,693,149
8	Cut Flowers	0603	996,416	927,202,015
9	Other Wood Articles	4421	662,696	17,096,947
10	Prepared Wool or Animal Hair	5105	0	62,665,732
11	Other Nuts	0802	48,982	232,901,371
12	Other Animals	0106	86,079	67,675,222
13	Pepper	0904	29,215	18,343,395
14	Raw Sugar	1701	8	1,140,039,544
15	Flavored Water	2202	412,670	70,372,513

Source: Growth Lab, Harvard CID, and The Observatory (product space/density data, including HTS labels), accessed December 19, 2013; GTIS (export data), accessed January 15, 2014.

Notes: Does not include Natural Resources sector, as defined by Growth Lab. [a] Ranked from closest to farthest products among the closest 15 products (i.e., 15 products nearest to the country's current capabilities) for all HTS 4-digit codes.

[b] Includes inter-African trade.

AGOA: Trade and Investment Performance Overview   233

Source: Growth Lab at the Harvard Center for International Development and The Observatory, http://atlas.cid.harvard.edu/ (product space and complexity data, including HTS labels).

Figure F.2. Cameroon: Product space and complexity metrics related to potentially competitive products.

Table F.3. Chad: Potentially competitive products based on product space metric

Density ranking[a]	Product	HTS-4 code	Chad exports, 2012[b]	All AGOA country exports, 2012[b]
			Actual $	
1	Halides	2812	0	5,064,697
2	Epoxides	2910	0	36,270
3	Precious Metal Compounds	2843	0	243,466,922
4	Nitrile Compounds	2926	0	1,385,915
5	Curbstones	6801	0	70,904
6	Plastic Pipes	3917	176,358	81,160,528
7	Rock Wool	6806	0	7,763,980
8	Glaziers Putty	3214	0	14,582,733
9	Building Stone	6802	0	24,243,031
10	Ethylene Polymers	3901	0	68,586,603
11	Blankets	6301	387	12,184,217
12	Chocolate	1806	7,295	102,897,241
13	Other Articles of Twine & Rope	5609	0	994,513
14	Twine & Rope	5607	4,681	15,047,940
15	Aluminum Bars	7604	1,219	11,114,964

Source: Growth Lab, Harvard CID, and The Observatory (product space/density data, including HTS labels), accessed December 19, 2013; GTIS (export data), accessed January 15, 2014.

Notes: Does not include Natural Resources sector, as defined by Growth Lab. [a] Ranked from closest to farthest products among the closest 15 products (i.e., 15 products nearest to the country's current capabilities) for all HTS 4-digit codes.

[b] Includes inter-African trade.

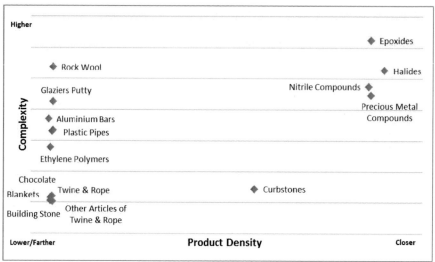

Source: Growth Lab at the Harvard Center for International Development and The Observatory, http://atlas.cid.harvard.edu/ (product space and complexity data, including HTS labels).

Figure F.3. Chad: Product space and complexity metrics related to potentially competitive products.

Table F.4. Côte d'Ivoire: Potentially competitive products based on product space metric

Density ranking[a]	Product	HTS-4 code	Côte d'Ivoire exports, 2012[b]	All AGOA country exports, 2012[b]
			Actual $	
1	Cocoa Butter	1804	250,203,279	442,378,826
2	Cocoa Beans	1801	2,720,889,629	6,294,341,705
3	Coconuts, Brazil Nuts & Cashews	0801	299,003,367	998,190,085
4	Rubber	4001	878,792,146	1,720,703,475
5	Bananas	0803	185,353,736	449,191,485
6	Cocoa Shells	1802	798,694	6,086,381
7	Cocoa Paste	1803	806,421,237	1,226,596,440
8	Cocoa Powder	1805	170,698,375	299,751,380
9	Manganese Ore	2602	23,427,345	2,304,760,898
10	Cassava	0714	1,453,699	36,217,158
11	Coconut Oil	1513	30,562,645	41,557,306
12	Palm Oil	1511	192,997,684	288,068,583
13	Accordions	9204	0	10,356
14	Copra	1203	0	26,308
15	Cloves	0907	0	82,534,204

Source: Growth Lab, Harvard CID, and The Observatory (product space/density data, including HTS labels), accessed December 19, 2013; GTIS (export data), accessed January 15, 2014.

Notes: Does not include Natural Resources sector, as defined by Growth Lab. [a] Ranked from closest to farthest products among the closest 15 products (i.e., 15 products nearest to the country's current capabilities) for all HTS 4 digit codes.

[b] Includes inter-African trade.

Source: Growth Lab at the Harvard Center for International Development and The Observatory, http://atlas.cid.harvard.edu/ (product space and complexity data, including HTS labels).

Figure F.4. Côte d'Ivoire: Product space and complexity metrics related to potentially competitive products.

Table F.5. Republic of the Congo: Potentially competitive products based on product space metric

Density ranking[a]	Product	HTS-4 code	Rep. of Congo exports, 2012[b]	All AGOA country exports, 2012[b]
			Actual $	
1	Cobalt Oxides & Hydroxides	2822	347,583	7,122,951
2	Plywood	4412	1,996,679	85,299,294
3	Wood Carpentry	4418	47,988	48,970,037
4	Shaped Wood	4409	1,162,801	32,624,726
5	Buckwheat	1008	0	6,751,317
6	Copper Wire	7408	0	110,750,764
7	Ground Nuts	1202	0	72,215,152
8	Honey	0409	0	7,707,846
9	Metal-Clad Watches	9101	1,201,584	8,931,567
10	Wool	5101	0	294,565,292
11	Other Wood Articles	4421	5,731	17,096,947
12	Dried Vegetables	0712	0	4,801,356
13	Cassava	0714	968	36,217,158
14	Dried Legumes	0713	0	361,812,983
15	Conveyor Belt Textiles	5910	0	1,395,513

Source: Growth Lab, Harvard CID, and The Observatory (product space/density data, including HTS labels), accessed December 19, 2013; GTIS (export data), accessed January 15, 2014.

Notes: Does not include Natural Resources sector, as defined by Growth Lab. [a] Ranked from closest to farthest products among the closest 15 products (i.e., 15 products nearest to the country's current capabilities) for all HTS 4 digit codes.

[b] Includes inter-African trade.

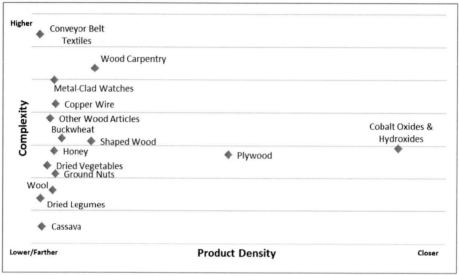

Source: Growth Lab at the Harvard Center for International Development and The Observatory, http://atlas.cid.harvard.edu/ (product space and complexity data, including HTS labels).

Figure F.5. Republic of the Congo: Product space and complexity metrics related to potentially competitive products.

Table F.6. Ethiopia: Potentially competitive products based on product space metric

Density ranking[a]	Product	HTS-4 code	Ethiopia exports, 2012[b]	All AGOA country exports, 2012[b]
			Actual $	
1	Dried Legumes	0713	125,741,514	361,812,983
2	Tropical Fruits	0804	2,959	317,693,149
3	Cassava	0714	6,033	36,217,158
4	Grapes	0806	0	747,028,881
5	Cut Flowers	0603	198,260,573	927,202,015
6	Ground Nuts	1202	145,190	72,215,152
7	Dried Vegetables	0712	90,708	4,801,356
8	Other Nuts	0802	39,296	232,901,371
9	Preserved Vegetables	0711	0	1,825,460
10	Raw Tobacco	2401	0	1,507,457,515
11	Frozen Vegetables	0710	2,034	28,798,196
12	Tanned Sheep Hides	4105	20,911,119	123,099,238
13	Building Stone	6802	4,635	24,243,031
14	Knotted Carpets	5701	7,312	2,172,639
15	Other Vegetables	0709	358,631	97,607,531

Source: Growth Lab, Harvard CID, and The Observatory (product space/density data, including HTS labels), accessed December 19, 2013; GTIS (export data), accessed January 15, 2014.

Notes: Does not include Natural Resources sector, as defined by Growth Lab. [a] Ranked from closest to farthest products among the closest 15 products (i.e., 15 products nearest to the country's current capabilities) for all HTS 4 digit codes.

[b] Includes inter-African trade.

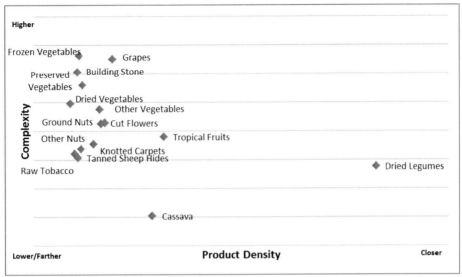

Source: Growth Lab at the Harvard Center for International Development and The Observatory, http://atlas.cid.harvard.edu/ (product space and complexity data, including HTS labels); USITC Dataweb/Customs (export data).

Figure F.6. Ethiopia: Product space and complexity metrics related to potentially competitive products.

Table F.7. Gabon: Potentially competitive products based on product space metric

Density ranking[a]	Product	HTS-4 code	Ethiopia exports, 2012[b]	All AGOA country exports, 2012[b]
			Actual $	
1	Plywood	4412	35,977,547	85,299,294
2	Shaped Wood	4409	532,915	32,624,726
3	Wood Carpentry	4418	668,760	48,970,037
4	Other Frozen Vegetables	2004	0	10,525,489
5	Other Wood Articles	4421	2,615	17,096,947
6	Metal-Clad Watches	9101	0	8,931,567
7	Ferroalloys	7202	0	4,150,403,383
8	Cassava	0714	0	36,217,158
9	Other Hides & Skins	4103	0	20,922,750
10	Antiknock	3811	2,921	7,284,069
11	Pearl Products	7116	0	72,996,623
12	Ketones & Quinones	2914	0	239,095,066
13	Precious Stones	7103	129	297,839,866
14	Neck Ties	6215	0	734,630
15	Essential Oils	3301	0	29,423,873

Source: Growth Lab, Harvard CID, and The Observatory (product space/density data, including HTS labels), accessed December 19, 2013; GTIS (export data), accessed January 15, 2014.

Notes: Does not include Natural Resources sector, as defined by Growth Lab. [a] Ranked from closest to farthest products among the closest 15 products (i.e., 15 products nearest to the country's current capabilities) for all HTS 4 digit codes.

[b] Includes inter-African trade.

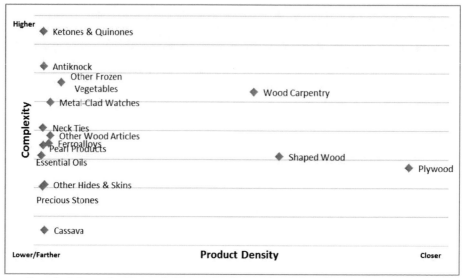

Source: Growth Lab at the Harvard Center for International Development and The Observatory, http://atlas.cid.harvard.edu/ (product space and complexity data, including HTS labels).

Figure F.7. Gabon: Product space and complexity metrics related to potentially competitive products.

Table F.8. Ghana: Potentially competitive products based on product space metric

Density ranking[a]	Product	HTS-4 code	Ghana exports, 2012[b]	All AGOA country exports, 2012[b]
			Actual $	
1	Cassava	0714	24,687,005	36,217,158
2	Cocoa Paste	1803	319,872,408	1,226,596,440
3	Cocoa Powder	1805	126,703,237	299,751,380
4	Pepper	0904	120,448	18,343,395
5	Tropical Fruits	0804	58,733,996	317,693,149
6	Plywood	4412	12,204,665	85,299,294
7	Shaped Wood	4409	6,681,355	32,624,726
8	Wood Carpentry	4418	1,541,785	48,970,037
9	Cut Flowers	0603	1,435,854	927,202,015
10	Dried Legumes	0713	5,096,020	361,812,983
11	Detonating Fuses	3603	500,116	58,282,464
12	Grapes	0806	11,644	747,028,881
13	Raw Sugar	1701	153,832	1,140,039,544
14	Prepared Wool or Animal Hair	5105	0	62,665,732
15	Precious Stones	7103	0	297,839,866

Source: Growth Lab, Harvard CID, and The Observatory (product space/density data, including HTS labels), accessed December 19, 2013; GTIS (export data), accessed January 15, 2014.

Notes: Does not include Natural Resources sector, as defined by Growth Lab. [a] Ranked from closest to farthest products among the closest 15 products (i.e., 15 products nearest to the country's current capabilities) for all HTS 4 digit codes.

[b] Includes inter-African trade.

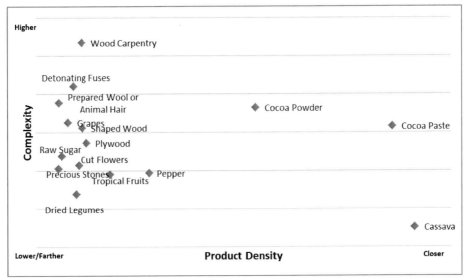

Source: Growth Lab at the Harvard Center for International Development and The Observatory, http://atlas.cid.harvard.edu/ (product space and complexity data, including HTS labels).

Figure F.8. Ghana: Product space and complexity metrics related to potentially competitive products.

Table F.9. Kenya: Potentially competitive products based on product space metric

Density ranking[a]	Product	HTS-4 code	Kenya exports, 2012[b]	All AGOA country exports, 2012[b]
			Actual $	
1	Cut Flowers	0603	613,213,959	927,202,015
2	Other Vegetables	0709	36,288,515	97,607,531
3	Cassava	0714	53,042	36,217,158
4	Tropical Fruits	0804	35,650,871	317,693,149
5	Dried Vegetables	0712	14,597	4,801,356
6	Raw Tobacco	2401	22,565,300	1,507,457,515
7	Fruit Juice	2009	14,694,494	259,667,402
8	Processed Fish	1604	34,097,469	1,076,310,494
9	Honey	0409	190,670	7,707,846
10	Non-Knit Active Wear	6211	5,977,599	18,812,010
11	Non-Knit Women's Suits	6204	75,296,357	205,008,852
12	Pepper	0904	512,361	18,343,395
13	Grapes	0806	55	747,028,881
14	Knit Men's Undergarments	6107	5,277	7,990,110
15	Non-Knit Men's Undergarments	6207	58,541	4,654,330

Source: Growth Lab, Harvard CID, and The Observatory (product space/density data, including HTS labels), accessed December 19, 2013; GTIS (export data), accessed January 15, 2014.

Notes: Does not include Natural Resources sector, as defined by Growth Lab. [a] Ranked from closest to farthest products among the closest 15 products (i.e., 15 products nearest to the country's current capabilities) for all HTS 4 digit codes.

[b] Includes inter-African trade.

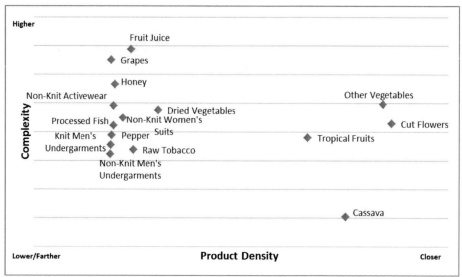

Source: Growth Lab at the Harvard Center for International Development and The Observatory, http://atlas.cid.harvard.edu/ (product space and complexity data, including HTS labels).

Figure F.9. Kenya: Product space and complexity metrics related to potentially competitive products.

Table F.10. Liberia: Potentially competitive products based on product space metric

Density ranking[a]	Product	HTS-4 code	Liberia exports, 2012[b]	All AGOA country exports, 2012[b]
			Actual $	
1	Cassava	0714	410	36,217,158
2	Non-fillet Frozen Fish	0303	307,635	850,988,814
3	Dried Legumes	0713	10,908	361,812,983
4	Tanned Fur Skins	4302	0	3,507,316
5	Cocoa Paste	1803	0	1,226,596,440
6	Metal-Clad Products	7114	0	1,082,545
7	Tanned Sheep Hides	4105	0	123,099,238
8	Plywood	4412	0	85,299,294
9	Metal-Clad Watches	9101	149,798	8,931,567
10	Shaped Wood	4409	534,148	32,624,726
11	Wood Carpentry	4418	0	48,970,037
12	Honey	0409	0	7,707,846
13	Wool	5101	0	294,565,292
14	Precious Stones	7103	3,882	297,839,866
15	Water	2201	0	6,721,012

Source: Growth Lab, Harvard CID, and The Observatory (product space/density data, including HTS labels), accessed December 9, 2013; GTIS (export data), accessed January 15, 2014.

Notes: Does not include Natural Resources sector, as defined by Growth Lab. [a] Ranked from closest to farthest products among the closest 15 products (i.e., 15 products nearest to the country's current capabilities) for all HTS 4 digit codes.

[b] Includes inter-African trade.

Source: Growth Lab at the Harvard Center for International Development and The Observatory, http://atlas.cid.harvard.edu/ (product space and complexity data, including HTS labels).

Figure F.10. Liberia: Product space and complexity metrics related to potentially competitive products.

Table F.11. Mali: Potentially competitive products based on product space metric

Density ranking[a]	Product	HTS-4 code	Mali exports, 2012[b]	All AGOA country exports, 2012[b]
			Actual $	
1	Raw Tobacco	2401	0	1,507,457,515
2	Dried Legumes	0713	76,362	361,812,983
3	Precious Stones	7103	1,535,015	297,839,866
4	Prepared Wool or Animal Hair	5105	0	62,665,732
5	Honey	0409	179	7,707,846
6	Buckwheat	1008	17,391	6,751,317
7	Cut Flowers	0603	24,434	927,202,015
8	Artificial Vegetation	6702	0	1,676,953
9	Tanned Sheep Hides	4105	13,340,805	123,099,238
10	Cassava	0714	174,667	36,217,158
11	String Instruments	9202	0	294,547
12	Jewelry	7113	2,724	207,169,552
13	Ginger	0910	124,134	53,875,138
14	Hat Shapes	6502	0	46,252
15	Footwear Parts	6406	0	8,654,746

Source: Growth Lab, Harvard CID, and The Observatory (product space/density data, including HTS labels), accessed December 19, 2013; GTIS (export data), accessed January 15, 2014.

Notes: Does not include Natural Resources sector, as defined by Growth Lab. [a] Ranked from closest to farthest products among the closest 15 products (i.e., 15 products nearest to the country's current capabilities) for all HTS 4 digit codes.

[b] Includes inter-African trade.

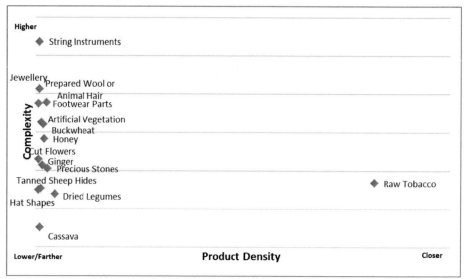

Source: Growth Lab at the Harvard Center for International Development and The Observatory, http://atlas.cid.harvard.edu/ (product space and complexity data, including HTS labels).

Figure F.11. Mali: Product space and complexity metrics related to potentially competitive products.

Table F.12. Mauritania: Potentially competitive products based on product space metric

Density ranking[a]	Product	HTS-4 code	Mauritania exports, 2012[b]	All AGOA country exports, 2012[b]
			Actual $	
1	Non-fillet Frozen Fish	0303	156,969,391	850,988,814
2	Processed Fish	1604	1,286,272	1,076,310,494
3	Other Hides & Skins	4103	36,184	20,922,750
4	Dried Legumes	0713	72,026	361,812,983
5	Prepared Wool or Animal Hair	5105	0	62,665,732
6	Wool	5101	0	294,565,292
7	Tropical Fruits	0804	6,527	317,693,149
8	Cassava	0714	2,148	36,217,158
9	Raw Sugar	1701	184,911	1,140,039,544
10	Precious Stones	7103	77,935	297,839,866
11	Tanned Sheep Hides	4105	1,636,209	123,099,238
12	Grapes	0806	0	747,028,881
13	Non-Retail Animal Hair Yarn	5108	0	5,754,306
14	Butter	0405	0	8,508,921
15	Other Carpets	5705	24,824	6,685,212

Source: Growth Lab, Harvard CID, and The Observatory (product space/density data, including HTS labels), accessed December 19, 2013; GTIS (export data), accessed January 15, 2014.

Notes: Does not include Natural Resources sector, as defined by Growth Lab. [a] Ranked from closest to farthest products among the closest 15 products (i.e., 15 products nearest to the country's current capabilities) for all HTS 4 digit codes.

[b] Includes inter-African trade.

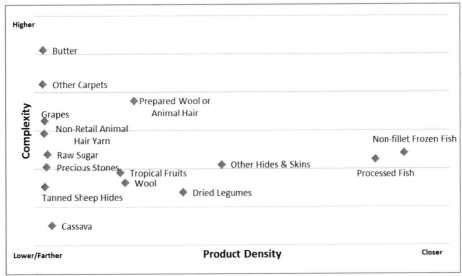

Source: Growth Lab at the Harvard Center for International Development and The Observatory, http://atlas.cid.harvard.edu/ (product space and complexity data, including HTS labels).

Figure F.12. Mauritania: Product space and complexity metrics related to potentially competitive products.

Table F.13. Mauritius: Potentially competitive products based on product space metric

Density ranking[a]	Product	HTS-4 code	Mauritius exports, 2012[b]	All AGOA country exports, 2012[b]
			Actual $	
1	Non-Retail Animal Hair Yarn	5108	446	5,754,306
2	Watch Straps	9113	13,098,943	13,541,069
3	Metal-Clad Products	7114	47,869	1,082,545
4	Precious Stones	7103	2,666,162	297,839,866
5	Knit Women's Suits	6104	48,702,266	180,975,812
6	Jewelry	7113	58,076,793	207,169,552
7	Tulles & Net Fabric	5804	2,914	821,143
8	Non-Knit Women's Shirts	6206	6,826,343	33,805,292
9	Watch Cases & Parts	9111	6,926	98,209
10	Imitation Jewelry	7117	7,989,671	23,145,112
11	Other Knit Garments	6114	3,717,778	18,259,233
12	Knit Sweaters	6110	80,355,711	198,046,240
13	Pearl Products	7116	9,771,069	72,996,623
14	Knit Babies' Garments	6111	3,821,235	21,608,987
15	Knit Men's Suits	6103	3,484,597	50,931,676

Source: Growth Lab, Harvard CID, and The Observatory (product space/density data, including HTS labels), accessed December 19, 2013; GTIS (export data), accessed January 15, 2014.

Notes: Does not include Natural Resources sector, as defined by Growth Lab. [a] Ranked from closest to farthest products among the closest 15 products (i.e., 15 products nearest to the country's current capabilities) for all HTS 4 digit codes.

[b] Includes inter-African trade.

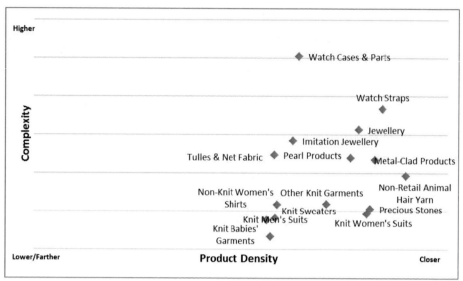

Source: Growth Lab at the Harvard Center for International Development and The Observatory, http://atlas.cid.harvard.edu/ (product space and complexity data, including HTS labels).

Figure F.13. Mauritius: Product space and complexity metrics related to potentially competitive products.

Table F.14. Mozambique: Potentially competitive products based on product space metric

Density ranking[a]	Product	HTS-4 code	Mozambique exports, 2012[b]	All AGOA country exports, 2012[b]
			Actual $	
1	Dried Legumes	0713	45,586,981	361,812,983
2	Ferroalloys	7202	0	4,150,403,383
3	Acyclic Alcohols	2905	717	241,922,048
4	Aluminum Wire	7605	0	2,913,145
5	Cassava	0714	57	36,217,158
6	Grapes	0806	0	747,028,881
7	Lead Oxides	2824	0	8,310,304
8	Other Nuts	0802	429,241	232,901,371
9	Hat Shapes	6502	0	46,252
10	Raw Tobacco	2401	234,793,750	1,507,457,515
11	Raw Sugar	1701	141,367,138	1,140,039,544
12	Heavy Pute Woven Cotton	5209	0	14,208,427
13	Ground Nuts	1202	8,224,943	72,215,152
14	Knotted Carpets	5701	15	2,172,639
15	Non-fillet Frozen Fish	0303	2,426,360	850,988,814

Source: Growth Lab, Harvard CID, and The Observatory (product space/density data, including HTS labels), accessed December 19, 2013; GTIS (export data), accessed January 15, 2014.

Notes: Does not include Natural Resources sector, as defined by Growth Lab. [a] Ranked from closest to farthest products among the closest 15 products (i.e., 15 products nearest to the country's current capabilities) for all HTS 4 digit codes.

[b] Includes inter-African trade.

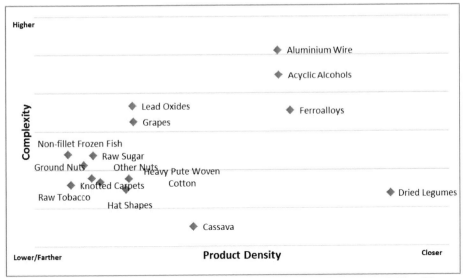

Source: Growth Lab at the Harvard Center for International Development and The Observatory, http://atlas.cid.harvard.edu/ (product space and complexity data, including HTS labels).

Figure F.14. Mozambique: Product space and complexity metrics related to potentially competitive products.

Table F.15. Nigeria: Potentially competitive products based on product space metric

Density ranking[a]	Product	HTS-4 code	Nigeria exports, 2012[b]	All AGOA country exports, 2012[b]
			Actual $	
1	Tanned Sheep Hides	4105	51,349,094	123,099,238
2	Cocoa Paste	1803	42,776,169	1,226,596,440
3	Knit Socks & Hosiery	6115	3,642	16,927,855
4	Wood Carpentry	4418	2,403	48,970,037
5	Shaped Wood	4409	236,961	32,624,726
6	Cassava	0714	1,053,930	36,217,158
7	Building Stone	6802	402	24,243,031
8	Cocoa Powder	1805	674,136	299,751,380
9	Packing Bags	6305	98,105	42,515,998
10	Dried Legumes	0713	3,023,053	361,812,983
11	Ground Nuts	1202	278,908	72,215,152
12	Knotted Carpets	5701	6,460	2,172,639
13	Grapes	0806	18,314	747,028,881
14	Raw Tobacco	2401	3,899	1,507,457,515
15	Non-Knit Women's Coats	6202	7,535	2,916,749

Source: Growth Lab, Harvard CID, and The Observatory (product space/density data, including HTS labels), accessed December 19, 2013; GTIS (export data), accessed January 15, 2014.

Notes: Does not include Natural Resources sector, as defined by Growth Lab. [a] Ranked from closest to farthest products among the closest 15 products (i.e., 15 products nearest to the country's current capabilities) for all HTS 4 digit codes.

[b] Includes inter-African trade.

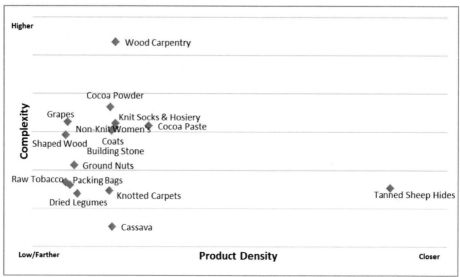

Source: Growth Lab at the Harvard Center for International Development and The Observatory, http://atlas.cid.harvard.edu/ (product space and complexity data, including HTS labels).

Figure F.15. Nigeria: Product space and complexity metrics related to potentially competitive products.

Table F.16. Senegal: Potentially competitive products based on product space metric

Density ranking[a]	Product	HTS-4 code	Senegal exports, 2012[b]	All AGOA country exports, 2012[b]
			Actual $	
1	Ground Nuts	1202	8,730,365	72,215,152
2	Plaiting Products	4601	208,391	4,671,440
3	Dried Legumes	0713	425,386	361,812,983
4	Other Hides & Skins	4103	561,377	20,922,750
5	Other Vegetables	0709	13,515,709	97,607,531
6	Honey	0409	246	7,707,846
7	Raw Sugar	1701	565,642	1,140,039,544
8	Tropical Fruits	0804	12,844,497	317,693,149
9	Non-fillet Frozen Fish	0303	136,666,925	850,988,814
10	Cassava	0714	204,916	36,217,158
11	Grapes	0806	20,968	747,028,881
12	Sauces & Seasonings	2103	963,413	102,426,791
13	Malt Extract	1901	3,490,334	33,244,518
14	Frozen Vegetables	0710	1,013,635	28,798,196
15	Detonating Fuses	3603	217,089	58,282,464

Source: Growth Lab, Harvard CID, and The Observatory (product space/density data, including HTS labels), accessed December 19, 2013; GTIS (export data), accessed January 15, 2014.

Notes: Does not include Natural Resources sector, as defined by Growth Lab. [a] Ranked from closest to farthest products among the closest 15 products (i.e., 15 products nearest to the country's current capabilities) for all HTS 4 digit codes.

[b] Includes inter-African trade.

Source: Growth Lab at the Harvard Center for International Development and The Observatory, http://atlas.cid.harvard.edu/ (product space and complexity data, including HTS labels).

Figure F.16. Senegal: Product space and complexity metrics related to potentially competitive products.

Table F.17. South Africa: Potentially competitive products based on product space metric

Density ranking[a]	Product	HTS-4 code	South Africa exports, 2012[b]	All AGOA country exports, 2012[b]
			Actual $	
1	Ferroalloys	7202	4,138,960,941	4,150,403,383
2	Manganese Oxides	2820	56,860,875	57,030,413
3	Other Nuts	0802	161,355,572	232,901,371
4	Chromium Oxides & Hydroxides	2819	24,475,104	24,478,452
5	Grapes	0806	698,313,934	747,028,881
6	Dried Legumes	0713	11,760,133	361,812,983
7	Prepared Wool or Animal Hair	5105	62,486,134	62,665,732
8	Manganese	8111	108,248,661	108,412,787
9	Raw Tobacco	2401	67,902,440	1,507,457,515
10	Detonating Fuses	3603	53,450,238	58,282,464
11	Lead Oxides	2824	7,848,816	8,310,304
12	Ground Nuts	1202	26,407,629	72,215,152
13	Wool	5101	286,967,296	294,565,292
14	Apples	0808	442,183,432	443,088,991
15	Hat Shapes	6502	39,648	46,252

Source: Growth Lab, Harvard CID, and The Observatory (product space/density data, including HTS labels), accessed December 19, 2013; GTIS (export data), accessed January 15, 2014.

Notes: Does not include Natural Resources sector, as defined by Growth Lab. [a] Ranked from closest to farthest products among the closest 15 products (i.e., 15 products nearest to the country's current capabilities) for all HTS 4 digit codes.

[b] Includes inter-African trade.

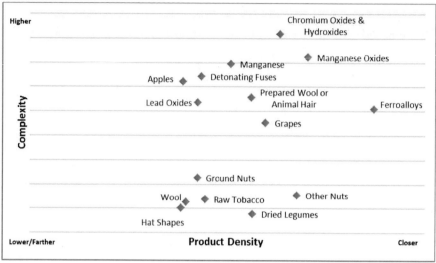

Source: Growth Lab at the Harvard Center for International Development and The Observatory, http://atlas.cid.harvard.edu/ (product space and complexity data, including HTS labels).

Figure F.17. South Africa: Product space and complexity metrics related to potentially competitive products.

Table F.18. Tanzania: Potentially competitive products based on product space metric

Density ranking[a]	Product	HTS-4 code	Tanzania exports, 2012[b]	All AGOA country exports, 2012[b]
			Actual $	
1	Cassava	0714	666,981	36,217,158
2	Pepper	0904	354,737	18,343,395
3	Raw Tobacco	2401	300,728,210	1,507,457,515
4	Dried Legumes	0713	104,275,707	361,812,983
5	Cut Flowers	0603	16,848,813	927,202,015
6	Knit Women's Shirts	6106	120,965	45,265,561
7	Prepared Wool or Animal Hair	5105	68	62,665,732
8	Other Vegetables	0709	155,658	97,607,531
9	Tropical Fruits	0804	793,654	317,693,149
10	Grapes	0806	147,117,026	747,028,881
11	Dried Vegetables	0712	5,378	4,801,356
12	Building Stone	6802	81,134	24,243,031
13	Curbstones	6801	0	70,904
14	Heavy Pute Woven Cotton	5209	225,189	14,208,427
15	Ground Nuts	1202	5,320	72,215,152

Source: Growth Lab, Harvard CID, and The Observatory (product space/density data, including HTS labels), accessed December 19, 2013; GTIS (export data), accessed January 15, 2014.

Notes: Does not include Natural Resources sector, as defined by Growth Lab. [a] Ranked from closest to farthest products among the closest 15 products (i.e., 15 products nearest to the country's current capabilities) for all HTS 4 digit codes.

[b] Includes inter-African trade.

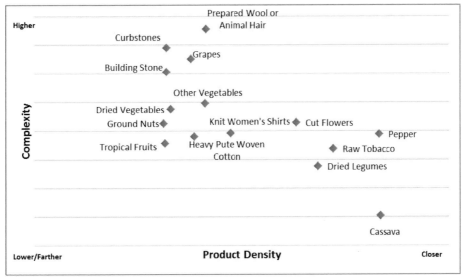

Source: Growth Lab at the Harvard Center for International Development and The Observatory, http://atlas.cid.harvard.edu/ (product space and complexity data, including HTS labels).

Figure F.18. Tanzania: Product space and complexity metrics related to potentially competitive products.

Table F.19. Togo: Potentially competitive products based on product space metric

Density ranking[a]	Product	HTS-4 code	Togo exports, 2012[b]	All AGOA country exports, 2012[b]
			Actual $	
1	Cassava	0714	128,767	36,217,158
2	Cocoa Paste	1803	0	1,226,596,440
3	Basketwork	4602	135,271	6,767,428
4	Artificial Vegetation	6702	0	1,676,953
5	Plaiting Products	4601	1,110,997	4,671,440
6	Ground Nuts	1202	1,299,788	72,215,152
7	Processed Fish	1604	24,679	1,076,310,494
8	Flavored Water	2202	1,841,242	70,372,513
9	Other Vegetables	0709	2,176,866	97,607,531
10	Fruit Juice	2009	134,533	259,667,402
11	Malt Extract	1901	798,474	33,244,518
12	Knit Women's Shirts	6106	8,991	45,265,561
13	Water	2201	3,000	6,721,012
14	Dried Legumes	0713	49,081	361,812,983
15	Sowing Seeds	1209	2,646	73,796,219

Source: Growth Lab, Harvard CID, and The Observatory (product space/density data, including HTS labels), accessed December 19, 2013; GTIS (export data), accessed January 15, 2014.

Notes: Does not include Natural Resources sector, as defined by Growth Lab. [a] Ranked from closest to farthest products among the closest 15 products (i.e., 15 products nearest to the country's current capabilities) for all HTS 4 digit codes.

[b] Includes inter-African trade.

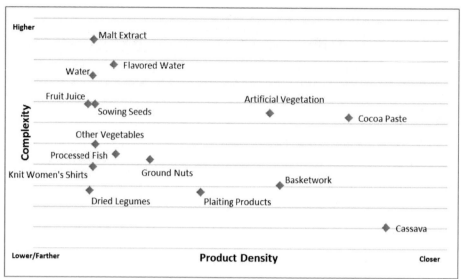

Source: Growth Lab at the Harvard Center for International Development and The Observatory, http://atlas.cid.harvard.edu/ (product space and complexity data, including HTS labels).

Figure F.19. Togo: Product space and complexity metrics related to potentially competitive products.

Table F.20. Uganda: Potentially competitive products based on product space metric

Density ranking[a]	Product	HTS-4 code	Uganda exports, 2012[b]	All AGOA country exports, 2012[b]
			Actual $	
1	Processed Fish	1604	124	1,076,310,494
2	Cassava	0714	954,748	36,217,158
3	Raw Tobacco	2401	74,670,052	1,507,457,515
4	Cut Flowers	0603	33,766,285	927,202,015
5	Tropical Fruits	0804	1,432,041	317,693,149
6	Non-fillet Frozen Fish	0303	9,494,239	850,988,814
7	Other Processed Fruits & Nuts	2008	81,880	271,350,925
8	Raw Sugar	1701	9,281,308	1,140,039,544
9	Tanned Equine & Bovine Hides	4104	20,224,076	170,141,982
10	Dried Legumes	0713	801,693	361,812,983
11	Honey	0409	14,990	7,707,846
12	Wine	2204	53,026	798,295,017
13	Wool	5101	0	294,565,292
14	Other Women's Undergarments	6212	1,074	15,657,510
15	Other Live Plants	0602	28,448,508	140,992,827

Source: Growth Lab, Harvard CID, and The Observatory (product space/density data, including HTS labels), accessed December 19, 2013; GTIS (export data), accessed January 15, 2014.

Notes: Does not include Natural Resources sector, as defined by Growth Lab. [a] Ranked from closest to farthest products among the closest 15 products (i.e., 15 products nearest to the country's current capabilities) for all HTS 4 digit codes.

[b] Includes inter-African trade.

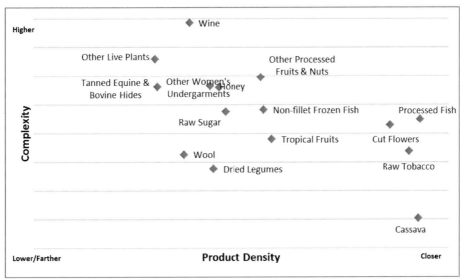

Source: Growth Lab at the Harvard Center for International Development and The Observatory, http://atlas.cid.harvard.edu/ (product space and complexity data, including HTS labels).

Figure F.20. Uganda: Product space and complexity metrics related to potentially competitive products

Table F.21. Zambia: Potentially competitive products based on product space metric

Density ranking[a]	Product	HTS-4 code	Zambia exports, 2012[b]	All AGOA country exports, 2012[b]
			Actual $	
1	Cobalt Oxides & Hydroxides	2822	197	7,122,951
2	Copper Wire	7408	102,171,896	110,750,764
3	Acyclic Alcohols	2905	0	241,922,048
4	Dried Legumes	0713	522,446	361,812,983
5	Detonating Fuses	3603	2,554,868	58,282,464
6	Raw Sugar	1701	90,117,062	1,140,039,544
7	Ferroalloys	7202	7,297,579	4,150,403,383
8	Other Processed Fruits & Nuts	2008	6,134	271,350,925
9	Other Vegetables	0709	2,746,208	97,607,531
10	Cassava	0714	111,417	36,217,158
11	Honey	0409	1,671,836	7,707,846
12	Tropical Fruits	0804	15,937	317,693,149
13	Wine	2204	15	798,295,017
14	Sowing Seeds	1209	184,197	73,796,219
15	Lead Oxides	2824	0	8,310,304

Source: Growth Lab, Harvard CID, and The Observatory (product space/density data, including HTS labels), accessed December 19, 2013; GTIS (export data), accessed January 15, 2014.

Notes: Does not include Natural Resources sector, as defined by Growth Lab. [a] Ranked from closest to farthest products among the closest 15 products (i.e., 15 products nearest to the country's current capabilities) for all HTS 4 digit codes.

[b] Includes inter-African trade.

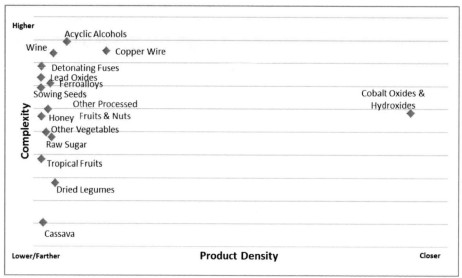

Source: Growth Lab at the Harvard Center for International Development and The Observatory, http://atlas.cid.harvard.edu/ (product space and complexity data, including HTS labels).

Figure F.21. Zambia: Product space and complexity metrics related to potentially competitive products.

APPENDIX G. BUSINESS AND INVESTMENT DATA

Table G.1. How SSA countries improved in governance in 2000–2012

Country	Voice and accountability	Political stability and absence of violence/terrorism	Government effectiveness	Regulatory quality	Rule of law	Control of corruption	Number of areas of improvement
Angola	√	√	√	√	√	√	6
Congo, Dem. Rep.	√	√	√	√	√	√	6
Liberia	√	√	√	√	√	√	6
Rwanda	√	√	√	√	√	√	6
Burundi	√	√	√	√	√		6
Djibouti		√	√	√	√	√	5
Sierra Leone	√	√	√	√	√		5
Zambia	√	√	√		√	√	5
Botswana		√		√	√	√	4
Congo, Rep.	√	√	√		√		4
Niger			√	√	√	√	4
Burkina Faso	√			√	√		3
Cameroon		√	√		√		3

Country	Voice and accountability	Political stability and absence of violence/ terrorism	Government effectiveness	Regulatory quality	Rule of law	Control of corruption	Number of areas of improvement
Cabo Verde	√			√		√	3
Comoros	√				√	√	3
Côte d'Ivoire	√	√			√		3
Equatorial Guinea		√		√	√		3
Ethiopia			√	√	√		3
Ghana	√	√		√			3
Lesotho	√	√				√	3
Mauritius		√	√	√			3
Mozambique	√	√			√		3
Namibia	√	√			√		3
Somalia			√	√		√	3
South Sudan		√	√	√			3
Swaziland	√		√		√		2
Tanzania	√	√				√	2
Uganda	√	√			√		2
Central African Republic					√	√	2
Guinea	√	√					2
Kenya	√				√		2
Malawi		√			√		2
Senegal		√		√			2
Seychelles			√	√			2
Sudan		√			√		2
Chad		√					2
Eritrea		√					2
Gambia, The				√			1
Guinea-Bissau				√			1
Nigeria				√			1
South Africa		√					1
Togo	√						1
Zimbabwe		√					0
Benin							0
Gabon							0
Madagascar							0
Mali							0
Mauritania							0
São Tomé and Principe							0
Total	22	29	17	22	25	14	129

Source: The World Bank World Governance Indicators (accessed March 4, 2014).
Note: √ = made improvement; South Sudan: only 2011 and 2012 data.

Table G.2. Rankings of SSA countries in ease of doing business and the numbers of areas of improvement in 2006–13

Country	Ranking in ease of doing business	Starting business	Dealing with construction permits	Getting electricity	Registering property	Getting credit	Protecting investors	Paying taxes	Trading across borders	Enforcing contracts	Resolving insolvency	Number of areas of improvement
Angola	178	√	√	√	√	√			√		no practice	6
Benin	175	√	√	√	√	√		√	√	√		8
Botswana	65	√	√	√		√	√		√	√		7
Burkina Faso	154	√	√	√	√	√		√	√	√	√	9
Burundi	157	√	√	√	√	√	√	√	√			8
Cameroon	162	√	√	√	√	√		√	√	√		8
Cabo Verde	128	√	√	√	√	√		√	√	√	no practice	8
Central African Republic	187	√		√	√	√		√	√			6
Chad	189	√	√	√	√	√		√				6
Comoros	160	√	√		√	√					no practice	4
Congo, Dem. Rep.	183	√	√	√	√				√	√		6
Congo, Rep.	186	√	√	√	√	√						5
Côte d'Ivoire	173	√	√	√	√	√		√	√			7
Equatorial Guinea	164	√	√	√		√			√		no practice	5
Eritrea	185	√		√	√				√		no practice	4
Ethiopia	124	√	√	√	√	√			√	√	√	8
Gabon	169	√	√	√	√	√		√				6
Gambia, The	148	√	√	√				√	√	√		6
Ghana	62	√	√	√	√	√		√	√	√		8
Guinea	179	√	√	√	√	√					√	6
Guinea-Bissau	181	√	√	√	√	√		√	√	√	no practice	8
Kenya	122	√	√	√	√	√		√	√		√	8

Country	Ranking in ease of doing business	Starting business	Dealing with construction permits	Getting electricity	Registering property	Getting credit	Protecting investors	Paying taxes	Trading across borders	Enforcing contracts	Resolving insolvency	Number of areas of improvement
Lesotho	139	√	√	√	√		√	√	√	√		8
Liberia	149	n.a.	n.a.	√	n.a.	n.a.	n.a.	n.a.	n.a.	n.a.	n.a.	1
Madagascar	144	√	√		√			√	√		√	6
Malawi	161		√	√	√			√	√	√	√	7
Mali	153	√	√	√	√	√	√	√	√	√		9
Mauritania	171	√	√	√	√	√		√	√	√	no practice	8
Mauritius	20	√	√	√	√	√			√	√		7
Mozambique	142	√	√	√	√	√	√		√	√		8
Namibia	94	√	√	√		√		√				5
Niger	174	√	√	√	√	√			√			6
Nigeria	138	√	√	√	√	√		√	√	√		8
Rwanda	54	√	√	√	√	√	√	√	√	√		9
São Tomé and Príncipe	166	√	√	√	√			√	√	√		7
Senegal	176	√	√	√	√	√		√	√	√		8
Seychelles	77	√	√	√	√			√	√		√	7
Sierra Leone	137	√	√	√	√	√	√	√	√	√		9
South Africa	41	√	√	√	√	√		√	√	√		8
South Sudan	184	n.a.	n.a.	n.a.	n.a.	n.a.	n.a.	n.a.	n.a.	n.a.	no practice	0
Sudan	143	√	√	√	√			√	√	√		7
Swaziland	120	√	√	√	√	√	√		√	√		8
Tanzania	136	√	√	√	√		√		√		√	7
Togo	159	√	√	√	√	√		√	√			7
Uganda	126	√	√	√	√	√		√	√	√	√	9
Zambia	90	√	√	√	√	√		√	√			7
Zimbabwe	168	√	√	√	√	√		√			√	7
# of countries improved		44	43	44	41	35	9	29	40	25	10	320

Source: The World Bank World Governance Indicators.
Note: √ = made improvement and n.a. = not available.

Table G.3. The improvement in openness of trade and investment policy regime in SSA countries over 2000–2013

Country	Trade freedom	Investment freedom	Number of areas of improvement
Angola	√	√	2
Benin	√	√	2
Botswana	√	√	2
Burkina Faso	√		1
Burundi	√	√	2
Cabo Verde	√		1
Cameroon	√		1
Central African Republic	√	√	2
Chad		√	1
Comoros	√	√	2
Congo, Dem. Rep.	√	√	2
Congo, Rep.	√		1
Côte d'Ivoire	√		1
Djibouti	√	√	2
Equatorial Guinea			0
Eritrea	√		1
Ethiopia	√		1
Gabon	√	√	2
Gambia, The	√	√	2
Ghana	√	√	2
Guinea			0
Guinea-Bissau	√	√	2
Kenya	√		1
Lesotho	√		1
Liberia	√	√	2
Madagascar	√	√	2
Malawi	√		1
Mali	√		1
Mauritania	√		1
Mauritius	√	√	2
Mozambique	√		1
Namibia	√		1
Niger	√	√	2
Nigeria	√		1
Rwanda	√	√	2
São Tomé and Príncipe	√	√	2
Senegal	√	√	2
Seychelles	√	√	2
Sierra Leone	√	√	2
Somalia			0
South Africa	√		1
Sudan			0
Swaziland	√		1
Tanzania	√	√	2

Country	Trade freedom	Investment freedom	Number of areas of improvement
Togo		√	1
Uganda	√	√	2
Zambia	√		1
Zimbabwe	√		1
# of countries improved	42	25	

Source: The Heritage Foundation Index of Economic Freedom.

Table G.4. The global ranking of SSA countries in Global Competitiveness Index and each pillar, 2012–13

Country	GCI	Institutions	Infrastructure	Macro-economy	Health and primary education	Higher education and training	Goods market efficiency	Labor market efficiency	Financial market development	Technological readiness	Market size	Business sophistication	Innovation
South Africa	52	43	63	69	132	84	32	113	3	62	25	38	42
Mauritius	54	39	54	87	54	65	27	70	35	63	109	41	98
Rwanda	63	20	96	78	100	117	39	11	49	113	128	70	51
Seychelles	76	47	42	79	47	31	70	48	94	66	142	87	93
Botswana	79	33	87	81	114	95	78	60	53	106	97	95	73
Namibia	92	52	59	84	120	119	87	74	47	104	120	102	101
Gambia, The	98	35	82	129	126	94	94	31	69	109	141	59	52
Gabon	99	67	117	9	128	122	126	63	106	86	110	141	136
Zambia	102	56	111	67	129	121	42	111	50	115	111	75	61
Ghana	103	75	110	108	112	107	76	97	59	108	70	101	95
Kenya	106	106	103	133	115	100	93	39	24	101	75	67	50
Liberia	111	45	115	82	130	114	40	61	74	132	144	62	54
Cameroon	112	107	125	59	118	115	89	58	105	126	87	104	79
Nigeria	115	117	130	39	142	113	88	55	68	112	33	66	78
Senegal	117	90	124	92	125	116	77	80	84	95	105	72	62
Benin	119	99	122	76	111	120	132	67	112	124	122	125	84
Tanzania	120	86	132	107	113	132	110	47	85	122	77	106	75
Ethiopia	121	74	119	114	116	134	120	87	129	140	66	129	114
Cabo Verde	122	57	114	121	71	99	105	126	121	90	143	118	120
Uganda	123	102	133	119	123	127	103	23	62	117	85	105	82
Mali	128	120	107	74	141	130	111	118	113	119	118	126	88
Malawi	129	76	135	136	124	129	112	43	75	134	123	115	99
Madagascar	130	136	137	95	110	133	115	54	138	135	113	122	106
Côte d'Ivoire	131	129	102	130	140	123	122	71	103	99	94	123	115
Zimbabwe	132	101	128	122	119	118	133	139	109	120	135	128	127
Burkina Faso	133	83	136	85	139	137	118	64	117	137	114	140	107
Mauritania	134	122	113	89	133	142	135	131	136	123	131	117	121
Swaziland	135	88	99	128	135	125	107	119	89	128	133	124	137
Lesotho	137	121	126	113	136	135	102	116	122	136	136	135	138

Table G.4. (Continued)

Country	GCI	Institutions	Infrastructure	Macro-economy	Health and primary education	Higher education and training	Goods market efficiency	Labor market efficiency	Financial market development	Technological readiness	Market size	Business sophistication	Innovation
Mozambique	138	112	129	125	137	138	124	128	134	121	101	131	122
Chad	139	140	140	45	144	140	141	95	137	143	112	138	113
Guinea	141	128	142	142	138	136	127	56	135	142	129	139	125
Sierra Leone	143	95	138	143	143	141	116	114	125	141	138	136	139
Burundi	144	142	141	137	127	143	139	112	144	144	140	143	140
Average	114	87	112	97	120	118	98	79	91	115	109	105	96

Source: The World Economic Forum, Global Competitiveness Index.

Table G.5. Number of new greenfield FDI projects by source country and year, 2003–13

Source country	2003	2004	2005	2006	2007	2008	2009	2010	2011	2012	2013	Total
United States	35	20	49	43	37	61	42	49	96	78	61	571
United Kingdom	37	15	28	35	22	64	70	59	80	82	76	568
South Africa	14	10	11	19	6	32	23	34	61	75	57	342
India	8	16	8	25	11	32	25	46	59	37	42	309
Germany	6	11	8	8	7	15	21	17	24	24	21	162
Portugal	4	7	4	10	18	36	26	21	24	4	5	159
Canada	22	11	31	11	5	21	12	10	15	11	8	157
France	5	8	11	11	8	21	26	12	17	16	17	152
Kenya	1	1	4	4	2	25	26	19	20	21	22	145
China	8	4	10	5	14	20	14	12	19	31	7	144
United Arab Emirates	3	2	6	11	12	16	7	5	14	25	19	120
Japan	4	7	12	4	5	5	13	9	22	13	21	115
Australia	9	5	17	10	6	15	13	9	12	7	10	113
Nigeria		2	3	7	2	21	19	13	18	5	21	111
Switzerland	4	4	3	8	4	8	15	19	8	11	12	96
Netherlands	5	2	4	3	3	8	6	8	11	9	10	69
South Korea	1	2	3	1	1	1	4	3	20	15	11	62
Spain	1		2	3	2	2	6	13	9	7	12	57
Sweden	3	4	2	4	2	9	5	6	4	7	4	50
Togo			1		6	10	10	3	12	2	4	48
Ireland	1	2	1	3	1	1	14	3	4	5	9	44
Russia	3	3	2	7	3	4	5	4	4	3	3	41
Italy	2	2	4	3	1	7	3	1	5	8	3	39
Luxembourg		3			2	5	4	6	9	5	3	37

Source country	2003	2004	2005	2006	2007	2008	2009	2010	2011	2012	2013	Total
Finland				4	2	3	2	3	3	18	1	36
Mauritius	1				2	1	6	9	11	3	2	35
Belgium	1	4			4	7	5	5	2	1	3	32
Brazil	1	2	1	2	3	5	6	2	6	3	1	32
Singapore	1	2		3		1	1	5	2	6	5	26
Malaysia	4		3	1	2	6	4	1	1		3	25
Egypt	1	1	2		1		5	7	1	3	4	25
Botswana				4			2	1	12	5	1	25
Israel		3	1	1	3	4		4	3		4	23
Norway	3	3	2	1	1	4		1	2	3	2	22
Hong Kong			2		2	2	1	1	5	2	5	20
Saudi Arabia	2			3	1	2	2	3	4	2	1	20
Zimbabwe	6	1				7	3	2			1	20
Tanzania					1	1	2	3	3	3	5	18
Qatar			1	4		5	1	1	2	3		17
Denmark		1	3			3	3	2		3	2	17
Kuwait	2	1		4	3	2	2	1				15
Côte d'Ivoire		1	3	1		1	2	1		1	2	12
Turkey	1	1			1	2	1	1	3		1	11
Ghana							1	1	5	2	2	11
Angola					1	2		3		1	4	11
Austria			1	2		1		1	1	4		10
Uganda			1		1	3	3	1			1	10
Taiwan		2		1			3		1	1	2	10
All other					5	23	21	18	13	27	24	173
Total	211	169	255	279	213	524	485	458	647	592	534	4,367

Source: Financial Times, FDI Markets database.

Table G.6. Numbers of greenfield FDI projects and investing companies in SSA, by source country, 2003–13

Source country	Number of projects	Number of companies
United States	571	365
United Kingdom	568	336
South Africa	342	169
India	309	160
Germany	162	104
Portugal	159	37
Canada	157	97
France	152	101
Kenya	145	54
China	144	88

Table G.6. (Continued)

Source country	Number of projects	Number of companies
UAE	120	80
Japan	115	65
Australia	113	74
Nigeria	111	38
Switzerland	96	43
Netherlands	69	54
Republic of Korea	62	23
Spain	57	38
Sweden	50	25
Togo	48	9
Ireland	44	24
Russia	41	29
Italy	39	25
Luxembourg	37	14
Finland	36	10
Mauritius	35	18
Belgium	32	19
Brazil	32	13
Singapore	26	14
Malaysia	25	17
Egypt	25	14
Botswana	25	9
Israel	23	17
Norway	22	20
Hong Kong	20	16
Saudi Arabia	20	15
Zimbabwe	20	11
Tanzania	18	12
Qatar	17	10
Denmark	17	14
Kuwait	15	10
Côte d'Ivoire	12	2
Turkey	11	10
Ghana	11	8
Angola	11	5
Austria	10	9
Uganda	10	8
Taiwan	10	8
Lebanon	8	5
Bermuda	8	7
Ethiopia	8	4
Mali	8	2

Source country	Number of projects	Number of companies
Pakistan	7	7
Tunisia	6	5
Bahrain	6	6
Cyprus	6	5
Vietnam	6	5
Indonesia	5	5
Namibia	5	3
Iran	5	4
Greece	5	5
Czech Republic	4	2
Romania	4	3
Zambia	4	2
Senegal	4	2
Thailand	4	4
Philippines	4	4
Algeria	3	2
Yemen	3	2
Cameroon	3	2
Congo, Dem. Rep.	3	3
Rwanda	3	2
Malawi	3	2
Libya	3	2
Morocco	3	1
Serbia	3	3
Jordan	3	3
Slovakia	2	2
Venezuela	2	1
Iceland	2	2
Lithuania	2	2
Cayman Islands	2	2
Sudan	2	1
Burundi	2	2
Mozambique	1	1
Moldova	1	1
Haiti	1	1
Eritrea	1	1
Bahamas	1	1
New Zealand	1	1
Hungary	1	1
Sri Lanka	1	1
Mexico	1	1
Gabon	1	1
Mongolia	1	1
Cuba	1	1

Table G.6. (Continued)

Source country	Number of projects	Number of companies
Poland	1	1
Malta	1	1
Estonia	1	1
Ukraine	1	1
Bulgaria	1	1
Argentina	1	1
Slovenia	1	1
Latvia	1	1
Chile	1	1
Total	4,367	2,467

Source: Financial Times, FDI Markets database.

Table G.7 Number of greenfield FDI projects and investing companies in SSA, by destination country, 2001–13

Destination country	Number of projects	Number of companies
South Africa	1,107	867
Nigeria	405	317
Kenya	319	263
Angola	308	150
Ghana	268	215
Tanzania	180	142
Uganda	169	123
Zambia	156	115
Mozambique	147	121
Botswana	96	76
Namibia	94	82
Rwanda	87	67
Ethiopia	85	77
Congo, Dem. Rep.	84	66
Zimbabwe	70	57
Mauritius	69	65
Senegal	63	57
South Sudan	60	42
Sudan	59	46
Côte d'Ivoire	57	50
Cameroon	43	34
Gabon	35	30
Sierra Leone	32	28
Madagascar	30	29
Mauritania	24	21
Guinea	23	22
Liberia	22	20

Destination country	Number of projects	Number of companies
Burundi	21	18
Congo, Rep.	21	19
Burkina Faso	20	18
Malawi	20	20
Mali	18	15
Swaziland	18	17
Equatorial Guinea	17	14
Djibouti	17	17
Gambia	16	12
Seychelles	16	16
Somalia	14	13
Togo	11	10
Chad	10	9
Lesotho	10	9
Niger	8	7
Cape Verde	8	5
Eritrea	7	4
Benin	7	7
Guinea-Bissau	5	4
Comoros	5	5
Central African Republic	3	3
São Tomé and Príncipe	3	3
Total	4,367	2,467

Source: Financial Times, FDI Markets database.

Table G.8. Number of greenfield FDI projects in SSA, by industry, 2003–13

Sector/industry	2003	2004	2005	2006	2007	2008	2009	2010	2011	2012	2013	Total
Financial Services	26	20	22	48	45	116	106	92	124	98	82	779
Communications	6	7	17	34	15	30	35	42	66	82	67	401
Metals	38	22	52	33	24	54	31	30	42	28	13	367
Business Services	6	8	13	17	14	23	29	37	42	73	70	332
Coal, Oil and Natural Gas	32	23	27	23	10	52	26	25	37	17	18	290
Food & Tobacco	12	8	13	12	9	19	33	29	45	38	39	257
Software & IT services	16	7	8	16	15	27	25	26	42	37	28	247
Transportation	4	5	11	8	4	10	30	15	22	26	23	158
Automotive OEM	6	6	14	15	4	15	15	16	28	16	11	146
Industrial Machinery, Equipment & Tools	1	1	4	3	5	12	21	17	18	31	10	123

Table G.8. (Continued)

Sector/industry	2003	2004	2005	2006	2007	2008	2009	2010	2011	2012	2013	Total
Hotels & Tourism	6	7	2	9	14	25	10	10	4	8	6	101
Chemicals	9	8	2	7	3	8	9	12	14	19	7	98
Minerals	8	9	15	4	9	15	10	8	12	5	1	96
Beverages	9	5	2	4		18	12	11	18	8	6	93
Building & Construction Materials	1	5	2	4	15	14	10	12	6	21		90
Textiles	7	7	2	2	2	6	5	12	15	7	20	85
Consumer Products	3	3	4	4	1	2	7	4	18	12	22	80
Alternative/Renewable energy	0	2	2	3	6	9	11	6	16	13	10	78
Real Estate	3	4	3	4	4	17	4	5	5	7	7	63
Consumer Electronics	2	5	4		3	3	2	3	10	8	14	54
Electronic Components	2	5	2		2	8	3	8	9	11		50
Pharmaceuticals	1		3	1	5	5	4	4	8	13	4	48
Automotive Components	1	3	4	4	1	4	7	5	4	3	2	38
Business Machines & Equipment	1	5	4	4	4	4		4	6	3		35
Healthcare				1		3	2	13	7	5	1	32
Warehousing & Storage		4	4	2	2	5	1	3		9		30
Paper, Printing & Packaging	6	1	1	4		1	2	3	2	1	5	26
Non-Automotive Transport OEM	2	1	1	2	2	3	2	5	4	2	2	26
Rubber	1	1	4		1	2	2	4	1	2	4	22
Plastics	1		1		1	1	1	5	3	4	2	19
Aerospace		1	3	2		4	1	1	1	2	3	18
Medical Devices	1		1	2	2					1	6	13
Leisure & Entertainment			1		2	2		3		4	12	
Ceramics & Glass	1		1			4	1		1			8
Engines & Turbines	1			1	1		2	1	1		7	
Wood Products	2					1	1				1	5
Biotechnology	1				1		1		1	1		5
Space & Defense							1		1	2		4
Semiconductors					1							1
Total	211	169	255	275	212	515	479	456	642	591	532	4,337

Source: Financial Times, FDI Markets database.

Table G.9. Number of M&A deals, by announced date and industry, 2000–13

Industry	2000	2001	2002	2003	2004	2005	2006	2007	2008	2009	2010	2011	2012	2013	Total
Communications, business, and computer services	13	8	5	18	24	43	42	34	40	26	31	38	32	41	395
Metals, mining, and agriculture	4	6	14	43	33	37	45	34	36	27	24	30	19	13	365
Financial services	2	1	3	7	9	10	14	16	24	6	8	13	9	16	138
Wholesale, retail, distribution	2	3	4	6	5	12	10	10	16	5	10	12	11	14	120
Food, beverages, tobacco	4	4	1	8	9	3	7	5	9	2	5	4	7	8	76
Chemicals, rubber, plastics, nonmetallic manufacturing	1	2	3	9	7	6	10	5	14	5	4	3	1	2	72
Machinery, equipment, furniture, recycling	1	3		7	5	3	10	12	9	1	5	3	2	8	69
Transport	1	1	1	5	2	5	11	6	4	2	3	7	4	2	54
Tourism	0	0	1	2	3	3	1	2	5	2	2	2	0	4	27
Construction	0	0	0	1	1	3	1	3	2	0	5	3	0	1	20
Publishing, printing	0	0	0	6	3	1	1	2	3	0	0	1	0	1	18
Gas, water, electricity	0	0	1	0	2	2	0	2	1	1	2	1	0	5	17
Textiles, wearing apparel, leather	1	0	0	1	2	0	2	0	1	3	0	0	0	0	10
All other	1	0	0	1	1	5	2	0	1	3	6	5	10	9	44
Grand total	30	28	33	114	106	133	156	131	165	83	105	122	95	124	1,427

Source: Bureau van Dijk, Zephyr M&A database.

Table G.10. Number of M&A deals in SSA, by EU member acquirer and sector of target, 2000–2013

Industry	United Kingdom	Netherlands	France	Germany	Luxembourg	Other	Total
Nonfinancial services	93	16	13	4	9	25	160
Metals & metal products	46	9	1	1	2	2	61

Table G.10. (Continued)

Industry	United Kingdom	Netherlands	France	Germany	Luxembourg	Other	Total
Primary sector (agriculture, mining, etc.)	33	5	6	1	4	6	55
Wholesale & retail trade	22	7	9	3	2	5	48
Food, beverages, tobacco	17	7	7	3	1	9	44
Banks	18	3	4	4	1	1	31
Machinery, equipment, furniture, recycling	8	2	2	7		9	28
Chemicals, rubber, plastics, non-metallic products	5	2	4	4	1	8	24
Transport	13	1	1	1		3	19
All other	33	6	6	3	5	9	62
Total	288	58	53	31	25	77	532

Source: Zephyr M&A database.

Table G.11. FDI inflows to South Africa, by source country, 2004–11 (million$)

	2004	2005	2006	2007	2008	2009	2010	2011	Total
Net foreign direct investment inflows	798	6,647	−527	5,695	9,006	5,365	1,228	5,807	34,019
Main origin of FDI inflows									
United Kingdom	7,036	7,940	2,698	2,211	2,412	1,550	4,002.2	8,756.4	36,606
Switzerland	−58	879	344	815	3450	−226	121.6	235.8	5,561
United States	480	82	159	1,000	306	410	779	722	3,938
Germany	578	476	666	782	−34	331	1,074.2	1,037.6	4,911
France	48	155	262	197	338	376	353.6	447.1	2,177

Source: African Development Bank.

Table G.12. China, number of greenfield FDI projects in SSA, by industry, 2003–12

Industry	South Africa	Zambia	Ethiopia	Angola	Kenya	Nigeria	Zimbabwe	Ghana	Sudan	Congo (DRC)	Other	Total
Communications	5	2	3	6	3	2	5	1	1	1	5	34
Metals	8	11					1	1		2	4	27
Automotive OEM	7	2	4		2				1		3	19
Coal, oil and natural gas				1		1		1	2		4	9
Building and construction materials	1					2					5	8

Industry	South Africa	Zambia	Ethiopia	Angola	Kenya	Nigeria	Zimbabwe	Ghana	Sudan	Congo (DRC)	Other	Total
Financial services	2	1	1	1	1			1			0	7
Chemicals	2	1								1	2	6
Industrial machinery, equipment and tools	3				1			1			0	5
Transportation	1							1	1		1	4
Consumer electronics	2				1						0	3
All other	5	1	3	2	1	4	1	0	0	1	4	22
Total	36	18	11	10	9	9	7	6	5	5	28	144

Source: Financial Times, FDI Markets database.

Table G.13. India, selected M&A transactions in SSA

Acquirer name	Target name	Target country	Deal value (million $)	Announced date	Completed date	Target industry
ONGC Videsh Ltd	Talisman Energy's Sudan Assets	Sudan	758	10/30/2002	3/12/2003	Oil and gas services
Bharti Airtel	Celtel Zambia Ltd	Zambia	499	5/20/2010	7/22/2010	Telecommunications
Videsh Sanchar Nigam	Sepco	South Africa	200	8/16/2005	8/16/2005	Telecommunications
Essar Group	Warid Congo	Congo	150	11/15/2009	11/16/2009	Telecommunications
Gremach Infrastructure Equipments and Projects	Osho Mozambique Coal Mining	Mozambique	100	9/26/2007	9/26/2007	Coal mining
Sesa Goa	Western Cluster	Liberia	90	8/6/2011	8/24/2011	Iron mining
Intelenet Global Services	Unnamed Mauritian company that owns Upstream and Travelport	Mauritius	75	12/3/2007	12/3/2007	Business services
Ranbaxy Laboratories	Be-Tabs Pharmaceuticals	South Africa	70	12/1/2006	12/1/2006	Pharmaceuticals
Sesa Goa	Western Cluster	Liberia	34	12/20/2012	12/20/2012	Iron mining
Godrej Consumer Products	Kinky Group	South Africa	33	4/1/2008	4/1/2008	Consumer products
Zee Entertainment Enterprises	Taj TV Mauritius	Mauritius	31	4/21/2010	4/21/2010	Television broadcasting
Global Steel Holdings Ltd	Delta Steel	Nigeria	30	2/24/2005	2/24/2005	Steel

Source: Zephyr M&A database.

Note: Under the first Sesa Goa-Western Cluster deal, Sesa Goa acquired a 51 percent stake in the company. Under the second deal, Sesa Goa acquired the remaining equity.

Table G.14. India, number of greenfield FDI projects in SSA, by industry, 2003–13

Industry	South Africa	Nigeria	Kenya	Tanzania	Mauritius	Ethiopia	Zambia	Ghana	Uganda	Other	Total
Financial services	13	2	3	13	2	2		1	3	7	46
Communications	2	4	7	1	1		1	1	3	18	38
Software and IT services	13	2	3		1		1	2	1	6	29
Automotive OEM	6	3	4			1	3	4		3	24
Coal, oil and natural gas	5	4	1		3		1			8	22
Healthcare		4	1	2	2	1	1	2	2	3	18
Business services	2	3	3	1	3		1	1		3	17
Metals	2	3		1	1		1	1		5	14
Industrial machinery, equipment, and tools	4		1	1				1		2	9
Pharmaceuticals		4	1	1		1			1	1	9
All other	21	6	8	6	4	11	6	2	3	16	83
Total	68	35	32	26	17	16	15	15	13	72	309

Source: Financial Times, FDI Markets database.

APPENDIX H. EU-SOUTH AFRICA FTA TARIFF COMMITMENTS

Table H.1. EU-South Africa tariff commitments: Industrial goods

European Community	South Africa
\multicolumn{2}{|l|}{Immediate elimination of duties on imports of all industrial products other than those listed.}
Annex II, list 1　Reductions to 75% of the basic duty on entry into force; to 50% after year 1; to 25% after 2 years; complete elimination after year 3.	Annex III, list 1　Reductions to 75% of the basic duty on entry into force; to 50% after year 1; to 25% after year 2; complete elimination after year 3.
Goods include, but are not limited to:　• Chemical products　• Textiles　• Wood　• Finished electronics　• Motor vehicles	*Goods include, but are not limited to:*　• Chemical products　• Textiles　• Glass products　• Consumer goods
Annex II, list 2　Reductions to 86% of the basic duty on entry into force; annual reductions thereafter to 72%, 57%, 43%, 28%, 14% in years 2–6; complete elimination after year 6.	Annex III, list 2　Reductions to 67% of the basic duty 3 years after entry into force; to 33% 4 years after; complete elimination after year 5.
Goods include, but are not limited to:　• Chemical products　• Textiles	*Goods include, but are not limited to:*　• Chemical products　• Rubbers and plastics

European Community	South Africa
• Motor vehicles	• Woods • Metals • Consumer goods • Heavy machinery and electrical equipment
Annex II, list 3 Reductions to 75% of the basic duty 3 years after entry into force; to 50% after 4 years; to 25% after 5 years; complete elimination after year 6; -or- Reductions to 67% of the basic duty 4 years after entry into force; to 33% 5 years after entry into force; complete elimination after year 6.	Annex III, list 3 Reductions to 90% of the basic duty 3 years after entry into force; annual reductions thereafter to 80%, 70%, 60%, 50%, 40%, 30%, 20%, 10% in years 5–12; complete elimination after year 12.
Goods include, but are not limited to: • Chemical products • Various metals (Reductions of duties on some steel products is carried out on an MFN basis, to arrive at zero duty in 2004)	*Goods include, but are not limited to:* • Electronic goods used in appliances • Paper products • Toiletries and cosmetics • Some finished furniture
Annex II, list 4 Complete elimination after a maximum of 10 years	Annex III, list 4 Reductions to 88% of the basic duty 5 years after entry into force; annual reductions thereafter to 75%, 63%, 50%, 38%, 25%, and 13% in years 7–12; complete elimination after year 12.
Goods include, but are not limited to: • Motor vehicles and parts — reductions beginning with 50 percent immediate reductions for specificproducts; with specific schedule forothers (determined at later dates)	*Goods include, but are not limited to:* • Chemical products • Paper products • Rubbers and plastics • Woods • Metals • Toiletries and cosmetics • Some finished furniture
Annex II, list 5 Review in year 5 for possible elimination.	Annex III, list 5 Progressive reductions according to specific schedule for goods. Parts of this list would also be considered for proposals for additional liberalization at a later date.
Goods include, but are not limited to: • Aluminum	*Goods include, but are not limited to:* • Vehicle parts • Tires • Textiles • Motors
	Annex III, list 6 Periodic review for additional liberalization.
	Goods include, but are not limited to: • Chemical products • Large components for vehicle manufacturing

Source: Compiled by USITC based on the original EU-South Africa Trade Development and Cooperation Agreement signed on October 11, 1999. The agreement was applied provisionally January 1, 2000; entered into force May 1, 2004.

Note: Certain tariffs or quotas applied to goods originating in the European Community as mentioned in these lists are subject to derogations of South African basic duties. These products are mentioned in the First Annex in the agreement.

Table H.2. EU-South Africa tariff commitments: Agricultural goods

European Community	South Africa
Immediate elimination of duties on imports of all agricultural products other than those listed.	
Annex IV, list 1 Reductions to 75% of the basic duty on entry into force; to 50% after 1 year; to 25% after 2 years; complete elimination after year 3.	Annex VI, list 1 Reductions to 75% of the basic duty on entry into force; to 50% after 1 year; to 25% after 2 years; complete elimination after year 3.
Goods include, but are not limited to: • Live animals • Meats • Vegetables • Tobacco products	*Goods include, but are not limited to:* • Meats • Vegetables • Processed food products (e.g., soups, pastas)
Annex IV, list 2 Reductions to 91% of the basic duty on entry into force; annual reductions to 82%, 73%, 64%, 55%, 45%, 36%, 27%, 18%, 9% in years 2–10; complete elimination after year 10.	Annex VI, list 2 Reductions to 67% of the basic duty 3 years after entry into force; to 33% after 4 years; complete elimination after year 5.
Goods include, but are not limited to: • Various kinds of milk, yogurt, and cheeses • Various fruit and vegetable products	*Goods include, but are not limited to:* • Meats • Vegetables • Processed products
Annex IV, list 3 Reductions to 87% of the basic duty 3 years after entry into force; annual reductions thereafter to 75%, 62%, 50%, 37%, 25%, 12% in years 5–10; complete elimination after year 10. A duty-free quota also applies to some articles in this list.	Annex VI, list 3 Reductions to 88% of the basic duty 5 years after entry into force; annual reductions thereafter to 75%, 63%, 50%, 38%, 25%, 13% in years 7–12; complete elimination after year 12. A duty-free quota also applies to some articles in this list.
Goods include, but are not limited to: • Flowers • Vegetable and fruit products	*Goods include, but are not limited to:* • Wheat products • Processed products (oils) • Fibrous goods • Tobacco products
Annex IV, list 4 Reductions to 83% of the basic duty 5 years after entry into force; annual reductions thereafter to 67%, 50%, 33%, 17% in years 7–10 ; complete elimination after year 10. A duty-free quota also applies to some articles in this list.	Annex VI, list 4 Periodic review.
Goods include, but are not limited to: • Meats and animal byproducts • Live animals • Cheeses • Fruits and vegetables	*Goods include, but are not limited to:* • Meat of bovine animals, swine, sheep, or goats, fresh, frozen, or preserved • Edible offal • Dairy products

European Community	South Africa
	• Sugar and confectionery • Flax • Hemp
Annex IV, list 5 Change in duty or quota schedules, but no elimination. Reductions of duties in certain processed goods could be in tandem with reductions in their basic products or by mutual concessions.	
Goods include, but are not limited to: • Processed dairy and confectionery products • Some processed agricultural products, food preparations	
Annex IV, list 6 Reduced duties as listed therein.	
Goods include, but are not limited to: • Cut flowers and flower buds • Fruits and nuts • Wine	
Annex IV, list 7 Periodic review.	
Goods include, but are not limited to: • Live animals • Meat and dairy products • Fruit and fruit juices • Wine • Grains	
Annex IV, list 8 No concessions, as the products are protected by EU denominations.	
Goods include, but are not limited to: • Cheeses, wine, and alcohol products	

Source: Compiled by USITC based on the original EU-South Africa Trade Development and Cooperation Agreement signed on October 11, 1999. The agreement was applied provisionally January 1, 2000; entered into force May 1, 2004.

Note: Certain tariffs or quotas applied to goods originating in the European Community as mentioned in these lists are subject to derogations of South African basic duties. These products are mentioned in the First Annex in the agreement.

Table H.3. EU-South Africa tariff commitments: Fisheries products

European Community	South Africa
Concessions apply after Fisheries Agreement to enter into force. All concessions to be fully implemented within 10 years from entry into force of the FTA.	
Annex V, list 1 Immediate elimination.	Annex VII, list 1 Duties on fisheries products to be eliminated in parallel with elimination of duties on corresponding products by the European Community.

Table H.3. (Continued)

European Community	South Africa
Goods include, but are not limited to: • Live fish • Fresh or frozen fish, excluding filets • Fish filets	*Goods include, but are not limited to:* • Fresh, frozen, or preserved fish, crustaceans, mollusks; caviar and caviar substitutes
Annex V, list 2 Tariffs eliminated in three equal annual stages beginning 3 years after entry into force of the Fisheries Agreement.	
Goods include, but are not limited to: • Live fish • Fresh or frozen fish, excluding filets • Fish filets and other fish meat • Live crustaceans, mollusks • Prepared or preserved fish, crustaceans, mollusks	
Annex V, list 3 Tariffs eliminated in equal annual stages starting at the beginning of the 4th year of the Fisheries Agreement.	
Goods include: • One type of live fish • One type of frozen fish • Fish filets and other fish meat • One type of prepared fish	
Annex V, list 4 Tariffs eliminated in equal annual stages starting at the beginning of the 6th year of the Fisheries Agreement.	
Goods include, but are not limited to: • One type of live fish • Fresh, frozen, or preserved fish, fish filets, crustaceans; caviar or caviar substitutes	
Annex V, list 5 Concessions to be reviewed.	
Goods include, but are not limited to: • Fresh or frozen fish • One type of fish filet • Prepared fish products	

Source: Compiled by USITC staff based on the original EU-South Africa Trade Development and Cooperation Agreement signed on October 11, 1999. The agreement was provisionally applied January 1, 2000; fully entered into force May 1, 2004; liberalization schedules were completed by 2012.

Note: The Fisheries Agreement has not yet taken effect.-

BIBLIOGRAPHY

Abebe, Bewket. "Not Simply 'Business as Usual' for Ethiopia's AGOA Ambitions." Addis Fortune (Ethiopia), August 11, 2013. http://allafrica.com/stories/201308122086.html.

Abuja, Nigeria: ECOWAS, 2011. http://www.spu.ecowas.int/wp- content/uploads/2010/06/ECOWAS-RSP-Thematic-Version-in-English.pdf.

AECOM International Development. "Priority Value Chains Assessment and Selection: Part One." Technical report prepared for USAID Southern African Trade Hub, 2011.

AECOM International Development. "Priority Value Chains Assessment and Selection: Part One." Technical report prepared for USAID Southern African Trade Hub, 2011. http://satradehub.org/home/priority-value-chains-assessment-and-selection-part-one.

African Cotton & Textile Industries Federation (ACTIF). "Competitiveness of the SSA Textile Sector Vs. Asian LDCs," 2010.

African Cotton & Textile Industries Federation (ACTIF). "Impact of AGOA on the Textile Industry in Kenya," November 2010.

African Development Bank (ABD). *Republic of Mozambique: Country Strategy Paper 2011–2015*. Tunis, Tunisia: ADB, 2011. http://www.afdb.org/fileadmin/uploads/afdb/Documents/Policy- Documents/Mozambique%20-%202011-15%20CSP.pdf.

African Development Bank (AfDB). *African Statistical Yearbook 2013*, 2013. http://www.afdb.org/en/documents/document/african-statistical-yearbook-2013-31680/.

African Development Bank Group. Kingdom of Lesotho: Country Strategy Paper, 2013–2017, February 2013. http://www.afdb.org/fileadmin/uploads/afdb/Documents/Project-and- Operations/2013-2017%20-%20Lesotho%20-%20Country%20Strategy%20Paper.pdf.

African Development Fund (ADF). "Macadamia Smallholder Development Project, Project Completion Report," April 2009. http://www.afdb.org/fileadmin/uploads/afdb/Documents/Project-and-Operations/Malawi.%20Macadamia%20Smallholder%20Development%20Project_EN.pd f.

African Union. "A Decade of African-US Trade under the African Growth and Opportunity Act (AGOA): Challenges, Opportunities and a Framework for Post-AGOA Engagement," November 2010. http://ti.au.int/en/content/challenges-opportunities-and-framework- post-agoa-engagement.

Aiello, Francesco; Federica, Demaria. "Do Trade Preferential Agreements Enhance the Exports of Developing Countries? Evidence from the EU GSP." University of Calabria Working Paper no. 02-2010, January 2010. http://www.ecostat.unical.it/RePEc/WorkingPapers/WP02_2010.pdf.

Aiello, Francesco; Paola, Cardamone. "Analysing the Impact of Everything But Arms Initiative Using a Gravity Model." Chapter 7 in *The Trade Impact of European Union Preferential Policies*, edited by Luca De Benedictis and Luca Salvatici. Berlin: Springer-Verlag, 2011.

Aiello, Francesco; Paola, Cardamone. "Analysing the Impact of Everything But Arms Initiative Using a Gravity Model." In *The Trade Impact of European Union Preferential Policies: An Analysis through Gravity Models*, edited by Luca de Benedictis and Luca Salvatici, 127–50. Berlin Heidelberg: Springer-Verlag, 2011.

AllAfrica.com, "Tunisia and WAEMU to Sign Free Trade Agreement." http://allafrica.com/stories/201309191176.html (accessed January 16, 2014).

Aluminum Federation of South Africa (AFSA). "Aluminum Industry in SA, Overview." Germiston, South Africa: AFSA. http://www.afsa.org.za/AluminiumIndustryinSA/Overview/tabid/119/Default.aspx.

Alves, Cristina Ana. "Brazil in Africa: Achievements and Challenges." In *Emerging Powers in Africa: Special Report*, edited by Nicholas Kitchen, 37–44. LSE IDEAS, June 2013. http://www.lse.ac.uk/IDEAS/publications/reports/pdf/SR016/SR-016-Alves.pdf.

American Chamber of Commerce in Morocco (Amcham Morocco). Trade and Investment Guide 2007, Part IV: Trade and Investment Regulations, 2007. http://www.moroccousafta.com/amchamguide.htm.

American Metal Market. "ENERGY WATCH South Africa turns a deaf ear … and promise into plight." April 1, 2008.

———. "Eskom declares power supply emergency." November 20, 2013.

———. "Eskom power plant delay endangers SA metal projects." October 31, 2011. AMM.com. "Pricing." New York: American Metal Market (AMM). http://www.amm.com/Pricing.html (accessed January 29, 2014).

Anderson, James E. "The Gravity Model." National Bureau of Economic Research Working Paper 16576, December 2010. http://www.nber.org/papers/w16576.pdf?new_window=1.

Anderson, James E; Eric, van Wincoop. "Gravity with Gravitas: A Solution to the Border Puzzle." National Bureau of Economic Research Working Paper 8079, January 2001. http://www.nber.org/papers/w8079.pdf?new_window=1.

Anganan, Villen. "Mauritius Exporters Switch Focus from EU to South Africa." *Just-Style.com*, April 29, 2013.

Asmah, Emmanuel; Stephen, Karingi; Mwangi, Kimenyi; Nick, Krafft; Zenia, Lewis; Nelipher, Moyo; John, Mutenyo; Laura, Páez; John, Page; Mekalia, Palilos; Ezra, Suruma; Olumide, Tatwo. *AGOA at 10: Challenges and Prospects for U.S.-Africa Trade and Investment Relations*. Washington, DC: Brookings Institute, July 2010.

Azzopardi, Tom. "Diversifying Chile's Exports." American Chamber of Commerce (Amcham) Chile. Business Chile Magazine, February 1, 2012.

Baldwin, Richard. "Global Supply Chains: Why They Emerged, Why They Matter, and Where They Are Going." In *Global Value Chains in a Changing World*, edited by Deborah K. Elms and Patrick Low, 13–59. Geneva: World Trade Organization, 2013. http://www.wto.org/english/res_e/publications_e/aid4tradeglobalvalue13_e.htm.

Bamber, Penny; Karina, Fernandez-Stark; Gary, Gereffi; Andrew, Guinn. "Connecting Local Producers in Developing Countries to Regional and Global Value Chains: Update." Organisation for Economic Co-operation and Development (OECD). Working Party of the Trade Committee. OECD Trade Policy Paper No. 160, December 3, 2013. http://search.oecd.org/officialdocuments/publicdisplaydocumentpdf/?cote=TAD/TC/WP(2013)27/FINAL&docLanguage=En.

Bartels, Lorand; Paul, Goodison. "EU Proposal to End Preferences of 18 African and Pacific States: An Assessment." Commonwealth Secretariat. Commonwealth Trade Hot Topics, issue 91, November 2011. http://www.secretariat.thecommonwealth.org/files/242343/FileName/TradeHotTopics91FINAL.pdf.

Bergstrand, Jeffrey; Scott, Baier; Eva, R Sunesen; Martin, H Thelle. *Ex-Post Assessment of Six EU Free Trade Agreements: An Econometric Assessment of Their Impact on Trade.* Copenhagen: Copenhagen Economics, February 2011.

Bermúdez-Lugo, Omayra. "The Mineral Industry of Namibia: Advance Release." 2011 Minerals Yearbook. Reston, VA: U.S. Geological Survey (USGS), April 2013. http://minerals.usgs.gov/minerals/pubs/country/africa.html#cf (retrieved February 4, 2014).

Bilal, San. "Count Down to Concluding EPAs: What's Really at Stake?" Talking Points (blog).

Bilal, San. "Trade Talks Set to Disrupt Africa-Europe Relations and Poison the Upcoming Africa- EU Summit." European Centre for Policy Development Management. Briefing Note no.002058, November 2013.

Bilaterals.org, "IBSA." http://www.bilaterals.org/?-IBSA-. (accessed February 6, 2014).

Borgenheimer, Rudi. "Motor Industry Development Program in South Africa." PowerPoint presentation, November 30, 2010. http://www.eibdconference.com/assets/files/Mercedes_RudiBorgenheimer.pdf.

Bouët, Antoine; Lionel, Fontagné; Sébastien, Jean. "Is Erosion of Tariff Preferences a Serious Concern?" Centre d'Etudes Prospectives et d'Informations Internationales (CEPII). Working Paper no. 2005-14, September 2005.

Brenton, Paul. "INTEGRATING the Least Developed Countries into the World Trading System: The Current Impact of EU Preferences under Everything But Arms." World Bank Policy Research Working Paper 3018, April 2003. http://elibrary.worldbank.org/doi/pdf/10.1596/1813-9450-3018.

Brenton, Paul; Mombert, Hoppe. "The African Growth and Opportunity Act, Exports, and Development in Sub-Saharan Africa." Washington, DC: World Bank, 2006. https://openknowledge.worldbank.org/bitstream/handle/10986/9288/wps3996.pdf?se quence=1.

Brenton, Paul; Mombert, Hoppe. "The African Growth and Opportunity Act, Exports, and Development in Sub-Saharan Africa." World Bank Policy Research Working Paper 3996, August 2006. http://www.wds.worldbank.org/external/default/WDSContentServer/IW3P/IB/2006/08/25/000016406_20060825122955/Rendered/PDF/wps3996.pdf.

Brenton, Paul; Takako, Ikezuki. "The Initial and Potential Impact of Preferential Access to the U.S. Market under the African Growth and Opportunity Act." World Bank Policy Research Working Paper 3262, April 2004. http://elibrary.worldbank.org/doi/pdf/10.1596/1813-9450-3262.

Bungu, Jerry. "Botswana Beef Exports Slump 89% after Exports to Europe Halted." Bloomberg, April 28, 2011. http://www.bloomberg.com/news/2011-04-28/botswana-beef-exports- slump-89-after-exports-to-europe-halted.html.

Bureau, Jean-Christophe; Raja, Chakir; Jacques, Gallezot. "The Utilization of Trade Preferences for Developing Countries in the Agri-food Sector." *Journal of Agricultural Economics*, 58, no. 2 (2007), 175–98.

Bureau, van Dijk. Zephyr Mergers and Acquisitions database (accessed January 7, 2014).

Business Daily Africa. "Textile Firms Resume Investments after AGOA Rule Extension," May 23, 2013. http://www.businessdailyafrica.com/Textile-firms-resume-investments-after- Agoa-rule-extension/-/539546/1863634/-/v4svtdz/-/index.html.

Business Innovation Facility (BIF), Equal Exchange, and Irish Aid. Malawian Macadamias 2010–2020.

Business Monitor International (BMI). Asian Investment in Africa: The Next Phase, October 2013, 2013.

Callebaut, Barry. "Barry Callebaut Inaugurates Second Cocoa Bean Processing Line in Tema Factory in Ghana>" News release, February 8, 2007. http://www.barry- callebaut.com/download.dhtml?url=/cms_files/N-3132-PDF_en.pdf,filename=Press%20release%20inauguration%202nd%20line%20Feb%2007%201.pdf.

Campbell, Keith. "Vale Now Active in Southern, Central and West Africa." MiningWeekly.com, September 2, 2011. http://www.miningweekly.com/article/brazilian-major-now-active- in-southern-central-and-west-africa-2011-09-02-1.

Candau, Fabien; Sébastien, Jean. "What Are EU Trade Preferences Worth for Sub-Saharan Africa and Other Developing Countries?" In *Trade Preference Erosion: Measurement and Policy Response*, edited by Bernard Hoekman, Will Martin, and Carlos A. Primo Braga, 65–102. Washington, DC, and New York: World Bank and Palgrave Macmillan, 2009. http://elibrary.worldbank.org/doi/book/10.1596/978-0-8213-7707-9.

Cardamone, Paola. "Trade Impact of European Union Preferences: An Analysis with Monthly Data." In *The Trade Impact of European Union Preferential Policies*: An Analysis through Gravity Models, edited by Luca de Benedictis and Luca Salvatici, 151–74. Berlin Heidelberg: Springer-Verlag, 2011.

Cargill. "Cargill Celebrates Five Years in Ghana and Renews Its Partnership with CARE to Support Sustainable Cocoa." News release, November 5, 2013. http://www.cargillcocoachocolate.com/wcm/groups/public/@ccc/@all/documents/document/na3080886.pdf.

Central Intelligence Agency (CIA). "Mauritius." *World Factbook*. https://www.cia.gov/library/publications/the-world-factbook/geos/mp.html (accessed January 16, 2014).

———. "South Africa." *World Factbook*. https://www.cia.gov/library/publications/the-world- factbook/geos/sa.html (accessed January 15, 2014).

Chemengich, Margaret. *Competitiveness of the SSA Textile Sector vs. Asian LDC Countries*. African Cotton and Textile Industries Federation (ACTIF). Nairobi: ACTIF, December 2010. http://www.cottonafrica.com/documents/ACTIF%20Report%20on%20Competitiveness%20of%20the%20SSA%20Textile%20Sector%20vs%20Asian%20LDC%20countries_2010. pdf.

Chemical Week. "Sasol Starts Up Acrylates Complex," April 7/14, 2004.

———."Shell Closes Louisiana MEK Plant," September 29/October 6, 2004.

Chemonics International. *Mauritius National AGOA Strategy*, 2013. http://www.competeafrica.org/Files/Mauritius_AGOA_Strategy_Final_May_2013.pdf.

China Business Insight. "China Outbound Direct Investment," February 2013. http://www.tusiad.org/rsc/shared/file/ChinaBusinessInsight-February-2013.pdf.

Chinembiri, Evans; Tinashe, Kapuya. "AGOA a Boon for South African Vehicle Exports." Engineering News, September 27, 2013. http://www.engineeringnews.co.za/article/agoa-a-boon-for-south-african-vehicle- exports-2013-09-27.

Christ, Nannette; Michael, J Ferrantino. "Land Transport for Export: The Effects of Cost, Time, and Uncertainty in Sub-Saharan Africa." *World Development*, 39, no. 10 (October 2011), 1749–59.

Chutha, Robert; Mwangi, S Himenyi. *The Africa Growth and Opportunities Act: Toward 2015 and Beyond*, Washington, DC: Brookings Institution, May 2011.

Cipollina, Maria; David, Laborde; Luca, Salvatici. "Do Preferential Trade Policies (Actually) Increase Exports? An Analysis of EU Trade Policies." Paper presented at the Agricultural and Applied Economics Association's 2013 AAEA and CAES Joint Annual Meeting, Washington DC, August 4–6, 2013. http://ageconsearch.umn.edu/bitstream/150177/2/CipollinaLabordeSalvatici_conf_MP acc2.pdf.

———. A Comparison between EU and US Trade Policies." Paper presented at the 12th Annual Conference of the European Trade Study Group (ETSG), September 9–11, 2010. http://www.etsg.org/ETSG2010/papers/CipollinaLabordeSalvatici.pdf.

Cipollina, Maria; Filomena, Pietrovito. "Trade Impact of EU Preferential Policies: A Meta-analysis of the Literature." In *The Trade Impact of European Union Preferential Policies: An Analysis through Gravity Models*, edited by Luca de Benedictis and Luca Salvatici, 91–109. Berlin Heidelberg: Springer-Verlag, 2011.

Cipollina, Maria; Luca, Salvatici. "Trade Impact of European Union Preferences." In *The Trade Impact of European Union Preferential Policies*: An Analysis through Gravity Models, edited by Luca de Benedictis and Luca Salvatici, 111–25. Berlin Heidelberg: Springer-Verlag, 2011.

Cirera, Xavier; Francesca, Foliano; Michael, Gasiorek. "The Impact of GSP Preferences on Developing Countries' Exports in the European Union: Bilateral Gravity Modelling at the Product Level." University of Sussex Department of Economics Working Paper no. 27-2011, 2011. https://www.sussex.ac.uk/webteam/gateway/file.php?name=wps27-2011-cirera-gasiorek.pdf&site=24.

CNN. "Lesotho Plans for Life without U.S. Trade Lifeline," February 15, 2011. http://edition.cnn.com/2011/BUSINESS/02/15/lesotho.textiles.aids.agoa/.

Co, Catherine Y; Ralitza, Dimova. "Preferential Market Access into the Chinese Market: How Good Is It for Africa?" Working Paper, October 13, 2013. (June version available at http://www.apeaweb.org/confer/osaka13/papers/Co_Catherine.pdf.

Cokayne, Roy. "Engine and Engine Part Exports Grow to R2.7bn Last Year." Business Report (South Africa), April 30, 2012. http://www.iol.co.za/business/news/engine-and-engine- part-exports-grow-to-r2-7bn-last-year-1.1285814.

Collier, Paul; Anthony, J Venables. "Rethinking Trade Preferences: How Africa Can Diversify Its Exports." Center for Economic Policy Research Discussion Paper 6262, May 2007. http://www.cepr.org/pubs/dps/DP6262.asp.

Commodity Import Approval Process, February 8, 2013. http://agoa.info/images/documents/5165/Commodity%20Import%20Request%20Proce ss-v2013.pdf.

Common Market for Eastern and Southern Africa (COMESA). *Annual Report 2011*. Lusaka, Zambia: COMESA, 2011. http://www.comesa.int/attachments/article/21/comesa_annualReport%202011_12_fin al.pdf

Conconi, Paola; Carlo, Perroni. Reciprocal versus Unilateral Trade Preferences for Developing Countries, September 2009.

Condon, Niall; Matthew, Stern. "The Effectiveness of African Growth and Opportunity Act (AGOA) in Increasing Trade from Least Developed Countries: A Systematic Review." Evidence for Policy and Practice Information and Coordinating Centre (EPPI-Centre) Report 1902, Social Science Research Unit, Institute of Education, University of London, March 2011. http://eppi.ioe.ac.uk/cms/LinkClick.aspx?fileticket=fwwVzZjUmFE%3D&tabid=2959&mi d=5542.

Cooke, FA Edgar. "The Impact of Trade Preferences on Exports of Developing Countries: The Case of the AGOA and CBI Preferences of the USA." Munich Personal RePEc Archive Paper no. 35058, June 2011. http://mpra.ub.uni-muenchen.de/35058/.

Corathers, Lisa A. "Manganese." *U.S. Geological Survey (USGS) 2008* Minerals Yearbook, October 2010.

———." *U.S. Geological Survey (USGS) 2011* Minerals Yearbook, May 2013.

Corathers, Lisa A. *Mineral Commodity Summaries: Manganese.* U.S. Geological Survey (USGS), January 2003.

———. *Mineral Commodity Summaries:* Manganese. U.S. Geological Survey (USGS), January 2008.

———. *Mineral Commodity Summaries:* Manganese. U.S. Geological Survey (USGS), January 2013.

Corathers, Lisa A. *Mineral Commodity Summaries: Silicon.* U.S. Geological Survey (USGS), January 2003.

———. *Mineral Commodity Summaries: Silicon.* U.S. Geological Survey (USGS), January 2009.

———. *Mineral Commodity Summaries: Silicon.* U.S. Geological Survey (USGS), January 2013. Corathers, Lisa A. "Silicon." U.S. Geological Survey (USGS) Minerals Yearbook, 2003.

———.U.S. Geological Survey (USGS) Minerals Yearbook, 2008, May 2010.

———.U.S. Geological Survey (USGS) Minerals Yearbook, 2012, December 2013. CPM Group. "Manganese Market Outlook," February 2012.

Cornell University. Legal Information Institute. "19 CFR 10.178a—Special Duty-Free Treatment for Sub-Saharan African Countries." http://www.law.cornell.edu/cfr/text/19/10.178a (accessed December 5, 2013).

Daily News (Tanzania). "Tobacco, Cashew Nuts Tanzania's Potential AGOA Export Bailout," August 22, 2013. http://www.dailynews.co.tz/index.php/features/21329-tobacco- cashew-nuts-tanzania-s-potential-agoa-export-bailout.

Davies, Elwyn; Lars, Nilsson. "A Comparative Analysis of EU and US Trade Preferences for the LDCs and the AGOA Beneficiaries." European Commission Directorate General for Trade Chief Economist Note 1, 2013. http://trade.ec.europa.eu/doclib/docs/2013/february/tradoc_150479.%201_February%202013.pdf.

Davies, Rob. Keynote address. Capturing the Gains Global Summit, Cape Town, South Africa, December 2012. http://www.capturingthegains.org/pdf/Rob_Davies_Keynote_CtG_Summit_Dec_2012.pdf.

De Backer, Steven. "Mining Investment and Financing in Africa: Recent Trends and Key Challenges." PowerPoint presentation. Webber Wentzel, March 2012. http://www.mineafrica. com/documents/2%20-%20Steve%20De%20Backer.pdf.

De Melo, Jaime; Alberto, Portugal-Perez. "Preferential Market Access Design: Evidence and Lessons from African Apparel Exports to the US and the EU." World Bank Policy Research Working Paper 6357, February 2013. http://elibrary.worldbank.org/doi/pdf/10.1596/1813-9450-6357.

Dean, Judith M; John, Wainio. "Quantifying the Value of U.S. Tariff Preferences for Developing Countries." World Bank Working Paper 3977, August 2006. http://elibrary.worldbank.org/doi/pdf/10.1596/1813-9450-3977.

Deloitte Automotive. *Navigating the Draft Automotive Production and Development Programme*, October 2012. http://www.deloitte.com/assets/Dcom- SouthAfrica/Local%20Assets/Documents/Navigating%20the%20Automotive%20Production%20and%20Development%20Programme.pdf.

Di Rubbo, P; Gabriele, Canali. "A Comparative Study of EU and US Trade Policies for Developing Countries: The Case of Agri-food Products." Paper prepared for the 12th Congress of the European Association of Agricultural Economists, Ghent, Belgium, August 2008. http://ageconsearch.umn.edu/bitstream/43961/2/118.pdf.

Dieye, Cheikh Tidiane. "How to Overcome the EPA Stalemate?" *Bridges Africa*, 2, no. 1 (March 2013).

Dinh, Hing, Vincent Palmade, Vandana Chandra, and Frances Cossar. *Light Manufacturing in Africa: Targeted Policies to Enhance Private Investment and Create Jobs*. Washington, DC: World Bank, 2012. https://openknowledge.worldbank.org/handle/10986/2245.

Dinh, Hing; Vincent, Palmade; Vandana, Chandra; Frances, Cossar. *Light Manufacturing in Africa: Targeted Policies to Enhance Private Investment and Create Jobs*. Washington, DC: World Bank, 2012. https://openknowledge.worldbank.org/bitstream/handle/10986/2245/672090PUB0EPI0067844B09780821389614.pdf?sequence=1.

East Africa Community (EAC). "Regional Frameworks for Development of Extractive Industries, Mineral Value Addition on the Way." News release, March 20, 2013. http://industrialization.eac.int/index.php?option=com_content&view=article&id=152:regional-frameworks-for-development-of-extractive-industries-mineral-value-addition-on-the-way&catid=40:press&Itemid=145.

East African Community. "EAC-EU Economic Partnership Agreement Negotiations Held in Brussels." Press release, January 30, 2014. http://www.eac.int/index.php?option=com_content&view=article&id=1474:eac-eu- economic-partnership-agreement-negotiations-held-in-brussels&catid=146:press- releases&Itemid=194.

East African Community. "EPA Negotiations on Course, EAC Interests Safeguarded—Amb. Sezibera," May 24, 2012. http://www.eac.int/index.php?option=com_content&view=article&id=1010:epa-negotiations-on-course-sg&catid=146:press-releases&Itemid=194.

Economic Community of West African States (ECOWAS) Commission. *Common Industrial Policy*. Abuja, Nigeria: ECOWAS, 2010. http://www.ecowas.int/publications/en/wacip/wacip_final_20100622.pdf.

———. *Regional Strategic Plan*. Abuja, Nigeria: ECOWAS, 2011. http://www.spu.ecowas.int/wp-content/uploads/2010/06/ECOWAS-RSP-Thematic-Version-in-English.pdf.

Economic Community of West African States (ECOWAS) Commission. *Regional Strategic Plan*.

Economist Intelligence Unit (EIU). "South Africa Trade: Trade Patterns and Regulations," February 15, 2013. http://www.eiu.com/industry/article/1010251685/south-xhtmlspan-classsearch-highlight-xmlnsxhtmlhttpwwww3org1999xhtmlafricaxhtmlspan-trade-trade-patterns-and-regulations/2013-02-15.

Economist. "Brazilian Companies Are Heading for Africa, Laden with Capital and Expertise," November 10, 2012. http://www.economist.com/news/21566019-brazilian-companies- are-heading-africa-laden-capital-and-expertise-new-atlantic-alliance.

———."Little to Fear but Fear Itself," September 21, 2013. http://www.economist.com/node/21586583/print.

Economist. "Ready to Take Off Again?" January 4, 2014.

Edelstein, Daniel L. "Copper." Mineral Commodity Summaries. Reston, VA: U.S. Geological Survey, January 2013. http://minerals.usgs.gov/minerals/pubs/commodity/copper.

Engineering News. "AGOA a Boon for South African Vehicle Exports," September 27, 2013. http://www.engineeringnews.co.za/article/agoa-a-boon-for-south-african-vehicle-exports-2013-09-27.

Equatorial Nut Processors Ltd. "About Us," 2013. http://www.equatorialnut.co.ke/aboutus.html.

Equatorial Nut Processors Ltd. "Our Certifications," 2013. http://www.equatorialnut.co.ke/certification.html.

Ernst & Young. *Ernst & Young's Attractiveness Survey*: Africa 2013, Getting Down to Business, 2013. http://www.avca-africa.org/wpcontent/uploads/2013/09/Africa_Attractiveness_-Survey_2013_AU1582.pdf.

EU Commission. "Opinion of the Commission regarding the Proposal for a Regulation of the European Parliament and of the Council amending Annex I to Council Regulation (EC) No 1528/2007 As Regards the Exclusion of a Number of Countries from the List of Regions or States Which Have Concluded Negotiations," May 3, 2013.

EU Commission. "Overview of EPA Negotiations," updated October 16, 2013. http://trade.ec.europa.eu/ doclib/docs/2009/september/tradoc_144912.pdf.

EU Commission. "Proposal for a Regulation of the European Parliament and of the Council amending Annex I to Council Regulation (EC) No 1528/2007 As Regards the Exclusion of a Number of Countries from the List of Regions or States Which Have Concluded Negotiations," September 30, 2011.

European Centre for Policy Development Management, April 26, 2013. http://www.ecdpm-talkingpoints.org/carry-on-pushing-forward-with-economic- partnership-agreements-epa-or-stop-them-all/.

European Commission (EC). "Trade: Countries and Regions; East African Community (EAC)." Brussels: EC, November 19, 2013. http://ec.europa.eu/trade/policy/countries-and- regions/regions/eac.

———. "Trade: Countries and Regions; Eastern and Southern Africa (ESA)." Brussels: EC, November 19, 2013. http://ec.europa.eu/trade/policy/countries-and- regions/regions/esa.

———. "Trade: Countries and Regions; South Africa." Brussels: EC, November 19, 2013. http://ec.europa.eu/trade/policy/countries-and-regions/countries/south-africa.

———. "Trade: Countries and Regions: Southern African Development Community (SADC)." Brussels: EC, November 19, 2013. http://ec.europa.eu/trade/policy/countries-and- regions/regions/sadc.

European Commission (EC). Eurostat database. http://epp.eurostat.ec.europa.eu/tgm/table.do?tab=tableandinit=1andplugin=1andlanguage=enandpcode=tec00055 (accessed various dates).

European Council, "2437th Council Meeting, Luxembourg, 17 June 2002," 29. http://www.consilium.europa.eu/uedocs/cms_data/docs/pressdata/en/gena/71044.pdf.

European Fresh Produce Association (Freshfel)—Southern Hemisphere Association of Fresh Fruit Exporters (SHAFFE) Secretariat. "Minutes of Freshfel-SHAFFE Citrus

Teleconference," April 22, 2013. http://www.freshfel.org/docs/citrus_wg/Minutes_of_Citrus_Teleconference_22_April.pdf.
European Union (EU) Commission. "Generalized System of Preferences." http://ec.europa.eu/ trade/policy/countries-and-regions/development/generalised- scheme-of-preferences/index_en.htm (accessed January 9, 2014).
Export Promotion Council of Kenya. "Trade Agreements." http://www.epckenya.org/index.php?option=com_content&task=view&id=50&Itemid=70 January 8, 2014.
Farmer's Weekly. "Making a Mountain out of Macadamias," February 11, 2013. http://www.farmersweekly.co.za/article.aspx?id=35299&h=Making-a-mountain-out-of-macadamias-.
Fasan, O. "Comparing EU Free Trade Agreements: Trade Facilitation." ECDPM InBrief 6F.
Ferrantino, Michael. "Policy Anchors: Do Free Trade Agreements and WTO Accessions Serve as Vehicles for Developing-Country Policy Reform?" Office of Economics Working Paper No. 2006-04-A, U.S. International Trade Commission, April 2006.
Financial Times. "Processing Capacity Grinds Cocoa Industry," December 17, 2012.
Financial Times. FDIMarkets database (accessed January 14, 2014).
Flatters, Frank. *The Economics of MIDP and the South African Motor Industry*. Queen's University, Canada, November 5, 2005. http://qed.econ.queensu.ca/faculty/flatters/writings/ff_economics_of_midp.pdf.
Flatters, Frank; Nnzeni Netshitomboni. *Trade and Poverty in South Africa: Motor Industry Case Study*. Trade and Poverty Project, Southern Africa Labour and Development Research Unit, University of Cape Town, 2006. http://www.tips.org.za/files/trade_flattersnetshitomboni.pdf.
Focus Africa, "Ethiopia." http://focusafrica.gov.in/Ethiopia_Trade_Agreement.html. (accessed January 15, 2014).
Fondel, BIT. "Silicon Metal," n.d. http://www.fondel.com/en/marketingen%20distribution/-downloads_2?page=3.
Frazer, Garth; Johannes, Van Biesebroeck. "Trade Growth under the African Growth and Opportunity Act." *The Review of Economics and Statistics*, 92, no. 1 (February 2010): 128–44.
Fulponi, Linda; Alejandra, Engler. "The Impact of Regional Trade Agreements on Chilean Fruit Exports." Joint Working Party on Agriculture and Trade, Trade and Agriculture Directorate, Organization for Economic Cooperation and Development (OECD), August 12, 2013.
Fung Global Institute (FGI), Nanyang Technological University (NTU), and World Trade Organization (WTO). *Global Value Chains in a Changing World*. Edited by Deborah Elms and Patrick Low. Geneva: WTO, 2013. http://www.wto.org/english/res_e/booksp_e/aid4tradeglobalvalue13_e.pdf.
Galan, Belem; Vasquez, I; Olajide, S Oladipo. "Have Liberalization and NAFTA had a positive Impact on Mexico's Output Growth?" *Journal of Applied Economics*, 12, no. 1 (May 2009), 159–180.
Gamberoni, Elisa. "Do Unilateral Trade Preferences Help Export Diversification?" HEI Graduate Institute of International Studies Working Paper, July 2007. http://graduateinstitute.ch/files/live/sites/iheid/files/sites/international_economics/shared/international_economics/publications/working%20papers/2007/HEIWP17-2007.pdf.
Geneva: International Trade Centre, 2012. www.intracen.org/WEDF-African-trade-for- web.

George, Edward. "Structure and Competition in West Africa's Cocoa Trade." Ecobank, November 21, 2012.

Gereffi, Gary; Olga, Memedovic. *The Global Apparel Value Chain: What Prospects for Upgrading by Developing Countries?* United Nations Industrial Development Organization (UNIDO) Sectoral Studies Series. Vienna: UNIDO, 2003. http://www.unido.org/fileadmin/media/documents/pdf/Services_Modules/Apparel_Val ue_Chain.pdf.

Gil-Pareja, Salvador; Rafael, Llorca-Vivero; José, Antonio Martínez-Serrano. "Do Nonreciprocal Preference Regimes Increase Exports?" World Bank Trade Brown Bag Seminar Paper, December 2012, http://siteresources.worldbank.org/INTRANETTRADE/Resources/Internal-Training/287823-1256848879189/65265081312911329405/SalvadorGilPareja_- GilLlorcaandMartAnezSerrano.pdf.

Gitau, Agnes. "Promoting Value Supply Chains in Sub Saharan Africa." *Kenya London News*, December 23, 2013. http://www.kenyalondonnews.org/?p=6403.

Glauser, James. "Acrylic Acid, Acrylate Esters and Superabsorbent Polymers." CEH Marketing Research Report, 2012.

Global Trade Information Service (GTIS). Global Trade Atlas (GTA) database (accessed various dates).

Global Trade Information Service, Inc. (GTIS). Global Trade Atlas database (GTA) (accessed January 24, 2014). http://www.gtis.com/english/GTIS_GTA.html (fee required).

Global Trade Information Service, Inc. (GTIS). World Trade Atlas database (accessed various dates).

Global Trade Information Services Inc. (GTIS). Global Trade Atlas (GTA) database (accessed November 22, 2013).

Godfrey, Shane. "Comment: Prospects for an African Clothing Industry?" *Just-Style.com*, June 25, 2013.

Government of Ethiopia. *Growth and Transformation Plan 2010/2011–2014/2015*. Addis Ababa, 2010. http://www.ethiopians.com/Ethiopia_GTP_2015.pdf.

Government of Malawi. Ministry of Industry and Trade. *National Export Strategy 2013–2018*.

Government of Rwanda. *Rwanda Handcraft Strategic Plan: Five Years (2009–2013)*. Kigali, 2009. http://www.minicom.gov.rw/IMG/pdf/Handcraft_strategic_plan_adopted_2009.pdf.

———. *Rwanda National Export Strategy*. Kigali, 2011. http://www.minicom.gov.rw/IMG/pdf/National_Export_Strategy.pdf.

Government of South Africa. Department of Trade and Industry (DTI). *Industrial Policy Action Plan: Economic Sectors and Employment Cluster, IPAP 2013/2014–2015/2016, 2013*. http://www.thedti.gov.za/news2013/ipap_2013-2016.pdf.

Government of South Africa. Written submission to the USITC, "Analysis of RSA Imports from the US." January 22, 2014.

Government of the United Kingdom (UK). Parliament. "Market Access for Exports from the ACP countries." Documents considered by the European Scrutiny Committee, October 26, 2011. http://www.publications.parliament.uk/pa/cm201012/cmselect/cmeuleg/428-xxxix/42808.htm.

Gradeva, Katerina; Inmaculada, Martínez-Zarzoso. "Trade as Aid: The Role of the EBA-Trade Preferences Regime in the Development Strategy." Ibero-America Institute for

Economic Research Discussion Paper No. 197, August 2009. http://wwwuser.gwdg.de/~fjohann/paper/DB197.pdf.

Greiner, Elvira O; Chiyo, Funada. "Methyl Ethyl Ketone (MEK)." CEH Marketing Research Report, 2012.

Grill, Bartholomäus. "Billions from Beijing: Africans Divided over Chinese Presence." *Spiegel Online International*, November 29, 2013. http://www.spiegel.de/international/world/chinese-investment-in-africa-boosts- economies-but-worries-many-a-934826.html.

Grynberg, Roman. "Botswana's Beef with the EU." *Mail & Guardian*, July 6, 2012. http://mg.co.za/article/2012-07-06-botswanas-beef-with-the-eu.

Grynberg, Roman. "Diamond Beneficiation in Botswana." *GREAT Insights* 2, no. 2 (February– March 2013). http://www.ecdpm.org/ Web_ECDPM/Web/Content/Content.nsf/0/A1D4CE6E1B7D4848C1257B1D004BE208?OpenDocument#sthash.pUlK31qH.dpuf.

———. "Some Like Them Rough: The Future of Diamond Beneficiation in Botswana." ECDPM Discussion Paper 142, March 2013. http://www.ecdpm.org/Web_ECDPM/Web/Content/Download.nsf/0/396A3B9ED5B580E3C1257B27004628C3/$FILE/DP%20142%20Some%20like%20them%20rough_Grynberg.pdf.

Grynberg, Roman; Masedi, Motswapong; Diana, Philimon. "Diamond Beneficiation and the WTO." *Manchester Journal of International Economic Law*, 9, no. 1 (2012), 2–22. http://heinonline.org/HOL/Page?handle=hein.journals/mjiel9&div=6&g_sent=1&collection=journals#6.

Gurmendi, Alfredo C. "The Mineral Industry of Peru: Advance Release." 2011 Minerals Yearbook. Reston, VA: U.S. Geological Survey, April 2013. http://minerals.usgs.gov/minerals/pubs/country/sa.html#br (retrieved February 4, 2014).

Haley, Stephen. "Table 60b." *Sugar and Sweeteners Yearbook Tables*. Economic Research Service, U.S. Department of Agriculture, January 15, 2014. http://www.ers.usda.gov/data-products/sugar-and-sweeteners-yearbook-tables.aspx.

Hartzenburg, Trudi; Samson, Muradzikwa. "Transfer of Technology for Successful Integration into the Global Economy: A Case Study of the South African Automotive Industry." UNCTAD/UNDP Global Programme on Globalization, 2002.

Hausmann, Ricardo; Cesar, Hidalgo; Sebastian, Bustos; Michele, Coscia; Sarah, Chung; Juan, Jimenez; Alexander, Simoes; Muhammed, Yildirim. *The Atlas of Economic Complexity: Mapping Paths to Prosperity*. Boston, MA: Harvard University, 2011.

Helman, Christopher. "Obama's 'Power Africa' Plan Greases Billions in Deals for General Electric." *Forbes*, July 1, 2013. http://www.forbes.com/sites/christopherhelman/2013/07/01/with-power-africa-plan- obama-to-grease-billions-in-deals-for-g-e/.

Heritage Foundation. "2013 Index of Economic Freedom: Trade Freedom." http://www.heritage.org/index/trade-freedom (accessed December 20, 2013).

Herz, Bernard; Marco, Wagner. "The Dark Side of the Generalized System of Preferences." *Review of International Economics*, 19, no. 4 (2011), 763–75.

Hidalgo, Cesar. "Discovering Southern and East Africa's Industrial Opportunities." Economic Policy Paper Series 2011. Washington, DC: German Marshall Fund of the United States, 2011. http://www.gmfus.org/galleries/ct_publication_attachments/Hidalgo_AfricaTrade_Jan11_final_web.pdf.

Hoekman, Bernard; Çağlar, Özden. "Trade Preferences and Differential Treatment of Developing Countries: A Selective Survey." World Bank Policy Research Working Paper

3566, April 2005. http://www.wds.worldbank.org/external/default/WDSContentServer/IW3P/IB/2005/04/21/000012009_20050421124442/Rendered/PDF/wps3566.pdf.

Hoekman, Bernard; William, J Martin; Carlos, A Primo Braga. "Quantifying the Value of Preferences and Potential Erosion Losses." World Bank Working Paper, July 2008.

Horticultural Crops Development Authority (Kenya). "Macadamia," February 21, 2014. http://www.hcda.or.ke/tech/fruit_details.php?cat_id=30.

Hulamin. "Hulett Alumium to Expand Capacity for High Value Products." News release.

Imara Africa Securities Team. "General Electric to Expand Its Investments in Africa." *How We Made It in Africa*, July 2, 2013. http://www.howwemadeitinafrica.com/general-electric-to-expand-its-investments-in-africa/27901/.

International Cocoa Organization (ICCO). *Annual Report*.

———. Quarterly Bulletin of Cocoa Statistics.

International Monetary Fund (IMF). *Regional Economic Outlook: Sub-Saharan Africa Building Momentum in a Multi-speed World*. Washington, DC: IMF, May 2013. http://www.imf.org/external/pubs/ft/reo/2013/afr/eng/sreo0513.pdf.

International Monetary Fund (IMF). *Trade Interconnectedness: The World with Global Value Chains*. Washington, DC: IMF, August 26, 2013. http://www.imf.org/external/np/pp/eng/2013/082613.pdf.

International Nut & Dried Fruit. *Global Statistical Review 2007–2012*. http://www.nutfruit.org/glob-stat-review-2011-2012_70816.pdf (accessed February 11, 2014).

International Trade Centre (Intracen). "Africa's Trade Potential: Export Opportunities in Growth Markets." Technical Paper. Geneva: Intracen, 2012.

International Trade Centre. *Africa's Trade Potential: Export Opportunities in Growth Markets*.

IRIN. "Madagascar: Textile Industry Unravels," February 24, 2010. http://www.irinnews.org/report/88224/madagascar-textile-industry-unravels.

Itano, Nicole. "U.S. Pact Lifts South Africa Car Exports." New York Times, July 9, 2003.

Jamasmie, Cecilia. "Vale Slashes Investment Budget for Third Straight Year to $14.8bn." *Mining.com*, December 2, 2013. http://www.mining.com/vale-slashes-investment-budget-for-third-straight-year-to-14-8bn-95369/.

Jean, Sébastien. "Assessing the Impact of the EU-Chile FTA on International Trade." UMR Economie Publique, INRA and AgroParis Tech. CEPII, Paris, April 30, 2012.

Jones, Vivian C; Brock, R Williams. *U.S. Trade and Investment Relations with Sub-Saharan Africa and the African Growth and Opportunity Act*. Congressional Research Service (CRS). CRS Report RL31772, November 2012. http://www.fas.org/sgp/crs/row/RL31772.pdf.

Journal of the European Communities, Partnership Agreement Between the Members of the African, Caribbean and Pacific Group of States of the one part, and the European Community and its Member States, of the other part, December 15, 2000.

Journal of the European Communities. Agreement on Trade, Development and Cooperation between the European Community and its Member States, of the one part, and the Republic of South Africa, of the other part.

Just-style. "European Economic Woes Hit Mauritius Textile Sector," December 1, 2010. http://www.just-style.com/analysis/european-economic-woes-hit-mauritius-textile-sector_id109568.aspx.

———. "Prospects for an African Clothing Industry?" June 25, 2013. http://www.just-style.com/comment/prospects-for-an-african-clothing-industry_id118021.aspx.

Just-Style.com. "European Economic Woes Hit Mauritius Textile Sector," December 1, 2010.

Kaplinsky, Raphael; Mike, Morris. "Chinese FDI in Sub-Saharan Africa: Engaging with Large Dragons." *European Journal of Development Research*, 21, no. 4 (2009), 551–69. http://www.palgrave-journals.com/ejdr/journal/v21/n4/full/ejdr200924a.html.

Karingi, Stephen, Laura, Páez; Derrese, Degefa. *Report on a Survey of AGOA's Past, Present and Future Prospects: The Experiences and Expectations of Sub-Saharan Africa*. Africa Trade Policy Center, Economic Commission for Africa, May 2011.

Karingi, Stephen; Laura, Páez; Derrese, Degefa. "Report on a Survey of AGOA's Past, Present, and Future Prospects: The Experiences and Expectations of Sub-Saharan Africa." Africa Trade Policy Centre Work in Progress No. 89. United Nations Economic Commission for Africa, 2012. http://www.uneca.org/sites/default/files/publications/atpcworkinprogress89.pdf.

Kaufmann, Daniel, Aart Kraay; Massimo, Mastruzzi. "The Worldwide Governance Indicators: Methodology and Analytical Issues." World Bank. Draft Policy Research Working Paper, Washington, DC, September, 2010. http://info.worldbank.org/governance/wgi/pdf/WGI.pdf.

Keck, Alexander; Andreas, Lendle. "New Evidence on Preference Utilization." World Trade Organization, Economic Research and Statistics Division, Staff Working Paper ERSD-2012-12, September 3, 2012.

Keck, Alexander; Andreas, Lendle. "New Evidence on Preference Utilization." World Trade Organization Staff Working Paper ERSD-2012-12, September 3, 2012. http://www.wto.org/english/res_e/reser_e/ersd201212_e.pdf.

Kennedy, Peter. *A Guide to Econometrics*. 5th ed. Cambridge, MA: MIT Press, 2003.

Kose, M Ayhan; Guy, M Meredith; Christopher, M Towe. "How Has NAFTA Affected the Mexican Economy? Review and Evidence." IMF Working Paper. WP/04/59, April 2004.

Kuhlmann, Katrina. The German Marshall Fund of the United States. Economic Policy Paper Series 2010. "A New US-European Approach to Trade and Development in SSA," 2010.

Kunda, James. "Zambia: Govt to Revive Textile Sector." *Times of Zambia*, September 3, 2013. http://allafrica.com/stories/201309040885.html.

Kuo, Chin S. "The Mineral Industry of India: Advance Release." 2011 Minerals Yearbook. Reston, VA: U.S. Geological Survey, January 2013. http://minerals.usgs.gov/minerals/pubs/country/asia.html#as.

Lazzeri, Thomas. "EU Wants to Force ACP Countries to Sign EPAs." Africa Europe Faith and Justice Network, 2014. http://www.aefjn.org/index.php/352/articles/european-commission-wants-to-force-acp-countries-to-sign-epas.html.

Lederman, Daniel; Çağlar, Özden. "U.S. Trade Preferences: All Are Not Created Equal." Central Bank of Chile Working Paper No. 280, December 2004. http://www.bcentral.cl/estudios/documentos-trabajo/pdf/dtbc280.pdf.

Lesotho Textile Exporters Association. "Lesotho Textile Industry." http://www.lesothotextiles.com/Pages/Lesotho-Textile-Industry.asp?lID=2 (accessed January 14, 2014).

Lilongwe: Ministry of Industry and Trade, 2013. http://www.malawihighcommission.co.uk/Malawi_National_Export_Strategy_Main_Do cument.pdf.

Linden, Greg; Jason, Dedrick; Kenneth, L Kraemer. "Innovation and Job Creation in a Global Economy: The Case of Apple's iPod." USITC *Journal of International Commerce and Economics*, 3, no. 1 (May 2011), 223–240. http://pcic.merage.uci.edu/papers/2011/InnovationJobCreationiPod.pdf.

Maastricht: European Centre for Development Policy Management, 2004. http://www.ecdpm.org/Web_ECDPM/Web/Content/Navigation.nsf/index2?readform& http://www.ecdpm.org/Web_ECDPM/Web/Content/Content.nsf/0/961144449C018863 C1256EE6002FAD2A?OpenDocument.

MacDonald, Alex. "Vale: Eyes $7B in Planned Africa Investments." Marketwatch.com, February 6, 2013. http://www.marketwatch.com/story/vale-eyes-7b-in-planned-africa-investments-2013-02-06.

Magyar, Michael J. *Mineral Commodity Summaries: Vanadium*. U.S. Geological Survey (USGS), January 2003. http://minerals.usgs.gov/minerals/pubs/commodity/vanadium/index.html#mcs.

Magyar, Michael J. *Mineral Commodity Summaries: Vanadium*. U.S. Geological Survey (USGS), January 2008.

———. "Vanadium." U.S. Geological Survey (USGS) Minerals Yearbook, 2004.

Makan, Ajay. "Oil Price Held High by Supply Disruptions." *Financial Times*, August 9, 2013. http://www.ft.com/intl/cms/s/0/6e91d54e-00e7-11e3-8918-00144feab7de.html.

Mattoo, Aaditya; Devesh, Roy; Arvind, Subramanian. "The African Growth and Opportunity Act and Its Rules of Origin: Generosity Undermined?" *The World Economy*, 26, no. 6 June 2003, 829–51.

May 4, 2012. http://www.thepacker.com/fruit-vegetable-news/shipping-profiles/South-African-citrus-importers-expect-strong-demand-150191325.html?source=related.

Mbora, Anne; Ramni, Jamnadass, Jens-Peter, Barnekov Lillesø. *Growing High Priority Fruits and Nuts in Kenya: Uses and Management*. Nairobi, Kenya: World Agroforestry Centre, 2008. www.worldagroforestry.org/downloads/publications/PDFs/B15956.PDF.

McKinsey Global Institute. Lions on the Move: The Progress and Potential of African Economies, June 2010.

Metal Bulletin. "Hulett Aluminum to Boost Rolled Product Output by 9%," February 21, 2005. http://www.metalbulletin.com/Article/1823301/Search/Hulett-Aluminium-to-boost-rolled-product-output-by-9.html?PageId=196010&Keywords=Hulett+9%25&-OrderType=1.

———. "Hulett Aluminum to Raise Rolling Capacity by 20%," October 12, 2006. http://www.metalbulletin.com/Article/1805901/Search/Hulett-Aluminium-to-raise-rolling-capacity-by-20.html?PageId=196010&Keywords=Hulett+20%25&OrderType=1.

———. "Hulett Invests for Growth," January 11, 2001. http://www.metalbulletin.com/Article/1446426/Search/Hulett-invests-for-growth.html?PageId=196010&Keywords=Hulett+Invests&OrderType=1.

Mevel, Simon; Stephen, Karingi. "Deepening Regional Integration in Africa: A Computable General Equilibrium Assessment of the Establishment of a Continental Free Trade Area Followed by a Continental Customs Union." Paper presented at 7th African Economic Conference, Kigali, Rwanda, October 30-November 2, 2012. http://www.afdb.org/fileadmin/uploads/afdb/Documents/Knowledge/Deepening%20Regional%20Integration %20in%20Africa%20A%20Computable%20General%20Equilibrium%20Assessment%2

0of%20the%20Establishment%20of%20a%20Continental%20Free%20Trade%20Area%20followed%20by%20a%20Continental%20Customs%20Union.pdf.

Mevel, Simon; Zenia, A Lewis; Mwangi, S Kimenyi; Stephen, Karingi; Anne, Kamau. "The African Growth and Opportunity Act: An Empirical Analysis of the Possibilities Post-2015." Joint publication of the Africa Growth Initiative at the Brookings Foundation and the United Nations Economic Commission for Africa, July 2013. http://www.brookings.edu/~/media/research/files/reports/2013/07/agoa%20beyond/130729%20agoa%202013webfinal.pdf.

Mevel, Simon; Zenia, Lewis; Mwangi, Kimenyi; Stephen, Karingi; Anne, Kamau. *The African Growth and Opportunity Act: An Empirical Analysis of the Possibilities Post-2015*. Washington, DC: Brookings Institute and United Nations Economic Commission for Africa, 2013. http://www.brookings.edu/~/media/research/files/reports/2013/07/agoa%20beyond/130729%20agoa%202013webfinal.pdf.

Mevel, Simon; Zenia, Lewis; Mwangi, S Kimenyi; Stephen, Karingi; Anne, W Kamau. *The African Growth and Opportunity Act: An Empirical Analysis of the Possibilities Post-2015*. Washington, DC: Africa Growth Initiative at Brookings, July 2013. http://www.brookings.edu/research/reports/2013/07/african-growth-and-opportunity- act.

Meyn, Mareike. "The EU-South Africa FTA and Its Effect on EPA Negotiations: An Examination of Some Options, Opportunities and Challenges Facing the BLNS Countries." Conference paper prepared for the European Community Studies Association in Southern Africa, "The Relationship between Africa and the European Union," University of the Western Cape, South Africa, January 22–23, 2004.

Mills, Greg. "Lesotho's Textile Industry Unravels." *Business Times*, September 4, 2011. http://www.thebrenthurstfoundation.org/a_sndmsg/news_view.asp?I=118474andPG=227.

MiningReview.com. "Vale Plans to Invest up to US$20 Billion in Africa," October 28, 2010. http://www.miningreview.com/vale-plans-to-invest-up-to-us-20-billion-in-africa/.

Ministry of Foreign Affairs of the People's Republic of China. "China and Ethiopia." http://www.mfa.gov.cn/eng/wjb/zzjg/fzs/gjlb/2984/t16506.htm (accessed January 8, 2014).

Minor, Peter; Marinos, Tsigas. "Impacts of Better Trade Facilitation in Developing Countries: Analysis with a New GTAP Database for the Value of Time in Trade." Nathan Associates conference paper presented at the 11th Annual GTAP Conference, Helsinki, Finland, May 7, 2008. https://www.gtap.agecon.purdue.edu/resources/downloa/4036.pdf.

Mobbs, Phillip M. "The Mineral Industry of Zambia: Advance Release." 2011 Minerals Yearbook. Reston, VA: U.S. Geological Survey, October 2012. http://minerals.usgs.gov/minerals/ pubs/country/africa.html#cf (retrieved February 4, 2014).

Morris, Mike; Cornelia, Staritz; Justin, Barnes. "Value Chain Dynamics, Local Embeddedness, and Upgrading in the Clothing Sectors in Lesotho and Swaziland." *International Journal of Technological Learning, Innovation and Development*, 4, no. 1–3 (2011), 96–119.

Mukherjee, Arijit; Leonard, FS Wang; Yingyi, Tsai. "Governance and Foreign Direct Investment: Is There a Two-way Relationship?" University of Nottingham, 2011. http://www.nottingham.ac.uk/economics/documents/discussion-papers/11-02.pdf.

Mupeseni, Kennedy. "Clusters Enhance Africa's Competitiveness." *Times of Zambia*, August 28, 2013. http://allafrica.com/stories/201308300212.html.

Naumann, Eckart. "The EU GSP Rules of Origin: An Overview of Recent Reforms." Trade Law Centre for Southern Africa Working Paper No. S11WP12/2011, November 2011. http://www.tralac.org/files/2011/11/D11WP122011-EU-GSP-Rules-of-Origin-Naumann-fin20111102.pdf.

Nelson, Andy. "South Africa Ships Almost 40,000 Tons of Citrus to U.S." *The Packer Online*, December 3, 2013. http://www.thepacker.com/fruit-vegetable-news/South-Africa- ships-almost-40000-tons-of-citrus-to-US-234311381.html?source=related.

Nelson, Andy. "South African Citrus Importers Expect Strong Demand." *The Packer Online*,

Nicita, Alessandro; Valentina, Rollo. "Tariff Preferences as a Determinant for Exports from Sub-Saharan Africa." UNCTAD Policy Issues in International Trade and Commodities Study Series No. 60, 2013. http://unctad.org/en/PublicationsLibrary/itcdtab61_en.pdf.

Nielsen, Lynge; Simplice, G Zouhon-Bi. "ECOWAS: Fiscal Revenue Implications of the Prospective Economic Partnership Agreement with the EU." World Bank Africa Region Working Paper Series number 103, April 2007.

Nilsson, Lars. "Comparative Effects of EU and U.S. Trade Policies on Developing Country Exports." European Commission Director General for Trade Working Paper, December 2005. http://trade.ec.europa.eu/doclib/docs/2006/september/tradoc_129998.pdf.

Nilsson, Lars; Nanna, Matsson. "Truths and Myths about the Openness of EU Trade Policy and the Use of EU Trade Preferences." European Commission Director General for Trade Working Paper, April 2009. http://trade.ec.europa.eu/doclib/docs/2009/july/tradoc_143993.pdf.

Nouve, Kofi. "Estimating the Effects of AGOA on African Exports Using a Dynamic Panel Analysis." World Bank Policy Research Working Paper Series, July 2005. http://papers.ssrn.com/sol3/papers.cfm?abstract_id=1026204.

Nouve, Kofi; John, Staatz. "Has AGOA Increased Agricultural Exports from Sub-Saharan Africa to the United States?" Michigan State University Department of Agricultural Economics Staff Paper 2003–08, September, 2003. http://ageconsearch.umn.edu/bitstream/11573/1/sp03-08.pdf.

Odenthal, Ludger. "FDI in Sub-Saharan Africa." Organisation for Economic Co-operation and Development. Working Paper No. 173, CD/DOC (2001)5, March 2001. http://www.oecd.org/development/pgd/1921651.pdf.

OECD. StatExtracts. http://stats.oecd.org. (accessed various dates).

Ofa, Siope V; Malcolm, Spence; Simon, Mevel; Stephen, Karingi. "Export Diversification and Intra-industry Trade in Africa." United Nations Economic Commission for Africa Draft, June 15, 2012. http://www.afdb.org/fileadmin/uploads/afdb/Documents/Knowledge/Export%20Diversification%20and%20Intra-Industry%20Trade%20in%20Africa.pdf.

Oil and Gas Journal. "EIA: U.S. to Approach Highest Petroleum Production Level since 1970," December 23, 2013. http://www.ogj.com/articles/2013/12/eia-us-to-approach-highest.

———. Worldwide Refining Capacities Report as of January 1, 2014. Special report, "Western Europe Leads Refining Contraction," vol. 111-12, Dec. 2, 2013.

Onguglo, Bonapas Francis. "Developing Countries and Unilateral Trade Preferences in the New International Trading System." Chapter 4 of *Trade Rules in the Making: Challenges in Regional and Multilateral Negotiations*, edited by Miguel Rodriguez Mendoza, Patrick

Low, and Barbara Kotschwar. Washington, DC: The Brookings Institution Press/Organization of American States, 1999.

Organisation for Economic Co-operation and Development (OECD). "A Policy Framework for Investment: Trade Policy." OECD Trade Policy Working Paper No. 19, 2005. http://www.oecd.org/investment/investmentfordevelopment/35488872.pdf.

Organisation for Economic Co-operation and Development (OECD). *Interconnected Economies: Benefiting from Global Value Chains.* OECD Publishing, 2013. http://www.keepeek.com/Digital-Asset-Management/oecd/science-and-technology/interconnected-economies_9789264189560-en#page1.

Organisation for Economic Co-operation and Development (OECD). *OECD Economic Surveys: Chile 2013,* October 4, 2013. http://www.oecd-ilibrary.org/economics/oecd-economic- surveys-chile-2013_eco_surveys-chl-2013-en.

Özden, Çaglar; Eric, Reinhardt. "The Perversity of Preferences: GSP and Developing Country Trade Policies, 1976–2000." *Journal of Development Economics*, 78, no. 1 (October 2005), 1–21.

Páez, Laura; Stephen, Karingi; Mwangi, Kimenyi; Mekalia, Paulos. "A Decade (2000–2010) of African-U.S. Trade under the African Growth and Opportunity Act (AGOA): Challenges, Opportunities and a Framework for Post-AGOA Engagement." African Trade Policy Center Work in Progress No. 81. United Nations Economic Commission for Africa, 2012. http://www.uneca.org/sites/default/files/publications/81.pdf.

Panagariya, Arvind. "EU Preferential Trade Policies and Developing Countries." *World Economy*, 25, no. 10, (November 2002), 1415–32.

Persson, Maria; Fredrik, Wilhelmsson. "Assessing the Effects of EU Trade Preferences for Developing Countries." Lund University Department of Economics, School of Economics and Management Working Paper 2006:4, June 26, 2006. http://project.nek.lu.se/publications/workpap/Papers/WP06_4.pdf.———. "EU Trade Preferences and Export Diversification." Lund University Department of Economics, School of Economics and Management Working Paper 2013:32, September 2013. http://project.nek.lu.se/publications/workpap/papers/WP13_32.pdf.

Pietermaritzburg, South Africa: Hulamin Ltd., October 11, 2006. http://www.hulamin.co.za/news/2006/October/hulett_aluminium_to_expand_capacity_for_high_value_products.htm.

———. "Official Opening of Rolled Products Expansion." News release. Pietermaritzburg, South Africa: Hulamin Ltd., December 11, 2009. http://www.hulamin.co.za/news/2009/December/official_opening_of_rolled_products_expansion.htm.

Pishbahar, Esmaeil; Marilyne, Huchet-Bourdon. "European Union's Preferential Trade Agreements in Agricultural Sector: A Gravity Approach." *Journal of International Agricultural Trade and Development*, 5, no. 1 (2008): 107–27.

Pitot, Roger. "The South African Automotive Industry, the MIDP and the APDP." NAACAM presentation, October 2011. http://www.automechanikasa.co.za/pdf/2013-docs/NAACAM.

Polyak, Désirée E. "Vanadium." *U.S. Geological Survey (USGS) Minerals Yearbook*, 2008, October 2010.

———. U.S. Geological Survey (USGS) Minerals Yearbook, 2012, October 2013.

Polyak, Désirée E. *Mineral Commodity Summaries: Vanadium.* U.S. Geological Survey (USGS), January 2013. http://minerals.usgs.gov/minerals/pubs/commodity/vanadium/.

Rabbobank. *Looking for Delta: How Global Companies Can Help Sub-Saharan Africa Reach Its F&A Potential*, October 2013. http://hugin.info/133178/R/1735308/581428.pdf.

Ramdoo, Isabelle; San, Bilal. "What Would It Take to Make an EPA Economically and Politically Feasible for Europe and Africa?" European Centre for Development Policy Management, Briefing Note No. 57, November 2013.

Reed, Stanley. "OPEC, Foreseeing No Glut, Keeps Oil Production Level Steady." *New York Times*, December 4, 2013. http://www.nytimes.com/2013/12/05/business/energy-environment/opec.

Reese, Jr; Robert, G. *Mineral Commodity Summaries: Vanadium*. U.S. Geological Survey (USGS), January 2002. http://minerals.usgs.gov/minerals/pubs/commodity/vanadium/.

Republic of Botswana. "Botswana Re-enters EU Market," July 5, 2012. www.gov.bw/en/PrintingVersion/?printid=9188.

Republic of South Africa. Department of Agriculture, Forestry, and Fisheries (DAFF). *A Profile of the South African Macadamia Nuts Market Value Chain*, 2012. http://www.daff.gov.za/ docs/amcp/macadamia2012.pdf (accessed February 11, 2014).

———. National Agricultural Marketing Council. *International Trade Probe*, March 2013.

Republic of Turkey, Ministry of Economy. Turkey's Free Trade Agreements. http://www.economy.gov.tr/index.cfm?sayfa=tradeagreements&bolum=fta&region=0(accessed January 9, 2014).

Reynolds, Kara. "The Erosion of Tariff Preferences: The Impact of U.S. Tariff Reductions on Developing Countries." American University, July 18, 2005.

Sapir, André; Lars, Lundberg. "The U.S. Generalized System of Preferences and Its Impacts." In *The Structure and Evolution of Recent U.S. Trade Policy*, edited by Robert E. Baldwin and Anne O. Krueger, eds., 195–236. Chicago: University of Chicago Press, 1984. http://www.nber.org/chapters/c5835.

Sauvant, Karl P; Padma, Mallampally; Geraldine, McAllister; eds. *Inward and Outward FDI Country Profiles*. 2nd ed. New York: Vale Columbia Center on Sustainable International Investment, 2013. http://www.vcc.columbia.edu/files/vale/content/Profiles_eBook_Second_ Edition_-_Oct_2013.pdf.

Seetanah, Boopen. "Inward FDI in Mauritius and Its Policy Context." Vale Columbia Center on Sustainable International Investment. Columbia FDI Profiles, April 30, 2013. http://www.vcc.columbia.edu/files/vale/documents/Mauritius_IFDI_-_April_30_-_FINAL.pdf.

SEMI. "Metallurgical-Grade Silicon Making Inroads in PV," n.d. http://www.semi.org/en/IndustrySegments/Materials/p044005.

Seyoum, Belay. "Export Performance of Developing Countries under the African Growth and Opportunity Act: Experience from US Trade with Sub-Saharan Africa." *Journal of Economic Studies*, 34, no. 6 (2007), 515–33.

Shakhashiri, BZ. "Chemical of the Week: Phosphoric Acid, H3PO4." www.scifun.org, February 6, 2008.

———. "Chemical of the Week: Sulfuric Acid, H2SO4." www.scifun.org, September 17, 2007.

Shi, Lin. "The Mineral Industry of Korea: Advance Release." 2011 Minerals Yearbook. Reston, VA: U.S. Geological Survey, May 2013. http://minerals.usgs.gov/minerals/pubs/country/asia.html#as (retrieved February 4, 2014).

Singh, Bharat P. "Nontraditional Crop Production in Africa for Export." In *Trends in New Crops and New Uses*, edited by J. Janick and A. Whipkey, 86–92. Alexandria, VA: ASHS Press, 2002. http://www.hort.purdue.edu/newcrop/ncnu02/v5-086.html.

Skully, David. "U.S. Tariff Rate Quotas and AGOA Market Access." Washington, DC: International Food and Agricultural Policy Council, 2010. http://www.agritrade.org/Publications/documents/USTRQsandAGOApolicyfocus_full.pdf.

South African Macadamia Nut Growers' Association. "Overview of the South African Macadamia Industry." http://www.samac.org.za/index.php/about-us/overview (accessed January 30, 2014).

Southern Africa Development Community (SADC). *Report of the Executive Secretary: Activity Report of the SADC Secretariat 2011–2012*. Gaborone, Botswana: SADC Secretariat, 2012. http://www.sadc.int/files/1613/7243/4333/SADC_ES_Report_2011-2012_web.pdf.

Spektorov, Yury; Olya, Linde; Bart, Cornelissen; Rostislav Khomenko. *The Global Diamond Report 2013: Journey through the Value Chain*. Bain & Company report, August 27, 2013. http://www.bain.com/publications/articles/global-diamond-report-2013.aspx.

Staritz, Cornelia. *Making the Cut? Low-Income Countries and the Global Clothing Value Chain in a Post-Quota and Post-Crisis World*. A World Bank study. Washington, DC: World Bank, 2011. http://documents.worldbank.org/curated/en/2011/01/13362258/making-cut-low-income-countries-global-clothing-value-chain-post-quota-post-crisis-world.

Suresh, Bala. "Sulfuric Acid." CEH Marketing Research Report 781.5000A, July 2012.

———. Stefan Schlag, and Yoshio Inoguchi. "Inorganic Color Pigments." CEH Marketing Research Report 575.3000A, February 2011.

Sy, Amadou. "Shifts in Financing Sustainable Development: How Should Africa Adapt in 2014?" Brookings Institution. Africa Growth Initiative, n.d. http://www.brookings.edu/~/media/Research/Files/Reports/2014/foresight%20africa%202014/08%20foresight%20sustainable%20development%20africa%20sy.pdf (accessed January 23, 2014).

Tadesse, Bedassa; Bichaka, Fayissa. "The Impact of African Growth and Opportunity Act (AGOA) on U.S. Imports from Sub-Saharan Africa (SSA)." *Journal of International Development*, 20, no. 7 (October 2008), 920–41.

Tagliabue, John. "An Industry Struggles to Keep Its Luster." *New York Times*, November 5, 2012. http://www.nytimes.com/2012/11/06/world/europe/antwerps-diamond-industry-tries-to-keep-its-luster.html?_r=0.

Ten, Senses. "Fair Trade Products," 2011. http://www.tensenses.com/products.php.

The Hague: TCC, March 2009. http://www.teacoffeecocoa.org/tcc/content/download/309/2079/file/Cocoa%20Barom eter%202009.pdf.

———. *Cocoa Barometer 2010*. The Hague: TCC, 2010. http://www.teacoffeecocoa.org/tcc/content/download/416/2948/file/TCC_COCOA_Bar ometer%202010%20(final).pdf.

———. *Cocoa Barometer 2012*. The Hague: TCC, 2012. http://www.cocoabarometer.org/Cocoa_Barometer/Download_files/Cocoa%20Barome ter%202012%20Final.pdf.

The Trade and Development Act of 2000 (Pub. L. 106-200). http://www.gpo.gov/fdsys/pkg/PLAW-106publ200/html/PLAW-106publ200.htm (accessed January 24, 2014).

Timmer, Marcel; Bart, Los; Robert, Stehrer; Gaaitzen, de Vries. "Rethinking Competitiveness: The Global Value Chain Revolution." Vox, June 26, 2013. http://www.voxeu.org/ article/rethinking-competitiveness-global-value-chain- revolution.

Trade & Industrial Policy Strategies (TIPS). "AGOA—Automotive Sector." http://www.tips.org.za/files/u72/agoa_automotive_sector_-_tips_use_this_version.pdf (accessed January 24, 2014).

TradeWatch. "The European Union's New Preferential Rules of Origin under the Generalized System of Preferences," March 28, 2011. http://tmagazine.ey.com/insights/the-european-union%E2%80%99s-new-preferential-rules-of-origin/.

Tralac Trade Law Center. "South Africa's Promotion and Protection of Investment Bill," November 20, 2013. http://www.tralac.org/2013/11/20/south-africas-promotion-and-protection-of-investment-bill/.

Tropical Commodity Coalition for Sustainable Tea Coffee Cocoa (TCC). *Cocoa Barometer 2009.*

Tse, Pui-Kwan. "The Mineral Industry of China: Advance Release." 2012 Minerals Yearbook. Reston, VA: U.S. Geological Survey, December 2013. http://minerals.usgs.gov/minerals/pubs/country/asia.html#as (retrieved February 4, 2014).

Twin. "Developing the Macadamia Sector in Malawi." http://www.twin.org.uk/projects/developing-macadamia-sector-malawi (accessed February 19, 2014).

U.S. Agency for International Development (USAID). East Africa Trade Hub. "AGOA Strategies Chart Course for Increased Exports," December 4, 2013. http://www.competeafrica.org/featured-content/agoa-strats-burundi-ethiopia/index.php.

———. *Mozambique Country Assistance Strategy 2009–2014.* Washington, DC: USAID, 2009. http://www.usaid.gov/sites/default/files/documents/1860/CAS_%202009-14.pdf.

———. *Removing Obstacles to Growth in Mozambique: A Diagnostic Trade Integration Study.*

U.S. Agency for International Development (USAID). *Kenya National AGOA Strategy*, June, 2012.

———. "Ten Senses Africa Ltd." http://www.competeafrica.org/partnership-fund/tsa/index.php (accessed February 21, 2014).

U.S. Department of Agriculture (USDA). Agricultural Marketing Service (AMS). *Fresh Fruit and Vegetable Shipments* 2000, March 2001. http://www.ams.usda.gov/AMSv1.0/getfile?dDocName=STELPRDC5061754.

———. *Fresh Fruit and Vegetable Shipments* 2013, February 2014. http://www.ams.usda.gov/AMSv1.0/getfile?dDocName=stelprdc5106575.

U.S. Department of Agriculture (USDA). Animal and Plant Health Inspection Service (APHIS).

U.S. Department of Agriculture (USDA). Foreign Agricultural Service (FAS). *Kenya: Macadamia Annual Report*, by Mary Onsongo. GAIN Report no. KE9025, October 1, 2009. http://gain.fas.usda.gov/Recent%20GAIN%20Publications/TREE%20NUTS%20ANNUAL_Nairobi_Kenya_10-1-2009.pdf.

———. Production, Supply, and Distribution (PSD) Database. http://apps.fas.usda.gov/psdonline/psdquery.aspx. (accessed March 3, 2014)

———. *Republic of South Africa: Citrus Annual, 2002*, by Patricia Mabiletsa. GAIN Report no. SF2014, May 24, 2002. http://apps.fas.usda.gov/gainfiles/200205/145683583.pdf.

———. *Republic of South Africa: Citrus Annual* by Nicolas Rubio. GAIN Report, December 14, 2012. http://gain.fas.usda.gov/Recent%20GAIN%20Publications/Citrus%20Annual_Pretoria_S outh%20Africa%20-%20Republic%20of_12-11-2012.pdf.

———. *Republic of South Africa: Citrus Annual*, by Nicolas Rubio. December 20, 2013. http://gain.fas.usda.gov/Recent%20GAIN%20Publications/Citrus%20Annual_Pretoria_South%20Africa%20-%20Republic%20of_12-20-2013.pdf.

———. *Republic of South Africa: Tree Nuts Annual*, by Linda Siphugu. GAIN Report, November 20, 2009. http://gain.fas.usda.gov/Recent%20GAIN%20Publications/TREE%20NUTS%20ANNUAL_Pretoria_South%20Africa%20-%20Republic%20of_11-20-2009.pdf.

———. *South Africa: Citrus Annual Report, 1999*, by Patricia Mabiletsa. GAIN Report no. sf9015, May 15, 1999. http://apps.fas.usda.gov/gainfiles/199906/25454675.pdf.

U.S. Department of Agriculture (USDA). National Agricultural Statistics Service (NASS). *Citrus Fruits: 2013 Summary*, September 19, 2013. http://usda01.library.cornell.edu/usda/current/CitrFrui/CitrFrui-09-19-2013.pdf.

U.S. Department of Commerce (USDOC). International Trade Administration (ITA). "African Growth and Opportunity Act." http://trade.gov/agoa/index.asp (accessed on November 20, 2013).

U.S. Department of Commerce (USDOC). International Trade Administration (ITA). Office of Textiles and Apparel (OTEXA). "Trade Preference Programs: U.S. General Imports by Category; 11/2013 Data; Total Textile and Apparel Imports (MFA)," January 2, 2014. http://otexa.ita.doc.gov/agoa-cbtpa/cat0.htm.

U.S. Department of Commerce (USDOC). Office of Textiles and Apparel (OTEXA). "Trade Preference Programs: The African Growth and Opportunity Act (AGOA)." http://web.ita.doc.gov/tacgi/eamain.nsf/d511529a12d016de852573930057380b/1e85488eb01fd2fd852573940049047d?OpenDocument (accessed November 26, 2013).

U.S. Department of Commerce. Bureau of Economic Analysis (BEA). Balance of Payments and Direct Investment Position Data, interactive database. http://www.bea.gov/iTable/iTable.cfm?ReqID=2andstep=1#reqid=2andstep=1andisuri=1 (accessed various dates).

———. "U.S. Direct Investment Abroad Tables." *Survey of Current Business*, September 2013, 207–249, tables 1–16. http://bea.gov/scb/pdf/2013/09%20September/ 0913_outward_direct_investment_tables.pdf.

U.S. Department of Energy (USDOE). Energy Information Administration (EIA). *Country Analysis: Angola*, February 5, 2014. http://www.eia.gov/countries/cab.cfm?fips=AO.

———. *Country Analysis: Nigeria*, December 30, 2014. http://www.eia.gov/countries/cab.cfm?fips=NI.

U.S. Department of Homeland Security (DHS). U.S. Customs and Border Protection (CBP). "AGOA Changes with Respect to Mauritania, Guinea, Madagascar and Niger Effective December 23, 2009, and January 1, 2010," January 4, 2010. http://www.cbp.gov/xp/cgov/trade/trade_programs/international_agreements/special_trade_programs/agoa_african_growth/agoa_chngs_2010.xml (accessed February 13, 2014).

U.S. Department of Homeland Security (USDHS). Customs and Border Protection (CBP). The African Growth and Opportunity Act. "What Every Member of the Trade Community Should Know About. . ." series. Informed Compliance publications, August 2003. http://otexa.ita.doc.gov/agoa-cbtpa/icp065.pdf.

U.S. Department of State (State Department) and U.S. Department of Commerce (USDOC), International Trade Administration (ITA), U.S. and Foreign Commercial Service (USFCS). *Doing Business in Namibia: 2013 Country Commercial Guide for U.S. Companies*. Washington, DC: U.S. State Department and USDOC, ITA, USFCS, 2013.

http://www.buyusainfo.net/z_body.cfm?dbf=ccg1%2Cbmr11%2Cmrsearch1&search_type2=int&avar=19999&country=Namibia&logic=and&loadnav=no (retreived February 4, 2014).

———. *Doing Business in South Africa: 2013 Country Commercial Guide for U.S. Companies*. Washington, DC: U.S. State Department and USDOC, ITA,USFCS, 2013. http://www.buyusainfo.net/z_body.cfm?dbf=ccg1%2Cbmr11%2Cmrsearch1&search_type2=int&avar=19999&country=South%20Africa&logic=and&loadnav=no.

———. *Doing Business in Zambia: 2013 Country Commercial Guide for U.S. Companies*.

U.S. Department of the Interior (USDOI). U.S. Geological Survey (USGS). *Mineral Commodity Summaries*, Washington, DC.

U.S. International Trade Commission (USITC). *Business Jet Aircraft Industry: Structure and Factors Affecting Competitiveness*. USITC Publication 4314. Washington, DC: USITC, 2012. http://www.usitc.gov/publications/332/pub4314.pdf.

———. *Export Opportunities and Barriers in African Growth and Opportunity Act-Eligible Countries*. USITC Publication 3785. Washington, DC: USITC, 2005. http://www.usitc.gov/publications/docs/pubs/332/pub3785.pdf.

———. Hearing transcript in connection with inv. no. 332-542, *AGOA: Trade and Investment Performance Overview*, January 14, 2014.

———. *Sub-Saharan Africa: Effects of Infrastructure Conditions on Export Competitiveness, Third Annual Report*. USITC Publication 4071. Washington, DC: USITC, 2009. http://www.usitc.gov/publications/332/pub4071.pdf.

———. *Sub-Saharan Africa: Effects of Infrastructure Conditions on Export Competitiveness— Third Annual Report*. USITC Publication 4071. Washington, DC: USITC, 2009. http://www.usitc.gov/publications/332/pub4071.pdf.

———. *Sub-Saharan African Textile and Apparel Inputs: Potential for Competitive Production*.

U.S. International Trade Commission (USITC). Commercial Availability of Fabric and Yarns in AGOA Countries: Certain Denim. USITC Publication 3950. Washington, DC: USITC, 2007.

U.S. International Trade Commission (USITC). *Electrolytic Manganese Dioxide from Australia and China*. USITC Publication 4036. Washington, DC: USITC, 2008.

———. Hearing transcript in connection with inv. no. 332-542, *AGOA: Trade and Investment Performance Overview*, January 14, 2014.

———. Interactive Tariff and Trade DataWeb (DataWeb)/U.S. Department of Commerce (USDOC). http://dataweb.usitc.gov (accessed various dates).

———. *Shifts in U.S. Merchandise Trade 2006*. USITC Publication 3940. Washington, DC: USITC, 2007.

———. *Silicon Metal from China*. USITC Publication 4312. Washington, DC: USITC, 2012.

———. Sub-Saharan Africa: Factors Affecting Trade Patterns of Selected Industries. USITC Publication 3989. Washington, DC: USITC, 2007.

U.S. International Trade Commission (USITC). *Export Opportunities and Barriers in African Growth and Opportunity Act-Eligible Countries*. USITC Publication 3785. Washington, DC: USITC, 2005. http://www.usitc.gov/publications/docs/pubs/332/pub3785.pdf.

———. Hearing transcript in connection with inv. no. 332-542, *AGOA: Trade and Investment Performance Overview*, January 15, 2014.

———.Interactive Tariff and Trade DataWeb (DataWeb)/U.S. Department of Commerce (USDOC). http://dataweb.usitc.gov (accessed various dates).

———. *Sub-Saharan Africa: Effects of Infrastructure Conditions on Export Competitiveness, Third Annual Report*. USITC Publication 4071. Washington, DC: USITC, 2009. http://www.usitc.gov/publications/332/pub4071.pdf.

———. *Sub-Saharan Africa: Factors Affecting Trade Patterns of Selected Industries, First Annual Report*. USITC Publication 3914. Washington, DC: USITC, April 2007. http://www.usitc.gov/publications/docs/pubs/332/pub3914.pdf.

———. *Sub-Saharan Africa: Factors Affecting Trade Patterns of Selected Industries, Second Annual Report*. USITC Publication 3989. Washington, DC: USITC, 2008. http://www.usitc.gov/publications/332/pub3989.pdf.

U.S. International Trade Commission (USITC). Hearing transcript in connection with inv. no. 332-542, *AGOA: Trade and Investment Performance Overview*, January 14, 2014.

U.S. Trade Representative (USTR). "Andean Trade Preference Act." http://www.ustr.gov/trade-topics/trade-development/preference-programs/andean-trade-preference-act-atpa (accessed February 13, 2014).

———."Caribbean Basin Initiative." http://www.ustr.gov/trade-topics/trade- development/preference-programs/caribbean-basin-initiative-cbi (accessed February 13, 2014).

———. *U.S.-Chile FTA: Final Text*, http://www.ustr.gov/trade-agreements/free-trade-agreements/chile-fta/final-text (accessed January 3, 2014).

———. U.S. Generalized System of Preferences Guidebook, July 2013.

———. "U.S. Trade Representative Michael Froman Comments on President's Decision to Suspend GSP Benefits for Bangladesh," USTR Press Release, June 2013. http://www.ustr.gov/about-us/press-office/press-releases/2013/june/michael-froman- gsp-bangladesh.

United Nations (UN). World Economic Situation and Prospects 2014. United Nations, New York, 2014. http://www.un.org./en/development/desa/policy/wesp/wesp_current/wesp2014.pdf.

United Nations Conference on Trade and Development (UNCTAD). "UNCTAD Asked to Identify Potential Supply Chains in Sub-Saharan Africa." News release, September 27, 2012. http://unctad.org/en/pages/newsdetails.aspx?OriginalVersionID=303.

United Nations Conference on Trade and Development (UNCTAD). UNCTADStat interactive database. http://unctadstat.unctad.org/ReportFolders/reportFolders.aspx?sCS_referer=&sCS_Cho senLang=en (accessed various dates).

United Nations Conference on Trade and Development (UNCTAD). *World Investment Report 2012*. Geneva: UNCTAD, 2012. http://unctad.org/en/Pages/DIAE/World%20Investment%20Report/WIR2012_WebFlyer.aspx.

———. *World Investment Report 2013*. Geneva: UNCTAD, 2013. http://unctad.org/en/pages/PublicationWebflyer.aspx?publicationid=588.

———. *Good Governance in Investment Promotion*. Geneva: UNCTAD, 2004. http://unctad.org/ en/docs/c2em15d2_en.pdf (accessed on December 17, 2013).

———. UNCTADStat interactive database. http://unctadstat.unctad.org/ReportFolders/reportFolders.aspx?sCS_referer=&sCS_Cho senLang=en (accessed various dates).

United Nations Economic Commission for Africa (UNECA). "AUC-ECA Launch Programme on Promotion and Development of Strategic Agricultural Value Chains in ECOWAS." News release, December 3, 2013. http://www.uneca.org/media-centre/

stories/auc-eca-launch-programme-promotion-and-development-strategic-agricultural-value.

———. *Making the Most of Africa's Commodities: Industrializing for Growth, Jobs, and Economic Transformation.* Addis Ababa, Ethiopia: UNECA, March 2013. http://www.uneca.org/publications/economic-report-africa-2013.

———. *Minerals and Africa's Development: The International Study Group Report on Africa's Mineral Regime.* Addis Ababa, Ethiopia: UNECA, 2011. http://www.uneca.org/sites/default/files/publications/mineral_africa_development_re port_eng.pdf.

United Nations Economic Commission for Africa (UNECA). *Assessing Regional Integration in Africa V: Towards an African Continental Free Trade Area.* Addis Ababa, Ethiopia: UNECA, 2012. http://www.uneca.org/sites/default/files/publications/aria5_print_uneca_fin_20_july_1.pdf.

———. *Making the Most of Africa's Commodities: Industrializing for Growth, Jobs and Economic Transformation.* Addis Ababa, Ethiopia: UNECA, 2013. http://www.uneca.org/sites/default/files/publications/era2013_eng_fin_low.pdf.

United Nations Industrial Development Organization (UNIDO). "Foreign Direct Investment in Sub-Saharan Africa: Determinants and Location Decisions." Working paper 08/2008, Vienna, 2008. http://www.unido.org/fileadmin/user_media/Publications/Research_and_statistics/Branch_publications/Research_and_Policy/Files/Working_Papers/2008/WP082 008%20For eign%20Direct%20Investment%20in%20Sub-Saharan%20Africa%20-%20Determinants%20and%20Location%20Decisions.pdf.

United Nations Industrial Development Organization (UNIDO). *Agribusiness for Africa's Prosperity.* Vienna, Austria: UNIDO, 2011. http://www.unido.org/ fileadmin/user_media/Services/Agro- Industries/Agribusiness_for_Africas_Prosperity_e-book_NEW.pdf.

United States Trade Representative (USTR). "African Growth and Opportunity Act (AGOA)." http://www.ustr.gov/trade-topics/trade-development/preference-programs/african- growth-and-opportunity-act-agoa (accessed on November 20, 2013).

———. "The African Growth and Opportunity Act Implementation Guide," October 2000. http://www.ustr.gov/archive/assets/Trade_Development/Preference_Programs/AGOA/AGOA_Implementation_Guide/asset_upload_file505_6510.pdf.

———. 2008 Comprehensive Report on U.S. Trade and Investment Policy toward sub-Saharan Africa and Implementation of the African Growth and Opportunity Act, May 2008. http://www.ustr.gov/sites/default/files/asset_upload_file203_14905.pdf.

———. "Generalized System of Preferences (GSP)." http://www.ustr.gov/trade-topics/trade-development/preference-programs/generalized-system-preference-gsp (accessed on November 20, 2013).

USITC Publication 4078. Washington, DC: USITC, 2009. http://www.usitc.gov/publications/332/pub4078.pdf.

———. *Textiles and Apparel: Assessment of the Competitiveness of Certain Foreign Suppliers to the U.S. Market.* USITC Publication 3671. Washington, DC: USITC, 2004. http://www.usitc.gov/publications/docs/pubs/332/pub3671/pub3671.pdf.

Van Engelen, Anton; Patrick, Malope; John, Keyser; David, Neven. *Botswana Agrifood Value Chain Project: Beef Value Chain Study.* Rome: Food and Agriculture Organization of the United Nations and the Ministry of Agriculture, Botswana, 2013.

Van Heerden, Oscar. "South Africa's Experience of the Trade, Development and Cooperation Agreement (TDCA) with the European Union from 1995 to 2005." Centre of International Studies, Cambridge University, June 2008.

Villarreal, M Angeles; Ian, F Fergusson. "NAFTA at 20: Overview and Trade Effects." Congressional Research Service, R42965, February 21, 2013.

Wang, Fangqing. "China's Textile and Clothing Firms Expand in Africa." *Just-Style.com*, December 18, 2012.

Washington Trade Daily. "US-Morocco Trade Facilitation," November 22, 2013.

Washington, DC: U.S. State Department and USDOC, ITA, USFCS, 2013. http://www.buyusainfo.net/z_body.cfm?dbf=ccg1%2Cbmr11%2Cmrsearch1&search_type2=int&avar=19999&country=Zambia&logic=and&loadnav=no.

Washington, DC: USAID, 2004. http://www.enhancedif.org/en/system/files/uploads/mozambique_vol_1_english.pdf.

———. West Africa Trade Hub. *Exports, Employment and Incomes in West Africa*. West Africa Trade Hub Technical Report #39, 2011. http://www.watradehub.com/sites/default/files/Multiplier%20Effects%20Study%20with%20annexes%2015.02.11.pdf.

Washington, DC: World Bank, 2004. http://siteresources.worldbank.org/INTWDR2005/Resources/complete_report.pdf.

———. Worldwide Governance Indicators database. http://info.worldbank.org/governance/wgi/index.aspx#home (accessed on December 17, 2013).

Webber, C Martin; Labaste, *Patrick. Building Competitiveness in Africa's Agriculture: A Guide to Value Chain Concepts and Applications*. Washington, DC: World Bank, December 2009. http://elibrary.worldbank.org/doi/book/10.1596/978-0-8213-7952-3.

Webber, Martin C; Patrick, Labaste. Building Competitiveness in Africa's Agriculture: A Guide to Value Chain Concepts and Applications. Washington, DC: World Bank, 2010.

Westbrook Resources, Ltd. "(Si) Atomic Number 14," n.d., http://www.wbrl.co.uk/silicon-metal.html.

Western Cape Citrus Producers Forum. "Summer Citrus from South Africa," 2013. http://summercitrus.com/profile/summer-citrus-from-south-africa.php.

Whalley, John. "Why Do Countries Seek Regional Trade Agreements?" Chapter 3 in *The Regionalization of the World Economy*, edited by J. Frankel. Chicago: University of Chicago Press.

Wilkinson, Fred. "King Citrus Mascot Promotes South African Fruit." *The Packer Online*. July 8, 2013. http://www.thepacker.com/fruit-vegetable-news/King-Citrus-mascot-promotes-South-African-citrus-214674331.html?source=related.

World Bank. Agriculture Value Added per Worker (constant 2005 US$) database. http://data.worldbank.org/indicator/EA.PRD.AGRI.KD (accessed December 11, 2013).

———. Logistics Performance Index: LPI Results 2012; Global Rankings 2012. http://lpisurvey.worldbank.org/international/global/2012 (accessed December 12, 2013).

———. "Trading across Borders." Doing Business Index, June 2013. http://www.doingbusiness.org/data/exploretopics/trading-across-borders.

World Bank. *The Business Environment in Southern Africa: Issues in Trade and Market Integration*. Vol. 1, *Summary*. Washington, DC: World Bank, December 31, 2010. http://www.wds.worldbank.org/external/default/WDSContentServer/WDSP/IB/2011/03/30/000356161_20110330001256/Rendered/PDF/587170v10ESW0g10312811110BOX358324B.pdf.

———. *Snapshot Africa: Benchmarking FDI Competitiveness in Sub-Saharan African Countries*. Washington, DC: World Bank, 2006. http://documents.worldbank.org/curated/en/2006/11/7440209/snapshot-africa- benchmarking-fdi-competitiveness-sub-saharan-african-countries.

———. *Snapshot Africa—Kenya: Benchmarking FDI Competitiveness*. Washington, DC: World Bank, 2007. www.fao.org/docs/up/easypol/506/snapshot_africa_kenya.pdf.

———. "Doing Business: A Joint Publication and Project by the World Bank and IFC; The Impact of the Regulatory Environment on Local Businesses around the World," 2013. http://www.doingbusiness.org/~/media/GIAWB/Doing%20Business/Documents/Miscellaneous/What-is-Doing-Business.pdf.

———. "Doing Business Economy Rankings." http://doingbusiness.org/rankings (accessed January 28, 2014).

———. "Doing Business Data." http://www.doingbusiness.org/data (accessed December 23, 2013).

———. World Development Indicators database. http://data.worldbank.org/data- catalog/world-development-indicators (accessed various dates).

———. *World Development Report 2005: A Better Investment Climate for Everyone.*

World Bureau of Metal Statistics (WBMS). "Aluminum, U.S.A.; 2. Semi Manufactures." *World Metal Statistics*. Herts, United Kingdom: WBMS.

———. "Metal Prices, London Metal Exchanges, Annual and Monthly Prices." *World Metal Statistics*. Herts, United Kingdom: WBMS, December 2003–December 2012.

World Cocoa Foundation. "Cocoa Value Chain: From Farmer to Consumer." http://worldcocoafoundation.org/about-cocoa/cocoa-value-chain/GO (accessed January 8, 2014).

World Economic Forum (WEF), World Bank, and the African Development Bank (AfDB). *The Africa Competitiveness Report 2013*. Geneva: WEF, 2013. http://www.weforum.org/reports/africa-competitiveness-report-2013.

———. The Global Competitiveness Report 2008. http://www.weforum.org/pdf/GCR08/Chapter%201.2.pdf.

World Economic Forum (WEF). Global Competitiveness Index: Country Rankings. http://www.weforum.org/issues/global-competitiveness (accessed December 12, 2013).

———. World Bank, and the African Development Bank (AfDB). *The Africa Competitiveness Report 2011*. Geneva: WEF, 2011. http://www.weforum.org/reports/africa- competitiveness-report-2011.

———. World Bank, and the African Development Bank (AfDB). *The Africa Competitiveness Report 2013*. Geneva: WEF, 2013. http://www.weforum.org/ reports/africa- competitiveness-report-2013.

World Steel Association. "Crude Steel Production, 1980–2012." https://www.worldsteel.org/dms/internetDocumentList/statistics-archive/production-archive/steel-archive/steel-annually/steel_yearly_1980-2012/document/Steel%20annual%201980-2012.pdf (accessed January 24, 2014).

World Trade Organization (WTO). "Textiles Monitoring Body (TMB): The Agreement on Textiles and Clothing." http://www.wto.org/english/tratop_e/texti_e/texintro_e.htm (accessed January 24, 2014).

World Trade Organization (WTO). Committee on Regional Trade Agreements. Factual Presentation: Free Trade Agreement between the EFTA States and the SACU States (Goods), Revision, March 24, 2010.

WTO. Trade Policy Review Body, *Chile: Trade Policy Review*, WT/TPR/S/124, December 4, 2003. http://www.wto.org/english/tratop_e/tpr_e/tp224_e.htm.

———. *Norway: Trade Policy Review*. WT/TPR/S/269, August 21, 2012. www.wto.org/english/tratop_e/tpr_e/s269_sum_e.pdf.

Zappile, Tina M. "Nonreciprocal Trade Agreements and Trade: Does the African Growth and Opportunity Act (AGOA) Increase Trade?" *International Studies Perspectives*, 12, no. 1 (February 2011), 46–67.

Zappile, Tina M. "Nonreciprocal Trade Agreements and Trade: Does the African Growth and Opportunity Act (AGOA) Increase Trade?" *International Studies Perspectives*, 12, no. 1 (February 2011), 46–67.

End Notes

[1] Public Law 106-200, May 18, 2000, 114 Stat. 251. Provisions in the Act referred to as the African Growth and Opportunity Act are set out in Title I of the 2000 Act.

[2] 19 U.S.C. § 3702.

[3] Ibid.

[4] These reports are provided in response to a letter from the USTR dated September 30, 2013, requesting that the Commission provide four AGOA reports under section 332(g) of the Tariff Act of 1930. The four reports, and their investigation numbers, are (1) 332-542, *AGOA: Trade and Investment Performance Overview*; (2) 332-544, *AGOA: Economic Effects of Providing Duty-Free Treatment for Imports*; (3) 332-545, *U.S. AGOA Rules of Origin: Possible Changes to Promote Regional Integration and Increase Exports to the United States*; and (4) 332-546, *EU-South Africa FTA: Impact on U.S. Exports to South Africa*. A copy of the letter from the USTR is contained in appendix A. The Commission's *Federal Register* notice announcing the institution of this investigation is contained in appendix B.

[5] Public Law 106-200, May 18, 2000, 114 Stat. 251. Provisions in the Act referred to as the African Growth and Opportunity Act are set out in Title I of the 2000 Act.

[6] 19 U.S.C. § 3702.

[7] Ibid.

[8] These reports are provided in response to a letter dated September 30, 2013 (received October 17, 2013), from the USTR, requesting that the Commission provide four AGOA reports under section 332(g) of the Tariff Act of 1930 (19 U.S.C. § 1332(g)). The four reports, and their investigation numbers, are (1) 332-542, *AGOA: Trade and Investment Performance Overview*; (2) 332-544, *AGOA: Economic Effects of Providing Duty-Free Treatment for Imports*; (3) 332-545, *U.S. AGOA Rules of Origin: Possible Changes to Promote Regional Integration and Increase Exports to the United States*; and (4) 332-546, *EU-South Africa FTA: Impact on U.S. Exports to South Africa*. A copy of the letter from the USTR appears in appendix A. The Commission's *Federal Register* notice announcing the institution of these investigations appears in appendix B.

[9] It should be noted that the terms "sub-Saharan African country" and "beneficiary sub-Saharan African country," and variations of each term, have different statutory meanings. AGOA defines the term "sub-Saharan African country" to mean the 49 countries listed in 19 U.S.C. § 3706, including South Sudan, which was added in 2012. AGOA defines the term "beneficiary sub-Saharan African country" to mean a country listed in 19 U.S.C. § 3706 that the President has determined is eligible for such designation under 19 U.S.C. § 2466a(a). In this report, the terms "AGOA beneficiary country" and "AGOA country" are used to identify an SSA country that has been designated eligible to receive AGOA preferences.

[10] See appendix C for a list of hearing participants.

[11] See appendix D for summaries of the positions of interested parties.

[12] The President's authority to designate an SSA country as a beneficiary SSA country is set forth at 19 U.S.C. § 2466a(a), 19 U.S.C. § 3703.

[13] 19 U.S.C. § 3704.

[14] Section 111(a) of the Trade and Development Act of 2000 (114 Stat. 257) added section 506A to title V of the Trade Act of 1974, codified at 19 U.S.C. § 2466a.

[15] The current AGOA provisions providing preferential treatment for certain textiles and apparel are codified at 19 U.S.C. § 3721.
[16] The AGOA Acceleration Act of 2004 (Pub. L. 108-274).
[17] As amended in 2004, AGOA defined the term "lesser-developed beneficiary sub-Saharan African country" to mean "a beneficiary sub-Saharan African country that had a per capita gross national product of less than $1,500 in 1998, as measured by the International Bank for Reconstruction and Development." Botswana and Namibia do not qualify under this definition. See 19 U.S.C. § 3721, historical and statutory notes. For a list of LDBCs under AGOA, see table 1.1.
[18] Before AGOA III, U.S. imports of apparel articles made with third-country fabric or yarns were subject to a cap, which was higher than what was specified in AGOA III. However, these caps have never been reached.
[19] AGOA IV amended section 112(c) of AGOA, providing for Commission investigations and determinations concerning whether fabric or yarn produced in beneficiary SSA countries was available in commercial quantities or "abundant supply" for use by lesser developed beneficiary sub-Saharan African countries in the production of apparel. The amendment specifically noted that certain denim fabric was available in the region. For more information about the abundant supply provision, including the Commission's investigations and determinations, see USITC, *Commercial Availability of Fabric and Yarns in AGOA Countries*, 2007.
[20] The Africa Investment Incentive Act of 2006 (Pub. L. 109-432).
[21] Miscellaneous Trade and Technical Corrections Act of 2004 (Pub. L. 108-429) amended AGOA and designated Mauritius as a lesser-developed beneficiary sub-Saharan country; however, AGOA IV did not continue to rant Mauritius this status.
[22] The Andean Trade Preference Extension Act, section 3 (Pub. L. 110-436).
[23] 19 U.S.C. § 2466a(a).
[24] For a list of the requirements, see 19 U.S.C. § 3703(a).
[25] 19 U.S.C. § 3703(a).
[26] 19 U.S.C. § 3703(b).
[27] 19 U.S.C. § 3706.
[28] Presidential Proclamation 7350, October 2, 2000.
[29] 19 U.S.C. § 2466a(a)(2).
[30] USITC, "Harmonized Tariff Schedule of the United States (2013)" (accessed March 11, 2013).
[31] 19 U.S.C. § 3722(a)(1)(A). A visa system is a government-industry process that demonstrates that the goods for which benefits are claimed were in fact produced in an eligible SSA country or countries according to the rules of origin that must be met to claim those benefits. USTR, "African Growth and Opportunity Act Implementation Guide," October 2000, 8.
[32] 19 U.S.C. § 3722(a)(1). The designated countries are listed in subchapter XIX of chapter 98 of the Harmonized Tariff Schedule of the United States (HTS), in which the treatment of textiles and apparel is set forth. See also USDOC, OTEXA, "Trade Preference Programs: AGOA" (accessed on November 27, 2013).
[33] 19 U.S.C. § 3721(c)(3)(A). In 2013, there were 39 AGOA eligible countries. The three AGOA beneficiary countries without LDBC status were Gabon, Seychelles, and South Africa.
[34] 19 U.S.C. § 3721(c)(3). See table 1.1.
[35] See section 2 for more information about trade under these programs. Also, see USTR, *2008 Comprehensive Report*, May 2008, 22.
[36] USTR, "Generalized System of Preferences (GSP)" (accessed on November 20, 2013).
[37] Designated beneficiary countries (whether or not least developing (LDBCD)) for GSP are listed in HTS general note 4; for AGOA as a whole, in HTS general note 16; and for the textiles, apparel, and luggage benefits, in U.S. note 1 and 2(d) of subchapter XIX of HTS chapter 98 (the latter note lists LDBDC beneficiaries). AGOA benefits provided in the HTS by means of GSP duty-free entry continue in effect for AGOA beneficiary countries during lapses in the GSP program.
[38] 19 U.S.C. § 2466a(b)(1).
[39] 19 U.S.C. § 2463(b). See also USDHS, CBP, *The African Growth and Opportunity Act*, August 2003, 3.
[40] USITC DataWeb/USDOC (accessed on December 31, 2013).
[41] This figure does not include imports under the tariff lines representing the special AGOA apparel and textile provisions.
[42] In 2013, GSP LDBDCs included 30 sub-Saharan African countries; 25 of them were AGOA beneficiary countries.
[43] USITC DataWeb/USDOC (accessed on November 20, 2013).
[44] USTR, *2008 Comprehensive Report*, May 2008, 22.
[45] 19 U.S.C. § 2463(c)(2)(D).
[46] 19 U.S.C. § 2466a(b)(2).
[47] 19 U.S.C. § 2463(a)(2).
[48] USTR, "The African Growth and Opportunity Act Implementation Guide," October 2000, 13.

[49] Before the Multi-Fiber Arrangement expired on January 1, 2005, the United States imposed quotas on the amount of textiles and garments that could be imported from developing countries. The textile and apparel articles imported under AGOA were exempted from such quota restrictions, although some are subject to a cap.

[50] 19 U.S.C. § 3721(g).

[51] 19 U.S.C. § 3721(b).

[52] 19 U.S.C. § 3721(c)(1). As noted above, U.S. imports of apparel made with third-country fabric are subject to a cap. However, in practice, the cap has never been reached, nor have trade levels come near to reaching the limits under the provision.

[53] 19 U.S.C. § 3721(c)(1)(B).

[54] Applied to textile and textile articles classifiable under chapters 50 through 60, or chapter 63 of the HTS. 19 U.S.C. § 3721(b)(8).

[55] USTR, "The African Growth and Opportunity Act Implementation Guide," October 2000.

[56] 19 U.S.C. § 3721(b)(3)(B).

[57] Although AGOA was signed into law in May 2000, the first U.S. imports to enter under AGOA were recorded in 2001.

[58] Table 1.1 provides a comprehensive list of AGOA-eligible countries by year.

[59] "U.S. imports from AGOA countries" refers to U.S. imports from AGOA-eligible countries in a given year, regardless of whether beneficiaries claimed preference for any products in that year.

[60] Including GSP for least-developed beneficiary developing countries, or LDBDCs. GSP LDBDCs are different from AGOA lesser-developed beneficiary sub-Saharan African countries (also abbreviated as LDBCs). See section 1 for more information.

[61] Authorization for the GSP program lapsed on December 31, 2010, causing duties to be applied starting on January 1, 2011 until its reauthorization on November 5, 2011. However, duties were subsequently refunded

[62] The United States imported $39.2 billion from AGOA countries under those tariff lines that were eligible for AGOA or GSP preferences in 2012. However, not all of these imports entered under AGOA or GSP. About 88.9 percent of these eligible imports, or $34.9 billion, entered the United States under AGOA and GSP (see table 2.1). About 0.1 percent, or $0.04 billion, entered the United States either NTR duty-free or under other duty-free programs. The remaining 11.0 percent, or $4.3 billion, entered the United States dutiable under NTR, and about $10.8 million of import duties were collected on these imports. USITC DataWeb /USDOC.

[63] "U.S. imports under AGOA" refers to U.S. imports from AGOA beneficiary countries for which AGOA preference is claimed.

[64] Out of a potential 6,757 HTS 8-digit tariff lines that are eligible for duty-free treatment under AGOA and GSP, AGOA countries exported to the United States under just 1,655 tariff lines in 2012. USITC DataWeb/USDOC.

[65] Crude petroleum is classified under HS2709 and subject to 5.25–10.5 cent duties per barrel (or 0.1 percent ad valorem equivalent) under NTR. U.S. imports of crude petroleum under AGOA are eligible for duty-free treatment. The leading AGOA country exporters of crude petroleum to the United States in 2013 were Nigeria ($9.9 billion), Angola ($5.9 billion), Chad ($2.4 billion), Gabon ($0.9 billion), and Congo, Rep. ($0.9 billion).

[66] Several factors contributed to the volatility of crude petroleum prices during this period. These include OPEC production and price limits; supply disruptions in Nigeria due to continued civil unrest; strikes in Angola and Nigeria by crude petroleum field workers over working conditions and pay; geopolitical tensions associated with events in Iran; increased demand in countries such as India and China; and the embargo on Syrian crude petroleum. Makan, "Oil Price Held High by Supply Disruptions," August 9, 2013; Reed, "OPEC, Foreseeing No Glut, Keeps Oil Production," December 4, 2013; U.S. Department of Energy, Energy Information Administration, "Short- term Energy Outlook," December 10, 2013.

[67] U.S. Department of Energy, Energy Information Administration, "What Drives Crude Prices?" January 8, 2014.

[68] U.S. Department of Energy, Energy Information Administration, "Petroleum Supply Monthly," January 30, 2014; Oil and Gas Journal, "EIA: U.S. to Approach Highest Petroleum Production Level," December 23, 2013.

[69] Naphthas are petroleum fractions similar to gasolines and kerosenes used in solvents and paint thinners or as a raw material in the production of organic chemicals.

[70] Textiles make up a small share of U.S. imports under AGOA.

[71] A U.S. tariff-rate quota of 12,000 metric tons is applied to tobacco imports from Malawi. The quota fill rate was about 70 percent on average during 2008–12. No other AGOA-eligible country is allocated a quota. U.S. Customs and Border Protection, "Historical Tariff-Rate Quota/Tariff Preference Level Fill Rates," (accessed February 25, 2014).

[72] For this discussion, utilization rates were calculated as the ratio of U.S. imports that claimed AGOA preferences to total U.S. imports from an AGOA country, regardless of whether those products were eligible for AGOA preferences. Another way of assessing AGOA utilization is to calculate the ratio of AGOA country exports that claim AGOA preferences to that AGOA country's exports of products eligible for the AGOA program. For an assessment of AGOA utilization calculated this way, see section 7.

[73] This growth represents the absolute difference between the value of imports in 2000 and 2013 and does not reflect nonlinear variations during the period.

[74] The order of profiles presented below is based on the amount of absolute growth in the value of U.S. imports from AGOA beneficiary countries between 2000 and 2013, beginning with the highest-growth group.
[75] USITC, *Import Restraints*, 2011, 3-2. For the purposes of this report, "regional supply chains" generally refers to regional production networks that are primarily located within SSA countries. Also, this section examines only traded goods.
[76] For the purposes of this report, the terms "supply chains" and "value chains" are used interchangeably, as they commonly are in the relevant literature. However, some authors have distinguished different concepts for each term. See, for example, FGI, NTU, and WTO, *Global Value Chains in a Changing World*, 2013; USITC, *Import Restraints*, 2011; Webber and Labaste, *Competitiveness in Africa's Agriculture*, 2009, 9.
[77] Davies, keynote address, 2012
[78] In addition, these chains use services such as financial and logistic services. USITC, *Import Restraints*, 2011, 3-2.
[79] USITC, *Import Restraints*, 2011, 3-2.
[80] See, for example, USITC, *Import Restraints*, 2011, 3-2 to 3-3; Linden, Dedrick, and Kraemer, "Innovation and Job Creation in a Global Economy," 2011; Timmer et al., "Rethinking Competitiveness," June 26, 2013; IMF, *Trade Interconnectedness*, August 26, 2013, 3; OECD, *Interconnected Economies*, 2013, 17. The example in the text references the GSC of the fifth-generation iPod.
[81] USITC, *Import Restraints*, 2011, 3-2.
[82] *Economist*, "Ready to Take off Again?" January 4, 2014, 23; USITC, *Business Jets*, 2012, 3-1–3-9.
[83] The U.S. firm LearJet was purchased by the Canadian firm Bombardier in 1990.
[84] Based on an automobiles example from USITC, *Import Restraints*, 2011, 3-37 to 3-39.
[85] For an example, see USITC, *Import Restraints*, 2011, 3-4 to 3-6; UNECA, *Making the Most of Africa's Commodities*, 2013, 82–83; Baldwin, "Global Supply Chains," 2013, 13–17.
[86] These firms supply multiple logistical services, which could include warehousing, distribution, tracking, and customs brokerage.
[87] It is common in the literature on value chains to talk about "lead firms." Lead firms are the controlling force in the GVC; they choose the location and number of suppliers, and oversee the chain to ensure suppliers meet appropriate standards and other requirements. UNECA, *Making the Most of Africa's Commodities*, 2013, 82–83.
[88] USITC, *Import Restraints*, 2011, 3-4 to 3-6; UNECA, *Making the Most of Africa's Commodities*, 2013, 82–83; Baldwin, "Global Supply Chains," 2013, 13–17; OECD, *Interconnected Economies*, 2013, 19–20.
[89] Baldwin, "Global Supply Chains," 2013, 16.
[90] UNCTAD, *Global Value Chains and Development*, 2013, 6.
[91] UNECA, *Making the Most of Africa's Commodities*, 2013, 80. The amount of foreign value-added content serves as an indicator of the extent of GSCs' linkages by industry. This content tends to be highest in basic industries (i.e., industries that make heavy use of primary goods such as metals, petroleum, rubber, and chemicals) and higher-tech industries, which often use component parts from many other countries in their assembly (such as communication equipment, televisions, radios, instruments, motor vehicles, and electrical machinery). OECD, *Interconnected Economies*, 2013, 25–27.
[92] Bamber et al., "Connecting Local Producers," 2013, 16. In GSCs in the extractive industries, the lead firms have the extraction rights. These lead firms have increasingly outsourced a number of production functions—including engineering, project management, and even exploration—to their suppliers.
[93] See for example, USITC, *Import Restraints*, 2011; Bamber et al., "Connecting Local Producers," 2013; UNECA, *Making the Most of Africa's Commodities*, 2013.
[94] Bamber et al., "Connecting Local Producers," 2013, 10–11.
[95] Bamber et al., "Connecting Local Producers," 2013, 11.
[96] For further information, see Bamber et al., "Connecting Local Producers," 2013, 29.
[97] UNCTAD, *Global Value Chains and Development*, 2013, 10; WEF, World Bank, and AfDB, *The Africa Competitiveness Report*, 2011, 18; UNECA, *Making the Most of Africa's Commodities*, 2013, 83. The highest participation in GSCs is found in east and southeast Asia, which is the world's primary region for export-oriented manufacturing and processing. UNCTAD, *Global Value Chains and Development*, 2013, 10–11.
[98] WEF, World Bank, and AfDB, *The Africa Competitiveness Report*, 2011, 18; WEF, Global Competitiveness Index: Country Rankings (accessed December 12, 2013).
[99] UNECA, *Making the Most of Africa's Commodities*, 2013, 83–84.
[100] International Trade Center, "Africa's Trade Potential," 2012, 5–9, 16.
[101] Dinh et al., *Light Manufacturing in Africa*, 2012, 23; UNECA, *Making the Most of Africa's Commodities*, 2013, 74; GTIS, Global Trade Atlas (accessed November 22, 2013); USITC, hearing transcript, January 14, 2014, 118 (testimony of Edward Gresser, Progressive Economy) and 189 (testimony of Steve Lande, Manchester Trade Limited, Inc.).
[102] Webber and Labaste, *Building Competitiveness in Africa's Agriculture*, 2010, 3; UNECA, *Making the Most of Africa's Commodities*, 2013, 74.
[103] Webber and Labaste, *Building Competitiveness in Africa's Agriculture*, 2010, 3; UNECA, *Making the Most of Africa's Commodities*, 2013, 74. According to UNECA, Africa deindustrialized during the 1980s and 1990s,

while Latin America and Asia became more industrialized as they took advantage of globalization. Between 1980 and 2009, SSA's share of GDP attributable to manufacturing value added fell from about 17 percent to 13 percent. This decline in industrialization is due to both historical legacy and policy failures, especially the structural adjustment programs (SAPs) in the mid-1980s, which are generally acknowledged to have failed in many areas, including improving value addition. (SAPs were World Bank and International Monetary Fund mandated policy changes, which included trade liberalization, macroeconomic adjustment and privatization).

[104] Dinh et al., *Light Manufacturing in Africa*, 2012, 5–7: USITC, *Trade Facilitation in the EAC*, July 2012; World Bank, Logistics Performance Index 2012; World Bank, "Trading across Borders," June 2013; UNECA, *Making the Most of Africa's Commodities*, 2013; WEF, World Bank, and AfDB, *The Africa Competitiveness Report*, 2011; WEF, World Bank, and AfDB, *The Africa Competitiveness Report 2013*, 2013, 8.

[105] SSA still has a majority rural-based population and work force; 65 percent of SSA's people live in rural areas, and 75 percent of the workforce works in agriculture. Webber and Labaste, *Building Competitiveness in Africa's Agriculture*, 2010, 2, 4; World Bank, Agriculture Value Added per Worker (accessed December 11, 2013).

[106] The World Bank assesses six factors for its LPI ranking, including efficiency of customs procedures, logistical competence, and infrastructure. Only five SSA countries ranked in the top half of the LPI 2012 ranking: South Africa, Benin, Botswana, Mauritius, and Malawi. World Bank, Logistics Performance Index 2012.

[107] World Bank, "Trading across Borders," June 2013.

[108] Christ and Ferrantino, "Land Transport for Export," October 2011; USITC, *Sub-Saharan Africa: Effects of Infrastructure*, 2009.

[109] WEF, Global Competitiveness Index: Country Rankings (accessed December 12, 2013). Only four SSA countries ranked in the top half of the GCI 2013–14 ranking: Mauritius, South Africa, Rwanda, and Botswana.

[110] For more information on the GCI ranking of SSA countries, see section 5.

[111] UNECA, *Making the Most of Africa's Commodities*, 2013; *Building Competitiveness in Africa's Agriculture*, 2010; Rabbobank, *Looking for Delta*, October 2013.

[112] This was done in detail in a study for the World Bank, which used SSA case studies to illustrate how "tools" can be used to increase SSA performance and productivity within agricultural/agroprocessing GSCs. Webber and Labaste, *Building Competitiveness in Africa's Agriculture*, 2010.

[113] For example, the history of SSA textile and apparel manufacturing highlights the importance of market access for manufacturing, as the region's participation in apparel GSCs has ebbed and flowed with access granted first through the Multi-Fiber Arrangement (MFA) and later through AGOA in conjunction with the third-country fabric provision. USITC, hearing transcript, January 14, 2014, 9, 20 (testimony of Ambassador Somduth Soborun, Republic of Mauritius), 188 (testimony of Steve Lande, Manchester Trade Limited, Inc.), 220 (testimony of Paul Ryberg, African Coalition for Trade).

[114] CIA, "South Africa" (accessed January 15, 2014); CIA, "Mauritius" (accessed January 16, 2014); GTIS, Global Trade Atlas (accessed January 16, 2014): Dinh et al., *Light Manufacturing in Africa*, 1: *The Africa Competitiveness Report*, 2011, 15. Most SSA heavy manufacturing exports also come from South Africa: 75 percent as of 2008. In 2008, 75 percent of SSA's "light" manufacturing exports, which tend to be labor intensive, also came from South Africa, with other significant sources including Botswana, Namibia, Mauritius, and Kenya. *The Africa Competitiveness Report*, 2011, 15, 19.

[115] For more information on foreign direct investment in SSA countries, see section 5.

[116] CIA, "Mauritius" (accessed January 16, 2014).

[117] South Africa and Mauritius both score 4.4 on the GCI, while the Southeast Asian regional average is 4.5. South Africa ranks 52nd out of 144 countries, and Mauritius ranks 54th. *The Africa Competitiveness Report*, 2013, 11.

[118] CIA, "South Africa" (accessed January 15, 2014).

[119] The different colors in figures 3.2–3.5 represent different stages of the GSC.

[120] UNECA, *Making the Most of Africa's Commodities*, 2013, 89; Spektorov et al., *The Global Diamond Report 2013*, August 27, 2013, 4; Grynberg, Motswapong, and Philimon, *Diamond Beneficiation and the WTO*, 2012, 12. The value of the diamond often determines the location where it is beneficiated.

[121] Taglia bue, "An industry Struggles to Keep Its Luster," November 5, 2012.

[122] UNECA, Making the Most of Africa's Commodities, 2013, 101; Grynberg, "Diamond Beneficiation in Botswana," 2013; Spektorov et al., *The Global Diamond Report 2013*, August 27, 2013, 17; Grynberg, Motswapong, and Philimon, *Diamond Beneficiation and the WTO*, 2012.

[123] UNECA, *Making the Most of Africa's Commodities*, 2013, 101; Grynberg, "Diamond Beneficiation in Botswana," 2013.

[124] Grynberg, Motswapong, and Philimon, *Diamond Beneficiation and the WTO*, 2012, 6; Grynberg, "Diamond Beneficiation in Botswana," 2013. De Beers had historically argued that Botswana did not have a comparative advantage in beneficiation, and the authors do find that beneficiating diamonds in Botswana is currently more expensive than doing so in low-cost centers in Asia. However, in the mid-2000s, De Beers dropped its objections for a number of reasons, including its diminished market power as its cartel ended, the fact that it is not directly involved in beneficiating diamonds, and the renegotiation of its leases on important Botswana

mines. Thus far, access to rough Botswana diamonds has offset the additional costs of beneficiating diamonds in country.

[125] The mines are operated by Debswana Diamond Company (Pty) Ltd, a joint venture between the government of Botswana and De Beers. DTC Botswana website, http://www.dtcb.co.bw/about_us.php (accessed January 23, 2014).

[126] Grynberg, "Diamond Beneficiation in Botswana," 2013.

[127] Grynberg, "Diamond Beneficiation in Botswana," 2013; UNECA, *Making the Most of Africa's Commodities*, 2013, 101.

[128] UNECA, *Making the Most of Africa's Commodities*, 2013, 101; Grynberg, Motswapong, and Philimon, *Diamond Beneficiation and the WTO*, 2102, 10. The Diamond Trading Company (DTC) is the trading arm of De Beers. DTC Botswana is a joint venture between De Beers and the Botswana government. The government of Botswana also owns 15 percent of De Beers. DeBeersGroup.com, DTC website, http://www.debeersgroup.com/operations/sales/diamond-trading-company/ (accessed January 23, 2014). For more information on DTC Botswana see the DTC Botswana.com website, http://www.dtcbotswana.com/about_us.php (accessed January 23, 2014); Grynberg, Motswapong, and Philimon, *Diamond Beneficiation and the WTO*, 2102, 10.

[129] Spektorov et al., *The Global Diamond Report 2013*, August 27, 2013, 17.

[130] UNECA, *Making the Most of Africa's Commodities*, 2013, 95. Cameroon is the sixth-largest producer.

[131] This is done through the Cocoa Research Institute of Ghana (CRIG). USDA, FAS, *Ghana: Cocoa Report*, March 15, 2012, 3.

[132] UNECA, *Making the Most of Africa's Commodities*, 2013, 145; USDA, FAS, *Ghana: Cocoa Report*, March 15, 2012, 5.

[133] Ibid.

[134] Regional markets generally want finished products, although the market for such goods is limited.

[135] UNECA, *Making the Most of Africa's Commodities*, 2013, 144–48.

[136] Zambeefplc.com website, "Our History," http://www.zambeefplc.com/zambeefplc/what-we-do/ (accessed January 23, 2014).

[137] These other products are milk, dairy products, eggs, edible oils, stock feed, flour, and bread. Zambeefplc.com website, http://www.zambeefplc.com/who-we-are/ (accessed January 23, 2014).

[138] Rabbobank, *Looking for Delta*, 2013, 31.

[139] Zambeefplc.com website, http://www.zambeefplc.com/zambeefplc/what-we-do/ (accessed January 23, 2014); Rabbobank, *Looking for Delta*, 2013, 31.

[140] Ibid.

[141] Ibid.

[142] Morris, Staritz, and Barnes, "Clothing Sectors of Lesotho and Swaziland," 2011, 98. Before South Africa entered these markets, both Lesotho and Swaziland had apparel industries, mostly established by Taiwanese firms. These Taiwanese firms primarily established production in Lesotho and Swaziland as part of their GSCs, in order to take advantage of U.S. market access offered first by the MFA, but especially by AGOA. However, a few Taiwanese firms now manufacture clothes in Lesotho and Swaziland for the South African market. Morris, Staritz, and Barnes, "Clothing Sectors of Lesotho and Swaziland," 2011, 97, 99.

[143] Morris, Staritz, and Barnes, "Clothing Sectors of Lesotho and Swaziland," 2011, 105, 107: USITC, hearing transcript, January 14, 2014, 208 (testimony of Paul Ryberg, African Coalition for Trade, Inc

[144] Morris, Staritz, and Barnes, "Clothing Sectors of Lesotho and Swaziland," 2011, 102: Chemengich, *Competitiveness of the SSA Textile Sec*tor, 2010, 43.

[145] Dinh et al., *Light Manufacturing in Africa*, 2012, 26, 41.

[146] UNCTAD, "UNCTAD Asked to Identify Potential Supply Chains in Sub-Saharan Africa," September 27, 2012. According to a similar study UNCTAD did for the leather and leather products sector in South Asia, the removal of tariffs and greater regional integration could boost intraregional trade of these products in South Asia 10-fold. FGI, NTU, and WTO, *Global Value Chains in a Changing World*, 2013, 323.

[147] Gitau, "Promoting Value Supply Chains in Sub Saharan Africa," December 23, 2013.

[148] Dinh et al., *Light Manufacturing in Africa*, 2012, 55.

[149] Although definitions differ, agroprocessing refers to the processing of raw materials derived from the agricultural, forestry, and fisheries sectors. The agroprocessing sector thus broadly encompasses agricultural products like staple crops (e.g., cassava), coffee, fruits, vegetables, fish, and meats, as well as processed products like vegetable oils, fruit juices, and other processed foods. For an overview of agroprocessing in SSA, including definitions and concepts, see UNIDO, *Agribusiness for Africa's Prosperity*, 2011, 28.

[150] UNIDO, *Agribusiness for Africa's Prosperity*, 2011, 44, 135

[151] UNIDO, *Agribusiness for Africa's Prosperity*, 2011, 44.

[152] UNIDO, *Agribusiness for Africa's Prosperity*, 2011, 154; AECOM International Development, "Priority Value Chains Assessment and Selection," April 2011, 21.

[153] UNIDO, *Agribusiness for Africa's Prosperity*, 2011, 52.

[154] Ibid, 51.

[155] Ibid, 66.
[156] Ibid., 81.
[157] COMESA, *Annual Report 2011*, 2011, 63–64.
[158] UNECA, "AUC-ECA Launch Programme," December 3, 2013.
[159] COMESA, *Annual Report 2011*, 2011, 63. The program, which ended in 2012, was an initiative of the European Commission and the African, Caribbean, and Pacific Group of States (ACP). The program aimed to reduce poverty and improve incomes and living conditions of agricultural producers in ACP countries.
[160] COMESA, *Annual Report 2011*, 2011, 63–64.
[161] ECOWAS Commission, *West African Common Industrial Policy*, 2010, 35, 38. For a list of potential agricultural and industrial products identified for development, see Annex I of the policy.
[162] SADC, *Report of the Executive Secretary 2011–2012*, 2012, 16.
[163] International Trade Centre, "Africa's Trade Potential," 2012, 10.
[164] Dinh et al., *Light Manufacturing in Africa*, 2012, 122.
[165] USITC, *Sub-Saharan Africa: Effects of Infrastructure Conditions*, 2009, 6-36.
[166] See Morris, Staritz, and Barnes, "Value Chain Dynamics, Local Embeddedness, and Upgrading," 2011, 101–102; Staritz, *Making the Cut?* 2011, 88–89.
[167] USITC, *Sub-Saharan African Textile and Apparel Inputs*, 2009, 3-20.
[168] Ibid.
[169] Staritz, *Making the Cut?* 2011, 88–89.
[170] USITC, *Sub-Saharan African Textile and Apparel Inputs*, 2009, xv.
[171] Staritz, *Making the Cut?* 2011, 90.
[172] USITC, *Sub-Saharan African Textile and Apparel Inputs*, 2009, xix–xx; Starlitz, *Making the Cut?* 2011, 75.
[173] COMESA, *Annual Report 2011*, 2011, 63–64.
[174] South Africa is one of the world's largest suppliers of all of the major ferroalloys. For a description of factors affecting growth in South Africa's exports of ferroalloys, see section 2 of this report.
[175] Government of South Africa, DTI, *Industrial Policy Action Plan 2013/2014–2015/2016*, 2013, 124.
[176] FGI, NTU, and WTO, *Global Value Chains in a Changing World*, 2013, 338.
[177] EAC, "Regional Frameworks for Development of Extractive Industries," March 20, 2013.
[178] ECOWAS Commission, *Regional Strategic Plan*, 2011; UNECA, *Minerals and Africa's Development*, 2011, 146-148.
[179] UNECA, *Minerals and Africa's Development*, 2011, 110.
[180] Ibid., 109.
[181] East Africa Trade Hub, "AGOA Strategies Chart Course for Increased Exports," December 4, 2013.
[182] Kunda, "Zambia: Govt to Revive Textile Sector," September 3, 2013.
[183] USITC, *Export Opportunities and Barriers*, 2005, D-4.
[184] In particular, the RCA index measures a good's share in a country's total exports relative to that good's share in world trade. For a more detailed description of RCA, see USITC, *Export Opportunities and Barriers*, 2005, D-4.
[185] USITC, *Sub-Saharan Africa (First Annual Report)*, 2007; USITC, *Sub-Saharan Africa (Second Annual Report)*, 2008.
[186] U.S. imports under AGOA of many of these products grew during the 2000–2013 period, as described in section 2 of this report.
[187] USITC, *Sub-Saharan Africa: Effects of Infrastructure Conditions*, 2009.
[188] USITC hearing transcript, inv. nos. 332-542, 332-544, 332-545, and 332-546, Edward Gresser, 119–20.
[189] USITC, *Export Opportunities and Barriers*, 2005; USITC, *Sub-Saharan Africa (Second Annual Report)*, 2008; USITC, *Sub-Saharan Africa: Effects of Infrastructure Conditions*, 2009.
[190] USITC, *Export Opportunities and Barriers*, 2005, 5-18; USITC, *Sub-Saharan Africa (Second Annual Report)*, 2008.
[191] World Bank, *Building Competitiveness in Africa's Agriculture*, 2010, 29–31.
[192] Ibid.
[193] Ibid.
[194] Ibid, 35–36.
[195] ECOWAS, *West African Common Industrial Policy*, 2010, 72.
[196] Skully, "U.S. Tariff Rate Quotas and AGOA Market Access," 2010, 2–3.
[197] USAID, West Africa Trade Hub, *Exports, Employment and Incomes in West Africa*, 2011, 6, 24.
[198] Ibid, 66.
[199] Ibid, 6, 24.
[200] UNECA, *Making the Most of Africa's Commodities*, 2013, 48.
[201] UNECA, *Assessing Regional Integration in Africa V*, 2012, 42; Mevel and Karingi, "Deepening Regional Integration in Africa," 2012, 16–22.
[202] Hausmann et al., *The Atlas of Economic Complexity*, 2011, 8. For a more detailed description of the product space methodology and its application to selected SSA countries, see appendix F of this report.

[203] Hidalgo, "Discovering Southern and East Africa's Industrial Opportunities," 2011, 15–18.
[204] Industry representative, interview by USITC staff, Washington, DC, January 13, 2014.
[205] USITC hearing transcript, invs. 332-542, 332-544, 332-545, and 332-546, January 14, 2014, Edward Gresser, 122.
[206] Minor and Tsigas, "Impacts of Better Trade Facilitation," May 2008, 17.
[207] Industry representative, interview by USITC staff, Washington, DC, January 13, 2014.
[208] For example, Swaziland was allocated 16,849 mt (raw value) and Malawi 10,630 mt (raw value) of the U.S. raw sugar import quota in fiscal year 2014. For the complete list of country-specific quotas, see https://www.federalregister.gov/articles/2013/09/18/2013-22641/fiscal-year-2014-wto-tariff-rate-quota-allocations-for-raw-cane-sugar-refined-and-specialty-sugar.
[209] Haley, Stephen, "Table 60b," January 15, 2014.
[210] The term "wholly obtained" is mainly used for natural products and goods made from natural products, which are entirely obtained in one country; it encompasses products extracted or harvested in a country and live animals born or hunted in a country. Commodities with imported parts or materials cannot be considered to be wholly obtained. World Customs Organization, http://www.wcoomd.org/en/topics/origin/instrument-and-tools/comparative-study-on-preferential-rules-of-origin/specific-topics/study-topics/who.aspx (accessed March 5, 2014).
[211] To achieve a double substantial transformation, the materials imported into the beneficiary country must be substantially transformed into a new and different intermediate article of commerce, which also must be transformed into the final article. The 35-percent value-content rule requires that the sum of (1) the cost or value of the materials produced in one or more of the beneficiary countries plus (2) the direct costs of processing operations performed in the designated beneficiary country must total no less than 35 percent of the appraised value of the merchandise at the U.S. port of entry. See section 507(a)2 of the Trade Act of 1974 (19 U.S.C. § 2466a) and HTS general notes 4(a) and 16.
[212] Industry representative, interview by USITC staff, Washington, DC, January 13, 2014.
[213] Grill, "Billions from Beijing: Africans Divided," November 29, 2013.
[214] *Economist*, "More than Minerals," March 23, 2013.
[215] *Economist*, "Little to Fear but Fear Itself," September 21, 2013.
[216] USITC hearing transcript, invs. 332-542, 332-544, 332-545, and 332-546, Amb. Somduth Soborun, January 14, 2014, 22–23.
[217] USITC hearing transcript, invs. 332-542, 332-544, 332-545, and 332-546, Edward Gresser, January 14, 2014, 120.
[218] Products were chosen for profiling here if they were both significant imports of the United States from non-AGOA countries and significant exports from AGOA. More precisely, a product was reported at the HS 6-digit level if the value of its exports to the world market from AGOA countries (excluding South Africa) exceeded $500,000 and if the United States had imported it in significant quantities globally but had imported less than $20,000 worth from AGOA countries.
[219] Unless otherwise noted, U.S. import data presented in this section are from USITC DataWeb/USDOC, and global trade data are from GTIS, World Trade Atlas database (accessed February 6, 2014).
[220] Fresh and frozen boneless beef are classified under HS subheadings 0201.30 and 0202.30.
[221] This includes all of SSA.
[222] Grynberg, "Botswana's Beef with the EU," July 6, 2012; Lomé Convention, 1975, http://ec.europa.eu/europeaid/where/acp/overview/lome-convention/lomeitoiv_en.htm.
[223] If sanitary conditions were met, imports from SSA countries would be duty free within quota only. Over-quota rates remain the same.
[224] Grynberg, "Botswana's Beef with the EU," July 6, 2012.
[225] The United States has a TRQ for beef that covers fresh and frozen beef carcasses, bone-in beef, and boneless beef. The country-specific aggregate quantity imported in a calendar year under the TRQ cannot exceed the following ceilings: Canada, no limit; Mexico, no limit; Australia, 378,214 mt; New Zealand, 213,402 mt; Japan, 200 mt; Argentina, 20,000 mt; Uruguay, 20,000 mt; other countries or areas (including all SSA countries), 64,805 mt. The within-quota rate for boneless beef ranges from 4.4¢ per kg to 10 percent ad valorem. The over-quota rate is 26.4 percent. In most years, there are no over-quota imports. USITC DataWeb/USDOC (accessed January 17, 2014).
[226] Copper ores and concentrates, unwrought forms (unrefined and refined), and waste and scrap thereof are covered under HS subheadings 2603.00, 7401.00, 7402.00, 7403.00, 7403.11, 7403.12, 7403.19, 7403.29, and 7404.00.
[227] Edelstein, "Copper," January 2013, 48.
[228] Tse, "The Mineral Industry of China: Advance Release," December 2013, 8.1, 8.6–7; Kuo, "The Mineral Industry of India: Advance Release," January 2013, 11.2.
[229] Mobbs, "The Mineral Industry of Zambia: Advance Release," October 2012, 43.1, 43.7–8.
[230] State Department and USFCS, *Doing Business in Namibia*, 2013; *Doing Business in South Africa*, 2013; and *Doing Business in Zambia*, 2013.
[231] EC, "Trade: Countries and Regions; South Africa," November 19, 2013.

[232] EC, "Trade: Countries and Regions; Central Africa," November 19, 2013; "Trade: Countries and Regions; East African Community (EAC)," November 19, 2013; "Trade: Countries and Regions; Eastern and Southern Africa (ESA)," November 19, 2013; "Trade: Countries and Regions; Southern African Development Community (SADC)," November 19, 2013; and "Trade: Countries and Regions; West Africa," November 19, 2013.

[233] Bermúdez-Lugo, "The Mineral Industry of Namibia: Advance Release," April 2013, 32.2, 7; Yager, "The Mineral Industry of South Africa: Advance Release," July 2013, 37.3, 18.

[234] Edelstein, "Copper," January 2013, 49.

[235] Gurmendi, "The Mineral Industry of Peru: Advance Release," April 2013, 17.3, 11; Edelstein, "Copper: Advance Release," July 2013, 20.3, 8.

[236] Certain fresh and frozen fish and shellfish are classified under the following HS subheadings: 0301.99, 0302.85, 0302.29, 0302.23, 0302.59, 0303.41, 0303.42, 0303.43, 0303.44, 0303.57, 0303.29, 0303.39, 0303.90, 0303.33, 0303.84, 0303.19, 0304.95, 0304.83, 0304.99, 0304.43, 0305.69, 0305.51, 0306.24, 0306.14, 0306.21, 0306.19, 0307.49, 0307.99, 0307.11, and 0308.19.

[237] Under the tariff shift rule, a good is considered sufficiently transformed when it is classified under an HTS code that is different from all non-originating inputs. Each program that uses this method has a unique set of tariff shift rules for all HS categories. See 19 C.F.R. part 102.

[238] *TradeWatch*, "The European Union's New Preferential Rules of Origin," March 28, 2011.

[239] Industry representative, telephone interview by USITC staff, January 6, 2014.

[240] Ibid.

[241] USITC hearing transcript, invs. 332-542, 332-544, 332-545, and 332-546, Amb. Somduth Soborun, January 14, 2014, 20; USITC hearing transcript, invs. 332-542, 332-544, 332-545, and 332-546, Paul Ryberg, January 14, 2014, 226–27.

[242] Miscellaneous fresh vegetables are classified under the following HS subheadings: 0708.10, 0708.20, 0709.20, 0709.30, 0709.60, 0709.93, and 0709.99.

[243] Singh, "Nontraditional Crop Production in Africa for Export," 2002.

[244] Ibid.

[245] USDA, APHIS, *Commodity Import Approval Process*, February 8, 2013, 4.

[246] For approved applications, the FAVIR (Fruit and Vegetable Import Requirements) database can be consulted at http://www.aphis.usda.gov/favir.

[247] Women's and girls' cotton blazers are classified under HS subheading 6104.32.

[248] *Just-style*, "Prospects for an African Clothing Industry?" June 25, 2013; *Just-style*, "European Economic Woes Hit Mauritius Textile Sector," December 1, 2010.

[249] Industry representative, interview with USITC staff, January 13, 2014.

[250] USITC DataWeb/USDOC (accessed January 30, 2014).

[251] Based on FDI data from UNCTAD, UNCTADStat database (accessed December 10, 2013).

[252] World Bank, *World Development Report 2005*, 2004, 20.

[253] Mukherjee, Wang, and Tsai, "Governance and Foreign Direct Investment," 2011, 1.

[254] IMF, Regional Economic Outlook, 2013, 1.

[255] Data for Somalia and South Sudan were not available.

[256] Based on data from the World Bank's World Development Indicators (accessed December 6, 2013).

[257] The latest data available from the World Bank World Development Indicators is 2011 for this measure.

[258] Based on the data from the World Bank, World Development Indicators.

[259] Ibid.

[260] IMF, *Regional Economic Outlook*, 2013, 3.

[261] Based on data from the World Bank, World Development Indicators (accessed December 6, 2013).

[262] Ibid.

[263] World Bank, Worldwide Governance Indicators (accessed December 17, 2013).

[264] Kaufmann, Kraay, and Mastruzzi, "The Worldwide Governance Indicators," September 2010, 2–3.

[265] UNCTAD, *Good Governance in Investment Promotion*, 2004.

[266] World Bank, Worldwide Governance Indicators (accessed December 17, 2013).

[267] Benin and Gabon are AGOA beneficiary countries. Madagascar lost its AGOA eligibility in 2010. Guinea-Bissau and Mali lost their AGOA eligibilities in 2013. Mauritania lost its AGOA eligibility twice over 2000–2013, though in 2013 it is again an AGOA beneficiary country. World Bank, Worldwide Governance Indicators (accessed on December 17, 2013), chapter 1, table 1.1.

[268] World Bank, Worldwide Governance Indicators (accessed December 17, 2013).

[269] Ibid.

[270] World Bank, Doing Business Indicators (accessed December 23, 2013).

[271] The 11 areas are starting a business, dealing with construction permits, getting electricity, registering property, paying taxes, trading across borders, getting credit, protecting investors, enforcing contracts, resolving insolvency, and employing workers. The overall ranking is based on the first 10 measures; the measure of employing workers is not included.

[272] Doing Business Indicators do not cover Djibouti and Somalia.
[273] World Bank, "Doing Business: A Joint Publication and Project," 2013.
[274] 2006 Doing Business Indicators are the earliest data available that are comprehensive and compatible with 2013 Doing Business Indicators. Doing Business Indicators do not have 2006 data for Liberia and South Sudan, so the changes mainly refer to the remaining 45 SSA countries.
[275] OECD, "A Policy Framework for Investment: Trade Policy," 2005, 2.
[276] Heritage Foundation, "2013 Index of Economic Freedom: Trade Freedom" (accessed December 20, 2013).
[277] Improvement over 2010–13.
[278] WEF, World Bank, and AfDB, *Africa Competitiveness Report 2013*, 2013, 4.
[279] WEF, *Global Competitiveness Report 2008*, 2009, 43. The 12 factors are identified in figure 5.1.
[280] The score range of GCI by country is 5.67 (best) to 2.85 (worst).
[281] Odenthal, "FDI in Sub-Saharan Africa," March 2001, 11.
[282] Ibid., 17–18.
[283] Ibid., 26–29.
[284] UNCTAD, UNCTADStat database (accessed October 29, 2013).
[285] Greenfield FDI projects are new investments by foreign investors, as opposed to acquisitions of, or equity investments in existing companies.
[286] BMI, *Asian Investment in Africa*, 2013, 17–18, based on data from UNCTAD, *World Investment Report 2012*, 2012.
[287] Sy, "Shifts in Financing Sustainable Development" (accessed January 23, 2014).
[288] Annual FDI inflows vary significantly from year to year, so the figures presented here show the average, for 2000–2012, of annual FDI inflows as a share of GDP. Commission calculations are based on data from UNCTADStat database (accessed October 29, 2013). Equatorial Guinea is not eligible for the AGOA program.
[289] Commission calculations are based on data from UNCTAD, UNCTADStat database (accessed October 29, 2013).
[290] EIU, "South Africa Trade," February 15, 2013.
[291] Sauvant, Mallampally, and McAllister, *Inward and Outward FDI Country Profiles*, 2013, 1047–48.
[292] Ibid., 1044.
[293] Ibid., 1049.
[294] Ibid., 1049–50.
[295] Ibid., 1054–6.
[296] AfDB, *African Statistical Yearbook 2013*, 2013, 278.
[297] See the Shell Oil website, http://www.shell.com.ng/ for details on the company's business activities in Nigeria.
[298] Sauvant, Mallampally, and McAllister, *Inward and Outward FDI Country Profiles*, 2013, 908–15.
[299] Comparison data for FDI inflows into SSA by source country/region are available only for 2003–2010. Data reflect the sum of FDI inflows for each period. "Other" includes SSA countries, particularly South Africa and Kenya, and non-SSA countries, including Japan, the United Arab Emirates, Canada, and Switzerland. "Other" was calculated by the Commission using total FDI inflows for each SSA country as reported by UNCTAD, and subtracting FDI outflows to SSA as reported by the official statistical agencies of the United States (USDOC, BEA), China (MOFCOM), and the EU (Eurostat). Official data are not available for Brazil or India. The EU reports data for all of Africa; Central and South Africa; and Northern Africa, so the SSA category used here is the Central and South Africa category. U.S. FDI outflows data are available for total Africa, and for individual countries within Africa. The SSA total reported here excludes the northern African countries of Algeria, Egypt, Libya, Morocco, and Tunisia, and reports the sum of available data for all other African countries.
[300] BMI, *Asian Investment in Africa*, 2013, 15.
[301] Data for greenfield FDI projects are only available beginning in 2003.
[302] Financial Times, FDIMarkets database; Bureau van Dijk, Zephyr database.
[303] Ernst & Young, *Ernst & Young's Attractiveness Survey*, 49; Imara Africa Securities Team, "General Electric to Expand Its Investments," July 2, 2013; Helman, "Obama's 'Power Africa' Plan," July 1, 2013.
[304] Total Africa data includes North Africa. USDOC, BEA, interactive FDI database (accessed January 17, 2014).
[305] Ibid.
[306] Financial Times, FDIMarkets database.
[307] Greenfield projects include four in software and IT services, two in financial services, and one in minerals. M&A transactions include one each in financial services, metals, transport, and other services, and one with no industry listed. Financial Times, FDIMarkets database, accessed January 7, 2014; Bureau van Dijk, Zephyr M&A database (accessed January 10, 2014).
[308] Seetanah, "Inward FDI in Mauritius," April 30, 2013.
[309] Sauvant, Mallampally, and McAllister, *Inward and Outward FDI Country Profiles*, 2013, 909–10.
[310] USDOC, BEA, *Survey of Current Business*, 226.
[311] Financial Times, FDIMarkets database.
[312] A table with more detail on U.S. greenfield FDI projects by industry sector and year is presented in appendix H.

[313] EC, Eurostat database (accessed December 16, 2013).
[314] Financial Times, FDIMarkets database.
[315] Ibid.
[316] Financial Times, FDIMarkets database.
[317] Ibid.
[318] Ibid.
[319] Alves, "Brazil in Africa: Achievements and Challenges," June 2013, 39.
[320] *Economist*, "Brazilian Companies Are Heading for Africa," November 10, 2012.
[321] Financial Times, FDIMarkets database.
[322] *Economist*, "Brazilian Companies Are Heading for Africa," November 10, 2012.
[323] Alves, "Brazil in Africa: Achievements and Challenges," June 2013, 41.
[324] *Economist*, "Brazilian Companies Are Heading for Africa," November 10, 2012.
[325] BMI, *Asian Investment in Africa*, 2013, 25; *Economist*, "Little to Fear but Fear Itself," September 21, 2013.
[326] Kaplinsky and Morris, "Chinese FDI in Sub-Saharan Africa," 2009, 555.
[327] Bureau van Dijk, Zephyr M&A database.
[328] Kaplinsky and Morris, "Chinese FDI in Sub-Saharan Africa," 2009, 563.
[329] Ibid, 561.
[330] Bureau van Dijk, Zephyr M&A database.
[331] Kaplinsky and Morris, "Chinese FDI in Sub-Saharan Africa," 2009, 557.
[332] Kaplinsky and Morris, "Chinese FDI in Sub-Saharan Africa," 2009, 560.
[333] World Bank, "The Business Environment in Southern Africa," 2010, 63.
[334] Sauvant, Mallampally, and McAllister, *Inward and Outward FDI Country Profiles*, 2013, 855, 859.
[335] Based on data for investment approvals by the Indian government. Sauvant, Mallampally, and McAllister, *Inward and Outward FDI Country Profiles*, 2013, 874.
[336] Bureau van Dijk, Zephyr database.
[337] Financial Times, FDIMarkets database.
[338] Ernst & Young, *Ernst & Young's Attractiveness Survey*, 2013, 5, 36; Financial Times, FDIMarkets database.
[339] UNCTAD, *World Investment Report 2013*, 2013, 42.
[340] Bureau van Dijk, Zephyr M&A database; Financial Times, FDIMarkets database.
[341] Ernst & Young, *Ernst & Young's Attractiveness Survey*, 2013, 5, 37. Oil and gas extraction projects accounted for only 3 percent of the total (based on data from the FDIMarkets database), although these projects likely account for a significantly greater share of total capital expenditures.
[342] Ernst & Young, *Ernst & Young's Attractiveness Survey*, 2013, 17.
[343] UNCTAD, World Investment Report 2013, 2013, 42.
[344] BMI, *Asian Investment in Africa*, 2013, 38.
[345] Ibid., 39–42.
[346] Services include activities such as marketing, business support services, and retail. Refining is included in manufacturing. Ernst & Young, *Ernst & Young's Attractiveness Survey*, 2013, 38.
[347] De Backer, "Mining Investment and Financing in Africa," March 2012, 6.
[348] Ibid, 7.
[349] Ibid.
[350] Industry representative, interview by USITC staff, Washington, DC, January 13, 2014.
[351] USITC, hearing transcript, January 14, 2014, 84 (testimony of Dennis Matanda, Manchester Trade Ltd.).
[352] BMI, *Asian Investment in Africa*, 2013, 52–55.
[353] Ibid, 56.
[354] USITC, hearing transcript, January 14, 2014, 47-48 (testimony of Girma Birru, ambassador of Ethiopia to the United States).
[355] USITC, hearing transcript, January 14, 2014, 152 (testimony of Edward Gresser, Progressive Economy).
[356] Financial Times, FDIMarkets database.
[357] BMI, *Asian Investment in Africa*, 2013, 63–68.
[358] Several Taiwanese investors quoted in the Godfrey article told the author that they would pull their companies out of Africa as soon as the program was ended, and given that the program was due to end in 2015, they would be unlikely to make any further investments in Lesotho or Swaziland. Further, uncertainty about AGOA renewal would lead some investors to relocate anyway. Godfrey, "Comment: Prospects for an African Clothing Industry?" June 25, 2013; Wang, Fangqing, "China's Textile and Clothing Firms Expand," December 18, 2012.
[359] USITC, hearing transcript, January 14, 2014, 289–90 (testimony of Stephen Lamar, American Apparel & Footwear Association).
[360] USITC DataWeb/USDOC, January 14, 2014.
[361] Godfrey, "Prospects for an African Clothing Industry?" June 25, 2013.
[362] World Bank, *Snapshot Africa—Kenya*, January 2007, 9.
[363] Industry representative, interview with USITC staff, Washington, DC, January 13, 2014.

[364] The reason why they are in Lesotho, says its local CEO Lin Chin Yi, is because of the duty and quota free access to the US market under the African Growth and Opportunity Act." Mills, "Lesotho's Textile Industry Unravels," September 4, 2011.
[365] Lesotho Textile Exporters Association, "Lesotho Textile Industry," (accessed January 14, 2014); Nien Hsing Textile Co. website, http://www.nhjeans.com/en/milestone.php (accessed January 14, 2014); Mills, "Lesotho Textile Industry Unravels," September 4, 2011.
[366] Wang, "China's Textile and Clothing Firms," December 18, 2012.
[367] Godfrey, "Prospects for an African Clothing Industry?" June 25, 2013.
[368] Godfrey, "Prospects for an African Clothing Industry?" June 25, 2013; Anganan, "Mauritius Exporters Switch Focus from EU," April 29, 2013; *Just-Style.com*, "European Economic Woes Hit Mauritius Textile Sector," December 1, 2010.
[369] World Bank, *Snapshot Africa—Kenya*, January 2007, 10, 15; Godfrey, "Prospects for an African Clothing Industry?" June 25, 2013.
[370] Industry representative, interview by USITC staff, Washington, DC, January 13, 2014.
[371] USITC, hearing transcript, January 14, 2014, 281–82 and 291–94 (testimony of Jaswinder Bedi, African Cotton and Textile Industries Federation, and Stephen Lamar, American Apparel & Footwear Association).
[372] USITC, hearing transcript, January 14, 2014, 291–94 (testimony of Jaswinder Bedi, African Cotton and Textile Industries Federation, and Stephen Lamar, American Apparel & Footwear Association)
[373] Bureau van Dijk, Zephyr M&A database.
[374] Capital investment values for most projects were not reported. Financial Times, FDIMarkets database.
[375] World Bank, "Snapshot Africa," 2006, 75–84.
[376] McKinsey Global Institute, Lions on the Move, June 2010, 1.
[377] USITC, hearing transcript, January 14, 2014, 39–40 (testimony of Ebrahim Rasool, ambassador of South Africa to the United States).
[378] African Union, "A Decade of African-US Trade," November 2012, 4.
[379] UNIDO, "Foreign Direct Investment in Sub-Saharan Africa," 2008. EBA refers to the EU's Everything but Arms preferential trade package offered to certain developing countries in Africa and elsewhere.
[380] Karingi, Páez, and Degefa, "Report on a Survey," May 2011.
[381] Engineering News, "AGOA a Boon," September 27, 2013.
[382] USITC, hearing transcript, January 14, 2014, 152 (testimony of Edward Gresser, Progressive Economy).
[383] CNN, "Lesotho Plans for Life without U.S. Trade Lifeline," February 15, 2011.
[384] Business Daily Africa, "Textile Firms Resume Investments," May 23, 2013.
[385] UNCTAD, FDI database (accessed on January 17, 2014); IRIN, "Madagascar: Textile Industry Unravels," February 24, 2010.
[386] Karingi, Páez, and Degefa. "Report on a Survey," May 2011.
[387] USITC, hearing transcript, January 14, 2014, 153 (testimony of J. Daniel O'Flaherty, National Foreign Trade Council); USITC, Hearing transcript, January 14, 2014, 158 (testimony of Katrin Kuhlmann, Corporate Council on Africa).
[388] Asmah et al., *AGOA at 10*, July 2010.
[389] USITC, hearing transcript, January 14, 2014, 17 (testimony of Somduth Soborun, ambassador of Mauritius to the United States); USITC, hearing transcript, January 14, 2014, 233 (testimony of Jaswinder Bedi, African Cotton and Textile Industries Federation); USITC, hearing transcript, January 14, 2014, 269 (testimony of Paul Ryberg, African Coalition for Trade); CRS, *U.S. Trade and Investment Relations*, November 2012.
[390] USITC, hearing transcript, January 14, 2014, 223–24 (testimony of Paul Ryberg, African Coalition for Trade).
[391] For more information on EPAs, see the section on EU EPAs later in this section.
[392] Other developing countries that had unilateral trade preferences but now have FTAs with the United States, such as Colombia, Peru, and CAFTA countries (Costa Rica, Dominican Republic, El Salvador, Guatemala, Honduras, and Nicaragua) were also potential case studies for this section. However, because of the recent nature of these FTAs, there is little information on the effects of these countries' transitions from unilateral preferences to reciprocal trade agreements in the economic literature. Despite recent strong growth in income and reduced poverty rates, Chile is still classified as a developing country by the United Nations Conference on Trade and Development. UN, *World Economic Situation and Prospects 2014*, 2014, 146.
[393] The UNCTAD website provides the following explanation of the rationale for GSP programs:
As stated in Resolution 21 (ii) taken at the UNCTAD II Conference in New Delhi in 1968,
"… the objectives of the generalized, non-reciprocal, non-discriminatory system of preferences in favour of the developing countries, including special measures in favour of the least advanced among the developing countries, should be:
(a) to increase their export earnings;
(b) to promote their industrialization; and
(c) to accelerate their rates of economic growth."
Under GSP schemes of preference-giving counties, selected products originating in developing countries are granted reduced or zero tariff rates over the MFN rates. The least developed countries receive special and

preferential treatment for a wider coverage of products and deeper tariff cuts. UNCTAD website, http://unctad.org/en/Pages/DITC/GSP/About-GSP.aspx (accessed March 16, 2014).

These programs also conform to the waiver initially granted by the GATT (the organization overseeing the General Agreement on Tariffs and Trade and precursor to the WTO) for a 10-year period in 1971 and made permanent in 1979. As explained on the WTO website, the 1979 "Enabling Clause" is "the WTO legal basis for the Generalized System of Preferences (GSP). Under the Generalized System of Preferences, developed countries offer non-reciprocal preferential treatment (such as zero or low duties on imports) to products originating in developing countries. Preference-giving countries unilaterally determine which countries and which products are included in their schemes." WTO website, http://wto.org/english/tratop_e/devel/e/d2legl_e.htm (accessed March 16, 2014).

[394] A list of GSP-type programs is maintained by the World Trade Organization http://ptadb.wto.org/ptaList.aspx (accessed November 15, 2013).

[395] Herz and Wagner, "The Dark Side," 2011, 25.

[396] As the term implies, reciprocal agreements are the product of negotiations between two or more parties, and in practice, the types of concessions vary significantly among agreements. Modern reciprocal agreements reflect in many ways the evolution of multilateral agreements, negotiated under the GATT and WTO, increasingly addressing nontariff issues, particularly in light of the decline in tariff rates. NAFTA agreement, https://www.nafta-sec- alena.org/Default.aspx?tabid=97&language=en-US (accessed December 18, 2013).

[397] The Trade and Development Act of 2000, sec. 102 (Pub. L. 106-200); Chutha and Kimenyi, "The Africa Growth and Opportunity Act," May 2011, 4.

[398] USTR, "Caribbean Basin Initiative."

[399] See 19 U.S.C. § 2463(c)(2)(A); see also USTR, *U.S. Generalized System of Preferences Guidebook*, July 2013, 8, 12.

[400] USITC, *U.S.-Chile Free Trade Agreement*, June 2003, xvii.

[401] Regulation (EU) No 978/2012 of the European Parliament and of the Council, October 25, 2012.

[402] Onguglo, "Developing Countries and Unilateral Trade Preferences," 1999, 3.

[403] Ibid.

[404] See, e.g., "Chile Protests Its Exclusion From U.S. GSP Scheme," February 4, 1988, http://www.sunsonline.org/trade/process/during/uruguay/gsp/02040288.htm (accessed February 13, 2014). U.S. legislation authorizing the U.S. GSP program prohibits the President from designating a country as a beneficiary developing country if the country "has not taken or is not taking steps to afford internationally recognized worker rights to workers in the country." 19 U.S.C. 2462(b)(2)(G).

[405] USTR, "U.S. Trade Representative Michael Froman Comments," June 2013.

[406] For example, the United States delayed implementation of its FTA with Colombia until Colombia's labor practices improved.

[407] See 19 U.S.C. § 2466a(a) and eligibility requirements in 19 U.S.C. § 3703. For more information, see section 1.

[408] Onguglo, "Developing Countries and Unilateral Trade Preferences," 1999, 2–3.

[409] A comprehensive review of the literature examining AGOA's performance is presented in section 7. Zappile, "Nonreciprocal Trade Agreements and Trade," February 2011, 61–62; Mevel et al. *The African Growth and Opportunity Act*, July 2013, vi.

[410] Herz and Wagner, "The Dark Side," 2011, 763.

[411] Aiello and Cardamone, "Analysing the Impact of Everything But Arms Initiative," 2011, 149. For more information about gravity modeling, see the section 7 section on the role of AGOA in increasing and diversifying exports.

[412] Meyn, "The EU-South Africa FTA," January 22–23, 2004, 9.

[413] African Development Bank Group, *Kingdom of Lesotho: Country Strategy Paper, 2013-2017*, February 2013, 6.

[414] Reynolds, "The Erosion of Tariff Preferences," July 18, 2005, 2.

[415] Bouët et al., "Is Erosion of Tariff Preferences," September 2005, 6.

[416] Keck and Lendle, "New Evidence on Preference Utilization," September 3, 2012, 2.

[417] WTO, Trade Policy Review Body, *Norway: Trade Policy Review*, August 21, 2012, vii.

[418] Van Engelen et al., *Botswana Agrifood Value Chain Project*, 2013, 29.

[419] Ibid.

[420] Beef exports from Botswana suffer from several problems in the EU market. In addition to stiff competition amplified by tariff erosion, exports declined substantially from February 2011 to May 2012, when EU inspections identified problems with Botswana's animal identification (traceability) system and EU standards of abattoir hygiene. Bungu, "Botswana Beef Exports Slump 89%," April 28, 2011; Republic of Botswana, "Botswana Re-enters EU Market," May 7, 2012; Van Engelen et al., *Botswana Agrifood Value Chain Project*, 2013 28, 30.

[421] Conconi and Perroni, *Reciprocal versus Unilateral Trade Preferences for Developing Countries, September 2009*, 3.

[422] Using that metric, Taiwan was the largest beneficiary. Sapir and Lundberg, "The U.S. Generalized System of Preferences," 1984, 205.

[423] Sapir and Lundberg, "The U.S. Generalized System of Preferences," 1984, 207, 223.
[424] Annual growth rates calculated by USITC staff from OECD, StatExtracts data series "GDP, US$, constant prices, constant PPPs, reference year 2005, millions." (accessed March 10, 2014).
[425] Kose et al., "How Has NAFTA Affected the Mexican Economy?" April 2004, 4-5.
[426] Data are for U.S. imports and exports. GTIS, Global Trade Atlas database (accessed January 2, 2014).
[427] Kose et al., "How Has NAFTA Affected the Mexican Economy?" April 2004, 5.
[428] UNCTAD, UNCTADStat database (accessed February 13, 2014).
[429] Villarreal and Fergusson, "NAFTA at 20," February 21, 2013, 4.
[430] Villarreal and Fergusson, "NAFTA at 20," February 21, 2013, 29.
[431] Kose et al., "How Has NAFTA Affected the Mexican Economy?" April 2004, 4.
[432] Galan and Oladipo, "Have Liberalization and NAFTA," May 2009, 161.
[433] Ferrantino, "Policy Anchors," April 2006, 10–11.
[434] Kose et al., "How Has NAFTA Affected the Mexican Economy?" April 2004, 5.
[435] Galan and Oladipo, "Have Liberalization and NAFTA," May 2009, 177–78.
[436] Sapir and Lundberg, "The U.S. Generalized System of Preferences," 1984, 206.
[437] Ibid., 207.
[438] Annual growth rates calculated by USITC staff from OECD, StatExtracts data series "GDP, US$, constant prices, constant PPPs, reference year 2005, millions." (accessed March 10, 2014).
[439] OECD, *OECD Economic Surveys: Chile 2013*, October 4, 2013, 32–33, 37.
[440] USTR, *U.S.-Chile FTA: Final Text*.
[441] Data are for U.S. imports. GTIS, Global Trade Atlas database (accessed January 7, 2014).
[442] UNCTAD, UNCTADStat database (accessed February 13, 2014).
[443] Azzopardi, "Diversifying Chile's Exports," February 1, 2012, 1.
[444] Over the last eight years (2005-2013), this percentage has increased about one point, as copper prices increased the value of copper relative to the value of other Chilean exports. GTIS, Global Trade Atlas (accessed March 11, 2014).
[445] Azzopardi, "Diversifying Chile's Exports," February 1, 2012, 1.
[446] Ibid.
[447] Fulponi and Engler, "The Impact of Regional Trade Agreements," August 12, 2013, 18.
[448] Ibid., 29.
[449] Ibid., 23-24.
[450] Ibid., 27.
[451] Ibid.
[452] WTO, Trade Policy Review Body, *Chile: Trade Policy Review,* WT/TPR/S/124, December 4, 2003, 25.
[453] Jean, "Assessing the Impact of the EU-Chile FTA," April 30, 2012, 16-17.
[454] Copper and ores were excluded from the analysis because the EU-Chile FTA was not expected to have an impact on these nondutiable products. Jean, "Assessing the Impact of the EU-Chile FTA," April 30, 2012, 18.
[455] Fulponi and Engler, "The Impact of Regional Trade Agreements," August 12, 2013, 5-6.
[456] Fulponi and Engler, "The Impact of Regional Trade Agreements," August 12, 2013, 6-7.
[457] Equivalence is defined as the acceptance of a partner's SPS measure as equivalent to one's own, even if different in many respects. Fulponi and Engler, "The Impact of Regional Trade Agreements," August 12, 2013, 18.
[458] Fulponi and Engler, "The Impact of Regional Trade Agreements," August 12, 2013, 18.
[459] GTIS, Global Trade Atlas database (accessed January 7, 2014).
[460] *Washington Trade Daily,* "U.S.-Morocco Trade Facilitation," November 22, 2013, 3–4.
[461] Amcham Morocco, *Trade and Investment Guide 2007,* 2007, 160.
[462] *Washington Trade Daily,* "U.S.-Morocco Trade Facilitation," November 22, 2013, 3–4.
[463] Two EU agreements in particular which set up cooperative committees on trade facilitation are the EU-Mexico FTA and the EU-Chile FTA. Fasan, "Comparing EU Free Trade Agreements," 2004.
[464] WTO, Committee on Regional Trade Agreements, *Factual Presentation: Free Trade Agreement,* March 24, 2010, 4.
[465] Journal of the European Communities, *Agreement on Trade, Development and Cooperation between the European Community and Its Member States, of the One Part, and the Republic of South Africa, of the Other Part,* Title 1, Article 1(c).
[466] Information on tariff disadvantage of imports from the United States is derived from a submission from the government of South Africa to the USITC, "Analysis of RSA Imports from the US." January 22, 2014. Trade flows may be affected by duties in place and may be substantially different in the absence of duties.
[467] EFTA includes Iceland, Liechtenstein, Norway, and Switzerland. SACU includes Botswana, Lesotho, Namibia, South Africa, and Swaziland.
[468] The text of the agreement can be found on the EFTA website, http://www.efta.int/free-trade/free-trade-agreements/sacu.
[469] No concessions were provided for basic agricultural goods (HS 1–24) from Norway. WTO, *Factual Presentation: Free Trade Agreement,* March 24, 2010, 10.

[470] Compiled by USITC. Trade flows may be distorted by duties in place and may have been substantially different in the absence of duties.
[471] The agreement will enter into force 30 days after notification by all signatory parties. "Preferential Trade Agreement between the Common Market of the South (Mercosur) and the Southern African Customs Union (SACU)," Article 36.
[472] Compiled by USITC. Trade flows may be distorted by duties in place and may have been substantially different in the absence of duties.
[473] *Journal of the European Communities*, "Partnership Agreement Between the Members of the African, Caribbean and Pacific Group of States and the European Community," December 15, 2000, Articles 36–37.
[474] EU Commission, "Overview of EPA Negotiations," updated October 16, 2013.
[475] The ESA states consist of Comoros, Madagascar, Mauritius, Seychelles, Zambia, and Zimbabwe. The EU negotiations for a trade agreement with the SADC involve Angola, Botswana, Lesotho, Mozambique, Namibia, South Africa, and Swaziland. An interim EPA with the East African Community involves Burundi, Kenya, Rwanda, Tanzania, and Uganda.
[476] European Council, 2437th Council Meeting, Luxembourg, 17 June 2002, 29, http://www.consilium.europa.eu/uedocs/cms_data/docs/pressdata/en/gena/71044.pdf.
[477] Kuhlmann, "A New US-European Approach," 2010, 6.
[478] One additional SADC country, Namibia, participated in negotiations but did not sign an interim EPA.
[479] EU Commission, "Proposal for a Regulation of the European Parliament," September 30, 2011.
[480] Bartels and Goodison, "EU Proposals to End Preferences," 2011, 3-4.
[481] EU Commission, "Generalized System of Preferences" (accessed January 9, 2014); Government of the UK, Parliament, "Market Access for Exports from the ACP Countries," October 26, 2011.
[482] Bartels and Goodison, "EU Proposals to End Preferences," 2011, 3-4; Lazzeri, "EU Wants to Force ACP Countries to Sign EPAs," 2014.
[483] Bartels and Goodison, "EU Proposals to End Preferences," 2011, 3.
[484] EU Commission, "Opinion of the Commission regarding the Proposal," May 3, 2013.
[485] East African Community, "EPA Negotiations on Course, EAC Interests Safeguarded," May 24, 2012. Additional negotiations are planned for March 2014. See East African Community, "EAC-EU Economic Partnership Agreement Negotiations," January 30, 2014.
[486] Dieye, "How to Overcome the EPA Stalemate?" March 2013, 17.
[487] Kuhlmann, "A New US-European Approach," 2010, 6.
[488] Nielsen and Zouhon-Bi, "ECOWAS: Fiscal Revenue Implications," April 2007, 12.
[489] Dieye, "How to Overcome the EPA Stalemate?" March 2013, 17–18.
[490] Kuhlmann, "A New US-European Approach," 2010, 6.
[491] *The revised Cotonou agreement*, http://ec.europa.eu/europeaid/where/acp/overview/cotonou-agreement/cotonou_trade_en.htm.
[492] Ramdoo and Bilal, "What Would it Take to Make an EPA Feasible?" 2014, 2.
[493] This section specifically covers to what extent AGOA countries export eligible products under AGOA or GSP preferences and not at the most favored nation (MFN) rate. Topics such as "exports of products not covered by AGOA" and "concentration of exports in a few sectors" are not included in this discussion. For more information on AGOA beneficiary countries' use of the AGOA program, see section 2.
[494] GSP LDBDCs are different from AGOA's lesser-developed beneficiary sub-Saharan African countries (LDBCs) in SSA. See section 1 for more information.
[495] This ratio includes AGOA-eligible products that claimed GSP preferences. The assumption is that in the absence of an identical preference under GSP, those products would otherwise claim preference under AGOA.
[496] Keck and Lendle, "New Evidence on Preference Utilization," September 3, 2012, 27.
[497] Ibid.
[498] Countries with utilization rates of less than 20 percent were Benin, Chad, Guinea-Bissau, São Tomé and Príncipe, Cabo Verde, Seychelles, Gambia, Mauritania, Eritrea, Rwanda, Niger, Guinea, and Uganda. Countries with utilization rates greater than 80 percent were Djibouti, Mali, Cameroon, Swaziland, Malawi, Madagascar, South Africa, Ethiopia, Ghana, Kenya, the Democratic Republic of the Congo, Nigeria, Mozambique, and Lesotho. For more information, see Brenton and Ikezuki, "Initial and Potential Impact," April 2004, 21, 35.
[499] Brenton and Hoppe, "AGOA, Exports, and Development," August 2006, 14.
[500] Countries with preference utilization rates of at least 98 percent in 2005 were Swaziland, Lesotho, Madagascar, Kenya, Malawi, Mozambique, Namibia, Botswana, Uganda, Ethiopia, and Gambia. Countries not utilizing preferences were Chad, Djibouti, Guinea-Bissau, São Tomé and Príncipe, and Seychelles. For more information, see Brenton and Hoppe, "AGOA, Exports, and Development," August 2006, 14.
[501] The Harmonized System is an internationally-recognized product nomenclature developed by the World Customs Organization that is used by many countries as the basis for customs tariffs and for purposes of collecting international trade statistics, among other uses. Various studies highlighted in this section conduct their analyses using HS product codes; the higher the number of digits, the more granular the analysis. For

[502] Dean and Wainio, "Quantifying the Value of U.S. Tariff Preferences," August 2006, 10.
[503] Ibid., 28–29.
[504] Countries not using benefits were Cameroon, Côte d'Ivoire, Senegal, Mali, and Niger. Countries with utilization rates of at least 95 percent were Ghana, Ethiopia, Lesotho, Madagascar, Malawi, and Mozambique. Countries with utilization rates between 80 and 94 percent were Botswana, Kenya, Swaziland, Cabo Verde, Tanzania, and Uganda. For more information, see Dean and Wainio, "Quantifying the Value of U.S. Tariff Preferences," August 2006, 10–11, 28–29.
[505] The authors do not list the countries with combined AGOA and GSP utilization of greater than 90 percent, although table 3 lists utilization by scheme for each country. Countries that achieved greater than 90 percent utilization in either GSP or AGOA were Cameroon, the Republic of the Congo, Côte d'Ivoire, Djibouti, Ghana, Kenya, Mauritius, Namibia, Senegal, South Africa, Swaziland, the Democratic Republic of the Congo, Ethiopia, Guinea, Mozambique, and Tanzania. Countries that did not utilize agricultural preferences were Benin and Niger. For more information, see Dean and Wainio, "Quantifying the value of U.S. tariff preferences for developing countries," August 2006, 15, 32–33.
[506] Bureau, Chakir, and Gallezot, "The Utilization of Trade Preferences," 2007, 185.
[507] Ibid., 194.
[508] These nine countries were Benin, Guinea-Bissau, Seychelles, Guinea, Chad, Uganda, Zambia, Rwanda, and São Tomé and Príncipe. At the same time, the authors note that these countries are producing and exporting products that already have a zero MFN duty rate. See Brenton and Ikezuki, "Initial and Potential Impact," April 2004, 18.
[509] Dean and Wainio, "Quantifying the Value of U.S. Tariff Preferences," August 2006, 9, 28–29.
[510] Ibid., 14.
[511] WTO Tariff Analysis Online, http://tariffanalysis.wto.org (accessed January 22, 2014). As noted earlier, MFN status is also called normal trade relations (NTR) in the United States.
[512] AGOA preferences were valued at less than 2 percent of the value of total exports to the United States for Angola, Burkina Faso, Benin, Cameroon, Djibouti, Chad, Congo, the Democratic Republic of the Congo, Ethiopia, Gabon, Gambia, Ghana, Guinea, Guinea-Bissau, Mali, Mauritania, Niger, Nigeria, Rwanda, São Tomé and Príncipe, Senegal, Seychelles, Sierra Leone, South Africa, Tanzania, and Zambia. All but seven of these countries had previously been eligible for GSP-LDBDC preferences, so AGOA provided little additional benefit for them. For most of the seven that were not eligible for GSP-LDBDC benefits, their exports were concentrated in products that had zero or very low tariffs, such as oil or cocoa beans. For more information, see Brenton and Hoppe, "AGOA, Exports, and Development," August 2006, 15.
[513] The value of AGOA preferences exceeded 10 percent of the total value of exports to the United States for Cabo Verde, Kenya, Lesotho, Madagascar, Malawi, Mauritius, Mozambique, and Swaziland. For more information, see Brenton and Hoppe, "AGOA, Exports, and Development," August 2006, 15.
[514] Dean and Wainio, "Quantifying the Value of U.S. Tariff Preferences," August 2006, 21; Brenton and Ikezuki, "Initial and Potential Impact," April 2004, 23, 27.
[515] Keck and Lendle, "New Evidence on Preference Utilization," September 3, 2012, 27.
[516] Candau and Jean, "What Are EU Preferences Worth?" 2009, 77.
[517] Ibid., 81.
[518] Bureau, Chakir, and Gallezot, "The Utilization of Trade Preferences," 2007, 183.
[519] Programs listed in parentheses refer to certain country groups. For example, GSP (LDC, ACP) for the EU refers to the utilization rate of GSP and other overlapping programs for countries that also qualified for preferences under GSP-LDC and ACP preferences under Cotonou. For more information, see Keck and Lendle, "New Evidence on Preference Utilization," September 3, 2012, 27.
[520] Because many schemes are overlapping, beneficiary countries can utilize various preferential regimes. As a result, defining utilization rates in isolation can lead to misleading conclusions about overall scheme utilization. Here the authors define "utilization rate" by the "best regime" available to a particular beneficiary country, or the ratio of all preferential imports from a set of beneficiary countries over all eligible imports from that country from any preference regime. For AGOA, this would include imports under AGOA and GSP, and in some cases under GSP for LDBDCs. For more information, see Keck and Lendle, "New Evidence on Preference Utilization," September 3, 2012, 8.
[521] The gravity model of trade is a theoretical framework used to estimate bilateral trade flows between two partner countries on the premise that country pairs with certain characteristics will tend to trade more with each other. In these models, exports are expressed as a function of each partner's economic size (typically gross domestic product (GDP)) and the distance between the two countries. Other explanatory variables are commonly added, including the presence of a common language between trade partners, a colonial relationship, tariff levels, trade agreements, or a common border, just to name a few. For more information on gravity models, see Anderson, "The Gravity Model," December 2010, or Anderson and van Wincoop, "Gravity with Gravitas," January 2001.

[522] Trade intensification is sometimes referred to as trade growth on the "intensive margin," while trade diversification is sometimes referred to as trade growth on the "extensive margin." Both terms are used in the literature.
[523] The author used a gravity model in a dynamic panel setting.
[524] Nouve, "Estimating the Effects of AGOA," July 2005, 17–8.
[525] In this case, the dependent variable is exports of product x from beneficiary country i to the United States in year t.
[526] Lederman and Özden, "U.S. Trade Preferences," December 2004, 15.
[527] Karingi, Páez, and Degefa, "Report on a Survey," 2012, 8.
[528] Ibid., 9.
[529] Brenton and Hoppe, "AGOA, Exports, and Development," August 2006, 3–4.
[530] Zappile, "Nonreciprocal Trade Agreements and Trade," 2011, 61.
[531] The author used an ARIMA variation of the gravity model.
[532] Seyoum, "Export Performance of Developing Countries," 2007, 523.
[533] Tadesse and Fayissa, "Time Impact of AGOA on U.S. Imports," 2008, 933.
[534] Condon and Stern, "The Effectiveness of AGOA in Increasing Trade," March 2011, 17.
[535] Gravity models are designed to predict positive values of trade, but trade data commonly contains zeroes, especially at highly disaggregated product levels. Not accounting for these zero trade flows is referred to as a "censoring problem," and can substantially bias coefficients to the point that they can lead to unreliable conclusions. For this reason, the overall model must be modified in some way, or a particular estimator should be used that takes into account these products for which no trade occurs.
[536] Cipollina, Laborde, and Salvatici, "Do Preferential Trade Policies (Actually) Increase Exports?" August 2013, 5.
[537] A Tobit model is a type of model that censors a regression sample in cases where the dependent variable cannot be measured or observed. In this case, the sample is restricted to positive trade flows in order to analyze how much AGOA caused trade values to vary from their predicted values. This method also allowed the authors to estimate the likelihood that the dependent variable (trade) would change from zero to a positive value. For more information, see Kennedy, *A Guide to Econometrics*, 2003, 284.
[538] Tadesse and Fayissa, "The Impact of AGOA on U.S. Imports," 2008, 934–37.
[539] A difference-in-differences model is an econometric method employed to measure the impact of a certain treatment wherein the impact is measured by calculating the difference between a group that received the treatment and one that did not, before and after the treatment. In this case, the triple difference-in-differences refers to differences in time (pre- and post-AGOA), products (products granted preferences under AGOA and products not granted preferences under AGOA), and countries (AGOA beneficiary countries and non-AGOA beneficiary countries). For more information, see Kennedy, *A Guide to Econometrics*, 2003, 414–15.
[540] Frazer and Van Biesebroeck, "Trade Growth under AGOA," February 2010, 133, 135–36.
[541] Ibid., 137.
[542] Seyoum, "Export Performance of Developing Countries," 2007, 523, 525.
[543] Ibid., 527–28.
[544] Cooke, "The Impact of Trade Preferences," November 2011, 18.
[545] Ibid., 31, 43.
[546] Nouve, "Estimating the Effects of AGOA," July 2005, 19.
[547] Ibid.
[548] Tadesse and Fayissa, "The Impact of AGOA on U.S. Imports," 2008, 932–33.
[549] Ibid., 929–931.
[550] Frazer and Van Biesebroeck, "Trade Growth under AGOA," February 2010, 135.
[551] Ibid.
[552] Ibid., 141.
[553] Ibid.
[554] The two countries for which AGOA was correlated with a statistically significant negative affect on apparel exports were Côte d'Ivoire and Senegal. For more information, see Frazer and Van Biesebroeck, "Trade Growth under AGOA," February 2010, 138.
[555] Frazer and Van Biesebroeck, "Trade Growth under AGOA," February 2010, 138.
[556] Cooke, "The Impact of Trade Preferences," November 2011, 43–4; Tadesse and Fayissa, "The Impact of AGOA on U.S. Imports," 2008, 933; Seyoum, "Export Performance of Developing Countries," 2007, 523.
[557] The authors estimate various specifications of the model, but their preferred estimator is the fixed effects Tobit trimmed least absolute deviation (LAD). They also estimated the model using ordinary least squares (OLS), Tobit, Eaton and Tamura (ET)-Tobit, and Poisson Pseudo Maximum Likelihood (PPML).
[558] De Melo and Portugal-Perez, "Preferential Market Access Design," February 2013, 21.
[559] Brenton and Hoppe, "AGOA, Exports, and Development," August 2006, 8.
[560] Ibid.
[561] Nouve, "Estimating the Effects of AGOA," July 2005, 19.
[562] Frazer and Van Biesebroeck, "Trade Growth under AGOA," February 2010, 141.

[563] Ibid., 138.
[564] Nouve and Staatz, "Has AGOA Increased Agricultural Exports?" September 2003, 12–13.
[565] Ibid., 13.
[566] Frazer and Van Biesebroeck, "Trade Growth under AGOA," February 2010, 141.
[567] Ibid., 138.
[568] Ibid.
[569] Tadesse and Fayissa, "The Impact of AGOA on U.S. Imports," 2008, 933.
[570] Ibid., 935.
[571] Ofa et al., "Export Diversification," June 15, 2012, 5.
[572] Ibid., 15.
[573] Páez et al., "A Decade of African-US Trade," 2010, 4.
[574] Frazer and Van Biesebroeck, "Trade Growth under AGOA," February 2010, 135.
[575] Ibid.
[576] Frazer and Van Biesebroeck, "Trade Growth under AGOA," February 2010, 135–36.
[577] Ibid., 136.
[578] Because the estimation was done on a country-product pair basis, this result does not suggest that there were no exports of these products from any AGOA country before the program. Rather, they mean that in these product categories, some countries that had not previously exported these products began to export them after the program's implementation. See Tadesse and Fayissa, "The Impact of AGOA on U.S. Imports," 2008, 934–37.
[579] Tadesse and Fayissa, "The Impact of AGOA on U.S. Imports," 2008, 934–37.
[580] De Melo and Portugal-Perez, "Preferential Market Access Design," February 2013, 20.
[581] Ibid., 21.
[582] Brenton and Hoppe, "AGOA, Exports, and Development," August 2006, 6–7.
[583] Karingi, Páez, and Degefa, "Report on a Survey," 2012, 12.
[584] Ibid., 13.
[585] Brenton and Hoppe, "AGOA, Exports, and Development," August 2006, 11-2.
[586] Some of those schemes outside of GSP are now defunct, including ACP preferences granted by the EU. Aside from those listed here, the remaining national schemes notified to UNCTAD include those of Belarus, Bulgaria, Estonia, New Zealand, Norway, Russia, Switzerland, and Turkey. http://unctad.org/en/Pages/DITC/GSP/About- GSP.aspx.
[587] In 2012, the EU remained the largest export destination for sub-Saharan Africa ($118 billion), but China is not far behind ($98 billion). Since 2007, China's share of sub-Saharan Africa's total exports has nearly doubled, from 12 percent to 23 percent. See GTIS, GTA database (accessed March 4, 2014).
[588] Persson and Wilhelmsson, "Assessing the Effects of EU Trade," June 26, 2006, 18.
[589] Ibid., 16.
[590] The authors suggest that this negative relationship could be the result of rules of origin or other administrative requirements under EBA with which LDCs may have a hard time complying. This would in theory explain a negative relationship, as the tariffs under EBA were not different from previous ACP arrangements, but cumulation requirements were altered. For more information, see Gradeva and Martínez Zarzoso, "Trade as Aid," August 2009, 28–9.
[591] Gradeva and Martínez-Zarzoso, "Trade as Aid," August 2009, 26, 28, 30.
[592] Ibid., 30.
[593] Pishbahar and Huchet-Bourdon, "EU's Preferential Trade Agreements," 2008, 116–17.
[594] Ibid., 119.
[595] The authors estimated a gravity model using a Poisson Pseudo Maximum Likelihood (PPML) estimator, noting that the alternative log-linearized OLS model may be biased because it is not defined for zero trade flows, and that OLS estimates may be biased and inefficient in the presence of heteroskedasticity, even when controlling for fixed effects.
[596] Countries with bilateral FTAs at the time of the analysis included Chile, Mexico, and South Africa. The authors explain that this result is likely due to the composition of South African exports, which accounts for about half of all EU imports from these three countries. Most imports are of base metals and mechanical appliances, which already have a very low preferential margin. As further evidence, when the authors excluded South Africa from the grouping, the coefficient estimate for FTA partners became positive and significant. Other groups for which positive trade effects were found (aside from ACP LDCs and ACP non-LDCs) include the Association of Southeast Asian Nations (ASEAN), Latin America, LDC non-ACP economies, and Mediterranean economies. See Nilsson and Matsson, "Truths and Myths," April 2009, 17.
[597] The authors do not report estimates for the other explanatory variables. For further information, see Nilsson and Matsson, "Truths and Myths," April 2009, 19.
[598] The EU uses the Combined Nomenclature (CN) system, which is comprised of the HS nomenclature explained above in footnote 10 and further EU subdivisions. For more information, see http://ec.europa.eu/taxation_customs/customs/customs_duties/tariff_aspects/combined_nomenclature/index_e n.htm.
[599] Cirera, Foliano, and Gasiorek, "The Impact of GSP Preferences," 2011, 12–15.

[600] Ibid., 12, 21.
[601] Since this analysis was conducted, the EU has revised its rules of origin for apparel for LDCs and now only requires single transformation to confer origin, which is similar to the rules of origin under AGOA. However, this provision is only applicable to LDC beneficiaries, meaning that major apparel exporters such as Kenya and Mauritius are not eligible for these less restrictive rules of origin. For more information, see Naumann, "The EU GSP Rules of Origin," November 2011, 8–9.
[602] Cirera, Foliano, and Gasiorek, "The Impact of GSP Preferences," 2011, 12.
[603] The authors estimated the gravity model using a Poisson Pseudo Maximum Likelihood (PPML) estimator.
[604] Cipollina, Laborde, and Salvatici, "Do Preferential Trade Policies (Actually) Increase Exports?" August 2013, 5.
[605] Ibid., 18.
[606] Although the author uses the term "textiles," the section referred to in the text are HS chapters 50–63, which include textiles and apparel.
[607] Cipollina, Laborde, and Salvatici, "Do Preferential Trade Policies (Actually) Increase Exports?" August 2013, 18.
[608] Ibid.
[609] Ibid., 20, 28.
[610] Cipollina and Salvatici, "Trade Impact of European Union Preferences," 2011, 121.
[611] These products were selected based on three criteria: LDCs were important exporters of the product, tariffs on these products were positive under GSP, and the product did not display inter-year tariff variability. Products meeting the authors' conditions were cloves, vanilla beans, coffee, crustaceans, and molluscs.
[612] EBA went into effect in 2001, but the EU offered specific GSP-LDC preferences before that time.
[613] Aiello and Cardamone, "Analysing the Impact of EBA," 2011, 145–47.
[614] Ibid., 148–49.
[615] Cardamone, "Trade Impact of European Union Preferences," 2011, 166–67.
[616] Ibid., 168–69.
[617] The different estimators used included ordinary least squares (OLS), least squares dummy variable (LSDV), Pseudo Quasi Maximum Likelihood (PQML), Negative Binomial Regression (NBR), and Zero Inflated Poisson (ZIP) regressions.
[618] Aiello and Demaria, "Do Preferential Agreements Enhance the Exports?" January 2010, 24.
[619] Ibid., 25.
[620] Co and Dimova, "Preferential Market Access into the Chinese Market," October 2013, 10–11, 25, 27.
[621] Fixed-effects settings control for unobserved, time-invariant characteristics of individual observations (such as one country's ability to do business more efficiently than another country), on the assumption that an individual effect is correlated with an explanatory variable. Random-effects models, in contrast, assume that these individual effects are not correlated with explanatory variables, and are thus part of the error term. For more information, see Kennedy, *A Guide to Econometrics*, 2003, 303–7.
[622] Cipollina and Pietrovito, "Trade Impact of EU Preferential Policies," 2011, 102.
[623] Ibid.
[624] Cipollina and Pietrovito, "Trade Impact of EU Preferential Policies," 2011, 102–3.
[625] Ibid., 107.
[626] Brenton, "Integrating the Least Developed," April 2003, 19–20.
[627] As noted above, EU apparel rules of origin for LDCs have since been revised and now require only single transformation.
[628] Brenton, "Integrating the Least Developed," April 2003, 19–20.
[629] The Tobit model is a sample selection model described previously. A probit model estimates the probability of a certain outcome based on a given set of explanatory variables. In this case, the dependent variable is the probability of a positive trade flow in a given product. For more information, see Kennedy, *A Guide to Econometrics*, 2003, 259–61.
[630] Gamberoni, "Do Unilateral Preferences Help?" July 2007, 22.
[631] Because the data straddled the line between when EBA was implemented in 2001, the author refers to these preferences as "GSP-LDC."
[632] These represent the results from the "best available regime" regression. When preferences were not treated as exclusive, EBA was estimated to have a statistically significant negative effect on export diversification. The author attributes this difference to the fact that the EBA beneficiaries that also received ACP preferences tended to use ACP instead of EBA, likely due to either nontariff barriers, restrictive rules of origin, or high administrative costs associated with accessing EBA preferences. See Gamberoni, "Do Unilateral Preferences Help?" July 2007, 16–18.
[633] Gamberoni, "Do Unilateral Preferences Help?" July 2007, 16.
[634] Ibid., 20–21.
[635] Gamberoni, "Do Unilateral Preferences Help?" July 2007, 21.
[636] As noted above, EU apparel rules of origin for LDCs have since been revised and now require only single transformation.

[637] Gamberoni, "Do Unilateral Preferences Help?" July 2007, 21.
[638] The authors use a Heckman sample selection specification for their model.
[639] Cipollina and Salvatici, "Trade Impact of European Union Preferences," 2011, 120–22.
[640] These sectors included footwear; articles of stone or ceramics; precious stones or metals; base metals; machinery; optical or photographic equipment, medical or surgical instruments, clocks and watches; and miscellaneous manufactured articles. See Cipollina and Salvatici, "Trade Impact of European Union Preferences," 2011, 120.
[641] Cipollina and Salvatici, "Trade Impact of European Union Preferences," 2011, 122.
[642] The authors used a fixed effect Poisson Pseudo Maximum Likelihood (PPML) specification of the gravity model.
[643] Persson and Wilhelmsson, "EU Trade Preferences and Export Diversification," September 2013, 17–19.
[644] Ibid., 21.
[645] The authors used a zero-inflated Poisson (ZIP) specification of the gravity model.
[646] Although the authors do not provide results with respect to specific trade preference regimes, bilateral trade flows representing all preference regimes are included in the data set.
[647] Cipollina et al., "Do Preferential Trade Policies (Actually) Increase Exports?" September 2010, 16–18.
[648] Ibid.
[649] Cipollina et al., "Do Preferential Trade Policies (Actually) Increase Exports?" September 2010, 16.
[650] Ibid.
[651] Davies and Nilsson, "A Comparative Analysis of EU and US Trade," February 2013, 14.
[652] Ibid., 13–14.
[653] Nilsson, "Comparative Effects of EU and US," December 2005, 12–13.
[654] Ibid.
[655] Collier and Venables, "Rethinking Trade Preferences," May 2007, 5.
[656] This is similar to the triple difference-in-differences methodology, but adds an additional dimension. In this case, the four dimensions are the difference in import market total apparel demand between the United States and the EU, differences in exporter relationship to the import market between the United States and the EU (including distance), differences in time (pre- and post-preferences), and differences in product (in this case, apparel relative to textiles).
[657] Collier and Venables, "Rethinking Trade Preferences," May 2007, 17–19.
[658] Ibid., 20.
[659] As noted above, EU apparel rules of origin for LDCs have since been revised and now require only single transformation.
[660] De Melo and Portugal-Perez, "Preferential Market Access Design," February 2013, 15, 21.
[661] As noted above, EU apparel rules of origin for LDCs have since been revised and now require only single transformation.
[662] Di Rubbo and Canali, "A Comparative Study of EU and US Trade Policies," August 2008, 7.
[663] Ibid., 8.
[664] Ibid.
[665] Bureau, Chakir, and Gallezot, "The Utilization of Trade Preferences," 2007, 191.
[666] Ibid., 194.
[667] Nicita and Rollo, "Tariff Preferences as a Determinant," 2013, 4.
[668] Cipollina et al., "Do Preferential Trade Policies (Actually) Increase Exports?" September 2010, 14.
[669] Ibid., 15.
[670] Cipollina et al., "Do Preferential Trade Policies (Actually) Increase Exports?" September 2010, 15.
[671] As noted above, EU apparel rules of origin for LDCs have since been revised and now require only single transformation.
[672] De Melo and Portugal-Perez, "Preferential Market Access Design," February 2013, 20.
[673] Ibid., 21.
[674] These data points are 2000–2001 averaged and 2010–11 averaged.
[675] Nicita and Rollo, "Tariff Preferences as a Determinant," 2013, 10, 16.
[676] Ibid., 16.
[677] Seyoum, "Export Performance of Developing Countries," 2007, 530.
[678] Ibid., 529.
[679] Brenton and Ikezuki, "Initial and Potential Impact," April 2004, 28–29.
[680] Tadesse and Fayissa, "Time Impact of AGOA on U.S. Imports," 2008, 939.
[681] Ibid.
[682] Frazer and Van Biesebroeck, "Trade Growth under AGOA," February 2010, 140.
[683] Nouve, "Estimating the Effects of AGOA," July 2005, 22–23.
[684] Condon and Stern, "The Effectiveness of AGOA in Increasing Trade," March 2011, 3.
[685] Brenton and Hoppe, "AGOA, Exports, and Development," August 2006, 12.
[686] Mevel et al., "AGOA: An Empirical Analysis," July 2013, 32.
[687] Ibid.

[688] Ibid.
[689] Páez et al., "A Decade of African-US Trade," 2010, 18–22.
[690] Páez et al., "A Decade of African-US Trade," 2010, 6. For more information, see Mattoo, Roy, and Subramanian, "The African Growth and Opportunity Act," 2003, 830.
[691] Páez et al., "A Decade of African-US Trade," 2010, 12.
[692] Karingi, Páez, and Degefa, "Report on a Survey," 2012, 20.
[693] Karingi, Páez, and Degefa, "Report on a Survey," 2012, 16–17.
[694] Karingi, Páez, and Degefa, "Report on a Survey," 2012, 20–23.
[695] Available online at http://edis.usitc.gov.
[696] Andriantiana Ulrich, minister of foreign affairs, Embassy of the Republic of Madagascar, written submission to the USITC, January 14, 2014.
[697] His Excellency, Somduth Soborun, ambassador of the Republic of Mauritius, USITC hearing transcript, 9–25, written submission, January 14, 2014, post-hearing submission to the USITC, January 16, 2014.
[698] Dr. Jose Luis Rocha, deputy minister of foreign trade, Republic of Cabo Verde, written submission, January 21, 2014.
[699] His Excellency, Girma Birru, ambassador of the Federal Democratic Republic of Ethiopia, USITC hearing transcript, 26–36, written submission, January 14, 2014.
[700] Her Excellency, Jean Kamau, charge d'affairs of the Republic of Kenya, USITC hearing transcript, 61–63.
[701] His Excellency, Abe Adefuye, ambassador and head of mission, Government of Nigeria, pre-hearing submission to the USITC, December 18, 2013.
[702] His Excellency, Ebrahim Rasool, ambassador of the Republic of South Africa, USTIC hearing transcript, 37–46, post-hearing submission, January 21, 2014.
[703] Government of South Africa, post-hearing submission, January 21, 2014.
[704] Paul Ryberg, president, African Coalition for Trade, USITC hearing transcript 220–229, written submission to the USITC, December 14, 2014.
[705] Jaswinder Bedi, chairman, African Cotton & Textile Industries Federation, USTIC hearing transcript 229–237.
[706] Ambassador Girma Birr of Ethiopia and Ambassador Somduth Soborun of Mauritius, joint written submission to the USITC, January 16, 2014.
[707] Stephen Lamar, executive vice president, American Apparel & Footwear Association, USITC hearing transcript 237–241.
[708] American Automotive Policy Council, written submission to the USITC.
[709] Thero Setiloane, chief executive officer, Business Leadership South Africa, written submission to the USITC, January 21, 2014.
[710] Paul Ryberg, CBI Sugar Group and Mauritius Sugar Syndicate, written submission, January 20, 2014.
[711] Members of the CBI Sugar Group include the sugar industries of Barbados, Belize, the Dominican Republic, Guyana, Jamaica, Panama, and Trinidad & Tobago.
[712] Peter Allgeier, president, Coalition of Services Industries, written submission, January 14, 2014, written submission, January 21, 2014.
[713] The Common Market for Eastern and Southern Africa, USITC hearing transcript 76–88, written submission to the USITC, January 14, 2014.
[714] John Cheh, vice chairman and CEO, Esquel Mauritius, written submission to the USITC, January 21, 2014.
[715] Katrin Kulhman, president, New Markets Lab, senior advisor, Corporate Council on Africa Trade Advisor, USITC hearing transcript, 89–99, written submission, January 14, 2014, post-hearing submission, January 21, 2014.
[716] Madelein Mkunu, CEO and president, Leading Women of Africa, written submission, January 21, 2014.
[717] Stephen Lande, president, Manchester Trade, USITC hearing transcript 99–115, written submission to the USITC, December 14, 2014.
[718] Buks Botes, marketing manager, Manganese Metal Company, Ltd, written submission, January 21, 2014.
[719] William Roenigk, senior consultant, National Chicken Council, USITC hearing transcript 241–250, written submission, December 17, 2013.
[720] Dan O'Flaherty, president, National Foreign Trade Council, USITC hearing transcript 138–146, written submission to the USITC, January 14, 2014.
[721] National Pork Producers Council, written submission to the USITC, January 22, 2014.
[722] Edward Gresser, director, Progressive Economy, USITC hearing transcript, 115–125, written submission to the USTIC, January 14, 2014.
[723] Rocky Mountain District Export Council, written submission to the USITC, January 20, 2014.
[724] Dr. Witney Schneidman, senior international advisor for Africa, Covington & Burling LLP and nonresident senior fellow, African Growth Initiative, Brookings, USITC hearing transcript, 212–220, and written submission, January 14, 2014.
[725] Scott Eisner, vice president, African Affairs, U.S. Chamber of Commerce, USITC hearing transcript, 125–138, written submission to the USIC, January 14, 2014.
[726] Julia Hughes, president, United States Fashion Industry Association, written submission, January 21, 2014.

[727] H. Michael Ligon, vice president, Universal Leaf Tobacco Co., written submission to the USITC, January 21, 2014.
[728] William Guyton, president, World Cocoa Foundation, written submission to the USITC, January 8, 2014.
[729] For detailed technical explanations of the analytical approach encompassing product space analysis and economic complexity, see Hidalgo and Hausmann, "The Building Blocks of Economic Complexity," June 30, 2009, 10570–75; Hidalgo et al., "The Product Space Conditions the Development of Nations," 2007; and Hausmann et al., *The Atlas of Economic Complexity*, 2011. Hausmann is a professor of economic development at Harvard Kennedy School's Center for International Development, and Hidalgo is an assistant professor at the Media Lab of the Massachusetts Institute of Technology (MIT).
[730] See below for additional information on standard data use and coverage, as well as the specific goods trade data sectors used for the information in this appendix.
[731] Hausmann and Hidalgo theorize that these results are explained by what they call productive knowledge or capabilities—the infrastructure, institutions, societal experience with similar production, and workers skilled in related types of production that are required to produce and then export new products. This productive knowledge goes beyond the traditional factors used by economists to explain production; i.e., capital and labor. Hausmann and Hidalgo theorize that a nation's base of productive knowledge must be expanded for the nation to move into production and export of new products.
[732] Bustos et al., "The Dynamics of Nestedness," April 2012.
[733] "Nearby" is a qualitative term to describe when two or more products require similar know-how to manufacture. If the unique productive knowledge (or capabilities) needed to make a specific good do not already exist in a country, it will prove highly difficult for the country to manufacture it. Instead, countries adapt existing capabilities to produce goods that require similar capabilities to ones already manufactured; these products are said to be nearby or in the adjacent possible. When a country has an abundance of nearby products, it has an easier path to capability acquisition, product diversification, and development. "Density," one of the metrics reflecting this concept, is defined below.
[734] Hidalgo and Hausmann, "The Building Blocks of Economic Complexity," June 30, 2009, 10570–75.
[735] "Product Complexity Index," one of the metrics reflecting this concept, is defined below.
[736] Hausmann et al., *The Atlas of Economic Complexity*, 2011.
[737] Hidalgo, *Discovering Southern and East Africa's Industrial Opportunities*, 2011, 3.
[738] Hausmann and Klinger, "Policies for Achieving Structural Transformation," 2009, 9.
[739] Ibid.
[740] In response to Commissioner Aranoff's question regarding expansion versus diversification and potentially competitive exports, Katrin Kuhlmann referred to this novel analytical approach, noting that "There's a model that a colleague of mine developed at MIT called the Observatory of Economic Complexity that looks at what countries are trading…." USITC, hearing transcript, January 14, 2014, 171 (testimony of Katrin Kuhlmann, president and founder, senior advisor, Corporate Council on Africa). For additional explanation of the use of product space analysis for export competitiveness assessment, see Reis and Farole, *Trade Competitiveness Diagnostic Toolkit*, 2012, 50–53.
[741] Government of Malawi, *National Export Strategy 2013–2018*, 2013, vol. 1, 7.
[742] Hidalgo, "Discovering Southern and East Africa's Industrial Opportunities," 2011.
[743] Ibid., 2–3.
[744] African Development Bank, "Comparative Study on Export Policies," 2012.
[745] Ibid., 6.
[746] MCC and Government of Liberia, "Liberia Constraints Analysis," September 2013, 114. Similar use was made of product space in a Tunisia study supported by the African Development Bank, the government of Tunisia, and the U.S. government (*Toward a New Economic Model for Tunisia*, 2013).
[747] Product space and complexity data (i.e., product density and product complexity metrics, as well as associated HTS 4-digit product labels) were sourced from the Observatory at Harvard Kennedy School Center for International Development (CID), based on analytical approaches initially developed by Hausmann and Hidalgo.
[748] Product labels have been developed by Growth Lab at the Harvard Center for International Development (The Observatory).
[749] For example, an uncompetitive product would be defined as having a revealed comparative advantage (RCA) measure of less than 5 percent. In particular, the RCA index measures a good's share in a country's total exports relative to that good's share in world trade. For a more detailed description of RCA, see USITC, *Export Opportunities and Barriers*, 2005, D-4.
[750] Most of the metrics are calculated using only countries that have reliable export data, exports of more than $1 billion, and population above 1.2 million.
[751] See discussion above on examples of the integrated use of product space and complexity analysis with other analytical tools by the African Development Bank, the MCC and the government of Liberia, and the government of Malawi to identify potentially competitive products.

[752] Whereas higher complexity values are associated with more complexity for a specific product, larger density values are associated with closer proximity (nearer) to a country's current export profile. The actual values have not been provided on the axes as the specific numbers are not intuitive, and the relative distance from current production capabilities and relative complexity is most useful for insight and potential policy analysis.
[753] Higher complexity values are associated with more complexity for a specific product. Larger density values are associated with closer proximity (nearer) to a country's current export profile.
[754] These broad economic development strategies include regional integration, export diversification to complement traditional export sectors, and production value addition (i.e., moving up the value chain).

INDEX

#

21st century, 216

A

accommodation, 118, 120
accountability, 109, 110, 252, 253
accounting, vii, 1, 10, 30, 50, 51, 105, 108, 117, 122, 124, 128, 221, 315
accreditation, 75
acid, 72
acquisitions, 23, 121, 122, 124, 131, 133, 135, 138, 139, 141, 143, 308
acrylic acid, 72, 73
ADC, 25, 88, 156, 160, 280, 307
adhesives, 72
adjustment, 219, 303
adults, 111
advocacy, 213
aerospace, 67
aflatoxin, 92
African economies, vii, 3, 173, 222
African Growth and Opportunity Act, v, vii, viii, 1, 2, 19, 21, 22, 26, 38, 82, 184, 186, 187, 188, 200, 273, 275, 277, 281, 284, 286, 287, 289, 290, 291, 293, 294, 296, 299, 300, 301, 310, 311, 319
age, 80, 280
agencies, 7, 14, 39, 77, 308
aggregation, 36, 37, 85, 163, 168, 228
agricultural exports, 37, 163, 170, 174, 176, 180, 184, 187, 188, 192, 194
agricultural market, 88
agricultural producers, 31, 305
agricultural sector, 72, 88, 153, 174, 176, 180, 192
agriculture, 7, 9, 15, 30, 36, 80, 83, 93, 94, 96, 120, 128, 132, 134, 135, 138, 139, 144, 148, 171, 177, 189, 192, 209, 221, 265, 266, 303

alcohols, 32
Algeria, 156, 261, 308
aluminium, 289
anchoring, 152
Angola, 8, 12, 16, 25, 28, 43, 50, 53, 54, 55, 60, 61, 62, 107, 109, 123, 124, 127, 128, 129, 130, 131, 132, 133, 139, 140, 143, 224, 229, 231, 232, 252, 254, 256, 259, 260, 262, 266, 267, 293, 301, 313, 314
animal husbandry, 94, 221
annual rate, 46, 107, 115, 125
annual review, 148
antidumping, 218
apparel industry(s), 22, 35, 45, 86, 120, 141, 142, 143, 144, 145, 207, 210, 215, 304
apparel products, 3, 4, 6, 15, 44, 45, 54, 62, 91, 163, 168, 169, 170, 172, 179, 181, 215, 231
apples, 92, 176, 178, 190
appraised value, 4, 44, 306
appropriations, 8
Argentina, 25, 150, 155, 157, 262, 306
ARM, 129
ASEAN, 316
Asia, 5, 19, 69, 80, 86, 102, 107, 112, 153, 302, 303, 304
Asian countries, 79, 120
asparagus, 105
assessment, 105, 167, 168, 183, 201, 202, 227, 273, 301, 320
assets, 115, 128, 275, 279, 296
Association of Southeast Asian Nations, 316
Austria, 25, 259, 260, 296
authority(s), 7, 84, 108, 218, 299
automobiles, 51, 81, 83, 129, 141, 158, 302
automotive sector, 118, 141, 144
awareness, 220

B

backlash, 140
Bahrain, 25, 156, 261
ban, 220
Bangladesh, 10, 143, 149, 157, 206, 295
banking, 117
banks, 118, 127
Barbados, 319
barriers, 6, 17, 24, 27, 33, 38, 41, 90, 96, 98, 102, 107, 112, 146, 149, 153, 160, 201, 208, 215, 219
barriers to entry, 17
base, 34, 51, 52, 56, 86, 89, 95, 117, 118, 227, 316, 318, 320
batteries, 70, 71
BEA, 22, 39, 121, 123, 124, 293, 308
beef, 44, 86, 102, 103, 104, 150, 159, 210, 275, 283, 306
Beijing, 283, 306
Belarus, 157, 316
Belgium, 25, 84, 105, 113, 259, 260, 279
benchmarking, 298
beneficial effect, 208
beneficiaries, vii, 2, 4, 6, 9, 14, 15, 33, 35, 37, 40, 55, 57, 60, 63, 68, 70, 101, 149, 163, 164, 165, 166, 170, 175, 178, 183, 184, 187, 193, 210, 211, 214, 217, 219, 300, 301, 317
beneficiary sub-Saharan African country, 41, 299, 300
benefits, vii, 1, 2, 3, 4, 5, 6, 8, 10, 11, 15, 35, 40, 42, 44, 69, 75, 80, 84, 85, 100, 101, 107, 146, 147, 148, 149, 150, 152, 153, 161, 164, 167, 170, 173, 183, 207, 213, 214, 215, 216, 218, 219, 220, 222, 223, 300, 314
beverages, 9, 37, 51, 52, 56, 78, 93, 115, 134, 135, 141, 168, 176, 186, 265, 266
bias, 168, 174, 177, 315
Bilateral, 157, 277
biofuel, 92
biomass, 130
BMI, 137, 276, 308, 309
bone, 306
Botswana, 6, 8, 10, 16, 22, 25, 31, 35, 41, 42, 43, 54, 78, 83, 84, 85, 102, 112, 114, 150, 155, 156, 159, 161, 172, 212, 224, 252, 254, 256, 257, 259, 260, 262, 275, 283, 290, 291, 296, 300, 303, 304, 306, 311, 312, 313, 314
brand image, 93
Brazil, 25, 27, 34, 39, 69, 106, 119, 128, 129, 130, 139, 150, 155, 157, 201, 221, 234, 259, 260, 274, 308, 309
breakdown, 50, 124, 132
Bulgaria, 25, 157, 262, 316

Burkina Faso, 16, 24, 32, 43, 54, 95, 110, 138, 224, 252, 254, 256, 257, 263, 314
Burundi, 16, 22, 24, 33, 43, 54, 96, 107, 112, 115, 144, 156, 160, 161, 224, 252, 254, 256, 258, 261, 263, 313
business environment, 21, 30, 82, 83, 109
businesses, 3, 7, 85, 88, 150, 152, 207, 220, 222
buyer(s), 63, 85, 86, 88, 211, 214, 215, 218

C

call centers, 143
Cambodia, 15, 206
Cameroon, 16, 24, 43, 51, 54, 60, 68, 123, 132, 139, 156, 157, 160, 161, 224, 229, 232, 233, 252, 254, 256, 257, 261, 262, 304, 313, 314
capacity building, 7, 8, 97, 102, 182, 183, 206, 207, 214, 215, 220, 221, 222
capital expenditure, 5, 309
capital flows, 117
capital goods, 143, 209
capital intensive, 209
capital markets, 150
carbides, 70
Caribbean, 17, 22, 23, 100, 107, 108, 113, 114, 146, 148, 150, 160, 165, 284, 295, 305, 311, 313
Caribbean nations, 100
cartel, 303
case study(s), 100, 102, 146, 147, 151, 175, 176, 303, 310
cashmere, 5, 45
casting, 71
catalyst, 70
category a, 58
CBP, 293, 300
CCA, 216
Central African Republic, 24, 34, 43, 117, 224, 253, 254, 256, 263
ceramic(s), 51, 264
certification, 81, 105, 207, 280
CFR, 202, 203, 278
Chad, 12, 16, 24, 43, 51, 54, 55, 107, 131, 224, 229, 233, 234, 253, 254, 256, 258, 263, 301, 313, 314
challenges, vii, 2, 10, 13, 14, 18, 87, 88, 89, 97, 106, 188, 207, 211, 217, 273
Chamber of Commerce, 204, 221, 274, 319
cheese, 94
chemical(s), 9, 29, 30, 32, 36, 49, 51, 52, 56, 70, 71, 72, 73, 96, 103, 127, 141, 159, 171, 172, 187, 218, 230, 302
Chicago, 290, 297
chicken, 86, 209

Chile, 35, 77, 103, 146, 148, 149, 152, 153, 154, 262, 274, 284, 285, 289, 295, 299, 310, 311, 312, 316
Chinese firms, 102, 131, 132
Chinese government, 131
chlorine, 70
CIA, 276, 303
city(s), 106, 212
citizens, 109, 110
civil service, 110
civil war, 109
clarity, 113
climate(s), viii, 21, 22, 27, 31, 33, 35, 38, 40, 106, 107, 109, 112, 144, 182, 201, 206, 220
clothing, 89, 134, 149, 182, 212, 220, 285, 291
CNN, 144, 277, 310
coal, 73, 90, 102, 119, 125, 128, 129, 133, 137, 141
coatings, 72, 73
cobalt, 129
cocoa, 9, 10, 30, 32, 47, 55, 67, 68, 69, 78, 83, 84, 85, 86, 96, 168, 214, 223, 230, 298, 314
cocoa butter, 32, 96
coffee, 32, 88, 96, 132, 168, 169, 175, 186, 190, 214, 304, 317
collaboration, 87, 89, 140
Colombia, 100, 101, 154, 310, 311
combustion, 56
commerce, 19, 83, 306
commercial, 5, 13, 33, 45, 95, 101, 103, 104, 105, 124, 139, 141, 153, 212, 300
commercial ties, 33, 101, 103, 104, 105
commodity, 131, 176, 280, 286, 289, 290
Common Market, 22, 23, 24, 25, 39, 88, 155, 156, 159, 204, 214, 277, 313, 319
communication, 118, 182, 214, 302
community(s), 92, 98, 113, 217, 219
community support, 219
comparative advantage, 23, 79, 96, 175, 179, 182, 209, 303, 320
comparative analysis, 193
competition, 7, 9, 69, 152, 179, 311
competition policy, 7
competitive advantage, vii, 1, 9, 14, 15, 29, 89, 215
competitive need limitations, 4, 44, 151
competitiveness, 10, 11, 27, 31, 38, 75, 81, 83, 85, 91, 96, 100, 107, 113, 114, 115, 183, 200, 218, 230, 291, 298
competitors, 87, 152, 175, 191, 218, 221
complement, 91, 216, 221, 321
complexity, 226, 227, 228, 229, 230, 231, 232, 233, 234, 235, 236, 237, 238, 239, 240, 241, 242, 243, 244, 245, 246, 247, 248, 249, 250, 251, 252, 320, 321

compliance, 35, 79, 149, 175, 183
composites, 112
composition, 12, 316
compounds, 70, 103
computer, 128, 135, 265
conception, 29, 78
conference, 287
conflict, 183
Congo, 12, 16, 43, 53, 54, 117, 131, 224, 225, 235, 252, 254, 256, 261, 262, 263, 266, 267, 301, 314
Congress, vii, 1, 2, 4, 6, 7, 8, 10, 13, 17, 18, 26, 27, 38, 42, 206, 210, 211, 217, 219, 223, 279
constant prices, 312
construction, 66, 67, 105, 110, 111, 128, 130, 136, 159, 230, 254, 255, 266, 307
consulting, 90
consumer goods, 70, 181
consumer markets, 144
consumers, 13, 71, 100, 134, 201, 223
consumption, 9, 10, 11, 12, 17, 29, 48, 67, 71, 77, 78, 82, 88, 103, 212, 224, 225
Continental, 286, 296
contract enforcement, 79, 88, 110
convention, 306
cooking, 92
cooperation, 102, 154, 155, 157
coordination, 21, 30, 81, 83, 84, 89
copper, 32, 96, 103, 129, 133, 139, 153, 218, 230, 280, 312
corruption, 41, 83, 109, 110, 149, 252, 253
cosmetic(s), 32, 92, 95, 269
cost, 4, 5, 22, 29, 31, 44, 63, 73, 79, 81, 83, 84, 86, 87, 91, 92, 94, 96, 97, 100, 104, 106, 110, 150, 180, 182, 207, 209, 214, 303, 306
Costa Rica, 310
Côte d'Ivoire, 24, 67, 68, 69, 85, 88, 139, 143, 156, 160, 161, 229, 234, 235, 257, 259, 260, 262, 314, 315
Cotonou Agreement, 160
cotton, 32, 51, 62, 78, 88, 89, 92, 93, 96, 97, 104, 105, 106, 142, 172, 187, 210, 214, 215, 230, 307
country of origin, 93
covering, 154, 163, 190, 200
criticism, 216
Croatia, 25
crop(s), 32, 88, 92, 93, 94, 97, 304
crude oil, 8, 12, 137, 167, 186
Cuba, 261
cultivation, 92, 93, 94, 139
culture, 31, 94, 95
Customs and Border Protection, 293, 301
Customs Union, 4, 23, 25, 36, 86, 103, 142, 146, 155, 156, 158, 286, 313

Cyprus, 25, 149, 261
Czech Republic, 25, 157, 261

D

data analysis, 170, 172, 184, 185, 186, 189
data set, 318
database, 34, 39, 64, 75, 77, 104, 116, 119, 121, 122, 125, 126, 127, 128, 129, 130, 134, 135, 136, 138, 140, 142, 259, 262, 263, 264, 265, 266, 267, 268, 275, 280, 281, 282, 293, 295, 297, 298, 306, 307, 308, 309, 310, 312, 316
deficit, 151
Delta, 86, 267, 290, 303, 304
Denmark, 25, 259, 260
density values, 321
Department of Agriculture, 290
Department of Commerce, 8, 18
Department of Energy, 62, 293, 301
Department of Homeland Security, 293
dependent variable, 315, 317
deposits, 71, 139
depreciation, 144
depression, 213
deregulation, 77
devaluation, 151
developed countries, 3, 4, 5, 12, 15, 17, 40, 41, 42, 45, 80, 139, 143, 146, 147, 149, 150, 160, 165, 174, 187, 189, 226, 310, 311
developed nations, 150
developing countries, vii, 1, 3, 27, 30, 39, 40, 42, 44, 47, 79, 80, 81, 82, 87, 102, 114, 146, 147, 150, 152, 163, 165, 177, 180, 182, 184, 185, 186, 189, 191, 192, 194, 195, 201, 213, 216, 219, 227, 301, 310, 311, 314
development assistance, 3, 14, 174, 190
development banks, 139
deviation, 315
DHS, 293
dialogues, 220
diamonds, 31, 32, 47, 78, 84, 85, 93, 96, 118, 303
dichotomy, 164
diesel engines, 212
diesel fuel, 60
differentiated products, 105
direct cost(s), 4, 44, 306
direct investment, 124, 125
disclosure, 111, 123
dislocation, 214
distillation, 61
distortions, 149
distribution, 18, 86, 95, 135, 212, 215, 265, 302

diversification, 22, 27, 36, 37, 39, 91, 96, 151, 163, 166, 171, 172, 177, 178, 181, 188, 189, 193, 201, 228, 315, 317, 320, 321
diversity, 94, 172, 228
DOC, 64, 288
Doha, 15
domestic demand, 50, 51, 65, 71
domestic economy, 80
domestic industry, 80
domestic investment, 112
domestic markets, 88
domestic resources, 152
dominance, 95, 213
Dominican Republic, 22, 164, 213, 310, 319
donors, 214
draft, 113
drawing, 113
drying, 95
dumping, 209, 218
duty free, 42, 44, 46, 47, 55, 74, 102, 141, 142, 146, 148, 158, 223, 306
duty-free, vii, 1, 2, 3, 4, 5, 6, 8, 10, 12, 14, 15, 17, 19, 22, 33, 40, 42, 44, 45, 46, 47, 59, 63, 76, 77, 86, 93, 101, 102, 103, 147, 150, 158, 159, 160, 163, 168, 182, 183, 201, 207, 210, 213, 214, 215, 216, 217, 218, 270, 300, 301
duty-free access, 3, 15, 33, 45, 86, 93, 101, 103, 150, 159, 216
duty-free treatment, vii, 1, 3, 4, 5, 6, 8, 10, 12, 14, 40, 44, 45, 47, 76, 101, 103, 147, 158, 201, 210, 218, 301
dyes, 72

E

earnings, 118, 178, 189, 310
East Asia, 101, 108, 114
Economic and Monetary Union, 157
economic assistance, 219
economic competitiveness, 214
economic cooperation, 7, 208
economic development, vii, 1, 3, 5, 10, 13, 14, 22, 29, 61, 80, 91, 98, 108, 146, 148, 152, 160, 211, 226, 227, 228, 230, 231, 320, 321
economic downturn, 50
economic empowerment, 216, 227
economic growth, 2, 3, 13, 42, 80, 85, 108, 139, 152, 155, 207, 208, 214, 216, 223, 310
economic integration, 14, 112, 183, 209, 223
economic landscape, 13
Economic Partnership Agreements, viii, 2, 156, 160
economic performance, 107
economic policy, 210

economic problem, 142
economic reform(s), 35, 152
economic relations, vii, 1, 13, 212, 220
Economic Research Service, 283
economics, 281, 287, 289
economies of scale, 59, 90, 92, 94
Ecuador, 100
education, 114, 215, 257, 258
educational system, 152
effective visa system, 42
egg, 218
Egypt, 24, 25, 102, 103, 156, 157, 227, 259, 260, 308
El Salvador, 310
electricity, 14, 32, 65, 85, 89, 90, 91, 96, 110, 254, 255, 265, 307
eligibility criteria, vii, 1, 3, 6, 13, 14, 22, 35, 41, 144, 149
eligible countries, 6, 17, 28, 29, 30, 42, 48, 49, 53, 56, 61, 64, 74, 76, 96, 99, 103, 106, 163, 164, 166, 183, 207, 210, 211, 212, 214, 219, 222, 225, 228, 229, 230, 300, 301
embargo, 61, 301
emergency, 274
emerging markets, 14, 50
employment, 10, 29, 80, 84, 97, 98, 118, 183
employment opportunities, 84
Enabling Clause, 311
endowments, 152, 229
energy, vii, 1, 8, 9, 10, 11, 19, 29, 31, 36, 49, 61, 65, 70, 81, 82, 83, 93, 96, 97, 125, 128, 140, 143, 144, 150, 168, 171, 186, 188, 207, 208, 209, 221, 264, 290
energy supply, 93
enforcement, 42, 109
engineering, 302
entrepreneurs, 220
environment(s), 7, 33, 81, 82, 92, 107, 108, 109, 110, 112, 113, 131, 145, 148, 152, 222, 227, 229, 290
environmental protection, 140
EPA(s), viii, 2, 14, 23, 36, 103, 146, 157, 160, 161, 162, 208, 211, 216, 221, 275, 279, 280, 285, 287, 290, 310, 313
Equatorial Guinea, 16, 24, 43, 107, 116, 117, 253, 254, 256, 263, 308
equilibrium, 22, 98
equipment, 21, 28, 29, 49, 50, 52, 53, 66, 85, 90, 122, 125, 130, 136, 141, 143, 159, 265, 266, 267, 268, 269, 302, 318
equity, 268, 308
Eritrea, 16, 24, 33, 43, 107, 139, 164, 224, 253, 254, 256, 261, 263, 313
erosion, 101, 150, 311
Estonia, 25, 262, 316

ethanol, 92
EU enlargement, 173
Europe, 19, 97, 100, 101, 106, 118, 120, 143, 153, 168, 170, 275, 285, 290
European Commission, 36, 161, 179, 278, 280, 288, 305
European Community, 22, 24, 156, 157, 158, 160, 268, 269, 270, 271, 272, 284, 287, 312, 313
European firms, viii, 2, 105
European market, 104, 105, 120
European Parliament, 280, 311, 313
European Union, viii, 2, 10, 14, 23, 25, 38, 79, 103, 106, 125, 162, 190, 191, 192, 273, 276, 277, 281, 287, 289, 292, 297, 307, 317, 318
evidence, 36, 82, 85, 167, 168, 169, 172, 184, 187, 188, 316
evolution, 2, 226, 291, 311
exchange rate, 79
executive branch, 7
exercise, 7, 85
expanded trade, 223
expertise, 90, 92, 128, 279
exploitation, 221
export competitiveness, 90, 215, 227, 320
export control, 207
export market, 76, 77, 96, 103, 105, 118, 172, 218
exporter(s), 6, 8, 9, 10, 11, 12, 15, 33, 47, 59, 64, 71, 75, 76, 77, 78, 85, 89, 100, 102, 103, 104, 105, 153, 154, 161, 170, 180, 188, 207, 215, 219, 223, 227, 301, 317, 318
export-led growth, vii, 1
extraction, 34, 92, 119, 120, 125, 128, 130, 131, 133, 136, 137, 138, 302, 309

F

factories, 63, 106, 143
farmers, 85, 88, 92, 94, 95, 207, 211, 223
farms, 92, 101, 105
FAS, 75, 77, 292, 304
fat, 97
FDI inflow, 22, 33, 34, 35, 112, 114, 115, 116, 117, 119, 120, 121, 123, 124, 125, 144, 145, 153, 266, 308
Federal Register, 39, 40, 44, 199, 299
feedstock(s), 60, 61, 67, 73
fertilizers, 154
fiber(s), 87, 94, 95
financial, 7, 33, 83, 108, 114, 115, 118, 124, 127, 128, 132-135, 139, 143, 151, 215, 302, 308
financial crisis, 151
financial incentives, 143
financial sector, 124

Finland, 25, 259, 260, 287
fires, 61, 92
fish, 32, 33, 88, 91, 93, 96, 99, 100, 101, 104, 153, 154, 207, 209, 211, 229, 230, 272, 304, 307
fisheries, 32, 96, 97, 160, 271, 304
fishing, 93, 104, 118, 120, 210
flat goods, 42
flexibility, 182
flights, 100, 106
flour, 88, 94, 304
flowers, 32, 33, 54, 91, 93, 94, 95, 96, 99, 100, 101, 230, 271
folklore, 5, 45
folklore articles, 5, 45
food, 9, 15, 67, 88, 93, 98, 102, 115, 120, 125, 128, 134, 135, 141, 164, 176, 184, 194, 270, 271, 275, 279
food industry, 176
food products, 98, 164, 194, 270
food safety, 15, 102
food services, 120
footwear, 4, 29, 32, 34, 42, 49, 91, 96, 100, 132, 141, 175, 181, 191, 210, 212, 228, 230, 318
force, 27, 36, 39, 147, 150, 153, 155, 156, 159, 162, 209, 268, 269, 270, 271, 272, 285, 302, 303, 313
Ford, 59, 118, 212
foreign affairs, 319
foreign aid, 117, 139, 140, 215
foreign assistance, 117
foreign direct investment, 13, 22, 23, 33, 37, 39, 77, 103, 106, 151, 182, 303
foreign exchange, 112
foreign firms, 80, 85, 121
foreign investment, 27, 38, 83, 106, 107, 113, 117, 118, 135, 140, 143, 151, 201
foreign policy, 6, 41
France, 15, 25, 34, 101, 105, 106, 114, 119, 120, 127, 128, 258, 259, 265, 266, 273
free trade, 3, 5, 23, 35, 98, 103, 145, 148, 152, 153, 154, 159, 164, 211, 213, 219
freedom, 27, 38, 110, 256, 257, 283
fruits, 9, 32, 76, 88, 94, 96, 153, 158, 168, 176, 186, 217, 230, 304
full capacity, 61
funding, 7, 8, 15, 18, 131, 139, 140
funds, 7, 8, 18, 124, 131
fungus, 92

G

Gabon, 12, 16, 24, 43, 51, 54, 55, 109, 123, 130, 133, 139, 164, 224, 229, 237, 238, 253, 254, 256, 257, 261, 262, 300, 301, 307, 314

GAO, 4, 13, 15, 18, 19, 219
GDP per capita, 108
General Agreement on Tariffs and Trade (GATT), 147, 151, 152, 311
General Agreement on Trade in Services (GATS), 158
General Motors, 118, 212
Generalized System of Preferences, vii, 1, 3, 6, 18, 23, 27, 38, 46, 163, 200, 281, 283, 290, 292, 295, 296, 300, 311, 312, 313
Germany, 25, 34, 106, 113, 117, 127, 258, 259, 265, 266
ginger, 230
global competition, 77
Global Competitiveness Report, 298, 308
global demand, 49, 50, 65, 67, 69, 75
global economy, 50, 208, 220, 223
global markets, 31, 87, 152, 155
global trade, 306
globalization, 303
goods and services, 27, 35, 39, 108, 112, 147, 148, 152, 160, 201
governance, 7, 33, 81, 83, 84, 107, 108, 109, 112, 209, 252, 285, 297
government procurement, 148
government revenues, 161
governments, 2, 6, 7, 39, 69, 78, 82, 87, 91, 102, 108, 115, 130, 220, 231
grades, 218
grading, 85
grants, 15, 102, 103, 221
gravity, 166, 167, 168, 169, 171, 173, 174, 175, 176, 177, 178, 179, 180, 185, 186, 188, 190, 191, 192, 193, 194, 311, 314, 315, 316, 317, 318
Greece, 25, 261
gross domestic product (GDP), 2, 3, 14, 16, 17, 23, 34, 80, 107, 108, 117, 134, 151, 152, 182, 303, 308, 312, 314
gross national product (GNP), 6, 42, 300
grouping, 227, 316
growth rate, 22, 56, 57, 80, 107, 108, 151, 152, 169, 312
Guatemala, 105, 310
guidance, 41
guidelines, 3, 118
Guinea, 16, 24, 43, 54, 128, 129, 130, 137, 139, 224, 253, 254, 256, 258, 262, 263, 293, 307, 313, 314
Guyana, 319

H

hair, 230
Haiti, 261

handbags, 32, 42, 89, 91, 93
harvesting, 97
health, 69, 75, 102, 114, 215
hemisphere, 103, 105
heteroskedasticity, 316
higher education, 83, 114
highways, 92
hiring, 140
history, 67, 173, 303
Honduras, 310
Hong Kong, 104, 149, 259, 260
hospitality, 144, 209
hotels, 144
household income, 97, 98
housing, 130, 209
human, 41, 81, 82, 83, 93, 149
human capital, 82, 83
human resources, 93
human right(s), 41, 149
Hungary, 25, 157, 261
hydrocarbons, 47, 128, 162
hydroelectric power, 133
hygiene, 311
hypothesis, 36, 177

I

Iceland, 24, 140, 155, 159, 261, 312
ID, 78
identification, 200, 201, 311
images, 277
IMF, 23, 39, 107, 284, 285, 302, 307
imitation, 93
impairments, 200
import sensitive, 3, 5, 15
improvements, 14, 33, 69, 79, 80, 96, 107, 109, 110, 111, 112, 140, 143, 144
incidence, 92
income, 44, 87, 97, 98, 108, 111, 146, 149, 150, 161, 179, 180, 194, 195, 221, 230, 291, 310
increased access, 150
independence, 110
India, 19, 27, 34, 39, 61, 83, 93, 102, 103, 106, 114, 119, 124, 129, 132, 133, 139, 140, 141, 143, 157, 201, 221, 258, 259, 267, 268, 285, 301, 306, 308
indigenous knowledge, 95
indirect effect, 35, 144
individuals, 200
Indonesia, 10, 69, 104, 106, 120, 139, 261
industrialization, 80, 98, 279, 303, 310
industrialized countries, 145, 164
inflation, 108, 114
informal sector, 80

infrastructure, 7, 14, 18, 21, 30, 31, 33, 34, 64, 81, 82, 83, 85, 87, 90, 93, 94, 96, 97, 100, 102, 105, 107, 113, 115, 118, 128, 129, 130, 131, 132, 133, 139, 140, 143, 144, 150, 183, 208, 209, 214, 215, 217, 220, 221, 228, 303, 320
ingredients, 32, 95
initiation, 171, 172, 182, 187
inspections, 311
institutions, 39, 80, 81, 90, 93, 94, 95, 108, 113, 114, 227, 320
integration, 14, 21, 27, 36, 38, 78, 82, 87, 89, 90, 98, 145, 155, 160, 200, 208, 209, 223, 231
intellectual property, 37, 79, 145, 147, 149, 155, 156, 182, 214, 222
intellectual property rights, 37, 79, 145, 149, 155, 156, 182
interest rates, 131
interference, 6
International Bank for Reconstruction and Development, 300
International Monetary Fund, 17, 23, 39, 284, 303
international standards, 149
international terrorism, 42
international trade, 179, 214, 219, 228, 313
internationally recognized worker rights, 41, 149, 311
intervention, 97
intra-regional trade, 14, 139, 208
investment capital, 112
investors, 2, 34, 35, 63, 105, 106, 108, 109, 110, 111, 112, 113, 114, 115, 117, 120, 122, 124, 125, 128, 130, 133, 134, 137, 139, 140, 141, 142, 143, 144, 145, 152, 206, 210, 211, 213, 217, 254, 255, 307, 308, 309
Iran, 61, 157, 261, 301
Iraq, 25, 156, 157
Ireland, 25, 258, 260
iron, 51, 64, 90, 102, 128, 129, 133, 137, 139, 158
irrigation, 92, 93
isolation, 314
Israel, 164, 259, 260
issues, vii, 2, 3, 7, 13, 14, 17, 87, 107, 118, 145, 147, 154, 155, 207, 214, 219, 230, 298, 311
Italy, 25, 114, 119, 258, 260

J

Jamaica, 319
Japan, 34, 79, 104, 114, 137, 140, 146, 173, 193, 258, 260, 306, 308
job creation, 98, 214, 216
joint ventures, 7
Jordan, 25, 156, 261

K

Kazakhstan, 157
kerosene, 60
Korea, 79, 103, 119, 137, 140, 146, 149, 157, 227, 260, 290
Kuwait, 25, 143, 149, 156, 259, 260

L

labor force, 17, 82, 130
labor market(s), 86, 113, 114, 152
labor shortage, 14
land acquisition, 139
languages, 103
Latin America, 23, 69, 107, 108, 113, 114, 152, 303, 316
Latvia, 25, 262
laws, 7, 35, 139, 148, 152
laws and regulations, 7
LDCs, 4, 5, 6, 12, 14, 15, 166, 167, 173, 174, 179, 183, 184, 185, 190, 193, 273, 278, 316, 317, 318
lead, 5, 79, 80, 84, 86, 88, 98, 100, 138, 148, 168, 174, 178, 181, 189, 212, 302, 309, 314, 315
leadership, 13, 88, 213, 221
Least Developed Countries, 19, 165, 275, 277
leather wearing apparel, 42
Lebanon, 25, 156, 260
legislation, vii, 2, 3, 6, 7, 8, 14, 19, 40, 113, 148, 149, 208, 213, 222, 223, 311
Lesotho, vii, 1, 10, 14, 16, 19, 22, 25, 28, 35, 43, 51, 53, 54, 55, 62, 86, 89, 141, 142, 144, 150, 155, 156, 160, 161, 224, 253, 255, 256, 257, 263, 273, 277, 285, 287, 304, 309, 310, 311, 312, 313, 314
lesser developed beneficiary countries, 200
liberalization, 155, 160, 162, 170, 182, 269, 272
Liberia, 16, 24, 43, 54, 109, 117, 123, 124, 137, 139, 140, 224, 227, 229, 240, 241, 252, 255, 256, 257, 262, 267, 308, 320
light, 14, 32, 33, 60, 87, 96, 212, 228, 303, 311
linear model, 193
liquefied natural gas, 32
liquidity, 144
Lithuania, 25, 261
livestock, 31, 88, 91, 94
living conditions, 305
loans, 102, 221
logistic services, 302
logistics, 79, 86, 87, 94, 215, 220
Louisiana, 73, 276
lubricants, 70, 71, 92
lubricating oil, 60
luggage, 42, 300
lying, 92

M

machinery, 29, 49, 59, 66, 85, 88, 136, 158, 217, 228, 267, 268, 269, 302, 318
macroeconomic environment, 83
magnitude, 181, 192
majority, 10, 15, 46, 51, 58, 62, 66, 74, 76, 83, 110, 116, 128, 135, 153, 159, 166, 167, 168, 172, 188, 303
Malaysia, 114, 120, 137, 139, 259, 260
management, 77, 79, 93, 94, 209, 302
manganese, 51, 70, 71, 217, 218
manufactured goods, vii, 2, 49, 83, 98, 151, 171, 226
market access, 17, 63, 81, 84, 102, 105, 106, 144, 145, 160, 161, 168, 181, 183, 188, 191, 193, 194, 207, 209, 215, 216, 220, 303, 304
market share, 63, 96
market-based economy, 41, 149
marketing, 75, 77, 79, 95, 97, 212, 309, 319
materials, 4, 44, 60, 79, 85, 89, 103, 176, 209, 306
matter, 200
Mauritania, 16, 43, 54, 103, 109, 138, 139, 164, 225, 229, 242, 243, 253, 255, 256, 257, 262, 293, 307, 313, 314
meat, 86, 98, 101, 218, 272
media, 110, 200, 282, 287, 291, 295, 296, 298
medical, 318
Mediterranean, 316
MEK, 72, 73, 276, 283
melting, 67
membership, 7, 35, 124, 151, 211, 216
Mercedes-Benz, 59
merchandise, 46, 306
mergers, 23, 122, 134, 135
meta-analysis, 173, 176, 177, 191
metallurgy, 64
metals, 21, 29, 31, 49, 50, 51, 52, 53, 56, 64, 70, 80, 90, 96, 128, 133, 135, 137, 269, 302, 308, 316, 318
meter, 291
methanol, 148
methodology, 36, 37, 113, 163, 178, 228, 305, 318
Mexico, 10, 25, 35, 79, 101, 103, 105, 146, 149, 151, 152, 261, 281, 306, 312, 316
Middle East, 93, 101, 141
mineral resources, 129
mission(s), 7, 220, 319
mobile telecommunication, 118, 133
modelling, 191
models, 186, 314, 315, 317

modernization, 215
modifications, 211, 216
Moldova, 261
mollusks, 272
momentum, 182
Mongolia, 261
Morocco, 25, 35, 146, 154, 156, 164, 227, 261, 274, 297, 308, 312
Mozambique, 8, 16, 25, 32, 34, 43, 54, 74, 89, 95, 97, 98, 112, 117, 123, 124, 127, 128, 129, 133, 137, 139, 140, 156, 160, 161, 212, 223, 225, 229, 244, 245, 253, 255, 256, 258, 261, 262, 267, 273, 292, 313, 314
Multilateral, 288
multilateralism, 19
multinational companies, 118, 143
multinational corporations, 90, 219, 220
multinational firms, 131
multiplier, 97, 98
multiplier effect, 97, 98

N

NAFTA, 23, 25, 35, 79, 101, 103, 105, 146, 148, 151, 152, 213, 281, 285, 297, 311, 312
Namibia, 6, 16, 25, 41, 42, 43, 54, 102, 103, 112, 132, 133, 142, 155, 156, 157, 159, 161, 212, 225, 253, 255, 256, 257, 261, 262, 275, 293, 300, 303, 306, 307, 312, 313, 314
national income, 108
national product, 42, 95
national security, 6, 41, 203
natural gas, 32, 34, 96, 119, 122, 125, 128, 129, 133, 136, 137, 138, 266, 268
natural resources, 2, 8, 21, 29, 34, 49, 78, 87, 90, 102, 115, 118, 133, 136, 140, 151, 226
negative effects, 113
negative relation, 37, 190, 316
negotiating, 26, 38, 146, 149, 160, 161, 162
negotiation, 27, 39, 40, 152, 157, 160, 201, 211
Netherlands, 25, 114, 119, 120, 128, 143, 157, 258, 260, 265, 266
New Zealand, 103, 150, 154, 261, 306, 316
Nicaragua, 310
niche market, 97
nickel, 138
nitrogen, 70
nontariff barriers, 26, 38, 112, 147, 175, 176, 317
North Africa, 36, 120, 131, 154, 308
North America, 23, 25, 35, 79, 101, 146, 152, 153, 212
North American Free Trade Agreement, 23, 25, 35, 79, 101, 146

Norway, 24, 102, 103, 114, 119, 150, 155, 159, 193, 259, 260, 299, 311, 312, 316

O

Obama, 2, 18, 19, 217, 283, 308
Obama Administration, 2, 19, 217
obstacles, 22, 26, 38, 89, 150
octane, 51
OECD, 23, 30, 39, 80, 81, 82, 131, 139, 152, 153, 154, 274, 281, 288, 289, 302, 308, 312
officials, 3, 13, 18, 149
oil, vii, 1, 6, 8, 9, 10, 12, 19, 54, 80, 83, 90, 92, 119, 120, 125, 128, 130, 132, 133, 136, 137, 138, 139, 172, 182, 209, 213, 214, 266, 268, 314
open economy, 120
openness, 112, 192, 256
operating costs, 109
operations, 44, 85, 86, 109, 112, 118, 129, 130, 203, 219, 304, 306
opportunities, 22, 82, 88, 89, 91, 96, 98, 107, 112, 118, 128, 140, 141, 144, 183, 188, 208, 216, 220, 227, 228, 229, 273
ores, 102, 103, 168, 306, 312
organic chemicals, 30, 56, 72, 73, 301
organic solvents, 73
Organization for Economic Cooperation and Development, 281
Organization of American States, 289
organize, 95
outsourcing, 80, 118, 143
overlap, 18, 180, 231
Overseas Private Investment Corporation, 7
ownership, 139, 143
oxygen, 70

P

Pacific, 22, 107, 108, 112, 150, 154, 160, 165, 274, 284, 305, 313
paints, 72, 73, 92
Pakistan, 157, 261
Palestinian Authority, 25, 156
palm oil, 120, 139
Panama, 319
Paraguay, 25, 150, 155
parallel, 271
Parliament, 282, 313
participants, 79, 104, 214, 299
penalties, 154
per capita income, 29
percentile, 109, 112

performers, 33, 109, 110
permit, 93, 110
Peru, 77, 103, 105, 283, 307, 310
pests, 85, 105
petroleum, 21, 23, 27, 28, 29, 30, 31, 32, 33, 34, 38, 46, 47, 49, 50, 51, 52, 53, 54, 55, 56, 57, 60, 61, 62, 73, 96, 98, 99, 106, 120, 124, 125, 128, 130, 133, 136, 137, 141, 165, 168, 187, 200, 202, 213, 224, 225, 288, 301, 302
pharmaceutical(s), 32, 72, 80, 95, 159, 171, 187
Philippines, 79, 106, 213, 261
phosphates, 129
physical properties, 64
pipeline, 133, 137
plants, 73, 85, 230
plastics, 32, 36, 72, 93, 134, 168, 169, 171, 172, 178, 186, 187, 265, 266, 268, 269
platform, 124, 144
platinum, 31, 47, 90
pleasure, 56
Poland, 25, 157, 262
police, 110
policy, 2, 7, 8, 14, 19, 26, 30, 35, 38, 81, 85, 89, 107, 109, 110, 112, 113, 118, 152, 167, 173, 179, 180, 193, 194, 195, 208, 209, 211, 212, 213, 216, 220, 222, 227, 229, 256, 280, 281, 295, 303, 305, 321
policy issues, 7
policymakers, 2, 182, 183, 216
political instability, 209
political system, 109
pollution, 73
polymers, 90
population, 120, 303, 320
port of entry, 77, 306
portfolio, 153
Portugal, 25, 34, 114, 127, 170, 172, 179, 181, 188, 193, 258, 259, 278, 315, 316, 318
positive relationship, 190
poultry, 132, 209, 218
poverty, 6, 41, 98, 149, 160, 211, 214, 220, 305, 310
poverty reduction, 6, 41, 149
power generation, 60, 125
predictability, 161, 207, 211, 222
preferential treatment, 5, 11, 19, 42, 45, 47, 148, 300, 311
preparation, 85
president, 4, 6, 7, 8, 13, 17, 18, 19, 26, 38, 40, 41, 42, 45, 148, 149, 204, 205, 207, 210, 213, 216, 217, 222, 295, 299, 311, 319, 320
President Clinton, 7, 26, 38, 42
President Obama, 6, 13, 17, 19, 41, 149, 207
price changes, 179
price competition, 179

primary products, 37, 78, 171, 176, 191
principles, 154
private investment, 91
private sector, 2, 7, 26, 38, 81, 83, 84, 85, 95, 110, 130, 167, 172, 188, 210, 215, 219
private sector investment, 2, 95
privatization, 152, 303
probability, 37, 153, 172, 177, 181, 188, 192, 193, 194, 226, 317
probit models, 194
procurement, 130
producers, vii, 1, 5, 10, 14, 15, 65, 69, 71, 77, 78, 85, 87, 88, 89, 97, 98, 100, 101, 102, 105, 106, 120, 159, 183, 209, 210, 211, 215, 217, 218, 219, 222, 223
product coverage, 17, 18, 164
product design, 79, 86
production costs, 67
production function, 81, 302
production networks, 29, 78, 89, 183, 302
professionals, 215
profit, 110, 111, 210, 220
project, 97, 109, 122, 129, 130, 131, 137, 139, 140, 220, 289, 302
property rights, 110
protection, 6, 33, 37, 41, 79, 107, 111, 113, 147, 149, 158, 182, 214, 292
public health, 221
public policy, 212
public sector, 21, 30, 83, 109
public service, 110
publishing, 13
pulp, 94

Q

quality assurance, 85
quality control, 75, 85
quality improvement, 75
quality standards, 153, 176
questioning, 164
quota free, 310
quotas, 4, 15, 35, 44, 63, 86, 101, 148, 206, 214, 223, 270, 271, 301, 306

R

raw materials, 21, 29, 31, 33, 78, 79, 80, 82, 85, 91, 92, 94, 95, 102, 103, 162, 171, 226, 304
reading, 229
real estate, 117, 118, 120, 135
real terms, 151, 152

reallocation of resources, 170
recession, 28, 46, 47
reciprocity, 219
recognition, 69, 154
recommendations, 13, 37, 162, 163, 182, 183, 207, 208, 210, 212, 222, 227
recovery, 152
recycling, 265, 266
refinery capacity, 60
reform(s), 14, 35, 145, 150, 151, 152, 161, 180, 183, 213, 216, 281
regional cooperation, 87, 160, 162
regional fabric, 41
regional integration, 14, 22, 26, 36, 38, 88, 91, 96, 98, 115, 160, 201, 208, 211, 214, 216, 221, 304, 321
regions of the world, 83
regression, 23, 174, 180, 181, 185, 187, 190, 191, 315, 317
regression analysis, 23, 190
regression model, 181
regulations, 94, 100, 102, 103, 109, 110, 112, 115, 158, 183, 216, 228, 279
regulatory agencies, 154
regulatory framework, 92, 113
relevance, 17, 189, 208
reliability, 100, 105
renewable energy, 34, 133
repair, 229
Republic of the Congo, 24, 25, 34, 54, 55, 102, 103, 106, 109, 117, 129, 130, 131, 132, 133, 139, 143, 157, 229, 235, 236, 313, 314
reputation, 105
requirements, 3, 4, 6, 31, 33, 40, 41, 42, 44, 45, 47, 81, 92, 93, 94, 102, 105, 149, 151, 154, 175, 182, 183, 189, 202, 203, 208, 219, 222, 300, 302, 311, 316
researchers, 78, 87, 226, 227, 228, 230
residues, 176
resins, 70, 71
resistance, 216
resources, 34, 35, 73, 78, 89, 90, 93, 94, 95, 102, 106, 108, 116, 133, 139, 140, 150, 161, 172, 287
response, 39, 46, 50, 87, 89, 113, 148, 215, 299, 320
restrictions, 5, 33, 65, 102, 112, 131, 149, 159, 175, 301
restructuring, 7, 35, 150, 152
retail, 79, 84, 86, 88, 106, 118, 130, 132, 135, 265, 266, 309
revenue, 139, 161
rights, 111, 113, 131, 147, 149, 154, 302
risk(s), 69, 79, 85, 92, 102, 105, 107, 109, 144, 153, 211, 213, 218

risk management, 85
rods, 218
Romania, 25, 157, 261
roots, 88
routes, 100, 105
rubber(s), 32, 47, 71, 72, 96, 134, 168, 265, 266, 302
rule of law, 6, 37, 41, 109, 113, 149, 182
rule of origin, 63, 210
rural areas, 303
Russia, 71, 76, 104, 138, 146, 157, 193, 258, 260, 316
Rwanda, 17, 24, 32, 33, 43, 54, 91, 95, 98, 107, 109, 110, 112, 114, 137, 143, 144, 156, 160, 161, 225, 252, 255, 256, 257, 261, 262, 282, 286, 303, 313, 314

S

sabotage, 61
safety, 102, 149, 150, 215
sales activities, 79
Saudi Arabia, 25, 156, 259, 260
scale economies, 31, 94
scaling, 216
school, 221
science, 98, 226, 289
scope, 18, 35, 145, 148
seafood, 32, 93
Secretary of Commerce, 45
security, 160
seed, 92
semiconductors, 80
Senate, 17, 18
Serbia, 261
service industries, 88
services, 7, 21, 30, 33, 34, 79, 81, 82, 83, 85, 90, 91, 93, 106, 108, 109, 115, 118, 124, 125, 127, 128, 130, 132, 133, 134, 135, 136, 137, 143, 154, 158, 160, 213, 214, 215, 216, 229, 263, 265, 267, 268, 302, 308
Seychelles, 17, 24, 25, 43, 54, 104, 107, 114, 156, 157, 161, 225, 253, 255, 256, 257, 263, 300, 313, 314
shape, 100
sheep, 270
shellfish, 104, 307
shortage, 89, 90
showing, 139
shrimp, 32, 96
Sierra Leone, 17, 24, 33, 43, 54, 107, 110, 137, 139, 144, 164, 225, 252, 255, 256, 258, 262, 314
signs, 112
silicon, 70, 71, 72, 297

silicones, 71
silver, 138
simulation(s), 183, 212
Singapore, 79, 139, 149, 154, 164, 259, 260
Slovakia, 25, 261
small businesses, 216
small firms, 173, 183
social programs, 69
social responsibility, 220
society, 110
software, 125, 127, 133, 308
solvents, 60, 301
Somalia, 17, 33, 34, 43, 107, 116, 117, 253, 256, 263, 307, 308
South America, 23, 25
South Asia, 120, 124, 304
South Korea, 227, 258
Southeast Asia, 82, 83, 113, 114, 120, 139, 303
Southern African Development Community, 25, 88, 156, 160, 280, 307
soybeans, 95
SP, vii, 1, 3, 6, 38, 46, 163, 296, 300, 311, 316
Spain, 25, 76, 113, 114, 258, 260
specialization, 80, 89, 94, 151, 179
species, 93, 95
specifications, 131, 177, 188, 190, 193, 315
speech, 13
spending, 13, 81
spillover effects, 168, 185
Sri Lanka, 143, 261
stability, 81, 109, 110, 115, 146, 152, 210, 211, 222, 252, 253
staffing, 7
stakeholders, 13, 78, 87, 88, 91, 97, 102, 220, 231
standardization, 94
state(s), 2, 7, 17, 24, 36, 63, 65, 69, 103, 109, 110, 129, 130, 137, 139, 146, 156, 158, 159, 160, 179, 209, 219, 222, 313
state-owned enterprises, 130
statistics, 39, 125, 130, 171, 296, 298, 313
steel, 32, 42, 51, 64, 65, 90, 96, 133, 158, 218, 269, 298
stimulus, 35, 152
stock, 93, 118, 131, 304
stock markets, 131
storage, 69, 70, 86, 89, 91, 92, 93, 94, 118, 134
structural adjustment, 303
structural reforms, 35, 152
structure, 13, 59, 206
style, 18, 284, 285, 307
sub-Saharan Africa, vii, viii, 1, 2, 6, 7, 8, 14, 18, 21, 24, 26, 27, 38, 40, 42, 67, 78, 96, 106, 114, 115,
117, 145, 162, 165, 166, 167, 173, 181, 182, 200, 201, 296, 299, 300, 301, 313, 316
subsidy, 59
subsistence, 94
substantially transformed, 306
substitutes, 272
substitution, 22, 175
Sudan, 6, 17, 24, 25, 33, 41, 42, 44, 54, 116, 131, 132, 133, 137, 143, 156, 157, 225, 253, 255, 256, 261, 262, 266, 267, 299, 307, 308
sugarcane, 92, 139
sulfur, 70
sulfuric acid, 71, 72
supplier(s), 28, 50, 51, 57, 58, 60, 62, 63, 64, 66, 68, 70, 72, 74, 76, 77, 78, 79, 80, 85, 86, 89, 100, 101, 104, 105, 106, 212, 215, 218, 302, 305
supply chain, viii, 21, 23, 27, 29, 30, 38, 40, 78, 79, 83, 86, 87, 88, 89, 90, 93, 100, 105, 200, 214, 215, 217, 221, 227, 231, 302
supply disruption, 61, 69, 301
support services, 309
Supreme Court, 210, 218
surplus, 151
survival, 181
sustainability, 69
sustainable development, 17, 216, 291, 308
Sweden, 25, 258, 260
sweeteners, 283
Switzerland, 24, 113, 117, 149, 155, 159, 193, 258, 260, 266, 308, 312, 316
syndrome, 219
synthesis, 167
synthetic fiber, 87
Syria, 25, 156

T

Taiwan, 63, 79, 115, 141, 146, 149, 259, 260, 311
Tanzania, 8, 17, 24, 25, 44, 54, 98, 102, 123, 127, 130, 132, 133, 137, 138, 139, 140, 142, 156, 160, 161, 172, 212, 223, 225, 229, 248, 249, 253, 255, 256, 257, 259, 260, 262, 268, 278, 313, 314
target, 7, 85, 97, 130, 265
tariff rates, 4, 112, 151, 168, 310, 311
taxation, 316
taxes, 111, 139, 208, 254, 255, 307
TCC, 69, 291, 292
TDD, 200
technical assistance, 7, 85, 87, 97, 183, 207
technical change, 2
techniques, 92
technological advancement, 113
technological advances, 29, 79

technological change, 79
technology, 94, 95, 118, 128, 133, 154, 214, 227, 289
technology transfer, 118
telecommunications, 34, 79, 81, 115, 117, 128, 132, 143
telecommunications services, 143
telephone, 39, 307
tensions, 61, 301
territory, 44
terrorism, 109, 110, 252, 253
terrorist activities, 6
textiles, 4, 6, 29, 31, 32, 34, 45, 49, 78, 87, 89, 94, 95, 96, 97, 98, 100, 101, 115, 120, 130, 134, 141, 142, 143, 145, 149, 150, 159, 161, 168, 170, 175, 177, 186, 189, 191, 207, 214, 227, 230, 277, 300, 301, 317, 318
Thailand, 104, 157, 227, 261
third country fabric, 186, 188, 206
third-country fabric, 5, 13, 36, 40, 41, 42, 45, 63, 96, 106, 141, 145, 170, 172, 188, 210, 211, 212, 214, 215, 222, 300, 301, 303
time frame, 50
time periods, 36, 163
time series, 178
tin, 168, 187
titanium, 90
Title I, 3, 299
tobacco, 9, 37, 44, 51, 52, 56, 93, 101, 128, 134, 135, 136, 141, 176, 214, 217, 222, 223, 230, 265, 266, 278, 301
Togo, 17, 24, 44, 54, 225, 229, 249, 250, 253, 255, 257, 258, 260, 263
total product, 129
tourism, 95, 117, 136
Toyota, 59, 118, 137
toys, 32, 80, 95
tracks, 46
trade agreement, viii, 2, 21, 22, 26, 27, 33, 35, 36, 38, 39, 40, 79, 101, 145, 146, 147, 148, 149, 150, 151, 152, 153, 154, 155, 157, 158, 159, 160, 164, 165, 166, 174, 176, 177, 186, 201, 310, 313, 314
Trade and Development Act of 2000, 26, 38, 291, 299, 311
trade benefits, 18, 22, 35, 40, 42, 144, 153, 219
trade creation, 172, 177
trade deficit, 108
trade liberalization, 3, 14, 59, 98, 303
trade policy, 7, 31, 83, 112, 166, 179, 180, 181, 192, 193, 194, 195, 220, 221
trading partners, 35, 92, 101, 145, 146, 150, 152, 153, 154, 181
traditions, 108

training, 83, 93, 114, 150, 152, 182, 212, 215, 221, 257, 258
transaction costs, 35, 81, 149
transactions, 112, 134, 140, 141, 143, 267, 308
transformation, 98, 101, 104, 163, 170, 179, 180, 227, 306, 317, 318
transparency, 13, 109, 112, 113, 154, 161
transport, 33, 58, 81, 83, 88, 89, 91, 92, 93, 94, 105, 134, 140, 207, 209, 308
transport costs, 33, 88, 92, 93, 105
transportation, 21, 28, 29, 31, 37, 49, 50, 66, 67, 69, 79, 81, 82, 83, 89, 92, 94, 100, 139, 182
transportation infrastructure, 31, 37, 89, 139
treaties, 113, 145, 158
treatment, 4, 6, 8, 12, 14, 40, 41, 42, 45, 85, 89, 101, 145, 148, 152, 153, 155, 156, 158, 159, 161, 179, 180, 201, 202, 300, 311, 315
Trinidad, 319
Turkey, 141, 143, 146, 155, 157, 159, 259, 260, 290, 316

U

U.S. assistance, 14, 208
U.S. Department of Agriculture, 105, 283, 292, 293
U.S. Department of Commerce, 22, 39, 220, 293, 294, 295
U.S. Department of the Interior, 294
U.S. economy, 46, 50, 151
U.S. Geological Survey (USGS), 275, 278, 280, 283, 285, 286, 287, 289, 290, 292, 294
U.S. Harmonized Tariff Schedule, 4
U.S. import trends, vii, 3
U.S. policy, 2, 151, 179, 180, 194, 195, 223
U.S. yarn, 5, 45
Ukraine, 262
UNDP, 283
uniform, 13
unions, 142
United Kingdom (UK), 25, 34, 105, 106, 114, 117, 119, 120, 127, 128, 138, 141, 143, 258, 259, 265, 266, 282, 298, 313
United Nations (UN), 19, 24, 39, 80, 82, 87, 88, 95, 98, 144, 146, 282, 285, 287, 288, 289, 295, 296, 310
United Nations Industrial Development Organization, 39, 144, 282, 296
unlawful transshipment, 4, 42
upholstery, 78
urbanization, 88
Uruguay, 25, 150, 155, 306
USA, 165, 185, 205, 218, 278
USDA, 75, 77, 292, 293, 304, 307

USGS, 72, 278

V

value-added requirement, 4
vanadium, 70, 71, 286, 289, 290
variables, 107, 108, 112, 167, 168, 173, 176, 177, 191, 193, 194, 314, 316, 317
variations, 163, 166, 178, 299, 301
varieties, 77, 92, 95, 172, 188, 227
vegetable oil, 88, 176, 304
vegetables, 30, 32, 56, 83, 88, 93, 94, 96, 99, 100, 104, 105, 168, 172, 186, 187, 217, 230, 270, 304, 307
vehicles, vii, 2, 9, 21, 28, 30, 46, 50, 51, 52, 55, 56, 58, 59, 96, 134, 141, 158, 168, 178, 210, 212, 217, 268, 269, 302
vein, 183
Venezuela, 25, 261
vessels, 56, 93, 104
Vice President, 204, 205, 212, 219, 221, 222, 223
Vietnam, 9, 10, 106, 261
violence, 109, 110, 252, 253
visa system(s), 45, 300
volatility, 28, 61, 301
Volkswagen, 59, 118, 127

W

waiver, 311
Washington, 17, 18, 199, 202, 203, 204, 205, 206, 208, 274, 275, 276, 277, 279, 283, 284, 285, 287, 289, 291, 292, 293, 294, 295, 296, 297, 298, 306, 309, 310, 312
waste, 67, 103, 306
wastewater, 89
watches, 42, 230, 318
water, 73, 81, 89, 92, 93, 94, 118, 207, 209, 265
water resources, 93
weakness, 50
wealth, 117
wearing apparel, 265
weather patterns, 92
web, 281, 283, 291, 293
welding, 51, 218

welfare, 80
West Africa, 18, 22, 24, 32, 85, 86, 88, 90, 95, 97, 120, 129, 132, 139, 143, 157, 160, 161, 276, 279, 282, 297, 305, 307
Western countries, 131
Western Europe, 103, 288
White House, 19
wholesale, 130, 135
wind power, 140
wires, 66
witnesses, 145, 202, 203
wood, 32, 92, 94, 96, 98, 153, 169, 181, 230
wood products, 32, 94, 96, 153, 230
wool, 5, 45, 230
work gloves, 42
worker rights, 6
workers, 11, 61, 80, 85, 90, 140, 149, 150, 223, 301, 307, 311, 320
workforce, 80, 87, 303
working conditions, 61, 80, 301
World Bank, 6, 32, 39, 42, 80, 82, 90, 97, 100, 107, 108, 109, 110, 111, 114, 115, 120, 139, 214, 253, 255, 275, 276, 278, 279, 282, 283, 284, 285, 288, 291, 297, 298, 302, 303, 305, 307, 308, 309, 310
World Customs Organization, 306, 313
World Development Report, 298, 307
World Trade Organization (WTO), 3, 4, 7, 13, 15, 18, 22, 28, 39, 82, 147, 150, 154, 160, 201, 218, 274, 281, 283, 285, 298, 299, 302, 303, 304, 305, 311, 312, 314
world trading system, 189
worldwide, 80, 103, 109

Y

yarn, 5, 18, 89, 141, 142, 300
Yemen, 25, 156, 261
yield, 176

Z

Zimbabwe, 17, 24, 25, 44, 89, 107, 116, 142, 143, 156, 161, 212, 223, 253, 255, 257, 259, 260, 262, 266, 267, 313
zinc, 138, 139